CENTRAL

T XAS

LONE ★ STAR
TRAVEL ★ GUIDE

CENTRAL
TEXAS

RICHARD ZELADE

TAYLOR TRADE PUBLISHING
Lanham • New York • Boulder • Toronto • Plymouth, UK

Published by Taylor Trade Publishing
An imprint of The Rowman & Littlefield Publishing Group, Inc.
4501 Forbes Boulevard, Suite 200, Lanham, Maryland 20706
http://www.rlpgtrade.com

Estover Road, Plymouth PL6 7PY, United Kingdom

Distributed by National Book Network

ISBN 978-1-58979-604-1 (pbk. : alk. paper)
ISBN 978-1-58979-608-9 (electronic)

∞™ The paper used in this publication meets the minimum requirements of American National Standard for Information Sciences—Permanence of Paper for Printed Library Materials, ANSI/NISO Z39.48-1992.

Printed in the United States of America.

CONTENTS

ACKNOWLEDGMENTS

In the thirty years spent putting together *Central Texas*, I've done a lot of listening, looking, and reading. Each experience, no matter how small, has increased in some way my understanding of Central Texas and subsequently has enhanced this book. For this I am grateful. But I owe special thanks to a number of people. I would like to thank the staff of the Center for American History at the University of Texas at Austin, who spent hours shagging down all the files and books I was forever requesting.

The Texas State Historical Association's *Handbook of Texas*, considered to be the gold standard for Texas history, was used as a reference for all the trips. Material for all the trips also came from the archives of the *Austin Democratic/ Daily Statesman* and the *Galveston County Daily News*, the *San Antonio Express, San Antonio Light, Llano News*, and others.

In putting together each trip, I found at least one book that proved to be a particularly valuable source of background information or quoted material. By trip, the books are as follows:

Riding the Fault: *History of New Braunfels and Comal County, Texas, 1844–1946*, by Oscar Haas; *Texas, with Particular Reference to German Immigration and the Physical Appearance of the Country*, by Ferdinand Roemer; *Tales from the Manchaca Hills*, by Edna Turley Carpenter; and *A Journey Through Texas*, by Frederick Law Olmsted.

Williamson County: *Land of Good Water*, by Clara Scarbrough; *Burnet County History*, by Darrell Debo; *Williamson County Centennial, 1848–1948*, by the Williamson County Centennial Committee; *The Fabulous Empire: Col. Zack Miller's Story*, by Fred Gipson; and *Culture of the Shin Oak Ridge Folk*, by J. Gordon Bryson.

Shiner-Lockhart Pilgrimage: *The History of Lavaca County*, by Paul Boethel; *Dr. J. B. Cranfill's Chronicle: A Story of Life in Texas Written by Himself about Himself*, by J. B. Cranfill; *With His Pistol in His Hand*, by Americo Paredes; *The Life of John Wesley Hardin as Written by Himself*, by John Wesley Hardin; *Earth Has No Sorrow*, by Dee Azadian; *On a Mexican Mustang through Texas*, by A. E. Sweet; *Do You Remember? Early Days in Luling, Texas by a Pioneer Citizen*, by Anne C. Huff Bridges; *Dog Ghosts on the Brazos: The Word on the Brazos*, by J. Mason Brewer; *Historical Lockhart*, by Zona Adams Withers; and *Historical Caldwell County: Where Roots Intertwine*, by the Mark Withers Trail Drive Museum.

The Wild West: *A History of Lee County Texas*, by the Lee County Historical Survey Committee; *Dog Ghosts on the Brazos: The Word on the Brazos*, by J. Mason

Brewer; *The San Antonio and Aransas Pass Railway*, by John W. Hedge and Geoffrey S. Dawson; *The Bastrop Advertiser*; *Evolution of a State*, by Noah Smithwick; *Coronado's Children*, by J. Frank Dobie; *Rip Ford's Texas*, by John S. Ford; and *Indian Depredations in Texas*, by J. W. Wilbarger.

Central Texas Stew: *Dr. J. B. Cranfill's Chronicle: A Story of Life in Texas Written by Himself about Himself*, by J. B. Cranfill; *William Bollaert's Texas*, edited by W. Eugene Holland; *Mills of Yesteryear*, by A. T. Jackson; *Driving Tour of Industry Texas*, by Anne Lindemann; *Guide to New Ulm*; *Consider the Lily: The Ungilded History of Colorado County*, by Bill Stein; and *Flaming Feuds of Colorado County*, by John Walter and Lillian Estelle Reese.

Many people have helped me over the years in assembling the material for this book. Their observations have made it truly special, something more than just another guidebook. Many are now deceased, but a bit of them lives on in these pages. Beginning with the first edition, back in 1983, my thanks go to Margaret Keidel, John and Edward Balcar, the Riskes, Gould Davis, Jimmy Nuckles, the Kliers, Mrs. Simek, Speedy, Emil, Joe, Cracker, Mr. Siems, Frank Wagner, C. W. Carlson, Clara Scarbrough, Max Theis, Red Casparis, Chuck Zelade, Irv and Mary Zelade, Susan and Jeff Reid, Brook Watts, Bill and Doris Bacon, Bob and Suzan Leggett, Kristin Brown, Odies Schatte, and Marianne Simmons. Thanks also to Emil Holtzer, Alton Koch, the Twin Sisters School Association, Rusty Vogt, Winnie Petty, and Walter Doebbler.

Subsequent edition thanks go to Marvin Finger, Andrew Sansom, Robin Giles, Edith Giles, Bill Stein, Buddy Rau, Louis Polansky, Helen Mikus, Joe Nick Patoski, Walt Falk, Gerald McLeod, Jim Shahin, Royce Nelson, and John Morthland.

Special, current edition thanks go to Curtis Clarke, faithful friend and driver, whose dedication and extra pair of eyes helped me concentrate on the finer details of updating, and Lisa Lach, indefatigable researcher on McDade and the Yegua Troubles, who helped me correct a number of previous misconceptions concerning that tragic feud.

My most heartfelt thanks go out to my deceased friend and mentor Anders Saustrup, who more than anyone else over the years helped me mold *Central Texas* into the substantial work that it is. His wealth of knowledge of Texas history and his dedication to historical accuracy saved me many times from potential embarrassment and made *Central Texas* more than just another guidebook.

INTRODUCTION

Texas, more than any other state, is the crossroads of America. Four major continental divisions come together here: the Rocky Mountains, the Great Western High and Lower Plains, and the Gulf Coastal Plains.

The farming woodland Caddos, the cannibal coastal Karankawa, the roaming Apache and Comanche hunters, and the desert cliff-dwelling Pueblos—all of them once called Texas home. The cultures of Old Mexico and the Old South, the Wild West, and the Great Plains met and sometimes clashed here. German, Czech, and Scandinavian émigrés of the nineteenth century flocked to Texas in search of a new and better life, much like the northern snowbirds of today.

Birds from all corners of the North American continent meet here, more than six hundred different species in all. Rocky Mountain and Eastern species of oak and pine converge uniquely in Texas which has at least five thousand species of plant life.

All these "roads" have led ultimately to Central Texas—the heart of Texas—resulting in a singular cultural, geographical, and physiological potpourri which manifests itself in foods like chicken-fried jalapenos and wurst tacos; pronunciations like "Purd'nallez" (Pedernales), "Gwaddaloop" (Guadalupe), and "Manshack" (Manchaca); Texas-German words and phrases like "der Outlaw," "der Bollweevil," "die Fenz" (the fence), "das Stinktier" (the skunk), "der Mesquitebaum," and "die Kuh dehornen" (dehorn the cow); and Czech-Texan words like "rencak" (rancher), "polkat" (skunk), "akr" (acre), and "barbekue" (barbecue). And only in the Hill Country of Central Texas will you see the sacred Enchanted Rock and the limestone fences, houses, barns, and Sunday houses of the old German Texans.

Then there is the Balcones Fault, that great crack in the earth which bisects the whole of Texas—separating the western upland from the coastal lowland—but which manifests itself only in Central Texas, dividing the region yet ultimately binding it together.

Hollywood has discovered Central Texas in a big way. *Leadbelly, Texas Chainsaw Massacre, Barbarosa, What's Eating Gilbert Grape, Hope Floats, The Newton Boys,* and *The Alamo* are just a few of the movies that have been filmed in our picturesque small towns and countryside since the mid-1970s. In the process, the movie companies have helped lengthen the life of a number of old buildings, with fresh coats of paint and other improvements. These improvements often included reproductions of old painted advertising on the buildings' exterior walls for soft drinks, chewing gum, and the like. Quaint, but not authentic.

Tradition has it that the name "Texas" derives from a Caddo language word meaning "friends" or "allies." And Texans are a pretty friendly bunch of people. Texas is also one of the most conservative states in the Union, and, Austin aside, Central Texas is as conservative as the rest of the state. As never before, this book attempts to explain both phenomena by exploring the rich, varied, complicated, and intertwined histories of the region's ethnic, racial, national, and socioeconomic groups.

The trips in this book are meant to reflect the one-of-a-kind diversity which is Central Texas. They take you out of the big cities, off the freeways and su-perhighways, away from the fast food franchises and shopping malls, and intro-duce you to the small towns and ghost towns, mountains and valleys, rivers and creeks, cafes and beer joints, and some of the fine folks of Central Texas—the wonderful sweet cream that always rises to the top of a bottle of whole milk. But like good whole milk, that which is uniquely vintage Central Texas gets a little harder to find each year.

Richard Zelade
Austin, Texas
October 2010

How to Use
This Book

We deliberately take to the tasty back roads so as to treat you to the most vivid flavors of Central Texas. Getting to wherever you're going is always at least half the fun.

While this book takes you far and wide across the heart of Texas, it is not a comprehensive guide to the area and does not pretend to be. Trips are organized along themes, and it has not been possible to include every town in the region.

Although Texas is now predominantly urban, small towns and the open country are still the state's bedrock and the strongest links to our traditional, unique Texas past. There is a distinctly different mentality to our back-roads communities, an informal order of things. Hours and days open for businesses, while usually reliable, are still left largely to the whim of the proprietor, who may just decide to take the day off, open late, or close early.

The hours and days of operation given are designed to be as accurate and as up to date as possible but should not be blindly be relied on. Places get sold, they close, or they burn down. Many places now have websites, which are usually useful for current information but are sometimes not updated as often as they should be. Calling ahead by phone is the surest way to confirm current hours of operation and other information.

Website addresses for restaurants, museums, visitor centers, and the like that have websites are given along with each attraction's phone number, with the exception of Texas state parks and natural areas. For information on all state parks and natural areas, go to the Texas Parks and Wildlife Department's website: www.tpwd.state.tx.us.

Another important thing that has changed since this book first came out in 1983, in addition to the ubiquity of websites, is the improvement in road names, signs, and numbering, mandated by universal 911 service. It's easier for me to publish concise, easy-to-follow directions now, but sometimes signs get knocked down or stolen, so it's still necessary at times to refer to local landmarks as direction aids.

Several of these trips can be easily done in one day, others take two days, and some can go either way. Distances are such that you should have to drive no more than thirty miles out of your way to find accommodations, since some of these small towns and villages have none. Usually towns with populations over one thousand do. The countryside is now conveniently dotted, more than ever, with bed-and-breakfast facilities, but these generally do not accept drop-ins. There is also considerable turnover in B&B inns. Call the local chamber of commerce for a current listing of B&Bs in the area you're interested in.

Each city or town's listing begins with the name of the county in which it is located, the best estimate of the current population, and the telephone area code.

Because of the Americans with Disabilities Act, most places listed are now wheelchair accessible or partially accessible. Call ahead to make sure. Wheelchair accessibility is indicated by the letter *W*.

You should always carry a good state highway map with you, such as the free Texas Department of Transportation map, available at the state travel visitor centers scattered across the state and at most local chambers of commerce and visitor centers. Mapsco's *The Roads of Texas Atlas* (www.mapsco.com) is my favorite travel companion; each public road, no matter how small, is shown and identified by its name and number, and many local landmarks, such as cemeteries, schoolhouses, community centers, and the like, are also identified.

If you just want to do part of a tour, or if you just want to visit a specific place, remember that about half of the towns and places in this book will be found on any good state highway map and are accessible by major highways.

With only a couple of documented exceptions, the road mileage in this book is over reasonably good to excellent paved roads. Perhaps fifteen miles are gravel, and these are generally well graded. They are sometimes rough and "washboarded" after bad weather, though.

Be careful when driving in rainy weather. Slow down on the winding roads, and be wary of low-water crossings. Any crossing with more than a few inches of running water can be dangerous, depending on the vehicle you are driving. When in doubt, "Don't Drown, Turn Around."

In concocting *Central Texas*, I blended history, personal observations, folklore, and trivia, and then spiced it up with a little geology, geography, and humor. I hope you have as much fun exploring Central Texas with this book as I had writing it.

Special Note: Due to the 2011 state budget crisis, the future of Texas state parks, including all state parks and natural areas in this book, was in doubt at press time. Please check the Texas Parks and Wildlife website for the latest status of each park or natural area.

RIDING THE FAULT

APPROXIMATELY 123 MILES

The Balcones Escarpment stretches from Del Rio to the Red River in a curved line across Texas. Invisible for most of its length, it rears up prominently from northwest of San Antonio to just beyond Austin, to a height of about three hundred feet above the prairie below. Several miles wide, the escarpment—which appears as a range of wooded hills to viewers on the prairie below—separates the Edwards Plateau from the Blackland Prairies and the Coastal Prairies. Its appearance prompted early Spanish explorers to call it Los Balcones—"The Balconies."

The Balcones Escarpment, a geologic fault zone consisting of many smaller individual faultings, was formed during a period of geologic turbulence over seventy million years ago, when there was a general downwarping of the earth's crust near the Gulf Coast and a moderate uplift inland. Over the years the older, harder rocks to the west have eroded much less than the younger, softer rocks to the east. The level of topsoil east of the escarpment is much thicker, thus supporting a greater amount of plant life. The fault line breaks across water-bearing formations passing beneath the Edwards Plateau to the prairie. Much of the water is forced to the surface by artesian pressure, resulting in such large and well-known artesian springs as Comal, San Marcos, and Barton Springs, as well as many smaller springs.

Because of increased consumption of Edwards Aquifer water (principally by the City of San Antonio) and droughts like the extended drought of the 1980s, flow from New Braunfels' Comal Springs nearly ceased several times during the 1980s, and in 1996 and 1999 as well. If the springs were to dry up, the blow to tourism in New Braunfels would be devastating, since the Comal River (as we know it) would cease to exist. Next to dry up would be the San Marcos Springs, followed by Austin's Barton Springs. San Antonio's once-famous San Pedro Springs dried up years ago. The water of the San Antonio River along San Antonio's famed River Walk is artificially pumped from the Edwards Aquifer.

RIDING THE FAULT

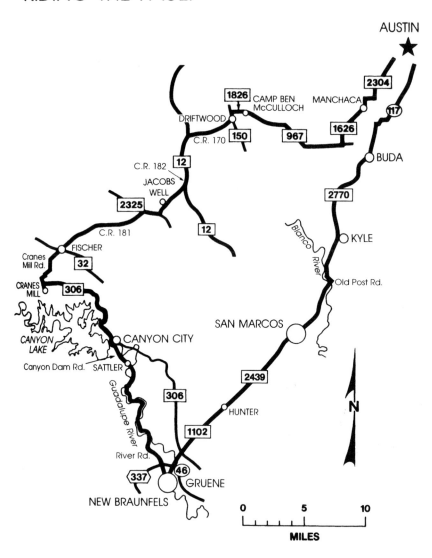

So enjoy the great springs of the region while you can, and be sure to conserve water so that future generations may enjoy them as well.

This trip carries you down the rocky eastern edge of the Balcones Escarpment to New Braunfels, home of the Comal River, Landa Park, and the Wurstfest. Before the Civil War, New Braunfels and San Antonio were the largest and most prosperous towns along the Escarpment. Austin, the capital city, was much smaller.

On the trip back to Austin, you travel along the escarpment's frontier with the flatter, richer Blackland Prairie, along the Old Stagecoach Road that ran from San Antonio to Austin. The trip begins at the Lady Bird Johnson Wildflower Center in far southwest Austin, near the intersection of Loop 1 and Slaughter Lane.

LADY BIRD JOHNSON WILDFLOWER CENTER

4801 La Crosse Ave. • Far southwest Austin • 292-4200 • www.wildflower .org • Tuesday through Sunday • Fee • W

Given our everlasting preoccupation with water (and the lack of it) in the region, it's appropriate that our trip begins at the Lady Bird Johnson Wildflower Center. Wildflowers are more than just beautiful; they are also practical problem solvers in a world that faces increasing shortages in—and quality problems with—soil, water, and air. Wildflowers and other native plants and grasses can provide beautiful, low-cost, ecologically balanced landscaping. Since wildflowers and native plants are used to surviving on their own, annual watering costs can be cut by 50 to 70 percent, and the need for fertilizers, pesticides, and herbicides is pretty much nonexistent.

Wildflower landscapes do best with minimal maintenance, requiring mowing only after the seed has set. The potential savings in labor, fuel, and equipment maintenance is great. When Mrs. Johnson broke ground for the Center in December 1982, she said that Texas alone, with its one million acres of state rights-of-way, could save $24 million a year if highway mowing could be reduced from four times to one time each year. By expanding its existing wildflower program in 1983, the Texas Highway Department saved 23 percent of its 1982 mowing costs of highway rights-of-way.

Wildflowers and native plants provide essential wildlife cover and food, and they stabilize critically disturbed areas such as construction and mining sites by preventing wind and water erosion. Many species of wildflowers thrive in poor soil that can support little else. Although twenty-five thousand species of wildflowers have been identified in the United States (five thousand grow in Texas), we actually know very little about them. Botanists have studied only several hundred species in depth.

The Wildflower Center is a private, nonprofit organization that educates the public about the ecological and aesthetic importance of native wildflowers and other native plants, trees, and shrubs. Botanists conduct experiments with various species and planting techniques, and they do research on the conservation and cultivation of native plants. The Center is a national clearinghouse for information on native plants and habitat. Fact sheets include how to establish a wildflower garden as well as propagation and seed collection tips. The center has spring and fall plant sales and gardening festivals, and it has advice on planting times and techniques. Educational programs, materials, and speakers are available for group presentations. Classes like wildflower watercolor painting, papermaking, wildflower photography, dyeing with native plants, and landscaping with native plants are regularly offered. Call for dates and information.

Attractions at the forty-two-acre Center along the Balcones Escarpment include a wildflower meadow and restored native prairie, as well as a half-mile-long nature trail. Display gardens contain "theme" plots that show different uses of native plants. The visitors gallery has exhibits that describe North American prairie, desert, and forest ecosystems; that show the medicinal, ceremonial, and agricultural uses of native plants; and that tell how to be better stewards of the earth.

Buildings are constructed of native sandstone, limestone, and recycled long-leaf pine and reflect the region's diverse architectural heritage: from the Spanish missions to the sturdy, boxy German farmhouses to western ranch houses. The forty-three-foot-tall stone observation tower offers great views. The Center pumps no water from the Edwards Aquifer; rooftop water runoff captured in specially designed cisterns takes care of the site's irrigation needs. A gift shop offers a wide variety of ecologically correct (EC) items. There's also a cafe. You can get married in one of the gardens or celebrate your anniversary in the visitors gallery, hold a conference in the 236-seat auditorium, or stage a fundraiser in the courtyard, but rental policies are EC.

From the Lady Bird Johnson Wildflower Center, head north on Loop 1, then east on Slaughter Lane shortly thereafter. In about three miles, turn right (south) on Manchaca Road (FM 2304).

MANCHACA

Travis County • About 5 miles from the Lady Bird Johnson Wildflower Center

A continuous chain of new subdivisions stretches uninterrupted out from Austin to Manchaca and beyond these days. This was not always the case. At the turn of the century, Manchaca was comfortably insulated from Austin by fifteen-odd miles and several stops on the International and Great Northern (I&GN) railroad, places with names like Vinson, St. Elmo, Korwin, and Kouns. The capital city, with all of its blandishments and temptations, was a good hour away by train, and over three hours distant if you chose to drive the wagon or surrey over the rattly, dusty Old San Antonio Road.

Manchaca is larger than you might first suspect, just judging from the highway signs. As old-time Manchacans will tell you, the Manchaca neighborhood stretches for a mile or so north of the present center, east to the Old San Antonio Road, and south very nearly to Buda, where the Manchaca Springs are located, near the old stage stop near Buda, which we will visit near the end of this chapter. Manchaca owes its existence to these springs, or what is left of them. Local legend tells us that a Colonel Jose Antonio Menchaca discovered the springs and subsequently camped there with his company of soldiers during the days following the Battle of San Jacinto. Menchaca and company had been charged with protecting early settlers from raiding Indians. Historical research doesn't back up this story, however. Not in question is Menchaca's existence; he came from a well-known Bexar family, he fought with the Texans at San Jacinto, and after the war he did command a cavalry company charged with protecting the republic's frontier from Indian depredations. The discrepancy lies in the fact that the springs were called Menchaca well before the revolution, no doubt named for someone else from the Menchaca family. At any rate, the spelling was corrupted slightly to Manchaca over the years, and the pronunciation was corrupted drastically to "Man-shack." Locally famous, the springs flowed "strong, clear, and 99 percent pure," in the words of an early inhabitant. Not surprisingly, they were a regular stop for travelers on the old Austin-to-San Antonio stage line.

With the coming of the I&GN in 1880, the neighborhood's center shifted northward from the springs to its present location. At 705 feet above sea level,

Manchaca station was located on the highest point of land between Austin and San Antonio on these old I&GN tracks. Its location on high ground meant maximum exposure to the cooling winds of summer and greater protection from the various plagues, chills, and fevers that always seemed to prey on bottomlanders.

Location on the railroad was highly prized. The railroad gave life and prosperity to towns like Manchaca and usually meted out death to the towns it bypassed, towns like Mountain City. Manchaca was a magnet to the area farmers, and Texas was overwhelmingly rural then. The daily comings and goings of the trains were social as well as business events, and much of the community's everyday life centered around the depot according to Edna Turley Carpenter:

> Old men and loafers met there to whittle, to pitch washers or horseshoes or quarters, or to chew tobacco and cuss the government; children romped and rode tricycles up and down the loading ramp; the telegraph operator gave out advance weather information; and those who were departing or expecting a visitor or a package from Sears, Roebuck and Company were present on legitimate business. But most came just for the fun of it, and the arrivals of the daily trains that stopped to take on passengers and freight were the high spots in the day for many colored and white folk alike. The trains gave people who had never been beyond the limits of Travis County a feeling of kinship with the outside world. It was a comfort not to feel hopelessly trapped. If one had the necessary money, and the hankering, it was possible to board a train at Manchaca in the morning, shop all day in Austin or San Antonio, and return before bedtime. The engineers were easily recognized by the individualistic toots they gave the whistles as the locomotives crossed Bear Creek bridge. Small boys were able to give realistic imitations of these toots. People checked their timepieces, if they were fortunate to own them, by a train's arrival. "The Sunshine Special was twenty minutes late today," you'd hear. Or, "The Katy Flyer has been right on the button every day this week."

It is hard to imagine such excitement over a train these days, but the train was the first and for a time the only means of breaking out of the isolation that was a way of life for rural Texans. The wonderment most of us feel toward commercial space flight or human-powered flight is perhaps comparable to the magic of the train for Texans around the turn of the century.

But despite the railroad's importance to towns like Manchaca, Buda, Kyle, New Braunfels, and so on, rail travel was far from safe, as illustrated by this *Austin Statesman* story dated July 5, 1883:

> The northbound passenger train telescoped with a freight train about four miles from Austin yesterday afternoon. The engine of the freight train broke down and was taken to Manchaca, and the train left on the track. While the freight train was standing there the northbound passenger came thundering along at the rate of 25 miles an hour. The disabled train was standing just around a curve from the approaching passenger, and the latter was on to the former almost before it was seen by the engineer. The trains were badly wrecked, but fortunately no one was killed and no one seriously hurt. Judge Devine had his hand bruised, and the engineer his nose skinned. The accident occurred near Korwin on the International and Great Northern railway switch. The conductor of the passenger train stated that the air brakes failed to work, and the train was helplessly unmanageable. The wreck was not cleared from the track until late this morning.

And this story is far from unique; there are dozens more like it on the stretch of the I&GN between Austin and San Antonio alone.

In 1958, Edna Turley Carpenter's sons, Tom and Buck Carpenter, described life in Manchaca at the turn of the century to Jane Hogan:

In Manchaca work was something to be discarded at the earliest opportunity, for it was considered a means of using one's life very poorly, almost a spiritual sickness. . . . At revival meetings there were Methodists, Presbyterians, Baptists, Catholics, Jews, Negroes, Mexicans, and whites—laborers and rich men—preachers and drunks; and it was a cinch for any of them to be saved, even if one fell out of a tree drunk during the preaching. Near our house watermelons red as a goat's behind going uphill and sweet potato vines as long as well ropes. Around the house peach trees in the back, pear trees on the side and plums in the front. Within the house dewberry pie and poke greens in the kitchen, and agarita berry wine and jelly and dozens of kinds of preserves lined up on the shelves under the staircase. Plenty of wood and water, cypress for the roofs, rocks for the fences, cedar bark to smoke on weekdays and Bull Durham on Sundays, and arrowheads to hunt. Don't forget the quiltings, kodaking with the girls, fish fries, ice cream suppers, parties with seven takings, and Dodson Park (practically donated by the colored butcher) used for picnics and baseball games by white and black alike. Most families ranged from seven to twelve in number. We keep thinking of Great-Uncle Milton Carpenter, who took one bath in the late spring and another in the early fall, and was a preacher, lawyer, doctor, and engineer—altogether a philosopher. What more could one man do? And our grandmother, Sue (McCuistion) Shepperd-McGuire-Carpenter-Hancock, who buried four husbands and had a favorite saying: "Life is just one devilment after another."

"It must be remembered that both the cultural and economic levels of this community were not very high," Edna said. "Few of the inhabitants had more than a high-school education, and many even less. Most people read little other than the daily newspapers and the Bible. Interest in the fine arts was practically nil. But they "didn't no more keer."

Manchaca's importance as a center of trade and civilization began to fade with the onslaught of the automobile and the great Texas highway system. Nowadays Manchaca has been subsumed by Austin suburban subdivisions. Manchaca's story is not unique. Texas is full of similar hamlets, places with names like Oatmeal, Grapetown, and Cain City. Keep this in mind as you roll through these spots; the countryside is full of ghosts.

DINING

RAILROAD BAR-B-QUE

727 FM 1626, about a quarter mile east of the intersection of FM 1626 with FM 2304 • 512-282-3288 • www.rrbbq.com • Open daily, lunch and dinner • Cr.

Here you will find very good mesquite-smoked pork ribs, sausage, chicken, and smoked turkey, plus the usual sides. You can get a chicken fried steak or fried catfish on weekends, but why? They have beer.

At FM 2304's termination, turn right on FM 1626. For the next 4.5 miles you teeter on the edge of the Balcones Escarpment. At the four-way intersection with FM 967, make a left turn west toward Driftwood on FM 967.

Not long after turning onto FM 967 is another one of those ghosts, Elm Grove, once a bustling village and the location of Hays County's largest public school in 1888.

The first few miles on FM 967 are now given over to suburban development, but after that, the pastureland you pass through on FM 967, as the Blackland Prairie gives way to the Hill Country, was the domain of King Cotton one hundred years ago. Cotton finally brought the full measure of civilization to this previously sparsely settled area. Cotton was an obsession with Texas farmers from the waning days of Reconstruction until the 1920s when the boll weevil, Johnson grass, urbanization, mechanization, falling prices, and a couple of strategically placed droughts, not to mention cotton's notorious land deple-tion tendencies, brought cotton farming to its knees. Cotton's disappearance around here was amazingly quick, as was the disappearance of row farming in general. But as crop farming bowed out, sheep and Angora goat raisers from the western edges of the Edwards Plateau moved right in. And now, only sixty-odd years later, this pastoral order is giving way to yet another order as the fleeing urbanites move in, seeking their own little patches of rural heaven.

Turn left onto FM 1826 when FM 967 comes to an end after 9.2 miles. Just after you turn onto FM 1826, you come to Camp Ben McCulloch and the Salt Lick.

CAMP BEN MCCULLOCH

FM 1826 • About 12 miles from Manchaca

Camp Ben McCulloch, located on scenic Onion Creek, began life as the annual summer meeting ground for the area's Confederate veterans. Their summer en-campment reunions became popular during the Gay Nineties, and since 1904, the region's Confederate veterans and their descendants have met here annually for a week of feasting and fun. The veterans named their camp for Confederate general Ben McCulloch. McCulloch died at the Battle of Pea Ridge, Arkansas, in 1862. He had earlier fought Indians on the Texas frontier under the com-mand of Captain Jack Coffee Hays, the namesake of Hays County. Many reunion-goers saw their first moving picture, ate their first cotton candy, and stole their first adolescent kisses here. The reunion was one of the few breaks in their isolated rural lifestyle. The reunion still comes off like clockwork each June as the grandchildren and great-grandchildren meet to renew old bonds. Cypress-shaded Onion Creek is very nearly as pleasant a place to take a dip as it was one hundred years ago. Incidentally, the great cypresses that once lined Onion Creek and the nearby Blanco River were a prime reason given by Presi-dent Lamar's 1838 Capitol Commission for locating the new republic's capital at Waterloo. The trees were worth more than the land was back then.

THE SALT LICK

FM 1826, across from Camp Ben McCulloch • 512-255-5638 • www.saltlick bbq.com • Open Wednesday through Sunday, lunch and dinner • No Cr. • W

The Salt Lick, which dates to 1969, is now as much a local institution as Camp Ben McCulloch. Brisket, ribs, and sausage, with traditional side dishes, served family style in a camp dining hall setting, is what draws eaters here. Cofounder Hisako Roberts' Japanese heritage is expressed in the barbecue sauce and the delicious coleslaw, which features toasted sesame seeds. The place can handle groups from thirty to two thousand. It's in a dry precinct, so bring your own beer and wine. The Salt Lick has grown into a little empire and in recent years has put up quite a stretch of rustic-looking cedar "worm" fence.

ANNUAL EVENT

JUNE

UNITED CONFEDERATE VETERANS REUNION

Camp Ben McCulloch • Week of the full moon • Free

The war ended well over a century ago, but descendants of Confederate veterans devote eight days each July to remember those veterans. Programs dedicated to remembering, fellowship, and dancing are the attractions. A carnival usually operates during the reunion, and there is a barbecue and soft drink concession and a cafe. Everything is free except food, carnival activities, and dances. The general public is welcome.

Continue west on FM 1826 from Camp Ben McCulloch. In just over a mile, turn left onto FM 150.

DRIFTWOOD

Hays County • 21 • About 2 miles from Camp Ben McCulloch

Driftwood: the name seems more appropriate for a Gulf Coast town. But keep in mind that millions of years ago this was the Gulf itself. To fully appreciate the name, you will do well to remember the suddenness and severity of flash floods in the region. Most of the year Onion Creek flows placidly along, becoming little more than a string of waterholes during anything approaching a drought. But when the Cen-Tex skies open up and send four or five inches of rain an hour crashing down onto the rocky countryside below, Onion Creek can turn into a rampaging, destructive wall of water. Trees, bridges, stock pens, and even houses can be uprooted by the water's force, landing wherever nature and chance deign. Such was the case in 1886, just when local cotton-gin owner and storekeeper Thomas Martin was attempting to get a post office established for the community that had grown up around his business enterprises. What would the name be? The current name, Liberty Hill, was out of the question. There was already a Williamson County post office with the same name. The men of the neighborhood gathered in front of Martin's house, located on the banks of Onion Creek, to come up with a name.

Inspired by a pile of drift caught up on a flat in front of Martin's house, one of the men suggested "Driftwood." Martin thought the name doubly appropriate, since he had used some driftwood to build his store. He died in 1901, and the new postmaster John Puryear moved his store and post office to the corner of FM 150 and County Road 170; Onion Creek flooded too often and too severely.

The limestone store building that now stands at the crossroads was built in 1915 to replace Puryear's wooden building, which had burned down. Across FM 150 from the store, the simple, white frame church building that houses the Driftwood United Methodist Church dates to 1884. It was built as a Methodist church. In 1911, the local Southern Baptist church building was destroyed, and the Methodist congregation invited the Baptists to share the use of their sanctuary (which they did until just a few years ago). The arrangement worked according to this formula: members of both faiths worshipped together each Sunday, but each denomination maintained its identity. The Methodists conducted services on two Sundays per month, the Baptists led worship the other two Sundays, and they alternated on fifth Sundays. "Union" Sunday school was conducted jointly by teachers of both faiths. Different denominations sharing a church building was a common practice in frontier days, but it is very rare today. The Baptists now have their own church just down the road.

Much like Manchaca, greater Driftwood is being rapidly swallowed up by suburban Austin.

Turn right onto Elderhill Road, next to the Old Driftwood post office and store.

Drivers take heed, for this is quintessential Hill Country roadway: up, down, twisting and turning back on itself, and barely tamed in places, but increasingly dotted with subdivisions and other types of development. Rubberneck at the beautiful countryside, but be prepared to dodge the stray cow or deer that may cross your path, or one of the many cars, trucks, and SUVs that now race along this road. Back in the days when roads were dirt and most folks drove Model Ts, Elder Hill on this road was the place to see exactly what your flivver could do. You'll know Elder Hill when you dip down it into the Gatlin Creek Valley.

Turn left after five miles onto Ranch Road 12, where the driving calms down a bit. Stay on Ranch Road 12 about five miles; then turn right on Jacob's Well Road and proceed 1.6 miles to a stop sign. Turn left and drive for 0.5 miles. Turn right on Pleasant Valley Road and right on Woodacre Drive. Proceed through the condominium complex over the low-water crossing on dry Cypress Creek. Watch for the gate on the right.

JACOB'S WELL NATURAL AREA

Wimberley Valley Watershed Association • PO Box 2534, Wimberley, Texas 78676 • 512-722-3390 • jacobswellspring@gmail.com • Free public tours every Saturday at 10 a.m. (except holidays); rain can cancel a tour • Donations welcome

Jacob's Well has been luring visitors—sometimes to their deaths—since it was first discovered in the 1840s. A natural well opening out of the bed of Cypress Creek, fed by the Edwards Aquifer, it was an important water source for early-day settlers, much like its biblical counterpart. Indeed, its discoverer was supposed to have uttered upon finding the well, "It is like unto a well in biblical times." The importance of Jacob's Well was underscored by the fact that it served as a corner point for four land grants. In more recent times, Jacob's Well has been part of a resort development and a favorite spot for divers, who are drawn to its jewel-like water. No one living knows where the well's narrow passage ultimately leads. Six have died trying to find out. Entrance to the underwater cave has been barred.

As interesting as the well is the man who originally surveyed most of the surrounding miles of countryside, Jacob De Cordova. De Cordova was born in Jamaica in 1808. Merchant, newspaperman, and master of five European languages and several Indian dialects, De Cordova moved to Galveston in 1837. He then moved to Houston and served in the Second Legislature as the Harris County representative. However, he decided that politics was not for him, so he packed up and headed for Austin, where he and his brother Phineas published a semiweekly paper called the *Texas Herald*. De Cordova was also a land collector, having bought over a million acres in land script by 1859. As "Publicity Agent for an Empire," he traveled Europe and the eastern United States lecturing on Texas and its many virtues. In addition, he published a map of Texas and several guidebooks for immigrants. His writings advocating Texas' claims to Rio Grande land at the time of the Compromise of 1850 were said to be vital in securing the $10 million paid to Texas for its claims to the land, territory that was later to make up parts of New Mexico, Colorado, Wyoming, Kansas, and Oklahoma. During the 1860s, De Cordova attempted to develop a power project on the Brazos River in Bosque County in order to establish textile mills and other industries. De Cordova's home east of New Braunfels was appropriately known as Wanderer's Retreat.

In 2010, the Hays County Commissioners Court purchased fifty acres of land adjacent to Jacob's Well that had been slated for high-density development, doubling the size of the Jacob's Well Natural Area and partnering with the Wimberley Valley Watershed Association (WVWA), which had purchased Jacob's Well and forty-six surrounding acres several years earlier in an attempt to preserve it for future generations. Like the other famous springs along the Balcones Fault, Jacob's Well is in danger of drying up permanently; it did so for three months in the summer of 2000 and again briefly in the summer of 2009.

Led by skilled docents, the tour takes you through fragile and highly diverse Hill Country terrain. Wear comfortable shoes and socks and dress appropriately. Some of the trail is shaded, and some is not. There are areas that involve an easy level of climbing, but there is a shorter accessible ADA-compliant walk. The hike takes approximately one hour. A picnic area includes a covered outdoor shelter. You are expected to pack your trash out, as per the practice of "leave nothing but footprints." You are responsible for your children at all times. Please consider their ages before coming to this site with its steep slopes and other natural hazards. You may swim at your own risk. There is no lifeguard. Pets and music players are not allowed.

From Jacob's Well, continue on Jacob's Well Road toward Fischer.

At the nearby Jacobs Well Cemetery, directly across from the entrance to "Wood Creek North," the stones date to the 1880s. It is peaceful and nicely shaded by cedars and live oaks.

Turn right on FM 2325 in another two miles, then left off FM 2325 after 1.5 miles onto the first paved road (Fischer Store Road) to reach Fischer. When the sign says "Keep Right," do so, for it means business as you twist and turn down to the crossing of the Blanco River.

FISCHER

Comal County • 20 • (830) • About 7 miles from the FM 2325/Fischer Store Rd. intersection

Traces of pre-barbed-wire rock fences herald your arrival at Fischer Store. Mr. and Mrs. Herman Fischer Sr. set down here in 1852. Fischer had been a banker in Germany. In 1853, they opened up a "commissary" in one end of their elongated log cabin. In just a few years, Fischer had a sizable freight operation going. Huge wagons, the semis of their day, pulled by five and six yoke of oxen— later by horses and mules—hauled goods to and from Johnson City, Blanco, New Braunfels, and smaller points in between. The post office opened in 1876, and a Fischer has always been postmaster. Herman, the banker-storekeeper, was known as "Store"; his brother Otto, a rancher, was nicknamed "Stock."

FISCHER BOWLING CLUB/NINEPIN BOWLING CLUB

First red frame building on the right as you enter Fischer • Open to the public every Saturday afternoon

Contrary to what you might think, Fischer is alive and kicking most nights of the week as balls roll and pins fly at the Fischer Bowling Club. Contact 935-2971 or 935-4420 for more information.

FISCHER DANCE HALL

Next door to the Fischer Bowling Hall

The bowling hall closes down on dance nights, when the venerable wood floors of the Fischer Dance Hall next door creak beneath the feet of couples two-stepping to the tunes of country bands like the Texas Top Hands. A one-eyed carpenter built the dance hall in 1898. It was used in the filming of Willie Nelson's movie *Honeysuckle Rose*. The Fischer Agricultural Society built and still owns both the dance and bowling halls. First established in the 1880s as a farmers association dedicated to the development and practice of improved farming methods, the Fischer Ag Society is now a recreational organization that anyone may join.

OLD FISCHER STORE AND POST OFFICE

Fischer Store Rd., at FM 484 • Open Thursday through Saturday • 935-4702

The present corrugated tin building was built in 1902 along the same simple, elongated lines as the original log structure. It served as a post office through November 1995, when the post office moved into the building next door. The gas station, which the current post office dislodged, is now located behind the old store building.

The old store is now a combination antique store and museum. The old wood-burning stove still dominates the center of the building. Inside the ancient post office cubicle, you'll see the aged, black-enameled safe still bearing the name "Herman Fischer" in gold gilt letters. Ancient cracker and coffee tins, boxes of locally collected rocks and fossils, barbed wire, and Fischer Store paraphernalia fill the turn-of-the-century shelves and display cases.

Herman Fischer built the house immediately behind the store in 1910. A national champion Lindheimer hackberry tree stood at the northwest corner of the house's yard until it died a few years ago. Hackberries are notorious for their short-livedness, but the local joke is that it died of "lead poisoning" from all the test bullets shot into it over the years by store customers.

The Fischer Haus B&B, a Victorian-era farmhouse built for Herman's son, Max Wilhelm "Willie" Fischer, his Elfrieda, and their eleven children, is set back behind the store to the right of his father's house. Family legend has it that the original log cabin store was torn down because it blocked Elfrieda's view of the countryside.

A little cedar log cabin built by the Dickens family in the days of Fischer Sr. sits in the Y of the road across from the store.

Veer right at the Y and take Crane's Mill Road south at the intersection with FM 32. When you come to a four-way intersection with a stop sign in about four miles, take FM 306 east (left).

CRANE'S MILL

Underneath Canyon Lake

Crane's Mill community now lies at the bottom of Canyon Lake. Crane's Mill once sat smack-dab in the middle of "Charcoal City," which stretched along the Guadalupe River valley from Sisterdale to New Braunfels. Charcoal City owed its beginnings to German settlers like J. B. Crain who fanned out from New Braunfels to tame the region starting in the 1850s. Civilization entailed clearing away the thick forests of Mexican juniper (cedar) and oak from their fields and pastures. When the Germans discovered that there was a market for charcoal—and Mexican juniper makes superb charcoal—they "burned" (made) charcoal during the time between planting and harvest. Once they were established, the German farmers started hiring drifters to help with the burning. The word went out, and by 1880 the rocky hills were filled with burners from as far away as England and Ireland. The charcoal kilns burned the year round, and the Guadalupe valley was almost always bathed in a smoky haze, redolent of burning cedar. In the days before public utilities, many city dwellers in San Antonio and New Braunfels depended on charcoal-burning stoves for cooking and for warmth, stoves that factories like the one in McDade, Texas, turned out by the boxcar load.

J. B. Crain built a mill here soon after he settled down. The name was anglicized to Crane when a post office was established before the Civil War. The community was also known as Engel's Crossing after the war, in honor of teacher and preacher August Engel, who moved here in 1870. He became postmaster of the reestablished post office in 1872. This crossing of the Guadalupe and its accompanying village are not the only communities killed off by Canyon Lake's creation in 1964. Prosperous farming hamlets like Hidden Valley and Mountain Valley have joined Crane's Mill, engulfed eternally (presumably) in the name of flood control.

CANYON LAKE

964-3341 • www.swf-wc.usace.army.mil/canyon • Open daily • Entrance fee

The next few miles along Canyon Lake are pleasant ones, particularly at sunset. Completed in 1964, the 8,230-acre lake is accessed by eight Army Corps of Engineers parks. Facilities are available for boating, fishing, swimming, water-skiing, scuba diving, picnicking, and camping (with fee). Commercial facilities around the lake include motels, restaurants, and marinas. Fishing is good for largemouth, white, and striped bass, and for channel, blue, and flathead catfish.

When you reach Canyon City after 9.5 miles on FM 306, take a right on Canyon Dam Road, just after the Canyon City sign.

The awesome earthen walls of Canyon Dam loom over you to the west, and a chastened Guadalupe River tumbles out of its little window on down toward New Braunfels. You can park on either side of the spillway and walk down the riverbanks for a look at the river.

Canyon Lake is deep, as far as Texas lakes go, and the water released through the dam's bottom gates is from the lowest reaches of the lake, which means that it is very cold—so cold that rainbow and brown trout live year-round in the stretch of river from Canyon Dam to Hueco Springs. They are not native to the river; before the construction of the dam, the habitat of this stretch of the Guadalupe was typical Texas warm-water stream, which is too hot in summer for trout. Now with the lake discharge, summertime temperatures of this stretch of the river seldom exceed eighty degrees, which allows the trout to survive. On the other hand, very few catfish or sunfish now live here; they prefer the warmer water. Trout are stocked in the river every winter by the Texas Parks and Wildlife Department. Trout fishing is year-round, but it is best from November through April.

SATTLER

Comal County • 30 • About 15.5 miles from Fischer

Sattler was founded by William Sattler in 1853, as German immigrants spread out across the Guadalupe River valley. Sattler has also been known as Mountain Valley and Walhalla. Walhalla is an ancient German pre-Christian word for "heaven." Much of Heaven—Walhalla—now lies beneath Canyon Lake. Sattler residents moved uphill when the lake came in.

Continue straight across FM 2673 at Sattler on what becomes River Road and go four miles, veering left at the intersection with Hueco Springs Road, about 1.5 miles past the fourth crossing

of the Guadalupe River by River Road. Less than two miles after this intersection, you come to Loop 337 and the outskirts of New Braunfels.

GUADALUPE RIVER

The emerald waters and powerful rapids of the lower Guadalupe, the sheer cliffs, and almost unnatural (for the region) verdancy of its banks have been magnetizing visitors and inhabitants since the first day the stream was discovered. Texas Indians, the Wacos and Tonkawas in particular, camped along the length of the river, especially at Waco (Hueco) Springs. Ferdinand Lindheimer recorded a meeting with some Tonkawas in 1846:

> There was a Tonkawa Indian Camp on the Guadalupe above New Braunfels which settlers often visited. One day there was a great celebration in the camp. The Tonkawas secretly had killed an Indian and were cooking the flesh. They took great pains to get the idea out of my head that they had killed a man. They said it was the flesh of a Waco Indian whom Americans had killed sometime ago; the flesh was smoked and it stank. . . . However the obscene exhibition of parts of the slain Indian's body distinctly showed that it had to do with fresh and not smoked flesh of mankind.

But the Tonkawas, according to some, were not averse to eating "aged" flesh; they rather prized it. In 1935, Mrs. Augusta Ervendberg Wiegraeffe told a San Antonio reporter,

> They [the Indians] always came with a flag of truce to show that they were friendly. The settlers wanted to show a friendly feeling towards the Indians too and decided to give them a big dinner. There was little in the way of food but the women did their best with the material at hand and were justly proud of what was a real feast for those times. The Indians came. They did not make use of knife, fork, and spoon, altogether they were dirty and disgusting and soon had devoured all the food. Leaving the table the Indians went down to the field to a semi-decomposed carcass of a horse and ate the meat.

Problems of a different sort face inhabitants along the river today. The alternately peaceful and wild beauty of the Guadalupe that so entranced Indians and early settlers continues to entrance river visitors today, as is obvious in the nonstop private and commercial development along the river between Sattler and New Braunfels. On summer days you can hardly see the river itself for all the tubes, rafts, canoes, and variously clad bodies inhabiting them, which form a continuous parade down the river. Somehow the Guadalupe manages to maintain a pristine appearance, if you can overlook the beer cans and related flotsam clogging its shoreline at various points. If you are a serious canoer or kayaker and you want to spend your summertime on the river enjoying it, not dodging all the tubers and rafters, hit the water by seven in the morning, no later than eight on weekends especially. It can be a real madhouse out here, on the river, alongside the river, and on the narrow winding River Road itself.

RIVERBANK OUTFITTERS

6000 River Rd. • Open April through October • 830-625-4928 • www
.guadaluperafting.com • MC, V

Located between the first and second crossings of the river on the River Road,
Riverbank Outfitters rents canoes, rafts, kayaks, and tubes and offers a shuttle
service back to your launch point. River levels and flow can vary, so call ahead
for conditions.

JERRY'S RENTALS

Located at the first crossing, Hueco Falls • 830-625-2036 • www.jerrys
rentals.com • Open daily in season

This long-established outfitter offers rafts, tubes, canoes, guided trips, shuttle
service, camping, showers, and a convenience store.

*When the River Road intersects Loop 337/SH 46, turn right. In slightly over a mile, you turn
left on California Boulevard, which is the second paved left after you pass Oakwood Baptist
Church and the New Braunfels water tower (on your right, on Loop 337).*

NEW BRAUNFELS

Comal County Seat • 50,000 (approximate) • (830) • About 14 miles
from Sattler

New Braunfels owes its name and existence to Prince Carl of Solms-Braunfels,
who as commissioner of the Adelsverein desperately searched for land on
which to settle thousands of German immigrants. The Adelsverein, or Mainzer
Adelsverein, or Verein zum Schutze Deutscher Einwanderer in Texas, or Verein, as it was variously known, was a society composed of ten rich German
noblemen who were interested in overseas colonization for economic and
philanthropic reasons. Through this "Society for the Protection of German
Immigrants in Texas" founded in 1842, these men hoped to make a profit by
settling Germans on land they purchased in Texas, assuming that land values
would go up as the colony tract was developed. They also counted on heavy
trade with their expatriate countrymen. At the same time, the noblemen would
be providing a safe and prosperous future for folk who otherwise would have
faced a bleak future in an overpopulated Germany.

By 1844, the Adelsverein had acquired title to the vast Fisher-Miller tract (located between the Llano and Colorado rivers), or at least thought it had. In reality, all it had was the right to settle the land, ownership of which remained with
the Republic of Texas. The land was extremely isolated and was inhabited by the
unfriendly Comanches. In addition, the soil was generally stony and infertile, the
rainfall meager and unreliable. No one from the Adelsverein (other than scouting
parties) set foot on the land before 1847, as incredible as it may seem. The two

agents sent by the Adelsverein in 1842 to scout for suitable land had not ventured beyond the fertile eastern half of the republic, the characteristics of which they naively attributed to the entire nation in their reports back to Germany.

More than five thousand optimistic Germans arrived at the Gulf Coast port of Carlshafen (Indianola) between the fall of 1845 and April of 1846. The Fisher-Miller Grant was too far away for them to settle immediately, so the colonization had to take place in steps. Prince Carl would have to find a place closer to the coast and civilization to function as a way station. If all of this sounds a little half-baked, it was.

The Adelsverein's offer to prospective immigrants was very attractive, and they had no shortage of applicants. Each single man was to pay $120, and each married man or head of a household $240. Each male applicant also agreed to cultivate at least fifteen acres for three years and to occupy his house for the same period. In return, the Adelsverein promised the immigrants free transportation to the colony; free land in the colony (160 acres for the single man, 320 acres for the family man); a free log house, provisions and all goods necessary to begin farming, supplied on credit until the second successive crop had been harvested; and numerous public improvements, including roads, mills, cotton gins, schools, hospitals, insane asylums, churches, and even the canalization of rivers. The Adelsverein proposed to do all of this with a total capital of roughly $80,000, apparently believing that they would realize great profits by retaining ownership of one half of the colony's land, land that, as has been said, they did not actually own.

Most of the society's funds had already been spent by the time Prince Carl arrived in the summer of 1844. Soon after his arrival in Texas, the prince realized the problems of moving thousands of immigrants from the port of Carlshafen (Indianola) to the Fisher-Miller Grant, a distance of over two hundred miles through untamed wilderness. He immediately began a search for land on which to build a way station for the immigrating colonists. After considering a variety of tracts, he wrote back to Germany telling Adelsverein officials that it would only be possible to establish a settlement on the southwestern edge of the grant during the first year. But there were many beautiful places to choose from between the Guadalupe and San Antonio rivers, Carl continued, and his favorite happened to be a four-league tract at the so-called fountains, located on the Austin-to-San Antonio road. Rich soil, lots of forest timber, water power, and proximity to the major settlements at San Antonio and Seguin were big pluses in its favor. Prince Carl also pointed out that it would be a good headquarters for the colonization projects, owing to its equidistant location from the coast and the upper portion of the Fisher-Miller Grant.

The land of the fountains belonged to the heirs of Juan Martin de Veramendi, a governor of Texas while it was under Mexican rule. During the last years of Spanish rule, the tract had belonged to Felipe Enrique Neri, Baron de Bastrop. In San Antonio, Prince Carl was directed to the Veramendi tract by the Swiss Texan Johann Jacob Rahm, who had fought on the frontier with Jack Hays' Texas Rangers. On Rahm's recommendation, Prince Solms purchased 1,265 acres from the Veramendi family on March 15, 1845, for $1,100, despite the fact that the Veramendi family was battling the heirs of the Baron de Bastrop in court over ownership of the tract. These acres lay on the Comal River, the "fountains" in Solms' report.

New Braunfels was founded on Good Friday, March 21, 1845, and named for Prince Carl's hometown of Braunfels. The town was founded on its present site on an omen. Prince Solms had been looking at several other sites on the Medina, San Antonio, and several other rivers in Central Texas. The prince wrote:

> I myself with a troop of twenty-five men proceeded inland to find a place suitable for a town and to make the necessary preparations and investigations, especially as to whether or not there were hostile Indians in that region. It was on such an excursion that I found snow on my tent one morning, which, though it could be rolled in the hand, by noon had melted. Taking this as a good omen, we established our German colony here to which I gave the name New Braunfels.

In gratitude for Johann Jacob Rahm's help in purchasing the Veramendi tract, Prince Solms appointed Rahm official butcher of the German Emigration Company and on May 14, 1845, gave him 4.5 acres of the tract on which to build the Rahm's Butchery. Later that year, on October 12, Rahm was shot dead by a man named Maertz from Wiesbaden. During a dispute between the two, Rahm fired his pistol at Maertz, who then pumped two rifle bullets into him.

COMAL RIVER

This 3.25-mile-long stream is the shortest river in the United States, and the springs feeding it were once among the four biggest in Texas. Now they are rivaled only by Aquarena Springs, the springs that feed the San Marcos River at San Marcos.

In olden times, Tonkawas, Wacos, Lipan Apaches, Karankawas, and other Indians camped near the springs. Spanish explorer Damián Massanet found a large group of Indians there when he passed through in 1691. Some early Spanish explorers mistakenly referred to the Comal River as the Guadalupe, and it was called the Guadalupe as late as 1727, but after Pedro de Rivera y Villalón identified the longer stream as the Guadalupe, the shorter was given the name Comal, Spanish for "flat dish."

Father Isidro Félix de Espinosa's diary during the 1716 Domingo Ramon expedition described the Comal springs:

> Soon we reached the passage of the Guadalupe which is made of gravel and is very wide. Groves of inexpressible beauty are found in this vicinity. We stopped at the other bank of the river in a little clearing surrounded by trees, and contiguous to said river. The waters of the Guadalupe are clear, crystal and so abundant that it seemed almost incredible to us that its source arose so near. Composing this river are three principal springs of water which, together with other smaller ones, unite as soon as they begin to flow. There the growth of walnut trees competes with the poplars. All are crowned by the wild grapevines, which climb their trunks. They gave promise already in their blossom for the good prospect of their fruit. The white and black mulberry trees, whose leaves were more than eight inches in length, showed in their sprouts how sharp were the frosts. Willow trees beautified the region of this river with their luxuriant foliage and there was a great variety of plants. It makes a delightful grove for recreation, and the enjoyment of the melodious songs of different birds. Ticks molested us, attaching themselves to our skin.

Despite the spring's beauty, the Spanish showed little interest in settling the area. The only recorded effort was San Francisco Xavier on the Guadalupe River, an unofficial, short-lived mission located at the site of present-day New

Braunfels. It was founded in late 1756 by Father Mariano Francisco de los Dolores y Viana, who had been the guiding force behind the defunct San Xavier missions on the San Xavier (San Gabriel) River near the site of modern Rockdale. In late January 1757, four Spanish families were living in jacals, and forty-one Indians were receiving religious instruction. Father Dolores sought to include the new San Xavier under the umbrella of Pedro Romero de Terreros' generous support for new missions in Apachería, or Apache territory. But the Guadalupe site, only forty-five miles from San Antonio, was outside the proposed mission field, which lay farther north near the present-day town of San Saba. Its exclusion created bitter feelings between fathers Dolores and Alonso Giraldo de Terreros, fellow missionary and cousin of the wealthy Don Pedro Romero. The mission was abandoned in March 1758, after the Comanches destroyed Santa Cruz de San Saba Mission, because Spanish authorities feared that the Comanches and their allies would next attack the unprotected San Francisco Xavier.

Early writer on Texas and geologist Dr. Ferdinand Roemer visited the Comal Springs with Ferdinand Lindheimer in 1846 or 1847 and wrote of his impressions:

We had to cross Comal Creek to get there . . . we came to a small, but extremely fertile plain on which dense patches of forests alternated charmingly with small enclosed prairies. A road made by the settlers for hauling the cedar trunks used in building their homes was the only sign of human activity. . . . We suddenly heard near us the murmuring of rapidly flowing water, and a few moments later stood at the most beautiful spring I had ever beheld. The natural basin, about forty feet wide, was of incomparable clearness and on its bottom, aquatic plants of an emerald green color formed a carpet. Low shrubs of the palmetto, which I had learned to know at a less attractive place, namely in the dismal swamps of New Orleans, lined the banks. An old live oak, decorated with long festoons of grey Spanish moss, spread its gnarled limbs over the basin. This however is not the only spring of the Comal; four or six more springs of even greater volume of even clearness, every one of them could turn a mill at its immediate source, all unite and form the Comal, which, unlike other streams, does not experience a gradual growth, but is born a sizeable stream.

Rutherford B. Hayes, who would become the nineteenth president of the United States, made a horseback trip through Texas in 1848–1849. He was impressed by New Braunfels: "Those fair-headed Teutons have built in a short three years the most prosperous, singular and interesting town in Texas. This is a German village of two or three thousand people at the junction of two of the most beautiful streams I ever saw, the Guadalupe and Comal. . . . The water is so transparent the fish seem hanging in the air."

In 1850, New Braunfels was the fourth largest city in Texas, behind San Antonio, Galveston, and Houston.

California takes you right into Landa Park, onto Landa Park Drive, across the Comal's headwaters.

LANDA PARK

Landa Park Dr., near downtown • 221-4370 • www.nbtexas.org • Open daily • Fees for picnic tables • W variable

Although the Comal's springs do not flow quite so forcefully these days, the river is still very nearly as beautiful today as it was in Roemer's time, as a stroll through Landa Park will reveal.

Landa Park is named for early New Braunfels industrialist Joseph Landa (1811–1896). Landa emigrated to Texas from Prussia, but unlike most of the other early settlers of New Braunfels, Landa was Jewish. His parents had wanted him to become a rabbi, so he ran away, first to England, and then to the United States. Landa came to San Antonio in 1844 and opened a store. But he didn't feel at home in San Antonio, so he moved to New Braunfels. He met and married Helena Friedlander during a trip to New York in 1851. In 1859, he bought the Comal Springs and surrounding land from William Merriwether, who had purchased the 480-acre Comal Spring Tract in 1847 from Maria Antonia de Veramendi Garza and her husband, Rafael Garza, and built a gristmill, sawmill, and cotton gin, all powered by the Comal's rushing waters. Landa greatly expanded this little industrial complex, eventually adding a grain elevator, electric plant, cotton-oil mill, and ice manufacturing plant. The river also provided the power for the town's woolen mills beginning in the 1870s, the start of a fabrics industry that would power the town's economy for well over one hundred years.

By 1862, the Landas had seven children and owned several slaves (which was a rarity among Texas Jews). Landa volunteered to serve in the Confederate military but was rejected because of a disability. When the Landas learned of the Emancipation Proclamation of 1863, they freed their slaves. The Knights of the Golden Circle, a secret antebellum organization that sought to establish a slave empire encompassing the southern United States, the West Indies, Mexico, and part of Central America, tried Joseph Landa in what amounted to a kangaroo court, convicted him of being an abolitionist, and ordered him to immediately leave the Confederacy or be hanged. So Landa fled to Mexico, leaving Helena in charge of the family and their businesses. She was nobody's patsy. One day, when an armed gang entered the Landas' store and demanded clothing and tobacco, she leveled a revolver at the men and threatened to kill the first man who touched anything. They left empty-handed.

During the Civil War, New Braunfels had a saltpeter-extract plant located in what is now Landa Park. It produced one hundred pounds of crystal saltpeter daily from bat guano gathered from nearby Cibolo Cave. The saltpeter was used to make gunpowder.

Joseph returned soon after the war's end and resumed building the family empire. The Landas lived their faith as best they could, despite being the only Jewish family in New Braunfels for many years. They usually worshipped at home, occasionally going by carriage into San Antonio to worship at Temple Beth-El. Son Harry Landa described the family's Seder observances, noting that the women first spent several weeks baking the matzoth, or unleavened bread. Several barrels of flour (at 196 pounds each) were necessary to make enough matzoth to satisfy the needs of fifteen family members and servants, in addition to their friends. Mrs. Landa also made sweet raisin wine. Joseph Landa led the Passover Eve ceremony, in English and Hebrew.

After the war, the gristmill grew and grew into the Landa Roller Flour Mill and Elevator, with a capacity of three thousand barrels of flour per week; the elevator could handle one hundred thousand bushels of grain.

By the 1890s "Landa's Pasture," as the present parkland was then popularly called, was a favored local picnic and festival ground. In 1897 (so the story goes), Helen Gould, daughter of I&GN railway magnate and robber baron Jay Gould, visited New Braunfels and was so impressed by the beauty of

Comal Springs and Landa's Pasture that she suggested the I&GN lay a spur line into the pasture. The railroad needed a recreation ground along the line, and Landa's Pasture was just the ticket. As soon as the Missouri-Kansas-Texas railroad reached New Braunfels, they also laid tracks into the park. In the days before the automobile, special excursion trains ran from as far away as Austin, and thousands of happy revelers filled the park on weekends. The Wurstfest complex is located here too.

A miniature train runs through the fifty-one-acre park. The Landa Park Aquatic Complex (350 Aquatic Circle, 221-4360, open Memorial Day through Labor Day, variable hours) houses three pools in one facility: a 1.5 million gallon spring-fed pool, a zero-depth pool, and the Bud Dallmann Olympic Pool for your fun in the water. The Comal Springs feeds the spring-fed pool and stays a constant seventy-two degrees year-round. The spring-fed pool has features such as the patented Wet Willie Slide, a rope swing, a zip line, and a zero-depth water play area with a mushroom waterfall.

The City Tube Chute (100 Leibscher Drive, 608-2165, open Memorial Day through Labor Day, variable hours) is located on the Comal River and is the longest tube chute in the world. The City Tube Chute offers family water fun, picnic areas, showers, dressing rooms, lockers, tube rentals, and personal flotation devices (PFDs). You can take a paddleboat ride on Landa Lake and see the Comal Springs.

The Panther Canyon Nature Trail is an excellent example of one of the faults in the Edwards limestone. The gently sloping pedestrian trail leads visitors approximately eight-tenths of a mile and back through the Balcones Escarpment. Hikers should allow at least one and a half hours for the hike. The William and Dolores Schumann Arboretum walking tour features over fifty species of trees. Guides for both trails are available at the Parks Department Office, on the corner of Landa Park Drive and Golf Course Road. During the summer, free Thursday night concerts are given on the park's dance slab.

The tranquil beauty of the Comal River is now overshadowed by the Schlitterbahn Waterpark, one of the country's most popular water parks. The river flows alongside Schlitterbahn, and the river's cool water is circulated through some of the park's rides. Some of the rides take riders into the Comal. In 1991, Schlitterbahn acquired venerable Camp Warnecke and in 1996 opened Blastenhoff and Surfenburg there, with Boogie Bahn surfing and uphill water coasters. You can stay overnight at the Resort at the Bahn (adjacent to the water park's main section) or at the Resort at the Rapids (next to Surfenburg). Call 830-625-2351; write to 305 W. Austin, New Braunfels 78130; or check out the website at www.schlitterbahn.com.

Continue through Landa Park on California, past the Wurstfest grounds and the prominent brown-brick ex-municipal power plant. California dead-ends into Landa Street (SH 46). Turn left on Landa, which soon becomes Seguin Street and takes you to New Braunfels' Main Plaza and the Comal County courthouse.

COMAL COUNTY COURTHOUSE

Seguin at San Antonio

The Victorian Gothic courthouse was built in 1898. The first session of the county court was held in 1846 in a room in the residence of Conrad Seabaugh, county clerk, which was located across the plaza from the current courthouse. The court continued to meet for several years in Seabaugh's room, paying him two or three dollars per month rent, until the county purchased its own property.

Visitors will find interesting old buildings scattered throughout New Braunfels, but the greatest concentration of vintage commercial buildings is in a two-block stretch of W. San Antonio Street (from the Main Plaza west to Hill Street and the railroad tracks). Most are two-story brick, really undistinguished, and simply styled, although much of the brickwork is expertly executed. New Braunfels was such a prosperous town during the first quarter of this century that many of the older, Victorian-era commercial buildings were torn down in favor of the buildings you see today. But a few pre-1900 commercial structures remain.

OLD GUADALUPE HOTEL

471 Main Plaza

New Braunfels' first hotel was the two-story Guadalupe Hotel, built in 1853 by Rudolph Nauendorf on a lot he purchased from J. J. von Coll. Jacob Schmitz bought the property in 1858, renamed it the Schmitz Hotel, and in 1873 added the third floor and balconies. Frederick Law Olmsted described New Braunfels and his pleasant stay at the Guadalupe Hotel during his visit to Texas in 1854:

> The main street of the town was very wide—three times as wide, in effect, as Broadway in New York. The houses, with which it was thickly lined on each side for a mile, were small, low cottages, of no pretensions to elegance, yet generally looking neat and comfortable. Many were furnished with verandahs and gardens, and the greater part were either stuccoed or painted. There were many workshops of mechanics and small stores, with signs oftener in English than in German; and bare-headed women, and men in caps and short jackets, with pendent pipes, were everywhere seen at work.
>
> We had no acquaintance in the village, and no means of introduction, but, in hopes that we might better satisfy ourselves of the condition of the people, we agreed to stop at an inn and get dinner, instead of eating a cold snack in the saddle, without stopping at noon, as was our custom. "Here," said the butcher, "is my shop—indicating a small house, at the door of which hung dressed meat and beef sausages—and if you are going to stop, I will recommend you to my neighbor, there, Mr. Schmitz." It was a small cottage of a single story, having the roof extended so as to form a verandah, with a sign swinging before it, "Guadalupe Hotel, J. Schmitz."
>
> I never in my life, except, perhaps, in awakening from a dream, met with such a sudden and complete transfer of associations. Instead of loose boarded or hewn log walls, with crevices stuffed with rags or daubed with mortar, which we have been accustomed to see during the last month, on staving in a door, where we have found any to open; instead, even, of four bare, cheerless sides of whitewashed plaster, which we have found twice or thrice only in a more aristocratic American residence, we were—in short, we were in Germany. There was nothing wanting; there was nothing too much, for one of those delightful little inns which the pedestrian who has tramped through the Rhine land will ever remember gratefully. A long room, extending across the whole front of the cottage, the walls pink, with stenciled panels, and scroll ornaments in crimson, and with neatly-framed and glazed pretty lithographic prints hanging on all sides; a long, thick, dark oak table, with rounded ends, oak benches at its sides; chiseled oak chairs; a sofa, covered with cheap pink calico, with a small vine pattern; a stove in the corner; a little

mahogany cupboard in another corner, with pitcher and glasses upon it; a smoky atmosphere; and finally, four thick-bearded men, from whom the smoke proceeds, who all bow and say "Good morning," as we lift our hats in the doorway.

The landlady enters; she does not readily understand us, and one of the smokers rises immediately to assist us. Dinner we shall have immediately, and she spreads the white cloth at an end of the table, before she leaves the room, and in two minutes' time, by which we have got off our coats and warmed our hands at the stove, we are asked to sit down. An excellent soup is set before us, and in succession there follow two courses of meat, neither of them pork, and neither of them fried, two dishes of vegetables; salad, compote of peaches, coffee with milk, wheat bread from the loaf, and beautiful and sweet butter—not only such butter as I have never tasted south of the Potomac before, but such as I have been told a hundred times it was impossible to make in a southern climate. We then spent an hour in conversation with the gentlemen who were in the room. They were all educated, cultivated, well-bred, respectful, kind, and affable men. All were natives of Germany, and had been living several years in Texas. Some of them were travelers, their homes being in other German settlements; some of them had resided at Braunfels.

The account they gave of the Germans in Texas was so interesting, and gratifying, that we were unwilling to immediately continue our journey. We went out to look at our horses; a man in cap and jacket was rubbing their legs—the first time they had received such attention in Texas, except from ourselves, or by special and costly arrangement with a negro. They were pushing their noses into racks filled with fine mesquit hay—the first they had had in Texas. They seemed to look at us imploringly. We ought to spend the night. But there is evidently no sleeping-room for us in the little inn. They must be full. But then we could sleep with more comfort on the floor here, probably, than we have been accustomed to of late. We concluded to ask if they could accommodate us for the night. Yes, with pleasure—would we be pleased to look at the room they could afford us? Doubtless in the cock-loft.

No, it was in another little cottage in the rear. A little room it proved, with blue walls again, and two beds, one of them would be for each of us—the first time we had been offered the luxury of sleeping alone in Texas; two large windows with curtains, and evergreen roses trained over them on the outside—not a pane of glass missing or broken—the first sleeping-room we have had in Texas where this was the case; a sofa; a bureau, on which were a complete set of the *Conversations Lexicon*; Kendall's Santa Fe Expedition; a statuette in porcelain; plants in pots; a brass study; a large pitcher and basin for washing, and a couple of towels of thick stuff full a yard and a quarter long.

At supper, we met a dozen or more intelligent people, and spent the later evening, with several others, at the residence of one of our accidental inn acquaintances. As I was returning to the inn, about ten o'clock, I stopped for a few moments at the gate of one of the little cottages, to listen to some of the best singing I have heard for a long time, several parts being sustained by very sweet and well-trained voices.

In the day time, I saw in the public street, at no great distance from a schoolhouse, a tame doe, with a band on its neck, to distinguish it from the wild deer, lest it should be shot by sportsmen. It was exceedingly beautiful, and so tame that it allowed me to approach, and licked my hand. In what Texan town, through which we have passed before, could this have occurred.

In the morning we found that our horses had been bedded, for the first time in Texas. As we rode out of town, it was delightful to meet again troops of children, with satchels and knapsacks of books, and little kettles of dinner, all with ruddy, cheerful faces, the girls especially so, with their hair braided neatly, and without caps or bonnets, smiling and saluting us—"*guten morgen*"—as we met.

HENNE HARDWARE COMPANY

246 W. San Antonio • 606-6707 • hennehardware.com • Open daily

Henne's cast-metal cornice is about as exuberantly Victorian as the downtown skyline gets. Louis Henne built this store in 1893, and certain newer inventory aside, the store still looks much the same inside as it did back then. An especially nice touch is the pair of "Louis Henne Co." stained-glass transom windows above the front doors. Henne's, in business since 1857, claims to be Texas' oldest hardware store.

OLD FIRST NATIONAL BANK BUILDING

278 W. San Antonio • Private offices

The First National Bank opened for business in September 1894. The bank's owners had budgeted $8,000 for its construction; the contractor built it for $13 under that budget. There was one attempted robbery in 1922. One bandit was killed, another wounded, and the third got away. The First National Bank moved over to the Main Plaza in 1931, and the building housed a variety of businesses before the current owners renovated it in 1982. Years of dull paint were removed, revealing the original bright-red-brick facade with carved white limestone accents. The original brick bank vault is still inside.

BRAUNTEX THEATRE

290 W. San Antonio • 627-0808 • brauntext.org

Neon and Art Moderne fans will appreciate the Brauntex's late 1930s sign and stucco-tile exterior. Touring shows and musical acts.

RAILROAD MUSEUM

302 W. San Antonio at the railroad tracks • 627-2447 • www.newbraunfels railroadmuseum.org • Thursday through Monday • Donations

The old 1907 train depot now houses the local Railroad Museum, which features displays of local railroad history and model railroad layouts. The museum's crown jewels are a 1942 0-6-0 Porter oil-fired steam locomotive and a 1950 MoPac caboose.

Getting the Galveston, Harrisburg, and San Antonio (GH&SA) Railway Company (which would eventually become the Southern Pacific Sunset Route) to run through New Braunfels and establish a station here on its way to San Antonio was a high priority for the town's citizens, so much so that the *Austin Democratic Statesman* snidely observed on November 17, 1876: "New Braunfels people must be stupendous asses when they pay $90,000 to induce Pierce [Thomas Wentworth Peirce—ed.] to build his road through their farms and yards and gardens. And the Hon. John Ireland sues the company for damages because it contracts its highway through his estate. But those Germans don't know how they will be ruined by the road and the judge does."

Major James Converse, construction engineer, had promised that a depot would be established within a half mile of the courthouse if he could get the requisite twenty acres of land. A number of prominent citizens, minus Ireland, had promised to give free right-of-way over their land. Despite the considerable inducements, the GH&SA line bypassed New Braunfels in favor of a more southerly approach into San Antonio from Luling via Kingsbury, Seguin, and Marion. New Braunfels would finally get its railroad in 1880, when the International and Great Northern passed through on its way from Austin to San Antonio.

NEW BRAUNFELS FIRE MUSEUM

Inside Fire Station No. 1, 100 block of S. Hill • Tours given when station is open

New Braunfels' fire department was founded in 1886 and is said to be the fourth oldest in the state. The museum displays firefighting equipment, tools, gear, and pictures that date to the department's founding.

FAUST HOUSE

361 W. San Antonio • Private offices

Just across the railroad tracks is the Faust House, built in 1905 by prominent local businessman John Faust, son of one of New Braunfels' first families. Besides its leaded-glass doors and stained-glass windows selected in Italy, the house was also acclaimed for its modern heating system, a steam boiler in the basement with floor radiators throughout the four-thousand-square-foot house. Those original doors and windows as well as the many elaborate light fixtures are still part of the house. Another treat is the inlaid parquet wood floor in the foyer along with the rest of the house's woodwork, which is mostly pine and is now free of its original dark stain. The carriage house out back has also been renovated.

FIRST PROTESTANT CHURCH (CHURCH OF CHRIST)

296 S. Seguin

Two blocks south of the Main Plaza, this simple Gothic church of ashlar-dressed limestone blocks was built in 1875. A log church was first built on this site in 1846. Its first pastor was the Reverend Louis Cachand-Ervendburg, who was appointed minister to the town's founding settlers by Prince Solms before they left the base camp at Lavaca Bay.

CHAMBER OF COMMERCE

390 S. Seguin • 800-572-2626 • www.nbcham.org • Open daily • W

The chamber of commerce has compiled a walking tour of historic New Braunfels. Most of the buildings on the tour are pre-1880. The *New Braunfels Herald-Zeitung* also publishes a free seasonal visitor's guide, which contains a historic-building tour and a schedule of events. You can pick up a copy at many local businesses and museums, as well as at the chamber. The chamber is located at the Civic Center, two blocks south of the square, at S. Seguin and Garden.

From the Main Plaza, go south on Seguin (SH 46) to Coll. Turn right onto Coll and go across the railroad tracks to Academy to get to the Sophienburg Museum.

SOPHIENBURG MUSEUM

401 W. Coll at Academy • 629-1572 • www.sophienburg.com • Monday through Saturday 10–4, Sunday 1–4 • Fee • W

The Sophienburg Museum is built on the hilltop site of Prince Carl's envisioned Fort Sophia (Sophienburg), which was to have been constructed for the protection of New Braunfels. The prince had a log cottage built here during the spring of 1845, and he lived here for a short time in grand style, raising the Austrian flag (there was no German flag) every morning and receiving guests in the full uniform of a Prussian army officer. The cottage, New Braunfels' first seat of government, was destroyed by the great hurricane of 1886, the same storm that wiped out Indianola (Carlshafen), the port of entry that the prince had established for the Adelsverein émigrés. Sophia was the name of Prince Carl's fiancée, and the prince returned to Germany in May 1845. By running home, Prince Carl missed the widespread sickness and pestilence that nearly destroyed the colony during the first two years following his departure. He left the Adelsverein's accounts hopelessly entangled and the coffers empty.

Because the Adelsverein was already heavily in debt, the five-thousand-plus Germans arriving at Carlshafen between the fall of 1845 and April of 1846 found themselves without adequate shelter and supplies. Furthermore, the recently erupted war between the United States and Mexico led to shortages of teamsters who could haul the colonists inland. The army was paying better wages than the Adelsverein. For six months, the immigrants had to camp on the cold, rainy, mosquito-infested beaches of Carlshafen, drinking bad water and eating little more than green beef. Small wonder then that hundreds died on the beach, and that in desperation hundreds more attempted to walk the distance to New Braunfels. Some went only as far as Victoria, Goliad, and Gonzales before giving up on their original dreams and settling down to make the best of it in these Coastal Plains towns. Many died along the way, and those who managed to reach New Braunfels brought disease with them. The first batch of colonists, who had come in the spring and summer of 1845 and therefore had missed the initial miseries of their compatriots, were now struck by the newly arrived pestilences. Between eight hundred and three thousand died; two or three expired each day in the little town. Prince Solms' successor, John O. Meusebach, did his best to whip the tottering finances of the colony into shape, but of the thirty-four thousand gulden sent him in 1845, all but a few hundred were spent paying off previous debts. He went everywhere to borrow money—unsuccessfully—hounded at every step by creditors, while society immigrants stacked up steadily at Carlshafen. Disheartened by the incompetence of Adelsverein officials in Germany and the deplorable conditions here in the

New World, Meusebach resigned his position in July 1847. The Adelsverein went bankrupt that same year.

Hermann Seele—an early New Braunfels farmer, lawyer, teacher, lay minister, mayor, state representative, Confederate major, and newspaper editor—wrote of the suffering he saw here during those miserable months of 1846:

> Every campsite between here and the coast and Indianola—and there were many, since the weather and roads, as well as the oxcarts, caused the overland journey to be filled with delays and to last many weeks—was marked with graves, ghastly milestones on the way that the German colonists of West Texas had to traverse. . . . I hurried through the forest camp, that upon closer inspection, held only too many sad scenes of sickness and death, in order to return to the ferry. As I passed a large tent, I heard a cry of distress.
>
> "Isn't there anyone here who will help us?" Looking into the tent, I caught sight of a family of nine persons bedded on the ground, moaning and groaning.
>
> I asked for pails, with which I brought up fresh water from the river. When I gave it to them, they drank greedily to still their burning thirsts, even though the water was neither clear nor cool.

Later that day, upon returning home, Seele fell into a fit of melancholia, to be aroused from it

> by the shouts of the children of a man who, with other immigrants, had set up camp on our land. He wanted to see me. He too lay sick of dysentery and dropsy and like others, suffered even more from homesickness. I went with the children to his bedside. With excitement and joy, the man extended his emaciated hand to me. His cheeks were lightly flushed, and his eyes were unnaturally bright. He wanted to let me know that he no longer suffered any pain, that he felt better and would soon be able to return to his beloved homeland with his family. Full of hope and joy, the wife and children listened to the father's words. From the recent, sad experience at the deathbed, I saw his end approaching. I hid my thoughts and spoke a few words of encouragement and sympathy. At home, however, I told my friends, "We must get up early tomorrow in order to dig another grave."
>
> Before sunrise the next morning, the sick man had quietly passed away. We dug his grave in the field and gently laid him to rest. Then we quietly said the Lord's Prayer for the dead man and his family.

What, exactly, did these poor unfortunates die of? Cholera was blamed by some. But others diagnosed the disease as scurvy of the mouth accompanied by dysentery. In the summer and fall of 1846, the terrible epidemic that had taken so many lives in Carlshafen and New Braunfels spread to Fredericksburg, where probably 100 to 150 persons succumbed to it. But not everyone who contracted the disease died from it.

William Hermes Sr., who came to Texas in 1846 and subsequently became a doctor, said in his later years that the colony's physician, a Dr. Schubert, had misdiagnosed the disease as scurvy of the mouth accompanied by dysentery and prescribed a remedy (eating lots of wild purslane, also called portulaca) that probably increased the number of deaths. Hermes came down with the malady and said that when he was studying medicine, he found the symptoms described in Schoenlein's *Pathology and Therapeutics*. Hermes claimed that the epidemic was caused by a disease then called petechial fever, or *Blutfleckenkrankheit*, as he called it in German (the word *petechia* means a small spot on the skin or mucous membrane caused by a minute hemorrhage and often seen in typhus). He noted that the warmer the weather became, the more the disease spread. The disease was marked by a very severe fever, caused by an extravasation of blood into surrounding tissues after a rupture of the vessels appeared on the body. Petechial fever is now more commonly known as cerebrospinal meningitis, an acute and often fatal infectious epidemic meningitis. Hermes believed that many of the afflicted would have survived had they been fed a diet of healthy, nutritious food, including fresh meat.

Dr. Schubert had been recommended to Meusebach in the spring of 1846 in Houston by Henry Fisher as a good doctor. Meusebach appointed him director of the settlement at Fredericksburg. He proved to be a very unsatisfactory director, in addition to his shortcomings as a doctor, and was disliked by a majority of the settlers. Late in 1846, without Meusebach's approval, Schubert assembled a company of men to go into the Fisher-Miller Grant. But he declined to cross the Llano River and returned to Fredericksburg, telling Meusebach that it was impossible to enter the granted lands because of hostile Indians. One of the last things Meusebach did before resigning as Adelsverein commissioner was to fire Schubert. Schubert then headed for Nassau Farm, which he had leased. Herman Spiess, who replaced Meusebach as commissioner general, later tried to oust Schubert from Nassau Farm, and in the process, a man named Rohrdorf was killed. Spiess and his men were brought to trial but were acquitted.

In 1886, New Braunfels was hit by the great hurricane that destroyed Indianola (Carlshafen). Gusts here reached eighty-five miles an hour, and several structures were destroyed. Others suffered major damage.

The Sophienburg Museum, which chronicles these difficult years and the happier ones that followed, is full of old New Braunfels memorabilia, tidily arranged, and is staffed by enthusiastic docents.

Two blocks west of the Sophienburg Museum is the von Coll House (at 624 W. Coll Street).

Jean Jacques von Coll, first lieutenant retired of the Duchy of Nassau, was the Fisher-Miller Grant's financial officer and led the first settlers to the Comal Tract in 1845. A year later, Meusebach sent von Coll to Fredericksburg to straighten out the mess caused by Schubert. After returning to New Braunfels, he was elected mayor, only to be killed shortly thereafter by an irate colonist who claimed that the Colonization Society had shortchanged him.

On New Year's Eve morning, 1846, placards were posted all over town that asked the populace to march on Meusebach's home and demand that he immediately fulfill the promises made to the colonists. A mob of about 150 persons armed with clubs and firearms gathered at the Sophienburg and sent a deputation to call on Meusebach. When the matter was not immediately resolved, the group crowded into Meusebach's home and uttered threats against Meusebach's life as the negotiations were carried on in an adjoining room. H. Fisher, who had arrived from Houston a few days before, and from whom the Verein "bought" the land, led the negotiations on behalf of the disgruntled colonists. After several hours of deliberation, the two sides came to an agreement wherein all immigrants would immediately receive deeds to the 160 or 320 acres promised in the grant. Fisher was charged with safeguarding the colonists' interests in drawing up the deeds. The surveying for these deeds would take place without delay, again with Fisher taking care of the colonists' interests. Meusebach was to resign his office but carry out its functions until his successor arrived.

When the results of the negotiations were announced, the mob cheered lustily and went home to celebrate. And two weeks thereafter, a surveying expedition left New Braunfels for Fredericksburg, where it would re-provision for the trip into the Fisher-Miller Grant proper, which neither Fisher nor Miller had ever seen.

To get to the Lindheimer Museum, take Seguin (SH 46) south from the Main Plaza, turn left on Garden, then right on Comal.

In case you can't find a copy of the seasonal visitor's guide or the chamber of commerce tour map, here's a simplified version of the route that will take you by most of the interesting old homes and buildings. It is about two miles long and can be walked or driven.

From the Lindheimer Museum, proceed up Comal (toward the courthouse) five blocks to the old Market Square. Go right at Market Square one block to Market Avenue. Turn left on Market, cross San Antonio, and turn left on Mill. Continue on Mill to Academy (four blocks). Turn left on Academy, go one block, and then turn left on San Antonio. After a short block on San Antonio, turn right onto Hill, which runs along the railroad tracks. Turn left onto Coll, cross the tracks, and turn right on Castell one block later. After three blocks on Castell, turn left on Jahn, follow its dogleg across Seguin, and turn left on Comal to complete the tour.

LINDHEIMER HOUSE

491 Comal • 629-2943 • nbconservation.org • Tours by appointment • Fee • W with assistance

Born and educated in Germany, Lindheimer left his homeland in 1834 as a result of his revolutionary political beliefs: the advocation of representative government and unification of the separate German states. Upon his arrival in the United States, Lindheimer wandered through a variety of occupations and latitudes. He volunteered for service in the Texas Republican Army after being shipwrecked in Mobile, Alabama, but the company of volunteers he joined arrived in Texas a day after the victory at San Jacinto. Prince Carl hired Lindheimer as a guide for the Adelsverein's immigrants. He led the first group of colonists to their raw new settlement at New Braunfels.

For his services, Lindheimer was deeded land on the Comal River, where he built a little cabin. Lindheimer collected much of the native Texas flora for Northern botanists, and he used the cabin as a base for his botanical explorations into the Texas wilderness. Over one hundred species or subspecies of Texas flora have borne his name in their botanical titles.

Lindheimer was one of the few white men the fierce Comanches regarded as a friend. The great Comanche war chief Santanta visited Lindheimer at his home on several occasions.

Lindheimer's intensive botany studies came to an end in 1852 when he became editor of the town's German-language newspaper. He built this house that year and published the *Neu-Braunfelser Zeitung* for twenty years. Lindheimer had a strong passion for freedom, truth, and right, and his views often brought him threats and abuse, especially during the Civil War. Although antislavery and pro-Union, he urged his readers to be loyal to their new country. To do otherwise would have been insane; Unionists elsewhere in the region were massacred for their beliefs. Lindheimer died here in 1879.

His home, now a museum, has been restored to look much as it did during his lifetime, a typical German fachwerk dwelling. Fachwerk (half-timbering) is an ancient construction technique employing wall frames made of studs and braces, with rocks or brick filling in the spaces between the squared timbers. Lindheimer's home was built from native cedar and limestone. The house is full of fine period furniture, much of it Lindheimer's. Some of the pieces were crafted by master cabinetmaker Johann Jahn. More examples of Jahn's work can be seen at the Museum of Texas Handmade Furniture.

To get to Conservation Square and the Museum of Texas Handmade Furniture, take S. Seguin (SH 46) south to its junction with Business US 81. Continue on Highway 46/81 to the intersection with Loop 337. Turn left onto Loop 337. In just a few yards, you will see signs for both Conservation Plaza and the Museum of Texas Handmade Furniture.

Turn right on Church Hill Drive and follow the signs a short distance until you reach the plaza and museum.

CONSERVATION PLAZA

Church Hill Dr. • **629-2943** • **www.nbconservation.org** • **Open Tuesday through Sunday** • **Fee**

Created and maintained by the New Braunfels Conservation Society, Conservation Plaza is a collection of early New Braunfels buildings (1849–1881) moved here in recent years. The crown jewel is the Baetge house, built in 1852 by Carl Baetge and originally located on the Demijohn Bend of the Guadalupe River near Sattler. Carl Baetge came to New Braunfels in 1850 with his wife Pauline, whom he met in Russia. A civil engineer, Baetge had been commissioned by the czar in the early 1840s to build a railroad linking the Winter Palace in St. Petersburg to the Summer Palace in Moscow, a distance of 420 miles. Pauline was a member of the Czarina's Court, and they were married upon completion of the railroad in 1846.

The Baetge house was faced with obliteration with the formation of Canyon Lake, so it was dismantled and later reassembled here. The house is of fachwerk construction, cedar timbers with homemade brick. This was plastered over inside and covered outside with cypress siding. The second story is unfinished inside, the better for the visitor to appreciate the handwork of construction. Some of the furnishings downstairs are original to the house, and many were made by hand in and around New Braunfels. Some of the drawings that Baetge made for the czar's railroad are on display upstairs.

Next to the Baetge house is one of the region's most interesting log barns, built by an immigrant named Welsch in about 1849. Each of the barn's three pens is built in an inverted pyramid fashion; that is, each wall slopes slightly outward (maybe one hundred degrees) from ground to roof instead of going straight up at a ninety-degree angle. The best explanation for this sloping was to keep the walls dry from the rain. The barn was originally located on Rock Street, which was the old road to San Marcos.

Also present are the Forke Store, built about 1865 by Jacob Forke on S. Seguin; the Haelbig Music Studio, built about 1850 by New Braunfels' first piano teacher; and the Star Exchange, also built about 1850 on S. Seguin. It first housed the Star Exchange and Billiard Room and later the *New Braunfels Herald-Zeitung*. Across the street is the 1870 Church Hill School, which is built of ashlar-dressed limestone blocks and is still in its original location.

Johann Jahn, one of New Braunfels' original settlers, was a Tischlermeister, or "master craftsman," and some of his furniture is on display here. The left side of his house dates to 1885; the other side was added a few years later. His adjoining cabinet shop contains some of his tools.

The Herman Blank and Seibold Houses (1855) are both examples of fachwerk construction.

HERITAGE VILLAGE AND THE MUSEUM OF TEXAS HANDMADE FURNITURE

1370 Church Hill Dr. • 629-6504 • www.nbheritagevillage.com • Closed December through January and major holidays • Fee

A few feet up Church Hill from Conservation Plaza, this museum showcases over seventy-five original pieces of furniture that were made by hand in Texas from the 1830s through the 1860s, including pieces by Johann Jahn, Franz Stautzenberger, and Heinrich Scholl. They populate the Andreas Breustedt house, built in 1858, which also contains other household artifacts common to the era, in a more-or-less homey atmosphere. The 1847 two-room dogtrot Reininger log cabin stands to the side of the Breusted house and is furnished in the style of the first settlers to arrive in New Braunfels. Other structures on the grounds are the Solms School, an early 1900s Comal County rural schoolhouse, and the Specht farmhouse.

OTHER MUSEUMS

SOPHIENBURG MUSEUM AND ARCHIVES

200 N. Seguin, in the old city hall building • 629-1572 • www.sophienburg .com • Open Tuesday through Saturday • Fee

The extensive archives include photos, handwritten original records, newspapers, maps, and oral histories pertaining to New Braunfels and Comal County. The archives are dominated by the leavings of the German immigrants, but they also contain material pertaining to all ethnic groups who have settled in the area since the 1840s. Exhibits portray local history.

WAGENFUEHR HOME AND BUCKHORN BARBERSHOP MUSEUM

521 W. San Antonio • 629-2943 • nbconservation.org • Open Tuesday through Sunday • Fee

Among the things on display in this old house and turn-of-the-century barber-shop are hundreds of hand-carved circus figurines and pictures made from rocks.

BAKERIES AND RESTAURANTS

Willie Gebhardt, the father of chili powder, perfected his creation in New Braunfels. In 1892, Willie opened up a cafe in the back of the Phoenix Saloon (193 W. San Antonio). Aiming to please his customers, he soon found out that chili con carne was a popular dish with New Braunfels's Germans. Gebhardt began to import ancho peppers from Mexico and figured out a way to dry them (in his mother-in-law's oven) and grind the peppers into a powder, which could then be easily used by the average cook. The year was 1894. He could make five cases of powder a week, and he sold it from the back of his wagon. Two years later, Gebhardt was grinding away down in a new factory in San Antonio. He invented most of the machinery to manufacture the chili powders. Gebhart also began canning ready-to-eat chili con carne in 1908 as well as tamales.

NAEGELIN'S BAKERY

129 S. Seguin • 625-5722 • www.naegelins.com • Monday through Friday 6:30–5:30, Saturday 6:30–5:00, closed Sunday • W

Naegelin's peach fried pies, bear claws, and cream puffs are just a few of their tasty offerings. Their loaves of white, whole wheat, French rye, and pumpernickel are cheap and tasty. All their pies are bargains, particularly the great coconut cream pie. Stollen, just like your German grandmother used to make, is a popular Christmas seller. They've been in business since 1868.

COOPER'S OLD TIME PIT BAR-B-Q

1125 N. Loop 337, just past the Guadalupe River bridge; turn right off Gruene Rd. • 627-0627 • www.coopersbbqnewbraunfels.com • Open daily

Cooper's New Braunfels is a carbon copy of the mother ship Llano restaurant, from the mesquite coals and giant pits to the array of meats on the menu. If you love the Llano original, you'll cotton to this clone.

LODGING

THE PRINCE SOLMS INN

295 E. San Antonio • 625-9169 • www.princesolmsinn.com

If Victorian is your pleasure, your choice should be the Prince Solms Inn, which was built in 1898 as the Eggering Hotel. The two-story brick Carpenter Gothic structure has been thoroughly restored and decorated in a very busy, very plush late-Victorian manner. Sit awhile in the downstairs parlor with books by Dickens or Doyle and slip back into another era. The inn has fourteen suites and rooms filled with antiques, and it has a homey atmosphere. Other amenities include a piano bar, full bar, and a variety of breakfasts.

Behind the inn is the Joseph Klein House, built in 1852 on the spot where the hotel now stands. It was moved to the back of the lot in 1898 to make way for the hotel.

THE FAUST HOTEL

240 S. Seguin • 625-7791 • www.fausthotel.com

If your tastes run more to Art Deco and Greta Garbo, your choice should be Faust. It first opened a couple of days before Black Friday in October 1929 as the "Travelers Hotel." Built by public subscription (like Fredericksburg's railroad) and equipped with all the latest luxuries, it was one of the finest hotels of its size in the state and was a source of civic pride. But despite its instant popularity, the Depression caught up with the Travelers in just a couple of years, and its operators went broke. It was saved from closure by Walter Faust Sr., local bank president, whose family originally owned the land where the hotel stands. Faust died shortly thereafter, and in 1936 the Travelers was renamed the Faust to honor him and his family. The hotel gradually slid downhill after World War II, but this trend was reversed starting in the mid-1970s. Under the present ownership, the Faust has been thoroughly refurbished and modernized without sacrificing much of the original beauty.

In contrast to the simple style of the building as a whole are the elaborate Spanish Renaissance details, such as the lavish stone carvings above the front entryways and first-story windows and the lobby's intricate Spanish tile floor. The Faust has sixty-one rooms, each with central air and heat, cable TV, and Wi-Fi/Internet as counterpoint to the iron beds, candlestick telephones, and flowery carpeting. Complimentary breakfast is available. The Faust Brewing Company, the only microbrewery in New Braunfels, is located in the hotel's original beer garden. The bar and tables are topped with Texas Pearl Granite surrounded in rich mahogany.

The Faust family's three-story Victorian mansion, which was displaced by the hotel, now stands half a block south and across the street at the corner of Coil and S. Seguin. It was moved there brick by brick.

ANNUAL EVENT

WURSTFEST

Ten days in very late October through early November; dates vary slightly year to year • Wurstfest grounds, adjacent to Landa Park, entrance on Landa St. • 800-221-4369 • www.wurstfest.com • Fee • W

New Braunfels is famous as the home of Wurstfest, a tribute to *Gemuetlichkeit* ("good times"), beer, and sausage that began in the early 1960s. Live music is played nightly in the cavernous Wursthalle, featuring polka bands. The fest's musical lineup also includes choral groups, mariachis, and C&W bands. Beer flows almost as prolifically as the nearby Comal Springs, and sausage is devoured by the mile. Weekend days are the best times for families with small children. The river-walk area provides a nice break from the madness inside. In any given year, Wurstfest weather can range from beautiful to cold, wet, and nasty; this is the time of year when fall's cool fronts finally begin to roll into Central Texas. It may be ninety degrees one day and fifty degrees the next. A final note of caution: Be careful not to overindulge on the German soda water and then drive; the law will be waiting for you.

In December 1908, Texas Prohibition laws closed New Braunfels saloons on Sundays for the first time ever in the city's existence. No acts of violence were recorded, but the *Dallas Morning News* observed that "Liberty was placed in a coffin, given an elaborate funeral, and conducted by a brass band and prominent citizens to her grave on the outskirts of the city."

During World War I, the nationwide surge of anti-German sentiment led some Texans to demand that New Braunfels' name be changed to a more appropriate, American name. The cooler heads prevailed in the end.

To leave New Braunfels, take E. San Antonio Street from the courthouse square across the Comal River. Turn left on Union Avenue, go nine blocks, and then turn right on E. Torrey until you come to the intersection with Gruene Road (about 0.75 miles). Turn left on Gruene Road and follow it into "downtown" Gruene, which is now actually within the New Braunfels city limits.

GRUENE

Comal County • 20 • (830) • About 4 miles from downtown New Braunfels

The Gruene area was first settled in the 1850s by the overflow from New Braunfels and was originally known as Goodwin. Cotton cultivation was introduced to New Braunfels and Comal County in 1852, and it quickly became the county's number-one cash crop. The land around Goodwin was prime cotton-growing country. Ernst Gruene and his two sons realized this and moved to Goodwin in 1872. Ernst had come to New Braunfels in 1845. One of Ernst's sons, Henry D. Gruene, became the town's namesake. A hustling entrepreneur, H. D. soon had twenty or thirty families sharecropping on the Gruene family's recently acquired acreage.

By 1878, Gruene had established the town's first mercantile store in the little white frame building that still stands across Hunter Road from the two-story, brick H. D. Gruene building. At that time, Hunter Road was a stretch on the Old Post Road, the main road between Austin and San Antonio. Shortly after the store was established, Henry Gruene built a cotton gin, which was powered by the waters of the Guadalupe River. The wooden structure burned in 1922. Its brick boiler house (the gin was converted to steam power in the early 1900s) now houses the Gristmill Restaurant, located behind the Gruene Hall.

Gruene next opened up a lumberyard and then a dance hall and beer garden in 1882. He also ran the post office and donated land for the local school. A blacksmith shop came along in the 1890s. By this time, eight thousand acres around Gruene had been planted in cotton. The town was growing, and so was H. D. Gruene's bank book, so much so that he decided to build his own bank, which he housed in the new (1904) two-story brick building that is still Gruene's most prominent landmark, next to the dunce-cap water tower. The structure also housed his store and post office. Gruene's original bank vault is still inside the bank wing, built of cinder-block-sized bricks and cast-iron doors, with "H. D. Gruene" inscribed in gold gilt thereon.

Gruene the man and Gruene the town prospered until 1920. That year, H. D. Gruene passed away. The boll weevil and pink bollworm came along and killed King Cotton, down to the last boll, in 1925. That disaster, combined with drought, falling cotton prices, and the land's decreasing productivity, caused a mass exodus of Gruene's cotton farmers, leaving the place a virtual ghost town until the mid-1970s when a new breed of tourism-oriented entrepreneurs moved in and saved the old town from destruction by developers. Gruene is now on the National Register of Historic Places. A number of antique, collectible, and specialty shops, along with restaurants and B&Bs, now call Gruene home.

GRISTMILL RESTAURANT

Behind Gruene Hall • 625-0684 • www.gristmillrestaurant.com • Open daily, lunch and dinner • Cr.

The restaurant operates out of the ruins of the brick cotton gin's boiler room that burned in 1922. Dine on chicken-fried steak, french fries, burgers, grilled chicken, and steak, and drink out of Mason jars while looking out over the scenic Guadalupe River.

GRUENE HALL

606-1281 • www.gruenehall.com • Open daily • W

Step inside Gruene Hall for a cold beer, and drink in the past. There is no escaping the memory of H. D. Gruene here, for even the front of the bar sports a metal plaque with his name embossed on it. Gruene family photos hang behind the bar. Back in the dance hall, seventy- and eighty-year-old advertising placards for New Braunfels businesses still hang. Some of the businesses they advertise are still hanging on, too. The beer garden is shaded by big cedars, under which picnic tables and old wagon hulks compete for space, and Christmas lights stay up year-round. Gruene Hall's owners advertise it as the oldest dance hall in Texas. The bands playing Gruene Hall are a mix of local country-and-western and regional rock-and-roll favorites.

LODGING

GRUENE MANSION INN

1275 Gruene Rd., New Braunfels, 78130 • 629-2641 • www.grueneman sioninn.com

Next door to Gruene Hall is the Gruene Mansion Inn, which is not a mansion but rather the spacious Victorian home that H. D. Gruene built for his family beginning in the 1870s. Originally one story stucco-over-brick, Gruene later added the second story, corner gazebo, and wraparound porches. Guests stay in any of several riverside "cottages" behind the house, which include H. D.'s converted corncrib and barn. All thirty units are furnished with antiques and handmade quilts. Some have kitchenettes.

From Gruene Hall, proceed north on Hunter Road, past the big brick H. D. Gruene building, which now houses an antique store, to reach Hunter.

In Comal County, there were mile posts along the post/stage road almost every half mile. Sometimes the mile post consisted of a number of cuts on a tree to mark the number of miles, but in Bexar County, the traveler had to guess how far it was to the next town.

In Bexar County, the roads law was not carried out as it should be. It was not carried out at all. Counties not half as rich, that didn't owe half as much money, with citizens not half as intelligent, had their roads fixed up better. You could travel all over Bexar County with a forty-horsepower telescope and not encounter a single mile post. Detectives could not find a mile post even if a reward were offered and the mile post was not armed. Strangers passing through Bexar County were best advised to carry along a guide post with them so that they could post it whenever they were in doubt about being on the right road.

On the stage road, there was not only an absence of guide posts, but in many instances the road was fenced by the property owners. The road's route changed about as often as a cowboy changed his socks, and each time, as the man said when he got two bad halves for a good dollar, it was a change for the worse. If you insisted on traveling the old road, you had to take down a barbed-wire fence, and if the property owner caught you, the road to New Braunfels might very well divert for a term in Huntsville. To find the new road required as much ability as that required of a Texas legislator. A simple board nailed to a post would have relieved much annoyance and caused a partial abatement in profanity. With the lack of system, the traveler enjoyed much flexibility. You could get to Austin around Cape Horn, or via Mexico City, New York City, or San Francisco, whichever you might prefer.

Turn right on FM 1102 to enter Hunter.

HUNTER

Comal County • 30 • About 7 miles from Gruene

Hunter started as a thousand-acre cotton plantation, operated by Major A. J. Hunter. The town was laid out and developed with the coming of the I&GN railroad in 1880. Major Hunter's daughter, Loulie, married E. M. House, who was to become one of the nation's leading power brokers during the first several decades of the twentieth century. House built Hunter into a major cotton-processing center. With cotton's fall, a new cottage industry grew up. Pablo De La Rosa moved to Hunter in the 1920s and in about 1926 started casting plaster of paris figurines for sale at the many roadside stands that were springing up along the new Texas highways. These figurines became big sellers, and soon everybody in town had some of De La Rosa's molds and was making statues of their own. The industry took a nosedive when the new highway went in around 1933, bypassing Hunter to the east (the present I-35 route).

Riley's Tavern, opened as soon as Prohibition ended in 1933, is currently Hunter's leading—and only—business. Old man Riley has been departed from our midst for the better part of two decades now, but his beer bar lives on, largely unchanged, with live music on the weekends.

From Hunter, turn right on FM 2439 at its junction with FM 1102 to reach San Marcos. You enter San Marcos on the Old Post Road (FM 2439) via Stringtown.

STRINGTOWN

Comal and Hays counties • Just outside San Marcos

Stringtown was founded in about 1850 by John D. Pitts and got its name from the six-mile string of houses that stretched along the Post Road from York Creek on the Hays-Comal county line to near Purgatory Creek, southwest of San Marcos. Pitts, who had been born at sea during his parents' trip from England to the United States in 1798, had grown up in South Carolina and Georgia. He was elected to the Georgia legislature in 1841, but he decided soon after to move to Grimes County, Texas. He persuaded his extended family in Georgia to join him, and in 1843, eleven Pitts families followed him to Texas. John D. Pitts served as adjutant general under Texas governor George Wood from 1848 to 1849. Pitts bought 1,500 acres of land here from his friend General Edward Burleson in 1850, and eventually much of his extended family settled along the San Antonio–San Marcos stage route. Pitts later organized the town of Pittsburgh, which later became the present-day town of Blanco. Pitts died in 1861, on his way from the state secession convention, and was buried in the Pitts family cemetery, located on your right, in the 3400 block of Hunter Road, aka the Post Road.

Pitts Cemetery began in 1850 with the burial of John Malone, the infant son of James L. and Eliza (Pitts) Malone and grandson of Eliza and John D. Pitts. Eliza Pitts was buried here in 1851. The cemetery was set aside by Pitts' sons-in-law, James Malone and Samuel Kone Sr., in 1875 and continues to serve as a burial site for the descendants of John D. and Eliza Pitts. It is closed to the public.

Situated as it was on the post/stagecoach road between Austin and San Antonio, Stringtown had its share of famous and infamous visitors. Sam Houston, Governor Oran M. Roberts, General Ed Burleson, University of Texas benefactor George Brackenridge, Bigfoot Wallace, and gambler/gunslinger/Austin city marshal Ben Thompson are all said to have left their respective marks here.

Two more young men—well known to all of us—are also said to have partaken of Stringtown hospitality. Old-timer Sam Kone told this story many years ago:

Two young men appeared at my father's gate one evening and asked politely for shelter for the night. They were gladly welcomed. The strangers took supper, stayed all night, ate breakfast, and upon leaving offered payment. They were met with the command "Stop again when you are passing this way." I had the honor of taking care of their very fine horses. A few months later, the pair returned through, but they were riding small mules instead of fine horses. We entertained them as before and later it was found out that we had hosted the James brothers, Jesse and Frank.

With each passing year, San Marcos creeps farther and farther south into Stringtown. Once in San Marcos, you enter the Hopkins Street Historic District, and you will notice the many stately, finely crafted old homes, built during the era when this was the main north-south highway and it was considered fashionable to have a house on the main drag.

SAN MARCOS

Hays County Seat • 51,000 (approximate) • About 8 miles from Hunter

Wonder Cave provides a rare opportunity to see the Balcones Fault.

WONDER WORLD/WONDER CAVE

1000 Prospect St., just off FM 2439/Hopkins St., about a mile south of downtown San Marcos; look for the signs on FM 2439/Hopkins St. and turn left (north) • 392-3760 • www.wonderworldpark.com • Open daily, except Christmas Eve and Christmas Day

Wonder Cave is billed as America's only commercial dry-formed cave. That means it was formed in a matter of seconds during an earthquake, during the creation of the Balcones Fault. It also means that you don't see any spectacular stalactite and stalagmite formations. You do see the Balcones Fault line running along Wonder Cave's ceiling and the waters of the Edwards Aquifer at the "wishing well." Don't go expecting to be visually dazzled; this is more of a thinking man's cave. It was discovered in 1896 when a water well was being drilled, and it housed a distillery and gambling den before the authorities shut down cave discoverer Mark Beavers' illicit operations. Public tours began in 1903 for a nickel a head. Wonder World also features an observation tower and a quaint little wildlife park stocked with llamas, all sorts of exotic deer, and other peaceful, feedable animals.

Once in San Marcos, FM 2439 dead-ends into SH 80. Continue straight on what is now SH 80 and follow its path to the courthouse square. At the square, turn left on Lyndon B. Johnson Drive, then right after two blocks onto University/Loop 82.

Here is some San Marcos trivia to chew on as you pass through town, beginning with some old legends:

- Once upon a time, an Indian maid, the chief's daughter, loved a boy far below her station. One bright spring morning, her lover was slain and laid to rest on the grassy banks of the San Marcos River with only the blue sky above as a coverlet. That night the moon and stars shone bright, and the chieftain's daughter fled in despair to the river bank where he lay. She said a prayer and then threw herself into the river so that she might be reunited with her lover. She was never found. A white water lily bloomed where she dove in.

- A beautiful Spanish maiden and her lover were captured by Indians near San Antonio and carried to their captors' camp near the head of the San Marcos River. Cognizant of their fate, the twosome flung themselves as one into the river and sank to their deaths.
- Near San Marcos, there is reputed to be a still-secret spot where Mexican brigands buried their plundered treasure as far back as the beginning of the nineteenth century. The gang was some eight hundred strong at one time, and their headquarters were located on the high hill later occupied by the Coronal Institute. From that spot, they preyed upon donkey trains passing from Natchitoches to Laredo on the Old San Antonio Road. These trains often carried gold and silver from the legendary San Saba and San Gabriel mines. Burying the loot nearby, they sent maps to their accomplices in Mexico showing the treasure's location. The maps have never surfaced, and no clues exist today as to the cache's whereabouts. But justice finally overtook the thieves. When they attacked one of the pack trains at the Blanco River crossing one day, they were repulsed by a large company of armed horsemen who drove them back to their roost and there killed most of the outlaws.
- Shortly after Dr. Caton Erhard opened San Marcos' first store in about 1848, Austin's Colonel John M. Swisher fell in love with the area's beauty while passing through on his way to Mexico and the war with Santa Anna. He returned to open San Marcos' second store, wherein he kept a barrel of whiskey with two faucets, one on the inside and one on the outside. Inside the store, whiskey was a dollar per quart; the same quart drawn from the outdoor spigot went for fifty cents.
- The year 1853 was known as "the year of the grasshopper plague," and a terrible drought prevailed for the next three years. Many cattle died of thirst and starvation, and for the first time stock raisers used prickly pears for cattle feed by burning off the thorns.
- The great hurricane of 1886 destroyed that year's entire cotton crop, and not another drop of rain fell until May 1887.
- Gold fever struck San Marcos in 1915 when old-time Arizona miner and San Marcos pioneer Jack Edwards discovered valuable ore in the old Burleson tract on the north edge of town. Assayed samples showed significant amounts of silver per ton, with traces of gold. A company was organized, but the operation proved unprofitable.
- Black gold fever struck San Marcos in 1922 when San Marcos pioneer D. D. Compton discovered oil flowing from his fifty-year-old water well. Experts estimated that if the well were pumped steadily it would yield five barrels of fine-grade paraffin oil a day. The oil was of such high quality that local motorists used it in their autos straight from Compton's well. With no refinery, Compton had to devise his own method of separating the oil and water. He bailed the oil and water mix from the well with a two-gallon galvanized bucket and poured it into a tub. A hole at the bottom of the tub was left open until all the water drained off and was then closed to retain the oil.

When University/Loop 82 comes to the T intersection a couple of blocks after turning onto it from LBJ Drive, turn left and follow University/Loop 82 past the Texas State University campus and Aquarena Springs; then turn left on the Old Post Road (County Road 140).

The road you have been traveling since you left New Braunfels is the old stagecoach route from Austin to San Antonio. Sources, including the *Handbook of Texas*, are somewhat contradictory in their details of early stagecoach service, but as best we can tell, in about 1847, the Texas United States Mail Line started a biweekly mail and passenger service between Houston and San Antonio via Washington on the Brazos, Independence, La Grange, Bastrop, Austin, and New Braunfels, using mud wagons (not the classic Concord stagecoaches we are used to seeing in the movies) pulled by mules. Mud wagons were lighter, smaller, plainer, and about one-third of the price of a Concord stagecoach, built for strength and endurance, not speed. Their only protection from bad weather and dusty roads were canvas side curtains, which could be rolled up and fastened. Mud wagons were good vehicles for the rough, rocky roads of Central Texas because of their lower center of gravity. Unlike Concord stagecoaches, which could easily mire down in mud, mud wagons, true to their name, could trudge on during bad weather.

Each wagon carried a sack of mail along with the passengers, and the journey took three days each way when the weather was good, the creeks and rivers weren't "up," and the "roads" were not muddy. In bad weather, the trip might take weeks, if it took place at all. If the mud was too deep, the stage just turned around and went home. Fares were not cheap: $20 for a one-way ride, or about $500 in today's money.

Stage stands were placed at twelve-mile intervals, and the mules were changed at each station. Each of these "stages" took about four hours to complete. A station stood in Stringtown, and the next one north stood beside the Blanco River, a ways upstream from the current road's Blanco River crossing on the north side of greater San Marcos.

In 1848, Messrs. Tarbox and Brown started a stagecoach service between Austin and San Antonio along the same road. In late 1845, the same firm of Brown and Tarbox had advertised a biweekly service by the Houston and Austin Mail Stage Line via Washington, Independence, La Grange, and Bastrop.

Bear left at the junction just north of the low-water crossing of the Blanco River. The road (you are now on County Road 136) hugs the Blanco for a few dozen furlongs. At this point, the Old Post Road is County Road 136. Although no longer the narrow winding strip of asphalt of decades past, the wider, better-paved road still twists and turns through relatively untouched countryside until you reach the southern outskirts of Kyle, which has been growing like kudzu vine since the late 1990s.

There were a number of stage robberies along this route, and the most famous of all took place about two miles north of the Blanco River crossing on April 7, 1874, at about dusk, when three armed men stopped the northbound coach from San Antonio. Among the eleven passengers were San Antonio's Bishop Gregg and George Brackenridge, president of the National Bank of San Antonio, on his way to open the Austin National Bank. After committing this robbery, the bandits rode off rather hurriedly toward the west. Their descriptions answered rather well to that of two of the James boys and one of their cohorts, a fellow named McCoy. It was even rumored that Belle Starr, dressed as a man, was one of the robbers.

But later that year, in August, Jim Reed, a stage and train robber, and husband of Belle Starr, was fatally shot near Paris, Texas, and on his deathbed he confessed to having robbed the San Antonio stage, absolving the James boys and Youngers of the crime. Nevertheless, the story of Jesse and Frank James having robbed the San Antonio-to-Austin stage persists.

NANCE'S MILL

Hays County • About 6 miles from San Marcos • Closed to the public

You are now passing through the old Nance's Mill neighborhood, which over-lapped the northern edges of San Marcos and the southern edges of Mountain City. Ezekiel Nance was a prime example of pioneer tenacity and enterprise. From about 1855 to 1885, he built and operated, at different times, five gins, five gristmills, a cotton mill, a sawmill, a shingle mill, and a beef packery on the banks of the Blanco River, three miles west of Kyle, all of which were swept down toward the Gulf of Mexico by the various overflows which came in those years.

In April 1858, Nance (with Edward Burleson Jr. and William Smith) was ap-pointed by the Hays County commissioners to locate a road from San Marcos to Nance's house on the Blanco River; from there the road ran on to Dripping Springs. A stage stop was established.

Nance was born in Tennessee in 1816. In the late 1820s, his family moved to a farm in Hempstead County, Arkansas. Orphaned soon after, Ezekiel lived with various relatives. In 1840, he married Luany Pate. They had two daugh-ters and four sons. Ezekiel was sheriff of Hempstead County before serving as treasurer of the State of Arkansas from 1848 to 1854. Luany died in 1852, and Ezekiel traveled to Texas seeking a homestead there. He selected a site at the junction of a small creek (which he named the Little Arkansas) and the Blanco River in Hays County. In June 1852, Nance acquired title to about ten thousand acres there. He later increased his holdings to more than fourteen thousand acres. He returned to Arkansas and married Martha Jane Alexander in April 1853 (they would have six children). That fall, Nance moved to Texas with his new wife, the five surviving children from his first marriage, his first wife's sister, and a number of slaves. One of the first things he did upon arriving was to put up a rock fence around his cropland to protect it from roving wild cattle. With his sons and slaves, Nance and his neighbors annually rounded up and branded wild cattle. On the Blanco River, Ezekiel built a dog-run house with a large fireplace at the end of each room. As his family grew, he added three rooms and covered the chinked log walls with cypress panels sawed at his mill; in 1994, the house still stood at its original site. He also built a smokehouse, slave quarters, a carriage house, and an additional two-room house for the eight boys in the family. Within five years, using slave labor, Nance had built a dam on the Blanco. Nance also built a blacksmith shop and tenant houses.

T. F. Harwell profiled Nance and his enterprises in the *Kyle News* on April 20, 1928:

> At that time, there were no conveniences of any sort. The early settlers had to undergo many privations and were hard put sometimes to get along. Some farming was going on, a good deal of food stuffs and a little cotton and corn were being grown, but there was neither gin nor mill, and in 1855 Major Nance erected a small gin and corn mill. The plant was exceedingly primitive, but it supplied a much-felt need and was patronized by people for many miles in all directions.

After a year or two the Blanco River one day got on a rampage and swept the mill and gin away. But Major Nance immediately replaced them, this time getting far enough from the river to be out of danger of overflow. This plant was also quite small and primitive.

When the cotton was hauled to the gin, it was carried in baskets to the gin stand, where a man fed it into the gin by hand. From the gin it was conveyed into what was called the "lint room." From the lint room it was carried again in baskets, to the press, which was separate from the gin. The press consisted of an oblong square box the size of the length and thickness of a bale of cotton, and perhaps fifteen feet high. The cotton was carried up a stairway to the top of the press and poured into it. By having a man in the press to tramp and pack the cotton, a sufficient amount could be gotten into it to make a bale. When this was done, the pressing started. A plunger, or packer, the size of the inside of the press, was fastened to the end of a large screw, perhaps four inches in diameter and fifteen or twenty feet long. This screw worked in a nut, or tap, with treads to fit. A long lever was attached to the upper end of the screw, one end slanting downward, reaching to within three feet of the ground. A horse or mule or ox was hitched to the lower end of this lever, a boy put on him, or behind him, to make him go, and around and around they went until the cotton was sufficiently pressed. When the bale was "tied out," the animal was turned in the opposite direction and again went around and around until the plunger reached the top.

Business soon increased until a larger gin was necessary. For the new plant, Major Nance moved back to the river and harnessed its waters for his power, considering the economy in power as more than offsetting the danger from overflow.

By this time, the settlement had grown to a considerable community. The post office was at Mountain City, where were also the nearest store and school. This was several miles away—too far for small children to attend school, so this little community built a small log house for school and church purposes. The population continued to increase and soon outgrew the log house, and in the early part of 1861, Major Nance had a rock building erected to be used for both church and school purposes as the log house had been. Into the masonry on the front of the building a small cross of dressed limestone was put, and beneath the cross a squared and dressed stone was placed, bearing the inscription "1861."

For many years, this building served the community for church and school. But when Kyle came into existence with the coming of the railroad in 1881, the town became the community center. Churches were built, and Blanco chapel was turned over to the Mexican Presbyterians who used it for several years. Later it was converted into a barn.

Major Nance did not enter the Civil War. Besides having passed the age of forty-five years, he and his neighbors considered that he would be of more service to stay at home and provide for their needs with his mill and gin. In about 1863, when everything that could not be grown or made at home was scarce and hard to get, Major Nance added a small cotton mill to his enterprises, making a very serviceable coarse cotton cloth. This mill's capacity was very limited, so he discontinued it after a year or so. In the latter part of 1863, Major Nance put his slaves to work fencing his land, thus putting several thousand acres under fence. This was the first large body of land fenced in this part of the state, and quite possibly in the entire state.

A great deal of wheat was then being grown, so Major Nance put up a flour mill. Later he added a sawmill and a shingle mill.

Following the close of the Civil War, cattle went down in price until it did not pay even to look after them, and some of the owners killed and skinned them for their hides. In order to furnish a market for the cattle, Major Nance conceived the idea of a beef packery. He went up the river about a mile from his other enterprises and put his idea into execution. He operated the plant a year or two, until 1869. He had sold a good deal of the barreled beef and had a large lot on hand ready to take to market when, with little warning, the Blanco River got on a rampage and swept away his beef packery and all his other enterprises. His barrels of beef were scattered along the waterways from here to the Gulf of Mexico.

He put up a small gin and mill in order to be ready for the next crop, and in October 1870, another rise, "which rose many feet higher than any other flood was ever known to reach," took away the gin, mill, and his cotton crop. Most men would have given up, but not Major Nance. He immediately erected another mill and gin in order that his neighbors might get bread and have their cotton ginned.

The 1870 federal census listed Ezekiel Nance, age fifty-four, with real estate valued at $15,000 and a personal estate of $5,000.

In late 1875 or early 1876, Major Nance, having apparently recovered from his former misfortune, began the erection of his next enterprise, by far the largest he had ever had. The roller process for making flour had come into use, and he put up a big roller mill. This he also built on the banks of the Blanco, but he so constructed it that it was able to withstand the onslaughts of the treacherous river. In its day, this mill served the people for forty miles in all directions.

On July 15, 1876, the *San Marcos Free Press* reported that Nance had ten thousand acres, with seven thousand acres under fence (mostly rock) and six hundred acres under cultivation, with two cotton gins, three shingle saws and one circular saw mill, and various other kinds of machinery, a blacksmith and other mechanics with shops on the ground, tenants and tenant houses, and so on. An excellent new schoolhouse had been added recently, and a new flouring mill had recently been put in operation. His cattle were nearly all of improved varieties.

But in the last years of Major Nance's operation of the mill, he fought a losing fight. The coming of the railroad placed him in competition with the larger mills, and the changing of the farming of the section from wheat to practically all cotton cut off his supply of raw material, so the business became unprofitable and was eventually discontinued, although not entirely until after his death.

One more venture, which was his last, Major Nance made in 1881—he built a gin in Kyle, the first to be built in the town. The Kyle gin proved profitable, but after a few years he sold it, and the new owner added an oil mill. It was destroyed by fire in the spring of 1909.

By 1883, Ezekiel Nance was the second-largest property holder in Hays County, with property valued at $36,000. He died in September 1885 and was buried in the Kyle City cemetery.

MOUNTAIN CITY

Hays County • 1,000 (approximate) • About 10 miles from San Marcos

The railroad's coming killed off Mountain City. In its heyday, from 1850 through 1880, Mountain City was a major stop on the Austin-to-San Antonio stage route, a regional supply center, and a gathering point for many of the great cattle drives of the late 1860s and 1870s. Mountain City's most illustrious citizen was Colonel W. W. Haupt, who came here from Alabama via Bastrop in either 1853 or 1857. A cotton planter, Haupt was an innovator as well, introducing the Essex hog and Brahma cow to the area, besides developing the Haupt berry, a cross between the blackberry and the dewberry. Haupt ran the region's first steam-powered cotton gin. In 1858, he decided to raise goats, beginning with the small, native "Mexican" goats. He quickly decided to improve and bought eight Angoras for $100. The Haupt goats he developed became a hit with Texas goat men. Haupt's ranch, store, hotel, and post office were the community's center, located across from the present-day Hays High School.

Miss Fannie Manlove, whose father was one of Mountain City's early settlers, wrote about the community's early history in the *Kyle News* on April 20, 1928:

> The original Mountain City community consisted of about twenty families, extended over a territory of about seven miles north and south and three or four miles in width. It might be said to have begun two miles west of where Kyle now stands and to have extended north to Allen's Prairie, a mile and a half west of the present location of Buda. The line of the present post road about marked the eastern boundary, while the west line was governed by the topography of the country.
>
> The first school building in the community was probably built about 1855. Pupils came from different parts of the country, and almost every home was a boarding house—the community spirit was strong, and intellectuality ran high. The advanced pupils were experts in math and Latin. The close of school was a great event in the community. All brought dinner, spent the day, and stayed for the night concert. Pupils were examined before the audience from the primer to the university courses. There were no graded schools there.
>
> There were many slaves in the community, and the masters, as a rule, Manlove said, were kind and the negroes happy. The night patrol seldom caught a culprit. On one occasion, "Uncle Steve," owned by Dr. Manlove, went to stake a horse near the timber for protection, as a norther was blowing, increasing as night came on. Uncle Steve lost his bearings as a blinding snowstorm swept the country. The next morning, his body was found a half mile from home by Bob Barton, then about twelve years old. The body was completely covered with snow with the exception of one hand.
>
> The first post office of the community was at the home of James Bunton. In 1858, it was moved to Colonel Haupt's store, and he named it Mountain City.
>
> During the Civil War, the greatest thrill was the coming of the stagecoach, driven by four to six large horses. As it passed the school building, the driver blew his horn vigorously. Men from all directions gathered at Haupt's store to hear the war news. Colonel D. E. Moore, having a strong voice, generally did the reading of the newspaper for the crowd. You can imagine the anxiety and excitement, for there were no telegraphs or telephones and no daily paper at the time.

All the young men went to war, leaving only the younger boys and middle-aged and old men at home. Mr. Ira Breedlove was the neighborhood squire and attended to all legal business. Dr. R. C. Manlove looked after the widows and orphans and did a general practice. His house was the home for wounded and sick soldiers and for anyone who was in need. One night he called to see a dying man, Mr. Powell, at or near Dripping Springs, who had been shot by Jayhawkers. Dr. Manlove met the Jayhawkers in the middle of Onion Creek and could hear their swords click. As he met them, he said, "Good evening, gentlemen," and all was well. He recognized some of the men, but it was not safe in those days to tell all you knew.

The Indians made a raid after the Civil War, coming as far down as the "Cross House" on the Kuykendall Ranch. One woman was scalped, but the Indians failed to use the tomahawk. Dr. Manlove dressed her wound every other day until she was entirely recovered.

But lawlessness reigned for a long time after the war. At one time, a widow, Mrs. Kate Black, was choked nearly to death by robbers trying to get her money. On another occasion, John Day was taken out of his home in the night and hanged three times from a large live oak tree. Day was thought to have considerable money, and did have it, and they were trying to get him to tell where it was. He told them, but they would not believe his stories.

One night shortly after the close of the Civil War, three traveling men camped for the night. One of the men had a fine horse which he staked near the camp. Feeling uneasy about the horse, he could not sleep, so during the night he decided that he would go and see about him. His comrades decided they would play a trick on him, so when the owner reached the horse, the men cried out "Indians!" The man rushed up and stabbed one of them, thinking he was an Indian. Dr. Manlove was called, but too late. The man died and was buried somewhere near Mountain City on the stage road.

Once, sometime in the 1870s, Dr. Manlove's buggy horse was stolen. The thief and horse were discovered by neighbors and chase was given. Both were shot near where Kyle now stands. The thief died, but the horse recovered. Finally things quieted down. The slaves had been freed, the carpetbaggers were gone, telegraph poles appeared, the iron horse came, and the early community disappeared.

But with the explosive growth of nearby Kyle and Buda that began in the 1990s, Mountain City enjoyed a revival as well and is now an incorporated municipality.

KYLE CABIN

Old Post Rd. • Open the third Saturday in September and on other special occasions

John Claiborne Kyle and his wife, Lucy Bugg, came to Texas from Mississippi in 1844 and built this cabin in about 1850. Built of squared-off cedar logs, this large four-pen cabin is the only one of its type left in Texas. Its central chimneys are also rare. The cabin is set back several hundred yards from the road and isn't immediately visible. About three miles after turning onto County Road 136, start looking for a sign that refers to the cabin, which will be on your left. The cabin is fenced in to protect it from vandals. It is about 0.3 miles south of the Kyle Cemetery, so if you pass the cemetery, you've gone too far.

As you continue up the Old Post Road toward the turnoffs to Kyle, you pass the old Kyle Cemetery on your right.

KYLE CEMETERY

Old Post Rd.

The first inhabitant here was an unknown young man whom cow hunters found hanging from an oak tree. Not knowing who he was, why he was hanging there, or who put him there, they buried the poor unfortunate under the oak. He was later joined by such notables as Texas Declaration of Independence signer Colonel John Bunton, W. W. Haupt, Claiborne and Ferguson Kyle, Ezekiel Nance, and Major Edward Burleson. One of the cemetery's most tragic burials was that of young Cora May Sloan.

On Saturday evening, May 13, 1882, as Austin excursionists bound for San Antonio on the I&GN stopped at Kyle for refreshments, they might have noticed a young girl, about sixteen or seventeen years of age, in attendance at the refreshment stand. As a reporter for the *Austin Statesman* wrote a few days later,

> Those who did will be somewhat astonished when this report presents to them the fact of her death—brought about by her own premeditated act. The name of the young woman was Cora May Sloan. Sometime during Sunday morning, and in consequence of some family matters, the girl received a slight chastisement (or perhaps only a correction) from her father, which made her very angry. Later in the morning she had an engagement with a young man in the neighborhood, to take a stroll. The young man failing to meet his appointment the girl went to his residence to ascertain the cause of his not coming.
>
> The young man not being at home, she asked the father if he (the son) was not going to keep his engagement with her; the father informed her that he did not know. She then asked him where his son was, and he replied that he thought he had gone out on the prairie somewhere. The girl upon hearing this immediately retraced her steps home and upon arriving there sat down and wrote a note giving her reasons for committing the rash act which caused her death. She put the note where it would be found and then took a large dose of strychnine. She was buried yesterday. From the wording of the note which she left, she must have written it in a fit of anger, as the language used was extremely harsh and bitter.

To get to Kyle, turn right on Center Street at the stop sign, off the Old Post Road. A left turn here takes you to the Nance's Mill community, but unfortunately the old Nance house and chapel are no longer accessible to the public. The road is gated and closed to the public after a couple of miles.

KYLE

Hays County • 32,000 (approximate) • About 11 miles from San Marcos

While Mountain City was dying, Kyle and Buda were springing up to take its place. The *Kyle News*, in an April 20, 1928, special edition, told the story of Kyle's first forty-eight years.

In the late 1870s, Jay Gould, the New York railroad builder, located his line of road through Texas. When he came down this way, he found that there was no town immediately on the proposed route between Austin and San Marcos—and of course one must be built. Town-building matters for the railroad company were in the hands of the New York & Texas Land Company, a corporation composed of stockholders of the railroad company. For the new town, they selected a gently sloping bit of prairie, nine miles north of San Marcos, and a short distance east of the hills—the railroad skirts the foot of the hills from Austin to San Antonio.

This land belonged to Captain Ferg. Kyle, whose father, Colonel Claiborne Kyle, was one of the first settlers of this region. Colonel Kyle furnished five sons to the Confederate Army, all in one company, Company D, Terry's Texas Rangers. All came home after the war and lived to be old men. Claiborne Kyle died in 1867. This community also furnished five other brothers, sons of Mr. and Mrs. James Stephenson, to the Confederate Army, and they too came home alive and lived to be old men.

Captain Kyle and the land company soon got together, and plans were made for a town to be named after the owner of the land. This was in 1879. The following year, Martin Groos, a surveyor, was employed to lay out the town, which he did in regular order, and just a half mile square, with wide streets; a park the size of a city block, the second block west of the railroad survey, was donated to the town.

A day was set, and lots were sold at auction. All the business lots, and many of the residence lots, were sold at good prices. The town grew rapidly from the time the railroad came, and soon the "Prairie City" became an important trading point. When the railroad came, almost the entire town of Mountain City moved bodily to Kyle, a small portion of it going to Du Pre, which later became Buda, which began building shortly after Kyle started.

When the railroad reached Kyle, a depot had not been built, and the station was opened up in a tent. S. M. Hopping, who was in the company's general offices at Palestine, and who was a telegraph operator, was sent to take charge of the station until a permanent could be gotten.

Lumberyards are necessary for town building. Knowing this, H. C. Wallace, a Rockdale lumber man, in February 1881, loaded his lumberyard, consisting of five cars of lumber and other building materials, and shipped it to Kyle. Before he could get located, however, J. A. Thompson, from some point in East Texas, shipped in a stock of lumber. Both opened up business here, but they later consolidated.

The first business house in the new town was a small wooden structure at the southwest corner of the public square, in which Tom Martin opened up a saloon. This business was established as soon as the town was laid out. In connection with the saloon was a meat market—the men could both eat and drink while they built the town.

And they especially did the drinking. Other saloons followed Martin's until finally there were four of them, and in spite of the fact that Kyle was never more than a village, they all had a liberal patronage, and their customers drank, gambled, and raced horses. They fought each other with regularity, cutting each other with their bowie knives and shooting each other up with their Winchesters and Colt 45s. A veteran of those early days reminisced, "It was 'dangerous to be safe' then. You'd better attend to your own business and keep out of others' affairs if you wanted to stay healthy."

D. A. Young built the first rock store building in Kyle, at the southwest corner of the square. The first dry goods store was opened by Otto Groos, who came here from New Braunfels. He later sold out to H. Hellman, a Jew who operated a general store here for many years, his business at one time being the largest in the county. Groos established the Kyle Bank, unincorporated, with $24,000 capital, in 1893. This bank was succeeded in 1911 by the Kyle State Bank, with a capital stock of $30,000.

The first newspaper, the *Kyle Weekly Nutshell*, was established in 1881 by A. L. Cashell, who later moved to Austin. Cashell gained some notoriety the following year as a defense witness in the murder trial of Austin city marshal Ben Thompson, who had gone down to San Antonio and killed Jack Harris, proprietor of the infamous Vaudeville Theater, on July 11, 1882. Thompson had accused Harris of swindling him of diamonds and money two years earlier in his gambling saloon adjoining the Vaudeville Theater, and Harris had threatened to kill Thompson since then.

When the hearing for Thompson's petition for bail began two weeks later, Thompson's defense was commenced by calling for Mr. A. L. Cashell of Kyle, newspaper proprietor, to prove that on about July 1 he saw Harris, who said, "I don't care a ——, if he comes to this town I will kill him, but I won't go to Austin for him."

While Ben was languishing in the San Antonio jail, having been denied bail in the Harris killing, his bad brother Bill decided to board a train at Kyle on October 28, 1882, and three officers with drawn pistols did not want him to. He drew his pistol and boarded the train. This was another instance when a full hand with bullets top beat three of a kind, two pairs, six card deal.

The Kyle Water Company built a waterworks in 1886, the water being pumped from the Blanco River a mile and a half away, as the crow flies.

The town was supported principally by farming and stock raising. The farmland is heavy black land, and cotton, corn, cane, maize, kaffir, and other feed crops all grew well, as did Irish potatoes, other truck, and most fruits. Berries like the Haupt berry did especially well. Cotton was the principal money crop until the 1920s when many farmers turned their attention to poultry and dairying in a trend toward diversification. Kyle was the heaviest cattle-shipping point between Austin and San Antonio in 1928, with commodious railroad shipping pens, including both "clean" and "dirty" pens, and a dipping vat.

In the same issue of the *Kyle News*, N. C. Schlemmer told of his early years in Kyle. Schlemmer was born near the town of Saarburg on the border between France and Prussia in 1854 and came to the United States in 1870.

In January, 1877, I came to Texas to visit a cousin at New Braunfels and subsequently held various positions with the I. & G. N. R. R. in Texas. I was stationmaster at Taylor from 1878 to 1880, before the M. K. & T. had reached that town, and when Taylor was the Eldorado of toughs and a regular hell-hole of saloons and gambling houses.

At Taylor I received the first call of fate, so to speak, to go to Kyle, through a friend, Col. Fowzer who had bought lots there when the town was laid off. He wanted me to go in with him and start in business there together, "on the ground floor," but I declined.

When the I. & G. N. R. R. had been built as far as New Braunfels and a station established, the company sent me there as agent. But while I had been waiting for an opening and undecided what to do, my friend Fowzer had induced me to make a tentative application for the post office at the prospective town of Kyle, which application was granted quickly, as I had no opponent, and the appointment was sent to me at New Braunfels, where I had already taken charge of the station. Of course I felt morally obliged to at least go and take a look at the new town. So on a dreary November morning in 1880, I got on a construction train at New Braunfels. A drizzling cold rain fell, and I felt miserably depressed when they dropped me on the open prairie somewhere between San Marcos and Austin, telling me it was Kyle. The depot had not been built and I was unable to find the town, but I thought it was perhaps due to my nearsightedness, and to the fog. Finally I espied a tough looking native at a distance, ran after him and asked the way to town. He pointed to the skeleton of a frame building in the distance, on the roof of which some men were working, and said that was all there was to it so far, however, that if I wanted a drink, I should go a piece farther on, where I would find a tip-top saloon and could get some good stuff. I followed his directions and went to the building in course of construction, where I found some old Taylor acquaintances at work building a hotel for my friend Col. Fowzer. They were camping on the open prairie near by and of course had no great modern accommodations to offer me, so we all decided to go to the saloon for refreshments and further deliberations. It was a wooden shack kept by a very polite and amiable man, and seemed to be the center of the town, or practically the town itself, for if there was another habitable structure near by I couldn't see it.

The proprietor was especially nice to me, seeming anxious to have me locate at the new town, and after setting up the crowd a few times, I withdrew to a corner of the saloon to eat a lunch of cheese and crackers, with a bottle of "Blue Ribbon," on a beer-keg. However, before I got through with my lunch, I was approached by a young man who introduced himself as W. E. Roach, at that time postmaster at Mountain City.

Mr. Roach explained that he had hoped to become the first postmaster of the town, but of course, if I already held the appointment, he would like to know it as soon as possible. Since he made a good impression from every standpoint and seemed popular with the inhabitants, I decided then and there to make all of them happy by resigning, or rather declining the appointment, as postmaster of Kyle. This decision met with the approval of the crowd, and after another farewell toast, I took the first freight train going south.

This all happened in the fall of 1880. In the spring of 1881 I was ordered to I. & G. N. headquarters at Palestine, to be informed that it was deemed to the best interests of the company to promote me from New Braunfels to their Kyle agency with a somewhat higher salary. However, I could not see it in the light of a pro-motion, and took an indefinite leave of absence. A few months later, I was offered the Overton station on the same road, which I accepted and held until the fall of 1884. Shortly after this, while stopping over at Houston, the superintendent of the Texas Express Company told me they had a vacancy in their office at Kyle, near Austin, and advised me to take it, in combination with some other kind of business in that promising new town.

At first I was shocked. But the next moment I realized for the first time, that, do what I would, I could not escape Kyle, that the powers that be, Fate, Provi-dence, Kismet, or whatever you may call it, had decreed and ordered, that I must go to that place, *nolens volens*, that it was written in the stars, so to speak, that I had to go there. And so I quickly resigned myself to the inevitable, and opened up a small grocery store, in a wooden shack on the center avenue in the city of Kyle, on Nov. 15, 1884, with the Texas Express Company's sign in front, as an ornament.

I had as my assistants a little later my brother Fred and a cousin, who afterwards established himself in the furniture business in Austin. At first we cooked our meals and slept in the back end of our shack, but, soon after the opening of the store, the Waters Pierce Oil Company gave me their distributing agency with warehouse in Kyle, and in January, 1885, I was also again appointed postmaster, with the endorsement of the leading citizens of the town. I rented the Rock Store building on Front Street, where the post office had been located, and in course of time enlarged the business to that of a general merchandise store. In 1890 I erected the large rock building, now occupied by the Schlemmer Mercantile Co., and had 17 men in my employ.

I married in 1889, and have four children all born and reared at Kyle where we continued to reside until 1904, when I turned the management of the business over to my brother, Louis, and entered the American Consular Service in Europe on March 13, 1905, as Vice-consul, and later Consul in charge, at Mannheim, Germany. On June 26, 1906, I was promoted to the consulate at Bergen, Norway. However for a number of reasons, I did not accept this very flattering appointment, but decided to return to Texas, and give my children a uniformly American education through American institutions, at Austin.

In July 1909, I was appointed postmaster at Austin by President Taft, which post I held four years. In the spring of 1916 we built a modern home on one of our farms, the former Vaughn place, about a mile northeast of Kyle, which we named "Elmhurst," on account of the grove of large elm trees surrounding the house. Here my good wife died on February 22, 1918, but I continued to make the place my home until after the tornado and terrible drought of 1925, when I turned all my properties over to my children.

Schlemmer died shortly after writing this article.

As you approach downtown Kyle, you pass, on your left, at 508 Center Street, the childhood home of the noted writer Katherine Anne Porter (famous for the novel *Ship of Fools*) who lived in Kyle as a young girl. The simple one-story frame ranch-style house is now affiliated with Texas State University.

The first sale of town lots took place on a summer day in 1880 under a spreading live oak tree, which still stands, branches drooping in its old age. The Kyle Auction Oak is located one block south of Center on Sledge.

The old Schlemmer Mercantile Company (now Center Grocery) still stands on Center Street downtown, as does the recently restored railroad depot, which still stands in its original location beside the tracks and serves as the city's visitor center.

For old-time Central Texans, it's hard to comprehend that the little old Kyle of not too many years ago is now a city of forty-thousand-plus inhabitants, and downtown Kyle is now referred to as "Old Kyle," versus the "New Kyle" which sprawls in all directions around it. In 2009, Hays County was the tenth fastest growing county in the United States, with just under 150,000 inhabitants.

Here are a few more interesting tidbits about Kyle before we leave:

- Towns across Texas were struck by railroad fever in the 1880s, and nearly every town of any consequence coveted its own line. Kyle was no different. On June 16, 1882, a resolution of the stockholders of the Kyle, Lockhart and Southern Railroad Company, authorizing the president to mortgage and sell stock to enable the company to complete the road, was filed in the secretary of state's office. Like many of its counterparts, the Kyle, Lockhart and Southern ended up going exactly nowhere. It is doubtful that surveying the line ever commenced.

- In 1882, the great presidential race between Grover Cleveland and Benjamin Harrison was overshadowed—in Kyle at least—by the election battle between Jim Hall and Boliver Greathouse for city constable. The night before the election, the local Mexican population was treated to a party at the expense of one of the candidates. They were furnished with eats and drinks, and after a night of dancing, those who were not too drunk, or dead from fighting among themselves, were shepherded at the crack of dawn to the polling place, handed fifty cents, and told to vote. Some did so two or three times. Several hundred people milled about for three days outside as election judges sweated over the final tabulations. The crowd allowed the judges no sleep during that time. In the end, Jim Hall won.
- Kyle was often the butt of Austin jokes, such as this one from December 24, 1882: "What is this city going to do, during the sitting of the legislature, in the way of lighting the streets? The moon cannot be depended on to shine every night, and when it does not shine the legislators will be in total darkness; and what is worse, they do not know the streets and man-traps as well as we do who browse around here year in and year out, and if they dislocate some of their precious necks while here, the balance may take offense or get frightened or something and cause the capitol to be moved to Kyle, or some other neighboring city, which would be very unpleasant."
- Kyle finally began to quiet down in 1898 when the saloons were voted out. With them went most of the bad eggs. Those who remained were too few in number to cause any trouble.
- One of Kyle's old Christmas Eve customs saw half of the town's boys and young men (up to about age twenty-one) lined up along one side of Main Street facing the other half along the other side of the street soon after dark. A furious firecracker and Roman candle war would then ensue. Many a coat and jacket were ruined from powder burns, and many an eye was blackened from the fistfights that often followed the pyrotechnical wars.
- Kyle was known as the "Jack Ass Capital of the World" in the early twentieth century because of the superlative stock grown by Max Michaelis and family. The Michaelis Ranch supplied mules to the U.S. military and mining companies and exported them to mines in South Africa and coffee plantations in Guatemala. Max's son, Max Jr., was also noted for introducing Charolais cattle to the United States in 1934. The ranch, located about four miles west of Kyle, at 3600 FM 150 West, is still in business, and the old ranch house built by Max Sr. still stands.
- Kyle had a woman mayor, Mary Kyle Hartson, from 1937 to 1946. She headed an all-female city government for four of those years.

DINING

RAILROAD BAR-B-QUE

107 E. Center St. • 512-262-4641 • www.rrbbq.com • Open daily, lunch and dinner • Cr.

They're located on the east side of the railroad tracks in what used to be a feed store, diagonal to the old depot on the west side of the tracks. It's the same ownership as the Manchaca location of the same name. They have good mesquite smoked brisket, pork ribs, sausage, chicken, and smoked turkey, plus the usual sides. You can get a chicken fried steak or fried catfish on weekends, but why? No beer.

Return to the Old Post Road (County Road 136) and continue north to Buda. Although Mc-Mansion-style residential development has reared its ugly head along sections of the road, especially just north of Kyle, there are still some pastures of tranquility along the way. At the intersection with FM 150, the Old Post Road becomes FM 2770. Once in Buda, turn left onto Main.

BUDA

Hays County • 6,000 (approximate) • About 8 miles from Kyle

The origin of Buda's name poses something of a mystery, although the most common explanation is that Buda is a corruption of the Spanish word *viuda* ("widow") and that the town was so named for the widow or widows who operated a hotel here in the early days. The other popular explanation is that the name Buda derives from Budapest, the capital of Hungary. In olden days, Buda and Pest were separate cities on either side of the Danube River. The Buda area was settled when Phillip Allen moved here in 1846 and began farming what was later to be called Allen's Prairie.

A town site was laid out in 1880 with the impending arrival of the I&GN, and the town was known as Du Pre for the first few years of its life, supposedly as a result of W. W. Haupt's supplications to railroad officials: "Do, pray, give us a depot." At any rate, Du Pre, or DuPre, or Dupree, was also being called Buda by 1887.

A great sale of lots for businesses or residences was held at Du Pre on April 2, 1881. The International and Great Northern ran a special excursion train that day and promised plenty of shade and water. "Bring your families and don't forget your lunch baskets," the ad in the *Austin Statesman* read.

On July 15, 1882, Du Pre held a grand Travis and Hays counties union picnic and barbecue. The International and Great Northern offered reduced rates for Austin pleasure seekers. The *Austin Statesman* reported on the grand event the next day:

> The train leaving at 7:30 yesterday was jammed and crowded, as were the coaches, so that the sleeper had to be thrown open, which was soon filled. Even then, a good many were left. There was some mistake as to notifying the proper officials about extra coaches, hence there were none placed on the train. In due time your reporter arrived on the grounds, which are located a short distance from DuPre station. There had already gathered a large crowd, and at the time of speaking, the large and spacious arbor was crowded with a large audience. There was some disappointment, and that no little, as the speakers announced for the occasion were, to a man, missing. However, a few men of some oratorical notoriety were present, and consented to occupy the time. Colonel Phil Claiborne's happy bits and facetious anecdotes raised peals of laughter. By the time he finished the sun had reached the meridian and in a short while dinner was commenced, which was the grand feature of the occasion. The table was a very large circular one, but not

near large enough to accommodate the two or three thousand people present. But the provision in the way of bread and barbecued meats was ample. I have never seen a finer lot of barbecued meat anywhere. The committee deserves great praise for the way in which every thing was arranged. Shortly after dinner, speaking recommenced. The after-dinner speeches found but few listeners. There was so much confusion under and around the arbor, and the wind was so high, that the speaking could only be heard by the few around the stand. The crowd moved and mingled together harmoniously, and passed off pleasantly the grand union picnic and barbecue between Hays and Travis county.

In an article titled "Buda in the Late Eighties" in the *Kyle News*, April 13, 1928, T. F. Harwell described life in Du Pre:

About May 1, 1887, a short while after I came to Texas, and while I was looking for a location, I visited Buda (then Du Pre), among other places. I put up at Mrs. Crizer's boarding house, better known perhaps, as the J. V. Allen Hotel. I stayed around Buda several days, walking up and down the street and talking to the folks, and I have not forgotten some of the people and the location of most of the business places.

Jim Goforth had a drug store and Dr. Robert Jameson officed with him. A little farther down, just past where the Birdwell rock store now stands [now the Old 1898 Store—ed.], were two stores, one of which was run by Tom Reagan, and the other by J. H. Schmidt, S. H. Nivens, and J. D. Talley.

Past these two stores was the Du Pre post office, housed in a small frame building, with Capt. L. D. Carrington in charge. Capt. Carrington was commander of Carrington's company, Rip Ford's regiment, in the Confederate Army. There was no business place between the post office and the Carrington Hotel. This hotel was said to be the most popular eating house on the I. & G. N. between St. Louis and San Antonio, and two or three trains stopped daily for meals.

"Budy, twenty minutes for supper," will be remembered as the familiar call of the train porters every evening, as the train pulled up opposite the hotel. In those days, the depot was about opposite where the bank building is now located. An incident comes to mind in connection with the Carrington Hotel: Dick Slack wanted to put up a lunch stand on the railroad right-of-way, near where the trains stopped, but under the company's agreement with Mrs. Carrington, they felt it would not be treating her right, so they refused permission. But he got a little farther back and put up his lunch stand and did some business, though it is perhaps an open question as to whether he made anything.

In June, '88, Mr. Hopping, who owned the thousand acres now composing the Watson farm three miles east of Buda, and which was nearly all in grass, offered me the foremanship of his hay baling outfit. I accepted the job, although I had never even seen a bale of hay pressed. But I didn't get fired, so guess my work was satisfactory. When he figured up the business, he said all he lost was what he didn't make.

I had little time for the social life. I had to "hit the ball"—no labor union hours for us. We worked from "sun to sun," and I, as foreman, usually had some extra work, for I must not only "maintain the dignity of my position," but also earn my dollar and a half a day, while the other boys only had to do a dollar's worth. About November, I went back to San Marcos, where I was then living, having saved about all my earnings.

In addition to all the standard businesses of a prosperous town of its day, Buda had a cheese factory and chamber of commerce. Buda also got natural gas service before San Marcos and other nearby towns did, because of one man.

52   CENTRAL TEXAS

Will Morgan grew up motherless in Buda, and the women of the town helped Dad Morgan take care of the boys. When Will got rich off oil and gas leases and had a set of plush offices in Houston, he used his influence to get gas lines to Buda in 1931, several years ahead of the other towns in the area.

More recently, Buda was the home of an artisans' colony during the 1970s. Several of the old commercial buildings are filled by antique-collectibles shops. Unfortunately, the most interesting of the lot, the Old 1898 Store, which was located in the old mercantile building on the corner of 200 Main at Loop 4, has been closed for several years now following the death of its owner, Austin geologist Carl Chelf.

CARRINGTON DRUG STORE

300 Main • Currently houses Memory Lane Antiques

One block north of the Old 1898 Store is Buda's most imposing downtown building, this stolid two-story orange brick box built in 1914 by prominent Buda druggist W. D. Carrington. He and his family lived upstairs, a common practice for the times.

Willie Kemp, in his entertaining memoir, *True Tales of Central Texas*, told the following story about W. D. Carrington:

> The first time I met Mr. Carrington I needed some medicine but had no money so I asked Mr. Carrington if he would take my check. At this time he knew Pa, but not me. I did not tell him who I was. He looked me over, then said you look honest, so I will take your check. After he saw my name on the check, he asked why didn't I tell him I was Louis Kemp's son. I told him that sooner or later Pa would not be around and I needed to stand on my own two feet.
>
> One day Pa went to Buda. While there he witnessed what he said was the hardest fought fist fight he ever saw, between W. D. Carrington and Tom Ruby. Pa said that both of these men were near the same age and sizes, that they evidently had had a falling out about something previously. Anyway, they met close by Mr. Carrington's drug store. When they met, no words were spoken. They rushed together, fighting violently, which continued until both men were so tired out they just stood there facing each other, not able to raise a hand, both still on their feet. Bloody, bruised, with black eyes and swollen lips. After resting a while and regaining their breath, Mr. Carrington, noble soul that he was, very gruffly said, "Tom, come into my drug store," which he did. Then they cleaned up and doctored each other's battered faces. At this time, Tom Ruby was the Constable, wearing a six shooter. Pa said that Mr. Carrington had one in his drug store, but neither one attempted to use their guns. Ever afterwards they were good friends.
>
> To my personal knowledge, Tom Ruby killed one man, named George Locke. It happened about 1913 or 1914. George was a local young man, high strung, impulsive, fool-hardy, vowing that he would not be "run over" by anyone, for he could take care of himself. Along about this time, spinal meningitis, a dreaded disease, broke out in Austin. It reached epidemic proportions, resulting in Buda posting a quarantine against people who went to Austin from returning to Buda. George Locke being young and not willing to abide by the quarantine, or thinking it was wrong to forbid anyone going to Austin to return to Buda, went to Austin and returned to his mother's home in Buda. Tom Ruby learned about George's travel, so, he being constable, went to the house where George was. George is reported to have come out of the front door with a six shooter in his hand. Both men began firing their guns. All of George's bullets went wild, missing Ruby. One

of these bullets went through the back door of Sherman Birdwell's grocery store [now the Old 1898 Store—ed.]. Ruby's bullets struck George Locke, killing him, as I understand, in his mother's front yard.

OLD BUDA BANK

312 Main (middle of the block)

This low-slung one-story brick building has housed an Indonesian restaurant and a newspaper. It started life, however, as the Farmers National Bank of Buda, and as such was the victim of one of Texas' most unusual bank robberies, back in 1926.

CARRINGTON HOUSE

320 Main

At the end of this block is the rambling two-story Carrington House of travelers' fame. Mrs. Carrington's hospitality was mentioned in print as early as 1886. By 1890, she had moved to Monterrey, Mexico, to manage the Topo Chico Hotel, located at the springs that still produce the famous mineral water of the same name. But by 1897, she was back in Buda running the Buda Hotel, claimed to be the only first-class hotel in Buda.

One day, during a cattlemen's convention in San Antonio, Mrs. S. A. Carrington served one thousand people en route to the convention on several special trains. The old hotel still stands (now a private residence) downtown. Sam Ealy Johnson, Lyndon's daddy, used to drive here from Johnson City in his buggy, park it, and ride the Sunshine Special up to Austin when the state legislature was in session. William Jennings Bryan and Governor Pat Neff came to Buda for a day of feasting and speechmaking in 1924.

Now, to the story of that 1926 bank heist. On December 11 of that year, Becky Bradley Rogers, a twenty-two-year-old UT graduate student and part-time stenographer for Attorney General Dan Moody, held up the Farmers National Bank. After an unsuccessful attempt to hold up the Round Rock Farmers Bank the previous day (the same bank Sam Bass had planned to hold up fifty years earlier), Becky walked into the Buda bank that Saturday morning posing as a newspaper reporter working on a story on the local farming economy. At noon, after all the day's customers had left, she pulled a .32 automatic on the cashier. With $1,000 tucked in her purse, she locked the cashier and bookkeeper in the vault and took off for Austin. The shocked employees were out of the vault in ten minutes and alerted the authorities. Reports had her headed for Fredericksburg, headed up the Old Post Road straight for Austin, and headed all over Central Texas. In reality she headed for Creedmoor, got stuck in the deep winter mud, got pulled out by an unsuspecting dairy farmer, and then drove leisurely into Austin where she mailed the money and gun to herself at a university post office box and dropped her muddy flivver off for a wash and wax. She was arrested by Austin police when she went to pick up her car. Everyone, the newspapers included, wondered how such a sweet and innocent-looking girl could have pulled off such a daring act. She pulled the job, she said, to finance treatment for her law student fiancé's "acute intestinal paralysis," but it turned out she was in debt to the Texas branch of the American Historical Association for $1,500, the result of a membership drive that failed.

Becky went through a series of sensational trials that ended in conviction and a fourteen-year sentence, reversal of the sentence on appeal, a second trial in La Grange that ended in mistrial, and a second mistrial verdict in a New Braunfels court, whereupon the state threw up its hands in frustration after three years of prosecution and dropped the case. Becky's long-suffering husband (she had been secretly married to him for some time before the robbery) served as counsel for the defense throughout the trial process. Following the dropping of charges in 1929, they dropped out of sight.

In the meantime, the Farmers National Bank had closed up. The bank had gotten its money back, but owner W. D. Carrington had seen enough: "When women start robbing banks I'm selling out." He did so in 1927 to the Austin National Bank. In the meantime, the bank was again robbed by a lone gunman, to the tune of $1,200. Shortly after its acquisition, Austin National Bank closed the Buda bank for good.

Local legend has it that Bonnie and Clyde robbed the bank. The only problem with the story is that Barrow didn't even meet Bonnie until 1930, three years after the bank had closed, and up to 1926, the year of the Buda bank robbery, Clyde's biggest crime had been stealing a rent-a-car to go see his girlfriend.

ANTIOCH COLONY

From the stoplight on Main Street, turn left on Live Oak/FM 967 and drive a half mile northwest. After crossing Onion Creek, take the first left (CR 148/ Cole Springs Road), then a right on CR 147, the Old Black Colony Road.

On February 1, 1859, Joseph F. Rowley, who had emigrated with his family from California to Texas, purchased 490 acres near Onion Creek, a mile northwest of Buda. After the Civil War, he sold tracts, at five dollars an acre, to former slaves for the purpose of establishing a farming settlement. Many of the freedmen came from Missouri. They founded Antioch Colony, named for the Turkish city, in 1870, ten years before the town of Du Pre was laid out. Ten to fifteen families lived in the community by the early 1870s. For years, the settlement was called the Black Colony—or worse—by whites living in the area. Farmers raised corn and other grains, cotton, and sugarcane, and mule-powered mills processed corn and bran and produced sorghum molasses. On July 15, 1874, Elias and Clarissa Bunton donated land for a school. Residents constructed a two-story building that soon served fifty-seven students as part of their own district, Antioch School District 5. The community's Mason Lodge and Order of the Eastern Star met in the school building. Citizens also established an African Methodist Church and the Antioch Cemetery.

The colony's men and women did whatever it took to earn a living, digging ditches, stone masonry, and doing domestic work for wealthy white families. Children shined white folks' shoes on Main Street for five cents a pair and worked alongside their parents in the fields. In the late summer and early fall, many families followed the cotton harvest around the state. All but the very youngest of children picked cotton.

With little hard money income, most families raised their own food, maintaining vegetable gardens and fruit orchards, raising chickens and other poultry, and raising and slaughtering their own cattle and hogs. They made their own butter and molasses. During the winter, when work was slow and food was short, the two white grocers in Buda sold them and other poor families supplies on credit, regardless of race.

Antioch Colony remained an active farming community into the 1930s and 1940s. Social life centered around the school and church, which had some seventy to eighty members. Until the 1940s, when a drinking fountain was installed in the colony's school, children carried jars of water with them from home. There was no running water at any of the homes, and only a few families could afford to drill a well. Most packed water from Onion Creek or bought it for twenty-five cents a barrel.

Telephone service had arrived in Buda in 1905 and electricity in 1927. But telephone and electric lines did not reach out to the colony until sometime after 1955, after most everyone had left the colony and fiercely segregated Hays County in search of better jobs. Much of the property was sold or lost after taxes went unpaid by absentee landowners.

The community pretty much became a ghost town. The church and the colony's school have long disappeared. There is little to see of the old days here anymore, save the Antioch Cemetery, which has about fifty headstones, and many more graves with no markers, dating back to the 1880s.

In the late 1970s, a few former residents returned to the colony and bought back the land of their ancestors. This slow rebirth of the colony has continued. LeeDell Bunton, a great-great-grandson of one of the founders, bought back part of his family land. In 1997, residents established the Antioch Community Church, and in 1999, approximately three hundred people attended the first Antioch Colony reunion. Local residents continue to maintain Antioch Cemetery, located on Old Black Colony Road. By 2000, some twenty people, members of three extended families and descendants of early settlers, lived in Antioch Colony.

ANNUAL EVENT

DECEMBER

BUDA FEST

Under the oaks in downtown Buda • First Sunday in December • Free • W

This Christmas shopping bazaar has arts and crafts, puppeteers, jugglers, musicians, and vendors.

Leave Buda on the first leg of Becky's getaway route. Follow Main/Loop 4 across the railroad tracks.

STAGECOACH PARK

880 Main St.

A few hundred yards after you cross the railroad tracks, you will see a sign for the City of Buda's Stagecoach Park. The one-story, ranch-house style white frame building is what remains of the old Onion Creek post office and stage-coach stop, said to date to about 1875 or 1876. Shaded by a grove of giant, ancient oaks, the stage stop was surely a cool and welcome rest stop on hot summer days. If you walk down the hill to the creek just below the Loop 4 bridge, you can see wagon and stagecoach wheel ruts carved into the limestone outcroppings in the creek bed.

The fifty-two-acre park has more than two miles of crushed granite trails, lots of open parkland, a playground, and a fishing pond with fountains. There is an amphitheater, a windmill with water flowing into a large catch basin reminiscent of the 1800s, a wildflower meadow, and dedicated wetlands preservation. Wildlife is abundant within, including deer. The park is equipped with restrooms, water, and electricity for the pavilion, which is available to rent for such things as family reunions and picnics, birthday parties, wedding receptions, and the like.

From the old post office and stage stop, continue for about a mile on Loop 4 (toward I-35) and turn left on the Old San Antonio Road (County Road 117), just west of I-35. Continue north on the Old San Antonio Road sixteen miles to reach Austin.

Incidentally, this road, the I-35 of its time, is believed to be the first paved rural road in Texas. Paving costs were paid by either the U.S. Post Office or the Agriculture Department, and the project was the first Federal Aid Project in Texas. Paving of this twenty-four-mile strip from the Travis County line through Hays County to the Comal County line was begun in 1915 and finished in 1919. It was also the first paving project of the newly created Texas Highway Department.

A good road was hard to find in Texas in 1919, where the old saying about "roads that are more hole-y than righteous" certainly rattled true. "Good roads," grumbled a turn-of-the-twentieth-century farmer in Bell County, "Come to Texas if you want to see good roads . . . good and sandy, good and rough, good and muddy."

Public roads in Texas were little more than improved trails in 1900; many were not much better than they had been in 1800. Texas law required that "first-class roads" be built between county seats, built on forty-foot rights-of-way and cleared of timber. Stumps less than eight inches in diameter were to be cut off at the ground, while larger stumps had to be rounded off so that wagon wheels could jounce off them easily. The little upkeep that occurred was done under the statute labor system, in which every able-bodied male was required to work on the roads a specified number of days per year. This practice had first begun in ancient Rome, had lasted in Europe through the Dark Ages, and persisted in Texas and other states into the early 1900s.

As early as 1894, the Dallas Commercial Club urged the construction of an all-weather roads system. The roads had changed little from the prairie schooner days. By 1905, there were 2,500 autos in Texas. Their drivers promoted good roads in their communities, and since many of them were businessmen, they worked on their commercial club colleagues to also support good roads. In 1903, the Texas legislature tried to create a Bureau of Highways to assist local counties with engineering advice on how to build good roads.

Around 1907, the automobile began making inroads in Texas. The legislature passed a law limiting auto speeds to eighteen miles per hour and requiring cars to stop to let horse-drawn vehicles pass if they signaled to do so. As auto travel increased, there was a mounting demand for hard surfaced roads. Motorists formed auto clubs in the cities, and statewide auto and good road associations followed.

Roads were built by counties using volunteers who donated at least three days of work annually, building dirt or gravel roads, using such primitive tools as the split-log drag. Legislators tried to create a highway bureau every session from 1903 to 1909 but failed. In 1910, Texas A&M University began offering a course in highway engineering.

In 1912, the Texas Business Men's Association recommended that a state highway department be created along the same lines that were later adopted when the legislature finally created the department. That year, forty road bond elections were held in Texas, twenty-six of which passed, totaling $2.37 million. The 1911 and 1913 legislatures authorized the creation of eighty-five county road systems and authorized the amendment of fifty-nine other county road systems.

In 1916, Congress passed the Federal Aid Road Act, which prompted a public cry for the creation of a state highway commission. Congress had appropriated $75 million to pay 25 percent of the construction cost of federally approved highway projects. Texas would receive $4.5 million of this aid if it created a highway agency to supervise expenditure of these funds. Chambers of commerce and drivers worked together to persuade state legislators to create the agency. In 1917, the first year of auto registrations, Texas had 194,720 motor vehicles. The Thirty-fifth Legislature created the Texas Highway Department and the Texas Highway Commission. The new agency began operations in June 1917 with ten employees.

Prior to 1917, all road-building activities had been on a county level, producing a system of unconnected roads. The Bankhead Act, enacted by Congress in 1917, provided for construction of the first paved highway to span the nation, including 772 miles in Texas from Marshall to El Paso. "Better Roads for Prosperity" was the road builders' slogan, and they worked hard to get communities and the state "out of the mud." But then the war slowed construction down to only highways vital to the war program.

J. Henry Martindale described a typical Central Texas county road working years ago in the *Austin Statesman*:

> The Commissioners Court named a road overseer in each community. For some unknown reason, these nonpaying jobs were sought . . . in the manner that people today hound their Congressman for a postmaster appointment. Perhaps it was because the road overseer was a person of distinction, looked up to by the folks of the community.
>
> Each male from 18 to 60 who lived on a farm had to contribute five days a year to work free on the roads in the area. Townsfolk rendered the same service on city streets.
>
> Usually the overseer would wait until the crops were laid by in July before he called the men out to work. The workers would arrive after the first flush of dawn,

bringing their lunches, hammers, hoes, crowbars, plows, grubbing hoes, and other tools. None worked hard enough to hurt himself. Frequently at the noon hour, there would be boxing, wrestling, and running matches. One day, two cousins put on a dandy fist fight.

Some of the "mainest roads" were kept up in another manner. Justices of the peace and county judges in those days could assess a penalty of working so many days on the county roads. Their overseer would usually . . . strut around wearing a big pistol or perhaps carrying a long rifle to see that the men kept busy.

During the 1920s, two points of view conflicted over the future of paved highway construction. The State Highway Commission advocated construction of major highways on a direct line through the counties, whereas many towns, counties, and chambers of commerce wanted to continue with the old practice of building highways through every village and hamlet along zigzag routes. Merchants feared that bypassing the small towns would rob them of customers. Previously, roads planned by county officials had been constructed without too much thought for connecting their roads with those of adjoining counties. Governor Pat Neff declared that hardly one hundred miles of continuous pavement existed anywhere in Texas. He deplored the fact that every good highway ended in a mud hole. In 1923, the legislature passed a law that highway intersections be marked to guide travelers along the right roads. A 1927 law specified that first-class county roads had to be forty feet wide, that all stumps over six inches in diameter be cut down to six inches of the road surface and rounded off, and that smaller stumps be cut smooth with the ground. By 1926, Texas had one million cars. In 1925, construction of a coordinated highway system began when the legislature gave the Highway Department total control of planning, building, and maintaining highways built with state and federal funds. County commissioners could no longer designate the route of state highways through their counties even though they had to pay 25 percent of highway construction costs. In 1932, the state and federal governments assumed all costs except rights-of-way.

This highway law of 1925, which gave the state highway commission total control, was meant to calm federal frustration with local officials. Frustrated by a lack of cooperation from local governing bodies, federal highway officials had announced in 1923 that they would withdraw all federal highway aid on January 1, 1926, unless highway designation and construction were placed in the hands of the state highway department. They gave the state two years to comply.

Many Texans feared federal usurpation and had to be shown and convinced that only supervision would be in federal hands. Initiation of highways, project design, and handling of materials would be done by the highway department. Chambers of commerce had to educate the public on the benefits of building a connected highway system. During the early 1900s, several bond issues to build road systems had been defeated because voters didn't see the benefit of spending a lot of money to build paved roads.

Motorists and improved highways begat the automobile tourist industry. Many of the early travelers stayed in hotels, spurring a boom in hotel construction. Others carried their own camping equipment. They camped in vacant lots on city outskirts. They spent money with local businesses during their stay, and so towns began to establish free tourist camps where folks could pitch their tent, make camp, and sleep under the stars. Sanitary conditions and safety soon became a problem, so garbage cans, toilets, electric lights, and police protection were often provided. Eventually, as costs increased, the camps began to charge twenty-five to fifty cents for registration. By 1922, Brady had opened a tourist camp on the outskirts of town. The city provided the property, the water and light company provided said services, and the chamber of commerce built a four-section camp house.

Soon cottages were constructed, and so tourist courts were born, which later begat motels.

ONION CREEK

About 5 miles from Buda

According to legend, somewhere near the Old San Antonio Road's crossing of Onion Creek, several miles north of Buda, is buried a kettle of Spanish gold and jewels, hidden in a drought crack by a Spanish army pack train under Indian attack. Many have searched, but none have found. This crossing is also known as Sasser Crossing, the place where a frontier bee hunter used to set his saucer of bee bait and lie in wait, hoping to follow the little bait taker back to its honey tree or cave.

Continue north on the Old San Antonio Road past the FM 1626 intersection and across Slaughter Creek to the junction with the I-35 frontage road. Turn right onto the southbound I-35 frontage road, then left a few yards up the hill onto the I-35 overpass, then left again onto the northbound I-35 frontage road. Take the South Congress exit (which comes up shortly), and follow the signs to take South Congress into Austin.

SOUTH CONGRESS AVENUE (AUSTIN)

Up until the construction of I-35 in the 1950s, S. Congress (US 81) was the main drag out of town. Back then, the Austin city limits didn't extend much farther than St. Edward's University (the campus stretched over 650 acres and contained a large farm in those days), and the stretch of S. Congress/US 81 beyond the city limits was a hotbed of whorehouses and honky-tonks.

Hattie Valdez was queen of the Austin madams, running two and three bawdy houses at a time. La Siesta Courts, and later the M&M Courts, were the best known houses in their day. Many Austin folk objected, but not much was done to shut the houses of ill repute down because the places had prominent customers and were relatively well behaved, for whorehouses. It was also suspected that the girls enjoyed more than just a friendly relationship with the forces of law and order. When Sheriff T. O. Lang took office in 1953, he immediately pledged to put the ladies of the night out of business and, true to his word, conducted raid after raid on the houses, but they just kept springing back up. The whorehouses suffered from the raids in the mid-1950s but weren't dealt a final blow until the 1960s, when the Tim Overton gang tried to muscle in on Hattie's business.

Tim Overton was a bear of a man. He had played football at the University of Texas, climaxing his stint as a Longhorn with a trip to the 1960 Cotton Bowl. Later that year, he and his brother Charles (who had already done time for burglary) were arrested on forgery charges. Tim soon expanded his repertoire to include bank robbery, whoremongering, and extortion. By 1965, he headed up a gang whose membership ranged from prostitutes to lawyers to two-bit gunmen to fringe members who were prominent Austin citizens. It was at this time that he decided to take over Hattie's, then located at the M&M Courts just outside the city limits. Overton went to Hattie and demanded that she install a pair of his girls. She refused, whereupon Tim brashly said, "We're taking over this town anyway, so we'll just take a percentage off the top of what you're taking in." Hattie promptly kicked him out, so Overton went to visit Sheriff Lang. Inside Lang's office, Overton told the sheriff that he was going to take things over, Hattie's included. Lang kicked him out at gunpoint. Undaunted, Overton began assembling a small army of hired guns. Hattie's backers in Austin got wind of Overton's plan and began assembling their own army. The Austin police were powerless since Hattie's was outside the city limits. Hattie's gunmen were ready and waiting for the Overton assault, but just as invasion was imminent, the Texas Rangers stepped in, sent everyone home, and closed the place down. This was the last straw for Hattie, and she retired for good after this episode. An Austin era had drawn to a close. The M&M Courts were torn down a few years later.

Tim Overton went to prison shortly after the Hattie fiasco. Released in 1972, he was gunned down in Dallas two months later.

ST. EDWARD'S UNIVERSITY

3001 S. Congress at St. Edward's Dr. • 448-8400 • W

Visible for miles atop South Austin's highest hill is the main building of St. Edward's University. Designed by noted architect Nicholas Clayton, this massive Gothic limestone structure was built in 1888–1889, was gutted by fire in 1903, and was rebuilt. The smaller Victorian Gothic limestone Holy Cross Hall was built after the fire. St. Edward's got its start back in 1872. E. Sorin, founder of the University of Notre Dame and superior general of the Congregation of the Holy Cross, bought four hundred acres here three miles south of the capitol. It began as a boys' school, with three boys enrolled by 1878. Holy Cross sisters performed the domestic chores, while Holy Cross brothers split the teaching and farming chores. A college charter was obtained in 1885, and enrollment grew rapidly thereafter, despite a tornado in 1922 that leveled practically every building on campus.

WILLIAMSON COUNTY

Set smack-dab in the heart of a state long accustomed to bragging on itself, Williamson County can make, in matters that are quintessentially Texan, a few sizable brags of its own.

Take King Cotton for example—"Gotta pick sum cotton ef it breaks my back"—in a state whose cotton crop has been called the most valuable crop grown in a single political subdivision in the world. Williamson County holds the all-time Texas one-year production record: 168,509 cotton bales produced in 1920, in the days when 70 percent of the Texas population depended on cotton for a living.

And take the weather—"If you don't like the weather in Texas, just wait a few minutes and it will change." More specifically, consider rain (or the lack of it), which every real Texan feels constrained to discuss at least once a day. Williamson County holds Texas' all-time one-day rainfall record: 23.11 inches at Taylor, September 6 and 7, 1921.

And what about cowboys—"Get along little dogey." Williamson County was home of Will Pickett, inventor (and arguably the greatest all-time practitioner) of the sport of bulldogging.

Then there were outlaws—"Some rob you with a six-gun and some with a fountain pen, but you'll never see an outlaw drive a family from its home." Sam Bass made a patch of Williamson County soil his eternal home under circumstances that made him legendary.

Williamson County's latest brag is that of phenomenal growth; it is one of the fastest-growing counties in the state, and it was the sixth fastest growing county in the United States in 2009, with nearly 395,000 inhabitants. In the late 1970s, Austin's explosive growth began to rub off on Williamson County along the I-35 corridor and US 183 North. By 1990, the county's population was 139,551; in 1995, it was estimated at 162,761. Georgetown (the county seat) and the once-sleepy villages of Round Rock, Cedar Park, and Leander

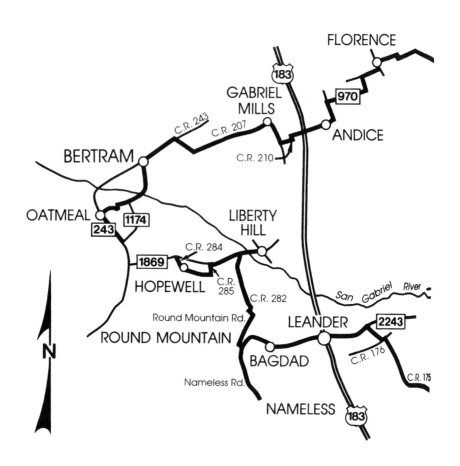

FLORENCE

183

GABRIEL
MILLS

970

C.R. 243

C.R. 207

ANDICE

C.R. 210

BERTRAM

OATMEAL

1174

LIBERTY
HILL

243

C.R. 284

1869

C.R.
285

HOPEWELL

C.R. 282

San Gabriel River

Round Mountain Rd.

LEANDER

2243

ROUND MOUNTAIN

C.R. 176

BAGDAD

C.R. 175

Nameless Rd.

NAMELESS

183

N

WILLIAMSON COUNTY

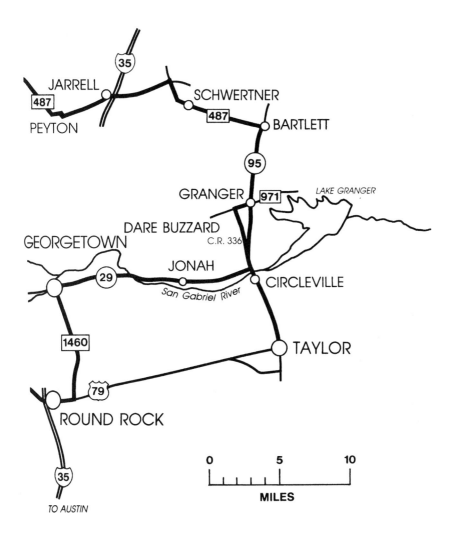

now have big-city conveniences and are beginning to experience big-city problems like drugs, gangs, and crime. This growth has created a trichotomy of suburbia versus small town versus rural life in what was already a dichotomous county. The suburban lifestyle has been winning lately, with the small-town and rural mindsets hanging on for dear life. Traditionally one of the state's most politically and socially conservative counties, Williamson County (particularly the western half of the county) is filling up with upwardly mobile urban refugees who are mostly fiscally and politically conservative, but often less so on social and personal-freedom issues.

Williamson County's posture astride the Balcones Fault makes this trip a delightful mix of rich, rolling, black-earth farmland and rugged Hill Country limestone. There is a reason for the tortured boundary line between Travis and Williamson counties: It reflects the dividing line between the watersheds of the Colorado and Brazos rivers. Williamson County's streams eventually empty into the Brazos, Travis County's into the Colorado.

This trip begins in the county seat, Georgetown, and ends in the heart of downtown Round Rock, Williamson County's largest municipality.

From I-35, take the SH 29 exit to reach downtown Georgetown and the courthouse square.

GEORGETOWN

Williamson County Seat • 42,000 (approximate) • (512) • About 11 miles from Round Rock

The first inhabitants of Georgetown were Tonkawa Indians, who drove buffalo off the high Tonkawa Bluff of the San Gabriel River just east of town and ran footraces around a five-hundred-yard track about four miles northwest of the present courthouse.

White settlers began to drift into the area during the early 1840s, when it was still a part of sprawling Milam County, and by 1847 the Brushy post office was located here. For the settlers living here, it was a long trip to the Milam County seat, Nashville-on-the-Brazos, where all legal matters were conducted. So in the early months of 1848, settlers in the western section of Milam County petitioned the Texas legislature asking for the creation of a new county, suggesting San Gabriel and Clear Water as possible names. The legislators created their county but named it after their esteemed colleague, Robert McAlpin "Three-legged Willie" Williamson. Legend has it that when the bill to create the "County of San Gabriel" came before the Texas Senate, Three-legged Willie arose and excitedly protested having any more saints in Texas. Willie never resided in the county named for him, but he traveled through it often.

A popular old-timer's story says that legislators voted to name the county for Williamson after he told the following tale on himself: A few years earlier, Colonel Frank W. Johnson had headed a surveying party that charted a ten-league land grant inside what would become Williamson County. Williamson was part of the surveying party. There were still great herds of buffalo on the scene, and on this particular day, Williamson determined to chase down one or more of the massive beasts. Colonel Johnson advised against the chase, for the ground was exceedingly wet, uneven, and full of holes. But Williamson was not to be denied and galloped off astride his horse. They were approaching full speed when his horse suddenly turned a somersault, throwing rider, gun, and crutch off into an inglorious heap. Once the horse was upright, it continued on after the buffalo. Williamson attempted to regain his equilibrium, but each time he stood up, his peg leg and crutch sank deep into the black waxy mud. After "swearing like an army mired in Flanders," he gave up and lay still in the mud until his horse was brought back to him some hours later.

Another version of the story says that every time he tried to stand up, a charging buffalo calf would knock him back down. He finally retaliated by shooting the calf from a prone position.

In May of 1848, the men entrusted with the task of locating the new county's seat of government met under a large live oak tree a few blocks south of the two forks of the San Gabriel to deliberate. As the men discussed possible locations, George Washington Glasscock Sr., a member of a land development firm with extensive area holdings, galloped up and made the following offer: if the commissioners would select this site for the county seat and name the town Georgetown in his honor, Glasscock would donate a 173-acre tract of land. "Paying due regard to donations of land" (which was required by law), the commissioners accepted Glasscock's proposition and thereby gained simultaneously a county seat and a new name. One of the commissioners, Washington Anderson, was a cousin by marriage to Glasscock. An Anderson family version of the story has Anderson proposing the land donation and town name to Glasscock, who consented after only a moment's hesitation.

Georgetown residents enjoyed few of life's amenities during the early years. Buffalo, bears, deer, wild turkeys, and Indians wandered at will through the little village. The first time a jail was needed, a wagon bed was turned upside down with the prisoner confined underneath, while the constable slept on top to prevent his escape.

In the 1850 census, Greenlief Fiske was listed as the county's largest taxpayer, paying taxes on $20,000 valuation. Fiske was also Williamson's first county judge. He had come to the area only four years earlier, settling on the South San Gabriel.

While conducting court in December 1854, Judge Robert Jones Rivers contracted pneumonia. He had been staying at the Ake Hotel, which was a log cabin built by John Ake in August 1848, the first house in Georgetown. When Rivers' condition worsened, Parson Stephen Strickland was summoned, and he told Rivers that his life was nearing its end. The judge asked that the curtain over his window be raised. Georgetown, according to an observer, "was then a mere hamlet on a hill, with almost limitless prairies stretching away on every side. There was a thin sheet of sleet on the ground and the brown and sere grass could be seen through it. Altogether it was a desolate and depressing scene." After gazing out the window for a while, Judge Rivers turned toward Parson Strickland and said,

Parson, I have always been a firm believer in the fitness of things and I have never been more forcibly impressed with this doctrine than I am at the present moment. I have been a great traveler in my day and time—have visited Europe, spent some time in the principal colleges, stopped at magnificent hotels, lodged in inns and taverns, and I tell you now, Parson, with all these experiences flashing before me, I know of no place that I can quit with fewer regrets than the new city of Georgetown and particularly this Ake Hotel.

Then, according to tradition, he turned his face to the wall and died.

After the Civil War, thousands of cattle pounded through downtown Georgetown on their long journey to the northern markets, bringing Georgetown its first real taste of prosperity. Three of the biggest cattle barons in the area were the Snyder brothers: Dudley, Thomas, and John Wesley. The foundation for their fortune was a huge herd of cattle that they had collected to drive east to the beleaguered Confederate garrison at Vicksburg. Vicksburg fell before they arrived, however, so the Snyders drifted back to Texas, awaiting orders that never came. At war's end, they slipped the herd across the Mexican border, where they sold the beeves for gold. They then returned to Williamson County, bought more cattle, and began driving them north. Innovative in many ways, the Snyders were unusual in that they did not permit their cowboys to drink, play cards, gamble, or swear in their presence.

When Round Rock became a railroad town in 1876, customers and merchants began to desert Georgetown for the tracks ten miles south. Apprehensive, the remaining Georgetown civic leaders got together, pooled their resources, and built a tap line from Georgetown to Round Rock. The line was built in 1878, and as a result the Georgetown economy rebounded.

Georgetown became famous for its "First Monday" trade-a-thons, which started soon after the Civil War. On the first Monday of each month, farmers would bring horses and cattle to the courthouse square to trade. Some visitors considered this event an excuse to go on a drinking spree. Others took it as an excuse to make some ethically questionable trades, and traders would touch up an old graying nag with shoe polish or lampblack to make it look younger. Many a cutting or shooting scrape resulted from these unsavory trades. First Mondays were so popular that horses were hitched in a continuous ring around the courthouse fence, and the streets were ankle deep in either dust or mud, depending on the weather.

Considerably more sedate today, the courthouse square is still interesting to see. In fact, with the removal of the 1960s facade of the now closed Gold's Department Store, it is one of the most complete and best-preserved courthouse squares in the state and is a Registered National Historic District. Georgetown calls itself the red poppy capital of Texas. For about a month (usually April) every spring, Georgetown gardens are awash with red poppy flowers. The tradition dates to World War I, when a returning soldier brought home some seeds from Flanders Field for his mother's garden.

Georgetown has three official historic districts. The Downtown Historic District is bounded by Rock Street to the west, Church Street to the east, Seventh Street to the north, and Ninth Street to the south. It includes the county courthouse and business district. The Belford National Register Historic District includes houses and churches along Austin Avenue and Main Street, between University Avenue and Nineteenth Street. It was named for Charles Belford, a turn-of-the-century builder who visited his construction sites wearing a suit and derby hat and carrying an umbrella, a piece of chalk, and a plumb bob. Of the eighty-one buildings in this eight-block district, seventy-three are at least eighty years old. The University Avenue/Elm Street National Register Historic District includes homes and churches on University Avenue between Myrtle and Hutto Road. It has twenty-two homes of interest, one of which was built for Buffalo Bill Cody's brother. It is notable for its large Victorian houses built in the 1890s on what had formerly been the Thomas Hughes Ranch.

Altogether, Georgetown has over fifty homes that have been deemed historic in one way or another, from grand mansion to shotgun shack; most are over one hundred years old. Most of these houses are located immediately east and southeast of the county courthouse in an area that includes the Southwestern University campus and extends below University Avenue to Fifteenth Street.

From SH 29, turn right onto Business US 81 (Austin Avenue) to reach the county courthouse.

WILLIAMSON COUNTY COURTHOUSE

Austin at 7th • Open Monday through Friday

The present Greek Revival courthouse was built in 1910 and is the county's fifth. Some of its charm disappeared when its massive marble pediment and roofline balustrade were removed in 1965, but the square's old oaks and pecans still stand guard, offering the weary traveler a bit of shaded rest on those hot Texas summer days. A number of historical monuments and markers dot the grounds.

M. B. LOCKETT BUILDING

119 W. 7th

Built in 1896, the Lockett building anchors this corner of the courthouse square. Built of field-dressed limestone blocks with a red brick facade, it features a pressed-metal cornice, a distinctive corner bay window, and a domed turret.

DAVIDSON GROCERY AND H. C. CRAIG BUILDINGS

115 and 117 W. 7th

Although distinctly separate structures, both turn-of-the-century buildings feature pressed-metal facades in good condition.

GEORGETOWN HISTORY AND VISITOR INFORMATION CENTER

101 W. 7th at Main • 863-5598 • www.visit.georgetown.org • Open daily 9–5, except Sunday 1–5 • W

Eager-to-help volunteers will direct you to a number of free or low-cost pamphlets and books about the area, which are available here.

OLD MASONIC LODGE

701 Main • Currently houses a restaurant

The old Masonic Lodge anchors the northeast corner of the square in its own impressive way. The most distinctive feature of this two-story limestone building is its tacked-on cast-metal second-story bay window and onion dome.

Shades of Baghdad! The Masons met upstairs and rented out the ground floor to a variety of businesses over the years until the building was sold in 1982.

DIMMIT BUILDING

719 Main at 8th

Another two-story limestone structure, the 1890s Dimmit building sports a cast-iron facade and full-length cast-metal cornice. The building is still owned by a descendant of the Dimmit family.

P. H. DIMMIT BUILDING

801 Main • Currently serves as an office building

Just across Eighth Street from the old Dimmit building is the P. H. Dimmit building. The P. H. Dimmit Company erected this Richardson Romanesque structure in 1901 as a hotel, but it was never used as such. It later served as a store, movie house, drugstore, office, and the like before undergoing renovation in 1960.

LESESNE-STONE BUILDING

102 W. 8th at Main

Built in 1884 and restored ninety-nine years later, this two-story building features some especially nice stonework and a pedimented metal cornice. Stone's Drugstore was the original ground-floor occupant and continued there for many years.

FIRE STATION

Main at 9th

A few yards south of the square is the restored two-story limestone building built in 1893 to house Georgetown's volunteer fire department (formed in 1884) and municipal operations. The building was constructed in an L plan around a metal standpipe that stood one hundred feet tall (fifteen feet in diameter) and held the city's water supply (234,000 gallon capacity). The fire department continues to occupy the building, although most of the city's municipal operations moved into the present city hall in 1971. The perimeter of the standpipe can still be seen in the pavement. The Firefighting Museum displays firefighting memorabilia and equipment from the past. Captain Emzy Taylor, of whom you will read more, helped found the department and served as chief.

OLD GRACE EPISCOPAL CHURCH/FOUNDERS PARK

Main at 9th

This whitewashed, wooden-frame, Carpenter Gothic-style church was built in 1881 at the corner of Main and Tenth. In 1955, it was moved to University Avenue, across from Southwestern University. By 1989, Grace's congregation had grown to the point that a new sanctuary was built. The Episcopal Diocese of Houston gave the old church building to the City of Georgetown, and in 1992 it was moved to its present site, one block from its original home. The building was restored and is home to the Georgetown Heritage Society's office and the Grace Heritage Center. Public restrooms are located behind the church.

Head west down W. Eighth, then north on Austin to complete this tour of the courthouse square and surrounding buildings of interest.

STEELE STORE/MAKEMSON HOTEL

800 Austin Ave. at W. 8th • Currently houses a variety of businesses

As early as 1848, a log cabin on this site served as Georgetown's first hotel and stage stop as well as its second post office. Construction of the present sprawling two-story limestone complex commenced in about 1870 and continued through about 1911. Previous users of the building included a dry goods store, a bank, and a hotel/boarding house.

OLD FARMERS STATE BANK/WILLIAMSON MUSEUM

716 Austin • 943–1670 • williamsonmuseum.org

An existing limestone building was remodeled in 1910 to house the Farmers State Bank; the result was a miniature Greek temple, with two massive Ionic columns, sandwiched into this stretch of Victorian buildings. In 1905, Farmers State Bank was one of the first three banks to receive a charter from the state of Texas. The bank moved out in 1962. The county bought the building in 1967. The building is notable for its black-and-white marble wainscoting, its twenty-foot ceiling with decorative, carved plaster molding, and its mosaic tile floor. Run by the Williamson County Historical Commission, the museum's rotating exhibits focus on local history and culture.

WINDBERG GALLERY

714-A Austin • 819-9463 • windberg.com

Georgetown is home to well-known landscape and still-life artist Dalhart Windberg. Here you'll find original paintings, limited editions on canvas, limited-edition prints, open-edition prints, and plates.

MILEHAM BUILDING

708–710 Austin

If you like pressed metal, you'll love the Mileham building, built in 1898. It sports a two-and-a-half-story pressed-metal facade, which came from the Mesker Brothers Company of St. Louis. The Mesker Brothers sold over five thousand storefronts nationwide between 1884 and 1907, and furnished decorative metalwork for many other Georgetown buildings.

DAVID LOVE BUILDING

706 Austin Ave. • Currently houses specialty shops

David Love was one of the area's earliest settlers. His name appears on the 1848 petition to form present-day Williamson County. He served as a county commissioner and was an original director of the Georgetown Railroad Company. In 1883, he built this two-story limestone and pressed-metal structure to house his dry goods store.

PALACE THEATER

810 S. Austin, just south of the square • 869-7469 • www.thegeorgetown palace.org

Built in 1926, the Palace Theater is the only Art Deco-style building in downtown Georgetown. It features community theater and live music.

WILLIAMSON COUNTY JAIL

312 Main, corner of Main and 4th • 3 blocks north of the courthouse square

Built in 1889, the old county jail was patterned after the Bastille, and with good reason. It was built during a time when cattle thieves and desperadoes still roamed the county and prisoners broke out of the old jail with impunity. Ironically, the first prisoner was one of its builders, who got a little too drunk while celebrating its completion.

From the courthouse square, take Main or Austin back down to University Avenue/SH 29. Turn left on SH 29 to leave town. SH 29 takes you past several substantial homes and churches, and the campus of Southwestern University, part of the University/Elm Street Historic District.

SOUTHWESTERN UNIVERSITY

University Ave./SH 29 at Maple • 863-6511 • W

Southwestern University traces its beginnings to 1840 and the creation of Rutersville College. The result of a merger of several colleges—Rutersville included—Southwestern opened for business in 1873. Despite its reputation as a respected institution of higher education, Southwestern retained some rough edges during its early days. Many of the male students carried guns, and at one point the school fathers ruled that all student guns must be checked in with the authorities. When one student who felt more comfortable with his gun on was asked to empty his gun, he responded by walking to the nearest window and firing until the chambers were empty. The faculty also maintained a running feud with the town's saloons; the savants accused the saloonkeepers of deliberately enticing the students and getting them drunk as revenge for faculty efforts on behalf of local option laws.

These days, though, the town and university get along fine, and Old Main, one of Georgetown's finest buildings, sits on campus facing SH 29.

One of Southwestern's most distinguished alumni was Jessie Daniel Ames. Born in Palestine, Texas, in 1883, Jessie Daniel moved with her family to Georgetown in 1893. She graduated from Southwestern in 1902 and went with her family to Laredo, where she met Roger Ames, an army surgeon whom she married in 1905. When he was assigned to New Orleans during a yellow fever epidemic, Ames sent Jessie home to live with her family, who had moved back to Georgetown and purchased the local telephone company. Roger's work took him all over the world, so they spent little time together; but they did have three children between 1907 and 1914, the year Roger died. Widowed at thirty-one, Jessie began to help her mother run the telephone company. Jessie Daniel Ames soon got into politics, organizing the Georgetown Equal Suffrage League in 1916. She was serving as state treasurer of the Texas Equal Suffrage Association in 1918 when the Texas legislature passed a bill permitting women to vote in state primaries. The suffragists had only seventeen days to register women to vote in the next primary; Ames and her cohorts registered 3,800 women in Williamson County. One observer commented on the sight of thousands of women pouring into the courthouse to register: "There's never been anything like it since." Mrs. Ames was a founder and first president of the Texas League of Women Voters, and one of the first woman delegates to state and national Democratic conventions. During the 1920s, Ames broadened her concerns beyond women's rights to black rights and interracial cooperation.

In 1929, she moved from Georgetown to Atlanta, Georgia, to become the national director of women's work for the Commission on Interracial Cooperation. A year later, she founded the Association of Southern Women for the Prevention of Lynching. By 1930, Ames realized that despite its long history in frontier America, lynching was largely a Southern phenomenon, a means of public intimidation designed to keep both blacks and whites in their respective places. She resented the widespread excuse that most lynchings were carried out in the name of chivalry and the protection of white Southern womanhood, and she discovered, in fact, that less than one-third of the 204 documented lynching victims between 1922 and 1930 were even accused of crimes against white women. Lurid descriptions of the crimes which the lynch victims were accused of, and equally lurid accounts of the lynchings and mutilations which often followed, served as a sort of "folk pornography" for the Deep South, printed in hundreds of Southern newspapers. Ames worked tirelessly for state and national anti-lynching legislation. By the early 1940s, Ames felt that the movement had been successful enough to allow the association to be dissolved. In 1944, she resigned from the Commission on Interracial Cooperation and went into retirement.

In 1969, Ames donated her library of more than 1,200 books to Southwestern University. She died in 1972 in an Austin nursing home. The spacious two-story frame home in which she and her family lived while in Georgetown still stands a block to the southeast off the courthouse square, at the corner of Farm and Tenth streets. It is not open to the public.

Southwestern University is also home to the Edward A. Clark Texana Collection, which is housed in the Smith Library Center. When Ed Clark (former U.S. ambassador to Australia and Texas attorney general and secretary of state) gave his private collection of about 2,400 volumes to Southwestern in 1965, it was described as one of the two greatest Texana collections in private hands. The collection has since grown to more than ten thousand items including more than seven thousand books which date from prerepublic days to the present. Parts of the collection may be viewed in the Special Collections Room at the Smith Library Center. It's best to e-mail for an appointment, libweb@sw.edu.

OLD MAIN

Southwestern University

Southwestern's Old Main, an immense cathedral Gothic limestone structure, was built in 1898–1900. The stonecutters employed to build it were the same Scottish artisans imported to build the new capitol in Austin.

Here are a couple of trivial tidbits for the ride out of town:

- In 1939, Georgetown came to be known as the Mistletoe or Kissing Capital of the world, when several local men began harvesting mistletoe for Christmas shipping.
- Texaco Oil Company had its beginnings in Georgetown when Judge R. E. Brooks and A. A. Booty organized the Texas Fuel Company. Brooks moved to Beaumont later that year, and in 1902 the Texas Fuel Company became the Texas Company, of which Brooks was treasurer and director.

From Southwestern University, head east on SH 29 toward Jonah.

DINING

WALBURG RESTAURANT

3777 FM 972; downtown Walburg (take I-35 north 4 miles to exit 268, then east 4 miles on FM 972 to Walburg) • 863-8440 • www.walburg restaurant.com • Open Wednesday through Sunday for dinner, call ahead for lunch hours

A bit of Bavaria, Texas-style, with German food and a beer garden with the lively polkas, waltzes, and two-steps of the Walburg Boys. The menu in this turn-of-the-century, ex-mercantile store is a mix of German and American food, like wiener schnitzel and chicken-fried steak, cordon bleu, and catfish. But try a house specialty like the sauerbraten, served with red cabbage and spatzle. Choose from several dozen varieties of German beer and wine.

Henry Doering, who built the place, founded the town of Walburg in 1883, naming it after his hometown in Germany. His mercantile store and the rich earth he offered for sale attracted dozens of German farmers, and by 1900 Walburg was a lively little town with a bank, a couple of churches and beer bars, and about a dozen other businesses. If you have time, drive north on FM 1105 about four miles (through Theon) to New Corn Hill to admire Williamson County's "cathedral on the prairie," Holy Trinity Catholic Church. Built in 1913, the brick church, with its distinctive twin towers, is modeled after the fourteenth-century Gothic Cathedral of St. Vitus at the Prague Castle in the Czech Republic. The bricks for the church were hauled in wagons. When they had to cross a deep mud hole, the men unloaded the bricks, crossed the wagon, and then reloaded the bricks. As you can see by the rolling countryside, it wasn't an easy drive. The parish was founded in 1889 to serve the area's German and Czech farm families. The name Corn Hill derives from the bountiful corn crops produced by area farmers.

OTHER ATTRACTIONS

INNER SPACE CAVERNS

4200 S. I-35, about 1 mile south of Georgetown at exit 259 • 863-5545 • www.myinnerspacecavern.com • Open daily, except Thanksgiving, Christmas Eve, and Christmas Day • Fee • W

Texas Department of Transportation drillers taking core samples for a proposed overpass discovered these caverns. Waters of the Edwards Aquifer carved them out over a one-hundred-million-year period. Remains of Ice Age mastodons, wolves, and saber-toothed tigers have been found inside the cave. Tours last about an hour. An inclined railway car takes you down into the caverns, and from there the trip covers less than a mile of relatively easy walking. Be prepared for brief periods of absolute darkness during the sound and light show. There is also a gift shop.

THE PAGE HOUSE

1000 Leander Rd., just west of I-35 at exit 260

The house was built in 1903 by J. M. and Olivia DeCrow Page. Boston-born J. M. Page had been a rancher, postmaster, and businessman in Georgetown since the early 1850s. Olivia died shortly after the house was completed, and the house was sold to her brother, Thomas DeCrow. The Polo Barn dates to the ownership of the Horace Weir family. During this period, polo became a popular sport in Texas, and in the 1930s, the Georgetown polo team was based in this big barn. It won several championships during this time.

AREA PARKS

SAN GABRIEL PARK

North shore of the San Gabriel River, north of downtown; take Austin/US 81 north • 863-9907 • parks.georgetown.org • Free • W variable

The North and South forks of the San Gabriel meet in Georgetown, and the town has taken advantage of its beautiful setting in this 320-acre park. You can swim and fish in the river. There are ball fields, a swimming pool, and picnic and cookout facilities. A trail leads to the beautiful Blue Hole.

LAKE GEORGETOWN

From Georgetown, take FM 2338 west about 4 miles to Cedar Breaks Rd.; then go south (left) to lake headquarters and Cedar Breaks Park • 863-3016 • Open daily • Fee • W variable

Lake Georgetown is formed by an Army Corps of Engineers dam on the North Fork of the San Gabriel River. Overlook is at the dam on the eastern end, off FM 2338. Three parks (Cedar Breaks, Jim Hogg, and Russell) have facilities for boating, fishing, swimming, hiking, picnicking, primitive camping, and RV camping. Two hiking trails run along the lake's north and south shores. The north-side trail is about five miles long; the south-side trail is about eleven miles long.

ANNUAL EVENT

JUNE

WILLIAMSON COUNTY SHERIFF'S POSSE RODEO

Last weekend in June • 746-4452 • www.georgetownrodeo.com • Rodeo Arena in San Gabriel Park • Fee • W

There is a parade, a dance, and several days of rodeo events.

After you leave Georgetown on SH 29 east, you enter the Blackland Prairies of Central Texas, some of the richest farmland found anywhere on earth. Although commercial development and subdivisions have crept several miles out of town now, swallowing up this fertile farmland a few miles from Jonah, the fields of cotton are interspersed with ones of milo, corn, and wheat. Except in time of drought, the pastures are usually green and the cattle fat.

Five miles east of Georgetown, you'll see a state historical marker. Near this marker, on the banks of the San Gabriel, the men of the ill-fated Santa Fe Expedition camped on their first night out. Aware of the heavy trade at Santa Fe, Texas president Mirabeau Lamar had determined to get a piece of the action. Texas needed trade, and it claimed jurisdiction over the Santa Fe area on the basis of an act of Congress in 1836. So Lamar determined to send an armed expedition north to establish a trade route from Texas to Santa Fe and to establish control of the New Mexico settlements. A call for volunteers was issued, and merchants were promised transportation and protection of their goods. The call was answered by 321 men and $200,000 worth of merchandise. Organized into five companies of infantry and one of artillery, the men loaded up their twenty-one ox wagons on June 19, 1841, at a spot just east of present-day Round Rock. Their first day's journey along the old Double File Trail took them all of ten miles, to this spot on the San Gabriel River.

The next day, the expedition resumed its journey north. The first few weeks of traveling through Central Texas were pleasant ones, filled with hunting and leisurely hours spent fishing. But things changed as they crossed the high arid plains. Losing their way, harassed by Indians, and hampered by insufficient provisions and water, the expedition reached Santa Fe only to be met by Mexican troops and convinced by a traitor in their midst to surrender. Exhausted and disheartened, the Texans surrendered without firing a shot. They were then marched to Mexico City and imprisoned; the survivors were released in April of 1842. Although the Santa Fe Expedition was an immediate failure, it stimulated an interest in Texas within both the United States and Mexico and formed a basis for Texas' claim to western territory.

After the marker, you cross the gravel-bottomed San Gabriel River. There is a low-water bridge just downstream that offers a nice view of the river; it's accessible by turning right on a little loop either just before crossing the river or after crossing.

Continue east on SH 29 until you approach the intersection with FM 1660 and Jonah. A few hundred feet before you come to the intersection, "Old Highway 29," a little paved lane, runs off to the right from SH 29 and enters "downtown" Jonah. This one-lane path is a patch of old SH 29 from the 1920s. Take the old road, or go to the intersection with FM 1660, turn right, and then turn left a block later. If you cross the San Gabriel River, you've gone too far.

JONAH

Williamson County • 60 • About 8.5 miles from Georgetown

When James Warnock and Joe Mileham built a gristmill on the San Gabriel in 1857, a community gradually developed around it. Mill and community were then called Eureka Mills. In about 1880, optimistic Eurekans applied for a post office with the pretty name Water Valley. It didn't float with the post office. They applied again with the name Parks, which the post office also brushed off. Community members gathered for the third time to pick a name. One of the most exasperated attendees remarked that, as far as picking a name acceptable to the post office was concerned, their hamlet's plight resembled that of Jonah in the whale. "So why not try Jonah?" someone suggested. They did, and the postal authorities approved.

Jonah grew up into a prosperous little cotton town with several doctors, a drugstore, a grocery store, and general merchandise stores. Nearby Willow Hole on the San Gabriel River was a popular recreation spot. But starting in 1921 with the great Williamson County flood, Jonah again entered the whale, so to speak. The demise of tenant farming and King Cotton added to the town's decline. The countryside depopulated. SH 29 bypassed Jonah to the north. A fire several decades ago destroyed most of by-then deserted downtown Jonah.

Three old store buildings and a greenhouse operation on the site of the old cotton gin are all that remain of downtown Jonah.

Turn left at the T intersection in front of the old store that now is home to the local fire department, following the convoluted path of the old highway. Immediately you cross a little concrete and angle-iron bridge dating from the 1920s, and then you immediately turn right again. In a few hundred feet, you rejoin SH 29, heading east toward Circleville. Continue east on SH 29 until it dead-ends into SH 95. Turn right on SH 95.

CIRCLEVILLE

Williamson County • 42 • About 7.5 miles from Jonah

The SH 95 bridge over the San Gabriel started life hundreds of years ago as a favored river crossing of Spanish expeditions. David McFadin settled nearby in 1846, but the village proper only dates to 1853, when the three Eubank brothers built their separate homes in a semicircle on the south bank of the river, hence the name Circleville. The town became an industrial center early on, with gins, tin and pewter shops, and a syrup mill. During the Civil War, the Confederacy built a factory to manufacture cotton cards—stiff brushes that made fluffy cotton into firm smooth battings to be spun into cotton or thread, quilted, or made into mattresses. The Union blockade made such industrialization necessary, since Texans could no longer easily trade their raw cotton for finished cloth.

Circleville began to decline with the development of Taylor in the 1880s and today is little more than a string of beer joints along the highway and stores that serve Lake Granger traffic. The Circleville Store serves barbecue brisket, pork ribs, Taylor sausage, and chicken (Saturdays only), which is acceptably good if you can't wait to get to Taylor for your 'que.

Continue south on SH 95 to Taylor (SH 95 becomes Main Street in Taylor).

TAYLOR

Williamson County • 15,000 (approximate) • (512) • About 5 miles from Circleville

Taylor owes its existence to the railroad. In 1876, when the International and Great Northern (I&GN) railroad was pushing its way south toward Austin, only a few scattered settlers lived on the prairies near the future site of Taylor. The Palestine-based Texas Land Company bought five hundred acres from an I&GN official and proceeded to plat a sixty-block town site. The first house was built in mid-May. A big lot sale was held in June 1876, even though the tracks of the new rail line were still a month away. Hopes were high for the new town, situated as it was on one of the great feeder branches of the Chisholm Trail and in the middle of one of the state's richest agricultural regions.

Taylor grew rapidly from the start, but life was not easy. Cattle drives passed right up Main Street through the middle of town, and water was available only from springs a couple of miles away. Those who made the trip peddled door to door dispensing the water from wagons. The inadequacy of this system was reflected during the fires of 1878 and February 1879. The 1879 fire, exacerbated by the strong winds of a norther that had blown through, destroyed twenty-nine buildings, leaving sixteen families homeless and thirty-four businessmen unemployed. Only four business houses were left standing. The town began to rebuild immediately, however, with brick and stone buildings replacing the earlier wooden ones. Then, in June 1881, a storm of hail and wind destroyed much of the town and crops for miles around.

First known as Taylorsville, the town was incorporated in 1882 as Taylor. That same year, Taylor drilled a well and built its first water system, in part to prevent future conflagrations.

N. C. Schlemmer came to Texas in 1877 and subsequently held various positions with the I&GN in Texas, including Taylor and Kyle (see the Riding the Fault trip). He wrote in 1928, "I was stationmaster at Taylor from 1878 to 1880, before the MK&T had reached that town, and when Taylor was the Eldorado of toughs and a regular hell-hole of saloons and gambling houses." He was not exaggerating—not too much, at any rate, judging by newspaper stories of the time.

April 23, 1879

NEAL CAIN KILLED. Passengers by yesterday morning's International train brought the news of the assassination of Neal Cain at his home in Taylorsville after dark Monday night. Some one fired a shot through the window of his residence after he retired, and Neal Cain is no more. He lived until six o'clock yesterday morning, suffering intensely. Neal Cain furnished some information which led to the arrest of two robbers in Houston, now in jail here, and the killing of the third, and the breaking up of the thriving gang that robbed the Circleville store, old man Jordan and Major Laurane, of this city, and the inference is that some one of the thieving party or a friend of it, fired the shot that ended the life of Neal Cain. His wife and children, in the room at the time, were unharmed, and there was no clue yesterday that pointed to the guilt of any one. It is also believed that one of the friends of the man whom Cain's brother shot and killed about a month ago did the shooting.

July 14, 1882

TAYLOR. About 9 o'clock last night W. F. Cook, a freight conductor running between Taylor and Palestine, shot and killed D. J. Healey, train dispatcher, in his office at this place, the ball striking him in the breast. He ran out of his office about 200 feet and fell, where he died in about five minutes, not speaking after being shot. Healey was formerly superintendent of telegraph for the International and Great Northern railway. Cook had been drinking and used very abusive language, provoking the quarrel. Marshal Olive, after a thorough search of the yards, procured an engine, and started north about 11 o'clock, and when about four miles north of Thorndale a man was discovered near the track, trying to signal engine with matches. Marshal Olive and posse hiding in the timber, the engineer stopped the engine and when the man was getting into the cab, he was discovered to be Cook. Marshal Olive demanded his surrender by the persuasion of a six-shooter in his face, when Cook kindly submitted.

Taylor's "Eldorado" time of toughs and hellhole of saloons and gambling houses ended with the killing of saloon keeper Ed Rousseau between ten and eleven o'clock Saturday evening, October 9, 1886, in his saloon.

Taylor City Marshal Tom Smith and Constable Ed Morris went to the saloon to arrest a man or quell a disturbance. Rousseau objected to the officers coming into his house for such purpose. He said he was capable of attending to his own premises and was responsible to the law in keeping an orderly house. A dispute or difference of opinion seemed to arise between him and the officers, and it was generally agreed that at about this point the shooting began. Rousseau was pierced with six or seven bullets and died almost instantly. No doubt there were bad feelings between Rousseau and the men. Both officers had previously had difficulty with him and claimed self-defense. There were a good many people in the saloon at the time of the dispute, but all agreed that when the shooting began, they were much too demoralized by the shooting to have any clear idea as to what transpired, other than wanting to get out of the place and escape danger.

A former Travis County deputy sheriff, Rousseau had a reputation as a brave and dangerous man who feared no one. He had shot and killed a black man in Austin under dubious circumstances in October 1878, and he then shot his own brother-in-law two months later in a dispute over whether Rousseau had mistreated his wife and her mother. He ran unsuccessfully for county sheriff in 1882. In 1883, he was convicted of assault and battery. In April 1884, he was tried for assaulting an Austin police officer but was acquitted. In August of that year, he was convicted of assaulting the co-owner of Austin's most prominent restaurant over the freshness of a glass of milk served to him.

A couple of weeks before his death, Rousseau had visited one of the most prominent whorehouses in Austin's whorehouse district. He had some words with one of the girls called "Dasie," and picking up a spittoon from the floor he struck her a fearful blow over the head, felling her to the floor. He was convicted of assault and battery, and fined ten dollars and costs. He left a wife and three children.

Taylor's economy received a boost when the Missouri-Kansas-Texas (MKT) railroad came to town in May 1882. On May 1, 1882, the last spike connecting the MKT with the International and Great Northern was driven, and Taylor looked forward to the grand benefits to be derived of international commerce, with the connection of the great east and the undeveloped resources of Mexico. An abundance of Piper-Heidsieck champagne and many refreshing kegs of lager and toasts made the day long to be remembered.

By 1890, the regional I&GN repair shops were located here, and a golden era was dawning. Dr. A. V. Doak established a mule-drawn trolley system to serve the townspeople and also built a pavilion (at 700 Sloan Street) with a seating capacity of one thousand. Dances, plays, concerts, religious revivals, skating parties, and even bicycle races and baseball games were held under its broad roof. It was sold and dismantled in 1900. Doak's ranch-style house, built in the 1860s, still stands at 600 W. Seventh Street.

By 1900, Taylor was the largest inland cotton market in the world. Taylor's principal streets were first paved then, too—not with gold, or even with brick, but with brick-sized wooden blocks. The parquetry has since been covered by asphalt.

The level prairie of gummy Bell clay—rich, black, and deep—that surrounds Taylor for miles and miles has long been the best cotton land in the world. Despite cotton's decline, Taylor continued to grow and today is home to some ten thousand people and two dozen industrial firms.

Over the years, Taylor has also produced several people of note, including Dan Moody, the youngest person ever elected governor of Texas. Moody was elected in 1927 at the age of thirty-four.

Taylor was also the hometown of Elmer "Pet" Brown, the 1914 middleweight wrestling champion of the world. Brown won his title in the Taylor City Hall auditorium, where he defeated Mike Yokel of Salt Lake City.

Will Pickett, "the Dusky Demon," inventor of the art of rodeo bulldogging, worked ranches around Taylor as a young man, and it was here that he perfected his bulldogging technique, displaying it for the first time at the Taylor Rodeo. At the turn of the century, the *Houston Post* classed Pickett as one of the "best and toughest of the new breed of folk heroes that dominated the American scene after the Civil War." The story then went on to describe Pickett's unique style, saying he would "leap from his horse onto a galloping steer, grab a horn in each hand and twist until the animal's nose came up. Then, like a bulldog, Pickett would grab the steer's tender upper lip in his teeth, let go of the horns and flap to one side, toppling the steer to the earth. . . . Pickett was as fearless as any cowboy who ever rode the range."

In the late 1880s, Thomas Pickett moved his family to Taylor. Bill worked for a number of area ranches. We'll learn more about Pickett later on this trip.

Elmore Torn, tireless promoter of the black-eyed pea and uncle of actor Rip Torn, also hailed from Taylor.

To reach the Dan Moody family home, turn right on Ninth and proceed one block west of Main/SH 95.

MOODY HOME MUSEUM

114 W. 9th at Talbot • 352-3463 • ci.taylor.tx.us • Open Sunday, Tuesday, Friday • Free • W variable

Once the residence of Dan Moody, governor of Texas (1927–1931), this two-story frame house (built 1887) with period furnishings. Dan Moody was born in this house on June 1, 1893. As Texas' youngest-ever attorney general (1925–1927), Moody established himself as a crusader against the Ku Klux Klan and government corruption. As governor, Moody continued his program of governmental reform, reorganizing the state prison and highway systems and creating the office of state auditor. He retired to private law practice at the end of his second term, declining to run for a third term. He emerged from political retirement in 1941 to run for the U.S. Senate, only to finish third against former governors W. Lee O'Daniel and James Allred. It was his only political defeat. Moody died at Austin in 1966 and was buried in the state cemetery.

From the Moody home, proceed south on Talbot.

ODD FELLOWS LODGE

120 W. 4th at Talbot

Many of Taylor's old brick business buildings still exist essentially unaltered, and this building is one of them. Built as the Odd Fellows Lodge in 1907, the two-story textured brick building features a pair of cast-metal Queen Anne porticos and elaborate diamond-pattern leaded windows, along with a castellated roofline and Alamo arch, which contains the date of erection (1907) and the inscription "IOOF" and the Odd Fellows' distinctive logo of three interlocked rings.

Proceed two more blocks to Second Street.

LOUIE MUELLER'S BARBEQUE

206 W. 2nd • 352-6206 • www.louiemuellerbarbecue.com • Open Monday through Saturday, lunch and dinner, or until sold out • No Cr. • W

When you reach Second, turn your head right and you'll catch sight of one of Central Texas' landmark barbecue joints, Louie Mueller's, which turns out an excellently flavored lean and tender brisket, a good-tasting though slightly greasy sausage, and a good lean flavorful steak. Mueller's homemade sauce is heavily laden with onion and is one of the tastiest to be found anywhere. The place serves only barbecue, although it is open during breakfast hours. If you feel like you're inside a gym that just happens to sell barbecue, well, you're right. The Taylor High basketball team played here for years before the Mueller family took it over. Beer.

THOMPSON BUILDING

201 W. 2nd • Currently houses Taylor Paint and Hardware

Directly across Second from Louie Mueller's is the Thompson building. A long, two-story, simply built structure of tan brick, the Thompson building is lifted from anonymity by its majestic cast-metal cornice, which features six turrets of varying heights, and cast-metal second-story-window architraves painted a bright, contrasting white.

TAYLOR BEDDING COMPANY

601 W. 2nd • 352-6344

Some of the cotton produced in Taylor went to the Taylor Bedding Company, which began business in 1903. Founder D. H. Forwood's dream was to use the area's cotton locally rather than shipping it away, so he started making and selling cotton mattresses. The business grew over the years, and now the makers of the Morning Glory mattress also manufacture furniture, mattress pads, and quilt batting. Texas' largest bedding manufacturer during the 1930s and 1940s, Taylor Bedding made 90 percent of the U.S. Armed Forces' mattresses during World War II. The plant ran twenty-four hours a day.

TAYLOR MEAT COMPANY

2211 W. 2nd (US 79 at the Loop) • 365-6358 • taylormeat.com • Open Monday through Saturday • W

Taylor has a healthy Czech population, and Taylor Meat Company makes a wide range of the smoked meats and sausages that the Czech Belt of Central Texas is famous for: pork and beef/pork links, liver sausage, ring bologna, wieners, head cheese, jerky, beef and cervelat "sticks," country-style bacon, hand-rubbed hickory-smoked hams, and even chorizo. Online shopping.

TAYLOR NATIONAL BANK

2nd and Main

Located at the northeast corner of Second and Main is the old Taylor National Bank building, one of the houses that cotton built. The millions of dollars that cotton injected into the Taylor economy are reflected in the three-story sandstone and brick building's stained-glass windows, polished marble columns, and inlaid tile entryway.

The Taylor National Bank was established in 1888 by C. H. Booth Sr. Booth had been a director of the First National Bank of Taylor established five years earlier, but he wanted the new bank to be a "people-owned" bank with a wide range of stockholders. The bank purchased this lot in 1888 for $4,800. However, construction of the Romanesque and Renaissance Revival styled structure, designed by prominent Austin architect A. O. Watson, didn't start until May 1894. The third floor and roof were used by the United States Weather Bureau from 1901 to 1930. The Taylor Refining Company took over the third floor from 1930 to 1939 when nearby Thrall experienced a short-lived oil boom. The Depression of the 1930s led to the merger of Taylor National Bank with First National Bank in 1931. The bank then became known as the First Taylor National Bank.

The bank building is just one of at least half a dozen notable commercial buildings clustered around this intersection that feature stained-glass windows and fine brick and tile work, most of which is obscured by years of dirt and drab paint. Downtown Taylor has not yet undergone a wholesale restoration like downtown Georgetown or Fredericksburg, although there are many buildings worth the effort. Most of Taylor's growth effort seems to be focused, regrettably, on strip development along SH 95 on the north side of town.

TAYLOR MOTOR COMPANY

E. 2nd at Porter

Neon, Art Moderne, and old car fans, don't pass up Taylor Motor Company. Cars aren't the attraction here, but rather the building itself. The white-stuccoed wraparound Art Moderne building is topped by its original round, revolving Buick-Chevrolet neon sign.

TAYLOR CAFE

101 N. Main, under the railroad bridge • 352-8475 • Monday through Saturday 7–11, Sunday 11–11 • No Cr. • W

Practically everybody has heard of Louie Mueller's. But one place you probably haven't heard of before is the Taylor Cafe, and owner Vencil Mares serves up the best ribs in town here, as well as some tasty lean sausage (from Taylor Meat Company), oak-smoked beef, stew, and plate lunches. The jukebox here has a good blend of country-and-western, polka, and Mexican selections. There is beer.

ANNUAL EVENT

AUGUST

TAYLOR INTERNATIONAL BARBECUE COOK-OFF AND RODEO

Murphy Park, on Lake Dr., 3 blocks west of SH 95 • Third weekend in August • 803-5855 • www.taylorjaycees.org • Fee • W variable

It's appropriate for a place known as the Barbecue Capital of the World to host the International Championship Barbecue Cook-off. Cooking categories include beef, poultry, sheep, goat, wild game, sausage, seafood, and sauce, in adult and junior categories.

To resume the trip, retrace your route from Taylor back up SH 95 to Circleville and the San Gabriel River crossing.

Barely a mile east of the SH 95 bridge across the San Gabriel is Comanche Peak, a high bluff on the south bank of the river where Indians were said to run buffalo over the edge.

Continue north on SH 95 toward Granger. Turn left on County Road 336, about three miles north of the San Gabriel River bridge. A highway sign directing you to Willis Creek Park and a big red prefab building with a white roof located on your right serve as a tip-off.

DARE BUZZARD

Williamson County • About 10 miles from Taylor

One of Williamson County's more uniquely named ghost towns, Dare Buzzard, also known as Dar' Buzzard, lies along County Road 336 along Opossum Creek, the first little stream you cross once you are on this road. It was a well-known village by 1856, when the *Georgetown Independent* urged a new mail route between Georgetown and Cameron via Dare Buzzard and other hamlets. There are a couple of stories as to how Dare Buzzard received its name. According to one story, a half-witted boy saw a buzzard flying overhead and pointed upward saying, "Dar' buzzard" ("There's a buzzard"). Others say the name was for a tavern so rough that even buzzards did not dare stay there. Take your choice. Nothing remains of Dare Buzzard today save a couple of old houses visible from the road.

Less than a mile past old Dare Buzzard, County Road 336 dead-ends into FM 971. Turn right on FM 971 to enter Granger.

GRANGER

Williamson County • 1,300 (approximate) • (512) • About 11 miles from Taylor

Folks first came to this area in the 1850s, attracted by cheap and fertile farm-land, but it took the Missouri-Kansas-Texas (MKT) railroad to actually see a town organized. When the "Katy" came through in 1882, Captain A. S. Fisher and W. C. Belcher laid out some of their land as a town, along the tracks and "around the station of Granger."

By 1884, a number of town lots had been sold here, and the nearby settlements at Macedonia and Dare Buzzard began to shrivel. Although the place was listed on some maps as Pollack, there is no evidence the village was ever called that by its inhabitants. But where the name Granger came from is the subject of a minor controversy. Some say the place was named to honor Civil War veteran John R. Granger. Others say it was named for the Grange, a popular nationwide farmers' organization of the time.

By the 1880s, and especially the 1890s, the rich land had attracted many European immigrants, especially Germans and Czechoslovakians, who became thrifty, industrious farmers. Granger was incorporated by 1891; it had a bank by 1894 and a newspaper by 1897. By 1893, Granger had its second rail line, the 15.5-mile Georgetown and Granger railroad. Promoted by Captain Emzy Taylor of Georgetown, this line was to connect with other lines that crisscrossed the state. Emzy's prominent merchant father Josiah had built the county's first two-story house in Georgetown. Josiah opened a bank in 1882 in Georgetown, helped organize both the Georgetown–Round Rock and the Georgetown–Granger railroad lines and started the town's waterworks. Financial problems resulted from expansion attempts, however, and Taylor committed suicide in Georgetown in 1895. The MKT finally bought the line and finished the tracks from Granger to Austin via Georgetown in 1904.

Granger today is a farm town, with a citizenry that is still of predominantly Czech extraction. It has declined from its glory days as a regional trade center, but nearby Lake Granger has helped stem the decline. The Blackland Co-op Gin is one of the county's few active cotton gins.

When FM 971 runs into SH 95, turn left, as per the signs. After two blocks, 971 veers off to the right. Turn left here onto W. Davilla. West of SH 95, Davilla's asphalt turns to red brick. You don't find too many brick streets left in Central Texas, and the two western blocks of Davilla are in great shape.

At the west end of town are the town's two Czech-heritage churches.

SAINTS CYRIL AND METHODIUS CATHOLIC CHURCH

W. Davilla at Brazos

Cyril and Methodius are two of the most popular saints in Czech Catholicism. These two brother missionaries came to Bohemia and Moravia from Constantinople spreading the Christian gospel. Many Czechs embraced the faith, and soon young Czech priests conducted services in the native tongue. Cyril and Methodius became known as the Apostles of the Slavonians. After several centuries under the Eastern (Greek Orthodox) branch of Christianity, Bohemia passed to the control of the Western, Roman Catholic branch, through the efforts of German missionaries sent to Bohemia by Rome. Masses were now conducted in Latin rather than in Czech. This Gothic-cathedral-style brick church dates to 1916.

GRANGER BRETHREN CHURCH

W. Broadway at Brazos, one block north of Saints Cyril and Methodius Church

Not all the Czechs who settled Texas were Catholic. One block north of, and in stark contrast to, the Catholic church, stands the Granger Brethren Church. The Brethren are a Protestant denomination that trace their origins to Moravia (in the Czech Republic today) and early Catholic Church reformer Jan Hus, who ultimately burned at the stake in 1415 for his efforts. This simple frame whitewashed church is very much in keeping with its members' beliefs about mankind's relationship with God.

The job of paving one-hundred-foot-wide Davilla Street took place in the summer of 1912. Granger's economy was booming. It was an important cotton marketing and shipping point for the region, boasting a combined cotton compress and cottonseed oil mill, an ice factory, a waterworks, and several banks. But after rainstorms, Davilla Street became a colossal mud puddle. When it was dry, traffic kicked up great clouds of dust. The weekly *Granger News* proclaimed, "Granger is said to boast the distinction of being the only city in the state of less than 5,000 inhabitants that has paved streets, or that is paving them." The Business League of Granger held annual "good roads and pavement celebrations" as part of its promotion of Granger as a progressive community. Ironically, the proliferation of the automobile diminished the importance of the railroad, upon which Granger had based its prosperity, and the community began to lose its population to larger cities and towns.

Retrace your path east across SH 95 onto E. Davilla. E. Davilla doubles as FM 971 as FM 971 leaves SH 95 and resumes its solo path eastward.

GRANGER CITY HALL

214 E. Davilla

Erected in 1908–1909, this two-story brick building originally housed Farmers State Bank. The bank closed in 1926, and the building became the Granger City Hall in 1929. Its shiny white corner cupola is reminiscent of one of the Kremlin's onion-shaped domes.

BOHUSLAV'S MARKET

204 E. Davilla

The signs outside are fading and pretty much illegible, but inside you'll find a meat case with Taylor wieners and some good, made-on-premises all-pork and all-beef ring sausage and beef jerky.

Davilla used to be lined with substantial and sometimes ornate brick buildings, but as the town declined, a number of them were vacated and torn down. One such victim was the Granger Opera House, which stood as a local landmark from 1905 until the mid-1970s. It was similar in appearance to the present Granger City Hall. Those that do stand are red brick and date to the very late nineteenth and very early twentieth centuries.

AREA PARKS

LAKE GRANGER

FM 971, about 8 miles east of Granger • 859-2668 • Open daily • Fee • W variable

This lake was created by damming up the San Gabriel River for flood control and water conservation purposes. It opened for fishing in 1981, having been well stocked with channel catfish and largemouth bass. There are thirty-six miles of shoreline. Friendship, Fox, Taylor, and Willis parks provide campsites, hookups (fee charged), picnic sites, swimming areas, boat ramps, and group shelters. Four wildlife areas also surround the lake.

From Granger, head north on SH 95 to Bartlett.

BARTLETT

Williamson and Bell counties • 1,700 (approximate) • About 5.5 miles from Granger

Despite farming's still-prominent contribution to the area economy, Bartlett continues to recede from the prosperity of its heyday. Its many charming, essentially unaltered brick downtown buildings still stand.

Settlers came here in the 1850s, but there was no identifiable town until 1882. John Bartlett, a postwar arrival, caught wind of the MKT's plans to build a railway through the area, and when the Katy surveyors came through laying out the right-of-way, Bartlett and J. E. Pietzsch donated land for the station and platted a town site. Lot sales began in late 1881, and by the time the MKT rails reached here in the summer of 1882, Bartlett's town was already a bustling village with several business establishments. John Bartlett and A. P. Clark erected the town's first building and engaged in the general mercantile business. Bartlett got its post office that fall, a newspaper in 1886, and a bank, organized by John Bartlett, in 1887. The town was incorporated in 1890.

Agricultural shipments out of Bartlett were so great that the big 1890s fire that destroyed Bartlett's early business district was looked upon as a blessing in disguise, for it brought about the construction of a more substantial brick business district.

The enormous cotton and foodstuff shipments out of Williamson County during these halcyon years led to the construction of the county's last railway, the Bartlett–Florence railway, chartered in 1909. Also known as the Dinky, the Bullfrog Line, and the Four Gospels Line, the railroad was chartered by non-county residents who believed the tremendous cotton traffic would make the line pay. They also thought they could soon sell the line to one of the county's existing railroads. The underfinanced Dinky ran into trouble from the beginning. The builders got only eleven of the twenty-three miles of rails laid before money ran out. After refinancing, the rails finally reached the western terminus at Florence in 1912. The Bartlett depot for the Bartlett–Florence was a leased, renovated house.

From SH 95, turn left onto FM 487, Bartlett's chief east-west axis, known in town as Clark Street. The two downtown blocks of Clark, between SH 95 and the railroad tracks, are still brick paved, as is Evie Street for a half block on either side of Clark.

On March 9, 1936, the Bartlett Electric Co-op became the first electrical co-op in the United States to provide electric power to its member customers. The town of Bartlett had enjoyed regular electric service since 1905, but in 1936 most farmers around Bartlett still milked their cows by hand, by the light of a kerosene lamp. They pumped their water, or the Aeromotor windmill did. Wives cooked on wood-burning stoves and scrubbed the laundry on a wash-board. There was no radio, and any electrical power a rural family enjoyed came from a noisy, smelly gasoline-engine-driven generator.

President Franklin Roosevelt signed an executive order creating the Rural Electrification Administration (REA) in May 1935 so that rural and small-town America might receive dependable, low-cost electrical power. By providing low-cost federal loans for power-line construction to the co-ops, the REA brought electric power to 90 percent of U.S. farmlands and small communities. Inspired by FDR's creation, Bartlett mayor Randy Miller went to Washington to lobby Congressman Sam Rayburn to sponsor the legislation to fund the REA.

Later that year, the REA lent $33,000 to Bartlett Community Light and Power, which later became the Bartlett Electric Co-op. The BCL&P built a fifty-nine-mile power line to serve Bartlett-area farmers. Power was supplied by Bartlett's municipal light plant, which had been built in 1934. The first operative section of the line served 110 homes.

The postholes for those first power lines were dug by hand, and it took eight men to set each thirty-five-foot pole into place. They were paid seventy-five cents an hour. Many of those first poles are still standing in and around Bartlett. Rayburn's REA funding bill finally became law two months after the Bartlett Co-op energized its first line, the first of its kind in the country. Today the Bartlett Co-op serves nearly five thousand customers with lines that spread over 1,500 miles.

Electrification was not enough to check the steady surge of urbanization, and commercial Bartlett declined. Downtown Bartlett's business buildings have not met the wholesale demolition that has flattened most of Granger's old business district. Clark's two downtown blocks comprise one of the nicest, intact, late-Victorian, brick, small-town business districts left in Central Texas. Like Smithville's business district, none of Bartlett's buildings are individually distinguished, but collectively they make a pleasingly picturesque whole, especially complemented by the brick street.

Bartlett's business district straddles the Bell-Williamson county line. The businesses on the north side of Clark are in Bell County; those on the south side are in Williamson. Several antique shops line downtown Clark Street now, and thanks to a recent movie filmed here, many of the old buildings have been spruced up. Several of the old buildings' alley walls sport old-style (but not original) painted advertisements for Coca-Cola, Wrigley's gum, and such.

BARTLETT NATIONAL BANK

Clark and Evie, one block west of SH 95

Jesse L. Bailey and his son, Charles C. Bailey, opened a private bank in conjunction with a mercantile business in Bartlett in 1898. J. L. Bailey and Son, Bankers, was replaced by the First National Bank of Bartlett in 1900. Essentially a Beaux-Arts Classicism building, the defunct bank's most outstanding features are its carved, wings-outstretched eagles, which line the building's street-side walls, flanked on either side by brickwork Ionic columns. The bank was surely the pride of the town when built.

Continue west on Clark/FM 487. One block west of the railroad tracks, on your left, is the old Bartlett Electric Co-op powerhouse.

BARTLETT ELECTRIC CO-OP POWERHOUSE

100 block of W. Clark at Emma, across from the police station • W

This red brick building houses the old municipal power plant built in 1934, which supplied power to that historic first REA line. The turbine room still has its original Fairbanks-Morse diesel electric generators. It's not open to the public, but you can peek through the door and windows.

Two blocks west of the railroad tracks and one block north of Clark is the old Bartlett school.

BARTLETT PUBLIC SCHOOL

Lucy and Bell

This castellated two-story Gothic schoolhouse is another good example of just how prosperous Bartlett was. The three-story hexagonal castellated turret located in the notch of the V-shaped school is the building's focal point. This is appropriate since the main entryway is through the bottom level of the turret. By 1907, Bartlett's five-room schoolhouse here proved inadequate to house the expanding student enrollment, so in 1908–1909, this multiwing brick building, designed by noted Austin architect A. O. Watson, was built here. When a new high school was erected in 1917, this building became an elementary and grammar school. The school closed in 1988. It now serves as a community activities center and museum which is open the fourth Saturday afternoon of each month.

From the school, double back to FM 487.

Pietzsch Street runs parallel to Clark, one block south. The five blocks of Pietzsch between Emma and Cotrell hold a number of large, old turn-of-the-century houses and two nice, old Victorian-era wooden church buildings that were not in use at press time, the 1899 First Presbyterian Church (Pietzsch at Lindemann) and, one block away, the Christian Church (Pietzsch at Alamo).

Proceeding out of town on FM 487, you pass the squat, Gothic-style Bartlett Methodist Church as well as several good examples of circa-1900 farmhouses. FM 487 follows roughly the route of the Bartlett–Florence railway.

Small as it was, the Dinky exerted great influence on the lives of the people and towns located along its path. It created new towns like Schwertner and Jarrell; it made a ghost town out of once-prosperous Corn Hill. Schwertner is the first town west of Bartlett on FM 487.

SCHWERTNER

Williamson County • 150 • About 5.5 miles from Bartlett

Schwertner was the Dinky's first depot west of Bartlett, a community settled in 1877 by Bernard Schwertner and his three boys, Frank, Edward, and Adolph. These Austrian immigrants farmed and ranched a huge tract of land stretching from Jarrell to Bartlett. The Schwertner family still owns much of this land, as is evidenced by all the ranch signs.

Adolph Schwertner built a gin here in 1903. When he heard of the projected railroad in 1909, Schwertner donated land for a town site. A depot, general store, dry goods store, hardware store, bank, meat market, blacksmith shop, and post office sprang up in short order. A doctor, saloon, lumberyard, and boarding house were soon added. Schwertner had its own brass band and a second cotton gin.

Today downtown Schwertner consists of one live tavern, several dead business houses, and the Schwertner State Bank.

A few yards west of "downtown" Schwertner, look to your left (to the south) and you can see a section of the Dinky's roadbed.

About three miles past Schwertner, on FM 487, atop the high ridge to your left overlooking Donahoe Creek, you'll see the old Primrose School, which once housed ninety-six pupils. The surrounding neighborhood was known as Lickskillet. Primrose/Lickskillet was a stone's throw from St. Matthew, the first of the "Four Gospel" flag stations on the Bartlett–Florence rail. These four stations between Bartlett and Florence were listed in official railroad records as Caffrey, John Camp, Atkinson, and Armstrong, but a religious lady gave the stops the names of the four respective New Testament gospels: St. Matthew, St. Mark, St. Luke, and St. John. Each flag station had a roof and benches—but no walls—and a picture frame, which contained the station's gospel name and appropriate verses from that gospel, hung from the rafters.

In spite of such divine guidance, the Bartlett–Florence Railway Company was financially plagued. It changed hands a number of times, finally becoming the Bartlett and Western railway. The Bartlett and Western owned two locomotives, ten freight cars, and two passenger cars, but as time passed, the coal-burning locomotives were replaced with gasoline motors. The passenger cars were designed like trolleys and could be caught almost anywhere along the line. Engineers outfitted a Fordson tractor with flanged wheels, allowing this "locomotive" to haul flatcars loaded with as many as 150 quarter-ton bales of cotton at one time. With the acquisition of the mail contract for northern Williamson County, the Bartlett and Western bought several Ford trucks, which were outfitted with railroad wheels and then used to haul the mail up and down the line. Small wonder that many folks along the line called it the Dinky. Its Bullfrog Line appellation was also well deserved; its cars were always jumping the tracks.

JARRELL

Williamson County • 1,400 (approximate) • About 7 miles from Schwertner

Jarrell is Williamson County's youngest town, and it owes its existence to the Bartlett and Western railroad. Jarrell's birth brought the demise of the once thriving village and stage stop of Corn Hill, so named in 1855 because of the fine corn crops the area produced. Corn Hill had a population of 500 and was home to a variety of businesses by 1910. When the Dinky railroad came along, however, instead of coming through Corn Hill, the tracks were laid a little over a mile to the north.

Real estate promoters O. D. Jarrell of Temple and E. C. Haeber of Bartlett purchased land along the railroad's right-of-way, platted a town, and held a sale of lots in December 1909. The new town site was located at the junction of the old stagecoach road (now I-35) and the new railroad. A saloon and two small stores were built almost immediately, but the nascent town lapsed into a coma when construction of the rails west from Bartlett bogged down.

But by the spring of 1911, the railroad had new owners and new capital, and a second lot sale was held in Jarrell. Residences were built, a bank and churches were organized, and the exodus from Corn Hill commenced. A man named Jim Hawkins slowly moved Corn Hill north to the new town, a process that literally took years, although the demise of Corn Hill was further hastened when local farmer S. A. Keeling bought a Case steam engine, which could move buildings in one-third the time required by mule power. By 1916, nearly everyone had left Corn Hill for Jarrell. Today only a crumbling building that used to function as a hotel stands at Corn Hill.

Jarrell's population has always been predominantly Czech and German hardworking, conservative farmers and ranchers.

Jarrell is located on the highest point of land along the highway between Oklahoma City and San Antonio, and just a few feet in elevation can make quite a difference in the winter. Years ago, a Georgetown postmaster used to win a regular supply of pocket money off this fact. During the norther season, he would take folks the thirteen miles up to Jarrell on the bet that it would have snow and ice, while Georgetown was warm and merely wet. He won so many times that he finally ran out of takers.

Jarrell today is most famous for the F5 category tornado of May 27, 1997, that struck the town, killing twenty-seven people. Double Creek Estates, a Jarrell subdivision, was wiped off the map, with all thirty-eight homes and several mobile homes destroyed. Many tornado experts considered the Jarrell storm to be the most violent tornado, in terms of damage intensity, they had ever seen.

These days, I-35 is Jarrell's chief industry, as evidenced by the string of roadside gas stations and package stores.

Cross under the interstate on FM 487 and follow its brief coupling with the southbound I-35 frontage road. Continue on 487 as it veers west from the interstate and Jarrell toward Florence.

FM 487 continues to follow the route of the Bartlett and Western in a general way, and occasionally you will catch a glimpse of its roadbed between Jarrell and Florence, where the last three gospel stops were located. The tracks west of Jarrell were on a difficult grade, so when heavy loads were pulled, the crew carried sand along, sprinkling it on the tracks to provide enough traction for the wheels to pull upgrade or to better control them on the downgrade.

After its initial financial problems, the railroad was acquired by career railroad man Thomas Cronin, who hailed from Palestine, Texas. Although Cronin never managed to transform the Dinky into anything more than just what its nickname implied, he at least made it a paying proposition until 1926. In that year, Cronin died, and Texas experienced a sharp decline in both cotton production and cotton prices. The price the Bartlett and Western received for hauling a bale of cotton fell from $1.59 a bale to forty-five cents. This was just a harbinger of the hard times to come. Cronin's daughter Marie came back from Paris to take over the railroad, giving up her career as an internationally known artist to do so. Her French styles and makeup were quite a shock to the stolid inhabitants of Williamson County, but she persevered here for a decade, struggling to keep her father's railroad alive. Finally she bowed to the inevitable and closed the line in 1935. The rails and ties were removed soon thereafter. Some say the rails were sold to Japan, where they were melted down and used against us in World War II; others say that Herman Brown of Brown and Root Inc. bought them. Neither story has been corroborated. Marie Cronin had planned to return to Paris and her career as an artist, but her eyesight was failing and she elected to remain at the family home in Bartlett, where she died in 1951. You can see an example of her work in the state capitol building in Austin: a portrait of Johanna Troutman, the "Betsy Ross of Texas."

PEYTON

Williamson County • About 6 miles from Jarrell

Six miles out of Jarrell, FM 487 runs close by Salado Creek, through the ghost town of Peyton. This hamlet was named for early settlers, the W. R. Peyton family. A store and post office were located here on the banks of the creek, and nearby was a half-mile straightaway track where local horse raiser Jay Owens trained his horses and where many an Owens horse raced other local equine speedsters. William Wilson operated the store, and one of his sons, James "Pinky" Wilson, wrote the lyrics to the "Aggie War Hymn" while in the trenches along the Rhine River at Coblenz in 1918. Persistent flooding caused the buildings along the creek to be moved or abandoned; nothing of Peyton is left here today but memories and a nice view of the Salado Creek. Salado is Spanish for "salty," which this creek is certainly not. Local plant life suggests that its name was accidentally interchanged with that of the Lampasas River; the Lampasas is salty, but its name means "water plant."

Gold was discovered just a few miles north of here in 1883, samples of which, in some instances, were assayed for as high as $2,500 a ton in gold. It was carried in a formation of decomposed limestone stained with oxide of iron. There was a great flurry of interest, which soon subsided after the field failed to show commercial possibility and evidence of trickery began to surface.

FLORENCE

Williamson County • 1,100 (approximate) • About 13 miles from Jarrell

Florence was settled in the late 1840s and early 1850s. It was originally called Brooksville. Some say early settler Enoch D. John named the hamlet after his hometown, Brooksville, Indiana. John built one of the area's first flour mills here. Others say that a man from Bastrop named Brooks set up a store here in 1853 and that the name derived accordingly. Indian attacks were still common in the early 1850s, and preachers usually kept a loaded gun close to the pulpit during Sunday services. When the post office was established in 1857, Brooksville became Florence, named for Brooks' daughter Florence or for Florence, Alabama, hometown of the first postmaster, Colonel Fisher, a retired lawyer. Or there's even the possibility the town was named for the daughter of Colonel King Fisher, the famous Texas pistolero.

Located on a feeder branch of the Chisholm Trail and surrounded by fertile cotton and wheat fields, Florence grew to be a prosperous little town. By the time the Bartlett–Florence railroad tracks arrived in 1912, Florence already had a bank, creamery, and cheese factory. There was even a college, the Florence College, from 1895 to 1903.

FM 487 becomes Main in Florence.

OLD CITY LIBRARY

Corner of Main and College

Main Street Florence today is a nice collection of mostly centenarian limestone buildings and some slightly newer brick ones, none of which are particularly distinguished. The most impressive of the lot is the old City Library, a two-story limestone building built as a drugstore in 1906 by J. F. Atkinson, son of prominent Florence merchant and early postmaster John W. Atkinson. Bigfoot Wallace used to travel down this street as a stagecoach driver on his way to Fort Gates, as Florence was on one of the early roads from Austin to Burnet and points west.

The Atkinson men were no shrinking violets. One Friday evening in September 1884, three men rode into Florence acting in a questionable manner and aroused the suspicions of several parties about town. Mr. J. W. Atkinson, suspecting something wrong, succeeded, during the evening, in removing some $800 or $1,000 from his store, leaving but a small amount in the safe. About dusk, the three men entered the store and, covering Mr. Atkinson with their pistols, demanded his money. At this point, Mr. Atkinson's son George walked into the store and, upon inquiring as to the cause of the row, was answered by a pistol being pointed at his head. He immediately raised the alarm, and the men opened fire on him and his father. With Mr. Atkinson still refusing to give up his money, one of the men jumped over the counter and seized two bags of silver, one containing $100 in Mexican money and the other about $35 in small change. One of the bullets struck the counter, glanced, and struck Mr. Atkinson in the head, but it did not do any damage more than scratching him. Mr. Atkinson was trying to discharge his pistol at the robbers, but it failed to revolve. By daylight Saturday morning, a number of men were on the trail after the daring thieves, John and William Atkinson among them. Failing to find any clue, they returned home. On Sunday morning, Mr. Atkinson's four sons, with the deputy sheriff of Williamson county, started again, and about eight miles from Killeen they saw three men who, discovering the posse, started to run and made for the brush. Being crowded, though, they took to the open country. Frank Atkinson, while in the brush, accidentally shot his horse and had to give up the chase. The deputy got lost in the brush, but the other three boys kept on the trail, and after running about a mile overtook one of them, and he gave up. Leaving one of the party in charge of the man, William and John Atkinson kept on after the other two, and nearing Killeen, the Atkinson boys commenced firing their pistols to alarm the town. Unfortunately there was but one horse saddled in town, and the owner refused to allow him to be used. By this time the robbers rode through the town, but in a few minutes over thirty men were on the trail. Mr. John Atkinson and his brother-in-law, Gus McDowell, kept in the lead and succeeded in running upon one of them about four miles north of Killeen. McDowell held him, and Atkinson followed the other about two miles, where he struck the mountain. The fugitive left his horse and took to the brush, and Atkinson ran by him. But Mr. Boyd, the constable, spied the man and made him hold up his hands. They were brought to Killeen and then carried to Florence to be identified.

They gave their names as B. T. Risner, Leander Risner, and Richard Only. There was some doubt as to whether they were the parties who committed the robbery, but they evidently were wanted somewhere, as they told very contradictory stories. They also answered the description of the parties wanted at Georgetown for attempted murder. So off they went to the county jail. Guilty until proven innocent was the rule across Texas at the time.

Continue on FM 487 until it dead-ends into SH 195; turn left on SH 195, then right a half mile later on FM 970, toward Andice. FM 970 stair steps its way west down to Andice through open high prairie.

ANDICE

Williamson County • 25 • About 7 miles from Florence

Andice was originally called Stapp, after Joshua Stapp, who built a log school/church building here in 1857, where Presbyterians, Methodists, and Baptists held joint, or "union," services. The name of the settlement was later changed to Berry's Creek. Two of Berry's Creek's residents were the Reverend William Isaac Newton and his wife. Their son Audice was born on January 5, 1899, and soon after this blessed event, Reverend Newton applied for a post office, requesting that it be named Audice. Postal authorities misread the name and approved the name Andice that fall, with Newton as postmaster. All that remains in Andice now are the old general store, which serves a Texas-class hamburger, and an old red brick school, which is now a community center.

When FM 970 crosses US 183, it becomes County Road 209. In about a half mile, the road forks. Take the fork that goes straight ahead, across the cattle guard. You are now on County Road 210.

This road takes you through rough ranching country, past the highest peak in Williamson County, Mount Gabriel (1,208 feet). Locally known as Pilot Knob, the peak served as a landmark to traveling Indians and explorers in early Texas. You can best appreciate its size relative to the gently rolling countryside by looking back over your shoulder in another four or five miles. The country here is very rough and sparsely settled, useless for farming and only marginally useful for stock grazing.

When County Road 210 dead-ends in the shadow of Mount Gabriel 1.3 miles later, turn right onto County Road 207.

If you were to turn left at County Road 210's dead end, you would very shortly enter the Loafers' Glory neighborhood. Nothing is there now. As quaint as the name sounds, it is not unique. Communities in Arkansas, Michigan, and North Carolina sport the same name. Loafer's Glory Apostolic Church was organized in 1908 after Wesleyan Holiness preacher George Sutton conducted a revival at Loafer's Glory School on Wilson Atwood's farm. Beginning in 1909, evangelist Fred Lohmann served as minister and conducted tent revivals that drew hundreds of people. A small frame sanctuary was erected in about 1910 on land donated by Jim Moore, who led the congregation until his death in 1917. Many ministers and missionaries originated from Loafer's Glory Church, which continued services until 1930.

While Noah Smithwick never visited Loafer's Glory, he got to know some of their spiritual brethren during his years at Mormon Mills, a few miles south of Burnet:

> There finally sprung up a sect in Backbone valley that discounted all others in spiritual manifestations. Protestant Methodists [Wesleyan Holiness is an offshoot of Methodism] they styled themselves, though just what the name implied I never learned. They had meetings every night, singing, shouting and going into trances, during which they spoke with tongues and played on imaginary harps, and, as a grand finale, springing to their feet and running as if pursued by the emissaries of Satan. Crowds of curious sightseers flocked to see the performance as though it were a circus.
>
> The men of the sect all felt themselves called to preach, and as the emoluments of office were not sufficient to support the whole neighborhood, they had to make up the deficit by hook and by crook. A whole batch of them were once summoned as jurors. One after another they arose and pleaded the statutes in their favor as ministers of the gospel. The judge finally arose and blandly inquired if there were any men in their neighborhood who were not ministers of the gospel. Shiftless at best, their hallucinations rendered them even more so; they had worked their credit for all it was worth and were almost on the verge of starvation. They had gotten into me for various amounts of breadstuffs and I decided to shut down on them, the more especially as crops were short that year and mill stuffs commanded cash.

One old fellow who had a large family had been particularly troublesome. Seeing him coming, I told the miller not to let him have anything more. With an empty bag in one hand and leading a thin, ill-fed looking little boy by the other, he assaulted my fortress with the usual request for a bushel of meal on credit, reciting the failure of his crop, which, by the way, he had neglected to plant, and the destitute condition of his family in consequence. Without daring to look at the child, I put on a severe look and replied: "I can sell every dust in the mill for cash, Mr. ———. It is therefore impossible to accommodate you." The poor creature turned away, and taking the little boy by the hand, said in tremulous tones: "Well, son, we might as well go." I involuntarily glanced at the child, whose appealing eyes were raised to my face; tears stood in the blue baby eyes, tears of hunger. "Here, John, give Mr. ——— a bushel of meal," I said to the miller. I never got a cent for the meal, but the joy that lit up that little wan, pinched face and sparkled through the tears in those little eyes amply repaid me. I knew that the father was improvident, but the child was not to blame for that. Verily, "the sins of the fathers," etc. That same man denounced me as an "infidel." "Well," said one of his neighbors, "he's better than you are anyway, for the Bible says, 'He that provideth not for his household is wuss'n an infidel.'"

Two miles and one ninety-degree turn later, you come to an intersection and a one-story limestone house. Turn right on County Road 236 by the house in order to reach the ghost town of Gabriel Mills.

GABRIEL MILLS

Williamson County • About 5 miles from Andice

Looking at this rough, thicketed countryside, it's hard to believe that a thriving community existed here as late as the 1920s. The only tip-off is the cemeteries that line the road. The first is the old Mount Horeb Church Cemetery, which is actually a string of family plots stretching along the road for several hundred feet. The road then takes a sharp bend to the right. Shortly thereafter you see on your right another cemetery, the Gabriel Mills Cemetery.

In the Bittick family cemetery, established in 1855, there is one particularly interesting stone, set off from the other, fenced-in markers. This rectangular limestone slab marks the final resting place of Elizebeth Simpson, whose crudely engraved marker reads: "ELIZABETH SIMPSON WAS BORNE APRIL THE 10 1831 AND DIDE SEPTEMBER THE 21 1864 AND REMEMBER AS YO AR PASING BY YO MUST DY AS WELL AS I." No one knows who Elizebeth Simpson was, but judging from the isolated position of the stone and the crude lettering, Simpson was probably a slave. The stone was moved inside the fence in the late 1980s. A hundred feet farther, you'll see a gnarled, spreading, centuries-old live oak tree. This is a hanging tree; from its branches were hanged two horse thieves well over one hundred years ago. It just goes to show that all hanging trees don't wither up and die.

Continue forward (east) on County Road 236 another mile, to the three-way intersection with County Road 209. Turn right here, onto County Road 209 (you cannot turn left). You are high atop the Shin Oak Ridge now, and the views to the west are great, stretching out some twenty miles. A quaint little Mexican cemetery with an open-air chapel and altar is on your right in about a mile, and shortly after, you come back to the old-time signpost and intersection with County Road 210 (the loop you have made is a little more than seven miles). In case you didn't notice it the first time around, take note of the old "worm" log fence, so named for the zigzag pattern in which it is constructed.

From here, continue as before on County Road 210 and County Road 207 to the one-story limestone house mentioned and turn left at the intersection with County Road 236.

The house was built from rock that previously had been used in the Brizendine Store at Gabriel Mills. Gabriel Mills was first settled in 1849 by Englishman Samuel Mather, who built a water-powered gristmill nearby on the North Fork of the San Gabriel River. Mather also did blacksmithing, and one of his early customers was the Comanche chief Yellow Wolf, who brought him some silver ore to be hammered into ornaments. Yellow Wolf offered to lead Mather to the source of the ore "three suns west," but Mather declined.

One building from the old days still stands, albeit miles away in Old Settlers Park in Round Rock. This cabin of squared logs and hand-hewn limestone was built in the early 1850s. It stood on property owned in 1850–1853 by Samuel Mather (1812–1878). The structure housed a church, a school, and the local Masonic Lodge before it became a dwelling.

More settlers joined Mather over the years. A church, school, and Masonic Lodge, collectively known as Mount Horeb, were erected here, although Indians continued to raid the settlement through the Civil War. Stores, a gin, cotton-and-wool-carding machines, and even a telephone exchange were established here in the following years. The town celebrated the erection of a great iron bridge across the North Fork of the San Gabriel River in 1893. But then the Masonic Lodge burned down. Nearby Bertram started to grow rapidly and began to lure businesses away. Then the schools were consolidated. People started moving away, and Gabriel Mills was literally a ghost town by the time of the Great Depression. The old iron bridge, damaged beyond repair by a flood in 1957, had to be torn down.

Gabriel Mills' famous native son was noted Indian fighter Andy Mather. The son of Samuel Mather, Andy was born here in 1851 and grew into a strapping six-foot-four-inch man. Indian fighter and Texas Ranger, Mather feared no one. Stories of his bravery abound. Mather was the first man to lasso a bear in Texas, killing it with his bowie knife. It was supposedly the biggest bear the state had ever seen. Another time, Mather was engaged in combat with a famous Indian chief. They exhausted their ammunition supply at the same time, whereupon the Indian started to flee the scene. Mather responded by lassoing the Indian around the neck, jerking him from his horse, and dragging him to death. Mather wore his blond hair down to his shoulders and was never seen without his spurs on. Mather's old friend Buffalo Bill Cody came to visit him once at Georgetown, and the longhaired pair of Wild West legends cut quite a figure together. Andy Mather died in 1929 and is buried in the Mather family plot in the Mount Horeb Church Cemetery. His stone is easily visible from the road. The Mather plot is the second plot up from the limestone house.

Continue your path west on County Road 236. In a few feet you will see the historical marker that tells the story of this vanished town and you'll cross the North Fork of the San Gabriel. The countryside stretches out a bit now, becoming sparsely treed grazing land. This marker is about 5.5 miles from Andice. When you enter Burnet County, Williamson County Road 207 becomes Burnet County Road 276.

In about four miles, this road dead-ends into another road. At this intersection by the Hutto Ranch, turn right onto Burnet County Road 274.

Now is as good a time as any to look back at Mt. Gabriel. You'll see why ancient travelers used it as a landmark. You can see the Bertram water tower ahead of you in the distance.

In a couple of miles, County Road 274 dead-ends into FM 243. Turn left on FM 243 to reach Bertram.

BERTRAM

Burnet County • 1,400 (approximate) • About 9 miles from Gabriel Mills historical marker

Bertram was a child of the Austin and Northwestern railroad, founded with the arrival of the rails in 1882 and named for Austin businessman Rudolph Bertram, a prominent railroad stockholder. The town of Bertram had its roots in the village of Cedar Mill thirty years earlier. Cedar Mill was located several miles south on a tributary of the South Fork of the San Gabriel River. When the route of the old Austin-to-Burnet road shifted northward, Cedar Mill moved to a spot on the river that the inhabitants first called Louis-town (in honor of their first storekeeper), and then South Gabriel. The village became prosperous. When news of the coming railroad drifted into town, progressive South Gabriel residents offered railroad officials $3,000 to route the tracks through their village.

By November 19, 1881, the engineering party of the Austin and Northwestern had crossed the South Gabriel a mile above the crossing of the wagon road leading from Liberty Hill to Round Rock. It was not yet determined where a depot would be located. By December 20, the first spike in the laying of the track was driven in Austin. South Gabriel really wanted the Austin and Northwestern and had secured the right-of-way for her part of the county. W. H. Westfall of Burnet had been in South Gabriel working on the matter and had seemingly succeeded in getting the company to run its line through South Gabriel. But by February 28, it was clear that their efforts were for naught. The Austin and Northwestern tracks went through north of South Gabriel instead.

So, the go-ahead merchants of South Gabriel decided to move their stores to the new depot and town site, and they and the townspeople just picked up and moved to the new town of Bertram en masse, just as they had earlier moved from Cedar Mill. Brothers Wild and L. R. Gray moved the entire town of South Gabriel (thirteen houses and two stores) two miles north to the railroad in two days. The Grays used thirteen yoke of oxen to accomplish this feat, and the entire town squeezed into one house during the two-day move.

By September 1882, the post office and W. A. Johnson's store were all that remained of the business part of South Gabriel. M. B. Lockett, Vaughan and Reilly, and the Grange store had all moved to the new town of Bertram. The merchants all expected to immediately buy and sell thousands of bales of cotton, as there were six cotton gins within eight miles of the place.

And so Bertram became a regional marketing center for farm and ranch products, cedar posts, and pecans. Thousands of carloads of pink granite rumbled through the town during its first decade of life, destined for Austin and the state capitol. Today Bertram is best known as home of the Oatmeal Festival.

BERTRAM SCHOOL

FM 243

Coming into Bertram on FM 243, you pass the two-story red-brick Bertram school. Bertram was in the middle of a cotton boom back in 1909, and this rock-solid schoolhouse with its topside bell tower reflects this era of prosperity. School sessions were structured around the cotton season then. The school closed in 1970, the result of a merger with the Burnet schools, but it has now reopened as Bertram Elementary School.

The popular Hill Country Flyer tourist train either stops at, or passes through, Bertram on weekends during season, and the old depot by the tracks adds a period touch to the scenery enjoyed by passengers. The original Bertram depot was torn down in 1964. This depot came from Orange Grove, Texas, and was built by the San Antonio and Aransas Pass railroad. Visit the website, www.austinsteamtrain.org, or call 477-8468 for up-to-date schedules and details.

As you cross the railroad tracks and SH 29, notice the Reed building across the highway, between Lampasas and Grange.

REED BUILDING

SH 29, between Grange and Lampasas

Tom Seldon (Tobe) Reed was a schoolteacher living in South Gabriel when the railroad came through. He decide to move his family to Bertram and open up a store, which would buy everything the farmer had to sell at the existing price and sell him everything he needed as cheaply as it could be purchased anywhere. His son, Tom, and brothers, Dave and Malcom, were partners in the store. They bought and shipped trainloads of cotton, cereal grains, and cedar posts. As the bank sign on the east side of the building indicates, they established a bank. Sometime in the early 1900s, the Reeds separated. Malcom went to Marble Falls. Dave stayed with the Bertram store. And Tobe and Tom moved to Beaumont, where they grew one of the country's largest importation firms, mostly of tropical fruit from South America. Malcom and Dave eventually moved to Austin and continued their cotton and cedar businesses, becoming very rich.

Built in 1905, the current Reed building is Bertram's most imposing business edifice. It is a two-story sandstone structure with a cut limestone-block facade. Inside you'll find high wood-strip ceilings, ceiling fans, a variety of old wood-and-glass cabinets and fixtures, and a nice turned-wood balustrade stairway leading upstairs.

In the alley behind the Reed building, you'll note an old tin-sided store whose lettered facade still reads "C. A. Newton Confectionery, Ice Cold Drinks, Cigars and Tobacco." It has been closed for years.

Next to the Reed building is the first new commercial building erected in Bertram (in 1884), a two-story building with cut limestone-block facade and limestone rubble walls. The stone was salvaged from the schoolhouse in the old South Gabriel community.

ANNUAL EVENT

SEPTEMBER

OATMEAL FESTIVAL

Downtown Oatmeal and Bertram • 355-2197 • www.bertramtx.com • Labor Day weekend • Most events free

Bertram's annual wingding is a bit of insanity known as the Oatmeal Festival, which used to be held in nearby Oatmeal. It got so big that most of the activities moved to Bertram. Events include an oatmeal cook-off and eat-off, an oatmeal sculpture contest, oatmeal box stacking, oatmeal bowling, the Hour of Oats, and such non-oat events as a footrace, barbecue, parade, and dances.

To leave Bertram, take SH 29 east, and then turn right onto FM 1174. You are bound for Oatmeal. About two miles after you leave Bertram, you cross the South Fork of the San Gabriel River. About a mile after you cross the river, you turn right on Burnet County Road 326 to reach Oatmeal.

After about three miles, this little road, which runs along scenic Oatmeal Creek, dead-ends into FM 243 at the whitewashed frame 1920s Oatmeal schoolhouse, which is now a community center.

OATMEAL

Burnet County • About 6 miles from Bertram

Oatmeal is the second-oldest settlement in Burnet County. A German family named Hafermehl (locally corrupted to Habermills) came here in 1849 by ox wagon and settled down for a season or two in the lush grasslands adjacent to the headsprings of Oatmeal Creek. Hafermehl translates into English as "oatmeal." Sometime after they had left, a local resident sent his sons out to look for strayed livestock, giving them instructions to "first look for them around Oatmeal Spring, then go down to the creek." The springs, creek, and community have been known as Oatmeal ever since. The "Oatmeals" were not heard from again until some descendants came back years later and tried to make claim and title to the family's original plot.

The fertile land along Oatmeal Creek attracted many settlers. By 1852, Oatmeal was a bustling village. Burnet County's greatest feud pitted the Oatmeal Creek faction against the Hamilton (Burnet) faction. Hamilton won. But this setback did not mean the end of Oatmeal. A post office was established here in 1853. The next year, John R. Scott arrived from New York via the California gold fields. Here at Oatmeal he planted Burnet County's first orchard and operated the county's first and only cheese factory.

An ardent Unionist, Scott was badgered and threatened by his secessionist neighbors once the Civil War started, so much so that he decided to flee to Mexico. He got only as far as the Colorado River between Marble Falls and Smithwick. There he was ambushed and shot by bushwhackers who robbed him of the $2,500 he was carrying and threw his body down "Dead Man's Hole."

Another prominent area citizen and staunch Unionist, John Hubbard, writer Noah Smithwick's son-in-law, was also robbed and murdered by bushwhackers. They threw his body into the water hole beneath the falls of nearby Cow Creek, which have since been known as Hubbard Falls.

After the Civil War, a colony of ex-slaves settled in the eastern section of Oatmeal community along Oatmeal Creek. Most of their homes were strung out in a line along Old Oatmeal Road, so the settlement was called Stringtown; it ceased to exist in the 1920s.

A few years ago, the state struck Oatmeal from its highway maps. Thanks to the Oatmeal Festival (see Bertram Annual Events), Oatmeal is back on the map.

From the schoolhouse, start back up County Road 326, the road you took to Oatmeal. After 0.2 miles you come to a Y in the road. You came into Oatmeal from Bertram on the fork to the left. Now, take the fork to the right as per the Oatmeal Church of Christ sign (County Road 327).

In a couple of hundred yards, you come to a brush arbor on your right and the Oatmeal Church of Christ just up the hill on your left.

OATMEAL CHURCH AND ARBOR

On Cty. Rd. 327 • Open only for Sunday services

The brush arbor dates to 1903. Its framework consists of cedar posts and poles, and its roof is cedar thatch. There are no walls. An arbor is a roof over one's head and nothing more, the simplest form of mass shelter. Arbors like this were the pioneers' first church buildings. As soon as they were settled in, they would build a log church building, then a frame, stone, or brick permanent sanctuary. The arbor would then be torn down or relegated to use during the hot summer months. Several dozen arbors still exist across rural Central Texas at places like Fitzhugh and High Grove, but they all have solid tin roofs and concrete floors. Here the afternoon sun trickles through the cedar thatch roof like raindrops falling from a tree after a storm, and the floor is packed earth, grassy green from disuse. Worshippers sat on a dozen straight-backed, uncompromisingly hard wooden benches—no chance of falling asleep here during the sermon. A bare lightbulb was the only concession to modernity. The Oatmeal Festival's gospel sings have traditionally taken place here at the arbor each Labor Day Sunday.

The church up the hill was built as a combination schoolhouse and church in 1869 for the lordly sum of sixty-five dollars. Except for minor repairs and a board floor, the simple rectangular limestone building looks just like it did in 1869.

From the church and arbor, continue east to the cemetery turnoff. Visit this neatly trimmed plot if you wish; otherwise follow the road's sharp turn to the left. You cross Oatmeal Creek in a few hundred feet. Turn left at the T intersection just beyond the creek crossing. You have just completed the Oatmeal loop and are back on the original road you took to get to Oatmeal. At FM 243 and the Oatmeal school, turn left and proceed south on FM 243. In about four miles, you come to the junction with FM 1174.

CEDAR MILL

Burnet County • About 3 miles from Oatmeal

This pretty little valley is the site of the old Cedar Mill community, located on the south fork of Oatmeal Creek and on what was once the main road from Austin to Burnet. When the road moved east in the 1860s, the people of Cedar Mill followed it, relocating first on the site known as South Gabriel and then moving to Bertram. Nothing remains of Cedar Mill today except a beautiful view.

Continue on FM 1174 south until you reach the junction with FM 1869. Turn left here onto FM 1869.

(If you went a couple of miles farther on 1174, you would cross a branch of Cow Creek. If you were to walk upstream a ways, which is not advised because this is private property, you would find dinosaur tracks in the rocky creek bed and the names of Captain T. D. Vaughan's Confederate Army company chiseled into the creek bank rocks.)

After about three miles on FM 1869, turn right onto County Road 285, and in a mile you come to the ghost town of Hopewell, where nothing but Hopewell Cemetery remains today.

HOPEWELL

Williamson County • About 6.5 miles from Oatmeal

Hopewell was settled in the early 1850s and was first called Burleson's Springs. The name Hopewell was derived from Hope, Arkansas, former home of several early settlers here, including the parents of Tom Seldon Reed. Located on one of the early routes of the Austin-to-Burnet road, Hopewell was plagued by Indian raids during the early years. Preachers kept their guns next to their Bibles on the pulpit; the men of the congregation also kept their firearms lapside. Indian attacks in western Williamson County increased during the Civil War because many of the settlers were off fighting, and northern traders had furnished the Comanches with the latest in firearms. The most brutal raid occurred here at Hopewell.

The Wofford Johnson family had spent the sweltering day of August 15, 1863, making molasses at the nearby Whitehead place. Returning home that afternoon, Mr. and Mrs. Johnson and their three children were ambushed by the Kiowa-turned-Comanche war chief Big Foot and his band. Wofford and his little girl were killed almost instantly in the dense dogwood thickets along Dog Creek. Mrs. Johnson galloped desperately for home but was shot down a few hundred yards later. The babe in her arms was taken for ransom. The Johnsons' oldest girl managed to escape and ran for help. Local Texas Ranger captain Jeff Maltby organized a posse and set off in pursuit of Big Foot and his band the next morning. The posse found the Johnson baby alive and unharmed on a cedar bush a few hours into their chase, abandoned by the fleeing Comanches. Maltby's posse got close enough to the Indians to identify Big Foot but were unable to capture the Indians when they leaped off a creek bluff and escaped into the darkness. Maltby spent the next nine years tracking down Big Foot and his lieutenant Jape. He finally confronted them in Runnels County in 1872. Captain Jeff and Big Foot drew simultaneously, but Maltby got his shot off first, breaking Big Foot's neck. In the meantime, Jape was fatally wounded by trooper Henry Sackett. Before he died, Jape confessed to the Johnson murders.

The Johnsons were buried in their wagon at the Hopewell Cemetery, which is now the only identifiable trace of the Hopewell community. Their common stone reads, "Wofford Johnson, Wife, and Little Dau, MASSACRED BY THE INDIANS, AUG 15 1863." They were the last Indian attack victims in Williamson County.

Church services here were first held under an arbor adjacent to the cemetery. After the war, a permanent sanctuary was built, followed by a school, gin, store, and Masonic Lodge, and a saloon that sold drinks by the dipper. Hopewell had a post office, for less than three months, in 1882. The town started to fade when the Austin-to-Burnet road made one of its many route adjustments. Now only the dead remain.

Continue south on County Road 285 from the Hopewell Cemetery. In less than a half mile, you come to an intersection with County Road 286. Bear left here on County Road 285. Around the bend and a couple of hundred feet later, County Road 284 veers off to the right, but you continue dead ahead on County Road 285. Soon you are treated to some nice views of Little Creek, off to your right. County Road 285 dead-ends at FM 1869 in another four miles. Turn right onto FM 1869 and go east about four miles to reach Liberty Hill.

Williamson County was home to a number of cattle barons during the last half of the nineteenth century. One of the classiest was Dave Harrell, who had a ranch between Hopewell and Liberty Hill. Harrell was Texas' first shorthorn breeder, and his bull Old Prince was the world champion shorthorn bull at the 1904 St. Louis World's Fair. A huge crowd gathered at the Liberty Hill depot to greet Harrell and the celebrity bull when they returned home.

LIBERTY HILL

Williamson County • 1,674 (approximate) • About 7 miles from Hopewell

Captain Cal Putnam was the first settler in these parts. He built a blockhouse near the present-day Liberty Hill in the early 1830s, when his nearest white neighbors were back at Hornsby Bend. The first settlement was located about three miles west on one of the two Austin-to-Burnet military roads. Baptist minister W. O. Spencer moved here in 1853 from Bastrop County, upon the death of his wife, and built his house where the second Austin-to-Burnet military road crossed the road between Austin and Fort Gates via Lampasas.

As a pastor, he was one of the community's most prominent inhabitants, and when Texas Revolution hero and U.S. senator Thomas Rusk stopped and made camp nearby one night in 1853, he was invited to stay at the Spencer residence. Rusk was a member of the Senate Post Office Committee and was touring the state looking for new post office sites. As Rusk rose from the breakfast table the next morning to thank his host for his splendid hospitality, he asked Spencer if there was any favor he might do for him. Spencer mentioned that there was not a single post office located on the road between Austin and Burnet, whereupon Rusk sat down and wrote out an order to his post office committee, requesting that a post office be established at this site and that W. O. Spencer be named its postmaster. Then he looked up and asked, "What shall its name be?" Spencer thought for a minute and then said, "These people around here are a peaceful, liberty-loving folk. I live upon a hill. I am fond of hills. Let's call it Liberty Hill."

After the Civil War, the village shifted slightly eastward with the stage road, and Spencer followed; his house operated as a hotel/stage stop from the 1870s until 1884. The town shifted again to its present site with the coming of the Austin and Northwestern railroad in 1882. In the summer and fall of 1881, everybody, and every town, between Austin and Burnet was eagerly awaiting the chosen path of the Austin and Northwestern, and the line's owners were playing this anticipation for all it was worth, asking the citizens of Liberty Hill for $10,000 cash, right-of-way, and a depot.

By December 18, Duncan G. Smith, the right-of-way agent of the Austin and Northwestern Railroad Company, had closed a contract with the people of Liberty Hill for the construction of the Austin and Northwestern railroad to that place, which assured Liberty Hill railroad communications with the balance of the world in a very short time. On April 14, 1882, the first regular passenger and freight train on the Austin and Northwestern pulled out of Austin for Liberty Hill. The railroad's arrival brought about an explosion in growth here, resulting in the string of brick and limestone business houses that still stands in downtown Liberty Hill.

Liberty Hill was for twenty-five years home to the Liberty Normal and Business College, which opened in 1885. Many families moved to Liberty Hill to enroll their children in the school, which was touted as the largest and most progressive normal in Texas. "Study is a pleasure and not a burden," its proprietors said. But the school fell on hard times and closed in 1910, and the two-story red-brick building was deeded over to the public school system.

In its heyday, Liberty Hill had three banks and two gins. It continued to prosper as a local shipping and marketing center until the decline of the railroad and area farming. The town experienced something of a revival in the 1970s when an investor restored many of the old buildings and touted Liberty Hill as a regional arts-and-crafts center. This boom has gone bust, but Liberty Hill has a magnificently restored downtown just waiting for some enterprising individuals to fill it.

From FM 1869, turn right on Loop 332 and park for a stroll downtown. Loop 332 is Liberty Hill's old main street.

GENERAL STORE

Corner of FM 1869 and Loop 332

This store is your starting point. There used to be old livery stables in back of the store.

OLD MASONIC LODGE

927 Loop 332

The next block of Loop 332 is a line of well-maintained, though mostly empty, two-story limestone and brick buildings. One of the best is the old Masonic Lodge, identified as such by a state historical marker. John Munro built this two-story limestone structure in 1883, operating a hardware store on the bottom floor. The Masons bought the top floor from him for their meeting hall. One of the banks, built in 1906, stands next door at 929 Loop 332.

Cross the street and begin the short stroll back to FM 1869.

STUBBLEFIELD BUILDING

1000 Loop 332 at Myrtle, north side

This is downtown Liberty Hill's oldest surviving structure, built by S. P. Stubblefield in 1871 of hand-cut limestone. The first floor houses a variety of businesses. The second floor was living space. Stubblefield, a Mexican-American War veteran, died in 1902; his family kept the building until 1907.

From downtown Liberty Hill, proceed east on Loop 332 to Liberty Hill High School and the international Sculpture Park.

SCULPTURE PARK

Liberty Hill High School grounds, Loop 332 at SH 29 • Open at all times • W

The late Mel Fowler was the driving force behind the International Sculpture Park, which features more than two dozen works by artists from America and Europe. Fowler lived and worked here for more than ten years before his untimely death in 1987 while in Italy. Three of the park's works are Fowler's; he loved to work in the Hill Country's native stone.

BRYSON STAGECOACH STOP

SH 29, 1 mile west of Liberty Hill • 512-630-4619 • www.forttumbleweed .net • Open to the public on a limited basis

John T. Bryson and his wife Amelia, prominent early settlers of the Liberty Hill community, left South Carolina in 1852 and settled in Washington County for one year before buying a strip of land along the south fork of the San Gabriel River near the crossing of the road from Austin to Burnet. They constructed this home in 1854, according to their grandson, J. Gordon Bryson. The Texas classic dog-run home was constructed of notched and fitted red cedar timber, lumber, and native stone chimneys. The milled lumber used on the floors, walls, and ceilings was hauled by oxen and wagons from a sawmill in the town of Cedar Break north of Bastrop.

It is said that the largest cedar trees in the world came from this brake, some of the logs being more than three feet in diameter. At some point after, John and Amelia Bryson and their family settled into their log homestead, near where the old Burnet and Lampasas roads forked.

The stagecoaches that ran on either of these military roads would stop at the Brysons' spring to water their horses. Given the need to have stage stops every ten to twelve miles, the Bryson homestead was ideally located.

To provide the extra water required by the stagecoach relay teams, the Brysons constructed two additional wells near their log barn.

As was the custom at all stage stops, the minute a stage coach pulled up to a halt in the front yard, the Bryson men unharnessed the team and fed, watered, and groomed the weary horses who had just completed their ten-mile run.

Meanwhile, Amelia would greet the passengers and driver with a pitcher of cool water from the spring.

Meals at many stage stops were often mediocre and limited to cornbread and sorghum syrup, "fry" (overfried bacon or pork belly), and bad coffee, but Amelia had a reputation as a gracious hostess and excellent cook, whose dinner table included seasonal fresh vegetables (or "put up" vegetables out of season), freshly baked wheat bread and cornbread served with freshly churned butter, fresh milk, smoked ham and sausage, beef, venison, fried chicken, and dessert.

In the morning, passengers breakfasted on hot biscuits and fresh butter, jellies and jams, eggs, bacon and sausage, fried potatoes, fresh spring-chilled milk, and of course piping hot coffee.

The privately owned property also contains the Round Rock Bank (1876) targeted by Sam Bass, an old general store from Stapp (present-day Andice, circa 1870), and a Pony Express station from Abilene.

Besides being a good cook, Amelia was also the community's midwife. Being good Methodists, they organized the area's first church and helped build a one-room log building in the Brysons' pasture in which to hold services; it also served as a schoolhouse.

The church that replaced it, much altered today, stands downtown at 101 Church Street, about a block and a half north off Main Street/Loop 332. Construction of a three-story building of native stone for use of the church, school, and Masonic Lodge was begun in 1870 on land given by T. S. Snyder. The upper stories were removed and choir space was added in 1905, wings were added in 1916, and a vestibule was added in 1954.

From downtown Liberty Hill, backtrack on FM 1869 across the San Gabriel River. Less than 0.5 miles later, you see a paved road running off to your left, the first paved left past the river. Turn left onto this road, which is identified by signs as County Road 282.

First you overlook the Little Creek valley. When the road forks for the first time, 0.5 miles from FM 1869, bear left.

As you leave Williamson County and the Shin Oak Ridge, County Road 282 rolls straight on past intersections with County Roads 284, 283, and 281. At this point, you are in the vicinity of the Jenks Branch Community, birthplace of Bill Pickett.

According to family records, Willie M. "Bill" Pickett was born on December 5, 1870, in the Jenks Branch Community. His father, Tom Pickett, came to Texas as a newly born slave, having been born on the road somewhere in Louisiana in October 1854, part of a party of South Carolinians moving to Texas: forty-eight whites and fifty-two slaves. The Barton family, to whom Tom Pickett's parents belonged, settled in Williamson County on the San Gabriel River below Liberty Hill and three miles from the Travis County line. The community they formed became known as Jenks Branch, named for Jinks Branch Creek, which runs into the San Gabriel, or for John W. Jenks and John W. Branch, two early landowners. After the war, most of the freed Barton slaves remained in the vicinity. The Barton family slaves bore the surnames Barton and Pickett.

Tom, who was of African, Anglo, and Cherokee extraction, married Mary Gilbert, whose ancestors were black, white, Indian, and Mexican, in 1870. They had thirteen children. Sometime in the early 1870s, the Picketts moved to Austin. Tom had a truck garden and sold his produce in the city. Bill finished the fifth grade, probably at Wheatville School near Twenty-fourth and San Gabriel. He was fascinated by cowboys and studied what they did. He listened to the stories told by his cousins who had worked on several of the great cattle drives organized by Thomas Snyder, brother of Dudley and John Snyder.

Bill was often late to school because he stopped along the way to watch cattle and cowboys at work. One day in 1881, he noticed a bulldog holding a cow motionless by her upper lip. Many early-day Texas ranchers used dogs to work wild cattle out of thickets, where they hid to avoid the cowboys. The dogs were usually half or more English bulldog and weighed fifty to sixty pounds. Their ancestors had been used in England for fighting or bullbaiting. There were heel dogs and catch dogs. The heel dog distracted the cow, nipping at the heels, and the catch dog moved in, locked in on the upper lip, and held fast until the cowboys could get the cow roped. The process was called bulldogging. As Bill watched, the bulldog finally released the cow and trotted off. This set Bill to thinking. A few days later, Bill grabbed a calf by the ears. It squirmed and bawled, trying to free itself. Bill chomped down on its upper lip, let loose of its ears, and threw it to the ground.

Another morning, on his way to school, he passed a group of Littlefield Cattle Company cowboys branding calves. They were having problems. Bill volunteered that he could hold the calves with his teeth. The cowboys got a good laugh out of this. One of them suggested that they let Bill try to hold one of the calves while they branded it. They roped and threw one of the largest unbranded calves and invited Bill to do his thing. He chomped down, and the calf barely moved as they applied the searing brand to its hindquarter. When Bill let loose, it scrambled up and rejoined the other calves. The cowboys were amazed and spread the word around Austin of Pickett's feat. He began to practice bulldogging cows and steers that ran wild in the mesquite brush, which was too thick to throw a lasso, so he would ride alongside the steer, lean over, jump from the saddle, grab it by the horns, twist its head, and throw it to the ground.

After Bill left school, he went to work as a cowboy. At age fifteen or sixteen, he started riding broncs on Sunday afternoon for spectators, passing the hat afterward for spending money. When he was sixteen, he was watching some cowboys trying to rope some wild steers near Austin. They weren't having much luck. Bill said that he could catch them and hold them with his teeth. They told him to go ahead and try. He caught and threw three steers in succession. Shortly after this, Bill was invited to go to a Confederate Soldiers Reunion in Nashville, Tennessee, to bulldog with a Wild West show. The attendees couldn't believe what they saw.

In the late 1880s, probably 1888, Thomas Pickett moved to Taylor. Bill worked for a number of area ranches. In 1890, he married Maggie Turner. Bill served as a deacon at the Taylor Baptist Church. In 1888, the first Taylor fair was held at the new fairgrounds. Tom and Bill gave a steer bulldogging exhibition. In the 1890s, Bill and his brothers organized the Pickett Brothers Bronco Busters and Rough Riders Association: "We ride and break all wild horses with much care. Good treatment to all animals. Perfect satisfaction guaranteed. Catching and taming wild cattle a specialty." They operated for several years and had a number of satisfied customers in the Taylor area.

Pickett was a patriotic American, despite the segregation that plagued his life; in 1898, he was a member of the Taylor Rifles, a one-hundred-man company affiliated with the Texas Volunteer Guard. The Taylor Rifles petitioned to serve during the Spanish-American War but were rejected in favor of a white cavalry company from Georgetown. The First Christian Church at 603 Talbot in Taylor still has a stained-glass window donated and installed by the Taylor Rifles.

Pickett had worked for Lee Moore, a rancher near Rockdale, who decided that there was money to be made from Bill's peculiar talent. He booked Pickett at county fairs and stockmen's association events around the state. Moore, naturally, took the lion's share of the gate while Pickett did all the hard work. In 1900, Moore took Pickett to Colorado and then to several other southwestern states until 1902, when Moore and Pickett parted ways.

Pickett then took up with Dave McClure, a well-known cowboy and promoter. The *Wyoming Tribune* breathlessly reported in 1904:

> The event par excellence of the celebration [Cheyenne Frontier Days] this year is the great feat of Will Pickett, a negro from Taylor, Texas. . . . Twenty thousand people will watch with wonder and admiration a mere man, unarmed and without a device or appliance of any kind, attack a fiery, wild-eyed and powerful steer, dash under the broad breast of the great brute, turn and sink his strong ivory teeth into the upper lip of the animal and, throwing his shoulder against the neck of the steer, strain and twist until the animal, with its head drawn one way under the controlling influence of those merciless teeth and its body forced another, until the brute, under the strain of slowly bended neck, quivered, trembled, and sank to the ground, conquered by a trick. A trick perhaps, but one of the most startling and sensational exhibitions ever seen at a place where daring and thrilling feats are commonplace.

Pickett measured just five foot seven inches tall and 145 pounds. What he lacked in size, he made up for with his powerful shoulders and arms.

The *Denver Post* quoted Pickett during Frontier Days: "Ropes is all right for to hang people with, but they gets in the way when ya wants to rope a steer."

In 1905, Pickett began working with the Miller Brothers' Big Round-Up, a Wild West show based on the 101 Ranch in the Oklahoma Territory that counted Tom Mix and Geronimo in its cast. Geronimo killed his last buffalo before a crowd of sixty-five thousand during a 101 Ranch extravaganza on June 11, 1905; it was barbecued and served to the press. Pickett's bulldogging followed the big dinner. The next day, Tom Mix rode a horse off a high bluff and into the flood-swollen Salt Fork of the Arkansas River for a movie camera, marking the beginning of his movie career. Mix and Pickett went on to become good friends.

In 1905, the Miller Brothers' show went to Madison Square Garden, where a young Will Rogers assisted Bill Pickett in his bulldogging act. On the first night, Pickett, on his horse, was positioned on one side of the chute with Rogers on the other side. The steer lunged into the arena and headed straight for the gate. Pickett's horse tore off after the steer but couldn't catch him. The steer took a flying leap and headed up the stairs that led into the grandstands. Pickett was right behind the steer, spurring his horse up the board steps, followed by Rogers.

They caught the steer on the third balcony of the grandstand; Rogers roped him by the horns as Pickett leaped from his saddle and piled onto the steer's head. As Pickett hung onto the horns, Rogers dragged the steer back down into the arena, and Pickett forced him to the ground. Zack Miller said Rogers was so thrilled by the experience that he decided to quit studying to be a lawyer. He'd be damned, he said, if he could stand around arguing a case in court when there was excitement like bulldogging to be had in this world.

Pickett also worked several weeks that year with Will Rogers in another Wild West show, for which Rogers performed rope tricks for fifteen dollars a week. The two became good friends, and Rogers would eat many a meal at the Pickett house.

In 1907, Pickett signed a contract with the three Miller brothers' (Joe, Zack, and George) newly formed 101 Ranch Wild West Show. In December 1908, the 101 Ranch Wild West Show went to Mexico City, where as a gimmick to draw spectators, Bill Pickett would try to bulldog a Mexican fighting bull. Accounts differ as to how well Pickett fared against the bull.

According to one version, a group of prominent Mexican matadors saw Bill bulldog a Texas steer. They weren't impressed. The Mexican press also criticized Pickett's work. The Millers challenged Manolo Bienvenida, a leading matador, to bulldog a steer. He agreed, but he never showed up. The Millers then proposed that Pickett would dog any bull the matadors chose. He was to fight the bull for at least fifteen minutes unless he dogged the bull flat on his back earlier.

The newspaper *El Imparcial* said that Pickett defeated the bull. The Pathe-Freres (Pathe Brothers) movie company filmed the battle in its entirety and showed the footage in theaters all over the United States in 1909, but it was lost sometime thereafter and has never been found.

Zack Miller's account, as recounted to Fred Gipson decades later, stated that Joe Miller challenged any bullfighter to do Bill's act. Joe would give a thousand pesos to the city's charity hospital if any bullfighter could bulldog a 101 steer Pickett style.

One man volunteered but then declined at the last minute in favor of a Mexican counterproposal betting five thousand pesos that Bill couldn't keep his hands on a Mexican fighting bull for five minutes. Bill agreed, on the stipulation that the Millers choose the bull.

It looked for a while like Bill would throw the bull. He was able to rock him till one forefoot came off the ground at each swing. The bull's neck muscles were tiring from Bill's weight.

The Mexicans grew incensed. When they saw that Bill was wearing the bull down fast, they began throwing whatever they could grab into the ring. A well-aimed quart beer bottle broke one of Bill's ribs. With that blow, Bill's grip loosened, and the bull lifted Bill high into the air and trotted around the arena, slinging Bill back and forth and slamming him into the wall. Four minutes had passed. Bill hung on through sheer stubbornness. Five minutes came, and Zack listened for the judges' bell. It didn't sound, not even when six minutes had passed.

That was enough for Zack, who wasn't going to let that bull kill Bill. Zack and a ranch hand galloped into the arena, snagged the bull's heels with their ropes, spread his legs, and threw him. Bill fell away from the bull and ran across the ring as fast as he could stagger—never once looking back—to check the injuries to his horse, who stood next to the wall.

A company of Mexican police galloped up and formed a protective line on either side of the 101 show participants. Zack took a look at the gore wounds to Bill's horse and cringed. But then one of the Mexicans from the show shouted, "Get me some bananas. I will cure him." Zack sent a boy to get some bananas. He rushed back with yellow ones. The man cursed the boy and sent him back for red ones. He then peeled them and shoved one banana into each of the gaping holes in the horse's rump. Incredibly, the wounds that should have killed the horse healed perfectly.

The troops escorted the show to its quarters. Joe angrily collected the five thousand pesos while the timekeepers apologized for their defective watches. From that day till the end of the sixteen-day run, the government had to keep troops posted to protect the show quarters from angry mobs.

Pickett spent most of the 1909 season recovering from his Mexico City injuries. He was back in 1910 as the 101 Ranch Wild West Show's star attraction. In 1913, the show sailed for South America. Experienced as he was on the "hurricane deck" of a wild Mexican mustang, Pickett was no sailor; the voyage was so rough that he and most of the rest of the passengers were seasick. Pickett said he never expected to reach Buenos Aires alive.

The show opened in 1914 in New York's Madison Square Garden and then went to Great Britain, where Pickett was well received. In 1915, boxer Jess Willard, who had just beaten Jack Johnson in Havana for the world heavyweight championship, joined the show. In 1916, Buffalo Bill Cody headlined the show. At the end of the season, the Millers sold the show. They and Pickett returned to the 101 Ranch.

At this point, Pickett had mostly retired from professional rodeoing, although he "came back" several times in the following years. He worked as a 101 cowboy until 1920, when he entered the Dewey Roundup and won the bulldogging competition. He then moved his family to Oklahoma City, where he worked at the stockyards and as a mill hand before returning to the 101 in 1924. He competed in a few rodeos each year, but not as many as he would have liked, because of segregation. In 1925, the Millers got back into show business, buying a circus and turning it into a Wild West show. Pickett was back in the saddle and back on the horns of the steers.

Not long thereafter, the 101 Ranch and Show began to fall on hard times; the show was losing money by the end of 1926 and continued to do so until it closed for good in 1931. The Great Depression hit the Millers, as it did everyone else. Believing the problems to be only temporary, they borrowed $500,000. But things only got worse in 1930. The show lost more money than ever and closed in August. One of the Miller brothers committed suicide. In September 1931, the 101 Ranch passed into receivership, and Zack Miller began to try to save at least part of the ranch. Pickett was there to help with the stock.

Maggie Pickett had died after a short illness in 1929, and Pickett was never the same again. He moved out of their house into a small house on the 101 and started drinking. The irony that she had died and he had survived, despite having broken or cracked most of the bones in his body at one time or another and losing at least several of his strong ivory teeth, was not lost upon him. She had often pleaded with him to give up bulldogging for the sake of his family.

Pickett died as he had lived, cowboying.

In March 1932, Fred Clarke, the 101's court-appointed receiver, announced a sale of the ranch's livestock, machinery, and everything else not tied to the ground. Zack Miller, bedridden, asked for twenty-four hours' time to separate his personal horses from the 101 property. The appeal was granted. That day he got a letter from Ida Red, a friend who had made it big in Africa. Miller decided that it was time to move to Africa with Ida Red. He called for Pickett, told him of his intentions, and asked Pickett to cut his horses out of the 101 stock.

Pickett offered to get rid of Clarke, but Zack demurred.

On March 19, Pickett had lunch and some choc beer and went to work cutting Miller's horses out of the 101 herd. It would be his last roundup. Accounts differ, but the end result was the same. One of the horses kicked Bill in the head and knocked him unconscious.

Pickett lingered for fourteen days, but he never regained consciousness. He died on April 2, 1932. On April 5, Will Rogers announced on his radio show that Pickett was to be buried that day on the 101 Ranch. Rogers went on to say that he and Pickett had been friends for many years, that he had enjoyed many times the hospitality of Bill and Maggie Pickett in their home, and that he greatly admired Pickett. "Bill Pickett never had an enemy; even the steers wouldn't hurt old Bill."

A black preacher from Ponca City conducted the service. According to *Fabulous Empire*, Bill's kin wanted him buried in a fancy store-bought satin-lined casket, even after Zack Miller told them that Bill had always wanted to be buried in a coffin built from the walnut timber growing on the ranch. They compromised by putting Bill in the fancy box, which was then placed in the wooden box.

Weak from illness, Zack Miller attended the funeral. When the preacher had finished, Miller said, "We're telling Bill goodbye. He's dead now and this is one time when a Negro and a white man are all the same. If there ever was a white Negro, it was Bill. His hide was black, but his heart was white. If all white men had been as honest and as loyal as this Negro, the world wouldn't be in the shape it's in today!" Zack Miller even wrote a poem to commemorate Pickett, called "Old Bill Is Dead."

Miller was never able to get his 140 horses cut out of the 101 stock sold at auction.

When County Road 282 enters Travis County, it is called Round Mountain Road. A yellow center stripe appears as you approach the Bingham Creek valley, and you are treated to some rugged, expansive Central Texas views. Gradually you dip down to the bottomland and the old Round Mountain community. It has no real organized center anymore. Your tip-off is the Round Mountain Baptist Church on your right.

ROUND MOUNTAIN

Travis County • 59 • About 9 miles from Liberty Hill

Round Mountain community took its name from a nearby summit; which summit is anybody's guess since there is no such peak on any existing map of Travis County. The hamlet centered around a school by the same name, which began life in the 1870s inside a log cabin. A new building was constructed in 1888 on land donated by local pioneer J. R. Faubion, and it remained in use as such until about World War II.

Round Mountain Road soon dead-ends into Nameless Road. To your right a few miles is the little community of Nameless. The area was first surveyed in 1853 and was well settled by the end of the Civil War. Families raised cotton or cut cedar posts and rails for sale elsewhere. In 1880 the citizens, who had begun to call their settlement Fairview, applied to Washington for a post office. The postal authorities nixed Fairview, along with the next five names offered. After the sixth rejection, the citizens lost their patience and told the postal authorities, "Let the post office be nameless and be damned." Hence the name. Although the post office here ceased to function in 1890, the place has been known as Nameless ever since. In 1884, Nameless had a district school that doubled as a church, a general store, and forty residents. It is said that an outlaw killed near Nameless is buried in the local cemetery.

Summer "camp" meetings were an annual highlight at Nameless. Hymn singing, food, and socializing abounded. Folks came to the week-long preach-a-thons from miles around. One summer, J. P. Colley, Nameless' postmaster, was ill but still insisted on attending the camp meeting. So his family tied his rocking chair to the wagon, and he passed away of a heart attack under the brush arbor as the congregation sang a song.

From Round Mountain, turn left on Nameless Road. In a few miles, as soon as you leave Travis County and reenter Williamson County, Nameless Road becomes FM 2243, and you enter the Leander city limits. When you have gone 5.3 miles from the Round Mountain/Nameless Road intersection, you come to the little community of Bagdad, which has been swallowed up by greater Leander, which has experienced the same phenomenal growth as Round Rock and Cedar Park since the early 1990s.

BAGDAD

Williamson County • About 5 miles from Round Mountain

You know you are in Bagdad when you come to a four-way traffic-light intersection with Bagdad Road. The Bagdad Cemetery is ahead of you and to your right.

Charles Babcock arrived here on Christmas Day of 1851. By 1854, he had surveyed a town site, and soon thereafter businesses began to grow up, for there was money to be made here. Bagdad was located on the Central National road, a military-public thoroughfare northwest out of Austin, halfway between Austin and Burnet's Fort Croghan. It was a popular stage stop and overnight stop. Babcock built an inn here to cater to the traveling trade, and even Robert E. Lee is said to have slept here.

The post office came in 1858. Babcock had named his town for the Old World trading city of Baghdad, anticipating a great commercial future for his strategically placed dream. Bagdad had a variety of stores, a boot shop, a marble yard, two schools, a commercial photographer's shop, silver and lead mines, and even telephone service by 1880. Bagdad eagerly awaited the arrival of the Austin and Northwestern railway and was gravely disappointed in April 1882 when the rails ran through a mile east at the new station called Leander. So gradually folks just moved over to the new town of Leander. The post office moved in 1882, and by 1900 Bagdad was a ghost town.

Turn right onto Bagdad Road for a few yards to reach the Heinatz store and home.

The only original buildings left in Bagdad today are the old Heinatz home and store. They were built by John Heinatz, who was also Bagdad's first postmaster, in the early 1850s. The home is privately occupied, and the old limestone store and post office serves now as a senior citizens' center. Remains of the old stage stand were just across the road from the Heinatz buildings.

Return to FM 2243 and turn right toward "old" Leander, past the old Bagdad Cemetery. Before you know it, FM 2243 runs into US 183 and you are in the middle of what was Leander's original business district.

LEANDER

Williamson County • 26,000 (approximate)

Leander, the successor to nearby Bagdad, owes its existence to the railroad. As the Austin and Northwestern tracks were pushing west toward Burnet, the railroad company sold town lots here on July 17, 1882. The rail magnates named the new town after Leander "Catfish" Brown, a company official. Bagdad's post office moved here that same fall. For years, Leander was a processing and shipping point for local cotton, wool, mohair, cedar, and limestone.

Leander is now just another bedroom town for Austin commuters. Not much is left of old Leander these days, just a limestone school building and a few smaller structures. Leander is now mostly new, dating back to the late 1970s.

To follow FM 2243's slightly convoluted path eastward, you turn right onto US 183. In a few hundred feet, you turn left on FM 2243. In these few hundred feet, you have seen old Leander. Shortly thereafter, FM 2243 crosses the 183-A toll road, and you come to the Davis Cemetery.

DAVIS CEMETERY/WEBSTER MASSACRE STATE MARKER

FM 2243 • About 1.5 miles from Leander

A mile and a half east of Leander on FM 2243, you see on your left the pioneer Davis Cemetery. The oldest grave dates to 1839, and tragically it is a common grave for the victims of the Webster massacre.

Their story goes as follows. On June 13, 1839, a group of seventeen people (fourteen men, a woman, a boy, and a girl) left Hornsby Bend east of Austin. They were heading for a spot on the North Fork of the San Gabriel River in what is now Burnet County, where they intended to settle. The group was led by John Webster, who had brought his wife and two children. The rest of their party—thirteen or so—were to join them at the site several days later. The grant of land was deep in Comanche country.

By August 19, the Webster ox train had come to Pilot Knob (Mount Gabriel today), which was only six miles from their land. At Pilot Knob, they spotted Comanche campfires nearby and decided to turn around. While crossing the South Fork of the San Gabriel River (a couple of miles north of here), one of the wagons' axles broke. The train camped there overnight while the axle was repaired. By sunup, they had reached Brushy Creek, where the Comanches were lying in wait for them. The settlers voted to fight and formed a wagon circle. It was a brave but hopeless fight, because the Comanches outnumbered them and had the surrounding thick timber for cover. The battle was over in a couple of hours. The Comanches had been following the settlers for miles on either side, just waiting for the right spot to attack.

All the men were killed; Mrs. Webster and the kids were taken prisoner. The Comanches spent the rest of the battle day divvying up the loot; that which they deemed useless they burned or otherwise destroyed. The grisly scene was discovered by one of Webster's surveyors, John Harvey, who had been delayed at Hornsby Bend. By the time he arrived, only skeletons remained. He also found burned wagons. Bullet holes and arrows riddled everything. Only one of the bodies could be properly identified, that of Milton Hicks, whose leg had been broken at the Battle of Anahuac. The bones were put into a common crate and buried. Upon hearing of a Texas-Comanche treaty, Mrs. Webster and daughter managed to escape and fled to San Antonio in 1840. Her son was repatriated six days later according to the terms of that Texas-Comanche peace treaty.

The Webster victims rest in the west corner of the graveyard, partially obscured by a thick clump of cedars. A state granite marker stands on the spot. The next oldest stone dates to 1856, and others display some interesting carvings and verse.

About 1.5 miles farther east on FM 2243, and a few hundred yards past Ronald Reagan Boulevard, turn right onto County Road 175.

Next you come to a Y in the road, formed by the junction of County Road 177 and County Road 175. Veer left, as County Road 175 goes eastward. Do not be misled into taking County Road 176, which you next encounter to your left almost as soon as you have executed the leftward veer. Continue straight ahead on County Road 175, toward Round Rock.

By this point, the road signs inform you that you are traveling on Sam Bass Road, the old San Saba Road. Then all of a sudden little Sam Bass Road becomes FM 3406, a four-lane drag strip built to handle the new commuter traffic. A half-mile later, you leave FM 3406 to return to Sam Bass Road, which enters Round Rock.

ROUND ROCK

Williamson County • 101,000 (approximate) • (512)

Anglo settlers began to inhabit the general Round Rock area during the 1830s. By 1850, an honest-to-God village had grown up here along the banks of Brushy Creek. In fact, the burg was first known as Brushy Creek. Thomas Oatts opened the first store and post office here in 1852; it was immediately followed by a stage stop and tavern. By 1854, postal authorities had deemed the name Brushy Creek too confusing. Faced with choosing another name, Oatts and friend Jacob Harrell thought a bit and then submitted the name Round Rock, after an enormous anvil-shaped boulder that sat in Brushy Creek by the creek crossing. The two had "spent many happy hours sitting on the rock and fishing." Other stores, mills, and houses followed. More businesses sprang up after the Civil War, including a cotton gin, newspaper, tombstone carver, and all the other usual businesses of a prosperous village. Round Rock prospered until 1876, when the International and Great Northern railroad came through a mile to the east. Thus Round Rock became "Old" Round Rock, and "New" Round Rock began to build alongside the iron rails. Old and New Round Rocks functioned as separate towns with separate post offices until 1891, when the Old Round Rock post office was abandoned. By this time, Old Round Rock was mostly deserted, and it stayed that way until the 1960s, when many of the remaining structures were restored. Today, the stretch of Chisholm Trail Road from Sam Bass Road to Brushy Creek is a historic district.

New Round Rock sprouted up as a tent city late in July 1876 on land belonging to Washington Anderson as the rails inched south toward Austin. The first sale of lots was on July 20 and drew between four and five hundred people. Businessmen from Austin, Georgetown, Old Round Rock, Rockdale, and McDade made purchases; twenty-six business lots were sold for a total of $5,125. The depot wasn't built yet, but already a little town of tents and board shanties had sprung up, and what a population was there—as rough and as harum-scarum a set as one would care to meet of a May morning or a winter evening. Gamblers and the frail and the fair were there en force, and the drinking of crooked whiskey and card playing were carried on without limit. They were there for the pleasure of the heavy force of men at work on the bridge across Brushy Creek.

A year later, over a dozen businesses were operating here. Some had moved from Old Round Rock; others had come all the way from Georgetown. That first year, a broom factory and a lime operation were established here, along with a newspaper, the *Round Rock Headlight*. But the new town, despite its prosperity, had no water service for years. Citizens bought their water from wagons that carted the wet stuff in from a spring east of town.

Round Rock was home to several cattle barons, including George Washington Cluck and his wife Harriet. When George drove a herd up to Abilene, Kansas, in the spring of 1871, Harriet was right there with him. So were their three children, the oldest of whom was seven. And Harriet was expecting number four in October. But in spite of a flooding Red River, cattle rustlers, and Indians, the Clucks and their herd made it safely to Abilene that fall. The herd was sold, the baby was born, and the next spring the Clucks moved back to Williamson County. They bought a new ranch with their profits, and that ranch eventually became the town of Cedar Park.

In 1970, Round Rock was a sleepy little farm and ranch community with a population of 2,800. By 1980, Round Rock's population was nearly 12,000; by 2009, it was over 100,000. Round Rock and Williamson County battle with Austin in the courting of business relocations and startups, and often win, most notably when Round Rock convinced Dell Computers to move out of Austin in 1993.

In September 1993, an *Austin American-Statesman* reporter observed that

> The 15 miles that separate Round Rock from downtown Austin might as well be 1,000. The two cities are opposites in many ways. The Austin City Council has swung from slow growth to pro-growth and back. Austin is characterized as the state's liberal enclave. Round Rock, a former bedroom community that has been aggressively pursuing commercial development, has a conservative, pro-business attitude that never wavers, no matter who sits on the City Council, say city officials. "There are more Rush Limbaugh fans in Round Rock than in Austin," said Round Rock City Manager Bob Bennett. "Round Rock is all the things Austin isn't." Round Rock's leaders believe these differences are the city's calling card.

Round Rock leaders liked this description of themselves so much that they posted the entire story on their website.

Round Rock was, in fact, an ambitious town pretty much from its beginning, at least beginning with the first railroad through town. And despite its present conservative bent, the Round Rock of old had its seamy side, as evidenced by these clips from the *Austin Statesman*:

> September 7, 1877
> They have a fancy-dance and boarding-house at Round Rock. The *Headlight* wants the "Institution" banished.

> December 23, 1880
> We learn that one Eugene Hall and another person, unknown, were on the warpath up around Round Rock Monday night, and while taking in the delectable village, rode up to a house occupied by demi-mondes, and firing through the window, seriously wounded a girl named Patterson and fatally shot one by the name of Fowler. The cause of the shooting is unknown and unprovoked. Hall was in Round Rock again Tuesday night, and swore he could not be arrested, and some dozen or more shots were exchanged by him and the officers. One of the balls took effect in Hall's leg, and he suddenly remembered he could be arrested, and cried right lustily for the officers to cease firing. The man who was with him when he shot the women gave himself up and turned state's evidence.

In 1881, when the owners of the Austin and Northwestern were having trouble collecting the construction money promised by Austin investors, Round Rock boosters did all they could to persuade them to build the line to Round Rock instead of Austin. But Round Rock failed to secure a detour of the road, even after offering the depot grounds, the right of way through Williamson County, and $15,000 in cash.

In May of that year, a gentleman from Round Rock told the *Austin Statesman* that "his town will beat Austin in trade and population in a couple of years, owing to the 'get up and get' of its people."

When Sam Bass Road takes a hard bend to the left, past Brandt Lane, and then Clark Street, you see on your left the old Round Rock Cemetery.

OLD ROUND ROCK CEMETERY

Clark and Sam Bass • W variable

This graveyard is most famous as the final resting place of the outlaw Sam Bass, but there is much else to look at here. As you enter this cemetery, you will immediately notice signs of segregation. The large Anglo section is straight ahead, while the Mexican section is to your left. It is a colorful area, contrasting strongly with the somber Anglo spread. Off to the back is the old slave and freedman's section, marked by a sign and historical marker. It dates to about 1851. Sam Bass and his confederate Seaburn Barnes lie buried along the cemetery's fence line, immediately adjacent to the slave section. Their placement here along the fence, between the Mexican and slave sections, was purposeful. Bass' current gravestone is a new one. Tourists chipped away the original stone. The old slave cemetery is full of broken bits and pieces of homemade stones. Only a few have legible inscriptions—crude, loving, and for the most part misspelled. It is the most pleasant section of the cemetery.

From the cemetery, continue on Sam Bass Road toward downtown Round Rock. This was the road on which the wounded Bass traveled in his attempt to escape Round Rock and the law back in 1878. Less than a mile later, you come to a four-way intersection with Chisholm Trail Road. I-35 looms in the background. Turn right here onto the Old Chisholm Trail; this really was part of the historic trail, as you will see.

OLD HOTEL AND TAVERN

Chisholm Trail at Poker Alley

On your right, at the corner of Chisholm Trail and Poker Alley, is an old hotel and tavern, which has been restored.

ST. CHARLES HOTEL AND THE OLD POST OFFICE

No. 8 Chisholm Trail at Emmanuel

Next on your right, at the corner of Chisholm Trail and Emmanuel, are the old St. Charles Hotel and the old Round Rock post office. The two-story St. Charles Hotel was built about 1870 and was for many years the home of Dr. William Owen, prominent local physician and businessman. The simple one-story limestone building next to it dates to 1853 and originally housed a mercantile store and post office operated by Thomas Oatts, Round Rock's first postmaster.

THE CANTINA

Next door to 4 Chisholm Trail

Back at 4 Chisholm Trail, the slim, two-story limestone building on the right from the St. Charles Hotel was once a boisterous tavern.

BRUSHY CREEK/THE ROUND ROCK

Chisholm Trail

In another few yards you cross Brushy Creek. One hundred plus years ago, herds of dusty market-bound longhorns and innumerable wagons crossed Brushy at this exact same spot. Look to your right as you cross and you can see the wagon ruts worn into the limestone creek bed. Immediately to your left, squatting in the middle of Brushy Creek between stone pillars of the old Georgetown railroad bridge, is the old Round Rock.

CITY PARK

This little park, with its life-size bronze statues, honors the role of the Chisholm Trail, the longhorns that trailed up it to Kansas, and the aforementioned Harriet Cluck, one of the few women cattle drivers.

EDWARD QUICK HOME

Chisholm Trail • Private residence

Just after you cross Brushy Creek, you see the old Edward Quick home, set back and well shaded on your left.

OLD ROUND ROCK STAGE STOP

901 Round Rock Ave., in the Commons Shopping Center

The old, limestone stage stop still stands just south of FM 620, a few feet west of what little remains of the Old Chisholm Trail.

To enter New Round Rock, turn left onto FM 620, which is called Round Rock Avenue inside the city limits.

Round Rock Avenue dead-ends at a five-way intersection that includes Main Street and Mays Street. You're downtown now, so find a place to park so that you can walk through Round Rock's old downtown, which is a historical district. Many of the older buildings have been restored to their original exterior appearance.

OLD BROOM FACTORY

N. Mays and E. Main • Office building

Round Rock's broom factory produced nationally acclaimed brooms for decades and decades. One of their brooms even won a gold medal for excellence at the 1904 St. Louis World's Fair. From 1887 until 1912, the brooms were manufactured in a building that still stands at the corner of N. Mays and E. Main. This structure, the Morrow building, was erected in 1876 of ashlar-cut limestone "bricks," with a smooth polished keystone door and window arches. After 1912, the structure housed a general store, furniture store, school, skating rink, and, most recently, an automotive repair shop.

Willie Kemp, in his entertaining memoir, *True Tales of Central Texas*, described how broom corn was grown at the turn of the century in the nearby village of Merrilltown:

> While living at Merrilltown, people were discouraged with raising cotton. Some turned to raising "Broom Corn." It grows to about six feet tall, makes a bushy head on top covered with seed. When it reaches a certain age, the heads are put in piles on the ground and left there a short while, then loaded on wagons and taken to the Broom Corn thresher, where the heads were held by the stem ends, a handful at a time, then the seeded ends were put in a position so that the thresher would thresh all seeds from the straws, then the threshed Broom Corn was laid out flat in rows on the ground to dry. It was left on the ground for the right length of time, then gathered and made into bales. These bales were sold to the Round Rock Broom Factory, which made the regular housekeeping brooms. Round Rock brooms were shipped to many stores within and without the state of Texas.

OTTO REINKE BUILDING

102 E. Main

Attached to the Morrow building is its soulmate, the Reinke building, built by merchant Otto Reinke in 1879. It, too, is two-story, built of ashlar-surfaced limestone, and has keystone window and door arches, yet the Morrow and Reinke buildings are distinctly different owing to their rooflines. The Morrow building features a fairly simple cast-metal cornice surmounted by a stepped ashlar limestone parapet, while the Reinke building has an arched pediment and graduated pedestals on either side.

OLD ECONOMY DRUGSTORE

202–204 E. Main

The north side of the 200 block of E. Main starts out strongly, with a string of three storefronts united by a common corrugated tin awning and identical, though separate, pressed-metal second-story facades.

The old Economy Drugstore has long since ceased to be a pharmacy. The vintage screen doors, high patterned-tin ceiling, and original wall cabinets and display cases are its most notable features. The building was built sometime between 1902 and 1909 and originally housed Round Rock Mercantile and then the Quick Pharmacy.

One of the Quick Pharmacy's most entertaining customers in the early days was Willie Kemp's older brother, Sam, a farmer in Merrilltown.

Every Saturday, summer, fall, winter, or spring, Sam went to Round Rock. There he got groceries, clothes, tools, harness or anything else needed. Whether the family were with him or not, Sam always on these Saturdays would go into "Quick's Drug Store and Ice Cream Parlor" and eat ice cream to his heart's content. His reputation for eating ice cream was known about far and wide. When he went to Quick's Ice Cream Parlor a crowd would gather to watch Sam Kemp eat ice cream. Many people would buy it as long as he would eat. At some of these settings he would eat most of a gallon. Of course, if he had to pay for it, he would eat a lot less. When others would buy the ice cream for Sam, they would unbeknown to him lay side bets as to how much Sam would eat. Sam really enjoyed these affairs and did his best to entertain the spectators. Sam ate so much ice cream each year that he had to pay for, that he opened up a charge account which he settled with his first bale of cotton in the fall.

PALM HOUSE

212 E. Main • 255-5805 • www.roundrockchamber.org • Monday through Friday 8–5 • Free • Currently houses the chamber of commerce and a museum

Sandwiched between the old Economy Pharmacy and the old city hall/library is the 1860-vintage Palm home, moved here from a rural location and renovated. T. J. Caldwell built this house, using home-quarried limestone for the walls and home-cut cedar for the rafters, foundation, and floor joists. His slaves did most of the work. The house is commonly called the Palm house because Sven and Mary Caldwell Palm bought the place in 1892. In its new location, the Palm residence houses the chamber of commerce and a small museum. Several informative booklets about Round Rock are available here, free or nominally priced.

TRINITY LUTHERAN COLLEGE

E. Main at College

Seven blocks east of the Palm house you encounter the old Trinity Lutheran College, which operated here from 1905 to 1929. When the college merged with another to become Texas Lutheran at Seguin, the graceful three-story Spanish Renaissance main building and other school buildings were taken over by the Lutheran Welfare Society. A historical marker tells the school's story.

NELSON-CRIER HOME

400 block of E. Main • Private residence

Heading back downtown, on the south side of E. Main you will encounter the Nelson-Crier home. Andrew Nelson was a prominent early Round Rock merchant, and his survivors built the three-story house over a five-year period, beginning with the year of Nelson's death, 1895. Its current Classical Revival facade dates to 1931. The house and yards take up an entire block.

NELSON BUILDING

E. Main and Lampasas

Back downtown, the John A. Nelson building stands on the corner of E. Main and Lampasas. Nelson built it in 1900 to house his hardware concern. Two-story limestone, with a full-length, top-to-bottom cast-iron and pressed-tin facade, the Nelson building is one of downtown Round Rock's most imposing structures.

SCENE OF THE SAM BASS SHOOTOUT

100 block of E. Main

Now that we're back at the heart of old downtown Round Rock, it's time to address the fate of the outlaw Sam Bass, whose "soft thing turned out rather serious," deadly serious, as we shall see, right here in the 100 block of E. Main on the afternoon of Friday, July 19, 1878. Bass and his gang had come to Round Rock to rob a bank. Previously they had limited themselves to holding up stagecoaches and trains, but now Bass and the boys were looking to move up in the crime world, but not too fast! They were hoping to cut their teeth on a "soft touch," a fat bank in a Podunk town.

When you stack Sam Bass up against other outlaws of his time, he cuts a mighty small figure. Born on an Indiana farm in 1851, Sam Bass was orphaned at thirteen. He came to Denton County, Texas, in 1870, where he found work as a cowboy and teamster. But Sam liked racing more than roping, and there was certainly more and easier money in the former. Sam had seen what hard work would get you, and what a good hand of cards or a fast horse would bring. The dime-novel glamour of the cowboy life wore off quickly for Sam, and when he acquired a four-legged streak of lightning known as the Denton Mare in 1874, he left the workaday world behind forever. Sam raced her all over Texas, Mexico, and the Indian Territory, winning every bet. But after two years of "swimmin' in grease," Bass could find no more takers, and he sold his fleet mare. He and friend Joel Collins drove a herd of cattle from San Antonio to Dodge City during the summer of 1876. With the profits from the drive, they decided to set themselves up as gold prospectors in the Black Hills of the Dakotas. They found no gold, and come the spring of 1877, Bass and Collins were broke and hungry. But they weren't about to go back to cowboying; you could blow an entire month's wages—twenty dollars or so—on one wild night in town, and then have to work hard for a month so you could blow it all again a couple of fortnights later.

A new friend named Jack Davis convinced them that robbing stages was an easier and quicker way to get gold. So they put together a gang, the Black Hills Bandits, and set to work. Their biggest job was the Union Pacific train robbery at Big Spring Station in September 1877. The take was $60,000, cut six ways. The gang split up after this hit, and Bass hightailed it back to Texas with his ten grand. Joel Collins and Bill Heffridge were subsequently killed in Buffalo, Kansas; Jim Berry was killed near Mexico, Missouri; and Tom Nixon and Jack Davis were never located. Never before and never again would Sam Bass have so much money.

Back in Denton County, Bass called on some friends and put together a new gang. The Sam Bass Gang commenced operations sometime during the winter of 1877–1878, robbing stages and trains across north Central Texas and generating big headlines. Often the headlines were bigger than the gang's take. The whole thing mushroomed to the point where the Bass Gang was blamed for every robbery across Texas in the spring of 1878.

Bass freely spent the little money he did get on fine clothes, saddlery, and the various other, more basic needs of life. Tales of Bass' generosity abound—a double eagle for a home-cooked meal or a dozen eggs or a couple of beers—but Bass had barely enough coin to buy a can of beans by the time he reached Round Rock. It was time to do or die—or starve, actually—for Bass.

Incredibly, Bass had not yet killed a single man. He firmly believed that discretion is the better part of valor, and he preferred to run rather than fight. With this attitude, robber Bass was in stark contrast to John Wesley Hardin and Rattlin' Bill Longley, neither of whom was a robber, and both of whom killed dozens of men and a woman or two.

In June, after two stage and four train robberies, Bass decided to move; Denton County was just getting too hot. The gang decided to move south to hit a bank, maybe in Waco, maybe in Belton. They'd figure out exactly where along the way. So off they went, down to Waco, Belton, Georgetown, and finally Round Rock.

Bass' fall at Round Rock was as much the result of politics as hot lead. In 1878, Texas was still recovering from the Reconstruction uproar. Most Texans despised their state government. Bandits and Indians roamed the state at will, and only the carpetbaggers and the bandits had any money. The people demanded that something be done about these brigands. The buck stopped with the Texas Rangers. Funded annually by the legislature, the Rangers realized that their jobs, their very existence, depended on bringing law and order—or at least a semblance thereof—to Texas, and bringing it fast. Newspaper editorials were already calling for some other type of peacekeeping force than the Rangers.

The Rangers needed a scapegoat, one brigand they could rub out quickly, so as to appease the wolves. Bass and his gang were hot news across Texas that summer, as evidenced by this bit of witticism in the *Galveston News* on June 8: "Bass is not any more afraid of being 'surrounded and held at bay' than a certain darky was afraid of work. He would 'lie down and go asleep alongside of him.'"

So the Rangers decided to hit upon Bass, and they set the wheels in motion by releasing Jim Murphy from prison. Murphy had been jailed for harboring Bass in Denton. Thinking his imprisonment unjustly harsh, Murphy made a deal with the Rangers. In exchange for his freedom, Murphy would play Judas; he would rejoin the gang and betray them into capture or death.

Bass was too easygoing and generous to be a good outlaw. He took Murphy back into his confidence, despite the warnings of other more suspicious gang members. Murphy talked Sam out of robbing the bank at Waco and into robbing the Round Rock bank. In the meantime, Murphy kept in touch with the anxious Rangers by surreptitiously mailed letters. While in Georgetown on July 14, Murphy managed to get word to the Rangers in Austin that Bass was headed for the Round Rock bank, and so the trap was set. That same Sunday evening, the gang rode the eleven miles down to Round Rock, setting up camp near the Old Slave Cemetery on the San Saba Road. Next morning, Bass and Frank Jackson rode into New Round Rock to case the town. Bass came back wanting to rob the bank that evening, but Murphy talked him out of the idea, suggesting they stay four or five days, posing as cattle buyers and thus allowing their horses to rest for the getaway. This would allow the Rangers plenty of time to set their trap. The boys decided to hit the bank on Saturday afternoon, July 20, and then made careful plans.

Sam rode into town on Thursday and came back a little disquieted. He had seen some men he thought were Rangers, despite their anonymous cowboy garb. He sent Jackson and Murphy into town the next morning for a second opinion. They found nothing, or at least that's what they told Bass. So Sam quieted his fears and decided that they should ride into town that afternoon to buy some tobacco and a few other odds and ends for their quick flight out of town. While they were there, they could also case the bank one more time and look for Rangers.

Bass, Jackson, and Seab Barnes rode into a seemingly deserted town; the afternoon was a scorcher, and anybody not in the shade was busy looking for some, Rangers included. Murphy had stopped back at the Mays and Black Store in Old Town, on the pretext of looking for Rangers there.

The Bass trio tied their horses up in an elm motte at the corner of Liberty and Lampasas (now a vacant lot) at about four o'clock. They rounded the corner onto Main Street and walked to Kopperal's Store at 101 E. Main. The bank was next door. The strolling gang did not go unnoticed. Travis County deputy sheriff Maurice Moore had seen them ride in and had noted their saddlebags and what appeared to be a six-shooter concealed under one of the men's coats. Bass and company were in turn scrutinizing Moore, who had been standing in front of the livery stable at 110 E. Main across the street from Kopperal's Store.

After the outlaws entered the store, Moore walked over to Williamson County deputy sheriff A. W. Grimes, an ex-Ranger, who was lounging nearby. He told Grimes of his suspicions. The two deputies walked over to the store. Moore hung out near the door, hands in his pockets, whistling. Grimes walked up to the strangers at the counter and asked carelessly of the one man if he didn't have a pistol under his jacket. "Yes," was the reply, and all three immediately drew and pumped Grimes full of lead. Gun still holstered, and the words "Don't, boys" still on his lips, Grimes stumbled back a few steps and fell dead by the door. Moore drew as the shooting started, and his fire was immediately answered.

Just the first few shots filled the air with blinding, acrid black-powder smoke, so the men were firing now at shadows and noises. Bass and company made it out the front door, but Sam's gun hand was shot up, and Moore sported a bullet in his left lung.

By this time, other men had heard the shooting and were running for the store, firing at the fleeing bandits, who were running for their horses. There was shooting from every direction. The outlaws made it through the livery stable and were running down the alley to their horses at the elm motte when the law's shots began to take deadly effect. Sam took a bullet in the back and through the liver, and Seab Barnes dropped dead in his tracks from a bullet in the brain, just as they reached the horses. The unscratched Jackson held off the law with one hand while untying Bass' horse and helping him mount with the other. He then mounted his own horse, and the two galloped away, Jackson holding up the ashen-faced and bleeding Bass to keep him from falling. They tore out to the north and west, crossing Brushy Creek near the Round Rock and passing Jim Murphy, who was sitting on the front porch of the Mays and Black Store in Old Town. They stopped at the graveyard camp and then headed north along the road to Georgetown.

Disappearing into a live oak thicket, Bass and Jackson were safe for the time being. Bass declared that he could go no farther, so Jackson helped him down and said he would stay with him: "I can match every one of them Rangers!"

"No, Frank, I'm done for," Sam said, and insisted that Frank save his own hide. Reluctantly, Frank obeyed, after first bandaging Sam up and tying his horse nearby, so that Sam might escape if he should feel better that night.

Come morning, the suffering Bass crawled out into a pasture and hailed a passing woodsman, begging the man to take him away into hiding, but the axman spooked and ran away. Thirsty, Bass staggered to a nearby farmhouse for water, but the woman there ran off without giving him a drink. The bloody Bass finally got some water from a road crew building the new Georgetown tap line from Round Rock to the county seat. Meanwhile, the Rangers had fanned out to find him. When they first saw Bass lying under a live oak tree, less than a third of a mile from where Frank Jackson had left him, the Rangers mistook him for a railroad hand and moved on past. A little later, the group's leader inquired of the section workers, who pointed out the dying Bass. Still in the dark as to the wounded man's identity, the Ranger leader approached Bass and asked, "Who are you?" Bass raised his left hand as a token of surrender and faintly called, "Don't shoot! I am unarmed and helpless. I'm the man you are looking for, I am Sam Bass."

The Rangers carried him back to New Town, where he was laid on a plain, low cot in a small plank shed, located roughly in what is now the parking lot between the old Mobil gas station and the frame Victorian house on Mays Street.

Dr. C. P. Cochran and A. F. Morris attended Bass and Moore.

Word was sent to Austin that Bass was in custody, but many there refused to believe the report, thinking it to be a political trick. The news of the capture of the great outlaw Bass almost displaced the state Democratic Party convention in public discussion. The theory of many in Austin being that possibly some political dodge was being played to help Hubbard caused a division of opinion as to the identity of the captured party. "Are you sure it is Sam Bass?" was asked over and again.

A special correspondent from the *Galveston Daily News* was quickly dispatched to Round Rock, and on arriving by train at 2 p.m. to report all particulars, and hearing that Bass was dying, he sought Major Jones quickly. One man, in whom Major Jones had confidence, but whose name could not be used then "for the best of reasons," identified Bass, satisfying Major Jones that it was the veritable Bass, and Jones showed the news correspondent a description which fit the man in custody. After hearing a brief review of the capture, the correspondent was conducted to the plank building where the prisoner lay breathing heavily. He asked him if he was Sam Bass and other questions, eliciting the following answers:

> I am Sam Bass; am shot to pieces, and no time to deny. There is a photograph of me, Joe and Joel Collins and J. E. Gardner, at old man A. G. Collins's house. Don't know anyone in Round Rock or any of the rangers now here. Did not know Jones was here. My men heard it on the streets casually. Had kept the run of reports of myself and party by reading the *Galveston News*. Had three men with me. Was not going to rescue Pipes and Herndon, two of the members of my gang who had earlier been captured. Never had anything to do with them. Was not with them when they robbed the trains, and intended to make a raise here on the bank, for I was out of money, and go to Mexico.

Bass made Deputy Sheriff Tucker a present of his gun. In talking with Major Jones, he admitted certain facts that comported with the testimony of witnesses at Austin, implicating him with Sam Pipes and Albert Herndon (both of whom had been arrested in April at A. G. Collins' house in Dallas, Collins being the father of Joel Collins) in train robbing. Bass denied ever robbing Texas stages, and he refused to blow on his pals.

When asked if he had any word for his people, he said his parents were dead and that he had two brothers, John and Linton, and four sisters. The two brothers lived at his birthplace, Mitchell, Indiana.

He admitted that he had been in the robbing business before. He robbed the Union Pacific express car, this answer being brought out by a question mentioning that event. Other questions of similar nature regarding names of his known accomplices in Texas he refused to answer, except in the one instance, when he fell into a trap and mentioned Pipes and Herndon.

The Rangers questioned Bass repeatedly about his Texas robberies, but he continued to refuse to give names or specific details. Sam clung to life through Saturday night and Sunday morning, refusing food, confession, or prayers. Thinking he was getting better, Bass suddenly pronounced, "The world is bobbing around"; then he lay back quietly for a moment, twitched his head wordlessly, and died. The day was July 21, 1878, Sam's twenty-seventh birthday.

"We thought we had a soft thing but it turned out rather . . . serious." The mortally wounded Bass summed up his entire life in that one sentence, regarding his final trip into Round Rock.

A number of people gathered to hold a wake for Sam Bass, and a local cabinetmaker worked all night to make a respectable coffin. Six paid black pallbearers loaded the coffin into a wagon. A small group of mixed colors trudged out with Bass' body to the burying grounds early next morning. As the procession made its way to the cemetery, its number grew by the hundreds. J. W. Ledbetter, a Methodist minister, joined the group and said a short prayer for Bass. At that moment, Frank Jackson galloped up, threw a clod of dirt on the grave in symbolic final tribute to his boss, and sped away. Sam's demise didn't even make the front page of the local paper, but all the same, legends began to grow about the goodhearted bandit, the Texas Robin Hood, the man betrayed by a man he called friend.

In 1879, his sister, Mrs. Sally Bass Hornbrook, visited the grave and had a pink marble marker installed, a base surmounted by a shaft. It was quickly chipped away by souvenir hunters.

His story was told, suitably embellished, in scores of dime novels, and in a song attributed to old-time cowboy John Denton. Long and sentimental, the ballad was sung by cowboys on the trail as a lullaby to their longhorned charges. Over the years, Bass has become revered as no other outlaw save Jesse James. How did such a feckless bandit become so beloved? After all, no town celebrates Bill Longley or John Wesley Hardin or Black Jack Ketchum Days, or names stores and cafes after them.

Perhaps his popularity lies in his failure. The average person can relate to Bass on a personal, fellow-mortal level. Bass never made a lot of money robbing, and what he made he gave away. He ran from fights rather than precipitating them. He was betrayed by a friend and died while casing his first bank robbery. In short, he was not a man to be feared, even if he wanted your money. He was just a lazy fellow who was smart enough to see that he could make easy money by waving a gun in the right direction. And once Bass was laid to rest, no one tried to resurrect him, like they did Jesse James, Bill Longley, or John Wesley Hardin.

The following observation from the May 31, 1879, edition of the *Galveston Daily News* offers some insight in the matter:

> Nor long since Bass's grave at Round Rock was decorated with flowers. Now Bass and his crowd were not remarkable for their piety, but in some respects they bore a strong resemblance to the apostles. Like them, they were pilgrims on earth, having no fixed place of abode. Like the apostles, they were despised of all men, and, like them, never forsook or denied their calling nor faith. They were frequently thrown into prison and suffered much tribulation, and, finally, they all came to untimely ends at the hands of the legally constituted authorities. Both were "fishers of men." The twelve apostles, however, were not raised in northern Texas.

Such words were never spoken with regard to the James gang, Longley, or Hardin.

Sam Bass was not the only world-infamous star associated with Round Rock. Homegrown boy Vander Clyde gained fame in Paris during the 1920s and 1930s as "Barbette, dazzling female impersonator aerialist."

As a young boy, Clyde became entranced with the circus, especially the aerialists, and he practiced walking on wires, fences, and anything he could find in Round Rock. Out of school at fourteen, he decided that he would become an aerialist. A fan of the Alfaretta Sisters, a family high-wire act, he learned that one of the sisters had died and that her survivors were looking for a replacement. With his mother's permission, Clyde auditioned and got the part. He dressed as a woman because female aerialists were supposed to be more dramatic. He later performed in Erford's Whirling Sensation, in which he and two others hung by their teeth from a revolving apparatus.

Clyde next decided to go it alone, developing a high-wire and trapeze act in which he appeared and performed as a woman and removed his wig to reveal his masculinity at the end of the performance. He took the act to Europe and played all Europe's major cities. Barbette became the talk of Paris and was befriended by members of both American café society and French literary and social circles. Writer Jean Cocteau was entranced by his combination of masculine strength and feminine grace and wrote a review of Barbette's act, "Le Numéro Barbette," in the July 1926 issue of the *Nouvelle Revue Française*. As described by Cocteau, Barbette's acrobatics became a vehicle for theatrical illusion. From his entrance, when he appeared in an elaborate ball gown and an ostrich-feather hat, to an elaborate striptease down to tights and leotard in the middle of the act, Barbette enacted a feminine allure that was maintained despite the vigorous muscular activity required by his trapeze routine. Only at the end of the performance, when he removed his wig, did he dispel the illusion, at which time he mugged and flexed in a masculine manner to emphasize the success of his earlier deception. To Cocteau, Barbette's craftsmanship, practiced on the fine edge of danger, elevated a rather dubious stunt to the level of art. Cocteau used Barbette in his masterpiece film, *The Blood of a Poet*, in which the bejeweled and Chanel-clad Barbette and other aristocrats applauded a card game that ended in suicide.

But tragedy struck in 1938. A fall and illness left Clyde almost totally paralyzed overnight. After a year and a half in hospitals, he came home to Round Rock to recuperate. Defying the doctors who said he would never walk again, Clyde walked the length of the town every morning, and then came home to one of his mother's huge breakfasts. By 1942, he was back in showbiz as aerial director of the Ringling Brothers Circus. He worked for almost every major American circus and is credited with inventing the aerial ballet spectacular that became a standard in every major American circus. He spent his last years in Round Rock, where he lived with his sister Mary Cahill. He died at home on August 5, 1973.

OLD MASONIC LODGE

Northeast corner of Mays and East Bagdad • Not open to the public

A block south of the Mays and Main Street intersection stands the old Masonic Lodge, built the same year as Sam's demise. The two-story limestone with brick cornice structure looks almost exactly as it did when it was built, and not much worse for wear.

Just a few feet south of the old Masonic Lodge, the railroad tracks that cross Mays Street were the site of one of the greatest tragedies in Round Rock history, an accident that brought about the law requiring buses to stop at all railroad crossings.

The Baylor University basketball team was traveling by bus on January 22, 1927, to Austin, where they hoped to avenge a 22–15 loss to the University of Texas Longhorns earlier that month. There were near-freezing temperatures and a heavy cloud of mist and fog blanketing the ground that morning. The wet road splattered mud across the bus' windshield, slowing the trip considerably. As the bus arrived in Round Rock on old State Highway 2 (now Business I-35), the journey had lasted three and a half hours. Creeping along at twenty-two miles per hour, the bus approached an open, level-grade railroad crossing downtown. The driver, freshman Joe Potter, was manually cranking the windshield wipers as he negotiated the unfamiliar road, unaware that the "Sunshine Special," a northbound, premier Missouri Pacific (still known as the International and Great Northern) passenger train, was barreling toward the crossing at sixty miles an hour. As the bus came within one hundred feet of the tracks, one of the passengers spotted the train and shouted a word of warning to the driver. With no time to stop the vehicle, Potter hammered the accelerator to the floor in an attempt to beat the train. The bus slid diagonally across the train's path, placing the back corner of the vehicle directly in front of the engine. The impact of the collision could be heard for miles. Ten of the passengers were killed and have been known ever since as the "Immortal Ten." State legislation was immediately introduced to construct overpasses or underpasses wherever state highways intersected with railroads. When U.S. Highway 81 was built through Round Rock eight years later to replace State Highway 2, the Texas Highway Department built the first railroad overpass in Texas.

DINING

ROUND ROCK DONUTS

106 W. Liberty • 255-3629 • www.roundrockdonuts.com • Open daily • W

This has been a Round Rock institution since 1926. The donuts are still made from scratch and fried fresh five or six times a day.

AREA PARK

OLD SETTLERS PARK AT PALM VALLEY

US 79, 3 miles east of downtown

To reach Old Settlers Park, go north on Mays from downtown to SH 79.

GREENWOOD MASONIC INSTITUTE HISTORICAL MARKER

Southeast corner of the intersection of Mays and SH 79

Sam Bass is not the only famous outlaw Round Rock can lay brief claim to. The Greenwood Institute, which was located about a quarter mile west of this marker, is best remembered as the alma mater of John Wesley Hardin. Brother Joe Hardin was studying law here in 1870 when his younger brother John, already on the run from the law, decided to join him in his studies. John Wesley camped in the woods near the school, and each afternoon Joe would bring his lessons, which John studied by the light of his campfire. As quick with words as with his gun, John Wesley Hardin purportedly received his diploma and a teaching certificate in record time. As a teacher during a brief career near Corsicana, it is reported that he received excellent attention and had no discipline problems.

Turn right on US 79.

About a mile down US 79, you see on your left a spacious old two-story double-galleried limestone house with an Indian lookout on top. This is the home Nelson Merrill built for his family in 1870. Born in Connecticut in 1810, he moved to Texas in 1837. According to his obituary, he almost immediately joined a company of rangers and fought Mexican attempts to retake Texas. In 1839, he raised his own company of rangers to give protection to the infant city of Austin and was elected captain. Merrill settled on Brushy Creek in Williamson County that same year, near the "fort" of earlier settler Dr. Thomas Kenney (Kinney), which was a picket compound (erected 1839) with two large gates to permit the entrance of wagons. Dr. Kenney and a few others, while out hunting, were attacked in their camp and were all killed by a band of Indians. Thus Captain Merrill was left to guard the outpost, between which and the Rocky Mountains there were no "American" settlements, yet he maintained his post, sometimes chasing the Indians and at others being chased by them. After years of toil and danger, the captain sold his place and settled in Travis County, at Merrilltown, named for him. While there, he served several terms as a county commissioner. Having purchased land on Brushy Creek, he sold his possessions at Merrilltown, moved back to Williamson County, established a farm, settled down to raising cattle, and built this spacious home. Why he added the Indian lookout is anybody's guess; by the time he built his house, there had been no Indian attacks in the area for more than five years. Perhaps it was out of nostalgia, like Charles Nimitz and his "steamboat" hotel in Fredericksburg. At any rate, he died here at home after a long and painful illness in January 1879.

Kenney's Fort served as the rendezvous for the troops of the ill-fated Santa Fe Expedition of 1841, and the archives of the Republic of Texas en route from Austin to Washington-on-the-Brazos, on the orders of President Sam Houston, were captured at the fort on December 31, 1842, and returned to Austin.

Palm Valley is named for Mrs. Anders Palm and her six sons, who settled here in 1853 on land that S. M. Swenson, a Swedish immigrant, acquired in 1838. Other Swedish immigrants soon joined them here along Brushy Creek. Swenson became a successful businessman just a few years after coming to Texas in 1838. As an immigration agent, he brought several hundred Swedes to Texas, most of whom settled in rural Travis and Williamson counties, in settlements named New Sweden, Manda, Lund, Hutto, and Palm Valley. The Palm family encouraged Swedish settlement in the area by assisting immigrants who arrived with little money, so Palm Valley became a focus of Williamson County's growing Swedish population. In 1876, the settlement became a stop on the International and Great Northern railroad. The Swedes were predominantly Lutheran; Lutheran church services were held in a log cabin built by A. J. Nelson as early as 1861, but nearby Palm Valley Lutheran Church was not formally organized until 1870. The present red-brick Gothic Revival church located west of the park was built in 1894.

The two-story Palm house (built about 1904), a barn and other farm outbuildings, and several old log cabins are on the grounds of Old Settlers Village, which adjoins Old Settlers Park at Palm Valley, which is a city park. Old Settlers Village pertains to the Old Settlers Association, a nonprofit organization dedicated to the preservation of cultural diversity in Williamson County. The cabins were donated to the Old Settlers Association in 1936. The Jacob Harrell family donated the little cabin, which once served as a one-room schoolhouse (with four students, according to records) and had a little porch out front.

The city park, which covers about three hundred acres, has a little lake, hike-and-bike trails, ball fields, and a disc golf course. It is located next to the Dell Diamond, home of the Round Rock Express baseball team.

ANNUAL EVENT

JULY

FRONTIER DAYS

Downtown and Old Settlers Park • July 4 • www.roundrocktexas.gov • W

July 19 was the day that Sam Bass was gunned down during an attempted bank robbery, and this day's celebration includes a reenactment of the fateful robbery, food, games, a parade, music, dances, and fireworks.

SHINER-LOCKHART PILGRIMAGE

Years ago, a group of Austin bicycle racers combined three of their favorite forms of entertainment—bike riding, drinking Shiner beer, and eating barbecue—into a single bike ride. Every other month or so, one of the guys would say, "Want to go to Shiner?" and immediately a spirited consensus sprang up, and the word was spread to everyone else. Those who could make it on the anointed day pedaled off en masse to our little Lavaca County mecca, the hospitality room at the Spoetzl Brewery, where the venerable Mr. Herbert Siems so ably dispensed the beer and little confidences. We could always count on a host of colorful local characters and employees to enliven our drinking, like Emil Vincik, Cracker Wallace, Joe Green, and Speedy Biel.

Emil came for the water, although his girlfriend usually sipped a Shiner. Well into his eighties, the irrepressible Emil never missed a dance, whether it was Friday night at the SPJST Hall or the big Labor Day Shiner Catholic Church Picnic.

Long, lean Joe Green was Shiner's oldest employee and the brewery's unofficial historian; Cracker Wallace was his nephew. Cracker, from our perspective, was one of the brewery's most important employees; he delivered the Shiner beer to Austin twice a week, plus ring sausage from Patek's Market if we asked. Speedy Biel was the brewery's congenial, easygoing sales manager. There was a family atmosphere that one rarely associates with brewing beer; we were on a first-name basis with the brewmaster, the kettle man, the bottle shoppers, the administrative staff, and, in short, everybody. In those pre-microbrewery days, the Spoetzl Brewery was the third smallest brewery in the country and pulled down just one-third of 1 percent of Texas' total beer sales. As small a niche as it was at the time, it seemed to satisfy everybody.

When our considerable thirsts were slaked, it was time to eat, and where better than Kreuz Market in Lockhart? So we racked up the bikes, and our

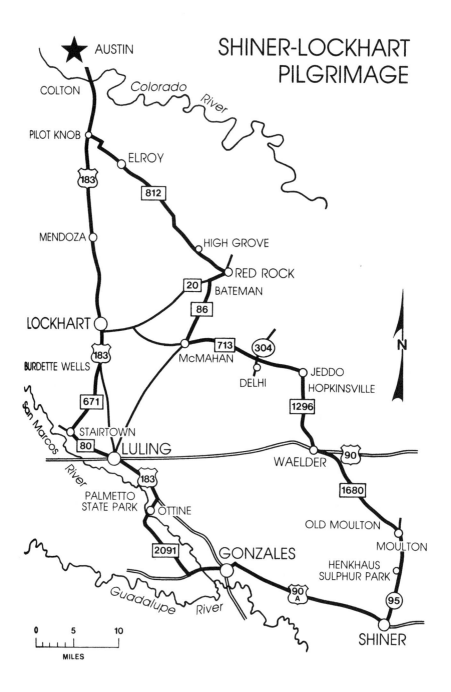

SHINER-LOCKHART PILGRIMAGE

AUSTIN

COLTON

Colorado River

PILOT KNOB

ELROY

183

812

MENDOZA

HIGH GROVE

RED ROCK

BATEMAN

20

86

LOCKHART

183

BURDETTE WELLS

671

713

McMAHAN

304

DELHI

JEDDO

HOPKINSVILLE

1296

N

San Marcos River

STAIRTOWN

80

LULING

WAELDER

90

183

1680

PALMETTO
STATE PARK

OTTINE

OLD MOULTON

MOULTON

2091

GONZALES

HENKHAUS
SULPHUR PARK

Guadalupe River

90
A

95

SHINER

0   5   10
MILES

designated drivers whisked us toward Lockhart. We sometimes detoured for pork ribs at Luling City Market, since there were no ribs at Kreuz and you could not count on getting Kreuz's pork loin past the lunch rush. Once at Kreuz, we wiped out the best of whatever meat was left. The traditionalists among us ate at the benches in the old, un-air-conditioned back room next to the pits, where sharp carbon-steel knives with worn-smooth wooden handles were chained to the tabletops for your dining pleasure. A sharp, well-pointed knife is the only eating utensil a real man needs.

The little brewery in Shiner isn't so little anymore, but it still begs visiting. Kreuz Market still carves up some of the state's best barbecue.

From Austin, take US 183 south toward Lockhart.

COLTON

Travis County • 50 • About 7 miles from downtown Austin

Just after you cross Onion Creek, south of the US 183/SH 71 intersection, you enter what was once the farming community of Colton. Donald and Jamine McKenzie, two Scottish immigrants, established in 1866 a community they called Cotton, an apt name, since the land yielded a bale of cotton to the acre in good years, thanks to the soil's wealth of volcanic ash, which had been spewed out millions of years earlier by nearby Pilot Knob. When the community applied for a post office, it was told to pick another name, and Colton it was. The first school was established in 1892 and was named Pine Knob, although this is not pine tree country and there are no old pines in the area.

PILOT KNOB COMMUNITY

Travis County • Just south of Colton

Pilot Knob community grew up at about the same time as Colton, as cotton farming enjoyed a strong spurt of growth from the end of the Civil War until the beginning of the First World War. Whole immigrant families, women and little ones included, labored long hours in the fields. But the cotton gins, general stores, and one-room schools are long gone, and the two little settlements have been swallowed up by Austin's relentless development.

PILOT KNOB

One mile west of US 183, just south of the FM 812 junction • Private property

Pilot Knob is the best known of several dozen volcanic craters and mounds that stretch along the Balcones Fault zone. The three rounded, knoblike hills that make up Pilot Knob rise up nearly two hundred feet higher than the surrounding countryside. Visible for miles around, Pilot Knob has been a guidepost for human travelers for thousands of years. Travelers on the Pinto and Chisholm Trails knew that they would soon reach the Colorado River and that a good place to cross was a shallow ford about where US 183 crosses the river today.

Pilot Knob was born about eighty million years ago, during the Cretaceous period, when most of modern-day Texas was covered by a shallow sea. Following the creation of the Balcones Fault zone from a belt of fractures in the earth's crust, hot molten lava from deep inside the earth pushed up through the sea water. Explosions caused by steam shook the sea's floor, and craters formed around these explosion vents. Ash, debris blown from the volcano, and lava filled the crater, creating a dome that rose above the sea floor. After things cooled off, reef organisms were attracted to the dome's irregular surfaces, and the reefs they formed were not unlike the coral reefs of the South Pacific and the Flower Gardens reef in the Gulf of Mexico. Beach rock formed where the waves lapped at the volcano's peripheries; this beach rock can be seen in nearby McKinney Falls State Park. The sea eventually receded, leaving Texas behind, and the exposed sea floor began to weather away to its current state. Pilot Knob's volcanic rock has resisted erosion better than the surrounding limestone. The hilltops of the knob are the exposed lava core itself, a volcanic rock called nephelinite, which is related to basalt.

Pilot Knob has long been regarded as a treasure mountain; people believed that riches had been buried here, or that diamonds could be found. The great diamond mines of South Africa are dug into similar geologic formations. In 1919, Professor J. A. Udden announced that the entire dome of the knob was composed of "nephelite basalt," also called "traprock," and that this was the toughest rock in Texas. Promoter Arvid Franke of San Antonio announced his high hopes for turning Pilot Knob into road-surfacing material. He said that he would build the crusher if the International and Great Northern Railroad would extend its tracks there. The railroad declined, and so the knobs still sit here.

Turn left on FM 812 toward Red Rock. In five miles, you come to Elroy.

ELROY

Travis County • 125 • About 5 miles from Pilot Knob

It is said that the land on which Elroy is located was once owned by an officer in Santa Anna's army, who traded it for a horse and saddle. The area saw its first permanent white settlers around Civil War times. The area was first known as Blocker's Pasture, or Driskill's Pasture, after its owner, Jesse Driskill, a cattle tycoon whose most enduring legacy is the Austin hotel that bears his name. Driskill eventually sold his pasture to a man named Tolbin, and after that the land began to be subdivided. A. A. Molund was the first to settle here permanently, in 1892.

At this time, the neighborhood was also known as Dutch Water Hole. It seems an old Dutch (probably a German) sheepherder camped with his flock here regularly on Maha Creek, where it makes its Elroy bend just east of the Elroy Hill and just south of FM 812. The creek was deep enough at the bend to be called a water hole, and one unfortunate day it was also deep enough to drown the old shepherd. The name floated.

Dutch Water Hole had a store and school by 1896, and soon the Water Holers were hankering for a post office. Prominent local healer and shopkeeper Dr. Black spearheaded the hamlet's drive. Dutch Water Hole was not an appropriate name, so Dr. Black solicited new name suggestions. This is where we lose track of the story for a bit. We know the postal service approved "Elroy," and Elroy it has been ever since, but we do not know how that peculiar moniker was coined. Local historian C. W. Carlson told me that Dr. Black asked Thomas Roy Miles, engineer at the local cotton gin, for his suggestion. The two put their heads together and came up with Miles' middle name, "Roy." But somewhere, somehow along the way, "El" was tacked on. Was it *el*, the Spanish word for "the"? Was it short for a name like Eldridge or Eleanor? Or was it short for Louis or Louise? No one knows anymore. Carlson believes that the store sign may have read "El Roy" at the turn of the century, but he's not sure. Such dual and even triple name combinations were common at the time and resulted in some of Texas' most colorful place names. But an aging Austin newspaper clipping declares that Elroy resulted from a switcheroo performed on a local settler's name: Leroy.

Elroy became a predominantly Swedish farming and ranching community and trade center. Its commercial importance began to decline in the 1930s, and the corrugated-tin hulk of the old Elroy general store on your right atop Elroy Hill has long stood vacant.

The land between Elroy and Red Rock on FM 812, while increasingly filling with urban refugees, is still relatively sparsely populated and given over mainly to ranching. As you draw closer to Red Rock, the color of the sandy loam gets progressively redder.

A little more than five miles past Elroy, and just after the FM 812/SH 21 intersection, you cross Cedar Creek. About five miles downstream (to your left) is the **village of Cedar Creek** (located on SH 21, 4.5 miles east of the FM 812/SH 21 intersection). This area was settled as early as 1832 by Addison and Mary Owen Litton. They were joined by others, such as Jesse Billingsley. In January 1842, a Methodist minister preached to a full house at the Owens home on Cedar Creek, and life in the community soon revolved around Methodist meetings. A post office opened in 1852. With the end of the Civil War, tensions between whites and blacks flared throughout Central Texas, most notably in the village of Cedar Creek. The area around Cedar Creek came to be heavily populated by blacks in the years immediately following the Civil War. Cal Thompson was a freed slave who became a leader among local African Americans after the Civil War. He purchased land in 1869 in the Cedar Creek community, at the suggestion of his former master, Marshall Trigg of Hills Prairie. Thompson eventually owned five hundred acres of the area's farmland and was described as "a Negro of much influence in the community." The African Americans of Cedar Creek formed a military organization called the Loyal League, with Sam Fowler as their captain. Every Saturday, the League would meet at the store, and some thirty or forty of them would drill up and down the road with their guns and other weapons. This activity diminished after an appeal by Jesse Billingsley to Governor Hamilton, but the hostility between the two factions continued.

In July 1874, Thompson was indicted for stealing some hogs, worth thirty dollars, from a white neighbor. Early in 1875, Thompson was found guilty of stealing hogs and sentenced to two years in the state penitentiary, despite strong testimony from men like his ex-master Trigg supporting Thompson's claim that the pigs had been stolen from him. His case was appealed to the Texas Supreme Court where the judgment was reversed and the case remanded. Thompson gave bond early in June 1875 and got out on bail.

The influence and power of the blacks in Cedar Creek grew throughout the 1870s and 1880s. In the May 1888 elections, two African Americans, Orange Weeks (Wicks) and Ike Wilson, were elected justice of the peace and constable, respectively, for the Cedar Creek precinct. Resentment between whites and blacks intensified. Some months later, an assault and battery complaint was filed against young Addy Litton (one of Frank Litton's sons), and Constable Ike Wilson came to the Litton home to serve the papers. Mr. Litton demanded that a white deputy do so. Wilson got Deputy Sheriff Holland to serve the papers. Litton's trial convened in a house near the Cedar Creek store on June 13, 1889. A group of white people, fearing the boy would not get a fair trial, went armed to the place of trial. The presence of many armed blacks caused the prosecuting attorney, Ed Maynard, to request a postponement. Judge Orange Weeks replied, "The white folks have had their day running this court, and some of the rest of us will have ours now. The case will proceed." A shooting fracas occurred when young Litton stepped outside for a drink of water, just after the case was given to the jury. Four men were killed at the scene, two blacks and two whites.

On October 19, 1889, the Bastrop County grand jury indicted a group of ten "colored men," including Ike Wilson and O. W. Wicks, for the murder of George Schoeff and Alex. Nolan, both white. Trials began on November 6, 1889, and the defendants pled not guilty. West Craft, a negro, testified for the state: "Wicks said for me not to go away; that he had me deputized to help protect the court; that we would bring the thing off directly, and that he wanted me to stay there, and wanted the negroes to hang together, and 'kill as many of the devilish white folks as they do of us.'"

The defense contended that the whites had threatened to interfere with the officers of the court, to rescue Addie Litton, to accomplish their purpose by force, and to kill Ike Wilson if necessary, that they congregated in large numbers under a mesquite tree a short distance from the house; that, when the jury retired to deliberate on the verdict, Litton left the house; that Constable Wilson followed, and called to him to await the verdict of the jury; that the whites then rose in mass, handed Litton a gun, and opened fire on Wilson; and that Wilson did not return the fire until he had been fired upon at least twice.

The jury didn't buy the defense's story. Convicted of murder in the second degree, O. W. Wicks was sentenced to twenty years in the penitentiary. The case was appealed to the Texas Supreme Court in 1890, which reversed the district court's judgment and remanded the case, observing, in part, "There was much conflict in the testimony as to which side, the whites or the blacks, began the difficulty which resulted so fatally."

Frustrated, the whites swore revenge on every black connected with the incident. A large exodus of blacks immediately followed. This incident incited riots in other areas, causing the deaths of many blacks. One by one they were murdered or they left the county. Two white men shot Thompson as he left Bastrop one day in 1890. At least one hundred white men saw the murder, but no one would tell who it was, the consensus being that he was "nothing but a trouble maker and both sides were glad he was killed," according to Jeptha Billingsley, Jesse Billingsley's son, whose family had owned slaves.

The *Bastrop Advertiser* was more sympathetic in recounting the killing in a February 1890 edition:

> While riding along the road from Bastrop to his home on Monday evening last, Calvin Thompson, colored, was shot down in cold blood by some unknown party or parties, two balls passing through his head, one through the temple and the other just above the eye. So far there is no clue whatever to the perpetrator of the dastardly act. He was a prominent colored man of the county, had accumulated considerable property, and possessed great influence with his race. By whom he was shot, or for what cause, is yet a profound mystery, and the officers have been unable to get any clue whatever, though a number of witnesses have been examined and the inquest is still held open for further evidence.

In 1884, Cedar Creek had a population of six hundred and was a shipping point for cotton and locally grown produce. The community's school, the Central Texas Normal Academy, had 101 pupils. But by 1914, Cedar Creek had dropped to 225 residents, four general stores, a gin, a tailor, a doctor, and a cattle dealer. Oil drilling in the area started in 1913, and in 1928, a pool was discovered four miles east on the Yost farm. Though not a major producer, the Yost oilfield yielded commercial quantities through the mid-1940s. The population climbed back to three hundred during these years but gradually declined afterward. A little over six miles past the FM 812/SH 21 intersection, you come to an intersection with FM 672. If you turn right (south) here and go another three miles, you will come to St. John Colony.

St. John Colony, located just inside Caldwell County, was begun in the early 1870s when the Reverend John Henry Winn purchased land here and founded the only independent black community in the county. After the Civil War, many former slaves remained in the area. By 1870, Caldwell County's black population was 38 percent of the total population.

Rev. Winn was looking for property that he and fourteen other families could purchase for their homes. He rode nearly sixty miles until he reached this place, which was two thousand acres of forest land. He found the Haynes and Harrison families living near Lytton Creek. Rev. Winn talked with Bob Haynes and Squire Harrison and asked if the property about their surroundings was for sale. They replied that it was. Because of the distance Rev. Winn had traveled, Haynes asked him to spend the night with him and his family. Early the next morning, Rev. Winn journeyed back to Webberville to tell his people that he had found the land for them. Rev Winn and the heads of the fourteen families journeyed to the new land. They cleared the land so they could build their homes. Each family bought from twenty-five to one hundred acres until they all had bought two thousand acres. After the first year, the colony began to grow spiritually and economically. It was named Winn's Colony after Rev. Winn. After the organization of the church in 1873 by Rev. J. H. Winn Sr., naming it St. John Missionary Baptist Church, the colony took on the same name.

The colony's cemetery is located on your left just before reaching the St. John Regular Baptist and St. John Landmark Baptist churches that constitute the community's center. The most famous citizen of the St. John Colony was

Azie Taylor Morton, born here in 1936. She served as treasurer of the United States from 1977 to 1981, the first African American ever to hold the post.

About twelve miles from Elroy, and about 0.5 miles past the intersection with FM 672, watch for the High Grove sign, which marks a paved county road. Turn left (north) here and go about 0.5 miles to reach High Grove.

HIGH GROVE

Bastrop County • About 12 miles from Elroy

The old whitewashed building doubled for years as the "white folks'" school and church and still hosts the High Grove Homecoming each May. The "coloreds" had to go to St. Lytton's School or St. John's School. Most everybody at High Grove moved to Red Rock in the 1890s.

Nearby, back on FM 812 and on your left, about two miles east of High Grove, and just after the Boyd Road intersection, start looking to your left. In less than half a mile, set in a grove of trees, are an old cabin and log outbuildings used in the filming of Gordon Parks' 1976 film, Leadbelly. The film crew was centered in Austin, and the movie can be said to have sparked the modern movie industry in Austin and Central Texas. Sonny Terry, Brownie McGhee, and Pete Seeger were among the musicians featured.
Continue eastward on FM 812 toward Red Rock.

RED ROCK

Bastrop County • 100 • (512) • About 16 miles from Elroy

The area around present-day Red Rock began to fill up with settlers in the 1850s. By 1859, a school had been established at Walnut Creek west of Lentz Branch, called Lentz Branch School. The community it served was called Walnut Creek or Lentz Branch until after the Civil War. Lentz Branch was named for William Lentz, killed at one of its water holes by the Indians. By the early 1870s, the community was also being called Red Rock.

Red Rock, which was also known for a while as Hannah—for an early local family of that name—was originally located several miles west of its present site, about where the cemeteries are now. The Old Red Rock Cemetery is off FM 812 to your right, down a dirt road (County Road 229) about half a mile. The newer cemetery is a mile closer to Red Rock on FM 812, on the left.

There are several different versions of how Red Rock got its name. One says the name owes to the red rock used by early settler James Brewer to construct the chimney of his cabin in the 1850s. Another says it refers to the red rock embedded in the banks of nearby Walnut Creek, where the old Waelder-to-Austin road used to cross. Early settlers would caravan to Austin once or twice a year to buy supplies, and the "red rock" crossing of Walnut Creek was one of the designated gathering points. In 1937, Lois Nellene

Turner said that "the man who named Red Rock was Sam Petty, because of a peculiar round red rock."

Red Rock has its own silver mine legend. Mexican miners were supposedly working a silver mine on a hill somewhere in the area of "Red Rock." The ore was low-grade, but over the years they had made and accumulated forty-three bars of silver at a smelter near the mine. Indians attacked, and all the miners were killed, one story says, with the bars hidden in a mine shaft. A variant of the story has one of the miners escaping death and years later (1870s) telling a Texas Ranger where the bars were hidden. The Ranger searched, but never found. "Red rocks" and "red hills" are associated with old Spanish mine stories in Llano and Menard counties. Remains of old mining and smelting activity have been found in the Red Rock area, but it may have been for iron, not silver. There is much iron ore in the area. There were iron mines worked in the nearby sand hills area, and a hill in the area is still called Iron Mound.

Red Rock was a prosperous community by the 1870s, with a post office and academies for young men and women. As was the case with many Texas towns, the Texas legislature passed a law forbidding the sale of liquor within a two-mile radius of the academies. On March 30, 1875, J. W. Bowen was indicted three times for selling liquor within two miles of Red Rock. Dr. Prince was indicted four times for the same offense.

Red Rock was a violent place during Reconstruction days. Andrew J. "Andy" Potter—the Fightin' Parson—was a circuit-riding preacher in those days. Potter's rounds took him to Red Rock to preach every so often, in spite of the young hellions' threats to shoot him or run him out of town. Potter always wore a pair of Colt 45s on his hips for just such occasions. While preaching at nearby Lytton Springs one Sunday, Potter was warned not to come to Red Rock on the next Sabbath. Potter replied that he would most certainly be there and that he expected a fine chicken dinner afterward. When he arrived the following Sunday, Potter laid his shootin' irons on the rude pulpit table in front of him and announced, "Now I sent word that I was coming to Red Rock to preach and I'm gonna preach. But I can shoot too. And if anyone wants a fight and starts one, we'll shoot it out." Potter preached his service and got his chicken dinner.

The life of a circuit preacher was not always fried chicken and pound cake for Sunday dinner, as this joke illustrates:

A circuit rider was conducting a prayer meeting out in a recently, thinly settled section where any event beyond the daily routine of staying alive was novelty. Everyone from miles around was present. At the end of his evening's message, the preacher asked of his audience: "Would all Christians please stand up?"

Not a soul moved.

"What! Not a friend of Jesus in the house?" he asked.

At which point one cowboy stood up declaring: "Stranger, I don't know who this Jesus feller is, but I'll stand up for any man that hasn't got any more friends than he has."

Prayer, like rain, was so foreign in some areas of frontier Texas that older children were puzzled at the sight. Jack Potter was requested to ask the blessing at one family's table before they ate dinner. As he bowed his head and humbly asked the blessing, a ten-year-old boy sat staring in wide-eyed amazement. He was so bewildered that when he saw Potter on the street the next day, he asked the Fightin' Parson, "Are you the preacher that talks to the plate?"

Feuds were a way of life in early Red Rock. Folks shot each other in the streets, on the highways, and in the fields they worked. Several dozen Red Rockers marched over to Cedar Creek to help their white friends in the big Loyal League shootout. Signs posted on the roads leading into Red Rock read: "Negroes/Troublemakers, don't let the sun set on you in Red Rock."

Blacks were not allowed to go into Red Rock unless they had some work to do for the white planters. But one man, Calvin Powell, would walk into town whenever he felt like it. The freed slaves had formed their own settlement at Walnut Creek, encouraged by their ex-masters, four men that included Trigg and McGehee. One of McGehee's ex-slaves, Ben Haywood, came to own four hundred acres. They started Pleasant Chapel AMEN Church just off Highway 20 near Walnut Creek Bridge.

Blacks all over the United States knew about Red Rock's warning signs, and long after the signs were gone (around World War II), blacks were afraid to be found in town after sunset. If they were detained past dark, they asked for a sympathetic white escort out of town. To this day, no blacks live in Red Rock; the closest black community is in St. John Colony.

Perhaps the community's antipathy toward blacks dated back to August 1860, when the *Texas State Gazette* reported,

> We learn from a gentleman just from Bastrop that the Negroes were foiled in a contemplated insurrection on Monday, 6th inst. The Negroes in Bastrop were suspected, from their conduct on Sunday, which led to the formation of a committee. Upon examination of the negro cabins on Walnut Creek, large quantities of arms and ammunition were discovered; in one cabin a keg of powder and new six-shooters, and in the other cabin various deadly weapons were found secreted.

A month later, George McKeon of Cedar Creek wrote the *Gazette* to say that his house had been set afire, blaming his own negroes or abolitionists.

Like the Knobbs country farther north in Bastrop County, it was a rare man in Red Rock who didn't have a killing or two under his belt, well into the twentieth century. And we're talking about pillars of the community too, not fly-by-night ruffians. Why?

Ask, and you'll get no answer better than "a man has to protect his own." Perhaps it has to do with the isolation of the place, far from the county seat or any other sizable town with law enforcement, in country where the roads were often rendered impassable for weeks at a time by deep red, sticky mud. The first paved road came through in the 1940s. Telephone service didn't come until after World War II. Such isolation attracted and bred an independent lot that made its own law. Folks don't kill each other anymore, but nobody's forgotten the past either. Visitors, of course, have nothing to fear; on the contrary, a pleasant conversation is easily commenced.

Family feuding predated the Civil War. In July 1858, John C. F. Hill and Frank Shepherd were arguing about the ownership of some stock. Hill stabbed Shepherd in the left shoulder and then skipped the country, leaving Shepherd's life in a very critical condition.

Legend has it that Frank James taught school here briefly, and wed a sixteen-year-old local girl by the last name of Pogue; their marriage was said to have lasted the weekend. He left when he heard that brother Jesse had been shot, thirsting for revenge. There isn't much to back up the story, although Frank was in Texas during the summer of 1881, staying off and on with his sister in North Texas. Where he went while not living with his sister is not known; while on trial in 1883, he could not recall anything of his Texas travels. He did go back to Missouri five months after Jesse's death to surrender to that state's governor.

Wild as Red Rock was said to have been, it held no attraction for seventeen-year-old Albert Kaduna, who came from Germany in 1879 to join his family in Red Rock. His parents and younger siblings had come to Texas in 1871. They settled near Walnut Creek north of old Red Rock, where they helped found Sacred Heart Catholic Church in 1877.

When Albert joined his parents here, he stayed only two weeks. He came in from the field with a team of mules, tied them up under a tree and left without saying a word. From Red Rock, he ended up in Split Rock, Wyoming, perhaps via an uncle in the cattle business. He worked with horses and as a cowboy. In his dotage, Albert told a nephew that he had trained and furnished horses for the Hole-in-the-Wall gang's getaways before he was arrested for assault with intent to commit robbery. He got four years in the state penitentiary.

Released in 1897, Al was arrested for holding up a store in Medicine Bow, Wyoming, in 1901. He pled no contest. While awaiting trial, he and three other prisoners escaped from the county jail, but he was recaptured three days later. He was sentenced to twelve years in the penitentiary and served nearly seven years before receiving a full pardon. In 1920, he briefly returned to Red Rock to collect his share of his late mother's estate and attend Mass at Sacred Heart Catholic Church with his family. He then returned to his ranch job near Split Rock. He died in 1941.

The area's scoff-Gods didn't push Parson Andy Potter around, but they had no problem burning the little Sacred Heart Church down to ashes one night in January 1891. A cryptic letter was found near the ruins:

BASTROP, TEXAS

My dear enimies—this being the reck day I will give you a notice that your out-fit is in slim show. By g—d I am this witch is my idea to do is to upset this, witch you will this morning find the ruins, please do not mention this to no body is it will cause you trouble the owner will please not say nothing for if you do h—ll is to pay By g-d to the dutch and marican catolic suns of B—s.

from a lover make out our names if you can

B. C.

H. S.

Family pride, stubbornness, and loyalty fueled the Red Rock feuds. At the height of the feuding, Gus Jung was running the Wilbarger Lumber Yard. He built coffins for local funerals. Two local men were feuding at the time and never missed the opportunity to take a shot at each other when they met. One day, one Mr. A was shooting at one Mr. B from inside the lumberyard's store, while Mr. B, at the side door, was trying to shoot at Mr. A within. Gus Jung, who had been out in the lumberyard, ran toward the store, as his wife, Emma shouted at him not to go over there, that he would be killed, to which Gus yelled back, "You go in the house. Do you think I'm going to let my two friends keep shooting at each other?"

He opened the front door and told Mr. A to put his gun on the counter and told Mr. B to push his gun through the side door. As he picked up both guns he scolded them, "You are both my friends and I can't have you shooting at each other."

The two feudists went peaceably home as Jung took their guns to the lumberyard where he kept them until both men had calmed down. But the feud revived, and eventually one shot the other down halfway between Bastrop and the nearby hamlet of Watterson.

One Saturday evening in February 1911, Will Smith, president of the Red Rock State Bank, grappled with Pierce Talley, who drew a pistol on him in the bank. Talley was shot five times. Smith was uninjured. Talley was sent to a hospital at San Antonio.

The Hoskins family of Red Rock feuded from without and from within. One Sunday morning in 1902, Louis Lunda (Lunday) was killed by John Hoskins at the latter's home near Red Rock. Lunda went to Hoskin's house, and thinking Hoskins asleep on the gallery, he picked up an ax and advanced toward him when Mr. Hoskins arose, stepped into the house, secured his gun, and shot Lunda. Revenge was late in coming: fourteen years.

John Hoskins was killed at Red Rock in August 1916 in front of Pester's Confectionary by a grandson, Norman Lunday, son of the late Louis, using a shotgun from inside the confectionary. Hoskins was fifty-five, and Lunday was either sixteen or eighteen, depending on who's telling the story.

Former Bastrop County sheriff I. R. "Nig" Hoskins was born in Red Rock in 1908, and long after, he explained that the 1902 killing resulted after granddaddy Hoskins and son-in-law Louis Lunday—Norman Lunday's father—had quarreled about whether Lunday's daughter should go pick cotton. She was twelve and didn't want to pick cotton. Granddaddy said he would take her home after a while, which didn't set well with her daddy. He came after Granddaddy Hoskins with an axe handle, cussing a blue streak. Granddaddy Hoskins blew him off the porch with a shotgun blast. Norman, Sheriff Hoskin's first cousin, was two when this happened. According to Sheriff Hoskins, Norman grew up on stories of his father's shooting, and when he turned sixteen, he decided it was time to avenge his father's death. So he shot his grandfather to death.

But according to contemporary newspaper accounts, there had been some trouble between grandfather and grandson for a couple of weeks previous to the shooting. Trouble was averted between these parties the previous week by the intervention of friends. They had been on friendly terms until a difficulty arose between them, in regard to the possession of Lunday's fourteen-year-old sister, whom Hoskins had reared. Lunday wanted her to live with his mother, and Hoskins wished to retain her at his home.

In 1952, I. R. Hoskins ran for sheriff. His opponents publicized the fact that his grandfather had been murdered in Red Rock in 1916 and about how rough a family Hoskins came from. His father came to Red Rock and told the town that he wanted to know who had brought Granddaddy Hoskins into this race, that he had been dead since 1916 and had nothing to do with this race. "Don't let me find out who's talking it," he warned, and he never found out.

"The old story was, way back there the law wouldn't go to Red Rock," Hoskins said. "They just wouldn't go out there. So, when I was elected back in '53, I got a call from Red Rock and I went out there. Course, I was raised in Red Rock, I run around there as a young kid, I married in Red Rock, and all, and I knowed everybody there. But I didn't go out there no 'bully of the woods' either. I went out there as a man and talked to this feller and told him the complaint I had. He was running a beer joint and selling beer to kids, and then they were gambling in the back of it. I just told him, 'If you don't quit it, now, I'm gonna have to come out here and catch you.' And he quit it. He wasn't no bully of the woods, either."

But Red Rock was a progressive little town, too. Cotton, corn, melons, and other truck crops grew well here, and when the Missouri-Kansas-Texas railroad came through the area in 1890, the merchants and most of the citizens of old Red Rock moved their buildings and homes to the present Red Rock. Red Rock soon had doctors, hotels, a drugstore, a bank, cotton gins, and all the other customary businesses of a regional trade center. There were from 1,600 to 2,500 bales of cotton ginned each year in Red Rock in those days. They had preaching in the school house until the three churches were built—first the Baptist, second the Christian, and third the Nazarene.

According to Gerald Hanna, there were always young men who were going nowhere riding through town. His father hired two of them one spring to work his fields. That fall, after all the harvest work was done, they prepared to ride on. As they left, one of the men asked his father if there was anyone he needed killed, since they were moving on, they would be glad to do the job for him.

By 1906, Red Rock had its first brick building, a source of pride for the entire town. Red Rock's bank was the largest between Smithville and Lockhart. The Black brothers showed Bastrop County's first talking pictures in the county's first real movie house, built in 1929. Earlier they had shown silent flicks in a makeshift, alfresco theater located in the back lot of the lumberyard.

Red Rock was resilient, too. Thirteen businesses burned in August 1918, and the town rebuilt.

In April 1919, all the business portion of Red Rock, except the bank and the railroad station, was destroyed by fire, which is said to have originated in the post office.

The downtown burned again in 1924 from the Liberty Garage (still standing, though no longer identified as such) down to the old depot, and everyone built again. Red Rockers were a proud, stubborn lot, particularly proud of their town baseball team. When asked if the New York Yankees might be able to beat the Red Rock nine, the answer was, "Not in Red Rock, they couldn't." The fame of the team was such that players were recruited to play for teams across the state, such as Edna in 1904, for a game with the powerhouse team from Ganado.

The Great Depression finally did Red Rock in. Although the discovery of oil during the 1930s brought another spurt of activity to the area, little remains today. The bank used to be on the corner as you entered downtown Red Rock. It collapsed to rubble in the early 1970s, and for years thereafter old men sat around cleaning salvageable bricks from the wreckage. Now even the rubble is gone.

RED ROCK GENERAL STORE AND FEED

201 Main, downtown Red Rock • 321-3360 • Open daily • No Cr.

Duncan Lentz ran this store from 1920 until his death in 1990, and could tell many stories of the area, if you knew how to get him to talk. Dunc is gone now, and the new owners have cleaned and repaired the building considerably, but held on to Dunc's old Coke cooler and put on display some of the old inventory and farm tools they found in the feed store, as well as the in-store-use "money" that Dunc's father coined and doled out for use by his customers from the early twentieth century through the early days of the Great Depression, in denominations from a penny to a dollar. Ask to see the little landscape mural on the feed store wall, painted in the 1930s by a hobo who got off the train one day, painted this, and then moved on.

From Red Rock, head south on FM 20. In a couple of hundred yards you pass through Bateman.

BATEMAN

Bastrop County • Just outside Red Rock

Bateman, settled in the 1880s, was named for an early resident. The coming of the Missouri-Kansas-Texas railroad in 1887 promised growth and prosperity, but the post office stayed open only from 1900 to 1904, and Red Rock instead became the area's shipping center.

Turn left on FM 86.

Ranching is still the economic mainstay of these thinly settled sandy-loam prairies, along with a little oil activity.

TAYLORSVILLE

Caldwell County • About 6 miles from Red Rock

Taylorsville, now more a memory than a village, was named for a local landowner and has no identifiable center.

Turn left on FM 713 at McMahan.

MCMAHAN

Caldwell County • 125

About ten miles from Red Rock, McMahan lies on Tinney Creek (also spelled Tenney), a branch of Plum Creek. The creek was named for Ambrose Tinney, who came here from Germany in 1831 and bought a league of land from the Mexican government for about nine cents an acre. Other families began to drift in during the 1840s. Sometime during the 1880s, D. W. Ellis established the area's first store, about 0.5 miles north of present-day McMahan at a place called Wildcat. Later a saloon was built on the east bank of Tinney Creek, just east of present-day McMahan, near the busy intersection of the Lockhart-to-La Grange and Red Rock-to-Luling roads. The saloon and surrounding neighborhood soon became known as Whizzerville: one of the saloon's regular patrons got so obnoxiously drunk one day that his neighbors set their dogs on him. The drunkard galloped away on his horse, but the dogs stayed glued to his horse's heels. The horse headed back for the saloon and, without stopping, lumbered through the saloon and out the back door, its half-senseless rider still hanging on. One patron remarked that the rider was sure "in a whiz," whereupon a local answered back, "This is Whizzerville." The name pleased hangers-on, and that's how the neighborhood came to be known.

In 1890, Ed McMahan built a store at the crossroads where McMahan now stands. Other businesses followed. A post office was established in 1896, but although locals favored the name Whizzerville, post office authorities rejected it. McMahan, Cole, Blundell, and Jeffrey were among the alternatives suggested; all were last names of prominent early settlers or merchants. Guess who won. R. W. "Bob" McMahan became first postmaster.

Several of the old commercial buildings still stand, including the old post office/general store, a one-story shotgun frame building with three bay windows separated by two sets of front doors. This facade style is not often seen in surviving buildings across the Hill Country. The old "McMahan, Texas" post office sign, which long hung from the porch, now hangs from the old feed store next door. The store closed during the early 1970s but reopened recently as the Whizzerville Inn.

FM 713 crosses Tinney Creek just after you leave "downtown" McMahan. McMahan is perhaps best known for its Southwest Texas Sacred Harp Singing Convention, an annual event that has attracted visitors from around the state, including James Michener, when he was researching his novel, *Texas*. Organized in 1900, the convention is held at the Bethel Primitive Baptist Church, located at the crossroads of FM 86 and FM 713.

The Saturday singing begins at 10 a.m., with a short break at 11 and dinner at noon. The singing resumes at 1 p.m. and lasts till 3 p.m. or later. The Sunday program is much the same.

Sacred harp singing, with its doleful minor chords and unusual harmonic patterns, is a far cry from modern church music. The songs reflect the hard times of Southern frontier life in the early 1800s, with the message that suffering is a natural and an endurable part of life, but with the promise that when this difficult life is done there will be joyful, eternal life with God in heaven.

Songs are sung a cappella; the "sacred harp" is the human voice singing hymns to God. Sacred harp, which is based on a four-note system (instead of the more common seven-note system), generally uses minor scales and segregates singers into separate groups based on voice parts. Some sacred harp melodies have been traced back nine hundred years to medieval Europe. At a singing, the main body of singers typically sits in blocks two or three deep and forms what is called a "hollow square," with the leader in the middle. The audience sits facing the square.

Sacred harp conventions and singing schools are not as widespread as before World War II, but they still take place throughout East Texas. The two oldest and largest meetings are McMahan's Southwest Texas Sacred Harp Singing Convention and the East Texas Sacred Harp Singing Convention in Henderson, organized in 1914.

DELHI

Caldwell County • About 8.1 miles from McMahan

Delhi, at the SH 304/FM 713 crossroads, is no longer listed on the maps, and not even the old folks know for sure how Delhi got its name. But according to several stories passed down, Delhi got its name from a traveling medicine man named Delhi. He stayed for a couple of months in the area putting on his shows. Since there was little else in the way of fun around here in those days, the young men from surrounding neighborhoods and settlements were always talking about going over to see Delhi, and so the name stuck long after the medicine man packed up his tent and stole away. The name dates at least as far back as 1879. A small church and school turned community center are located a ways south on SH 304.

Delhi's most famous citizens are the Black family, founders and owners of the also-revered Black's Barbecue in nearby Lockhart. Edgar Black Sr. was a rancher and ran a general store in Delhi before relocating to Lockhart, where he opened Northside Grocery and Black's Barbecue in 1932. Black served two terms as Caldwell County judge before his death in 1962. Edgar Black Jr. was born in Delhi in 1925; in 1948, he entered the family business.

JEDDO

Bastrop County • 75 • About 5 miles from Delhi

Jeddo is another ghost town. Established after the Civil War, it was originally called Hallmark's Prairie, after an early settler, John Hallmark. Dr. J. B. Cranfill's memoir describes life here in the years following the Civil War.

Cranfill was ten years old when his family moved here from Gonzales County during the week of Christmas 1868, at a point about equidistant from Gonzales, Bastrop, Lockhart, and La Grange, on the main roads from Lockhart to La Grange and from Bastrop to Gonzales. The nearest post office was Hopkinsville, Gonzales County, five miles away. With the establishment of a post office in 1874, the community became known as Jeddo, but folks continued to call the neighborhood Hallmark's Prairie well into the twentieth century.

Like nearby McMahan, Hallmark's Prairie was a Primitive Baptist stronghold. Primitive Baptists were also called Hardshell Baptists. The Hardshell Baptists believed in what they call "foot washing," basing this belief on the thirteenth chapter of John. Most of the preachers that he knew in his boyhood were Hardshell Baptists. There was a whole family of Bakers from McMahan who were preachers, and Baker family members are still active in the Bethel Primitive Baptist Church there.

The Cranfills worshipped at a nearby "rawhide lumber" church. Rawhide lumber was sawed from oak trees. It worked beautifully when green, but when the lumber dried under the heat of the summer sun, it warped in every direction and in every conceivable fashion. For that reason, it had to be nailed very securely. If it were not thus nailed when green, it never could be nailed, because a nail can't be driven through a rawhide lumber plank after it seasons. This church had a pine lumber floor and pine lumber seats, many of which did not have any backs to them.

Services began at about eleven in the morning and closed sometime in the afternoon, depending on the number of preachers present and the time it took for the Lord's Supper and the foot washing. Folks always very carefully washed their feet before a foot washing and put on the cleanest and best pair of socks they had.

Many strangers came down Hallmark's Prairie way to witness the foot-washing exercises, but many of those who came to scoff remained to pray. Many misunderstandings and embryo feuds were settled on these foot-washing occasions. No man could ever allow an enemy to kneel and wash his feet, and no man could ever remain an enemy of the man whose feet he had washed. Sounds like Red Rock could have used some Hardshell Baptists in their midst.

Those old frontier men carried their guns and revolvers everywhere they went. Cranfill's father, in the frontier times, slept with a pistol under his pillow and took his arms with him into the pulpit and laid them beside the Bible. No one knew when an attack would be made by the Indians, and those old-time Texans believed that "self-preservation was the first law of nature." While Cranfill the elder believed profoundly in predestination, he resembled another old Primitive Baptist preacher who was preparing to go one Sunday morning to a church where he was to preach, and before he left he took down and checked his gun for the trip. His son twitted him:

"Father, if you believe in predestination, why are you afraid of Indians?"

"Ah, my son," he replied, "I did not know but what the Lord had predestinated that I should kill an Indian today."

A wave of indignation swept over the old Texans when the first six shooter law was passed in 1873. "When the six shooter law was passed, there was a coincident order empowering negroes to be policemen. Many of the negroes were equipped with arms and the white men were deprived of arms. The old Texans ignored the law almost universally, and the result was that a good many negroes and some white men lost their lives," Cranfill stated.

During this period, a Democratic barbecue was held on Hallmark's Prairie, at which future governor Joseph D. Sayers of Bastrop was the principal speaker. A white Republican had taken black policemen there to keep order and to see that the white men were not armed. When Sayers arose to speak, he looked around, and spying the white Republican, began to denounce him by name and added: "I want Mr. —— to understand that I am here on this ground armed. I have a pistol in each one of my pockets, and I defy him and all his Negro police to disarm me. The first man that approaches me to disarm me I shall shoot dead on the spot, and I know that my friends here will finish up the balance of the bunch."

No one tried that day to disarm Sayers or the other Democrats who were present.

In the spring of 1874, Cranfill bought some much-craved books from the neighboring Scoby boys, and told the following tragic story about them.

The Scoby boys and their father had come from Massachusetts to Texas in the spring of 1873 after Mrs. Scobey died. Mr. Scobey felt a call from God to teach a Negro school and built a little two-room cabin near the Cranfill farm.

Gathered there each day, for free tuition, were a score or more of little black boys and girls, and no teacher ever worked more earnestly to impart knowledge to the young. Scobey had no friends except the blacks; a few white Christian men sympathized with his efforts to do good, but they scarcely dared to claim him as a friend.

By May 1874, he had been teaching at the little school about a year. State and county elections were to be held that November. Bastrop County had many black voters. A story spread that old man Scoby was doing all he could to carry Bastrop County for the "Radicals" with the Negro vote, despite the fact that he never left his little place.

A mob formed and started for Scoby's home on a moonless night in May. Before they decided to kill him, they became wild with liquor at a wayside saloon. In those days the Southern mob and Southern barroom were inseparable. There was never a sober mob. Spell "murder" backward and you have "red rum"!

From the saloon, the mob swept on. Hushed and silent, they drew near the little cottage gate. The old schoolteacher was fast asleep. The mob halloed, and the old man, thinking some belated cowboy had lost his way, sprang to the door and out into the yard, where, with a Christian welcome in his heart and on his lips, he was shot to death.

"Kind neighbors came next day and buried old man Scoby out in his little farm. His murderers were never known, and no effort was ever made to find them out. The two boys sold off the books and furniture, almost gave away the little farm, and left for parts unknown."

Cranfill's memory was a little faulty as to dates, but not to the basic facts of the killing; according to contemporary newspaper accounts, the murder took place in early February, and Scoby had evidently just announced himself as a Republican candidate for the state legislature. He had been arrested once for horse stealing but had finally been acquitted. He was about sixty years old at the time of his death.

Cranfill described the old South Texas way of celebrating Christmas.

On our way down to Alum Creek on Christmas Eve of 1875, we met several of our neighbor boys who were headed for Jeddo, where they gathered at Asa Bellamy's blacksmith shop and began to fire off anvils. In those days, the anvil-firing went on until late at night, and sounded like distant cannonading. Another way of making night hideous was to bore auger holes in the giant oak trees, fill these auger holes with powder, leave a fuse, and after igniting this fuse, to get out of the way and watch the powder blow the giant tree to atoms. Many of the beautiful oaks of which Bastrop County boasted were thus despoiled. In some places, it looked as though a tornado had passed through the land, or that lightning had shattered these lions of the forest.

Jeddo's closest claim to infamy was Christopher Columbus "Jud" Nite, born in 1869 in the sand hills near Jeddo. The Nite family soon moved to Gonzales County, where brother Jim Nite was born in 1871. Of eleven children, Jud and Jim became outlaws. We can't be sure of what crimes they committed because they were closemouthed and used aliases. They hired men to bring them supplies and horses while they were hiding.

Jud married Ida Quinney in 1890, becoming Bill Dalton's brother-in-law. Jim didn't marry, but being handsome, he had many women friends. At one point, he stole a Mormon's furniture and ran off with his wife.

The Nite brothers ended up in Oklahoma after robbing some banks in northeast Texas. In Ardmore, the law shot and killed Dalton, but the Nites escaped and went back to South Texas.

On August 6, 1896, Fayette County Constable Charley Null was riding to the precinct courthouse at Muldoon through a pasture when he was shot and killed, probably on his way to obtain a warrant for the arrest of Bunk Stagner, head of a local ranching family who apparently engaged in cattle rustling as a sideline. Bunk was immediately suspected of participating in the murder. Jim and Jud had been in the area at the same time and were also suspected of the murder. Stagner was ambushed and killed by a small group that included two of Null's sons just over a month later.

In January 1897, the Nites stole a herd of cattle in Kimble County and drove them to McCulloch County and sold them. On February 1, Kimble County sheriff Jones heard that the Nites were back in his county. He started after them with a posse and found them in Menard County at dusk on February 5. They waited until daybreak to attack. As they rode in, a small dog in camp started to bark, and Jud jumped up out of his bedroll and started shooting and running. Jim lay in bed and fired. Jud was fatally shot in the head; Jim was shot through both hips and had one leg broken and was shot in the arm. Jim Nite was taken to Junction for trial and was sentenced to seven years in the pen, under the alias John Underwood. His true identity was determined while he was in prison, and he was taken to Longview for trial for a bank robbery and got life. While in Tyler in February 1899 appealing the life sentence, he escaped from jail. He was recaptured near Carlsbad, New Mexico. Back in prison, he admitted that he and Jud had killed Charlie Null for $500, paid to them by a man he would not name, in the back room of a Smithville saloon. Jim was eventually pardoned and moved to Tulsa where he courted a widow with a fourteen-year-old boy who didn't like Jim. He got into a fight with the boy and the boy's friend, son of the local druggist. Jim and the druggist had a few subsequent words, but there was no trouble.

A couple of days later, Jim was walking past the drugstore, and the druggist asked Jim to come in and inspect a six-shooter that he had traded for. They walked in, the man got the gun out of the box, and he shot Jim in the heart. The druggist first said it was an accident, but later he said that he killed him because he was afraid of him.

The post office closed in 1927. The Jeddo school is gone. Even the two general stores serving ranchers through World War II have disappeared completely.

At Jeddo, FM 713 runs out and you must turn right on FM 1296.

HOPKINSVILLE

Gonzales County • About 2 miles from Jeddo

No trace of Hopkinsville remains today. Founded by D. S. Hopkins in the 1850s, Hopkinsville was a farming community that grew into a cattle town after the Civil War. Herds bound for Kansas via the Chisholm Trail gathered here. By the time J. B. Cranfill's family arrived at nearby Hallmark's Prairie, Hopkinsville boasted a post office, grist mill, saloon and school, and the Hopkinsville Academy, which the Cranfill boys attended for several years.

While the Cranfill boys were attending the academy, a traveling overland country circus came to Hopkinsville. Among the many engaging attractions was a man who had never had any arms. This man could load and shoot a pistol, could write with his toes, and could perform many other wonderful feats with his feet.

Settling feuds by killing was common but not Hollywood style, more like the following cowardly murder at the little Hopkinsville saloon. A stranger had come to Hopkinsville a few days before, was given a name, and secured work. He was up early that morning and went to the saloon for a drink. A man pursuing him rode into town, hitched his horse, inquired for the man, was told where he was by some unsuspecting citizen, and hastened over to the saloon, where he found the man he wanted. He at once opened fire on him without giving him a chance for his life and put five or six bullets in him. The man died instantly, and the murderer coolly mounted his horse and galloped away. No one ever learned the real name of the murdered man or of the murderer. Nothing serious was done to capture him.

When Hopkinsville was bypassed by the railroad, the townspeople moved to Waelder.

WAELDER

Gonzales County • 950 (approximate) • (830) • About 9 miles from Jeddo

Waelder sprang up with the arrival of the Galveston, Harrisburg, and San Antonio (GH&SA) railroad in 1874 and was named for Jacob Waelder, a German immigrant who came to San Antonio in 1852. Veteran of the Mexican War of 1848, newspaperman, and lawyer, Waelder served three terms in the Texas legislature before the Civil War and did a stint in the Confederate Army. After the war, Waelder labored extensively for the state's railroad interests. GH&SA officials named the town Waelder in honor of their hardworking company attorney.

Bolivar Ward arrived in Waelder on July 4, 1874, and gives us a vivid description of this new railroad terminus town:

As the clown in the circus proclaims, as he enters the arena, "Here we are." Waelder is to-day the terminal of the "Sun Set Route" viz., the Galveston, Harrisburg, and San Antonio Railroad. We leave Flatonia, the terminus of ten days ago, behind us, and proceed westward twelve miles and reach this place. Place, did we say? Yea, a place in the woods, the gin-mill, the gambling hell and pitfalls being predominant at the present writing. But few business homes are here, though the noise of the hammer, the saw cutting planks, the axe displacing trees—all tend to indicate that in a few days, Waelder will be a town of some importance. The scenery from this station is not to be seen to-day; too many trees displace the view.

All here is in the busy turmoil of life, each one is trying to gather in some of the filthy lucre that floats in this, as in all terminus of railroads. Seven miles of iron have been laid from here San Antonio-ward. In three weeks more Harwood will be reached: Waelder then sinks quietly to a station, and the glory of poor grub, no beds, rows, riots and rumpuses sink into the past.

Our intentions being good, we immediately upon our arrival last night rushed for a tent and supped good enough. Now how shall we make out for a bed, without having the canopy of heavy for an immediate, as it were, covering. The fertility of the brain is generally good. We fertilize our brain and bring into play a car, not a Pullman, though our mail route agent friend, Leonhard, pulled us over to sleep, perchance to dream.

A nice bed, at the expense of the government, was afforded me—two M. T. mail sacks. We lay our wearied limbs thereupon. A little window was observed at the foot of our couch. Plank short, limbs long, out of the window go our feet, for a foot, and truly, it was a feat to get those feet through.

We are acquainted with a superintendent of a railroad "out West"; he is lengthy, his feet are muchly. If he had had that bed that night, trees in close proximity to the track on which our car was anchored would have had to be cut down to enable him to rest in quietude. He is a *hardy* man, however, and would have put up with the inconvenience indulged in by your correspondent.

By May 1877, life in Waelder was fairly quiet, with the adoption of prohibition. The notable exception had occurred two months earlier, when the Reverend Frank Green, presiding elder of the African M. E. Church for this district, was fired on and wounded. The cause, like the identity of those who did the shooting, was not ascertained. But the value of a black man's life, even a man of the cloth, did not count for much more in Waelder than in any other part of Texas at the time. Waelder's population was only about a hundred, but the town's seven business houses were all doing a good business with area farmers.

By 1900, Waelder was Gonzales County's second largest town. Waelder still possesses a number of well-kept Victorian homes.

Turn right on FM 1115 when FM 1296 dead-ends. After five blocks on FM 1115, you come to US 90 and the main crossroads of Waelder. There are also some more nice Victorian houses on Avenue D (if you go straight beyond where FM 1296 turns east).

MILLER'S STORE

US 90, one block east of FM 1115

The old R. L. Miller store is identifiable by the historical medallion on the wall. First established in 1866, Miller's was until the 1980s your typical general store, selling everything from horseshoes to sardines to televisions to crockery. A hat and dress shop was located upstairs during Waelder's heyday. In those days, Miller gave every newborn boy a pair of pants with an attached card that stated that these pants were to be worn on the boy's first birthday, compliments of Miller's Store. Those were also the days when local boys would wait for the sack of liquor on the Saturday train from Flatonia. Then they would "relax" a bit with their bottles and shoot up whatever came to mind: the sky, the awning, each other, or anyone else foolish enough to come downtown on a Saturday night. Before it was removed several years ago, you could still see some of the bullet holes in Miller's awning.

ANNUAL EVENT

SEPTEMBER

FIESTA GUACAMOLE

City Park • www.cityofwaelder.org • Labor Day weekend, Saturday and Sunday • Free except dinner

Do chili cook-offs leave you cold? Then try the St. Patrick's Church Fiesta Guacamole, where you—yes, you—could become the world's champion guacamole masher. Besides Sunday's world championship guacamole mash-off, this Mexican-style celebration includes a carnival and midway, homemade Mexican food, a parade, and lots of hot dance music.

Take US 90 east out of Waelder.

The fading and peeling car lots and business establishments littering the road out of town testify to Waelder's prosperity through the pre-interstate era, when US 90 was the traveler's route from Houston to San Antonio. The interstate highway system has crippled or killed dozens of towns like Waelder, much as the railroads did to towns like Hopkinsville a hundred years ago. At the edge of town, turn right on FM 1680 to Moulton.

OLD MOULTON

Lavaca County • About 12 miles from Waelder

Soon you reach the venerable white frame church that is the surviving total of Old Moulton, the "Queen of the Prairies," so named for its blackland prairie soil that produced bumper crops. In 1834, the Winters family walked most of the way from Mississippi to East Texas, a two-month trip. In 1852, they settled here on the Lavaca River and named their settlement Moulton after their Mississippi hometown. So goes one story. Others say Moulton was named for an early settler. Still others say the name came from a traveler who said the area's live oak mottes reminded him of his hometown of Moulton in Alabama. At any rate, Moulton prospered as a farming community and supply stop on the Chisholm Trail. From 1874 to 1895, it was the home of the Moulton Male and Female Institute, which boasted one of the state's top music departments. The great hurricane of 1886 blew the academy and most of the town down. Locals started to rebuild, but the San Antonio and Aransas Pass (SA&AP) railroad came along in 1887, two miles east of Old Moulton, on its way from Yoakum to Waco. The exodus to the new town site alongside the tracks began that same year. The institute was rebuilt in Old Moulton and hung on there until 1895, when the founder's widow tired of the business and moved to San Antonio.

MOULTON

Lavaca County • 950 (approximate) • (361) • About 14 miles from Waelder

SAINT JOSEPH'S CATHOLIC CHURCH

Church at Pecan, off FM 1680

Saint Joseph's Church and cemetery greets you as you enter Moulton. Built in 1924, the church's interior has recently been restored to its original classic Gothic style with long, narrow nave, side aisles supported by ten columns, stained-glass windows, and chancel.

In a couple of blocks after you pass Saint Joseph's Catholic Church, you come to an intersection with FM 532. Turn left here to reach downtown Moulton, which runs alongside the railroad tracks. As you approach downtown, you can see that much of old "new" Moulton remains.

Even a fleeting perusal of the two commercial blocks of Main Street reveals that Moulton was once a prosperous, bustling town. All the buildings are built of brick or sandstone, in a rainbow of colors and styles. The collective, mostly continuous rooflines on each block take your eyes on a crazy, roller coaster ride.

Main Street parallels the tracks but is set back a ways up the hill, away from the smoke and dust and general hubbub that used to surround the depot. Between Main St. and the tracks are the rusting cotton gin and sprawling warehouse that were once bursting with bales.

OLD BOEHM STORE

Main at Moore

This sandstone building is one of Moulton's oldest business structures, built in 1906. Ed Boehm started a saloon and general store on this corner in 1887. Boehm was a recently arrived refugee from Moravia via Russia. Russia's governmental restrictions and popular ignorance had disgusted Boehm. A college graduate, he worked for fifty cents a day upon his arrival in the New World in order to establish a grubstake. Many of his hardworking and hungry Moravian friends joined him here during the next few decades.

The stone used to build the store was quarried a couple of miles west of Moulton at the old Maurin Quarry. New Moulton continued as "Queen of the Prairies" until tenant farmers and the one-crop (cotton) farming system began to fade from the scene. As cotton played out, Moulton became Texas' leading garlic production center for a few years preceding World War II.

WAGNER'S DEPARTMENT STORE

106 S. Main

Step in and step back in retail time here. Frank Wagner opened this store at the end of World War II, and the store's fixtures and inventory are a fascinating mélange of old and new: boat-sail cloth pants and shirts for the 1940s are stacked next to the latest boot-cut Levis and Wranglers. A peek in the display windows alone takes you back fifty years in time. And none of the old stuff is used, mind you. Frank's philosophy was: It'll sell sooner or later, even if it's fifty years later. Frank passed away a decade or so ago, but the store opens on weekends for your shopping enjoyment.

Frank Wagner remembered that the whole town reeked of garlic at harvest time as the trackside warehouses were filled with the pungent root. By 1939, Texas was second only to California in garlic production. But the garlic boom faded, as did the smell of garlic, and by the late 1960s, it was just a pungent memory.

MOULTON PUBLIC LIBRARY AND MUSEUM

102 S. Main • Open Monday through Friday

On display are early city and county photos and documents that document the town's German-Czech heritage. There are also rotating exhibits.

Moulton's most famous son is musician Adolph Hofner, born here in June 1916. When he was ten, the family moved to San Antonio. Of Czech-German heritage, Hofner first gained fame as the leader of a South Texas western swing band that rivaled Bob Wills in popularity, at least around San Antonio. He recorded his first songs in 1935. After World War II, he returned to his roots and began playing a unique, delightful blend of Czech and German polkas and waltzes, and western swing music. He's been called the Bing Crosby of Texas swing. Much of his work was recorded by Charlie Fitch's Sarg Records in Luling. The easiest way to get acquainted with Adolph's music is to pick up a copy of an Arhoolie/Folklyric CD titled *Texas-Czech Bohemian & Moravian Bands Historic Recordings, 1929–1959*. Among the songs he does is "The Shiner Song," which is a Texanization of the old Czech standard, "Farewell to Prague." The CD also features another band from just down the road in Shiner, the Joe Patek Orchestra.

PAVLA'S TAVERN

114 S. Main • Open daily • 596-4449 • No Cr.

Pavla's Tavern was built in 1922 and has changed little in appearance over the years. You'll enjoy the antique bar and cheap beer.

MAIN BAR

111 N. Main • Open daily • No Cr.

Now called Scooter's, the Main Bar was a great vintage place to stop for a cold one, open since 1925, with beautiful wire-frame bar stools, pressed-tin ceiling, linoleum domino tables, and cheap beer.

Moulton has dozens of late Victorian/pre–World War I homes still standing, mostly along W. First, W. Second, and Arnim streets, all of which run parallel to Main.

Up at the corner of North Street and W. Second, on the north end of Moulton, is the old Sam and Will Moore Institute, now part of the Moulton Public School System.

SAM AND WILL MOORE INSTITUTE

North St. at West 2nd

In December 1898, a group of leading citizens met and decided to try to re-establish the old Moulton Male and Female Institute that had ceased to exist a few years earlier, and if successful to call it the Samuel and William Moore Institute. They prepared a memorial and presented it to Will Moore, who was now living in Houston, and the different heirs of Sam Moore, asking for their cooperation in an effort to erect a suitable building to use as a college.

When this two-story brick Greek Revival-style school was built in 1901, it was the pride of the region. Will Moore and Sam Moore's survivors donated the land plus half of the cost of building the school. The remaining construction money was raised by the rest of the town. Dedication day was celebrated with a parade, concerts, speeches in Czech, German, and English, a big barbecue, and a ball.

KLOESEL'S STEAKHOUSE AND BAR

101 E. Moore • 596-7323 • Open daily, lunch and dinner

The Moore Hotel was located here from 1889 to 1940. In 1940 it became Ed's Market and Grocery, and in 1942 it was converted into a restaurant. There is also a full bar and dance floor.

To leave Moulton, return to FM 532 (Moore Street), cross the railroad tracks, and turn right on SH 95 toward Shiner.

PATEK'S MARKET

FM 532 at SH 95 • 596-7116 • Open daily • W

Patek's makes and sells some of the best sausages and smoked meats to be found anywhere: wieners, chicken sausage, pork sausage, pork and beef sausage, bacon, and summer sausage. Every Saturday they make and sell barbecue brisket, chicken, pork ribs, and pork steaks.

As you speed away from Moulton, toss your head back at Moulton's water tower, built in 1917 and brought to Moulton in 1935. Moulton has called it the second-tallest water tower in Texas; it's one of the tallest, at any rate.

HENKHAUS

Lavaca County • 60 • About 5 miles from Moulton

Henkhaus, which lies along the old SA&AP line and off the highway to the west a mile or so, is another one of those many faded Texas farm villages. It was named for its founder, a Mr. Henkhaus from Shiner. In its prime, Henkhaus boasted a store, a dance and beer hall, a cotton gin, and the Evergreen School.

SHINER

Lavaca County • 2,200 (approximate) • (361) • About 10 miles from Moulton

You are now in sight of Shiner, which had its genesis as the little hamlet of Half Moon (located a mile or so west of present-day Shiner), which grew up, some say, as early as during the Civil War days. One explanation for the name, Half Moon, came from the peculiar half-moon shape of the stand of timber surrounding a little trading post and community center. Of course in those days most of this area was treeless prairie, waist-high in sage and buffalo grass.

According to the group Historic Old Town Shiner, the first settlers arrived in 1884 and settled under a live oak knoll called Half Moon, after its earlier name as an Indian campsite.

We do know for sure that the Half Moon post office was established in 1885.

In 1887, the San Antonio and Aransas Pass (SA&AP, or SAP) railroad began laying track from Yoakum to Waco, and Henry B. Shiner donated 250 acres of choice land, including the right-of-way and grounds for the depot. Half of this land he retained by taking alternate lots and blocks.

The first train came through in August 1887. As was the case with so many other hamlets and villages bypassed by the railroad, Half Moon settlers moved to the new site. The new town was known for a time as New Half Moon, but on March 1, 1888, the new town officially became known as Shiner, after its benefactor.

Henry's father, Peter Shiner, came to this country from Prussia and settled in New Orleans, where he met and married Miss Emma Hemmes. In 1846, they removed to Victoria, Texas, where Henry B. Shiner was born in February 1848. In 1860, Mr. Shiner moved with his family to San Antonio, where he continued to reside until his death, which occurred in 1882. Henry B. Shiner at eighteen was sent to Soule's commercial college at New Orleans. On the completion of the course there in 1867, he returned to Texas and engaged in cattle raising in Lavaca County. In 1870, he drove his first herd north to Abilene, Kansas. In 1876, Mr. Shiner bought the J. H. Harris home of one thousand acres on Rocky Creek. Here he remained with his family and continued to buy land, which he had enclosed and used for pastures. After acquiring some eight thousand acres, he embarked in the cattle business on an extensive scale. In 1882, cattle reached the highest price ever known in this country and sold for from eighteen to twenty-five dollars a head, and cattle raisers reached the zenith of their prosperity. Mr. Shiner now commenced selling his Lavaca County land in small tracts, at seven to eight dollars an acre, to German and Slavic immigrants, and reinvesting in McMullen County, where he established a ranch of forty thousand acres of splendid pastureland.

Knowing several years in advance of the railroad's plans to build a road through the region, Shiner saw the chance to make a bundle off his Lavaca County landholdings by settling the waves of German and Slavic immigrants entering Texas on his lands. But he needed the railroads to make his promotion work; the farmers would need cheap, fast transportation for their crops. He made a deal to split his profits with the SA&AP railway.

Mr. Shiner held on to about five hundred acres of land in the immediate vicinity of Shiner, which was divided up into small farms. In 1893, Shiner told the *Galveston Daily News*: "The Germans and Bohemians who have settled up this country have made it blossom as the rose. They are the best farmers in the state and you need about 1000 more of them here."

The area saw its share of lawlessness and tragedy in those turbulent early days.

In the 1890s, it is told, a young drifter, barely nineteen, murdered a local wealthy landowner for his money. A vigilante posse was organized, and after thirty hours they tracked the boy into a rough area just east of present-day Shiner, called "the Boundary." The boy and his horse were exhausted, out of water, and out of food. When he looked behind him, he could see his pursuers and the glint of the setting sun on their gun barrels. The posse drew nearer, and finally at the top of a hill, the boy's horse dropped dead. The young killer disentangled himself and stood calmly but defiantly, rifle in hand, facing his pursuers. The posse halted just out of his range to consult among themselves and then started slowly toward the young man, uncertain of what he meant to do. The group halted just within shooting range, and their leader, a brutish man and experienced killer, shouted, "Do you want to give up?"

"No, I don't—shoot if you want to. I want to die like a man and will shoot the first man who comes a foot nearer," was the boy's defiant response, as he braced himself for the inevitable.

The leader stepped forward, rifle cocked, and shouted, "Surrender or I'll shoot the hell out of you." He swung his rifle to shooting position as he spoke, his men and the boy following suit. Their shots rang out as one, and the posse captain fell forward, shot dead through the heart. The vigilantes stood silent for a moment and then started to move, some toward their leader, and others toward the boy, who lay "gasping, his chest torn by the rifle fire, trying desperately to raise himself from where he had fallen. His life ebbed away as his life blood poured upon the ground and with it he paid his penalty under the law."

The survivors buried their captain and the boy in a common grave, "a few yards from the creek and near a clump of live oaks" and then galloped away into the night.

Of course, such occurrences were not uncommon here in the "Free State of Lavaca," so named because of Lavaca County's habitual lack of respect for whoever held the reins of government at the time. In 1835, the Lavacans resisted the Mexican government. In 1860, the county voted almost unanimously for secession; four years later, it was denouncing Jeff Davis and his war. In the 1880s, Lavacans fought barbed wire, railroads, and land monopolists. From 1910 to 1916, the county was a hotbed of socialism, and in 1920, county voters bolted the Democratic Party gubernatorial ticket in favor of impeached governor "Gentleman Jim" Ferguson. Throughout Prohibition, Lavaca County vehemently resisted its enforcement. Lavaca County's Germans and Czechs loved their beer, as evidenced by this chestnut of a joke:

A local option election had been held in a predominantly German Lavaca County precinct, and the election judge was counting out the votes. "Vet, vet, vet, vet . . . ," he droned. Then suddenly frowning, he said, "Dr-r-ry." He continued, "Vet, vet, vet, vet, vet . . . " until his eyebrows bristled and he exclaimed, "The son-of-a-gun—he voted twice!"

But back to Shiner.

The town soon began to prosper, in spite of the fires that raged across the prairies and through Shiner during those early years.

Early one morning in November 1894, the town was startled by a tremendous explosion, which proved to be another safe robbery. Mr. F. Wilks was the first one on the street. He called on some of his neighbors for assistance. Arming themselves, they proceeded toward A. G. Wangemann's store to investigate. While turning a street corner, Mr. J. C. Blohm was confronted by three men with drawn pistols, who opened fire on him but did not hit him. Mr. Blohm returned the fire but did not know whether he struck one of the robbers or not, as they ran off. Upon entering Wangemann's store, Mr. Blohm found the safe cracked and the whole inside a seething mass of flames. The robbers, after opening the safe, had set the store on fire to obliterate their deed, and the whole block burned. Mr. Wangemann lost all his books, accounts, and notes, which were burned in the safe. R. Wolters lost five buildings, an entire loss, with no insurance. George Segeller's Saloon, the Elite restaurant, the *Shiner Gazette*, and a saddle shop were also destroyed; most of these establishments were uninsured.

The robbers only obtained about one hundred dollars, as the burglar-proof chest in the safe was not disturbed. There was no clue as to who the robbers were, as there were no suspicious characters about town the day before the explosion. Shiner rebuilt again.

In the true stubborn tradition of the Free State of Lavaca, Shiner had two schools in those days, both named the Shiner School. This caused considerable confusion, since the schools were in the same school district. One dated back to the Half Moon days of 1884; the other came with the new town. Neither school would change its name. Shiner No. 1 and Shiner No. 2 was the best compromise they could strike, until the day No. 1 caught fire and Fred Bunjes was the big hero in saving the school. Shiner School No. 1 was officially called the Bunjes School from that day on, but to most of the natives it was still Shiner No. 1.

As you enter Shiner, you see on your left the Kaspar Wire Works. Shiner was a cotton town from the word go, but in 1898, farmer August Kaspar began a factory that endures to this day and is still family owned and run. In 1895, Kaspar figured out a way to recycle all the smooth wire discarded by local ranchers and farmers, in favor of the more effective barbed wire, into something useful and cheap. Using a pair of pliers, he hand wove the smooth wire into corn shuck baskets and horse muzzles for personal use. When neighbors saw them, they wanted some, and soon Shiner's leading stores were selling his products. By 1905, it was a full-time job, and so Kaspar moved into the town of Shiner.

With the decline in demand for baskets and muzzles, the wire works began to make florist easels, coat hangers, gym baskets, shopping baskets, shelving, display racks, and newspaper vending machines and racks. Kaspar Wire Works went on to become the largest producer and renovator of newspaper racks in the world. Their newspaper racks can seen be seen in towns and cities across Texas, and their lockers and gym baskets still serve in hundreds of schools. Today the product line includes thousands of wire, sheet metal, stainless steel, and tubing products, such as racks, displays, medical fixtures, computer frames and stands, food handling utensils, and even the quaint, old-style benches for sale at the Spoetzl Brewery gift shop across the highway.

Shiner is still very much a Czech-German community. As late as 1963, in the local phone book, names like Busch, Cervenka, Janak, and Goetz predominated. There was but one Smith and no Jones in the directory; one Sanchez but no Garcia. You don't hear Czech or German spoken on the streets anymore, but what's left of the older generation still speaks it at home and in the still popular "old-time" music.

The churches still hold the soul of Shiner and dominate the Shiner skyline, along with the Spoetzl Brewery. Many local youth attend the local Catholic twelve-year male and female academies. There are no real mansions in Shiner, but there are few bug tussle shacks either, which befits a town that calls itself the "Cleanest Little City in Texas."

San Francisco, Kansas City, New York City, Los Angeles, Dallas, Houston, and even Detroit—all have their iconic songs, songs that define the city. Not many small towns in Texas can make the same claim, Luckenbach being perhaps the best known and Dumas ("Ding Dong Daddy from Dumas") the least known. But Shiner has its own anthem, "The Shiner Song," popularized by the late, great Joe Patek Orchestra of Shiner.

> When we left Shiner, the sun was shining.
> When we left Shiner, the sun was shining.
> There was plenty of beer and lots of food.
> There was plenty of beer and lots of food.
> When we left Shiner, the sun was shining.
>
> When we left the brewery, the barrels were empty.
> When we left the brewery, the barrels were empty.
> And we were drinking and having a good time.
> And we were drinking and having a good time.
> When we left the brewery, the barrels were empty.
>
> When we left Prague, the sun was shining.
> When we left Prague, the sun was shining.
> There was plenty of beer and lots of food.
> There was plenty of beer and lots of food.
> When we left Prague, the sun was shining.

Right across SH 95 from the Kaspar Wire Works is the Spoetzl Brewery.

SPOETZL BREWERY

603 John Hybner Way • 594-3383 • www.shiner.com • W variable

The brewery referred to in "The Shiner Song" began business in June 1909 when a group of prominent local businessmen organized the Shiner Brewing Association, capitalized to the tune of $6,000. J. H. Huebner was among the first directors, and Herman Weiss, of Galveston, was the first brewmaster. The group had bored an artesian well that yielded water just fifty-five feet from the surface, providing the water that the brewery still uses. In 1913, the association built a new and commodious beer and ice vault.

In 1914, the association leased the operation to Kosmos Spoetzl and Oswald Petzold of San Antonio, with an option to buy in 1915. They first named their business the Home Brewing Company, renaming it Petzold and Spoetzl when they exercised their option to buy in 1915. When Spoetzl bought out Petzold in 1918, he changed the name to the Spoetzl Brewery.

Born in Bavaria in 1873, Spoetzl worked his way through the Augsburg Brewery School and then worked at several breweries in Munich and in Bohemia to gain additional knowledge and experience. Spoetzl spent five years in Cairo, Egypt (where he brewed Pyramid beer), but decided he didn't like the climate, so he moved to Canada. On his way to Saskatchewan, he caught pneumonia. At that point, he decided that Texas looked better and headed for the United States, ending up in San Antonio. That was in 1914. In San Antonio, he read a newspaper ad placed by a little community brewery in Shiner, searching for someone to rent the facility. The local owners were better at drinking beer than brewing it. Spoetzl leapt at the chance and moved to Shiner, where he put all the knowledge and experience at his command into his beer. Soon he bought the brewery outright.

Kosmos Spoetzl had a simple marketing philosophy: A good beer will sell itself. So he set out to brew the very best beer he could. That done, he had to make sure that people drank it. Spoetzl knew that once a man had tasted his Shiner beer, he would buy it. So he bought a Model T, and with a couple of kegs iced down in the back, Spoetzl and his dog bumped across the rolling, fertile prairies that surround Shiner, roping in thirsty farmers and travelers and then plying the adults with ice-cold beer and the kids with silver coins.

Spoetzl produced just one beer, officially called "Old World Bavarian Draft," which was a heavy, dark, all-malt German lager that spoke eloquently to his mostly Czech and German audience. The Volstead Act of 1918 put many breweries out of business, but Spoetzl hung on, selling ice, brewing near beer, and storing deer carcasses. But stories abound as to the not-so-near beer that escaped from here. Joe Greene, now deceased, was the brewery's unofficial historian and Methuselah, having first started work here in 1930. He worked here over fifty years. Average employee tenure here is twenty-five years; they evidently like what they do for a living.

But back to the near beer; Joe Greene had this to say, for the record: "We just made the beer like we always had, then reboiled it to get the alcohol out and please the Federal men." The reboiling process regularly engulfed the rest of town with its distinctive sour mash stink. The Spoetzl Brewery trucks started rolling again the very minute that Prohibition ended in Texas (one minute past midnight on September 15, 1933), carrying "Shiner Beer—Full Strength, Fully Aged," to towns like Praha, Muldoon, Dime Box, Nickel Community, and the Sandies, and on to San Antonio. Spoetzl, as a rule, never went much more than seventy miles out of his way in any direction for business, although he did have a distributor as far west as Kerrville beginning in 1935, when he donated the beer for the festivities marking the inauguration of officers of the two local American Legion posts. Kosmos was a regular visitor to Kerrville, probably, like so many others, for his health.

The end of Prohibition also brought an increase in production, and the brewery now employed between thirty-five and forty people during the winter, adding on a few more people during the thirstier summer months. Spoetzl also changed the name (but not the recipe) of his beer to "Texas Special Export" and began bottling it for the first time in the familiar "export" bottle (neophytes call it a longneck).

Slowly but surely, the brewery grew over the years. Business improved so much with the end of Prohibition that by the end of May 1935, extensive additions to the brewing plant had been completed, which doubled production capacity.

Spoetzl's home was across the street from the brewery, and having a fondness for animals, he kept deer, goats, sheep, dogs, peacocks, ducks, geese, pigeons, guinea pigs, and cows on his place.

The brick Spanish Revival brew house and office building were built in 1947. Kosmos died in 1950, and his daughter Cecilie—"Miss Celie"—inherited the brewery and was for a time the only female brewery owner in the country. She named her son-in-law, H. C. Leach—a Canadian fighter pilot and war hero—as brewery manager. She didn't exactly rock the boat with radical changes. Shiner did not appear in no-return bottles until 1958, and wasn't canned until 1970, four years after Miss Celie sold the brewery to a group of New Braunfels businessmen. But she continued to live across the street from the brewery in a pink brick house that has since been moved elsewhere.

Kosmos' conservative influence was such that after fifty years, the recipe of Texas Special Export remained unchanged. He had been fiercely, colorfully, idiosyncratically protective of his beer. "Water's for washing your feet," he had long ordained. "If you want to drink, drink Shiner beer." Whenever he caught someone salting his beer, he would snatch the salt shaker away and say thunderingly, "If my beer needed salt, I would have put salt in it."

But times and tastes were changing toward lighter beer, and the new owners began experimenting with the recipe until they came up with Shiner "Premium" beer. They also upped the brewery's capacity to seventy-two thousand barrels per year. But despite the change in recipe and brewing capacity, Shiner remained every bit as much a handmade and naturally brewed beer as it was in 1915. It's still brewed with artesian water from the original well drilled for the brewery.

Shiner Premium has given way to Shiner Blonde, and the brewery's bread-and-butter brand is now Shiner Bock. Bock is traditionally an early spring beer, and brewery records indicate that bock was brewed here as early as 1917. Its popularity (and year-round production) owes to the old Austin hippie scene. Shiner Premium became a popular beer for members of the Austin counterculture during the early 1970s, for a variety of reasons (including the low price). But when a seasonal shipment of Shiner Bock rode into town in about 1975, it was love at first quaff. By 1978, Spoetzl was brewing Bock the year round, chiefly to slake the Austin market's prodigious thirst. Beer bars in traditional Shiner territory (remember Kosmos' seventy-mile radius rule) almost exclusively stocked Shiner Premium; Bock was an Austin thing.

So much has changed since then; microbreweries have sprung up like yeast all over Texas and the rest of the country. Shiner is no longer the only "Little Brewery" in Texas, although it's still far from being a giant. While major brewers can produce up to 3.5 million cases per day, Shiner produces about 750,000 cases per year. Shiner is no longer just a Central Texas phenomenon; you can buy it all over Texas and in a number of major American cities now. And now there's a host of Shiner boutique beers, including Shiner 101, which is probably the closest in taste to Kosmos' original, stout brew.

But the old saying still applies, mostly: "Our Beer Goes through Thousands of Quality Czechs Each Day."

Brewery tours are given Monday through Friday. The hospitality and gift room is open Monday through Friday and features the original copper brew kettle on display.

From the Spoetzl Brewery, continue south on SH 95 to downtown Shiner. As you approach the junction with US 90A, you see old downtown Shiner on your right.

As in Moulton, most of Shiner's old business houses line the railroad tracks for several blocks. The elaborate brickwork on these buildings testifies to Shiner's turn-of-the-century prosperity.

Turn right on US 90A, cross the tracks, and turn right on Seventh Street.

WILLIAM GREEN BUILDING

103 N. 7th

The William Green building, built in 1911 by prominent local businessman William Green, is one of downtown Shiner's most impressive buildings. Inside is a towering, mirrored bar back. It currently houses Shiner Restaurant and Bar, 594-2898, www.shinerrestaurant.com.

SHINER OPERA HOUSE

7th at Ave. D • Check www.shinertx.org for calendar

Back in the Gay Nineties, a town wasn't fully civilized unless it had an opera house. Shiner's opera house was built in 1895 by William Wendtland and Louis Wagener. The opera house was upstairs, with the Opera House Saloon downstairs. The saloon was succeeded by a variety of other businesses over the years, but the opera house has remained in use. A community dinner theater group now performs upstairs several times a year.

Shiner calls itself the "cleanest little city in Texas," and if you drive around a bit through the residential environs, you'll probably agree. Many of the immaculate homes date back to the town's founding.

SAINTS CYRIL AND METHODIUS CATHOLIC CHURCH

312 S. Ludmila, just off US 90A and just east of the US 90A/SH 95 intersection • Open for services • W

This red-brick Romanesque Revival-style church, dedicated in 1921, towers cathedral-like over Shiner. The lovely stained-glass windows were imported from Bavaria. You'll also enjoy the towering altar and statuary. The dome-ceiling murals of Jesus alone in prayer are the crowning touch.

PATEK'S GROCERY AND MARKET

224 S. Ave. E • US 90A, next to Saints Cyril and Methodius Catholic Church • 594-3171 • www.shinersmokehouse.com • W

Patek's makes an interesting variety of link sausages and smoked meats on the premises, including green onion pork sausage, low-salt sausage, Polish- and Italian-style sausage, all-pork and all-beef sausage, red hot links, beef wieners and bologna, and beef jerky. Homemade breads, egg noodles, and kolache fillings, including poppy seed, are also sold. You can even buy tapes and CDs of many of the region's Czech bands, including the Patek Orchestra, one of Texas' most famous Czech bands.

The Patek Orchestra dates to John Patek's arrival in Shiner in 1895. This family orchestra recorded for Decca during the 1930s, then switched to Martin Records in San Antonio. A versatile group, they even played Mexican polkas. The band's demise thirty years ago was a blow to music lovers; its performance at the annual Shiner Catholic Church picnic was a popular tradition for dancers and listeners alike.

MUSEUMS

EDB MUSEUM

800 block of US 90A • 594-4180 • www.shinertx.org • Open Tuesday, Thursday, and Saturday • W variable

This museum is centered around the 1895 Louis Ehlers cigar factory and the 1853 Green family house. The cigar factory produced several different types of stogies, including the Becky Brown, Katy Lee, and Good Company. Five union men rolled them and were paid a penny for each cigar they rolled. One of Shiner's early, prominent businessmen, William Green Jr., was born in the rustic, dogtrot house, which was originally located in the nearby Winnton community. He ran a post office and general store here for eight years.

EDWIN WOLTERS MEMORIAL MUSEUM

306 S. Ave. I • 594-4180 • www.shinertx.org • Call for hours or visit website • Donations accepted

The museum's collections reflect the ethnic diversity of Shiner's history as well as the area's natural history, including an antique gun collection and old-time country store.

HISTORIC OLD TOWN SHINER

594-3999 • www.shiner-oldtown.org

This organization exists to preserve the heritage of Shiner. Of chief interest to tourists is its annual Shiner Historic Homes Tour in November.

LODGING

THE OLD KASPER HOUSE

219 Ave. C • 594-4336 • www.oldkasperhouse.com • Cr.

This bed-and-breakfast inn is situated in a restored Victorian home, two blocks east of SH 95, between the Kaspar Wire Works and the SH 95/US 90A intersection. They have eight units, private baths, and a full breakfast.

ANNUAL EVENTS

APRIL

TRADE DAY

Downtown • 594-4180 • www.shinertx.org • Third Saturday in March • Free • W

Antique show and dealers, arts, crafts, food, livestock, and almost anything else sellable or tradable that's legal can be found here. Dozens upon dozens of dealers set up for business, encouraged by low booth prices. Consequently, Shiner Trade Days are better attended and more interesting than those of other towns.

JULY

HALF MOON HOLIDAYS

Green-Dickson Park • 594-4180 • www.shinertx.org • Friday and Saturday nearest July 4 • Admission fee to dances • W

The people of Shiner have been celebrating the Glorious Fourth since at least 1892, when the *Shiner Courier* reported that "the saloon men of Shiner will have charge of the bar at the 4th of July picnic and the proceeds will go in a benefit to the Catholic church."

Today, street dancing and beauty pageants happen at night; footraces, tugs-of-war, outhouse races, and such take up the day.

SEPTEMBER

SHINER CATHOLIC CHURCH PICNIC

American Legion Park, 102 S. Ave. G • 594-3836 • www.sscmshiner.org • Sunday before Labor Day • Admission fee to dances, dinner

Every rural Catholic church in Texas has some kind of festival or picnic, and this is one of the oldest and biggest. It dates back to 1897. Up to ten thousand locals and visitors attend the affair, dancing to the polka music of such favorites as the Shiner Hobo Band. Dancing—polka and country—runs from noon till midnight, and revelers can take a break at the various games, the bazaar, the auction, or horseshoe pitching. Dinner is the other big attraction, with Shiner Picnic Stew, sausage, fried chicken, and all the trimmings. Mass is conducted early that day to leave plenty of time for fun. A similar picnic is held on the Sunday of Memorial Day weekend in May.

Prior to the establishment of the big September church picnic, Shiner held a Volksfest celebration a little later in the month of September, with political speeches in the day and swinging with the fair ladies of Shiner in the mazy waltz on the big wooden dance platform in the evening.

From Shiner, continue west on US 90A toward Gonzales.

As we leave Shiner, we would do well to remember that times have not always been happy and gay here, but we should also remember that no matter how dark the times may have been, someone has always managed to scratch out some humor in the face of even the worst of tragedies. To wit, in this vicinity just after the Civil War—so the story goes—a man named Martin was passing through, bound for Brownsville from Fayette County with a load of cotton. He had a man with him to help drive the team of horses. At nightfall, the pair camped on a nearby creek. During the night, the hired hand split Martin's head open with an axe as Martin slept. The murderer then skedaddled with Martin's money. The grisly scene was discovered the next morning, a posse was organized, and the killer (or a reasonable facsimile thereof) was apprehended and taken back to the scene of the crime. There by the creek, the hired hand was dispatched to his fate from the high branch of a stout tree. As was the custom of the time, the corpse was left hanging as a warning to others. Later that day, one of the posse members mentioned to an ex-slave that the lynched man had been left wearing a fine felt hat, with a four-bit piece still in his pants pocket. Times being what they were, the freedman headed at dusk for the hanging tree, only to find his victim hanging out of reach. He found a chunk of wood nearby, which when stood upon enabled him on tippytoe to reach the dead man's pocket. Feeling the coin deep in the pocket, he made one final stretch to grasp the coin and in doing so knocked the block of wood over. There he hung by his one hand, which was buried in his dead compatriot's pocket. Try as he might, he could not extricate his hand, and so he dangled there for the rest of the night. His cries for help attracted passersby the next morning who released him. As he fell to the ground and the four-bit piece rolled free, the man vowed never to steal anything again. The tree is said to have withered away and died, as is supposedly traditional with hanging trees.

A little more than nine miles from downtown Shiner, just before you cross Peach Creek, you'll see a historical marker and a gravel road (County Road 361) running to your right, which takes you to the Sam Houston Oak and the historic Braches home, located a few hundred feet north of the highway.

SAM HOUSTON OAK/BRACHES HOME

General Sam Houston and his little army rested under the spreading branches of this huge, ancient live oak a week after the Alamo fell in March

1836. It was the first rest stop of the Runaway Scrape. The Texians had just burned Gonzales, and the flames could be seen from Houston's camp here.

The two-story plantation house you see was built in the 1840s or 1850s. It replaced a log house built in 1831 by Judge Bartlett D. McClure and wife Sarah Ann McClure. Its size and full, two-story Greek Revival gallery was quite rare for the era and bespoke the Braches' wealth during those hardscrabble times, when many Texans were living in cabins or tents. The big house became a stopping place for stagecoaches, wagon trains, and mail carriers. After Judge McClure's death in 1842, Sarah Ann married Charles Braches, a representative in the Republic of Texas congress. Braches had conducted a literary and music school in Mississippi before coming to Texas. Soon after his arrival here, he became an influential citizen and leader. The plantation house became a cultural center for this section of the state. Because of vandalism, the house has been closed to the public.

The noted travel writer Frederick Law Olmsted passed through here on a trip to Indianola on the coast in 1854 and described the sorry state of this, one of the state's major roads (the same one traveled by German immigrants to New Braunfels and Fredericksburg only a few years before), round about the Peach Creek crossing:

We passed cotton fields again, and wagons loaded with cotton. One carrying eight bales, drawn by ten very lean oxen, was from San Marcos, bound to the coast. The teamster, who was on horseback, told us his best day's work was ten miles. Across the wet hog-wallow prairie of the latter part of the day, the road was very heavy. In the creek, near which we made our camp, was a cotton team stalled, and it was late at night before the whipping and swearing came to an end. While we were at breakfast in the morning, the teamster drove by his cattle, which had strayed away in the night for better pasture, and stopped to ask our assistance. He had cut trees for fulcrum and lever, and thought with our help be should be able to get out. We worked for an hour under his guidance, covering ourselves with mire, but effecting nothing. A man appeared on horseback, who added his forces. After perceiving that our combined efforts would not suffice to raise the wheel, he said, "Stranger, I'll give you my advice. I'm sick, and not able to help you much. I'm going now to see a doctor. But your wagon isn't very badly stalled, sir. The mire is not deep here. That wheel is on the gravel now. I'll tell you what's the matter; your cattle are too weak. Now you take them all out, and give them a feed, and turn them out to graze till another team comes up, and they'll have to help you, because there isn't room to get by. And I'll tell you what I'll do. I'll call at the overseer's (of roads), and tell him you sent for him to help you. He's got plenty of teams and hands, and if he don't come, you return him (to the County Court), because he's no business to leave a place like this in the road." With that he mounted, and rode on. We did the same, the teamster offering us no thanks, but shouting after us, "What'll you take for that mule?"

We saw again along the road to-day many dead cattle. The herds were miserably poor in flesh. Most of the carcasses were of working oxen, usually from the carts of Mexicans, who give their teams no corn, depending entirely upon the pasturage.

Toward night, we entered on the great level prairies of the coast. Here we met a gang of negroes, three men, two women, and two boys, under guard of a white man and a very large yellow mastiff. The negroes had each some article to carry, one an axe, another a rifle, another a kettle, a fourth led a horse, to whose saddle were fastened a ham, a coffee-pot, and a buffalo robe. This last, undoubtedly, would be the white man's covering at night, the negroes having no extra clothing.

They were evidently slaves consigned to some planter in the interior, probably by his factor in New Orleans, as part of the proceeds of his crop.

They were much fagged, and sullen with their day's walk. The prospect before them was a boundless flat prairie, with a cold north wind, and rain threatening. They were evidently intending to camp upon the open prairie, as for eight miles we had passed no house. Before midnight, a severe rain-storm did, in fact, commence.

Drawing closer to Gonzales, about twelve miles out of Shiner, you pass by the turnoff to the old Maurin Quarry, which supplied sandstone for buildings in Shiner, Moulton, Gonzales, Flatonia, and surrounding communities. It operated from 1883 to 1908 and was established by Firmin Maurin from Marseilles, France.

Just after the junction of US 90A with FM 532, take Spur 146 into Gonzales. Spur 146 becomes St. Louis Street within the city limits. St. Louis takes you to the Gonzales County courthouse. The 1913 iron-truss bridge in the park on your right as you come into town originally crossed the San Marcos River west of town in the Oak Forest community before being relocated here for a pedestrian and bike trail.

GONZALES

Gonzales County Seat • 7,200 (approximately) • (830) • About 18 miles from Shiner

Gonzales proudly calls itself the Lexington of Texas, where on October 2, 1835, defiant Texian irregulars battled Mexican troops sent to take possession of a small brass cannon. The gun had been sent to the settlement four years earlier as protection against Indian attacks. Mexican authorities feared that the colonists might use the cannon against them. The Texians buried the cannon in a peach orchard. But then they disinterred the piece, mounted it on oxcart wheels, and filled its barrel with pieces of chain and scrap iron. On October 2, the Texians crossed the Guadalupe River to confront the Mexican force, which had halted on the west bank of the river. Flying a crude flag with a picture of the cannon and the words "Come and Take It" emblazoned thereon, the Texians attacked, killing one Mexican soldier. Both sides realized that war was now inevitable and retired to their respective home bases. The Texians stepped back to Gonzales and began to prepare for their siege and capture of San Antonio de Bexar.

Gonzales started life in 1825 as capital of Green C. DeWitt's colony of Anglo-American settlers, named for Rafael Gonzales, a native of San Fernando de Bexar and governor of the state of Coahuila y Texas. Gonzales was abandoned in the summer of 1826 after an Indian attack. On July 4 of that year, most of Gonzales' citizens had gone up to Burnham's Crossing on the Colorado River for a big celebration. While they were gone, the Indians attacked. They killed one man who had stayed behind and then plundered and burned the village. Upon their return, the survivors promptly fled back to Burnham's Crossing and other more established settlements. New settlers began rebuilding the village in 1827.

In his book *A Trip to Texas in 1828*, José María Sánchez described his visit to Gonzales in April of that year:

We made haste the following day, and a little after six we started on our way. At about one or two o'clock we reached the Guadalupe River and crossed on a ferry boat, while the carriage and the wagons forded the stream. The road lies along rolling country covered with woods, and the meadows we met from time to time present to the eye of the imaginative traveler all the beauty of wild nature. When one sees the herds of deer fleeing, inhales the perfume of numerous flowers, and listens to the singing of the birds, the soul seems to revel in an unknown joy; and those who have a romantic heart seem to be transported to an enchanted country, or to be living in the illusory Arcadia. The heavy woods that form the banks of the Guadalupe whose pale blue waters run silently to the Gulf of Mexico are seen on entering the vast plain covered with grass and flowers. How this calm contrasted with the passions that surged in my wretched heart! On the eastern bank of this river are built six wooden cabins inhabited by three North American men, two women and two girls of the same nationality, and a Mexican, all of whom form the village of Gonzalez [*sic*]. On seeing the tranquility which these peaceful inhabitants enjoy in contrast to the passions that wreck our souls in the populous cities, an involuntary sigh escaped my breast just as one of the girls, who was barely more than ten years old, and whose beauty made her attractive, came out to offer me a seat with that charming grace that only innocence can lend. Her kindness, so rare among those of her nationality, the sight of her roselike face and her bare little feet, and the recollection of human misery which at this moment crowded my mind, moved me strangely, as I thought that perhaps some day a daring hand would pluck rudely this flower of the desert, and then tears would come to wither the face where now joy and smiles dwell. These thoughts permitted me only to thank her and I returned to our camp to wait for slumber to come and deaden the bitter thoughts of the afternoon.

In 1832, Gonzales was officially laid out as a town, in the Spanish style, with a central cluster of five public squares in the form of a cross, and an elaborate gridiron of streets and lots.

Gonzales was the only town to answer William B. Travis' pleas for reinforcements at the besieged Alamo; it sent thirty-two men to martyrdom. On March 11, 1836, Sam Houston arrived to take command of the Texian Army volunteers here. Then the bad news from the Alamo and Goliad reached Gonzales. So, on March 12, the Texian Army burned Gonzales to the ground and retreated east. This was the beginning of the Runaway Scrape. After the Texian victory at San Jacinto, Gonzalans returned, and the town became the county seat of newly formed Gonzales County in 1837.

In June 1837, when a "Citizen of Ohio" passed through Gonzales on his way to San Antonio, he found a settlement still in ruins after the Runaway Scrape. Many of Gonzales' inhabitants had not yet returned, but the Citizen from Ohio did run into one memorable character whom he described in an Ohio monthly called the *Hesperian*:

During the day, we were pressed by a person of singular and marked character who at the age of seventy retained all the boyish feelings of youth to go with him to see a specimen of growing corn. The old man had banished himself from a comfortable home on the banks of the Mississippi to wander upon the outskirts of Texas, from motives of personal security. From long-established habit, it would be impossible for him to express a sentence upon any subject, no matter how free from all excitement, without uttering as many oaths as there were necessary and unintelligible words. Each sentence was prefaced by a singularly connected string of profanity which compelled the listener to wait a considerable time before he could form any idea what was to follow. He informed me that he had not slept in a house for a number of years and when asked the reason replied by saying that he could not do so without 'catching a cold.'

When Robert Williamson was a circuit court judge for the Republic of Texas, Gonzales County was part of his circuit. Court met under a spreading live oak tree, and the bar of justice was a rough-sawn plank laid across a couple of whiskey kegs. The judge sat on a nail keg. Williamson sat down and leaned his rifle and walking stick against the oak tree. He laid out his law book and gavel on the plank and pronounced court in session. The spectators got rowdy and the more and louder the judge called for order in the court, the rowdier they got. But Willie wasn't intimidated. He reached for his long rifle, laid it on the table, cocked the hammer and put his finger to the trigger. There was suddenly a deafening silence.

"This court is coming to order," Willie pronounced, "and if it doesn't come to order right now I am going to by God kill somebody and I'm not particular who I kill."

Court quickly came to order and did so every session thereafter, especially when Williamson presided.

Z. N. Morrell, a Baptist preacher who fought the Comanches at Plum Creek near present-day Lockhart in 1840, was living on the Guadalupe River in 1841, preaching in area communities. One night he was preaching at a schoolhouse four miles above Gonzales. Several men stood guard at the doorway, and others at the rear sat with their guns across their knees.

"I preached with unusual liberty; the attention was undivided; many earnest prayers were offered for our protection in the midst of difficulties and dangers, and some praised God aloud."

Morrell dismissed the congregation, and before they had begun to depart for home they heard a gun fired a few hundred yards distant, followed by the "shrill Indian whistle." Morrell warned the faithful to proceed with caution to their homes. Since the way home for everyone was the same for some distance, Morrell's oxcart, carrying his and two other families, took the lead. They began to sing a hymn to chase away the gloom: "On Jordan's stormy banks I stand, and cast a wishful eye to Canaan's fair and happy land, where my possessions lie."

It was a lovely moonlit night, and the group rolled along, confident that "God would protect His company of worshippers to their homes."

The next morning, everyone assembled after the news was received that a man had been killed. About two hundred yards from the schoolhouse where they had worshipped, they found the terribly mangled, bloodstained body of Dr. Witter, a prominent local physician. They buried him as best they could, raising a little mound "over the body of a learned infidel, who refused to go to meeting, though it was so close to his house."

In February 1846, German scientist Dr. Ferdinand Roemer passed through Gonzales in his way from Houston to New Braunfels. He was not impressed by what he saw: "About thirty to forty poor, dilapidated frame houses and log cabins were scattered about on the level plain. The resources of the place seemed to be in keeping with its cheerless aspect. No sugar, coffee or other necessities could be bought in the entire place—nothing but bad whiskey."

Baptist preacher Z. N. Morrell had been warmly received in Gonzales in 1841, but the following incident, as recorded in the *San Antonio Texan*, shows that not all flavors of Christianity were so warmly received: "During the past week a Mormon Missionary has been holding forth in Gonzales. At his last meeting there, he pulled off his coat and rolled up his sleeves—which, alas! caused a stampede of the lady part of his audience. Soon after, he was escorted around the town to the music of tin horns, cow bells, etc., and told to leave ere the dews of night were kissed by early dawn, and he did nothing shorter."

That missionary was John Ostler, and he was one of two Mormon elders "mobbed" (as they put it) in Gonzales. On the afternoon of June 19, 1856, Ostler and Morris J. Snedaker, on their way to Port Lavaca, entered Gonzales and stopped at Goss' tavern. With Goss' help, Ostler and Snedaker got permission to preach at the courthouse. They soon created a great curiosity throughout town.

Upon the request of some fellow area Mormons, the pair went to DeWitt County for a preaching. Not long after their return to Gonzales, they found that local curiosity had turned to anger and hatred, as Snedaker wrote:

"They of different sects was all afraid against him on doctrine but they soon began to find out they had bad tools to work with and resorted to another kind: tar, pistols, guns, Bowie knives, clubs etc., etc."

Ostler had a preaching obligation on July 8. He had arisen to speak when there was a roaring of horns and the ringing of bells, and a mob painted all in black marched into the courthouse and through the large congregation gathered there, with their pistols and bowie knives, and took Ostler by force.

They led him up and down the streets of Gonzales, as if he were some great beast, yelling loud, "A Mormon from Salt Lake! Hurrah! Here a Mormon right from Salt Lake."

After they had exhibited him for several hours, they let him go, saying that he must leave the town by the next morning or he would get a fine coat of tar and feathers. He tarried just long enough to tell Snedaker where to find him. Then he started in the night for Grimes County by way of Port Lavaca. Snedaker, who had been sick in bed for several weeks, decided to ride over to an ally's place where he could continue to recuperate in relative safety before making his escape.

At nine that evening,

There was one of the most dreadful noises I ever heard broke loose. Horns, bells, cowbells, and some of the loudest yelling I ever heard. The door was soon encircled with a ring that they had formed, being some 25 or 30 in number all painted up as black as a thundercloud. Then this dreadful conglomerated noise ceased. A tall straight pretty form person stepped forward in profound order and a general manner as spokesman saying, "We are the princes of Belzibubb right from the dominion of hell and we have come to see if our friend is here. Is he here? Oh yes, there is our friend. We have at last found you. Come now friend. We have a long journey ahead. It is time we was off. We must go."

He stepped forward, with a belt 'round him with pistols and Bowie knife and was followed by two or three more who came rushing in.

They pushed Snedaker's host aside and pulled Snedaker from the bed. He did not resist. They got him out the door in his stocking feet, "whereupon I was escorted by the princes of belzibubb with a nigger at each arm over the gravel, stones and prickly pears together with other prickers on the road and through the bushes around that neighborhood for 3 1/2 miles, exhibited before three or four dwelling houses with the loudest yelping, blowing and bell ringing I ever heard."

Doubled over in weakness and trying to pick all the thorns and spines from his feet as they dragged him from house to house, Snedaker pleaded for mercy and was rewarded with hair pulling and unmerciful kicks.

"They would grab me by the hair and pull my head back while at the same time my arms was held by these niggers as if in a vise and these fellows whose faces was blacker than a thundercloud would take turns kicking me and forcing me along until we came to a large jack oak tree," where the princes decided to give Snedaker a breather.

As a black man wailed away on an old fiddle, the kidnappers formed a circle and powwowed with a bottle of liquor they passed around until they felt Snedaker was fit to walk again. The dark demons, black men, and Snedaker stumbled along as before until they reached another jack oak, where he saw ten saddled horses in a circle, held by one man in the center.

They let Snedaker lie down and rest while they sat in council and imbibed more liquor until they got up and took Snedaker back to the point of his abduction, where they saddled his horse and forced him aboard. They rode awhile before stopping. He begged his captors to let him lie on the ground, "whereupon they caught me by the feet and jerked me along for a number of rods over the rough ground with my head and shoulders thrashing upon the ground, saying, 'You damned heretic. You ought to be killed.'"

A stranger who heard Snedaker's pleading for rest came to see what was going on but was ordered back by the gang, and he quickly made tracks. The gang forced Snedaker onto his saddled horse and ordered him to ride ahead of them. He complied with their order; "Here they would whip my horse and make him jump which hurt my head most wonderfully. I would still plead with them to have mercy on me; they would whip the harder."

They ruddered him around all night, going to every house and grog shop in those parts. Many of the houses had dogs, and as Snedaker and the princes drew near, they "would come roaring as if to eat us up."

But when the company would break loose with their horn blowing and bell ringing, "the dogs would curl their tails between their hind legs and run for their life, scale the fence and make their way under the house and not a whist could be heard from them."

Herds of cattle, horses, and hogs ran for their lives, "as if the devil had kicked them in the end."

They came to another large jack oak at about dawn. The princes ordered Snedaker off his horse, whereupon they dismounted and surrounded him,

and then abused me in a shameful manner. And then spit tobacco spit upon me until I was unaccountable. Here they ordered me to mount my horse. I was about used up but succeeded after many kicks and thumps upon me. Here I was ordered to return to the road and never be seen in that part again if I wanted to live.

After I had started one of those princes came with a club 9 or 10 feet in length and gave a blow that would have straightened me prostrate upon the ground had not the club broke in three pieces. Here it knocked me blind though I succeeded in sticking upon my horse.

He looked back after traveling a short distance to see them holding conference, no one in the saddle. He spurred his horse and hurried away, until he reached a little grove of trees to the right of the road. He stopped to listen, but heard no one following him, so he dismounted, threw down his saddle for a pillow and his blanket for a bed, and "fell upon my blanket, got my head upon my saddle and I was as independent as anybody and was unaccountable rich with tobacco spit."

After many denials of food and shelter, he reached Grimes County on July 30, 1856, where he found Ostler.

Others found Gonzales to be a more welcoming town. Czech immigrants began settling Gonzales County around 1850, and the town of Gonzales today has a distinctive Czech flavor, down to the polka music show each weekday on KCTI AM 1450 (www.kcti1450.com).

The citizens of Gonzales County supported the Confederate cause during the Civil War with pretty much the same enthusiasm as they had the Texas War for Independence. And as it drew to its end, some chose to leave rather than to surrender.

The end of the war and the announcement of the Emancipation Proclamation on June 19, 1865, in Galveston was received with relative equanimity. According to the *Gonzales Inquirer* at that time,

> The order of Gen. Granger, liberating the slaves in Texas, has been pretty generally carried out by our citizens. But few have expressed any regret at their loss; indeed, the real majority appear perfectly reconciled at the new order of things, believing that, with proper regulations, the change will be greatly to their advantage. All the negroes, with a few exceptions, wisely concluded to remain at their old homes, upon the same terms as heretofore, or for small wages. The few who preferred shifting for themselves, soon realized that their freedom was not what their imaginations had so beautifully pictured, and some quietly returned to their former homes. There has not been exceeding a dozen lounging about the streets at any one time.

Like most Texas towns, Gonzales was destitute at the end of the Civil War, as the following story illustrates: Jim Towns was born on the Guadalupe River in 1852 in a log cabin on land granted to his grandfather for services to the Republic of Texas. Right after the end of the Civil War, his mother told him, "Jim, hitch the oxen to the cart and take a load of roasting ears to Gonzales and trade them for something to eat. Anyway, bring back a sack of salt."

It took him a day and a half to reach Gonzales. Once in Gonzales, he spent a day driving around and around trying to sell or trade off the roasting ears. Finally he swapped a few dozen roasting ears to a traveling photographer for a tintype picture of himself. "It was a sad looking picture, for I had cried a lot over my dismal failure. It seemed there was not a dollar's worth of money or a spoonful of salt in Gonzales. I was forced to go back home without anything but the roasting ears and the tin-type. On the whole trip I did not eat anything but corn roasted in ashes."

Beginning in 1869, Towns made seven or eight trips up the Chisholm Trail. He was in Abilene when his uncle Phil Coe was killed by Bill Hickok. He was on a George Littlefield drive in 1873. Towns and ten men went to Columbus to pick up 3,150 steers from Shanghai Pierce and the Stafford brothers. Bob Stafford told him after delivering the cattle that they would never get those steers out of the country. "We've sold and delivered these old scalawags so many times that we're getting ashamed to look at them. They get away from everybody who tries to drive them off. You never saw such a bunch for stampeding and when they hit one of these breaks they are gone."

Towns said that his men were man enough to handle this bunch all the way to the Indian Agency at Fort Sill. Stafford recommended that he buy insurance and guaranteed that the herd would run on him before they had gone one hundred miles.

The herd got the habit of running every night around eleven o'clock. Nevertheless, Towns got them to Fort Sill and delivered to Colonel Hunter of the Indian Agency. It took all day and into the night to cut and classify the herd. Towns felt compelled by honesty to advise Hunter: "They are a bad lot. We bought them a-running, we have driven them clear across Texas a-running, and you can see for yourself that we delivered them a-running. Unless you post your men and ring herd them [keep them going in a circle] tonight, you will be running at eleven o'clock."

Hunter replied that he had bought and handled more Texas cattle than the young Towns had ever seen. "My men will take care of them all right. Here are a few more cigars for your good intentions."

When fellow cowhand Dunn Houston went to bed, he asked Towns to wake him up at eleven because he wanted to hear those steers run at "some other fellow's expense." Sure enough, Towns woke Houston at eleven to tell him that hell was popping. "The last we heard of those old mossy-horns, they were still a-running."

But as Reconstruction began to set in, Gonzales proved to be as inhospitable to carpetbaggers as it was to Mormons.

After the war, the Freedmen's Bureau was established in Texas, putatively to help ex-slaves transition to lives of freedom. Schools were set up across the state, including Gonzales, to provide freedmen with a basic education. Early in 1870, the Reverend Joseph Welch, state superintendent of the Freedmen's Bureau schools, complained to his superiors that on one recent night, as the teacher was about to close the Gonzales night school, "A party of five or six men, disguised, attacked him with revolvers and after beating him unmercifully threw him into the river, and threatened to drown him but didn't do it."

Gonzales was also home to Texas' most notorious pistolero, John Wesley Hardin, during the years following the Civil War. Hardin was officially credited with thirty killings, give or take a few. But the late Frank M. Fly, longtime Gonzales County sheriff and justice of the peace, begged to differ: "He admitted to 48 and I personally know of several he didn't admit. I don't doubt that Wes Hardin killed any less than 100 men." Such renowned shootists as Wild Bill Hickok, Ben Thompson, and Bill Longley avoided any direct confrontation with Hardin's guns.

Wes Hardin was already an experienced killer and wanted man when he settled in Gonzales County at the behest of his kin here, the Clements family. Hardin had been on his way to Mexico in order to avoid Governor E. J. Davis' state police, but he decided to stay here when cousin Manning Clements assured him he would be safe from arrest. Besides, the Clementses were in particular need of Hardin's expertise. They and most of the rest of Gonzales and neighboring DeWitt counties were in the middle of the Sutton-Taylor feud, the longest and bloodiest feud in Texas history.

The feud began on Christmas Eve 1868 when Deputy Sheriff William Sutton shot Buck Taylor and Dick Chisholm to death following an argument over a horse sale. The Taylors and their friends were unreconstructed Rebels and a thorn in the side of the carpetbagger government in Austin. The Taylors had already whipped Union soldiers sent to tame them, and after the Christmas killing, Governor Davis sent a contingent of his state police to try again.

The captain of the carpetbagger force was special officer Jack Helm. Helm and his gunners were known as "regulators," and they joined forces with Sutton and "the law" to bring the "outlaw" Taylor bunch to their knees. In practice there was little difference between the law and the lawless; ambushes and lynchings were the regulators' favored tools.

Helm's past was a shrouded one. Some folks said he was a Confederate veteran and that one day after the war's end he had shot dead a freedman sitting on a fence for doing nothing more than whistling "Yankee Doodle." Governor Davis dismissed Helm in the fall of 1870 on misconduct charges; earlier that year, he had arrested two of the Taylor clan on trivial charges and then shot them. But Helm remained active in the feud as sheriff of DeWitt County. After Helm's dismissal, the regulators became known as the Sutton party.

By the time of Hardin's arrival in 1871, the feud had grown into a little civil war involving hundreds of men. There was no remaining neutral. You picked a side or you left the country. Hardin avoided the fire awhile by heading a Clements herd of longhorns up the Chisholm Trail to Abilene, Kansas, killing six men along the way. While in Abilene, he tamed Ben Thompson and Wild Bill Hickok and killed three more slow drawers. He was drawn into the feud on his return to Gonzales County. As Hardin continued to add notches to his gun, Governor Davis became determined that his police would get rid of the gunslinger. Blacks in Austin and Gonzales were of the same persuasion. Fifty of them congregated on the Gonzales courthouse square in the fall of 1871 to ride down south into Clements country, shoot down Wes and his friends, and burn their houses. Word of this posse got to Hardin and the Clements clan. They urged the vigilantes to come on down because "a warm reception" had been arranged. Despite warnings from some of Gonzales' more levelheaded white men, many of the black vigilantes rode down into the area known as the "Sandies." Hardin met them alone, killing three and sending the rest hurrying back to Austin and Gonzales.

It was here that love complicated Wes Hardin's life. Hardin married Jane Bowen, who had ties to the Taylor party. Wes was determined to settle down in southern Gonzales County. This resolution lasted only a few months. By September 1872, he was in the Gonzales County jail on murder charges. Less than a month later, he was out, courtesy of a sharp file and an obliging jailer.

By this time, the Sutton-Taylor feud was at its height. Pitkin Taylor, the elderly patriarch of the Taylor clan, had been ambushed and shot in an especially dastardly way. He died a lingering, painful death, and the Taylors were out to kill—by any means possible—every Sutton confederate they could find. Hardin traveled to Wilson County to kill Jack Helm. Mission accomplished, Hardin decided to move his family and cattle up to Comanche County. Upon arriving there, he killed the deputy sheriff of neighboring Brown County at a horse race in Comanche. All the men in Brown County were soon on his heels, and the Hardin bunch was on the run again. Wes got away, but his dear brother Joe and four friends were not so lucky. The posse shot two of them dead and hanged the other three.

Hardin ran to Florida, killing six more men along the way. He and his family lived in secrecy there for several years before Texas Rangers captured him at Pensacola in 1877. The following year, John Wesley Hardin was sentenced to twenty-five years in the state pen at Huntsville for the killing of Deputy Charles Webb in Comanche.

While in the pen, Hardin made repeated attempts to escape, he studied law and the Bible, and he gradually became a model prisoner. He was released in 1894, just a year after his wife's death. Admitted to the bar after his pardon was granted, Hardin settled down in Gonzales with his two children to practice law. He attended the Methodist church regularly, shunned gambling halls, and didn't drink. The only problem was he couldn't make a living. Folks wouldn't hire him; his earlier reputation haunted him. Drawn into politics, Hardin campaigned hard for a friend running for county sheriff, vowing to leave the county if the other candidate—who was an old enemy—was elected. Hardin's enemy won, and Hardin made good on his promise, moving to El Paso. Again he tried to lead the decent life, but his old reputation refused to let him be. He began to frequent gambling halls and drink.

In the spring of 1895, Hardin went into the hospitality business, announcing in the *El Paso Times:* "I have bought an interest in the Wigwam Saloon and you who, whether in El Paso or elsewhere, that admire pluck, that desire fair play, are cordially invited to call at the Wigwam where you will have everything done to make it pleasant for you. All are especially invited to our blowout on the 4th."

His new career was short-lived. While in one of El Paso's gambling dens, Hardin was shot by City Constable John Selman, who deliberately gunned Hardin down from behind on August 19, 1895, possibly because Selman thought that Hardin had invested in the Wigwam money that he owed to him. Hardin was forty-two years old.

Hardin had killed his first man at age fifteen, but he was not your typical desperado. Coming from one of Texas' oldest and most respected families, Hardin was believed by many to be a man more sinned against than sinning. He was a handsome, well-mannered man who considered himself a pillar of society. He robbed no banks, and he stole no horses in his career. Hardin maintained from the beginning that he never killed anyone who did not deserve it and that he always shot to save his own life.

What of the Sutton-Taylor feud? Suttons continued to kill Taylors, and Taylors continued to dispatch Suttons. Even the Texas Rangers failed to break the feud. By 1876, though, the Suttons, many of whom were peace officers, had the upper hand, and the feud pretty much came to an end. There were hardly any Taylors left. But the Sutton party boys occupied themselves with other forms of mischief, and guns spat lead throughout Gonzales and DeWitt counties into the first decade of the twentieth century.

In spite of the bloodshed, Gonzales County prospered. Cotton was king, and the county also became one of the state's leading poultry and cattle producers. A few million turkeys and chickens saved Gonzales from the full ravages of the Great Depression. In 1936, Gonzales proudly proclaimed itself the first-ranking turkey-producing county in the nation. Gonzales County no longer rules the roost nationally, but it still leads Texas in chicken and egg production. And abandoned chicken farms have a new lease on life as commercial mushroom farms. Mushrooms thrive in chicken manure.

Life was good to many people in Gonzales, starting in the 1880s. The town is filled with much history and Victorian architecture—public, commercial, and residential. Downtown Gonzales has a number of interesting buildings and shops, so park somewhere on the courthouse square and perambulate. The greatest concentration of antique and specialty shops is on St. Joseph.

GONZALES COUNTY COURTHOUSE

St. Joseph at St. Louis • 672-2435 • Open Monday through Friday

J. Riely Gordon, responsible for several other grand Texas county courthouses, designed this three-story Romanesque Revival courthouse. It was built in 1895 of red brick from St. Louis and is laid out in the form of a Greek cross with a central stairwell inside adorned with ornamental ironwork. Firmin Maurin, owner of the nearby Maurin Quarry, supervised construction. The final price was $65,000. The roof was originally slate; it was replaced with red tile in the 1950s. The basement had a dirt floor until 1958, when cement was poured. The Seth Thomas clock was installed in 1896 and cost $900. It ceased to work during the 1920s, and there is a gallows-humor explanation for why. The last man to hang from the Gonzales County jail gallows was Albert Howard in 1921. Toward the end of his stay on earth, Howard became obsessed with the hours he had left, marking their passage by the toll of the courthouse clock. He swore his innocence, as many in his position have, and proclaimed that his innocence would be borne out by the courthouse clock, which would never again keep the correct time. The four faces fell out of sync and remained that way for decades until 1990, when Henry Christian spent his time and $11,000 to repair it.

GONZALES COUNTY JAIL MUSEUM, VISITOR INFORMATION CENTER AND CHAMBER OF COMMERCE

414 St. Lawrence at St. Joseph • 672-6532 • www.gonzalestexas.com • Jail and visitor information center open daily • Chamber of commerce open Monday through Friday • Free • W

The old jail, located on the square, was completed in 1887 and served said purpose until 1975. A registered historic landmark, the jail now houses the chamber of commerce and a museum. The upstairs cell block and first-story jailer's quarters, as well as the lunatics' cell and dungeon, where the only light and air comes from holes above the door, remain intact. Six legal hangings took place in or near the county jails, the first being held outside. The most prominent hanging took place in 1878 when four thousand people, including newspaper reporters from across the state, came to Gonzales to see Brown Bowen, brother-in-law of John Wesley Hardin, take the fatal plunge. The permanent, upstairs gallows were built in 1891, and the last hanging took place there in 1921. The original gallows was dismantled in 1953 or 1954, but a replica has been installed in the original location upstairs. It stands amid the prisoners' cells—not a pleasant sight to wake up to each morning. But such sobering practices were deemed necessary in earlier days. The fortresslike jail took two years to construct and was built to hold between 150 and 200 prisoners, in case of riot.

One such riotous episode occurred in 1901, involving the celebrated Tejano outlaw, Gregorio Cortez, whose story is told in the museum.

Gregorio Cortez was born in 1875 near Matamoros. In 1887, his family moved to Manor, near Austin. From 1889 to 1899, he worked as a farmhand and vaquero in Karnes, Gonzales, and nearby counties, which gave him a valuable knowledge of the region and terrain. He had a limited education but could speak English. He married Leonor Diaz in 1890, and they would have four children. Cortez was considered a handsome, likeable young man.

In 1900, Gregorio and his brother Romaldo decided to settle down and farm on their own. W. A. Thulemeyer, who owned a large ranch in Karnes County, rented some of his land to the brothers. The year 1901 was their first as renters, and by June they had a good corn crop in the making.

On the afternoon of June 12, 1901, Karnes county sheriff W. T. Morris appeared at Gregorio's house; Atascosa county sheriff Avant had asked Morris to help him locate a horse thief from Atascosa County who had been trailed to Karnes County. Sheriff Avant did not know the man's name. The only information Morris received was that he was a "medium sized Mexican with a big red broad-brimmed Mexican hat." Morris followed a trail to Kenedy, in Karnes County, and on the morning of June 12 he began to check up on local Mexicans who had acquired horses in recent weeks.

Deputies John Trimmell and Boone Choate accompanied Morris, with Choate acting as interpreter. But Choate's Spanish was limited. Through Choate, Morris questioned various Mexicans in Kenedy, including Andres Villarreal, who told them that he had recently acquired a mare by trading a horse to Gregorio Cortez. So Morris decided to visit Cortez.

When the lawmen arrived, the Cortez brothers were resting on the front porch. Romaldo got up to greet the lawmen. Choate's poor job of interpreting led to a major misunderstanding between Cortez and Choate. After speaking with the lawmen, Romaldo told Gregorio, "Te quieren" (literally "They want you," a common way of saying in Spanish, "Somebody wants to speak to you"). But Choate interpreted this to mean, "You are wanted," and that Gregorio was the horse thief they were seeking.

Choate apparently asked Cortez if he had traded a *caballo* ("male horse"), to which Cortez truthfully answered no, because he had traded a *yegua* ("mare"). Choate failed to make the distinction.

When Gregorio said no, Sheriff Morris approached the Cortezes, telling Choate to inform Romaldo and Gregorio that he was going to arrest them.

Whereupon Cortez said, *"No me puede arrestar por nada"* ("You can't arrest me for nothing"), which Choate understood as "No one can arrest me."

At this point, Morris shot and wounded Romaldo, narrowly missing Gregorio. Gregorio responded by shooting and killing Morris. He then fled the scene on foot, toward Gonzales (and then possibly Manor), some eighty miles away. The authorities promptly jailed Leonor and the children, Cortez's mother, and his sister-in-law. Romaldo was captured and jailed.

Posses were organized and began searching for Cortez. His name was soon on the front page of every major Texas newspaper. During his escape, Cortez stopped at the Robledo family house near Belmont. Gonzales County sheriff Richard Glover and his posse found Cortez at the home on June 14 and attacked. In the ensuing gunfight, Glover and a man named Schnabel were killed, and two members of the Robledo faction were wounded. Upon Glover's death, Deputy Frank Fly became sheriff of Gonzales County.

Cortez escaped again and walked about ten miles to the home of a friend, who lent him a horse and saddle. Cortez then headed toward Laredo. The hunt for "sheriff killer" Cortez intensified. The *San Antonio Express* claimed that Cortez headed "a well organized band of thieves and cutthroats." The *Seguin Enterprise* denounced him as an "arch fiend." Governor Joe Sayers and Karnes County citizens offered $1,000 for his capture.

The posses searching for Cortez involved hundreds of men, including the Texas Rangers. Cortez found it difficult to evade capture around Laredo since many of the lawmen hunting him were Mexican Americans, such as Sheriff Ortiz of Webb County and Assistant City Marshal Gomez of Laredo.

While anti-Cortez sentiment grew, so did the numbers of his sympathizers, who regarded him as a hero evading the evil "rinches." Some Anglo-Texans even came to admire Cortez: the *San Antonio Express* touted his "remarkable powers of endurance and skill in eluding pursuit."

Mexican Americans in Gonzales, Refugio, and Hays counties experienced retaliatory violence. After a search described as "one of the greatest manhunts ever pulled off in South Texas," Cortez was captured near Laredo after an acquaintance led a posse to him on June 22, 1901. By the time Cortez was captured, at least nine persons of Mexican descent had been killed, three wounded, and seven arrested.

Once he was captured, a legal defense campaign began. Letters of support were published in newspapers as far away as Mexico City. Funds for Cortez's defense were raised through donations, *sociedades mutualistas* (mutual-aid societies), and benefit performances. Cortez went through numerous trials, the first of which began in Gonzales on July 24, 1901. Eleven jurors found him guilty of the murder of Schnabel. The jury gave him a fifty-year sentence for second-degree murder. The defense's attempt to appeal the case was denied.

Unsatisfied with the verdict, a mob of three hundred men tried to lynch Cortez. After receiving a tip that the lynch mob was forming, Sheriff Fly locked himself in the jail with Cortez. At midnight, the mob attempted to pick the lock and then began ramming the door with a telephone pole. Fly saved Cortez's life by confronting the crowd with drawn pistol through a barred window and convincing them that he would defend Cortez to the death. The next day, Fly and Cortez took the train from Gonzales to San Antonio.

Shortly after the verdict, Romaldo Cortez died in the Karnes City jail. On January 15, 1902, the Texas Court of Criminal Appeals reversed the Gonzales verdict. The same court also reversed the verdicts in trials held in Karnes and Pleasanton.

In April 1904, the last trial was held in Corpus Christi. By the time Cortez began serving life in prison for the murder of Sheriff Glover, he had been in eleven jails in eleven counties. While in prison he worked as a barber. Cortez also enjoyed the empathy of some of his jailers, who provided him the entire upper story of the jail as a "honeymoon suite" when he married Estefana Garza of Manor in December 1904.

Attempts to pardon him began as soon as he entered prison, and the Board of Pardons Advisers eventually recommended a full pardon. Governor Oscar Colquitt gave Cortez a conditional pardon in July 1913. Once released, Cortez thanked those who helped him recover his freedom. Soon after, he went to Nuevo Laredo and fought with Victoriano Huerta in the Mexican Revolution. He married for the last time in 1916 and died shortly afterward of pneumonia.

His story inspired many variants of a *corrido*, or ballad, called "El Corrido de Gregorio Cortez," which appeared as early as 1901.

Folklorist Americo Paredes popularized the story of Gregorio Cortez in *With His Pistol in His Hand: A Border Ballad and Its Hero*, published by the University of Texas Press in 1958. A Texas Ranger angered by it threatened to shoot Paredes. Cortez's story gained further interest when the movie *The Ballad of Gregorio Cortez* was produced in 1982.

A well-documented and extensive historical guide and tour of Gonzales is available here free of charge. The historical trail is well marked by "Come and Take It" signs. Since the accompanying interpretive guide put out by the chamber of commerce is free and so nicely detailed, only a few of its highlights will be touched upon here.

RANDLE-RATHER BUILDING

427 St. George

The Randle-Rather building was built in 1897. This elaborate three-story Roman Revival structure was constructed of locally made natural-clay bricks. Featuring ground-level Roman arcades, and second- and third-level balconies with Tuscan columns on either side, and topped by a square tower with Roman arched windows, the Randle-Rather building is a study in balance and beauty. A variety of businesses have been housed here. The third floor was devoted to the K. D. (Keep Dry) Club, the region's foremost social club. Their Christmas ball here was the height of the social season; the women dressed in their finest silks and satins, and the gentlemen were attired in "full dress with frock-tailed coats."

Gonzales has many beautiful old homes. On St. Louis Street are the Old Gonzales College (820 St. Louis), the Rather House, and the Kennard House. Construction on Gonzales College's first building began in 1851, with stone hauled in from nearby Peach Creek. Classes started in 1853. There were separate male and female colleges. School enrollment peaked at 276 students in 1859–1860. The college granted a four-year degree. The Civil War disrupted the college's progress, and the school continued to decline during Reconstruction. The college property was eventually sold to the city, and the buildings became part of the local school system. In 1890, W. M. Atkinson, a graduate of the college, bought this building and remodeled it, using stone from the Maurin Quarry.

The Rather House (828 St. Louis) was built in 1892 for Charles Rather, a prosperous Gonzales County cotton planter and partner of the Randle-Rather building, on the grounds of the old Gonzales College. The two-story house is built of Louisiana cypress and Bastrop pine. The Rathers moved to Austin in 1910, and the house has gone through a succession of owners. It has recently been restored.

The Kennard House (621 St. Louis) is a good example of the Queen Anne architectural style of the late Victorian period. This frame two-story house was built in 1895 by Mr. and Mrs. James Kennard. The house's original corner tower with third-story open arcade has survived, and the restored house still looks like it did one hundred years ago.

The two-story, twin-turret William Buckner Houston home (621 St. George) took three years to build. Mrs. Houston was an artist and painted the parlor ceiling in a manner reminiscent of the Bishop's Palace in Galveston, and she also painted a mural on the dining room walls. The house has been recently restored and opened as a B&B.

The elaborate red-brick Victorian Lewis-Houston Home (619 St. Lawrence) took James Dunn Houston four years to build. He finished it in 1899 and then sold it in 1900 to Mr. and Mrs. George N. Dilworth. Their widowed daughter, Margaret Dilworth Lewis, moved into the house with her parents and stayed until her death in 1950. They had plenty of room. The house has fifteen main rooms, five bathrooms, and an indoor conservatory. Each room has its own fireplace.

Gonzales has many attractive postbellum and Victorian homes. Notable are the multigabled Bell house (ca. 1900, 803 St. Lawrence); the J. B. Wells house (ca. 1885, 829 Mitchell, limited-hours museum, the Gonzales chapter of the Daughters of the Republic of Texas is the custodian, contact Gonzales chamber of commerce for more information); and the Sheriff Frank Fly home (ca. 1914, 827 St. Joseph). Fly was also a personal acquaintance of John Wesley Hardin during Hardin's attempt to establish a law practice in Gonzales after his release from the penitentiary.

OTHER MUSEUMS AND HISTORIC SITES

GONZALES MEMORIAL MUSEUM

414 Smith at St. Louis • 672-6532 • www.gonzalestexas.com • Tuesday through Saturday, Sunday afternoon, closed Monday • Donations accepted

Built in the Texas centennial year (1936), the museum is a good example of the Texas brand of Art Moderne architecture, built from native limestone. The museum honors the "Immortal Thirty-two," who answered Travis' pleas for help at the Alamo, and the "Old Eighteen," who held off the cannon-demanding Mexican troops at the Battle of Gonzales. The museum also has many items pertinent to the history of Gonzales and Texas, such as the original "Come and Take It" cannon.

THE EGGLESTON HOUSE

1300 St. Louis, east of the Gonzales Memorial Museum • 672-6532 • www .gonzalestexas.com

The Eggleston House, built by Horace Eggleston in the 1840s, is Gonzales' oldest standing structure. Built of hand-hewn burr oak logs, it has plank floors whipsawed by Eggleston's slaves. The windows of this dogtrot cabin were originally made of paper liberally coated with bear grease or hog lard, which made the paper more translucent. The cracks in the walls were chinked with moss and clay.

CANNON FIGHT BATTLEGROUND

Off SH 97

The cannon fight took place south of town. Several monuments and markers explaining the battle and the events leading up to it are located along US 183 as you head south out of town. The battle site itself is located six miles west of US 183, off SH 97 near Cost. At the large bronze-and-granite monument dedicated to the Texan participants in the battle on SH 97, turn right on Park Road 95 and continue to the banks of the Guadalupe River and another monument to those determined men. Then retrace your tracks back to Gonzales and the courthouse.

PIONEER VILLAGE

US 183, as it leaves Gonzales for Luling • 672-2157 • Open Tuesday through Sunday • Fee

Gonzales' pioneer past is preserved in these nineteenth-century buildings collected from around the county. The 1830s Greenwood log cabin was probably built as a slave cabin and then became a sharecropper's house. Instead of clay or mud chinking, chunks of wood filled in the gaps between logs so that they could be removed for better ventilation in summer. The double-pen Knowles-Townsend log house (1840s) is distinctive for its lack of the almost universal dogrun and for its central chimney. The Samuel Gates house (1856) was built of elm and oak logs and then covered with expensive, imported cypress boards. The blacksmith shop dates to the 1860s, the Schindler barn to the 1870s. The Hamon church was built by the people of the nearby Hamon community in the 1870s. First a Presbyterian church, then Baptist, it is notable for its slanted floor, built so that the worshipers in back could see better. The two-story Muenzler house serves as museum for a growing collection of early area artifacts and memorabilia.

The old Oak Forest schoolhouse features an old-time doctor's office in one end and a typical school in the other. There is a working blacksmith shop and broom factory. A smokehouse, hog pen, and old-style vegetable and flower garden add to the authenticity.

Started in the late 1980s, the Pioneer Village grows and evolves yearly. In 1994, the St. Andrews house, former slave quarters, was moved here. Historical reenactments are held here several times during the year.

Adjacent to the Pioneer Village is the site of Fort Waul, a short-lived Confederate fort built early in 1864 to protect Texas from a possible Yankee attack up the "River Route" that led from Victoria on the coast and ran through Gonzales to San Antonio. It was also to be used as a grain depot. It was an earthen fortification measuring 750 feet by 250 feet. The fort was named for Thomas N. Waul, a South Carolina native who came to Texas in 1850 and established a plantation on the Guadalupe River in Gonzales County.

Waul was famous as a spellbinding orator with a dramatic flair. After marrying a rich woman, he retired from his law practice to his plantation home. During the spring of 1862, he roamed central Texas raising a group of fighters in a magnificent ambulance drawn by four fine back mules. His oratory on the courthouse squares made even the children want to join the Confederate Army.

The primed volunteers converged at Brenham to formally organize Waul's Legion. This group of approximately two thousand men served in Mississippi in 1862 and 1863. Much of the legion was captured at Vicksburg in July 1863. The artillery battery was captured in April 1864 after the Battle of Mansfield. After being paroled, legion members returned to Texas for reorganization and served until the end of the war at Galveston and at other points on the coast. Waul returned to his plantation after the war but later moved to Galveston. He died in Greenville in 1903.

The San Marcos River joins the Guadalupe just out of town, and Waul's plantation lay along the River Route that led to San Antonio. Waul's neighbors were the Littlefield family, the most famous of whom was George Washington Littlefield, who eventually moved to Austin and became an early patron saint of the University of Texas.

In the fall of 1850, Fleming Littlefield located himself on several hundred acres on the Guadalupe, fifteen miles above Gonzales. He soon bought several thousand more acres; ran horses in the Sandies, west of Gonzales; and opened a store in Gonzales. He died in January 1853. Mrs. Littlefield closed the store to manage his estate, and by 1860 the Littlefield properties consisted of the original Fleming Littlefield place, the nearby Charles White place, and the home place, situated in the fork of the Guadalupe and San Marcos Rivers. Fleming's son, George, joined Terry's Texas Rangers and rose to the rank of company commander, the youngest in his regiment. He fought at Shiloh, Perryville, and Chickamauga. After being wounded at Mossy Creek, Tennessee, on December 26, 1863, George Littlefield went home. At Mossy Creek, he had been promoted to major, a title by which he was addressed after the mid-1880s.

At the end of the war, Mrs. Littlefield told her slaves that she didn't own them anymore and they were free to leave. Most of them elected to stay. They were given each a horse and fifty dollars, some beef cattle, and collectively a schoolhouse/church on two acres.

George began to manage the family business. But the great flood of July 1869 destroyed what was shaping up to be a fine cotton crop. Almost ruined, Littlefield began to explore alternatives. He decided to trail horses and cattle to market. He began his first drive in the spring of 1871.

When Littlefield went out to buy cattle, he sometimes carried so much silver and gold that it came close to breaking the wagon. In 1877, the two sacks of silver and gold, along with the major, mashed the buggy springs down on the axles, and the boys accompanying Littlefield had to pick up some old cow bones and push them under the springs to support the load.

He got into the banking business via a store he opened in Gonzales with some partners. One day, a grocery drummer dumped $5,000 of gold on the floor of the store and asked them to exchange his money for funds the store held in New York City. They agreed on a fee and decided to make banking part of their mercantile activities, keeping the money in a safe. They eventually added a rail to fence off their bank "office"; they then added a cage and began banking according to accepted style.

SANTA ANNA'S MOUND

J. B. Wells Park • 2301 CR 197 • Take US 183 south out of Gonzales, cross the Guadalupe River, and turn right onto CR 197 into J. B. Wells Park • 830-672-3192 • www.cityofgonzales.org

This 169-acre city park contains a large mound or hill formed of pebbles, a thousand or so feet from the Guadalupe River. On the top of this mount are several small groves of scrubby, umbrageous live oaks. On the eve of October 2, 1835, the Mexican troops under the command of Santa Anna encamped on the summit of this mound, ever since known as Santa Anna's Mound. A mile-long crushed limestone hike and bike trail circles the mound.

DINING

GONZALES FOOD MARKET

311 St. Lawrence • 800-269-5342 • www.gonzalesfoodmarket.com • Monday through Saturday

Oak-mesquite smoked brisket, ring sausage, chicken, ribs (pork, beef, and most notably lamb, highly recommended!), pork steaks, pork chops, and a variety of sides make this place a worthy alternative to any barbecue place in Luling or Lockhart.

LODGING

ST. JAMES INN

723 St. James • 672-7066 • www.stjamesinn.com

Local cattle baron Walter H. Kokernot had this three-story, four-square style house built in 1914. It has thirty rooms and nine fireplaces. It is now a B&B. Each bedroom has its own bathroom and fireplace. A full "gourmet" breakfast is served in the formal dining room. Checks and credit cards are accepted. Write to 723 St. James, Gonzales 78629.

ANNUAL EVENT

OCTOBER

GONZALES COME AND TAKE IT DAYS CELEBRATION

Town square, 414 St. Lawrence • 888-672-1095 • www.gonzalestexas.com • First weekend in October • W

The activities commemorate the famed battle cry of the opening skirmish of the Texas Revolution, highlighted by a parade, a rodeo, an arts-and-crafts show, an antique show, a historical pilgrimage, a reenactment of the battle, tours of historical homes and the Pioneer Village, and street dances.

PARKS

LAKE WOOD RECREATION AREA

Go 5 miles west from Gonzales on US 90A, then 5 miles south on FM 2091 • Open daily

The Lake Wood Recreation Area (thirty-five acres) offers access to Lake Wood and the Guadalupe River. The San Marcos River enters the Guadalupe downriver from the park. Gonzales is ten miles (four leisurely hours) downriver from the park; the river is navigable by canoe the whole way. Lake Wood covers 488 acres. The average depth is eight feet; in places, the riverbed is thirty feet deep. For anglers, there are bass, catfish, crappie, rough, and baitfish. There are RV full-hookup sites, as well as tent campsites in a big pecan grove, restrooms with hot showers, and picnic facilities. There is a boat ramp and docks.

From the Gonzales courthouse square, take St. Louis Street west to US 183. Turn right (north) on US 183, continuing until you reach the intersection with US 90A, where you turn left. After about 3.5 miles on US 90A, turn right on FM 2091 to reach Palmetto State Park and Ottine.

PALMETTO STATE PARK

78 Park Road 11 South; FM 2091, about 14 miles from Gonzales • 830-672-3266 • www.tpwd.state.tx.us • Open daily • Fee • W variable

Palmetto State Park (270 acres), named for the tropical dwarf palmetto (Sabal minor) plant found here, hugs a crooked bend of the San Marcos River and also has a four-acre oxbow lake. The unusually luxuriant vegetation and sulphur springs have drawn naturalists from all over Texas for well over a hundred years. The SA&AP railway ran weekend excursion trains here at the turn of the century, when the place was known as the Ottine Swamp. Many people believed the spring waters had medicinal powers.

The land was acquired from private owners and the City of Gonzales beginning in 1934 and was opened in 1936. This is an unusual botanical area where the ranges of eastern and western species merge; diverse plant and animal life abound. The dwarf palmetto grows in profusion, along with many other plants not seen elsewhere in the Southwest. White-tailed deer, raccoons, armadillos, squirrels, and numerous birds live in the park.

The springs are actually now extinct, but two artesian wells supply the same warm, sulfur-laden water (with its distinctive smell) to different areas of the park. Activities include camping, hiking, fishing, pedal boating, and swimming. Palmetto's Wild Outdoor Adventure and Ecology Program for eight- to twelve-year-old children is offered the first two weeks of June.

The San Marcos River runs through the park. You can put in at Luling City Park and travel fourteen miles to Palmetto, portaging around one dam along the way; or put in at Palmetto and take out at Slayden bridge, 7.5 miles downriver. You can make a two-day trip from Luling City Park to Slayden bridge with an overnight in Palmetto along the way. It is strongly recommend that boaters wishing to camp overnight at Palmetto call the central reservation center. Texas

Parks and Wildlife Department recommends that people should not paddle the stretch of river from Luling to Palmetto State Park, until this situation has been rectified. Please contact the park for more details. Take-in and take-out points are limited; the river is mostly bordered by private land. There are no rapids, but almost always a steady current. Rentals are available at Spencer Canoes (512-357-6113) in Martindale. Check river conditions at the park or at Spencer's. You can fish for perch, catfish, and bass. Camping is permitted, and there is more than a mile of hiking trails. The Texas State Park store rents pedal boats and sells firewood and other sundries. Overnight guests should make reservations two to three weeks ahead of time, March through November.

Just past the park headquarters, on your right is the old white-stucco-with-red-tile-roof hospital, from the healing water days.

To reach Ottine, turn left at the stop sign (where FM 1586 turns into a county road), as per the Ottine Cemetery sign, just past the park headquarters.

OTTINE

Gonzales County • About 13 miles from Gonzales

Ottine owes its existence to Adolph Otto who settled here in 1879. Otto built a cotton gin shortly after his arrival, and a community grew up around it. "Ottine" is a combination of the names of J. A. Otto and his wife, Christine. The old, slowly deteriorating store/post office (now closed) is a piece of classic, turn-of-the-century Texas. There are several nice old Victorian-era houses along the way and scattered about the old store.

From Ottine, take either Park Road 11 through Palmetto State Park or FM 1586 to US 183, which is about two miles from Ottine. Turn left (north) on US 183 to reach Luling. Park Road 11 has a nice scenic overlook along the way to US 183.

US 183 begins to parallel the tracks of the Southern Pacific Railroad as you enter town. Back in the days before TV and radio, when the only book most homes had was the family Bible, folks entertained themselves by telling stories, often about each other. Many a Texas community had its own folk heroes, like Pecos Bill, Judge Roy Bean, Strap Buckner, Andrew Jackson Potter, and Gregorio Cortez. Among the blacks around Luling, there was Unkah Aaron, tales of whom were recorded for posterity in J. Mason Brewer's *Dog Ghosts and Other Texas Negro Folk Tales*. Unkah Aaron and Aunt Hetty lived on a farm about eight miles out of Luling, along these Southern Pacific tracks. At age ninety-eight, so the stories go, Unkah Aaron was as spry as a sixteen-year-old, still cutting firewood and plowing his fields, never sick a day of his life and never complaining about life's little setbacks.

One day, a white man asked Unkah Aaron why he could still get around like a teenager, and Unkah Aaron replied, "Ah don' dig up de pas', an' Ah don' tote de future."

One Saturday, Unkah Aaron rode his mule, Old Joe, into Luling to sell some eggs, butter, and frying-size hens, so that he could buy Hetty some cornmeal so she could make cracklin' bread, and some sugar for their coffee. As he rode home, some boys met him just before he reached the house, shouting, "Unkah Aaron, we come to tell you dat yo' house done burnt down wid all yo' things in hit whilst you was down to Luling."

"Yeah, chilluns, Ah knows," Unkah Aaron replied. "Ah ain't worried so much 'bout the house, but Ah sho am sorry for de chinches and the fleas."

Like many other farm families—white, black, or Hispanic—Unkah Aaron and Aunt Hetty were dirt poor.

One cold winter day, with the woodpile low and a norther blowing in, Unkah Aaron went to his pasture to cut some firewood. He brought a coon sandwich and peach butter biscuit sandwich for lunch and whacked trees until dusk. He collected the best wood and started for home. At that point, two boys from the neighboring farm ran up bellowing, "Unkah Aaron, Unkah Aaron! We jes' comed to tell you dat Aunt Hetty doned died."

"Oh yeah, is dat all?" replied Unkah Aaron. "De way y'all was hollerin' an' a-yellin', Ah thought sump'n' done railly happen."

After Aunt Hetty died, Unkah Aaron got lonesome. He listened for the Southern Pacific trains' whistles as they got to the railroad crossing just before his farm, and he would go out and sit on the steps of the little two-room house he built after the first one burned down and watch the trains roll by. He liked all the trains that passed by, but his favorite was one called the "Yellow Belly," which was painted yellow up front and had a whistle that Unkah Aaron was especially partial to. It passed by about noon every day, running between Houston and San Antonio. The train always slowed as it got to a curve at the crossing near Unkah Aaron's farm.

Unkah Aaron liked that train so much he decided one day to stop it and try to do some business with the crew. The next day as it approached, Unkah Aaron stood by the tracks waving his red handkerchief for the train to stop. The engineer ground the train to a halt, jumped out, and asked Unkah Aaron why he stopped the train.

Unkah Aaron looked him straight in the eye and asked, "You wanna buy a possum?"

"Hell, no! I don't want to buy no possum, and you get the hell off this railroad track right now!" the engineer exploded.

About this time, the conductor, who had jumped off the passenger coach wondering why Unkah Aaron had stopped the train, walked up and said to the engineer, "Leave Uncle Aaron be. I'll buy his possum."

Turning to Unkah Aaron, he asked, "How much do you want for the possum?"

Unkah Aaron bowed his head, somewhat embarrassed and replied, "Ah don' know. Ah ain't caught 'im yit."

After the end of the war, ex-slaves learned that though they were now legally free, many white Southerners were doing everything in their power to keep blacks powerless, immobilized, and landless.

When the last federal troops left the South in 1877 and Reconstruction gave way to renewed racial oppression, a former slave named Benjamin "Pap" Singleton began urging blacks to form their own independent communities in the West. Those who followed his advice called themselves "Exodusters," comparing themselves to the ancient Israelites of the Old Testament, because they believed the West would prove their promised land.

Soon these early Exodusters' hopeful letters home were being read aloud in black churches across the South, and in the spring of 1879, word spread that the federal government had set all of Kansas aside for former slaves. The rumor was false, but it sparked a genuine Exodus that brought more than fifteen thousand African Americans into Kansas within the next year.

Between November 1879 and March 1880, between three thousand and four thousand African Americans left Texas for Kansas, including approximately one thousand families from south central Texas, some of them white. Land owners and their families tried to do the work formerly done by field hands and house servants; young men from Missouri and other states and some older blacks rented land or hired out.

"Kansas seemed like an ideal place for people who were disillusioned with the black codes that had been passed in the South, the meanness of the Ku Klux Klan, the meanness of the sharecroppers who really weren't sharing the way they had agreed, and these are the people who paid five dollars, five bucks to Pap Singleton to come up the river to a new life in Kansas," said Bertha Calloway.

Singleton wasn't doing it for purely altruistic reasons. Like a lot of great westerners, he was a land speculator and hoped to make a fortune. But he did have a vision of a place where people of color could breathe free.

Not all Southern blacks chose to go to Kansas. Some refused to go out of fear of the unknown. As one ex-slave wrote, "I have a littel place and I Dont want to Brake up to Do better and Do worse." Some were simply reluctant to forsake their old homes, as was the freedman who said, "We feel sorry to think that we have to leave our fathers', mothers', wives' and children's dust and flee into other states to make a living."

This mass migration lasted little more than a year, dying out almost as quickly as it had begun.

The following song was written from the view of an ex-slave who chose to stay in the South even as his neighbors vacated their homes to go to the Kansas promised land. Originally called "De Little Cabins All Am Empty Now," the song was written as a dialect piece by Thomas P. Westendorf in 1881.

> Oh, this heart of mine am breaking with grief 'tis granted now,
> And I never will be happy any more.
> There are cabins in the valley, and cabins on the hill,
> And the green grass is growing 'round the door.
> Can't you hear the owls a-hooting in the darkness of the night?
> It brings a drop of sweat out on my brow.
> Oh, I feel so awful lonesome, I fear I'll die from fright,
> Since the little cabins all are empty now.
>
> Oh, they say they've gone to Kansas, where they say there's better times,
> But they will have to learn how to plow
> Just the same as in old Dixie, where they're wont to win their dimes;
> What's the use of living when there ain't no joy combined?
> Chorus
>
> Oh, the little 'tater patches are growing high with weeds;
> The melon vines they all have gone to waste;
> And the melons that were on them have rotted off and died,
> 'Cause there's no one left around to get a taste.
> Chorus

The emigrants came back from Kansas ragged, footsore, weary, and hungry, complaining,

They never give us no land, jus' made us plow and plant wheat in the fall. What us know about wheat?

Git kivvered up wid snow, cain't eat it; old mule cain't eat it. Ain't no sweet taters ner black eye peas in de bin; got to buy everything 'cause everything belong to somebody: take anything us need, say us steals, got to work out a fine or lay in jail. Ain't had no shoes ner no new close since befo' de wah. Whut yu all gwine do wid us?

The prodigals were received back into favor and put to work at the kind of jobs they knew best, paid wages, and if they took something they were dealt with "according to the offense."

"It began to look like white, Indian, negro, and Mexican Texans had found their place in the sun, and prosperity would be ours again. The railroad was coming from the east. Surveyors, promoters, and right-of-way men were with us in large numbers," said Calloway.

LULING

Caldwell County • 5,400 (approximately) • (830) • About 8.5 miles from Ottine

Folks have said—for the better part of one hundred years—that to get to Luling all you have to do is follow your nose. Oil and gas wells have kept Luling's coffers full, but they have also filled the air with a sulphury reek endured by natives and visitors alike for over sixty years. You are advised of your entry into Luling by a miniature oil derrick atop a sandstone pedestal bearing the inscription, "Luling Oil Since 1922."

Texas knew no Luling before 1874; the place was just a sleepy little farming and plantation neighborhood.

Leonard Corder Huff came to Caldwell County from Georgia before the Civil War, after selling a gold mine in Cass County, Georgia. He brought his large family and a score of slaves (whom he called his "people," never using the word "slave") in his own vehicles, with a drove of horses and cattle, across the country to the estate in Caldwell County previously bought for him by his agent, William Haggerty. He had four thousand acres of land here and other assets to the value of $65,000.

Huff, thinking "to whom much is given much is required," educated orphan children with his own children, he bought whole families of negroes rather than separate parents and children, and he lost one hundred slaves by the Emancipation.

Huff's wagon trains transported his and his neighbors' corn, cotton, and other produce to the coast for transshipment by water to Galveston, New Orleans, and New York, or for export to Europe.

The post office was at Prairie Lea to the west and Atlanta to the east—until W. R. "Bill" Johnston's store, with Masonic Lodge upstairs, was established at the confluence of Salt Branch and Plum Creek. Johnston's store carried a line of staple and fancy dry goods, hardware, and groceries—including barrels of molasses, vinegar, and whiskey, which was sold by the quart, gallon, five gallons, or more, but a drink was free.

It was a great joke to shift the vinegar and whiskey barrels and hang the tin cup on the wrong barrel. No Mason ever told his fellow members of the exchange. Joe Johnston was always present for the Masonic meetings, with his eight hound dogs, Marcus, Aurelius, Americus, Vespuccius, Julius, Caesar, Nip, and Tuck. Sometimes the names of Nip and Tuck were changed to Ulysses and Grant, with the saying "Grant got mixed up with a bull dog" (referring to Confederate general Joseph Johnston).

The Johnstons were cousins of Confederate general Joseph Johnston and came to Texas after Sherman's march through Georgia.

Living on Plum Creek was an extended family from Mississippi. The wife of Dr. Davis had a sister who married a "person from the North" named Jordan. Jordan built a log cabin just the other side of the Plum Creek crossing, called it a doggery, and sold strong drink. He allowed white and black boys to pitch horseshoes and play poker, seven-up, and other card games together on the premises.

After the Civil War, a local group of the "Ku Kluxers" was organized and met at the "Big Gate" of Colonel Huff's field. Because the Big Gate was a quarter of a mile from any of the buildings, no one at Huff's house ever saw anyone arrive at the gate. After meeting, the well-disguised horses and riders left by twos, threes, or fours to "patrol" the country and appear at any gathering of ex-slaves, carpetbaggers, or other troublemakers who they thought preferred stealing to work. This organization was also called "Patrollers" ("Patter Rollers" by the blacks), and the blacks had a song about them with the following chorus:

> Run nigger, run, patter roller get yo'
> Run nigger, run, it's almost day.

Judge Mackey of the Federal Bureau held court near Prairie Lea. He did his utmost to put an end to the lawless practices of the Reconstruction period, but it was impossible. Every grown man wore a pistol when he left home and was not considered well dressed without one.

Many wealthy planters like Huff went broke after the Civil War and lost their properties. Despite losing all his slaves, Huff refused to give up his gracious lifestyle. Take the wedding of his son, Thomas. H. Huff, and Miss Louranie Scoggins. The young couple and a score of attendants and friends went to Colonel Huff's for dinner after the service.

The menu included baked Virginia ham, roast pork, yams, fried chicken, giblet gravy, new potatoes, peas, cabbage slaw, gherkin pickles, plum jelly, butter, biscuits, grape jelly, peach, plum, and apricot preserves, white cake, pound cake, sillabub (an old English drink), wine, and coffee.

Then there was the ball at Colonel Huff's on San Jacinto Day, 1873. Approximately fifty of the country's young people attended. The young ladies wore full skirts with several embroidered, tucked, and ruffled petticoats, floor length, the bodice part of the dresses having a round neck and short puffed sleeves. Their dresses were of silk, mull, India muslin, or tulle. They were ruffled, flounced, embroidered, and of all the springtime colors. The men wore Prince Albert suits of broadcloth, with soft white linen shirts and fancy brocade or pique vests. At the neck, they wore the customary stocks and cravats.

The furniture had been removed from the big front room and the wide front hall for dancing. The piazza, or "front gallery," was for promenading. Two violinists and a banjo player furnished lively music for the Virginia reels, double square dances, and that very new dance, the varsouviana ("Put Your Little Foot"). Some of the country boys executed some extra fancy steps in dancing the reels, cutting pigeon wings, and "Chicken in the Bread-tray."

Small cakes and Madeira wine were served at midnight. This was the last formal entertainment, as Colonel Huff was already in failing health.

He died on July 29, 1873. When the estate was settled, it was insolvent, and his home plantation became the Chapman farm. His younger children were now dependent on their older, married brother and sisters. His second wife, Martha Meriwether Huff, and her daughters and sons, moved into Luling with her mother, Mrs. Martha Marshal Williams Meriwether.

Life began to change forever in the early 1870s with the news that the Galveston, Harrisburg, and San Antonio railroad (which would eventually become part of the Southern Pacific system) was coming from the east to San Antonio. Surveyors, promoters, and right-of-way men arrived in large numbers. Railroad stockholders wanting to see about their investments and their South Texas land made lengthy visits.

Lawyers, engineers, and surveyors arrived and secured board and lodging in the vicinity. Colonel Thomas Wentworth Peirce, president of the GH&SA Railway Company, and Major James Converse, construction engineer, came on an inspection tour. Many of the railroad company's stockholders came to Luling—or San Marcos, as it was first called, owing to its location on the San Marcos River—to inspect their holdings. Among these was a Scotch noble-woman, Lady Leah Cahar, with her footman in livery. The lady called herself a sportswoman and was fully equipped for all of these activities, wearing a hunter's green short-skirted riding habit with derby hat and high-topped laced boots. She rode about accompanied by a man from the livery stable from which the horses were obtained.

She dressed for dinner, and both of her dinner dresses and ball gowns were of fine silk, satin, or velvet, were décòlleté, and had extremely long trains perfectly fitting her (and her tilter bustle). She created a sensation when she went the two blocks to the Orchard Hotel to six o'clock dinner, with the footman walking along behind holding up her train. Gallant Drs. Van Gasken and Blunt and others soon replaced the footman, teaching the lady that American escorts carried a lady's train with her hand on his left arm and were proud to do so.

Her footman's livery looked like the colonial farmer costume, with the same kind of coat, stock, lace ruffles at the wrist, knee breeches, silver buckles at the knee, white silk stockings, black low-cut shoes, large silver buckles at the instep, hair brushed back and tied "in a club" on the nape of the neck, and a tricornered hat; only this man wore gold earrings.

The construction crew moved from the other side of Harwood on Peach Creek. The section house was moved to Salt Branch. This was a small town in itself, having bridge builders, Irish pick and shovel men, drivers of teams or plows and scrapers, hangers on, and so on. One foreman rented a three-room log house from the Huffs for his wife and small girls, saying the camp was too rough. Major Converse and another foreman were in the Huff home. It was definitely understood that a town would be built at Josey's Store.

Josey's Store was owned by a Jewish immigrant family from Bavaria who settled here just after the Civil War. Joseph Josey (1821–1889) had made a deal in the early 1870s with Galveston, Harrisburg, and San Antonio (GH&SA) railway officials to build a station for their new westbound line on his land, offering the railroad twenty-five acres. The station was to be located smack-dab in front of his store, or so he thought. A town site had been laid out, and Josey had been selling land to sooners since 1873 in anticipation. The budding settlement was already being called Joseyville. But the railroad officials decided to route the tracks a little differently, and when the first all-passenger excursion train from Galveston rolled in on the evening of September 8, 1874, Josey's Store was located on what would become the far outskirts of Luling.

One of the excursionists described their welcome:

> Here we met with a cordial reception, and a large crowd, embracing all colors and nationalities, were in waiting at our stopping place. Speeches of welcome were made by Mr. E. Lewis, Mr. Burgess and Mr. Cook.
> Luling is a city in embryo. The rude yet majestic old oak has fallen, the thick, shrubby mesquite has been cleared away, and it seems not difficult at this time, to discern the outlines of the long drawn and principal avenue, the din of the hammer, the clatter of workshops and the hum of a busy spirit is heard long after nightfall. In the morning we welcome the music again. Here we see life in its every form and variety—the frontier boy upon his mustang pony and wide brimmed hat, the city gentleman, the man of less polish, the educated and the uneducated. In our sleepers we spent the night, and early next morning took leave of this young, yet fast growing place to return to Galveston.

At high noon exactly that day, halfway between Sixth and Fifth avenues, Lady Cahar drove the silver spike, saying, "This is the center of town I name Luling." People from Prairie Lea and some other places refused invitations to go home with the citizens, saying, "We have never eaten in a hotel and we can visit you some other time. It was a great day!"

The station at Luling opened on September 10.

On November 28, 1874, "D. R." wrote enthusiastically to the *Galveston Daily News*:

> The town of Luling is to-day the fastest little town in the state, and is frequently spoken of as *the red-hot town*, and the life and times here can be truly compared to the mining days in California.
> The post oak forest four months ago was the borne and habitation of the panther, bear and deer is to-day, covered with a thriving town and an incorporated city numbering about five hundred houses with a population of two thousand five hundred, and some of the buildings would reflect credit on the Queen City of the Gulf. There are about one hundred and fifty business houses, thirty-one of which are bar rooms, five hotels, five livery stables, one bank, and restaurants and boarding houses in abundance.

For a year or so, Luling served as the terminus of the GH&SA railway, and the place roared. Folks called it the wildest town in America. Dogtown, just west of Luling, was known to offer every vice known to man. Luling had no local government in those days, only county and state law haphazardly enforced by a few deputies. Judge Lynch settled more than a few cases. They say Sam Bass, Wes Hardin, Jesse James, the Younger Brothers, King Fisher, Texas Jack, and Austin's onetime marshal Ben Thompson visited Luling during those lawless days. Journalist Alexander Sweet, a visitor to Luling in those early days, recorded the following impressions:

About noon we arrived in Luling, which, a short time ago was the terminus of the San Antonio Railroad, and it remained so for almost a year. It was a type of the town created by the railroads in their progress through Texas. Its history would read like a chapter from the biography of the man with the wonderful lamp,—its site, one day the feeding-ground of the jackass-rabbit and the home of the *coyote*; a month hence, a wooden town of a thousand inhabitants. Where *then* the rattlesnake aired his poisonous fangs, *now* the denizen of the music-hall exhibits her equally dangerous blandishments. *Then* the wild beasts of the field, as their instincts and necessities taught them, made war on each other with the weapons nature furnished: *now* human beasts (gamblers and roughs), prompted by the devil and bad whiskey, destroy each other with the deadly derringer and the murderous bowie-knife.

In one short month the howling wilderness is transformed, by the nervous energy and resistless enterprise of the railroad pioneer, into a town of a hundred houses, where beer is sold, billiards are played, the gentle tiger is bucked, and the strange woman holds her court; where the scattered ragments of the Third Commandment darken the air, and the sound of the pistol shot is monotonously frequent,—a pandemonium of vice, folly, and sin, where the struggle for gold, and the viler passions of men, blot out the better part of man's nature,—a place where a drink of whiskey costs twenty-five cents, a poor cup of straight coffee the same amount, and a badly cooked dinner, served on a rough pine table without a cloth, costs a dollar,—a spot where all manner of trades and professions are represented, where the bedbug luxuriates, and even the book-agent lurketh around, with his brazen check burnished more elaborately than usual, to meet the exigencies of the situation. So moves the car of progress; so the "star of empire westward takes its way," and civilization's march is onward toward the gateway of the setting sun.

Walking up the straggling streets, we find the houses in irregular rows, and fronting on the streets at every possible angle of incidence. The houses are mostly of the dry-goods box style of architecture, the fronts covered with roughly painted signs for the purpose of letting the world know the proprietor's business, and how badly he can spell. Here is a restaurant where the owner advertises "Squar Meals at Resonable Figgers, and Bord by the Day or Weak;" next, a Chinese laundry; then a beer-saloon; across the street a gun-shop; next to it a saloon; then a bakery, a saloon, another saloon with billiards, a lumber-yard, a dance-house, a restaurant, a free-and-easy, a saloon, a shooting-gallery, a faro-bank, a grocery, a saloon and hotel, a ten-pin alley, a concert-hall; and so on to the end of the street. Queer and suggestive signs some of these whiskey-dens have,—"The Sunset," "The How-Come-You-So," "The Panther's Den;" and on one, in a North-Texas town, is inscribed the legend, "Road-to-Ruin Saloon—Ice-cold Beer 5 cts. a Skooner."

While passing the Dew-Drop-Inn saloon, we were startled by several pistol-shots being fired in quick succession inside the house, and only a few feet from us. Assuming a safe position behind a convenient cotton-bale, we awaited the development of events. A loud-talking crowd was in the saloon. The crash of glass, and the fragments of billiard-cues that came whizzing out of the door, indicated that somebody was raising Gehenna inside. As the shooting ceased, the crowd came pouring out, carrying the limp form of a man who was shot in the leg, had a bullet in his left lung, and was bleeding profusely from a knife-cut on the neck. Inquiry elicited the information that he was a cowboy, who, being on a "high lonesome," entered the saloon, and incontinently began discharging his six-shooter at the lamps and mirrors behind the bar. This, it seems, is a favorite pastime with the high-spirited cattle-kings in their moments of enthusiasm. The role had been enacted, however, with such frequency, of late, that it began to pall on the taste of the spectators.

What was at first a tragedy, exciting and dramatic, was now but a vapid piece of very weak comedy of questionable taste and doubtful propriety. So thought the barkeeper; and he emphasized his views by placing a few bullets where he thought they would do the most good, and have the most mollifying effect. The wounds were fatal. The playful cowboy died, and, as a bystander remarked, "never knew what hurt him."

The barkeeper was never tried. In less than twenty-four hours this "difficulty," as it was called, passed out of the public mind in the light of a fresh and more interesting incident of a like character, where two men were killed, and one woman dangerously wounded.

So long as a town remains the terminus of a railroad in Western Texas, it presents the characteristics described. The roughest of wild frontiersmen and desperadoes congregate there. It is what is called, in the classic vernacular of the country, "a hoorah place." As soon as the terminus is located ten or twelve miles farther west, a new town springs up, the rowdy element moves out of the old one, half of the houses are moved off to the new town, and the place, wrecked and dismantled, is left to the few people who came to stay. It is then that the real progress and civilization begins. Brick houses take the place of the wooden ones carried away; the bulletholes in the doors and shutters are filled with putty; the brazen noise of the music-hall is hushed, and in its stead the voice of the Methodist circuit-rider is heard singing the songs of Zion.

In the hotel where we were stopping, there was a guest whose name, as the register showed, was Joseph P. Maxwell, but who was better known among his associates and the people of the town as "Monte Joe." He had been in Luling about 3 months. No one knew where he came from, and no one cared to know. He had stepped off the train one morning, had registered at the hotel, and in 3 days afterwards was on speaking terms with one-half of the male population of the place.

In a town like Luling, society was not exacting. A stranger was not required to exhibit credentials, nor to state who his grandfather was, as a condition of entrée into society. In fact, society was of a mixed character,—if it had any character at all,—and could not afford to be particular.

A man named Lewis Ginger was riding the stage to San Antonio one day in 1874 or 1875 with two nuns and a man named Rowdy Joe Lowe, husband of Rowdy Kate and the proprietor of a saloon, a dance hall, a gambling hall, and a crew of dancing girls in Luling. He was telling his fellow travelers about how a jury of twelve good men had recently acquitted him of murder, "without leaving their seats," for having rid the town of a lowdown skunk.

The four-horse stage was rolling at a respectable clip when all of a sudden the lead horses turned in their tracks and brought the coach to a lurching stop. The driver yelled out, "Great guns, what a rattler!" It was more than eight feet long and as big around as the leg of a good-sized man, with twenty rattles. Its rattling could be heard at least two hundred yards.

Rowdy Joe said, "Just watch me cut that fellow's throat." He pulled out his Colt 45, stepped within about fifteen feet of the monster, and almost severed the head with one shot.

Things were so bad that in March 1875 in the state legislature, Representative Leonidas Jefferson Storey of Lockhart presented a petition of the citizens of Luling stating that the town was infested with lawless and desperate characters, that the mayor was in jail, that there was nobody to try drunks and downs, and so forth, and asking the legislature to help them out and to send a supernumerary from the legislature over.

But by December 1875, a new terminus station had opened at Kingsbury, twelve miles to the west.

As the railroad moved westward toward San Antonio, the construction crews and fly-by-nighters moved with it. Luling quieted down and kept growing, even though it wasn't a pretty place. Neighboring townsfolk were wont to say, "Luling has sand, fleas, grass burrs, and so many new people it's hard to tell who is what." Dogtown became Ragtown, Luling's "colored" community.

By the end of November 1874, a local correspondent bragged to the *Austin Daily Statesman* that two thousand bales of cotton, and three thousand pounds of hides daily, had been shipped since September 15. The town was incorporated; it had a population of 2,500 and 150 business houses, including hotels, banks, livery stables, and stores of all kinds.

Beginning in 1875, the tent dwellers, bridge builders, and troublemakers were moving with the railroad to Dorn's Ford on the San Marcos. By 1877, the greater number of the town's nightspots were replaced by other business places. One of the music and dance halls became Collins and Johnston's private bank. A great majority of professional gamblers and other undesirable citizens had followed the railroad west. However, some who gambled remained, along with the wild young men who left town on running horses after sowing their "wild oats," yelling like Comanches. "Judge Lynch" continued to solve cases, such as the unknown man hung on the Salt Branch bridge.

Still, by February 1877, Luling was described as one of the most moral, Christian, and churchgoing towns in all Western Texas and was now known for its quiet and good order. A correspondent of the *State Gazette* reported that there had been fewer violations of the law in Luling than in any other railroad town in Texas of its age, size, or surroundings, as proved by the records of the justice and district courts. City offices were most vigilant, and liquor had been voted out of Luling and the rest of Caldwell County, for a while anyway. Only one man in the county chose to fight the local option law—a Mr. Munster of Luling. The other saloon keepers closed out stock and went into other lines of business. The prohibition of liquor was no doubt brought on by tragedies such as the following in Lockhart: On the evening of August 17, 1876, rapid firing was heard in the vicinity of the Granger Saloon. A number of men repaired to the spot, where they found a man dead on the walk, shot in the heart. It proved to be a man who had come in from the Cardwell Springs in the morning and who gave his name as Wash Perry. He had been drinking heavily during the day and was said to have attacked several persons with a knife a short time before he was killed.

Although Luling's justice of the peace declared that he had fined more men for drunkenness since, than prior to, local option's passage, the *State Gazette* correspondent saw no evidence of drinking, nor where the opportunity to drink was. On the contrary, churches and schools were flourishing, men of families were moving in every day, and women and children went unattended at all times and in all localities without fear or hindrance.

There are several stories regarding the origins of Luling's name. One is that it was the maiden name of Thomas W. Peirce's wife; another is that it was named for a Judge Luling. A more entertaining story involves a Chinaman, Ling Lu, who came along with the railroad crews as a laundry man. A generally easygoing man, Ling Lu didn't stand for certain things, such as being called a girl (on account of his pigtail), being asked if he were Mexican or black, or being asked if he used his mouth and teeth to dampen shirts for ironing. Ultimately, Ling Lu—or Lu Ling as he was sometimes called—cut his hair short and adopted the name John Chinaman. He stayed in this town for ten years without once leaving. In addition to his laundry service, Lu Ling ran a message service and offered the town's first indoor toilets as an adjunct to his laundry shop.

But the cold, hard truth is that Luling derived its name from Charles Luling, a wealthy and influential banker of New York City, a personal and particular friend of Mr. Peirce, the president of the Galveston, Houston, and San Antonio railroad.

Luling served as a gathering point and supply center for cattle drovers on the Chisholm Trail. It also was the railroad end of a freight road that ran to Chihuahua, Mexico. A stage service ran between Luling and Austin, via Lockhart.

In 1880, Joseph Josey gave up merchandising and moved his family to a new "brownstone" home on Railroad Avenue. Herman Josey and his cousin Herman Golesticker returned from college in New York and were active in promoting the Josey market garden and in selling town lots.

In 1889, a second railroad, the San Antonio and Aransas Pass, was built through Luling, connecting it with Lockhart and Shiner.

The railroad may have birthed Luling, but the town took no guff from either Southern Pacific (SP) or the SA&AP. In 1890, engineer Andy Williams came on a special car to stand trial for running his train through the corporate limits faster than six miles an hour. After hearing the evidence, Mayor Walker imposed a fine of twenty-five dollars on the defendant.

That year, Luling had an opera house, two hotels, and a population of two thousand, and it was anticipating completion of a system of waterworks, electricity, and another ice factory. The number of residents fell to 1,349 by 1900 but increased again to 1,502 by the 1920s.

Cotton ruled the local economy until the momentous year of 1922. On August 9 of that year, Edgar B. Davis' Rafael Rios No. 1 well blew in, opening up an oil field twelve miles long and two miles wide. Davis had discovered oil where geologists had sworn there was none. For a while it had looked as if the experts were right; the first six wells Davis' United North and South Oil Company had drilled were dry. But Davis was a man of faith and a man of mission. Deeply religious, Davis believed that God had directed him to come to Luling to deliver the city and Caldwell County from King Cotton's monopolistic grip on the area economy.

Edgar Davis was six foot three inches and weighed 350 pounds in his prime. Instead of going to Harvard to play football, he had taken a six-dollar-per-week job in a shoe company, working his way up to company treasurer. After a nervous breakdown in 1908, he traveled the world for year. In the Far East, he became interested in rubber and later persuaded the General Rubber Company to let him buy several large rubber plantations to manage for the company. He became a company director and left the rubber business a decade later, worth $3.5 million.

By 1922, his brother Oscar and friends had some oil leases near Luling. They asked Edgar to check the leases even though Edgar had no experience in oil. He learned that the experts thought there was no oil in the county. But Edgar had a hunch. By the summer of 1922, he had drilled six dry wells and had started a seventh. At that point, he had no phone, no office furniture, an overdrawn bank account, and unpaid workers. But finally, in August, the seventh well came in. By 1924, the field was producing fifty-seven thousand barrels daily, or eleven million barrels per year. Four years later, he sold out.

Luling roared again during those hectic oil days, as Deputy Sheriff Tom Brown remembered: "Many a night I put 35–40 men in jail. Weekends you never went to bed. Friday, Saturday, Sunday you might as well stay up all night."

Davis had given away most of his rubber millions before coming to Luling, but when he became rich again he resumed his generous ways. Early in 1926, Davis sold his field to Magnolia Oil for $12.1 million. And he set out to give it all away. That June he threw the biggest barbecue Luling has ever known. Davis invited fifteen thousand people from three counties. To feed them, Davis purchased six tons of beef, two thousand fryers, five thousand pounds of lamb, seven thousand cakes, innumerable barrels of ice cream, and truckloads of soda. But where would he hold the event? Obviously he couldn't hold it in one of his smelly, dirty oil fields, so he bought 140 acres on both sides of the San Marcos River. One bank was for whites, the other for blacks. The total bill for the bash was $4 million. Five managers were given $200,000 each, and all employees got bonuses commensurate with the time they had spent working for Davis, amounting to between 50 and 100 percent of their total accrued salaries. Davis also gave Luling a golf course and gave Luling's blacks their own athletic club-house, among many other gifts. He established the Luling Foundation in 1929, a demonstration farm of over one thousand acres, operated for the advance-ment of all facets of agriculture. He sponsored three annual scenery painting competitions that cost him $65,000.

He spent $1.5 million over two years to finance a play about reincarnation named *The Ladder*. It was a failure of colossal proportions. One critic called it "a large, richly upholstered piece of nothing at all," while a kinder soul merely noted that producer Brock Pemberton "presented quite a long play." It tanked on Broadway after first foundering in Stamford, Detroit, and Cleveland. Davis tried to hire Eugene O'Neill to doctor the play, but O'Neill didn't even ac-knowledge the offer.

Davis invested on hunches, several of which paid off, as we have seen. But the investment hunches he made with the remainder of his oil fortune failed him. Massachusetts, where Davis had previously lived, still regarded him as a citizen and sued him for back taxes. After years in court, the state won a $700,000 judgment. So, in 1935, Davis went bankrupt.

He continued to live in Luling and with donated money from townspeople made something of an oil field comeback, but the money he earned was out of reach because he had never settled the lawsuit he lost to the Commonwealth of Massachusetts. His weight dropped to 200 pounds. He became Luling's lead-ing bridge player. Untroubled by the highs and lows in his life, Davis died in Galveston in 1951 and is buried here, revered as Luling's number-one citizen.

Back when he was giving his wealth away, he had said, "I have no right to any of this money. I'm called a success, but there's as shadowy a line between success and failure as between sanity and insanity. When I share my money I'm just equalizing things a little."

Luling was also home for thirty years to another one of Texas' more unique adopted sons. Julius Myers—the last town crier in America to ply his trade—moved here from New York City at age sixteen for health reasons. His com-mercial pronouncements echoed through the streets of Luling until he moved to San Antonio in 1912.

The September 18, 1929, edition of the *Victoria Advocate* noted his passing: "Julius Myers, famous town crier of San Antonio, and a most colorful figure, died in his sleep of a heart attack Wednesday. From 1912 until about two years ago, when city officials banned him from street ballyhooing, Julius was seen daily on downtown thoroughfares. He was one of the few town criers in America and was known as such to thousands of tourists."

There are dozens of pump jacks within the city limits of Luling. Perhaps you noticed, as you drove into Luling on US 90/US 183, the mosquito pumpers strung out every few feet along the railroad tracks, painted up as grasshoppers, mules, crows, melon eaters, and such. The chamber of commerce (www .lulingcc.org) commissioned local artists to create moveable characters.

Luling's oil may help keep Texas and America moving, but more dear to most Texas hearts and palates are Luling's watermelons. One of the state's leading watermelon producers, Luling celebrates its most delicious product each June with the Watermelon Thump.

Davis Street, Luling's main business thoroughfare, parallels US 90 along the north side of the railroad tracks. Continue a short distance on US 90, past the intersection where US 183 turns north, and turn right on Avenue N. Cross the tracks and park in one of the shaded parking stalls that are located between Davis and the tracks.

Take a stroll down Davis. Downtown Luling doesn't have the architectural charm of Gonzales, but it has lures of its own.

Downtown Davis Street still retains most of its early to mid-twentieth-century charm, down to the old "Stop" and "Keep Right" stop signals embedded at the intersections of Davis and Laurel, and Davis and Pecan. Made more than eighty years ago in Lockhart, these low, round cast-iron domes, called "turtles" back in the day, are a charming reminder of the days of Model Ts and open-car motoring in general, and were once common in towns across Texas and the rest of the country.

The concept was that one or two of these "turtles" should be placed at each of the four corners of the business blocks, and one at other streets leading into the town's highways, giving travelers of the highway the right-of-way through town. All that was needed at first was to have several traffic officers to "learn" the people how to observe these stop signals. The idea was, for instance, that a car going south on Laurel must come to a complete stop before entering onto Davis (then the highway street), the same with a car coming from the south on the same street.

At the corner of Davis and Pecan, someone has removed enough stucco from the side of the Allen building so that we may all enjoy the old painted advertisement for Battle Axe Plug Tobacco.

CENTRAL TEXAS OIL PATCH MUSEUM

421 E. Davis • 875-3214 • www.oilmuseum.org • Open Monday through Friday

The name says it all; the heady history of the area's oil industry is preserved with examples of equipment, photos, and the like. All in all, the museum does a good job of depicting life in the Oil Patch from about 1925 to 1950. It is housed in the imposing Walker Brothers building, built in 1885 or 1886 as a mercantile store by J. K. and W. B. Walker not long after their arrival in Luling.

SARG RECORDS

311 E. Davis

Still standing at press time was the small building housing Sarg Records, run by Charlie Fitch until his death in 2006. One of the great undersung heroes of Texas music promotion, Fitch was a sergeant during World War II, hence the name. In business since 1953, with more than 150 singles and three albums under his belt, Fitch was one of the few record executives who can say he said no to Willie Nelson. He often told the story, with no remorse, of the day in 1954 when Willie sent him a demo tape in hopes of getting a contract with Sarg.

"Nobody, but nobody, would have recorded it, so I just threw the tape in the corner, where it stayed for years. It wasn't recordable, just two times two stuff, you know. Willie was a deejay back then, and the tape he sent me had been recorded over that day's stock market report, so the last song trailed off into the last of that day's stock market quotes. He sent it to me and said, 'If you like it, tell me. If you don't like it, tell me. It won't hurt my feelings.'"

Fitch's 150-odd singles included records by artists such as Cecil Moore, Homer and Gene and the Westerners, Arnold Parker and the Mustangs, Adolph Hofner and the Pearl Wranglers, the immortal Cajun Link Davis Sr., and even San Antonio rock-and-roller Sir Douglas Sahm, back in 1953 when he was just a twelve-year-old local prodigy known as "Little Doug." "Real American Joe" and "Rollin', Rollin'" are the record's two songs; it is a collector's item, as is Link Davis Sr.'s 45-rpm single, "Big Houston," backed by "Cockroach." But Fitch's most prolific and interesting artist was Adolph Hofner (see Moulton). A look at the names of just a few of his recordings with Sarg reveals his musical versatility: "Longhorn Stomp," "Bandera Waltz," "Westphalia Waltz," "Shiner Song" ("Farewell to Prague"), "El Rancho Grande," "Julida Polka," "Kansas City," "Rockin' and a Boppin'," "Cotton-eyed Joe," "Spanish Two-Step," "Dude Ranch Schottische," "Krasna Amerika/Beautiful America Waltz," and "Steel Guitar Rag." Fitch was also a jukebox distributor, and some of his classic oldies could still be seen through the display window at press time.

DINING

CITY MARKET

633 E. Davis, near US 183 • 875-9019 • Monday through Saturday 7–6 • No Cr. • W

Brisket, pork ribs, and ring sausage are served up in the little enclosed pit room at the back of the market. The brisket is lean and tender and good. The link sausage is also tasty and less greasy than most. Accolades go to the pork ribs: succulent, meaty, and with a slightly sweet, smoky flavor. One regular patron from Houston was once overheard to say of the ribs, "Sometimes I take $40 worth of ribs home to the kids. They eat on them 'til they're full, run around for a while, then dig in again." Your meat is served on the traditional brown butcher paper with crackers or white bread. You eat in the front room, where beer, pop, potato salad, slaw, and beans are sold. Grab a bottle of their special homemade sauce and dig in.

LULING BAR-B-Q

709 E. Davis • 875-3848 • Open daily • W

Luling Bar-B-Q's main advantage over the City Market is that it is open Sundays, when many tourists visit Luling, and it serves many more side dishes. Otherwise, the meat is of the same stellar quality, including the succulent little loop sausages.

OTHER ATTRACTIONS

FRANCIS-AINSWORTH HOUSE

214 S. Pecan • 875-3435 • www.ainsworthhouse.com • B&B

Dr. Sidney Joseph Francis settled in Luling in 1889 after earning a medical degree from Tulane University. Dr. and Mrs. Francis had a modest frame house constructed on this corner in about 1896; it was enlarged in 1916 to its present size. Prior to Francis' death in 1935, his youngest daughter and her husband, H. Miller Ainsworth, moved into the house. The house remained in the Ainsworth family until 1989, when it was deeded to the city of Luling. It was a museum until 2003, when it was sold and transformed into a bed-and-breakfast. It has a full-service restaurant and can be rented for special events.

LULING FOUNDATION AGRICULTURAL DEMONSTRATION FARM

523 S. Mulberry • 875-2438 • www.lulingfoundation.org • Call or visit the website to arrange a tour

Edgar Davis established this model farm to promote alternative agriculture to the farmers of Caldwell, Gonzales, and Guadalupe counties in an attempt to free them from the evils associated with a one-crop agricultural system. A free, public institution, it shows the advantages of diversified livestock and agricultural operations and has a number of educational programs and several annual and topic-specific field days. The farm currently measures 1,123 acres; eighteen soil types are found. There are 5.5 miles of San Marcos River frontage. You can buy fresh produce at the office.

LULING JEWISH CEMETERY

N. Hackberry near Newton St.

Thanks in part to Joseph Josey, Luling had a sizeable Jewish community, large enough to have its own cemetery, although no rabbi was ever hired or synagogue organized. And as we shall see, Luling's early propensity toward violence extended to the Jewish population as well. William Finklestein was the first unfortunate to be buried in the Jewish cemetery, in 1879, killed in a quarrel that began over a sale at his store. His widow borrowed four dollars from William's family to buy a barrel of apples and supported herself and their four children by making pies and jellies. It is said that Jesse James and company stayed with her on two occasions, paying $500 for room and board. True or not, she did well enough to send her boys to college and to give substantial dowries to her daughters. In 1876, Reuben and Sarah Jacobs settled in Luling. They tried to keep kosher, but the kosher meat they ordered from San Antonio often arrived spoiled. A hot-tempered cattle buyer, Reuben once killed a man with his fists after the man pulled a knife on him. His eldest daughter was murdered by her first cousin when she refused to marry him. What happened to him is debatable; one account says he escaped by hopping a train, while another says he was taken away by a vengeful mob.

Most of the Jews who settled in small Texas towns were Orthodox by training and culture. But very quickly they either moderated their religious practices or moved to the city. Keeping kosher and observing the holy days, festivals, and other rituals was inconvenient or impossible. For shopkeepers, it would have been economic suicide not to work on the Sabbath, which was the biggest trading day of the week, when all the farmers and ranchers came into town to buy and sell goods. Jews were happy to be here. Whatever conditions and compromises they encountered, it had been far worse in Germany, Eastern Europe, and Russia.

Reform Judaism, which began in nineteenth-century Germany, was the ideal compromise for Jews trying to survive and prosper in small-town Texas: saving their identity as Jews but discarding the imperative of "mitzvot," living a Jewish life. By 1910, there was a Jewish presence in many county seats and trading towns in the state, often in the form of a Hebrew Free Loan or other self-help society, subscribers to the Jewish Publication Society, or a cemetery.

Jewish farmers and ranchers were a rarity. Few of the Jews had owned land in Europe or had otherwise accumulated much wealth. Most of the Jews who immigrated to Texas went into business for themselves. Anyone with a horse and wagon could make a living: hauling freight, carrying trunks from the train station, moving households, peddling fruits and vegetables, or as a junk man picking up discarded articles. It was easy to pick up scrap metal, paper, rags, slaughterhouse by-products, and other scrap nobody wanted, and to then clean, sort, grade, and assemble it in commercially viable lots. They were always on the lookout for new markets for whatever scrap they found. During the Luling oil boom, salvage dealers sold used steel, pipe, and drums for the oil industry.

Many of the Jewish immigrants began as backpack peddlers of goods acquired by selling their possessions at the port of entry, which was usually Galveston. Trade routes, railroad lines, new towns, established communities, and relatives who had already arrived drew Jewish settlers to diverse areas of Texas. When the peddler found a hospitable community that offered the potential for earning a livelihood, he would set down roots, open a small store, and establish a chain linking him to his supplier at the port of entry.

In turn, as relatives arrived, they were sent out as peddlers from the new location to newer areas, where they opened stores. A family could get into the retail grocery business for as little as $200, in a fifteen-foot front store with living quarters in the back, and a daily replenished stock of fruit, vegetables, and a few staples. With $500, you could open up a dry goods store with a stock of "workingman's" clothing and a cigar box for a cash register. Business was cyclical, commensurate with the area's cotton crop or other agricultural seasons. Merchants often carried customers until their crops or animals were sold. No one wanted to lose a sale, so Jewish merchants were more than eager to please their customers, offering low prices, a friendly sales style, and special service.

The Luling Jewish Cemetery contains about one hundred graves, including those of the Joseys and Louis Goodman, known as "the Rabbi with the five wives." Three of them are buried alongside Goodman here. One of Joseph and Fannie Josey's five children was Noah, so named because he was born during a flood. Fannie was placed atop a raft of cotton bales and towed to higher ground where she safely gave birth.

BLANCHE PARK

US 183 at Fannin • Open at all times • Free • W

The shotgun-style log cabin in this little park is notable for its dovetail notch construction, which is a comparative rarity in Texas. Reverend William Johnson (1822–1889), a farmer and Baptist minister who came to Texas in 1833, built this cabin near Tenney Creek (eleven miles northeast of Luling) in the 1870s. Dr. Thomas Benton Coopwood (1860–1932) used the cabin as his office in the late 1890s. Coopwood served as Caldwell County's health officer for more than thirty years. The cabin was moved here in 1972 and restored.

ZEDLER'S MILL COMPLEX

San Marcos River at SH 80, south of town

The current Zedler's Mill Complex dates to the late 1880s, when Fritz Zedler began rebuilding the mill that burned down just after he had purchased it in 1888. The mill, which was built in 1874, had been destroyed several times by floods. Zedler was born in Prussia in 1840 and came with his family to Texas in 1852. He began hauling mail and freight at the age of eighteen across southern Texas. He served briefly in the Confederate Army, moved for a year to Mexico in 1863, and eventually established a mill in Gonzales County in 1872. In 1890, the mill began supplying water to Gonzales and electricity thereafter. The Zedler home, built in 1900, was considered to be one of the finest in the area at the time. Fritz Zedler died in 1932. The mill ceased operations in the 1960s. The sawmill/gristmill/cotton gin complex, most of which dates from 1900 to the 1920s, is one of the most complete in existence in the state and is slowly being restored.

ANNUAL EVENT

JUNE

WATERMELON THUMP

Downtown • 875-3214 • www.watermelonthump.com • Last full weekend in June • W variable

The Watermelon Thump pays tribute to the area's sweetest crop. A parade, Watermelon Queen coronation, dance, food booths, arts-and-crafts show, fiddling contest, golf tournament, and grand champion watermelon auction are among the activities. The winning melon has fetched over $3,000 in the past. The season's biggest melons tip the scales in the sixty- to eighty-pound range, slightly smaller than the ninety-plus-pound grand champs grown in McDade, but sweetness counts more than size, Luling growers retort.

From the City Market in downtown Luling, go north on US 183 two blocks and turn left on SH 80, which is also called Austin Street. In about 5.5 miles you'll come to Stairtown and an intersection with FM 671. Turn right on FM 671.

STAIRTOWN

Caldwell County • 35 • About 5.5 miles from Luling

The dozens of wells that you see and smell and hear pumping away are working Davis' original golden field. The original Rios No. 1 well is located along FM 671, 0.8 miles off SH 80. The rotten smell is hydrogen sulfide, which is a by-product of production.

BURDITT WELLS

Caldwell County • About 10.5 miles from Luling

Caldwell County has a number of historic springs, mostly mineral laden (calcium, sodium bicarbonate, fresh to slightly saline, hard, alkaline, high chloride, and nitrate content). Mineral and sulphur springs abound in this section of the county, and folks often picnicked at them. One of the most popular springs was Burditt Wells, now known as Mineral Springs and located in the Joliet community. Dr. H. N. Burditt discovered the springs in about 1870 and built a resort with a large hotel. Invalids afflicted with scrofula, rheumatism, erysipelas, ulcers, malarious fevers, liver complaints, derangements of the spleen, jaundice, dyspepsia, dropsy, affliction of the kidneys, constipation, Bright's disease, piles, and so on, were drawn in great numbers here. The waters were claimed to be antibilious, cathartic, diuretic, alterative, and tonic. The hotel, now long gone, served those who wished to take the waters for an extended period. There were dances and baseball games.

The water was bottled and sold nationwide. In August 1876, the Baker, Graham and Company drugstore in Austin was advertising Burditt's Sour Well Water. This "very valuable medicinal water" contained sulphate of magnesium, sulphate of alumina, free sulphuric acid, a little chloride of sodium, and a trace of iron.

The San Antonio and Aransas Pass railroad (locals called it the SAP) stopped here on its daily run between Lockhart and Yoakum. The waters of Burditt Wells were particularly prized, and families would often pack a picnic lunch, ride the train down in the morning, and return home on the evening run. In June 1890, the Burditt Wells property was put up for sale by virtue of a decree of the District Court of Caldwell County between the heirs of Dr. H. N. Burditt, deceased. The resort and the well dried up in the 1930s, as did curative-water resorts all over Texas and the United States.

Not much is left at the Mineral Springs these days save a tranquil, shady cemetery and church. The SAP tracks, which roughly paralleled US 183 and FM 671, were pulled up years ago. The Mineral Springs are near the church on the south bank of the west fork of Plum Creek, about 250 meters east of FM 671. They are also known as Cardwell Springs and Rogers Springs, although the original Cardwell Springs were about three miles from the Burditt resort and sported their own hotel, a large, roomy frame building, some fifty by one hundred feet, situated convenient to the well and springs—two in number. Many visitors chose to camp in the adjacent woods. Mr. Rogers made mineral salts by evaporating the spring water and then sold them. The water was believed to have curative powers but was strong, harsh, and with an unpleasant taste.

Continue north on FM 671 toward Lockhart, which runs into US 183. Continue north on US 183 to Lockhart.

LOCKHART

Caldwell County Seat • 12,000 (approximate) • (512) • About 15 miles from Luling

Lockhart was originally known as Plum Creek and had a post office by 1847. Named in 1848 for surveyor and Indian fighter Byrd Lockhart, on whose land the town was laid out, Lockhart became county seat for the newly organized Caldwell County.

Nearby Plum Creek was the scene of the Battle of Plum Creek, where a volunteer army of Texans, including Mathew "Old Paint" Caldwell, Edward Burleson, and Ben McCulloch, decisively defeated a band of marauding Comanches on August 12, 1840. The Comanches had swept down the Guadalupe River valley that summer, pillaging, plundering, and killing. The rampage was their revenge for the Texans' deadly duplicity at the Courthouse Fight in March 1840, where, under pretense of peace talks, Comanches were lured into a San Antonio building and a number of them were slaughtered. After leveling Linnville in Calhoun

County, the Comanches began to retreat westward, hotly pursued by the Texans. The warriors suffered heavy casualties on the banks of Plum Creek and were never again to be a serious threat east of the Balcones Escarpment.

But there were occasional raids. According to Tom Gambrell of Lockhart, just before the Civil War, twenty Indians swept down from the north. They drove a wagon filled with plunder, including a lot of silver items. The raiders captured a white woman and took off along the eastern bank of Clear Fork Creek, which runs south about two miles west of town. The settlers soon set off in pursuit. The Indians couldn't go very fast with their wagon of treasure, so they unhitched the horses, emptied the silver into the creek, left the wagon there, and fled with the woman on horseback. The settlers found the wagon and continued the chase. The raiders had turned southwest and were approaching the steep hills and valleys that surround Round Top Mountain some eight miles southwest of Lockhart. Indians used to light signal fires atop Round Top Mountain to alert their comrades. The whites were only a half mile behind the Indians when they entered this rough country. The Indian carrying the woman knocked her off the horse with a tomahawk blow to the head so that he could escape into the brush in time. The woman was dead when the whites reached her. The Indians navigated the brush better than the whites, so they escaped.

The white settlers buried her close to town, and the grave, neatly arched with stones, lies close by the Lockhart–Prairie Lea highway, about 1.5 miles out of town. The whites didn't search for the silver that evening, but they went to the creek the next day to look. They found nothing but took the wagon. Others came to search over the years, dredging, seining, and gouging the bottom, but in vain. Some say the Indians sneaked back that night to retrieve the silver, others say it sank into the muddy mire. A number of the pursuers swear that they saw the silver tumble into the water, but no trace of the treasure was ever found.

George Hindes moved to Caldwell County from Mississippi with his parents at the age of eleven in 1855. He first visited Lockhart on Christmas Day 1855, and he described the experience: "In those days Lockhart was wild and woolly, a wide-open town, where whiskey and every other kind of 'blue ruin' flowed freely. That day I saw a Mr. Perry kill a Mr. Cabaniss with a knife. It was a frightful experience. My curiosity caused me to ask what caused the trouble, and I was told it was whiskey. Then I went strong for prohibition and was never intoxicated in my life."

In the years following the Civil War, Lockhart was a principal staging center for herds starting up the Chisholm Trail. In fact, Lockhart's Colonel Jack Myers really marked out most of what was to become known as the Chisholm Trail when he drove a herd up to Abilene, Kansas, in 1867. A distinguished Civil War veteran (hence his title) and California forty-niner, Myers drove his first herd of cattle up to Salt Lake City. On his way home, he stopped in Kansas at Junction City. There he met Joseph McCoy, a northern entrepreneur who had dreams of shipping thousands of Texas beeves east and north from Kansas via the rapidly expanding railroads. It was a marriage made in heaven; McCoy agreed to build loading pens, a hotel, and all the other facilities the trail drivers would need. He asked only, "If I build these pens, will you bring me 25,000 head of cattle a year?" "We will bring you a million head a year," Myers answered. Myers was true to his word, going home to spread the gospel and gather up a fresh herd. He was the first to reach McCoy's new city. Millions of Texas beeves followed in his wake. Myers died in 1874 and is buried in Lockhart Cemetery.

The flavor of those cowboy times is echoed in a Depression-era mural in the Lockhart post office (217 W. Market Street), "The Pony Express Station," painted by John Walker in 1939.

Lockhart enjoyed a reputation as a tough town. During Reconstruction, several incidents of racial violence prompted the stationing of federal troops at Lockhart and Prairie Lea, and clashes between federal soldiers and local residents led to considerable ill feeling. Military authorities seized and destroyed or mutilated court records at Lockhart. When Unionists in Prairie Lea complained that freedmen and Union men were being outraged and murdered by "reconstructed Rebels," Governor Throckmorton sent a military force there in the spring of 1867 to maintain order. W. C. Phillips wrote Governor Throckmorton that "during my short stay here, I have seen freedmen run down by horsemen, run out of town, and shot at. On December 8 [1866] I saw a freedman whipped because he addressed a young man as Tom instead of 'Mas Tom.'" He also said that on another occasion, Nelson Smith, a freedman, was shot down because he refused to give his flask of whiskey to two unreconstructed Rebels.

By 1870, Lockhart had gained a reputation as the place where they killed a man every day. Every building on the square was a saloon or grocery store (that sold liquor) at one time or another. On Saturday, area farmers, ranchers, and cowboys poured into town to buy supplies or to fritter away their meager wages. Merchant Sam Glosserman reminisced several decades later,

Everyone came to town on Saturday and what they wanted was a red bottle of soda water or a bottle of beer and Kreuz barbecue. People used to go around and around walking around the square, having the time of their lives, fighting and boozing.

This was really a wild town—one of the wildest in the U.S. This was the wildest town in Texas; I used to stand on Dad's corner and see killings, one after another. I saw police beat people over the head. I remember one guy clubbed a man to death with an axe handle right on that corner.

Old-timer Geoffrey Wills remembered,

They had the White Caps [Ku Kluxers] organization. Everyone packed a six-shooter. We had a high sheriff, but that's the way he run this town. This town was considered a desperado town. It had sporting houses, wide-open gambling places, and all those things. People would never come through this town and they would by-pass it on account it was so bad. My parents told me it was nothing to wake up Sunday morning and find two or three men dead . . . find them in the alley dead, I was born in 1908 and it was still going on.

In 1950, ex–trail driver Berry Roebuck, then ninety-four years old, pointed to the courthouse square and told a San Antonio newspaper reporter, "I've seen many a man killed on that square. A good gun used to be the law there."

Even the chickens weren't safe; one day, a drunken cowboy shot dead all the cluckers running around the courthouse square.

Small wonder, then, that on November 5, 1884, the *Lockhart Register* declared:

The pistol law is one of the best on the statute books of the state. Some are in favor of making the carrying of them a penitentiary offense. If the full penalty of the law as it is was given to the offenders, there would not be so much of the outrageous shooting and concomitant evils. Some would carry pistols if it was a hanging offense. One hundred dollars from these each time they were caught would soon bring a halt to many who are going down the downward road to trouble.

Lockhart was even peripherally involved in the Taylor-Sutton feud. In March or April 1868 or 1869, depending on the source you read, William Sutton, a deputy sheriff, led a posse from Clinton in DeWitt County in pursuit of a gang of horse thieves, including Charles Taylor, who had fled to Bastrop. The posse caught the men on the street in Bastrop, and in front of Crow and Jones' dry goods and general merchandise store, they killed Charley Taylor and captured another accused horse thief named James Sharp, whom they shot or hanged near Lockhart on the return journey as he was "trying to escape."

Caldwell County deputy sheriff B. B. Sullivan was shot and killed on July 7, 1876, while attempting to arrest a crime suspect at a local store. As Sullivan attempted to handcuff the suspect, the man, Dick Allen, pulled a revolver from his boot and shot the deputy. Sullivan, who was just twenty-four at the time of his death, was survived by his wife. He is buried in Lockhart City Cemetery. Allen was later arrested by the Hays County sheriff. He was convicted of Deputy Sullivan's murder and sentenced to hang. When citizens learned that the suspect might have the conviction overturned on appeal, on the night of October 23, 1876, a body of armed men went to the jail at Lockhart and, overpowering the guard, took out the prisoner Dick Allen and hanged him. But great indignation was expressed by many other citizens at this outrage, not that they felt any sympathy for Allen. These good citizens preferred to see Allen hanged by law, the jury convicting him having reflected the sentiments of a people opposed to mob law.

J. W. Montgomery, one of Caldwell County's most well known and estimable citizens, who had served with Waul's Texas legion during the Civil War, was shot and instantly killed on the streets of Lockhart on October 11, 1899, by his son-in-law, Ed Larimore. There was a huge crowd on the streets following the shooting, and great excitement prevailed.

Gunfights were not the only miseries that plagued Lockhart. Early in 1879, a tornado at Lockhart hit the eastern portion of the town, destroying forty buildings, including the Masonic Hall and several churches. One or two people died, according to contemporary accounts.

Understandably, most Lockhart folks at the turn of the century got skittish when they heard any noise that sounded even remotely like gunfire. So panic gripped downtown Lockhart one hot, dusty late afternoon in July 1904 when local blacksmith Emil Seeliger and one of his sons, Alfred, came bumping and backfiring toward the freshly graveled courthouse square in his homemade horseless carriage on his inaugural run. Folks all over the square ducked for the nearest available cover, according to J. Henry Martindale, Caldwell County treasurer and historian. They were sure that the feuding was raring up again. Pretty soon the city marshal peeked up and told everyone it was safe to come out; it was just Seeliger and the hossless wagon he'd been building for two years. Seeliger built it out back behind his blacksmith shop, which stood a few feet north off the courthouse square, at 106–110 N. Main, where stands now an orange-with-white-trim brick building (built in 1896). Seeliger had been reading magazine stories about these marvelous new machines, and being of a mechanical turn of mind, he set about to build the first automobile manufactured in Texas, despite the ribbings he got from his friends who came by to visit during the construction process.

Heads began to pop out to gaze upon Seeliger's wondrously strange contraption. He had spent $125 building his car, $60 of which went to buy its four 28 × 2.5 inch tubeless motorcycle wheels. Seeliger acquired a one-cylinder upright engine and located it under the seat; it delivered power to the rear wheels via three bicycle-chain drives. The gas tank formed the backseat. The gas line led to an old-fashioned gas-mixture carburetor salvaged from an old gasoline launch. Two dry-cell telephone batteries made up the ignition system. Acetylene lights were used for night driving. Seeliger built the steering mechanism out of a shotgun barrel and a pair of bicycle handlebars. To steer the car, you turned the handlebars in the direction you wished to go. With a body built from trap buggy plans, the "Seeliger Special" topped out at fifteen miles per hour, getting fourteen miles per gallon. Seeliger bought his gasoline at the local drugstore, by the five-gallon can, at thirty-five cents a gallon (no tax).

But back to that historic afternoon. George Chilton, a sewing machine agent, had hitched his big pair of grays to a telephone post in front of the crowded Silver King Saloon and had gone in for a drink, a talk with friends, and a "perfect ending for the day." But then Seeliger appeared on the streets, and all the horses were suddenly terrified by this belching, fire-breathing beast. The horses and Chilton's light delivery wagon bearing two brand-new sewing machines went bounding down the street. The wagon hit a pothole, and one of the sewing machines bounced off the wagon, wrapping itself around a light post. Another few feet, another pothole, and the second heavy machine went flying off as Chilton ran after his wagon, already ruing his losses.

The patrons of the Silver King emptied the place to see their horses and wagons careening down the street.

The news of Seeliger's automobile made the wire services, and the dispatch that went out from Lockhart across the state declared that Lockhart's citizenry was cosmopolitan and democratic, in that the first automobile was owned by a blacksmith and not a capitalist.

On another of his early drives several months later, he passed the Lockhart public school at recess time, and not surprisingly, the children broke out after it in a veritable stampede, followed by their teachers. They didn't run very far, for at that time the car had a habit of stopping every few hundred yards. But when it started again, many of the students started after it again, refusing to be herded in by the teachers. Emil's car became so popular with the schoolchildren that they referred to the Seeliger family as "Automobeligers."

Seeliger even ran his horseless carriage on the railroad tracks. Considering the roads of that era, he doubtless got a smoother ride along the rails. Emil Seeliger's machine eventually ended up on the scrap heap, as he felt it had no historic value. As the numbers of automobiles increased, Seeliger decided to devote all of his time to auto repair. Seeliger's blacksmith shop was replaced by a larger brick building that housed Lockhart's first auto repair garage.

Seeliger's automobile was not the only harbinger of the new age confronting Lockhart's citizens. The town installed its first water system in 1900, and shortly thereafter, county commissioners voted to convert the new courthouse's broom closets into water closets. The county judge said such luxuries were foolish extravagance; there were outhouses behind every saloon in town. But he was voted down, and the toilet facilities were installed. Evidently they were an immediate hit; after the first month's water bill, the judge ordered all the bathroom doors chained and padlocked, so enraged was he at the size of the bill. It took legal action to get them unlocked.

At the turn of the twentieth century, blacks composed nearly 40 percent of the voting population of Caldwell County, and in the summer of 1904, they organized and announced their intention of promulgating a county Republican Party ticket composed of solely black candidates. At the same time, they denounced Democrats and preached racial equality.

There are two accounts of what happened next. According to the July 28, 1904, *New York Times*, on July 27, a committee of the county's well-known citizens called upon John Larremore, the negro chairman of Caldwell County's Republican Committee, and other local negro leaders, fearing a race war, so critical had the conditions become. The negroes, anticipating the white committee's visit, refused a conference and denounced the whites. A fight was started, and in the struggle, Larremore was shot and killed, and four of the others were captured. Caperton was insolent, and the committee punished him. The others were ordered out of the county. Further trouble was feared.

Another version of the incident states that "a mob of masked whitecappers killed a negro and seriously injured another that day. They first visited Tom Caperton, took him from his home and severely beat him and then went to John Larremore's house and tried to break in. His wife opened fire, which the whitecappers returned. After the fusillade Larremore was found dead in the hallway of his house."

White paranoia had been fueled by the fact that Lockhart even had its own black newspaper, the weekly *New Test*, established in 1893 and edited and published by Henry Clay Gray. By 1899, according to the *National Newspaper Directory*, the four-page weekly (published Saturday, annual subscription two dollars) boasted a circulation of eight hundred, equaling that of the white *Lockhart Phonograph*, and fifty more than the white *Lockhart Register*, the predecessor of today's *Lockhart Post Register*.

A member of the 1883 class of Fisk University, with a B.A. and B.D. from Oberlin College in 1885, Gray was considered to be an "uppity nigger" by white Texans of his day, most famously by that enemy of Baptists, Catholics, and Christianity in general, William Brann, "the Iconoclast."

In volume 4 of his collected works, Brann calls Gray "a smart nigger now loafing around the white man's hen coop and tater-patch somewhere in South Texas. He has written a piece 'about the Apostle' and sent a marked copy to his Baptist brethren in Waco. Henry is a mulatto, which argues that somewhere in his ancestry there was a white bum and a black bawd; still he is the moral equal and social superior of alleged white men who act as sewers for his intellectual offal."

On February 13, 1909, a black man, Richard Miller, walked into Kreuz Market in an intoxicated state and started using bad language. When proprietor Alvin Kreuz, son of founder Charles Sr., reprimanded him, Miller cursed Kreuz, whereupon Alvin hit him over the head with a wagon spoke. Miller was removed to a nearby drugstore, where he died within fifteen minutes. Kreuz waived examination and was released on bond. He was not punished.

Today Lockhart is considerably more sedate than in days past, but resurrected old-timers would have no trouble picking their way around the square. The new and modern downtown of one hundred years ago is the quaint and historic downtown that visitors find so delightful to stroll today. Lockhart's historic district contains six full blocks and parts of three other blocks. Most of the eighty-four buildings are commercial.

To get to the historic district, turn left off US 183 onto San Antonio Street and go two blocks.

One of the most controversial sagas in Lockhart's history began in 1998, when it was announced that Kreuz Market, the holy grail of Texas barbecue, would be moving from its sacred position just off the courthouse square, as a result of a family quarrel.

The building that became world famous as Kreuz Market was opened as a meat market in 1885 by a man named Swearingen. Charles Kreuz Sr., a cattleman who had just moved to Lockhart from Hunter, bought it and opened Kreuz Market in 1900, selling groceries, fresh meat, and barbecue on Saturday, cooking up whatever raw meat remained at the end of the week. By 1914, Kreuz was a retired stockman, having left the business to his sons, Teddy and Alvin, and his son-in-law, Hugo Prove. The weekend business proved so good that in 1924, his sons built bigger pits and began buying meat just for barbecue. But the market still operated as a full-fledged grocery store.

In 1935, fifteen-year-old Edgar "Smitty" Schmidt began working for the Kreuz brothers, sweeping floors and such. In 1948, he bought the market from Alvin, Teddy, and Hugo and left the name like it was. The barbecue grew with time, in even more legendary proportions as the grocery business trailed off. Around 1982, he sold the business, but not the building, to his sons, Rick and Don. Smitty died in 1990, leaving the building that housed Kreuz Market to his daughter Nina.

After several years, brother tenant and sister landlord could no longer get along. Hence the move to north Lockhart in 1999, with twice as many pits as before and seating for at least seven hundred. The original Kreuz Market building reopened as Smitty's (named for Edgar), a barbecue restaurant just like Kreuz Market.

At any rate, go pay your respects to the original Kreuz Market location, even if you choose not to eat at Smitty's. From the front door of the original Kreuz Market, look down the alley in front of you, and you can see "N. O. Reynolds Saloon" still painted on the alley side of the old brick building that opens onto the courthouse square (108 E. Market). The building (and sign) dates to 1890, when it was built for Louis Halfin.

Louis Halfin had a sister by the name of Pauline Halfin, who married Fred Bloom. Pauline Halfin ran the saloon, a rare occupation for a woman during an era when decent women didn't even walk into saloons. One of her regular customers, Morgan White, an honest farmer but a bit of an overindulger, was accused of insulting Pauline. Friends of Morgan sent word to him that Louis Halfin and Fred Bloom were planning to kill him for his impertinence. Soon after, Morgan came to town, walking down the sidewalk toward the saloon with a musket. "Louis Halfin was shooting from an upstairs window and nailed Morgan through the head on the sidewalk with a Winchester, shot his brains out and men walked on [the brains] out on the sidewalk," Geoffrey Wills related.

The N. O. Reynolds of "N. O. Reynolds Saloon" was Nelson Orcelus "Mage" Reynolds, noted Texas Ranger. His birth certificate states that Reynolds was born in Pennsylvania in 1846, but he always called himself a Missourian by birth. At any rate, he served in the Confederate Army during the last year or two of the Civil War. His nickname, "Major" or "Maje," is said to derive from an incident in which a small Confederate band under his command captured a force of Union soldiers and took much-needed arms and clothing from them. Reynolds appropriated the Union major's heavy coat, earning his nickname. Reynolds came to Texas in 1872. He joined the Texas Rangers on May 25, 1874, under the command of Cicero R. "Rufe" Perry in Blanco County, where he served with Scott Cooley, mentioned in the *Lone Star Travel Guide to Texas Hill Country*. He went on to serve under such well-known leaders as Dan W. Roberts and Neal Coldwell. For a time he served with the escort of Major John B. Jones.

He campaigned against Indian raiders, but his most famous exploits were in action against white outlaws. He served briefly with the Frontier Battalion in Mason County but quit the Rangers for a brief time rather than pursue his dear friend Scott Cooley, former fellow Ranger of Company D turned outlaw. On July 28, 1877, with a very small force, he ended the Horrell-Higgins feud of Lampasas County when he arrested the leader and ten other members of the Horrell faction. He was given command of the newly formed Company E in recognition of his accomplishment. As Company E commander, he transported and guarded John Wesley Hardin during one of his several incarcerations in the Travis County Jail, as well as Johnny Ringo. Reynolds then moved on to San Saba County in 1878, where he helped quiet, at least for a while, that county's difficulties. He arrived in Round Rock too late to take part in the street battle that destroyed the Sam Bass gang, but one of his men arrested the mortally wounded Bass.

Reynolds retired from the Ranger service in late 1879. He was elected sheriff of Lampasas County in 1886 and 1888, and he later engaged in private business in Lockhart and in Orange and Brazoria counties. He married Irene T. Nevill in 1882 in Austin. Reynolds, called the "Intrepid" by fellow legendary Ranger James B. Gillett, died on March 1, 1922, and is buried in Center Point with thirty-one of his fellow Texas Rangers.

CALDWELL COUNTY COURTHOUSE

Courthouse square

This immaculate Second Empire courthouse is one of the state's most photographed and has been in several recent Hollywood movies. It was in built in 1892 of stone from nearby Muldoon with red Pecos sandstone trim for $65,000. The original four-way Seth Thomas clock in the tower was vandalized and replaced by an electric clock in the 1950s. In 1992, a 1916-model Seth Thomas clock, which is very similar to the original, was restored and installed in the clock tower. Restoration of the building was completed in 1999.

On February 19, 1915, Caldwell County sheriff J. Henry Franks and Lockhart City marshal John L. Smith got into a fight at the county courthouse. Smith had been a deputy sheriff under Franks and had run against him for sheriff. Smith reportedly cursed and abused the sheriff, who went to his office and got a shotgun. The two men opened fire, and Franks killed Smith. Sheriff Franks was released under a $3,000 bond.

On the evening of May 12, 1915, Franks was returning from a motion picture show to his residence in the county jail when an assassin hiding beneath a cotton platform at the railway depot fired two shotgun blasts at him. The first missed and struck a telegraph pole, but the second shot struck the sheriff in the back, neck, and shoulder, killing him instantly. Other county sheriffs and Texas Rangers came to Lockhart to investigate the assassination. The Caldwell County Commissioners Court and the Texas governor posted a reward of $750. The Texas Rangers arrested two men, but the charges were dropped. The killer of Sheriff J. Henry Franks was never apprehended, and the case remains unsolved. He was survived by his widow and a young daughter. Franks rests in Lockhart City Cemetery next to his wife.

EMMANUEL EPISCOPAL CHURCH

118 N. Church at Walnut • 398-3342 • Sunday 9–1

A block west of the courthouse square is the Emmanuel Episcopal Church, which has the oldest continually used Protestant church building in Texas. A simple, unpretentious structure, it is easy to miss. Don't make that mistake. The congregation was organized in 1853, and the building was completed in 1856. The sanctuary's two-foot-thick concrete walls are a mixture of sand, gravel, Lockhart caliche, ash, water, and cow manure. The ceiling timbers are hand-hewn cedar. The floor is made of locally quarried and highly polished limestone slabs. The altar, chancel rails, and window frames are also originals, hand carved from native walnut. Federal troops used the church as a horse stable during Reconstruction days.

A few feet south of the church, at 112 N. Church, is Holter's Feed Store, which was built in 1902 as Masur Brothers Hardware. The Masurs' original painted advertisements, as well as a more contemporary "Coca-Cola 5 ct." ad, are still visible on the south side of the building.

The Joseph Masur family, related by marriage to Susanna Dickinson, the "Messenger of the Alamo," came to Lockhart from Germany in 1873. Joseph Sr., a blacksmith, established a shop just behind the present three-story building. In 1880, Joseph set his sons up in the furniture and hardware business, and they built the building which now stands on Church Street. Lockhart had no Catholic church when the Masurs arrived in Lockhart, so they furnished a temporary building where Mass could be celebrated. In 1933, the Masurs sold 265 acres southwest of town to the city of Lockhart for a public park; this became Lockhart State Park.

FIRST CHRISTIAN CHURCH

W. San Antonio at S. Church, 1 block west of the courthouse square • 398-3129

The First Christian Church in Lockhart was organized in 1852. The present Gothic structure was completed in 1898 at a cost of $28,000, a tribute both to God and the skilled brick masons who built it. An excellent example of bichromal brickwork, which is now enjoying a revival of sorts in and around Austin, this sanctuary features a combination of flat-sided red brick and textured ivory brick, which looks like limestone from all but inches away. The numerous arches and rounded half columns and caps are further testament to the bricklayer's skills. All the church's windows are stained-glass memorials.

And, as long as we're here, let's take a moment to reflect on the strange passing of Texas' most unusual man of God, "Fightin' Parson" Andy Potter (also see

Bastrop, Winchester, and Buescher State Park). It was in the year of our Lord 1895, on Sunday evening, October 21, in a little country church just outside Lockhart at Tilmon, and "as Fighting Parson Potter raised his hands in a closing prayer, the lights of the little church were suddenly blown out by a strong gust of wind, and when the lamps were relighted the audience gasped to see the preacher lying dead in the pulpit. As the lights had gone out, so had gone out the life of Texas' most picturesque preacher. Fighting Parson Potter's wish—that he might die in his pulpit—had been granted." Potter was buried in Walnut Creek Cemetery near Lockhart.

J. Henry Martindale told the following version of Potter's dramatic passing to the *Lockhart Post-Register*: On the night of his death, he finished a sermon at Tilmon and then said, "Brethren, I have always stated that I wanted to die in the harness. Here of late I have been feeling bad and I would not be surprised if the end was near." Barely having said this, he pitched forward, dead. He was buried at the Bunton Cemetery, near Dale.

His obituary on October 26, 1895, read in part: "Mr. Potter was well known in Bastrop County, where he had lived during the fifties. He had long been an itinerant preacher of the Methodist church on the Texas frontier and has had many startling adventures with Indians and desperados. He had acquired a widespread reputation for his fearlessness and devotion to his ministerial work, and was most generally known as the 'fighting Methodist parson.' His body was sent to Goldthwaite for burial."

Regardless of where he was finally planted, Parson Potter was certainly well known in this region, and stories about him abounded. Years earlier, he gave notice that he would be preaching at eleven o'clock on a certain day at a certain schoolhouse on Plum Creek in Caldwell County. He arrived early at the place, wearing his six-shooter and carrying a rifle across his saddle. Somewhat to his surprise, he found a group of men already gathered there. They were a boisterous bunch who had gathered to race horses and gamble.

Potter asked the leaders when the races were supposed to start.

Eleven o'clock, they answered.

Did they know he was going to preach there at eleven?

Yes, they did.

Potter asked where the track was.

In front of the schoolhouse, the men replied.

When did they set the time for the races?

After they heard there was going to be a gathering for the preaching.

Potter announced his plans: "At eleven o'clock I am going to stand up facing the open door of this house and start holding services. On the table in front of me, full cocked, will be this rifle and right by it, also cocked and ready for close action, will be this six-shooter. The first man of you that rides past the door on his horse I'm going to shoot daylight into. Now if you had set your date for the horse races before I had announced services or if the dates had conflicted unintentionally, I would have been willing to divide time with you. As it is, I have the rights and I am going to stand up for them."

He began preaching at eleven. Nobody rode by on the racetrack because all the racing men were inside the schoolhouse listening to his sermon.

According to Martindale, at the end of the war, Potter returned to Lockhart. The Presbyterian church had no pastor, and even though Potter was a Methodist, he filled the pulpit until a Presbyterian minister was found. Soon after the war, he was invited to preach in a Walnut Creek community about twelve miles from his home at Dale. Before he got there he was told that a former pastor had been run off by bullies. Potter got there about an hour before services were scheduled to begin. He found a large congregation present, including the men who had made the threats. Potter walked up to the pulpit and placed his Bible there, with a revolver on either side. He then told the bullies on the front pew that he had come to teach the word of God and understood that he would have to fight in order to do so. He then said that he didn't want to fight, but that he didn't mind doing so if necessary. He preached unmolested, and after he finished, the rowdies shook his hand and invited him to dinner. Many of them became Christians.

ALBION HOUSE

604 W. San Antonio

This ample, two-story Neoclassical mansion exemplifies the prosperity that Lockhart enjoyed during the King Cotton years. The house was built in 1898 by Albion Chew, a local businessman and land developer, and his wife Birdie. Chew owned a lumberyard, so the materials used to build the house were of top quality: mostly heart pine, with some cypress. A four-year restoration earned the house an award from *Southern Living* magazine in 1998.

DR. EUGENE CLARK LIBRARY

217 S. Main, one block south of the courthouse square • 398-3223 • Monday through Friday 10–6, Saturday 9 to noon

Also impressive is the Clark Library, Texas' very first city library, built in 1900. A Tulane graduate, Dr. Eugene Clark practiced medicine here from 1883 to 1896. Clark left Lockhart to pursue graduate studies in Europe. He died in his hometown of New Orleans in 1898, leaving $10,000 to the city of Lockhart for the construction of a public library. The library cost $6,000 to build and is modeled after the Villa Rotunda in Vicenza, Italy. Beautiful stained-glass windows are trimmed in walnut and walnut shutters cover the windows. The ceiling is white embossed tin, bearing brass gooseneck light fixtures. Ascend the narrow, winding iron staircase to reach the narrow, horseshoe-shaped second-story gallery, where you can better appreciate the Victorian interior. It is said that President William Howard Taft gave a speech here.

CALDWELL COUNTY HISTORICAL MUSEUM

315 E. Market St., 1 block east of US 183 and the courthouse square • 398-9643 • www.lockhart-tx.org • Open Saturday and Sunday

This little brick castle was built after a 1908 election in which the county's voters approved a $25,000 bond sale to finance it. The jailer's quarters were on the first floor. The upper floors have fifteen concrete and steel cells. One cell rises from the center of the jail. The gallows were supposedly removed as recently as the 1930s. Located inside the old county jail, the museum features the Mildred

Vaughan Memorial Room, the Country Store, an 1890 kitchen, the Pioneer Room, early photographs, and other Texas memorabilia.

ANDREW LEE BROCK CABIN

Lions Park, on US 183 across from the HEB supermarket • Open daily

Andrew Lee Brock came to Caldwell County in 1849 and married Rebecca Wayland in 1850. Her daddy gave the newlyweds two hundred acres of land on the Clear Fork branch of Plum Creek. That year, he built the cabin that is now located in this small city park. He later became a successful businessman and built a grand home that had the county's first bathtub. A number of buildings on the courthouse square were built by Gus Birkner for Andrew Lee Brock.

By 1830, there were a couple of cabins and a trading post at Lockhart Springs on the northeast side of modern Lockhart. They were close to Plum Creek and close to the 1840 battle site. In the 1870s, Lockhart was famous among Central Texas towns for the number of flowing springs it had. Several fern-draped springs were located in the park near the Brock cabin but had dried up by 2009. The most important of the Lockhart springs are Storey Springs. They are on private property in the 300 block of N. Commerce, but they can be seen from a small city park located at the north side of the bridge over a small creek into which the springs empty.

The springs are named for Leonidas Jefferson Storey, the thirteenth lieutenant governor of Texas. Born in Georgia in 1834, he came to Texas in 1845, first to Gonzales and then to Lockhart in 1847. He studied law, was admitted to the bar, and began practice in Lockhart. During the 1850s, he advocated Texas' right to secede while questioning whether that was the best solution for the state's problems. But with the war, he helped recruit the county's first regiment, and he served as second lieutenant of Company B, Twenty-sixth Texas Cavalry, fighting to the end of the war and reaching the rank of captain.

He came back to Lockhart and practiced law until 1872, when he was elected to the House of Representatives. He was reelected in 1874. Two years later, he was elected to the Senate and served two terms. In 1880, he ran for lieutenant governor. He only served one term but remained active in the state Democratic Party. In 1892, Governor Hogg appointed him to the newly created Railroad Commission, on which he served until his death in 1909, at which time he was chairman of the commission.

There are many complaints of the dirty and vicious politics of today, but they pale beside those of days long past, such as the day Sam Houston spoke at Storey Springs. During his unsuccessful campaign for the governorship in 1857, Sam Houston spoke one sultry afternoon from a platform erected in a grove near Storey's spring. Soldiers who had fought under him at San Jacinto, and their kin, comprised a large portion of his audience. Uncharacteristic of orators of the time, Houston was not formally dressed, but instead was clad in a long coarse linen duster that reached nearly to his ankles, loosely fitting linen pants, no vest, and low quartered shoes. His shirt was unbuttoned to the point that the audience could see the hair on his chest, thick as a buffalo mop, according to Judge Alexander Terrell ("Recollections of General Sam Houston," *Southwestern Historical Quarterly* 16, no. 2), one of Houston's political opponents, who was present that day. Terrell had never seen Houston speak in public before so informally attired, "but his erect bearing, the majesty of his appearance, his deep-toned, commanding voice, impressive gestures, and perfect composure made a lasting impression" upon Terrell. That impression was deepened when he denounced the state Democratic executive committee, of which Terrell was a member.

While Houston was speaking, Judge William Simpson Oldham rode up. A lawyer and politician, Oldham had moved to Austin in 1849 from Arkansas, hoping to beat a mild case of tuberculosis and revive his political fortunes, which had suffered as of late in Arkansas, due in part to financial scandals with which he was associated.

Oldham took from a large pair of saddlebags two volumes of the *Congressional Globe*, a serial publication that contained the congressional debates of the Twenty-third through the Forty-second congresses (1833–1873). The audience standing in front of the platform, wondering what was going on, began to restlessly move about. In response, Houston said, "Be still, my friends, be still, I will report the cause of this commotion." Stepping to the rear of the platform and looking over, he turned back to his audience and said, "It's Oldham, only Oldham. I'll tell you what he is doing." After looking to the rear again he faced the audience and loudly said, "He is opening some books, but they are not the bank books he stole and sunk in White River, Arkansas."

Terrell was standing by Oldham's side. Oldham bit in two the cigar he was smoking and said, "He wants to provoke an attack and have me assassinated." Oldham knew the devotion of Houston's friends, Terrell said, and how a personal difficulty between the two would terminate.

Referring again to Oldham, Houston said that a paper issued by the state Democratic executive committee appointed by "some conspirators at Waco" stated that the committee intended to handle him "without gloves." Houston paused and then drew a pair of heavy buckskin gauntlets from the pocket of his duster and put them on with a rhetorical flourish, saying, "That paper is too dirty for me to handle without gloves." He then drew the paper from his pocket and read that portion that declared that all traitors should be defeated, and that with the defeat of Houston they would "add to theirs a name of fear that traitor knaves shall quake to hear." He then threw the paper to the floor and exclaimed: "What! I a traitor to Texas! I who in defense of her soil moistened it with my blood?" He then took several steps, limping on the leg wounded at San Jacinto, and continued, "Was it for this that I bared my bosom to the hail of battle at the Horseshoe—to be branded in my old age as a traitor?"

The effect could hardly be described, according to Terrell. A wave of sympathy swept over the audience, and his old soldiers wiped tears of indignation from their eyes with red bandana handkerchiefs. Houston then proceeded to read off the names of each member of the executive committee, including Oldham and Terrell, denouncing them in turn.

Luckily for Oldham and Terrell, no blood was shed that day.

LOCKHART STATE PARK

4179 State Park Rd.; to reach the park, go 1 mile south of Lockhart on US 183 to FM 20, then southwest on FM 20 for 2 miles to Park Road 10, then 1 mile south on Park Road 10 • 398-3479 • Open daily • Fee • W variable

Lockhart State Park is on 264 acres west of Lockhart. The park was constructed by Civilian Conservation Corps (CCC) workers between 1935 and 1938 and was opened as a state park in 1948. Activities include picnicking, camping, fishing, hiking, nature study, a nine-hole golf course, 1.5 miles of hiking trails, and a swimming pool. Clear Fork Creek yields bass, catfish, and sunfish. There is also a Texas Park Store.

DINING

In the fiercely contested battle for the title of Barbecue Capital of Texas, Lockhart is arguably the champion; in *Texas Monthly*'s exhaustive 1997 search for the best barbecue in Texas, three Lockhart establishments made the prestigious Top Fifty.

BLACK'S BARBECUE

215 N. Main, just off the courthouse square • 398-2712 • www.blacksbbq .com • Open daily, lunch and dinner • DS, MC, V, checks accepted • W

Black's claims to be the state's oldest barbecue operation run by one family, since 1932. The cooking method has remained unchanged over the years: post oak is used to indirectly smoke the meat, which is seasoned only with salt and pepper. The brisket cooks for twenty-four hours. The tasty beef-and-pork sausage is homemade. The pork ribs are meaty; chicken appeals to the cholesterol conscious. The sides are numerous but uninspired; cobbler for dessert is better. They have a cafeteria-style serving line and beer. Decor is a combo of Texas license plates and Longhorn horns.

CHISHOLM TRAIL BBQ

1323 S. Colorado (US 183) • 398-6027 • Open daily, breakfast, lunch, and dinner • No Cr. • W

This unpretentious spot is a good barbecue backup when Kreuz Market is closed. Like Black's, it is popular with locals for its vegetable and salad offerings.

KREUZ MARKET

US 183 (west side) across from the cemetery, north of the railroad tracks • 398-2361 • www.kreuzmarket.com • Monday through Friday 7–6, Saturday 7–6:30 • No Cr. • W

Kreuz Market's beef brisket, shoulder, and prime rib eloquently speak for themselves. Many folks' personal favorite is the pork loin chops. Kreuz doesn't barbecue ribs; they barbecue the entire loin, bone in, and slice off the thick, lean, tender chops to your order. You will even succumb to devouring their thin, crisp, succulent outer layer of fat and gnawing the bones as a final nod to gluttony. Be advised that the chops are a popular item and are usually gone at the end of the lunch rush. Their homemade ring sausage is good but a bit greasier than most.

Saturday lunch at Kreuz is a pan-humanic experience. Hundreds of folks stream through at noon, lining up dozens deep to buy their meat. You take your choice of white bread or crackers, and the meat cutters pile it all on brown butcher paper. Some take it home; most eat it in the dining room. Young and old, black, brown, and white, rich and poor, locals and tourists, farmers, professionals, and blue collars are all elbow to elbow chowing down at the broad, long picnic-style tables. Accoutrements include pinto beans, fresh and pickled jalapenos, white onions, tomatoes, and avocados. Wash it down with cheap beer or pop.

SMITTY'S

208 S. Commerce • 398-9344 • www.smittysmarket.com • Open daily • W

The name may be different, but for many people, this is still Kreuz Market, down to the old brick building and pits, the traditional oak wood fires, and great tasting meats. According to "Smitty" Schmidt in 1976, when Charles Kreuz bought the market, housed in a sheet-metal structure, he chose to barbecue indoors instead of cooking in the traditional outdoor, open pit style. The market met with such success that the old metal building was torn down in 1924, and the market was rebuilt in the same location and expanded to include dining space. By 1935, Kreuz barbecue was a regular feature at football team banquets and other dinners held in Kreuz dining rooms.

In 1937, *Meat Merchandising* magazine ran a photo of Teddy wrapping what looked to be a large roast. The short article in the local paper also noted that "Kreuz Bros. Company Market is regarded as unique by many people coming to Lockhart." During World War II, the fame of Kreuz sausage and other barbecue spread worldwide, and even the most imprecisely addressed letters managed to make it to the market, thanking the boys for their "hot gut" sausages and the best barbecue in the world. One of their secrets was using only corn-fed beef, for its firmness and lack of moisture.

Unlike the new Kreuz Market, Smitty's is open for a few hours around lunchtime on Sundays, a blessing for Sunday drivers who want a touch of Lockhart's "real thing."

ANNUAL EVENT

JUNE

CHISHOLM TRAIL ROUNDUP

City Park • 398-2818 • www.chisholmtrailroundup.com • Second weekend in June

Features arts and crafts, food vendors, carnival, barbecue and chili cook-offs, washer tournament, and much more.

SIDE TRIP

BRIDGES OF CALDWELL COUNTY

This diversion takes you over several quaint old bridges, including an iron trestle bridge that is at least one hundred years old. It also takes you through Tilmon, although the church where Parson Potter preached to his death no longer stands. Be forewarned; this trip is for the adventurous only, as much of it is over rough, gravel road. Do not attempt it in rainy weather or if you have a low-clearance vehicle.

From downtown Lockhart, backtrack south on US 183 until you reach the intersection with FM 20. Turn left here, and then in just a few feet, turn right onto FM 1322. Take FM 1322 from Lockhart down to Brownsboro Community. Turn left on County Road 194 (Clear Fork Road). The Clear Fork Baptist Church, which you pass, has held services since 1850, making it Caldwell County's oldest church. At FM 86, turn left and proceed a few feet to the intersection with County Road 146; then turn right and continue east on County Road 146, which doglegs its way to an intersection with County Road 141 (Tenney Creek Road). Go right here. After one short dogleg, you come to an intersection with County Road 154 (Silver Mine Road), which leads you past the Hardshell Cemetery, filled with primitive, handmade tombstones. After another couple of doglegs, turn left on County Road 145A (Vinehill Road). When County Road 145A reaches the intersection with FM 3158, turn left on FM 3158 to reach Tilmon (where the Fightin' Parson, Jack Potter, died). The church no longer stands, but the old schoolhouse and community center remain. When you come to the intersection with FM 86, turn right, and when SH 86 intersects with FM 713, turn left, and then left on SH 20 to return to Lockhart.

Hardshell was presumably named for the Hardshell Baptist sect. Primitive, or Hardshell, Baptists objected to organized mission societies, Sunday schools, Bible societies, and seminaries as both unscriptural and a threat to congregational independence.

In July 1876, Dick Allen shot and killed Bud Sullivan at Hardshell. Allen fled west and was captured by cow hunters near Dogtown (near Luling). He was brought back to Las Buros, where he escaped and headed for the San Marcos River. He met two cow hunters, who took him prisoner. But Allen got their gun and shot them both dead. He was captured not long thereafter in the Blanco bottomlands by Hays County sheriff Rhoe and jailed in Lockhart.

From Lockhart, take US 183 north and continue on toward Austin.

Today Lockhart has only one gin and is more famous for its cottonseed breeding farms, started here in 1882 by A. D. Mebane, than for its cotton. Over the years, Mebane puttered and tinkered in his experimental plots, finally developing his world-famous Mebane Triumph cottonseed, characterized by great drought resistance and up to 40 percent greater yield than other contemporary seed strains. Mebane's Triumph revolutionized the cotton industry. As you head toward Austin on US 183, you see a few of the roadside fields still planted in King Cotton.

Many of these fields are now thick with mesquite. Ranchers, farmers, and motorists who suffer flat tires from its sharp thorns may hate it, but to others, mesquite has been quite valuable. Indians processed the bean pods into soup, bread, and beer. Cabeza de Vaca was the first European to record the fact that the natives not only ate the pulpy mesquite pods when they ripened, but also made them into a flour. He described the process in a book published in 1540.

A more recent cookbook, *Regional Cooking* (1947), contains the following mesquite-bean cake recipe similar to the old Indian recipe: Gather mesquite beans when they are very ripe. Spread them out in the sun until they are dry. Find a stone about a foot long and very narrow. Using that stone as a pestle, grind the beans on another flat stone until you have achieved a flourlike consistency. Sift the flour to get out all the hulls and trash. Take as much flour as you will need, pour just a little water in it, and stir. Then leave it out in the sun to dry a little. Then mix in enough water to make a stiff dough. Cut the dough into little cakes and set them out in the sun until very dry. They are then ready to be eaten with coffee or milk or to be stored for future use.

The mesquite served as a food of last resort to the traveler and also as a coffee substitute. Mesquite wood has been made into firewood, bows, arrows, fence posts, house lumber, road-paving logs, flooring, furniture, and even a cannon. A sticky gum exuded from the tree was used for mending pottery cracks and as a hair preparation that would dye hair jet black and kill cooties at the same time. Stephen Austin even advised his colonists to look for the biggest mesquite on their land and drill their water well there. It was erroneously thought that the mesquite pointed the way to sweet, shallow water.

Farming manuals from the 1890s advised that the mesquite

> bean is nutritious, fattening livestock. This tree is taking possession of prairie tracts and gradually rendering the land more valuable. The whole body of wood is also rich in tannin, thus rendering it as a good tanning material. It is said, indeed, to be better than any of the old popular materials, as it better preserves the leather. The bean is very nutritious as feed for horses and cattle. Generations of farm and ranch children have chewed on the sweet beans, especially during Texas' various farm depressions, when mesquite beans were the closest thing to candy they could afford. [The tree] has spread rapidly over the prairies within the past few years and now furnishes firewood in many localities where a few years ago there was not a stick of any kind of fuel to be found.

Ranchers and farmers hate mesquite because it chokes out precious grazing grass; hunters love it because doves love it. Ranchers and farmers hate mesquite because it's nearly impossible to kill off (its long taproot makes it practically drought proof and impossible to dig out); woodworkers love its handsome pink-to-black burl and shadings. Deer, javelina, rabbits, and birds depend on the tree for food and shelter.

But perhaps mesquite's noblest use is as barbecue wood. It imparts a unique taste to the meat that is preferred by many, but not all, Texans.

Big for a mesquite is about twenty feet tall and perhaps a couple of feet in diameter. Most mesquite trees are little more than big bushes, and this recalls an old Texas joke. It seems a group of horse thieves were nabbed by a posse and "invited" to attend a necktie party. But being civilized men, the posse members allowed the brigands to choose the species of tree from which they wished to swing. Most of the men opted for the more beautiful and romantic oaks, elms, cypresses, and pecans. But one smart thief chose a mesquite. Since the posse were men of honor, they had to give the cagey crook a reprieve when they couldn't find a mesquite tall enough to get his feet off the ground.

Since 1980, mesquite has been "discovered" by the world at large. Mesquite grilling is in big-city restaurants from coast to coast. Practically every charcoal manufacturer now offers mesquite-tinged briquettes. Landscapers extol its gnarled lacy-leafed beauty in yards and rock gardens. The tree has its own fan club, Los Amigos del Mesquite, whose several hundred members devote their resources to educating the public about the mesquite tree and its uses.

About 3.6 miles north of Lockhart, you come to an intersection with Caldwell County Road 221, which leads to the ghost town of Polonia, about three miles west of US 183.

POLONIA

Caldwell County

Polonia was a small, rural Polish community first settled in 1891. The three-acre tract of land for the Catholic church that was the center of Polonia was deeded to the Catholic Diocese of San Antonio in 1894, and thus the Parish of Sacred Heart was formed. A small frame church was built. By 1900, approximately twelve Polish families were farming in the area. At one point, Polonia had a church, two schools (one for whites, the other for Mexicans), a cotton gin, a blacksmith shop, and a general store. Polonia declined in the 1930s because of the failing family-farm economy. The Catholic church was razed in 1939. The Polonia Community Cemetery is the last reminder of the once vibrant village. The hilltop view from the cemetery of the surrounding countryside is nice.

MENDOZA

Caldwell County • 50 • About 10 miles from Lockhart

The little hamlet of Mendoza, near the intersection of US 183 and SH 21, is the home of the Headless Woman of Mendoza, one of Central Texas' better-traveled "haints." The story of this unfortunate woman is a variant on the ancient tale of "La Llorona" (the weeping woman). The tale of La Llorona has been told in many forms in many different places. The sad story of the Headless Woman of Mendoza goes something like this:

Once there was a woman who had two children. She didn't love them and neglected and mistreated them. She was having too much fun dancing and going to parties. First one child, and then the other, died from her neglect. But she felt no remorse and continued to lead a gay life. On her way home from a party one night, the car in which she was traveling crashed, and she was decapitated. When she died, she had not confessed her sins or repented of her ill treatment of her children. So now she appears on roadsides all over the area grieving for her children and looking for her head. She is doing penance for her sins. Travelers who stop to pick her up often do not notice anything amiss with the shapely dark figure in the shawl until they look into her eyes and find none.

The Mendoza area was mostly open rangeland until the 1870s. A school had been built by 1878; it also doubled as a church. The school and community around it were known as Rest. A Baptist preacher from Lockhart would ride up to Rest one or two Sunday afternoons a month to conduct services. But during these early days, like in Red Rock and Llano, Rest wasn't very peaceful. Since this was still largely ranching country, there were a lot of cowboys in the area, and the unwashed among them diverted themselves on preaching days by roping and then pulling the shutters off the church windows during service, or they would sit on the front row jangling their spurs or snoring loudly. Peace finally came to Rest when Mr. Jim Gaddis rode in to preach. He had heard of the cowboys' rowdiness, and he wore his six-shooters to church. Like the Reverend Andy Potter, Jim Gaddis laid down one pistol on each side of the Bible on the lectern and announced that everyone would be respectful during church or he would gladly meet the offenders outside afterward. He got no takers. Sometime during the 1880s, for reasons nobody remembers, Rest's name changed to Mendoza.

From Mendoza, continue on US 183 north about twenty miles to Austin.

Coming back into Austin, just after you pass Pilot Knob (the geographic formation) on your left, you come to the intersection with McKinney Falls Parkway, which leads to McKinney Falls State Park.

MCKINNEY FALLS STATE PARK

5808 McKinney Falls Parkway; take McKinney Falls Parkway from US 183 straight to the park entrance • 243-1643 • Open daily • Fee

McKinney Falls State Park is a 744-acre park named for Thomas F. McKinney, who was one of Stephen F. Austin's first three hundred colonists. Sometime between 1850 and 1852, McKinney bought this property at the falls on Onion Creek, where he became a prominent breeder of racehorses. McKinney even had his own private track. His large two-story home, stone fences, and the first flour mill in the area were built with slave labor. The stabilized ruins of McKinney's homestead and those of his trainer's cabin are in the park. Information on McKinney and the history of the park's land use is interpreted in the Smith Visitor Center.

Within the park, you can see evidence of Pilot Knob's volcanic activity. The wide stretch of rock at the Onion Creek falls is limestone mixed with volcanic rock; the park also has outcroppings of basalt and green clay, which was originally volcanic ash.

Camping, hiking, road and mountain biking, picnicking, fishing, and wildlife observation are among the park's activities. The busy season is March through November.

La Llorona sometimes appears along the Colorado River on dark nights. One day she took her two children here and drowned them. She never repented, and so she comes back to the river at night, wailing for her children. Some say she has a seductive figure and the face of a horse. Others say she is dressed in black, with long hair, shiny tinlike fingernails, and the face of a skeleton. Still others say she is dressed in white, with the face of a bat. Perhaps you'd like to find out for yourself.

THE WILD WEST

APPROXIMATELY 160 MILES

Feuds blanketed Central Texas like a crazy quilt after the Civil War. They were of all shapes and sizes: ethnic, interfamily, rancher versus farmer, old-timer vs. newcomer, confined to a single community or county or spilling out over a several-county region. About all they had in common were violence and the spilling of blood outside of the law. Some of the grandest feuds were between extended families, such as the Sutton-Taylor feud of south central Texas, the Horrell-Higgins feud of Lampasas County, and the Townsend-Stafford-Reese feud of Colorado County.

German farmers and ranchers faced off with Anglo-American ranchers who had emigrated from the American South in the Mason County Hoodoo War. In southern Bastrop County, newly freed blacks from Cedar Creek battled unrepentant white Rebels from neighboring Red Rock.

The bloodiest, longest-lived, widest-spread, most complicated and least understood feud sprawled across Williamson, Lee, and Bastrop counties and lasted for at least twenty years after the end of the Civil War, or perhaps longer, depending on when you think it began and ended. It was such a complicated feud that it really doesn't have a name as such, except perhaps "the McDade Troubles," the climax to the feud.

A more proper, encompassing name would be the "Yegua Troubles." *Yegua* is Spanish for "wild mare," and wild horses were found in abundance along the three creeks that bear their name: West, Middle, and Yegua creeks. The gang of cattle rustlers said to have caused all the problems in the region was called the "Yegua Notchcutters." But the origins and story of the Yegua Troubles is as wild and tangled as the land itself and the impetuous people who settled it.

The Reconstruction years following the Civil War whipped Texas into a feverish turmoil. The railroads, aided largely by Yankee capital, began their conquest of Texas during the Reconstruction years. The railroads were the harbingers of an industrial revolution that kept Texas in a state of ebullition long after the despised "bluebellies" and carpetbaggers went home. Violence

223

THE WILD WEST

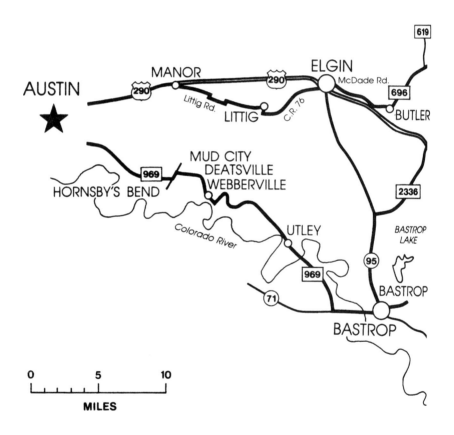

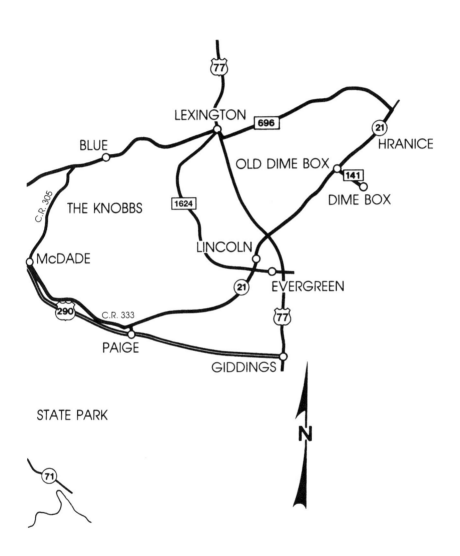

LEXINGTON

696

BLUE

OLD DIME BOX

21

HRANICE

C.R. 305

THE KNOBBS

1624

141

DIME BOX

McDADE

LINCOLN

77

EVERGREEN

21

290

C.R. 333

77

PAIGE

GIDDINGS

STATE PARK

N

71

often accompanied the sudden prosperity the iron rails brought, and for some years violence and prosperity fed upon each other. Towns lucky enough to be located along railroad lines were almost guaranteed immediate prosperity; they were also almost guaranteed a measure of lawlessness.

Regardless of where you were from, the fall of 1865 and the winter and spring of 1866 were pretty grim eating in most of Texas. Confederate money and bonds were now worthless, so tens of thousands of Southern folks had literally nothing of value to spend. "Many members of both the lawless and the lawful groups had been old friends and neighbors all along until the younger generation started the depredations which turned friend against friend and neighbor against neighbor. It was heartbreaking for some of the vigilantes to have to deal with these boys, but there was nothing else to do. Killing had to be stopped," explained G. K. Martin, whose father was one of the Yegua vigilantes.

Some members of the lawless group were newcomers, or "nesters," who wandered into the Yeguas after the Civil War and began roping up wild cattle and pigs so they would have something besides dirt to eat. According to old-timer John Knox, the nesters formed gangs and rounded up big herds of cattle they rustled from area ranchers and farmers and drove them to the nearest market. The "old-timers" reported the thefts to the sheriffs in Brenham, Caldwell, and Bastrop, but it didn't do much good. The country was so rough that the sheriffs were afraid to come looking for rustlers because of the possibility of ambush.

By 1866, lynchings were already so common that boys gave directions to travelers with reference to the number of dead men hanging near critical intersections. After each lynching, people from the neighborhood were called to see if anyone could recognize the dead man or men. Often no one could, and folks just assumed that the hanging was done by local citizens who took the law into their own hands or by a group of citizens from another county who caught up with their prey and dispatched them on the spot.

This trip takes us through a section of Central Texas that saw both extraordinary prosperity and extraordinary trouble in the first few decades following the Great War, courtesy of Reconstruction and the iron horse.

The Houston and Texas Central (H&TC) railway was the first railroad to link the state capitol of Austin with the rest of the world, arriving on Christmas Day 1871. It was a long time in coming. The Civil War had halted railroad construction projects all over Texas. The H&TC grew out of the Washington County Railway Company, which was incorporated on February 2, 1856. By October 1, 1860, a line of railway extended from Hempstead to Brenham, a distance of 21.3 miles. The company was sold to the Houston and Texas Central Railway Company. The Houston and Texas Central Railway Company began work from Brenham reaching Ledbetter, Fayette County, in January of 1871, and Giddings, Lee County, in May 1871. Construction reached a point near McDade in September 1871, and a point near Manor, Travis County, in November 1871. Much of the roadbed of the Houston and Texas Central Railway was built by convict labor, which used wheelbarrows to build up the dirt work of the roadbed.

Leave Austin via US 290 east. At Manor, take Spur 212 right into town.

MANOR

Travis County • 5,800 (approximate) • (512) • About 8 miles from Austin

Manor, like many small Texas towns, was on the eclipse from the 1920s until recently. But at the turn of the century, Manor was bustling, the second largest city in Travis County. King Cotton and Manor's location on the railroad were the reasons. The surrounding fields with their rich, black, waxy earth produced a half bale of cotton to the acre, and it took three gins to process the fall crop. H&TC locomotives hauled away fifteen thousand bales in a good year. Before the advent of World War I, Manor boasted a couple of banks, a newspaper, and electric streetlights, not to mention a mostly brick downtown.

The town dates to 1850, when James Manor moved here from nearby Webberville. By 1859, the town was one of Travis County's largest and was commonly known as Parson's Seminary, after a girls' school located where Manor Junior High School now stands. Manor was also known as Wheeler's Store before the H&TC came through in 1871. The name Manor was adopted thereafter, in honor of James Manor.

Manor was not immune to the white-on-black violence that plagued Bastrop and Caldwell counties after the Civil War. In September 1876, Billy Freeman, a white man, killed Marshall Johnson, a black man, supposedly in self-defense. Johnson was called a "quarrelsome character," who had threatened Freeman's life and said he would burn the town of Manor. Johnson was just one of several "rough characters of the colored persuasion at Manor who had worn out the patience of the people at that place, and unless they made themselves scarce they, too, would be killed." Freeman was not arrested.

In 1887, young Gregorio Cortez and his family moved to Manor, and it is said that after he killed Karnes County sheriff W. T. Morris in 1901, he was on the run to Manor until he had a shootout with posse pursuers near Gonzales, whereupon he turned south toward Laredo, where he was finally captured.

As you enter town on Spur 212, you pass, on your right, the Bloor mansion. Built in 1897 and 1898 by Alfred Bloor, a prosperous cotton buyer, and his wife Martha, the Bloor Mansion is Manor's most architecturally distinguished residence, with its distinctive tower with conical roof, a blend of the Queen Anne and the Colonial Revival styles. In 1878, Alfred and Martha and their children moved to the Manor area from Pennsylvania. The family settled in a log house about three miles south of Manor, near present-day Lake Walter Long. They later built a more comfortable home near the cabin and lived there until moving here in 1898.

The brick for the house came from the Elgin Pressed Brick Company. Alfred died the following year, but his wife resided in the home until her death in 1928. The property stayed in the family until 1951, when it was converted into a rest home for the elderly. The house became a private residence again in 1960.

Downtown Manor is considerably quieter now than it was during its pre–World War I heyday. The old bank building, at the corner of Parsons and Lexington/Spur 212/FM 973, is a restaurant. Old downtown Manor consists of a block of brick buildings along the south side of Parsons Street between Lexington and San Marcos streets. The most impressive of these is the one-story, red-brick J. F. Nagle building. Most of Manor's businesses are along US 290, including Cafe 290.

DINING

CAFE 290

11011 US 290 at Loop 212 • 278-8780 • www.texascafe290.com • Open daily, breakfast, lunch, and dinner • W

Stepping into Cafe 290 is like stepping into a 1940s cafe. They take great pride in their chicken-fried steak, but they also serve grilled steaks and chicken, fried chicken and catfish, Tex-Mex specialties, burgers, and more. Homemade pies, cobblers, and other goodies are for dessert. Breakfasts are Southern style and ample. They have beer.

TEXAS TRADITIONAL BBQ

910 Caldwell at US 290, just east of 290 Cafe; look for the sign • 799-4279 • Open daily lunch, dinner • Cr. • W

The stars here are the beef ribs and pork steaks, although acceptable brisket, pork ribs, chicken, turkey breast, and Elgin sausage are served. The owner learned his chops at Elgin's Southside Market. Friday is chicken-fried rib-eye steak day.

Leave Manor by heading east (away from Austin) on Parsons/Spur 212. This is old Highway 20, the main highway between Austin and Houston during the days of flivvers and bathtub gin. Continue on Old Highway 20 after Spur 212 veers north (to the left). A couple of miles east of Manor, the road comes to a T intersection. Turn right here onto Littig Road, which crosses the railroad tracks a few feet later and then makes a hard left to the east. Out here, Old Highway 20 is also called Littig Road. While cotton is no longer king, it is still grown in many of the fields along this road.

LITTIG

Travis County • 37 • About 8 miles from Manor

The sleepy hamlet of Littig, a predominantly black community, was first called Bittig, supposedly in honor of early settler and Manor merchant, J. W. Bitting (note the difference in spelling), who donated land for the community school in 1889. The school, and later the community, became known as Littig. Why "Littig"? The July 19, 1883, *Austin Statesman* reported that "Mr. G. W. Littig, a popular conductor on the main line of the Houston and Texas Central railroad, registered at the Raymond [hotel] yesterday." It's also possible that in those pre-typewriter days, when all documents were recorded by hand and the finer points of spelling were oft ignored, Bittig might have become Littig, as one recorder would misread and misspell the writings of an earlier recorder. At any rate, in 1944, Mrs. Annie Rucker Baker became one of the first black postmistresses in Texas, sponsored by Congressman Lyndon Johnson.

Once in Bastrop County, the old highway is called County Road 76. A couple of miles past Littig, you come to another T intersection, marked by a yield sign and a Southwest Stallion Station sign. Turn left here onto the old Elgin River Road, the old settlers' route from Webberville to what we now call Elgin. Soon you enter Elgin.

ELGIN

Bastrop County • 9,800 (approximate) • (512) • About 6 miles from Littig

Elgin has been known by a variety of names (some very colorful) since the first white settlers moved to the area in the 1840s. By 1845, Young's Settlement, also known as Perryville, had been established two and a half miles south of the site of present Elgin on land granted to Elizabeth Standifer in 1829 as a member of Stephen F. Austin's "Little Colony." Standifer's daughter and son-in-law, Sarah and John Litton, built their home on this land, along with Michael Young and several of Standifer's sons. The churches and the local Masonic Lodge used the name Perryville, possibly for Perry Young, who was Michael Young's son.

The little community was also called Hogeye. There are at least four entertaining explanations for the origin of this name: (1) Area residents were often invited to the Litton home for community dances. "Hogeye" was the name of a popular, bouncy fiddle tune of the day, the only tune a slave belonging to John Litton knew how to fiddle. He might be heard sawing away at this ditty at dances or during any spare moment in the day, hence the name Hogeye. (2) Better hogs were raised here than in surrounding communities. (3) The eyes of one of the community's men had a peculiar, porcine expression. (4) The community was named for the symbolic eye of the Masonic order, which according to historian W. Walworth Harrison looked "to some of the unlettered natives" like a hog's eye.

The name Hogeye was a source of endless mirth to the hamlet's neighbors, especially the "sleek sophisticators" of Austin. On December 30, 1876, an *Austin Democratic Statesman* reporter "started out to interview someone, and coming up on a gentleman from the city with the classic name of Hogeye, we attempted to pump a few views out of him, but we found pretty dry pumping. After adjusting his spectacles and clearing his throat, he sagely reported that the chickens out in his neighborhood had gone into mourning because the weather had frozen the grasshopper eggs."

Lickskillet was another name given to the settlement in those early, often-meager pioneer days when there were only a few homes in the area, and a visiting traveler often had to "lick the skillet" to get his dinner.

Litton was appointed the first postmaster of Young's Settlement in 1849, and so the Litton home became the community's post office as well as a station along the Concord Stage Line. He served as postmaster until 1855, when he resigned to develop his property. Litton's eldest daughter, Martha Ellen Litton Turner, was postmistress at Young's Settlement during the Civil War. Litton eventually settled his family on a tract of land at the headwaters of Little Sandy Creek northeast of Young's Settlement, in the first house in the area built entirely of sawed lumber. He died of acute appendicitis in 1856 and was buried in the State Cemetery in Austin.

At one time in the 1850s or 1860s, Perryville had a saloon, a general store, two blacksmith shops, a grocery, and twelve to fifteen households. One unusual business venture, begun in 1866, involved camels. Bethel Coopwood and Enon Lanfear bought thirty-two "U.S. government surplus" camels and attempted to use them to carry mail and other items between San Antonio, El Paso, Chihuahua City, and Los Angeles. They sold the camels to circuses and fairs when the venture failed.

In 1871, the newly arrived H&TC established a flag stop called Glasscock several miles north of Young's Settlement, and residents began moving their homes and businesses toward the railroad flag stop, located just west of present-day Elgin. The Young's Settlement post office was discontinued in December 1872, and that community slowly declined. The new town laid out with the coming of the railroad was named to honor H&TC land commissioner Robert Morris Elgin. Most of the towns along the Houston and Texas Central railroad were named for an H&TC official or promoter.

Elgin was a Tennessee native and descendant of the American patriot Robert Morris. He came to Texas in the early 1840s and settled at Brenham, where he was deputy county clerk for Washington County. He served in the Mexican War of 1848, after which he went to Austin and took a position in the general land office, where he remained until after the Civil War, when he removed to Houston and became land commissioner of the Houston and Texas Central railroad.

But some locals like to tell another story. When the H&TC began laying tracks through here, some of the neighborhood folk did not want a railroad, including a Mr. Miles. He headed up the Miles Gang, who announced publicly that they didn't want a railroad and weren't going to have one. The railroad tracks came on through anyway. Once or twice, the Miles Gang tore up the tracks, which were promptly repaired. Finally, the first train into the new station was announced. The Miles Gang swore they would "shoot the lights out of it."

This train was late in arriving at Glasscock station. It was already dark when the train passed through Miles' territory, so the engine headlight and passenger coach lanterns had been lit. The Miles Gang was waiting east of town, and when the train roared by, they roared too, shooting out all the train's lights. Mission accomplished, the Miles bunch slipped into the thick post oak thickets. The next evening, they were shooting at the train again. It got to the point that whenever the train approached Miles' thickets, the conductor would warn all the passengers to "lay low; we're in for hell agin." Eventually the Miles Gang ceased their nefarious activities, but the spot continued to be known up and down the line as "Hell agin," commonly pronounced "Hell 'gin." The station-master knew that not many town lots would sell in a place called "Hell 'gin," but he was also loath to give up a name so rich in connotations. So he struggled with it awhile and further corrupted the corruption to "Elgin."

Perhaps the shoot up referred to in the above legend is the one that took place on the evening of August 11, 1874, near Elgin. Some fourteen shots were fired in all, indicating that several shooters were involved. Two or three of the shots passed through the windows and side of the sleeping car, causing the panic-stricken passengers to fall down into the seats to save themselves.

Conductor Smith Parr was of the opinion that no robbery was intended, as the train had just started after taking on wood. The identity of the shooters was unknown, and it was publicly speculated that revenge on the Central company was their motive.

With regard to the "Miles Gang," the reality is that the family patriarch, W. P. Miles, was a fairly respectable man; he was active in area politics in the 1870s as a member of the Hogeye faction in the Bastrop County Democratic Party, the Elgin Grange, and he served as an election officer in Hogeye (1873) and as Precinct Four county commissioner (1879). In 1873, he was the Democratic candidate for Precinct Four county school director but narrowly lost to the Republican candidate, George Warren.

But his boys walked on the wild side.

On May 22, 1875, Theo Miles, son of W. P. Miles, deliberately shot down and instantly killed Job Lewis from the door of his saloon in Elgin. The parties had been at outs for some time. Miles surrendered at once to authorities and was placed under a $2,000 bond. Interested parties worked hard to keep the affair from the public, but only for so long. The killing had no lasting effect; by March 1881, Theo Miles was constable of Bastrop County Precinct Four. He died in July 1883, in Austin, where he had been living. His wife was from Austin.

On the evening of January 29, 1878, just after dark, two unknown men rode up in front of the saloon that sixty-year-old W. P. Miles was running in Elgin and shot him through the window. He was sitting at his desk writing at the time. Thinking him killed, the men rode away without being recognized. They did not kill him, however; five of the shots took effect in his left shoulder and back, causing a painful but not dangerous wound. A feud had existed for several years, since the shooting of Job Lewis by Theo Miles, and it had been feared all along that it would result in further casualties. Miles had been often advised by friends to leave Elgin on account of anticipated trouble and threats, but the advice was not taken. Suspicions rested on certain parties, but no arrests were made.

On May 25, 1876, the *Austin Statesman* reported that two men were hung to a tree with their own stake ropes and their hands tied behind them, on the head of Dry Creek, near the Bastrop and Williamson county lines a few miles from Elgin station. Their names were not known, but they were believed to be from East Texas, based on belongings found on the men and their saddles. They had money on them (about three dollars), so they hadn't been robbed.

On the evening of April 6, 1884, Walter Miles mortally wounded Harry Taylor, son of Dr. W. A. Taylor of Elgin. An old feud existed between young Miles and young Taylor. There are several versions of the killing, and all agree that Miles had been in town that evening and had become somewhat intoxicated, and that the two men had not been on speaking terms for over a year. From here the accounts scatter in widely different directions. I have chosen to relate the version told by Harry's uncle, J. M. Taylor. Harry had been over to see a neighbor, and on his way back home, about dark, he overtook Miles, who had been up the lane a piece and was riding slowly. Taylor passed Miles near the Miles house, and just as he passed, Walter said, "You God damned son of a bitch, you shall not pass me again," and jerking out his six–shooter, he fired but missed. Then Taylor, seeing that Miles was going to kill him, threw himself down on his horse and begged him for God's sake not to kill him. Miles fired a second time, and the ball struck him in the center of the back and came out the front. Taylor was not aware that his life was in danger and was not armed at all, having only a small pocketknife, and that was broken. When the shooting was over, little Jimmie Brooks went over to see what was the matter. As he rode up to Walter Miles' house, Miles backed up against the gate with a Winchester in hand, which he drew down on the boy and cursed him and told him that he was going to kill him. And would have done so then, only Jimmie begged for mercy, and an old black man begged for him, which saved his life.

Miles took to the brush on horseback. No efficient steps were taken to arrest him; in fact, the next morning after the shooting, Miles rode over to the town looking for someone else he wanted to kill before leaving town. The general consensus was that Miles possessed some very noble traits of character, and were it not for strong drink—the bane of this community—he would have been a good citizen. Taylor lived for eight hours and was buried on April 8.

This killing was the straw that broke the camel's back. A few days later, owing to the recent killings and a general disregard for law and order, making the impression abroad, justly, that Elgin was a hard place to live at, a mass meeting of the citizens of the town and community, to consider the best methods of protecting society, preventing depreciation of property, and stamping out lawlessness in all its forms, was called by notices being posted around town for a night meeting at the M. B. Church South, and for the short notice given, a goodly number were present. The meeting was calm and dispassionate, but one could observe depicted upon the faces of those sturdy men a determination to see that law and order was observed in the future. The question was then raised as to whether the defunct corporation should be exhumed and resuscitated (incorporated with its founding, Elgin had subsequently disincorporated), or whether a demand should be made of the precinct officers who lived there for a more faithful and exact discharge of their duty, which latter was adopted. During the discussion, the past action of the officers was handled in a respectful but condemnatory manner, whereupon A. J. Poe, Justice of the Peace, having been called upon for his views, stated that if the citizens would sustain him and give him a proper constabulary force, he would see that law and order were maintained, which the entire assemblage agreed to do. Mr. Robert. H. Miles, the present constable and Walter's brother, was requested to resign, which he did in a very pleasant, willing manner. Dr. R. H. Burleson was solicited and endorsed by the entire audience to act as special deputy sheriff until a constable could qualify, which he agreed to do. Dr. Burleson was considered a cool, deliberate man, and as fearless as a lion, and one that would discharge the duties of the office regardless of friend or foe.

Once he had resigned his post, Robert Miles took flight to join his brother. He had been indicted for the slaying of a black man at a recent dance in Elgin, and for various smaller crimes, and had been arrested after his resignation in April by officers in Elgin, but by a bold dash he had succeeded in making his escape. The story was that he had gone to a dance party and had called up a black man to him and told him he was going to kill him. The man got on his knees and begged for his life, but the cold-blooded villain killed him without mercy while he was pleading.

The two brothers were captured in North Platte, Nebraska, about six weeks later and were brought back to Texas by Bastrop County deputy sheriff Will Scurry. The return of the Miles boys for trial stirred things up considerably in Elgin and the rest of Bastrop County.

Walter was denied bail in his habeas corpus trial shortly thereafter.

Late in June 1884, Walter Miles appealed to the state court of appeals from the judgment of the court below that denied him bail with regard to the Harry Taylor murder charge. The appeals court, following its former rulings in this respect, declined to comment upon the evidence but held that the court below had acted correctly in refusing bail to the appellant and affirmed the judgment.

At the same time, Robert Miles appealed from a judgment allowing him bail in the sum of $5,000 with regard to the charge of murdering the black man at the dance in Elgin, and the court deemed the evidence sufficient to hold him under the above named bail. The appeals court, after carefully reviewing the evidence, held it sufficient to say that the bail demanded was under the circumstances reasonable, and the judgment was affirmed.

Walter Miles' trial for the Taylor murder was held in late October 1884. He had languished in jail ever since. Interest in the case was great, and the courtroom was full, a number of ladies being present, which was a bit out of character for the times. We can only speculate as to their interest. After more than a day's deliberation, the jury found him guilty of murder in the second degree and sentenced him to twenty-five years in prison.

Robert Miles was tried and convicted of murder, but he appealed his case in May 1885. The appeals court reversed his conviction. At his retrial in November, the prosecution dropped all charges against him.

But that was not the end of Bob Miles' career in violence. One evening in July 1894, a difficulty occurred on First Street in Taylor in front of the Silver King saloon in which George Steadman, formerly a locomotive fireman on the Katy south of Taylor, was shot and instantly killed. Four shots were fired, two of which struck the victim, one in the bowels and the other breaking an arm and entering the left side. Soon afterward, Bob Miles surrendered to the officers and admitted that he had done the shooting. It seemed that for some time, past differences had existed between the two, Miles accusing Steadman of stealing some money from a gambling table which he conducted above the saloon. This accusation was denied by Steadman in bitter and abusive language, and thus the matter stood until the night when the two met with the result as stated. Miles was taken to the Georgetown jail. Steadman was of one of the most respected families of Taylor. Miles was a married man with a family residing at Elgin.

The road to peace in Elgin had been a long and bloody one. But by the fall of 1884, the *Bastrop Advertiser* was noting that "Elgin though formerly infested with outlaws, has been purged and the place filled with enterprising citizens. The selection of Dr. Rufus Burleson as deputy sheriff of Elgin is a wise move on the part of the law abiding citizens of that locality. A man of fine judgment, with plenty of nerve and bravery, he will soon bring order out of chaos, and the people should not be slow in lending him every assistance needed."

Elgin began to prosper as an agricultural center and shipping point, particularly after 1886 and the arrival of the Missouri-Kansas-Texas railroad (commonly referred to as the MKT or Katy), which hauled produce north. Hundreds of carloads of melons were shipped out yearly, as well as thousands of bales of cotton. Brick buildings, a sure sign of prosperity in those times, came early and in great numbers to Elgin. Even the old cotton gin you pass on the way into town is brick. Elgin was a center for brick production by the dawn of the twentieth century. Downtown Elgin is still predominantly brick, although the brick streets are now paved over with asphalt.

In 1894, the thriving Elgin Pressed Brick Company, which made six or seven different shapes of finishing brick, had shipped its product to Fort Worth for its courthouse, to Gonzales, and to other points. The plant had a capacity of 25,000 bricks per day, and the four kilns could each burn 250,000 bricks at once. The clay was secured near the yard, and McDade lignite coal was used as fuel. The plant had formerly used northern coal, one carload of which equaled two carloads of McDade lignite, but the owners had found that the McDade coal produced satisfactory results and was cheaper than wood.

Once in town, the River Road becomes Central Avenue.

Downtown Elgin still looks much as it did in 1916 at the apex of its prosperity. Old downtown Elgin is now a certified historical district, from Brenham Street on the south side to Fourth Street on the north side, Avenue A to the west and Avenue F to the east. Elgin has one of the best and largest vintage business districts still standing anywhere in Texas, one that straddles both sides of the railroad tracks. There are two blocks worth of brick commercial buildings on the south side of the tracks along and behind Central Avenue; most, unfortunately, are abandoned or barely hanging on.

The first of these historic buildings as you enter town is the old P. Bassist building (201 Central Avenue at S. Avenue C), which dates to 1906. The second story of Philip Louis Bassist's red-brick pride and joy served as Elgin's opera house; Lily Langtry is said to have performed here. The ground floor has housed a variety of businesses over the years, including Bassist Produce and the Elgin post office.

The east wall of the old (1900) Schroeder Grocery at 119 Central Avenue, at S. Avenue C, still cheerfully urges "Enjoy Bright and Early." Next door (117 Central) is one of Southside Market's many past homes. Elgin is famous for its "hot gut" sausage, and Southside Market is the granddaddy of all the local sausage stuffers. William Moon established the Southside Market in 1882 on what is now FM 1704. By 1886, the market had moved to 117 Central. It continued to move around until it settled for a half century at 109 Central in 1944; Southside Market is now located on US 290, and the south side of Elgin hasn't been the same since.

The humble little board-and-batten wooden depot building on your left next to the tracks is the original (1872) H&TC freight depot.

Elgin has one of the largest collections of painted wall advertisements in Central Texas. Here on the south side of the tracks, you can still read the fading old advertisements painted on several of the commercial buildings, such as the south wall of the two-story, former "RIVERS BROS. MERC. CO." building at Austin and S. Main, which sold "Royal Shoes" in the good old days. In the alley behind Schroeder Grocery (119 Central Avenue at S. Avenue C), you can see a circa 1900 Star Tobacco mural painted on the north wall of the building across the alley from Schroeder's. Look through the shop windows at 106 N. Main (the 1901 Dildy/Webster building), and you'll see two old, black-and-white painted wall advertisements dating to the turn of the century that were recently uncovered during a building restoration. One ad advertises a grain and feed company; the other touts Owl brand cigars, complete with a big white owl.

Central Avenue dead-ends into Main Street. Turn left here to see the north side of the historical district. Main Street is the principal thoroughfare in downtown Elgin.

North of the tracks, Main Street is in better shape: many of the old buildings have been restored, there are new businesses in them, and a number of long-time local businesses are still active.

In the Elgin post office (21 N. Avenue C), western and Depression-era art aficionados can see and enjoy the mural "Texas Farm," by Julius Woeltz, 1940.

ELGIN DEPOT MUSEUM AND ARCHIVE (OLD UNION DEPOT)

14 Depot Ave. at Main • Open Tuesday through Saturday 2–5 • 285-2000

Sandwiched in between the railroad tracks and the first block of business houses on the east side of N. Main is the red-brick Union Depot, built about 1903. It served as the local passenger depot for about sixty-five years. It underwent an eight-year, $500,000 restoration before reopening as a train museum in 2002.

A. CHRISTIAN SALOON

Depot Ave., facing Union Depot

A. S. Christian bought this lot for $300 in 1897 and built a saloon (one of seven in Elgin at the time), which he named A. Christian Saloon. According to an old story, the saloon (whose name was painted in large letters on the side of the building to attract thirsty passengers from the eight passenger trains that stopped in Elgin every day) drew the attention of a Bible salesman passing through town, who detrained and rushed into the saloon to congratulate its proprietor on his fine establishment. The salesman beat a hasty retreat when he realized that being a "Christian" had nothing to do with the den of iniquity he found inside.

ELGIN CHAMBER OF COMMERCE

114 Central Ave. • 285-4515 • www.elgintxchamber.com • Open Monday through Friday • W

This is your best source for visitor information.

CITY CAFE

19 N. Main • 281-FOOD • Open daily, breakfast, lunch, and dinner • W

City Cafe is one of the better small-town cafes in Central Texas. The building dates to about 1890 and is said to be the second brick building built downtown. It first housed a general store and drugstore, then a barber shop and bakery; it has housed a cafe since 1910. City Cafe serves the old standards like chicken-fried steak, plus some surprises.

MILLER BROTHERS BUILDING

32 N. Main at E. 1st

The most impressive building on the north side of the tracks is the two-story, red-brick with tan-brick accents Miller Brothers building. The building dates to about 1890, with a 1911 addition. It was home to Elgin's second bank, the Merchants and Farmers State Bank. The bank's original vault is still inside. It still has its stained-glass front door and transoms.

NOFSINGER HOUSE

310 N. Main

Dr. I. B. Nofsinger built this Queen Anne-styled house with local brick in 1906. Born in Kentucky in 1864, Nofsinger came to Texas as a young man and practiced medicine in McDade before moving to Elgin in 1900. His house symbolizes Elgin's turn-of-the-century prosperity, when the town grew from 832 people in 1890 to 1,709 people in 1910. The house is now Elgin City Hall.

Continue north on Main to Elgin Memorial Park. Along the way you'll see several more substantial old homes from Elgin's golden era.

OTHER ATTRACTIONS

ELGIN ANTIQUE MALL

195 US 290 • 281-5655 • Open daily

A number of dealers are located inside, and the inventory constantly changes. They have furniture, glassware, and all sorts of specialty collectibles.

DINING

MEYER'S ELGIN SMOKEHOUSE

188 US 290 • 281-3331 • www.cuetopiatexas.com • Open daily, lunch and dinner • W

Here in the Sausage Capital of Texas, Meyer's sausage is a worthy alternative to Southside Market's "hot guts." The beef brisket and pork ribs also stand up to their Southside competition. All the usual barbecue side dishes (plus cream corn) are available. Meyer's Elgin sausage is now sold in a number of major supermarkets across greater Central Texas, Houston, and the Dallas–Fort Worth metroplex.

SOUTHSIDE MARKET

1212 US 290 • 281-4650 • www.southsidemarket.com • Open daily • W

Southside Market makes the sausage that made Elgin sausage famous. Besides the sausage, Southside Market serves up pork and beef steaks, beef and pork ribs, beef brisket, and mutton. The pork steak is plastic-fork tender and peppery—and in its own way easily the equal of the pork chops from Kreuz Market in Lockhart or Cooper's in Llano. The side dishes are good too. What's missing is the ambience of the market's old location downtown on Central Avenue, on the south side of the tracks. The building that now houses the market used to be a bank.

ANNUAL EVENT

JUNE

Western Days • Elgin Memorial Park • 285-4515 • Fourth weekend in June
Events include parades, dances, a rodeo, a fun run, and an arts-and-crafts fair.

To leave Elgin, return to Main Street at the railroad tracks. Go south on Main, past the intersection with Central Street, and take the first possible left turn, onto Brenham Street, which turns into County Road 106, aka the old McDade Road.

After leaving town, the land to your left (this is the old Miles Gang territory) is East Texas overgrown, while to your right, the old H&TC railroad tracks run past new ranch-style houses, old crumbling farmhouses, and gravel pits on the way to Butler.

BUTLER

Bastrop County • About 6 miles from Elgin

Butler is a company town and dates back to the railroad's arrival in 1871. Michael and Patrick Butler came to Austin in the early 1870s and started a brick factory soon after. The business prospered, and Butler bricks were used all over Austin: in the old city hall, in the capitol building, and in the streets of downtown Austin. Upon their discovery of good clay here on Sandy Creek, the Butlers began moving their operation out here, beginning with a plant built in 1903. Naturally, all of the company's buildings and dwellings are made of brick.

As you enter Butler, you cross some railroad tracks and pass the entrance to the brick works on your left. A few feet later, you come to the intersection with FM 696. At this point, you could continue straight ahead on the old highway to McDade, but instead, turn left on FM 696 and head toward Lexington. On your left, as you cross Sandy Creek, you will see more of the brick works, and then the pits where the clay is excavated. The countryside on both sides of the road for the next several miles is dominated by a recently started, controversial, and undeniably ugly lignite coal-mining operation.

Five miles from Butler, you come to an intersection with FM 619, going left (north) to Taylor. If you turn left, you soon enter Williamson County and the western fringes of the old Jim Olive family ranch. Jim's son, Isom Prentice "Print" Olive, would light the fuse to what became the Yegua Troubles, the great feud of the Yeguas.

Print Olive was born in 1840 in Mississippi, the son of James and Julia Brashear Olive. When Print was three, the family moved to what is now the southeastern corner of Williamson County, on Brushy Creek near West Yegua Creek. The area was thinly settled and prone to Indian raids. Williamson County would not be created until 1848.

They built a log cabin and were soon good friends with their neighbors, the Lawrences. They were a popular, outgoing family, giving parties and inviting their neighbors who lived up and down Brushy Creek. Jim set up a store near his home at a place called Cross Roads, later called Lawrence Chapel. Mrs. Olive, her daughters, and her daughters-in-law all went to church, but not the boys. Julia and sisters were Methodists; Jim never forced the boys to attend church. They were close as a family, fiercely loyal and gentle with friends, but showing no mercy to enemies. Jim Olive remained a respected citizen all his life; not so his sons.

Print Olive received some basic education, but most of his school years were spent on the open range of his family's ranch, roping cattle, especially mavericks with no brand, to build their herd. Not that cattle were worth much, but they were free for the taking, and the heavily forested, rough country wasn't fit for anything but running hogs, horses, and cattle.

James and Julia had nine children, including sons Prentice, Thomas Jefferson "Jay," Ira Webster, Marion, and Robert. James and Julia and their daughters were gentle, but not the boys, especially Print and Bob, who always seemed to be fighting with someone. Print seems to have been paranoid, and Bob was always in trouble. As he grew of age, Print developed a taste for fast company, liquor, poker, and gunplay, the opposite of everything his father stood for. But his doting mother usually managed to hide Print's indiscretions from James.

The creek bottoms and adjacent hills in the southeastern part of Williamson County were covered with an almost impenetrable growth of cat's claw, chaparral, cactus, wildrose, mesquite, and other spiny growths that seemed an impassable barrier. There were places where it would have been difficult to see a bull elephant with a spyglass. Such wild country attracted a wild breed of humanity.

In February 1856, Mormon elder Morris J. Snedaker (see Gonzales), on a mission from Salt Lake City, passed through Lexington and was halted by rain in Olive territory. He received a hearty invitation to stay and preach to the folks in the neighborhood, which was so newly settled that it as yet had no church or schoolhouse. Thomas Stevens, who had the largest home in the settlement, said he would provide a room for Snedaker's preaching. Stevens was a very rough-spoken man who told Snedaker they all needed a good preaching to, "for they was a damned rough set in that neighborhood and all of the God damned preachers had forsaken us. I think there might be something done in this neighborhood if you preach right."

Stevens sent one of his boys around the neighborhood circulating the news that a lecture would be given at his house by a reverend Mormon elder from Salt Lake next Sabbath at two o'clock. When Sunday came, it was still raining, as hard as Snedaker had ever seen it rain. Notwithstanding the rain, Stevens' house was filled.

According to the account given by Snedaker,

As they waited for the Word, they were busy talking about trading horses, swapping forms, cattle catching, deer hunting, etc., etc., and smoking tobacco.

Every man was talking very earnest and it came about time for me to do a little talking. I called the house to order. One of Mr. Stevens' hound dogs came into the house. He told him to go outdoors. The dog didn't understand. He repeated it again and again. Finally he got up and swung his long leg back with a heavy foot on the end of it and took the dog right back of the forelegs and as it was a hound he made a big noise and fairly deafened all in the house.

He then took the dog by the nape of the neck and tail, then sent him outdoors headlong for more than a rod. As it was clay ground and still raining very hard, the dog slipped about one rod and yelped like all things. He got up and ran under the house and there yelled like all things a' shaking. What a noise for about ten minutes. After the noise ceased the news came that the dog was dead.

I, however, opened the meeting, then commenced preaching. I thought I must make some comments about the dog to start on. This set them a'laughing. This, however, gave me a pretty good start and I thought I talked to them about ten minutes but was little more than 3/4 of an hour.

After he finished, Stevens told him that his doors were welcome for Snedaker to preach as much as he wanted to, then turned around to his neighbors and said, "By God, that is as good preaching as anybody can do. We are a damned wicked set here and need preaching to. They all call us a godforsaken set but I think we can be reclaimed."

"They came up to me," Snedaker wrote in his diary, "and wished me to preach again to them. I thought I preached all I knew and more, too."

But he concluded to return again to them later that season to preach, and the next day he continued on his journey north, across Brushy Creek.

Money was scarce in the Yeguas before the Civil War, so scarce that their circuit-riding preacher, the Reverend Daniel Morse, was paid in livestock, which he said was better than money.

Print Olive joined the Confederate Army and fought at Shiloh (where he was wounded in the hip) and Vicksburg, where he was captured in 1863. Paroled after promising that he would no longer bear arms against the United States, he went to the Confederate port of Galveston where he loaded and unloaded blockade runner ships until the end of the war. When not working, he drank, gambled, and got into fights.

Print, like thousands of other Civil War veterans, returned home at war's end, hardened by all the suffering he had endured. But the experience would serve him well, because he knew he would have to fight, ruthlessly if necessary, to profit from the only marketable asset abundant in Texas at the time, cattle. Folks said of him, "He don't scare."

Print decided he was going to get rich off cattle. When he got home, Print partnered with his brothers Thomas, Bob, and Ira and began rounding up the unbranded, wild longhorns that had proliferated during the war, and in 1866, they commenced to driving their herds to Kansas. Their cowboys could drink as much as they wanted as long as there was no drunkenness and they were able to ride the next day.

The Olive pens were built north of Brushy Creek near Thrall, and from these pens the Olives loaded cattle to ship by rail after 1876.

On February 4, 1866, Print Olive married Louisa Reno. Five children were born to this couple. To his family, Print was a loving husband, father, and provider. The marriage almost didn't come off; a few days before the wedding, Print caught Rob Murday driving Olive-branded cattle to Hogeye. Murday said he was driving cattle for a neighbor of the Olives, John Franklin "Turk" Turner. Print Olive shot and wounded Murday.

Turk Turner was the son of Mann Turner, who came to Texas from Tennessee. Mann and his wife had four boys, Allen, Jerry G., John Franklin (Turk), and Jerry T. Mann died in 1862 in Little Rock while serving in Confederate Army. His widow married N. B. Tanner. After he died, she married Horace Alsup in 1872. And so Turk and the other Turner boys became the stepbrothers of Horace Alsup's boys, of whom we shall hear more.

This shooting, then, could be considered the opening shot in a range war that would last twenty years over three counties and kill dozens of people. It would soon spread beyond the Olives and their immediate neighbors and attain a life of its own apart from the Olives, who fled to Nebraska in 1876 and 1877.

The Olive Brothers saw the influx of newcomers as a major threat to the way of life enjoyed by cattlemen like themselves who considered the government-owned land their property. The early cattlemen who had free range on the open prairies considered Olive a savior in the beginning. Print and the Olive boys took the lead in trying to rid "their land" of the troublesome newcomers, taking the law into their own hands to protect their property.

In January of 1867, Print was hauled into court to face charges of assault with intent to kill in wounding Rob Murday. But Murday, who was now an Olive employee, failed to appear against Print.

The Olives would be in and out of court constantly during the next ten years, mostly on assault charges filed against them. In 1867 alone, there were thirty-six cases in Williamson County involving the Olives, including one for Print pistol-whipping a cowboy in a saloon; in that case, charges were not pressed, and the case was dismissed. The worst punishments handed down by judge or jury were one-dollar fines.

In 1870, Bob Olive, age fourteen, was charged with theft of a colt from Sampson Connell of Georgetown, who was a friend of James Olive. Charges were dropped.

Early in 1870, Print Olive shot it out with a young Lee County rancher, variously known as Dave Fream, Deets Phreme, and D. R. Frame, after Print discovered him driving a herd containing Olive-branded steers. Olive cut his steers out, unmolested, and drove them home. Then he came back and goaded Fream into a fight, whom he suspected of earlier attempting to ambush Bob Olive. Fream died, and Print suffered a gunshot wound in the left shoulder. Olive was indicted, but the trial was postponed until March 1872. A friendly judge at the district court in Georgetown threw the case out of court when Olive's lawyers found "evidence" that Fream was the leader of a band of rustlers known as the Yegua Notchcutters.

To celebrate, the Olives gave a big community dance at their ranch, and then the Olive brothers hit the trail with a herd to Kansas.

Print Olive found himself playing poker with fellow budding cattle baron James Kenedy (son of Mifflin Kenedy of the King Ranch) in Ellsworth, Kansas, in July of 1872. During the game, Olive caught Kenedy cheating, threatened to kill him, and ran him out of the game. The next day, Kenedy caught Olive in the Ellsworth Bar and opened fire, screaming, "You son of a bitch, now you can cash in your checks." Kenedy shot Olive in the hand, groin, and thigh and would have killed him if not for the intervention of "Nigger Jim" Kelly, one of Olive's most esteemed cowboys. Kelly shot Kenedy in the leg, knocked him to the floor, and took his gun. Olive soon recuperated and returned to Texas.

Back home, more and more folks were beginning to complain about the Olives, even some of the "old guard" free-range ranchers who had earlier supported Print. It seems that the Olive herds, particularly Print's, were always increasing while other stockmen's herds were shrinking. Print attributed it to working harder than anyone else. But others did not see it that way.

There were rumors of cleverly altered brands, accusations and counter accusations. Print circulated a warning that anyone seen riding or driving an Olive horse or cow would be shot on sight. When several Olive horses were mutilated, Bob held a man at gunpoint for information about the cuttings.

Print said repeatedly that no one would convict him for shooting cattle thieves. When he ambushed three men that he claimed were driving Olive cattle in 1875, he killed two of them and wounded W. H. McDonald. He was indicted for intent to murder, but the indictment made no mention of the two dead men. The original indictment disappeared, and Print pled guilty to simple assault and was fined one dollar. The charge of intent to murder McDonald was again put on the docket, and on January 4, 1876, witnesses refused to testify against him. So Print and Jay Olive pled guilty to assault and battery and simple assault and were fined a dollar each. The bailiff of the district court at Georgetown complained, "The Olives are in and out of court as much as I am."

Late in February 1875, Print, Jay, Ira, and Bob heard that some supposed rustlers were at the Rockfront Saloon in McDade, and Print stepped in to give them some "straight talk." They included Cal Nutt, Gus Zeitler, and Dock and Lawson Kelley.

Night riders had ridden into James Olive's ranch, hamstringing one of his finest saddle horses and cutting the tongues from two others. The mutilated animals had to be destroyed. Bob told his father it was the Cal Nutt gang. Henry Hoyle had seen them riding south.

N. B. Ware was a young man who cow hunted with the Nutts. Bob went off searching for Ware. On December 17, 1875, Ware was riding with Pete Zieschang when Bob Olive intercepted them. Zieschang ran off, but Bob kept Ware at gunpoint until Print got there to ask him some questions. Ware told Olive that the Kelley brothers did the cutting, but that it was Cal Nutt's idea, seeing as how Olive had threatened him.

On January 3, 1876, Print's trial for the attempt to murder W. H. McDonald began. But Allen E. Wynn and James Williams didn't show up for the prosecution. Allen Wynn was Print's nephew, while Williams was an old friend.

Bob tracked down and killed Lawson Kelley, who he claimed was hired to kill him. "It was a fair gun fight," Bob said. Nevertheless, Bob was charged on January 25, 1876, and was given a four-man guard for his protection from Dock and his friends.

Print pistol-whipped and beat up Peter Zieschang and Ernest Poldrack, two German immigrants who objected to the Olives' cattle trail passing over their land.

In 1876, Allen Wynn, who was a cotton farmer in the Knobbs community, was attacked and robbed by a group of men while on his way to Bastrop to get medicine for a sick member of his family. Wynn, pretending to be dead, overheard someone say, "Thad, do you think he is dead?" To Wynn and the Olive clan, "Thad" could only be Thad McLemore of Lee County. This robbery is said to have led to the infamous Pat Airhart Dance and Lynching of 1877.

In March 1876, Print Olive rode upon a scene of two beeves being skinned in Lee County. He shot and killed Turk Turner and the old man with him, James H. Crow. Some sources say he wrapped each of them in a hide with the Olive brand showing. The bodies were taken to Hogeye for burial. The *Statesman* said Crow's son found the bodies. They were found several hundred yards apart. Turner had long been regarded as a lawless, dishonest character and desperado, but old man Crow, though he had a son in the penitentiary, was not so regarded. The gentleman from McDade who furnished this information said that in the last three to four months, twelve persons, all thieves and desperados, had been killed in that country within a radius of twenty-five miles, and the gang still wasn't wiped out.

By this time, emotions were so high that Print and Ira talked of moving to Nebraska or Wyoming. Jay wasn't interested in moving but thought that Print and Ira should get Bob out of Texas. The Olive women wanted this too.

On the night of August 1, 1876, a group of fifteen to twenty men led by Grip Crow, son of James Crow, attacked the Olives at their cattle pens several miles from their houses. Jay was killed, and Print was wounded in the hip, along with several of the Olive's cowboys. According to contemporary accounts, Jay's body was riddled from head to foot by nineteen bullets, with one eyeball torn completely out. The Olives evidently fired back with some success, for the next day a black man was brought into Austin for treatment of gunshot wounds received during the attack; a gun and considerable blood were found at the point from which the Olive camp was fired upon.

The Olives believed, from the inscription on a watch found at the scene ("To Fred from Mother, Christmas 1860"), that Print's supposed best friend, Fred Smith, was involved. Soon after the fight, according to the story told in Harry Chrisman's *Ladder of Rivers*, Print caught Smith crossing Brushy Creek in the Lawrence Chapel area with a wagon full of household goods. When Smith was across, Olive said to him, "Draw when you are ready, Fred." Smith made his move. Print shot him through the bridge of the nose, killing him instantly. Olive disposed of the body, and the story was kept quiet. Since Smith's body was never found, no proof existed that Smith was dead, and no charges were brought.

After the attack on the Olive camp in which Jay was killed, the *Bastrop Advertiser* wrote words to the following intent:

> Something must be done to put a check upon the lawlessness now reigning supreme throughout Texas, and if the Legislature and Governor refuse to protect the people, it is the duty of all good citizens to rise in their might and suppress this great nuisance. The prosperity of our State, justice, and mercy require that something be done, and that speedily. Every neighborhood should call a general meeting of its citizens, from which meeting no good man should absent himself, and there let the matter be talked over and some proper course marked out by which all may be protected in their rights as citizens, and let the guilty be brought to punishment. Let every difficulty, every disturbance of any kind, be sifted to the very bottom, and "let no guilty man escape."

On September 5, a gentleman from up about Taylor told the *Austin Daily Statesman* that the "war spirit" between the Olive and Smith parties was still at fever heat, and that blood and thunder might be looked for at any time.

Public sentiment, at least among the newspapers, seemed to favor the Olives. On August 8, 1876, the *Austin Statesman* opined,

The Olives are stockmen and have long suffered at the hands of horse and cattle thieves. Several months ago they gave out that they would kill anyone they found skinning their cattle or riding their horses and not long after that they found old man Crow and Turner and killed them in the woods near McDade while skinning a beef with the Olive brand. Crow had a son who had served one or more terms in the pen and he accused the Olives of killing his father and threatened to avenge his death. Since that time it is said that he was head of a band of roughs and desperados and this crowd was suspected of committing the horrible tragedy perpetrated on the Olive brothers and their employees on the night of August 1. The Olive brothers were said to be upright men with many warm friends in the vicinity of where they lived and that it was quite probable that further bloodshed and trouble would follow.

Would not it have been better that the Olives, instead of killing on the spot persons meddling with their stock, should have arrested and turned them over to the civil authorities, and had them punished in the regular way? Thirty years ago the regulators and Moderators held a carnival of blood and violence in Texas, and house-burnings and assassinations for revenge did not cease for ten years.

After Fred Smith's sudden disappearance in August 1876, two armed black men named Banks and Donaldson arrived at the Olive ranch, at Post Oak Island, as the neighborhood was then called, on September 7. They dismounted and asked Print's wife for water. Heading for the house, Banks inquired as to the whereabouts of Print, who had heard the conversation from inside the house and came out with his rifle asking the men their business. The men explained they were out hunting stolen horses. Olive demanded to know why they asked Mrs. Olive about her husband's whereabouts. He believed that the rustlers sent Banks and Donaldson. Becoming scared, Banks jumped for his horse and was shot dead, while Donaldson was bullwhipped and run off.

District court was set to convene on September 18. J. P. Olive was brought into town on September 12 under arrest for the murder of Red Banks. He was admitted to bail for $3,500. No inconsiderable excitement was said to exist in the Olive neighborhood, originating in this and previous troubles. Upon the serving of the writ by Deputy Sheriff Tucker, Olive said he would not go with him without a strong guard; he was certain he would be attacked by his enemies and killed. He had some twenty men with him at his house when Tucker and one assistant arrived, and Tucker acted as the emergency of the occasion suggested itself to him. He summoned a number of men to accompany him with the prisoner to Georgetown, taking a circuitous route. The next day, another party of armed men approached the outskirts of town. This party had with them two witnesses, colored, who were to appear against Olive. They considered the lives of these witnesses in danger from the Olives. The members of this party were said to be good citizens of that portion of the county. They did not come into town but remained somewhere near the outskirts. Both parties were quiet and orderly, and each was desirous that the law should take its course. Robert Olive and Samuel Carr were also under arrest for the murder of Dock Kelley (colored) on September 10, also at Post Oak Island. On their examination before esquire Morrow Tuesday, there was no evidence to implicate the Olives in the murder, and they were bound over, as required by law, in the sum of $250 each. The famed Captain McNelly's company of Texas Rangers would not have been out of place stationed about Post Oak Island, folks declared.

There were now two camps of men camped within two miles of Georgetown, about two miles from each other on two roads, one company of about sixty men, the other of about forty. The general opinion of neutral parties was that the Olive brothers were desperate men and had their adherents in the country, and that they were at comity, and had been for years, with another family, equally desperate. The company of forty men were the friends of the Olives and were awaiting the verdict of the jury; if it were against the Olive boys, they would sally into town and take them from the officers of the law. The company of sixty men was organized to prevent these results, and to see that the law was vigorously executed. The men in each company stated that they were all law-abiding citizens and were organized for no bad purpose, but simply to see that the law was vindicated.

Print was indicted for murder and assault with the intent to kill on September 22, 1876, with trial on October 1. Officials at Georgetown set up a special patrol to keep peace during the trial, since the Olives always had a group of friends attending their trials to make sure their man got a fair trial. Print was found not guilty on both charges. The charges on Fred Smith's murder had been dismissed, since no body was ever found.

By now even the Olives' friends were alarmed by Print's excessive drinking and fighting. They encouraged Print to move on. Even Mrs. Olive suggested a move to new country, like Nebraska. Brother Ira had been in the Colorado-Nebraska area for some time.

Bob Olive then went after Cal Nutt, who had worked for Fred Smith. He found and killed Nutt at the Rock Front Saloon in McDade in December 1876. Bob, on the run after killing Cal Nutt, was sent to Nebraska ahead of the rest of the family to contact Ira Olive and scout out a suitable range. Because he was on the run, Bob assumed the name Bob Stevens, the name by which he would be known while in Nebraska.

But before Bob left, there was one more bit of mischief to be done. In early November 1876, he carried off a little black boy, about six years old, from southern Bastrop County, which would provoke the lynching of John Black, who was accused of killing the boy. Two black men would be hanged in Bastrop County late in 1878 for Black's lynching, ironically on the same day that Bob Olive's body reached Elgin from Nebraska, where he had been killed in a shootout with supposed rustlers. Bob was buried at Lawrence Chapel.

Print had one more summons to attend in Georgetown on March 28, 1877, but the charges were dismissed and he split for Nebraska. But even after the Olive brothers were gone, their surrogates carried on their bloody work. On September 6, 1877, in the Sam Haynes Saloon at Round Rock, George Adams, an Olive cowboy, shot Old Bill Turner, a relative of Turk Turner.

Print Olive settled in west central Nebraska after bringing up his herd in the spring of 1877. He began complaining about rustling at the same time the country began filling up with settlers. Olive had brought most of his cowboys to Nebraska. One day, Ira severely berated one of the Mexican herders because he found two horns knocked from the cattle, whereupon the Mexican drew a knife. Ira shot him dead, paid the man's widow well, and all was kept from the law, but not from the other cowboys or the local ranchers. Before long, Print was informed that he had moved in on grass saved for winter range by cattlemen who had claimed the region for years. That, combined with his reputation for trouble, forced him to move on to the Dismal River area. Before long homesteaders and the little ranchers who ran cattle on government land were told that this was Olive land and to stay out. Print was soon referred to as Nebraska's richest rancher. He was high-handed, overbearing, and bulldozing, just like in Texas. Ami Ketchum and Luther Mitchell were two homesteaders who did not scare out. In November 1878, Bob Olive and a posse rode up to the Ketchum house and demanded that those inside surrender. Bob was now a deputy sheriff and had a warrant for the arrest of Ketchum and Mitchell on dubious evidence. Shooting broke out, and Bob was killed. Ketchum and Mitchell were caught and turned over to Print Olive who immediately hanged the two men in a most gruesome manner, after first shooting a begging Mitchell. The bodies were later cut down, doused with whiskey, and set afire. A cowhand buried the two men a few days later. Olive was found guilty and was sentenced to the penitentiary for life. After twenty months in jail, Olive won a new trial in his home district, where he was acquitted. Nearly broke from his many trials, suffering the winterkill of half his herd, and roundly disliked, Olive moved his operations to Dodge City, Kansas, where he cosigned a note for Joe Sparrow. Joe paid the money back, all except for ten dollars, which Olive had to make good. Print and Sparrow argued over the ten dollars on more than one occasion. Finally, Olive threatened Sparrow. On August 6, 1886, Sparrow gunned down Olive in Trail City, Colorado.

About three miles past the FM 696/FM 619 intersection, you come to an intersection with Lee County Road 305, which is also marked by a sign for the Knobbs Springs Baptist Church. Off to your right are the four hillocks known as the Yegua Knobbs. Turn right on Lee County Road 305 to reach the Knobbs country.

THE KNOBBS

Lee County • About 11 miles from Butler

You might as well throw your compass away out here for all the good it will do you; the ferruginous sandstone that composes the Knobbs will cause its needle to flutter about wildly, rendering it useless. Back 130 years ago, the Knobbs were not a good place to get lost. Following the war, this area was a favorite hangout for rustlers, murderers, and other ne'er-do-wells, and with good reason. The county seats and the sheriffs were a good twenty miles and half a day's ride away, and the thickly wooded hills and valleys made good hideouts.

These same hills and valleys made scratching out a living from the soil even more difficult than it already was. Boys from the Yegua Knobbs were known as "notchcutters," although it is not clear whether the name referred to the notches in their gun handles or the notches in the trees they used as trail markers through the dense thickets of the creek bottomlands. The name "Yegua Notchcutters" first surfaced at the beginning of the Civil War, when a group of volunteers from the area, comprising Company F of the Fifth Texas Cavalry, called themselves the Yegua Notchcutters.

Lee County was created in 1874 from pieces of Burleson, Washington, Bastrop, and Fayette counties. The Knobbs area of Lee County came from Bastrop County. The theft and unrest before the creation of Lee County involved the corners of three counties, each sliver of county far removed from the sheriff and county seat.

The first sheriff of Lee County was James McKowen, one of the area's early settlers, and by now a wizened, white-haired old man. He seems to have been ineffective in curbing area crime, as evidenced by this April 1, 1876, editorial in the *Austin Statesman*:

> If the sheriffs of several counties of Texas, authorized as they are to call out the posse comitatus, were removable by the governor, there would be infinitely better order maintained in western counties. Now and then a sheriff is chosen by the disorderly elements of society. His sympathies are with those that delight in excitements of rapine, violence, and disorder, and there is no local restraint upon ebullitions of villainy and crime is openly riotous. If Gov. Coke's hand were mailed with iron force enough to choke the official life out of sheriffs of counties in which murderers go unwhipt of justice, murders would soon be very rare.

McKowen was succeeded in 1876 by Sheriff Jim Brown, who quickly proved to be a man of action, as the *Statesman* noted on May 11, 1876: "We admire the intelligence of the people of Lee County. They elect the right sort of sheriffs. Achilles was not more invulnerable than the sheriffs of Lee. The last one they created over there was shot last week and penetrated by nine buckshot but he still lives unawed, unterrified, and unkilled. His name is Jim Brown and they can't knock the black out."

In 1922, S. J. Speir wrote about his memories of the youth at Yegua Knobbs around 1877. His country was divided into three communities, Coon Neck, Hogeye, and Yegua Knobbs. He lived in Coon Neck, the westernmost settlement. The boys of the communities were antagonistic toward each other over the region's pretty girls. The Hogeye boys called the Coon Neck boys "red necks" and "hillbillies." They called the Yegua Knobbs boys "Yegua Notch Cutters."

> When we had a dance, them Yegua Notch Cutters would come in and dance with spurs on their boots, pants in their boot tops, big white hats on, and a red handkerchief tied around his neck. Sometimes a Yegua Notch Cutter's spurs would get tangled up in a girl's dress and throw her down on the floor. This would cause a fight. The boys would go outside and fight it out with their fists while the girls circled round and clapped their hands like a dog fight was on. If a boy pulled a knife or gun, he was called a coward. The other boys would gang on him, take his knife or gun away from him and make him fight it out with his fists, or back down. When the fight was over, they all went back in the house and started up the dance again. Among the Yegua Notch Cutters was more good fiddlers than any place on earth.
>
> The Hogeye boys were fighters and made us Coon Neck boys stand around. Coon Neck boys were more likely to steal your watermelon or chicken. Coon Neck never turned out any Abe Lincolns or King Solomons, but could boast of not turning out any desperados or bad men.

Many Southern spirits and pockets were empty after the Civil War. For many, rustling and robbing seemed to be the easiest way to make a living, and a well-aimed gun often served as a morale booster as well as a quick and easy method of settling accounts. A human life, even one's own, seemed to have less value after the great conflagration. The words of Confederate veteran Dan Hensley, about to be hung by Knobbs-area vigilantes for rustling a yearling calf, may help us to understand these unsettled times:

> Now gentlemen, as you know, I have just come home from fighting in the war. I found my wife and family almost starved to death and I could not find any of the

few head of stock, oxen, cows and canes, steers or hogs that I had to leave behind when I was forced to go to war. I have been gone about four years and, as you know, if I didn't go, I would have been shot. And to fight in a war, as so many others did, that was not any of my business, since I never did believe in slavery and also was too damn poor to own one.

I'm what is called "poor white trash," just cluttering up the countryside. We came here to try all over again but the slaveholders have the money, the best land and most land, the best and most animals and equipment, besides the cheap slave labor. It has been hard for us to live because no one cares whether we live or die. Mostly they would rather see the latter.

I know the slaves have been mistreated, but on the other hand, being property of the rich people, they were fed and housed and taken care of that way to which we had to fend for ourselves and which was worse than the slaves this way because we had neither the tools or the skills to build a decent home or farm with. Just as they say, "root, hog, or die."

As you know, if the slaveholder had as many as three slaves he did not have to serve in the Confederate Army; but if he did, he was commissioned as an officer and you know how many Privates of us poor white trash there was. Now the officers stayed behind us, directing us and shooting anyone in the back who faltered or tried to leave. I have had to kill other humans or be killed and I am so damn tired of it all, till I don't give a damn what you do.

Although I would like for you to examine your conscience and if there is a man in this crowd who had not so much as stolen one yearling or hog, then let him whip this worn-out horse out from under me.

The man's words rang true to the posse, so true that by the time he had finished, most of them had gone shamefacedly home. The last man to leave was honorable enough to remove the "convicted" man's noose and untie him. Most vigilante incidents did not end this way, however.

There was an unwritten law that if a man were caught stealing a cow, he would be shot on the spot, and it was often carried out. Almost anything went in this deadly game.

Practically everyone in the Yegua Knobbs neighborhood lost some cattle, according to G. W. Martin. The rustlers operated mostly at night according to a well-planned system. The country south and southeast of Taylor along the Brushy Creeks was covered with undergrowth. Stolen cattle could be concealed easily with comparative safety, and the rustlers, well armed, did not hesitate to shoot "suspicious" intruders.

A man rode up to my grandmother's house one day and asked her if there were any cattle for sale in the neighborhood. She told him no, that the Olives had stolen all the cattle in the community and that she did not know of any cattle left in the country. He turned, smiled, and rode away. She later learned that she had been talking to Print Olive, said by some to be the arch cow-thief in Texas.

Before barbed wire, it was an easy matter to round up several cows in a bunch and take them out of the country and there change the brands by adding a mark to the old one, or by cutting another bit in the ear. This was a big business, and many a person became a wealthy and "respectable" rancher by this means.

Some of the outlaws tried to get my father to join them, but he told them he had to care for his widowed mother and his sisters. Some of them told him that if he ever got into trouble to call on them and they would get him out. My father managed to keep their friendship, although he would not associate with them. They little suspected that he was a member of the law enforcement group. He told me that the committee never called on him to take part in any of the executions, for which he had always thanked his God.

Faced with increasing lawlessness and the inability of the law to deal with the problem, certain citizens in the area had formed the Knobbs Committee in 1875. It would function for eight years. This vigilante group worked with similar committees from neighboring settlements like McDade, Bastrop, Oak Hill, and Giddings. Executions were handled by groups from outside the area where the crimes were committed. Membership in these committees was secret; to be a known member was to court death by those you were after. Members met at night in a variety of wooded locations, using whistles, grunts, and throat clearings for signals. Action came by a simple majority vote. Even prominent citizens were involved, for these were truly desperate times. They claimed that they tried to avoid sanctioning innocent men, but some who were killed had done nothing more than harbor a friend or relative wanted by the vigilantes.

For instance, in 1900, the Martins were in the midst of cotton-chopping time when a stranger rode up on a big, fine horse looking for work. Daddy Martin put him to work. He was a good hand and earned his pay. When the season was over, he collected his pay and rode away. A short time later, the Martins learned that he had stolen the horse he was riding. The man was tried, convicted, and sent to the penitentiary. If this had happened in 1880, Martin might have been lynched for aiding and abetting a horse thief, albeit unwittingly.

The original list of committee signees, as published in the *Galveston News*, included men from the Highsmith, Billingsley, Bryce, Armstrong, W. H. Hasley, Stephens, McLemore, Lawhorn, French, Null, Hughes, Martin, Allen, Nash, Ransom, Turner, Jewel, and Lane families, many of whom were the kin of the outlaws the vigilantes would later hang.

Most all the Knobbs men—vigilantes and outlaws—feared for their lives during these years. It was unsafe for the menfolk to leave the house after sunset, so the women answered the door, milked and fed the cattle, and brought in firewood for the evening. Some families put up heavy curtains made of dark material to obscure all movements within the house. This practice brought misery on hot summer nights, since the curtains let in none of the cool evening breezes. Some men even wore their wives' nightgowns and caps to further obscure their identities. But occasionally all these precautions were in vain; at least one man was dragged from his home one night and lynched.

A letter from the Thornhill family of Bosque County to the Turners of the Knobbs in June 1876 illustrated just how bad things were: "You said there had bin a great deal of hanging and killing going on in your country. It must be horrible country you live in. You wanted to know if there was fussing up here. They are all peasble in our own country. Men seem to be glad to see one another."

In open country, outlaws and vigilantes employed the same methods of waylaying their victims. The favored tactic was for at least two and sometimes up to five men to secret themselves at opportune places along the road on which the victim was to travel. If the first ambush failed, someone on down the line would be successful.

At least one prominent vigilante got so nervous about his work that he moved to Victoria County for the rest of his life. On his deathbed in 1918, Elias K. Stanley, known as K. Stanley to his vigilante friends, admitted to assassinating Horace Alsup in 1879. But his deed, however justified it may have seemed at the time, gave Stanley a case of the nerves that he couldn't shake. One hot day, he was walking along the road near his house, with a loaded, percussion-cap rifle over his shoulder. Suddenly he heard a shot fired close by from an unseen assailant. He began to run like a scared rabbit. When he finally stopped, he took a look at his gun and saw that it had fired the terrifying shot. The heat of the day had set off the cap. Shortly thereafter, he sold out and moved to Victoria County where he lived until his death.

K. Stanley's early life had been brutal and tragic. Elias Kavanaugh Stanley came to Texas with his family at three years of age from Mississippi. In 1849, the family moved to Webberville, where his father Elias owned a blacksmith shop and was murdered in 1852. His widow and children moved to Sand Fly, in Burleson County, and then Knobbs Springs, where she married Rueben Ransom.

Despite the rough-and-tumble nature of the area, parts of the Knobbs country were (and are) quite beautiful, such as the Knobbs Springs. According to the Lee County Historical Survey Committee:

> From under the base of the first [northern] Knobb, on the west side, once gushed a spring, and it solved the water problem for the early settlers. . . . Being the sole water supply for the settlement, it was a community responsibility to keep the spring clean. A reservoir about five feet across and five feet deep was dug and walled up with split post oak logs. Surrounding the area where the spring bubbled from the hill was a blackberry thicket set in seepy quicksand. A hollow log was pushed back under the berry vines and water poured through it in a clear beautiful stream. People came with barrels on sleds and in wagons to haul water. They stretched covers over the barrel tops and fastened them down with ropes or hoops to keep the water from sloshing out. In the summertime women from the neighborhood would bring their washings, children, lunches and melons and spend the day scrubbing and gossiping.

Their flow is now greatly reduced and they are hard to reach since some of the old roads have been closed.

The Knobbs are sparsely settled these days, and there is little to remind us of those turbulent times, except the old cemetery next to the new church building about three miles down this twisting road from FM 696.

Turn around and double back to FM 696. Continue east on FM 696. If you want to cut this trip by approximately half, don't double back to FM 696, but continue south on Knobbs Springs Road. In about seven miles, you'll reach McDade. Take it easy driving this road. It twists and turns constantly and is booby-trapped with lots of potholes.

BLUE

Lee County • About 11 miles from Butler

Blue was originally known as Blue Branch, named for the waters of Blue Branch Creek. By 1879, a half dozen or so Blue men had been waylaid and killed by unknown assailants. Depending on whom you listened to, these unfortunate men had either been brigands or upright men. At any rate, several of them had been found bound in cowhide.

Horace Alsup was assassinated near his home on the Yeguas, Lee County, about eight or ten miles from McDade, in mid-October 1879. The killing was done from an ambush about noon by an assailant who remained unknown until former Lee County vigilante K. Stanley confessed to the killing on his death-bed years later. Alsup is buried in the Burns Cemetery at Blue in an unmarked grave. A good man at heart, he had nevertheless harbored his sons Drew and Wade, his son-in-law Young Floyd, and various of their friends whenever the boys got in trouble with the law, which seemed to be pretty often according to Bastrop County court records; so often, according to one source, that the boys decided they ought to leave the county. But before they left, Wade Alsup, Young Floyd, and company wanted to have a little fun.

So on Wednesday evening, June 27, 1877, five or so of them saddled up and headed for a dance in old Blue at Fiddlin' Pat Airhart's (also spelled Erhart) place near Blue Branch Church in Lee County. Some say they had planned to kill Pat and ride off into the night. Not that they had anything against Airhart; they just didn't want to leave the county without a parting shot. Little did they know that the party was a trap set specially for them.

This dance has become a legend over the years, and there are many versions of the story, which sometimes agree and often differ. Here are the "facts" as originally reported by the *Austin Statesman* on June 29, 1877:

> The news reached this city yesterday of the hanging of three or four men at Mc-Dade Wednesday night. Fifteen disguised men called at a house where a dance was going on, and presenting guns, commanded the men they wanted to walk out, and when they did so they were all taken away and hung on the same tree. One report said that the men hung were bad characters and cattle thieves, and another said they were men of good reputations, and that their hanging grew out of the shooting of a man by Sheriff Brown. They were young men and citizens of Lee County.

The *Austin Statesman* followed with more details on July 4:

> On the night of the 27th instant a party of between 15 and 20 well-armed men in masks rode up to the house of Mr. D. P. Airhart, where a sociable dance was being participated in. Some of them entered the house, pistols in hand, and ordered Mr. Airhart to call the names of all the men present, which he did. The mob expected to find seven men; certain parties at the place, and as the names were called out four of these being present. They were invited out and taken in charge by the remainder of the mob, who then took them off about 500 yards and hung them all to one limb. The names of the parties were Wade Alsup, John Kuykendall, O. B. S [sic] and Y. G. Floyd. It is said that these men were noted thieves, which was probably the cause of the hanging.

Years later, old "Aunt" Rose Price, who worked for Airhart, spoke of the men's atrocious manners that night. "Massa Pat wan' ready f'um to eat yit—hadn' eben ax 'em. Dey cum in and fell in dem cakes and pies and slop coffee all ov' da table. Lor' hit look like a storm been in dere. I wuz dat mad I cudda hit 'em ov' da haid wid a cheer."

The list of names of the men the vigilantes wanted included Wade Alsup, Young Floyd, Blake Scott, John Kuykendall, Ab Kaneman, and Sol Wheat. Kaneman escaped through a window; Wheat wasn't at the dance. Alsup, Floyd, Kuykendall, and Scott were hustled outside, and one of the masked vigilantes told Airhart to keep fiddling and keep the rest of the folks dancing till sunrise. Only then could the dancers stop and go home. As the four started off in the custody of the posse, Kuykendall remarked to one of his comrades, "Another trip to Giddings, boys." His more knowledgeable friend replied, "We will never see Giddings." Truer words were never spoken. The departing dancers found the four next morning, swinging from the stout limb of a tree on Blue Branch, about five hundred yards from Airhart's place. Apprised of his close call, Airhart is said to have traded his fiddle in for a Bible and become a preacher.

Jeptha Billingsley, in an article titled "McDade Lynchings Fifty Years Ago Remembered," published in the *Elgin Courier*, May 21, 1936, explained his family's version of what brought about the necktie party:

> Allen Wynn, a well-known and highly respected citizen living near the Knobbs, had brought some cotton to town and did not return home until that evening. After he had gone about four or five miles out and had crossed the Yegua and had come to the far edge of the dense wooded bottom, he heard two men climbing up into the back end of his wagon. In a moment they had caught hold of his shoulders, pulled him backward from his seat, beat him in the face and taken his money away. Allen recognized the men, and gave the information to a Vigilance Committee that had been formed.
>
> The men who had attacked and robbed him were occasional visitors at the home of Pat Erhart who lived near the Blue community, so it was agreed that Pat, who was a fiddler and frequently gave dances in his home, should announce that he'd have a dance. The Committee were confident that "their men" would be present. The dance took place as planned and while Pat was swinging the bow of the favored tunes, some member of the Committee quietly put in his appearance and called out the desired men one at a time. Five of them were spotted, but one of them managed to make his escape unseen and was not present when his final summons came. It was not long before the dancers became conscious that muffled proceedings were going on, and gradually some of the more curious men excused themselves and went out doors to investigate, and it wasn't long before the news was received that four of the community undesirables had been hung on a tree. That naturally put an early stop to the dancing, and much excitement and feeling of fear took place in everyone's heart—no one knew just when the confederates of these men would put in their appearance and have their revenge—perhaps, even on innocent persons.

According to another story told to Bemus Turner (a relative of Turk Turner) by Bemus' father, Pat Airhart was a wealthy bachelor who often entertained with lavish dance parties. He had a nice home, two servants (Aunt Rose and Steve Price), and a well kept farm. He dressed well and could play many instruments including organ, fiddle, banjo, and guitar and was known as a singing teacher. He came to McDade often because he kept his money with George Milton. The vigilantes decided to hold a special dance at Pat's house on June 27, 1877. Three weeks before the dance, Pat drove to town to buy supplies for the party, including a barrel of whisky from the Nash brothers' Rock Front Saloon. He visited with George Milton and Dr. Vermillion and issued a general invitation to his dance, three weeks hence. Milton donated a gallon of his best whiskey for the vigilantes.

A huge crowd came, the largest ever. The music started at 8:30, and folks danced the square dance, pigeon wing, and waltz before the first intermission an hour later. Steve Price was a carpenter but could also play the fiddle and banjo, so he entertained while Pat checked in the guests' weapons. His parties were known for their orderliness. All weapons, even knives, were confiscated and locked by Pat in a shed.

At about 2 a.m., the house was surrounded by masked vigilantes armed with shotguns and Winchesters. They handed a list of names to Pat, who read them out: Wade Alsup, John Kuykendall, Young Floyd, Blake Scott, and Jim Floyd. All answered save Jim Floyd, who was outside when the vigilantes rode up; he split the scene.

Were they bad characters or young men of good reputation? They had all been arrested on various charges, including cattle theft and malicious mischief, but had gotten off.

Blake Scott was the son of Joseph Blake Scott who would serve as U.S. postmaster of McDade from 1881 to 1884. Joseph Blake Scott had a reputation of being "a fine man," and Blake was his son from a marriage prior to his marriage to Mrs. Elizabeth J. Wiggins Hollingshead.

Elizabeth J. Wiggins Hollingshead and her first husband, Elijah Hollingshead, had a daughter, Emma "Emily" Hollingshead. With Scott's marriage to Elizabeth Hollingshead, Emma became stepsister to Blake. Love blossomed, and Emma Hollingshead and Blake Scott, her stepbrother, were having a great time at the Pat Airhart dance near Blue Branch on June 27, 1877. They were very fond of each other. Everyone was square dancing when the masked men appeared in the doors and windows with their guns, calling out the names of Wade, Blake, John, and Young. As he answered his call, Blake whispered to Emma, "So long, Emma."

And what became of Pat Airhart? Lee County old-timer and chronicler John Knox said that Airhart decided to become a preacher after the lynching. He began studying the Bible and joined the Baptist Church. He eventually became an evangelist and held revival meetings at surrounding towns in a large tent. He preached out of the Bible in simple language. His message spread, and he moved his crusade around the state by train and then to other states.

At any rate, by 1912, it appears that he had settled in Kerr County, where the name Rev. D. P. Airhart appears on a number of marriage records as officiating minister.

Blue once had a chair factory and several stores serving area farmers. Nowadays it is just a sleepy little ranching community. Prominent Texas potter Ishmael Soto is currently Blue's most illustrious resident. His shop is located a ways up a red gravel road, marked by a simple sign reading "Soto 4.6 miles."

The countryside begins to stretch out a bit as FM 696 approaches Lexington, Lee County's oldest town.

LEXINGTON

Lee County • 1,200 (approximate) • (979) • About 9 miles from Blue

San Jacinto veteran James Shaw rode up this way in 1837 looking for a place to settle down. His war service entitled him to a league of land; the new republic had no cash money with which to pay its soldiers. In need to water late one afternoon, Shaw traced a buffalo trail to a clear running spring. A band of Indians was already camped there. Boldly, Shaw decided to ride up to them rather than take flight. They turned out to be friendly Tonkawas, who let Shaw drink his fill and then gave him some of the buffalo meat they were roasting. Shaw named the creek Indian Camp Branch and started staking out his league of land the next day. He built a log cabin with a rock chimney, which also served as post office and schoolhouse, for he was postmaster and teacher between surveying jobs.

Shaw's next encounter with Indians was not as peaceful. Huddling around the campfire one night after the passage of a blue norther, Shaw and the surveying party he headed were attacked by Indians. They sent a shower of arrows into the camp, one of which struck Shaw in the knee. Unable to rise, he was seconds away from being scalped by two knife-wielding Indians when a burly Irishman rushed the pair and knocked them unconscious. He carried Shaw to safety while the other surveyors fought off the marauders.

Other settlers came to live nearby, and their community was known as String Prairie, because it strung out for about ten miles along the narrow band of blackland prairie that runs from Bastrop County through Lee County almost to the Trinity River in East Texas. In 1850, the locals got together and laid out a town site, naming it Lexington after the Massachusetts village of Revolutionary War fame. When Lee County was created in 1874, Lexington bid to become county seat, but that honor went to Giddings, located on the H&TC railroad. Lexington got its railroad in 1890, and with the arrival of the San Antonio and Aransas Pass railroad, the whole of Lexington picked up and moved the short distance to its present location. String Prairie was just a memory as folks moved into town. Cotton ruled the Lexington economy during this era, to be supplanted later by ranching and peanuts, and recently by oil. Lexington sits on the oil-rich Austin Chalk, as does the rest of Lee County.

You will see the Lexington city limits sign as you enter town on FM 696. This section of FM 696 is called Seventh Street within town. Less than a half mile past the city limits sign, FM 696 meets Loop 123. FM 696 turns right here to join Loop 123 (Rockdale Street within the city limits). Follow Rockdale four blocks (less than a half mile), turning right on Third Street to reach downtown Lexington and the city square.

LEXINGTON CITY SQUARE

3rd, Wheatley, 4th, and Main

The square is located two blocks south of Rockdale. Most of the town's business establishments still surround the square. Lexington prides itself as a God-fearing town. Not surprisingly, all of the town's bars were segregated, side by side, on the far west side of the square. The spacious city square today holds the town water tower and not much else. Lexington's founders had envisioned a much grander function for it, intending that the Lee County courthouse sit here. But, as we know, Giddings won the election. Lexington may not have the courthouse, but it does have the Lexington Museum. And while the museum isn't nearly as impressive as the Lee County courthouse, it's at least as interesting.

LEXINGTON MUSEUM

Main at 4th, next to the city square • W variable

Three log buildings make up the Lexington Museum. The Guthrie cabin is the oldest of the lot, built in 1846 by George Washington Guthrie, who fought at San Jacinto and in the Civil War. It was moved here from its original location on the old stage road to Austin. Lawyer Ephraim Roddy built the other cabin in 1850. The Fowler family added on to it in the 1870s. The log farm building was moved here from a site on FM 696. Attached to it are two walls from the old iron calaboose in Giddings, where Rattlin' Bill Longley spent his last days. More on Longley later.

SNOW'S BBQ

516 Main • 773-4640 (Saturday only) • www.snowsbbq.com • Open Saturday morning only, until the meat runs out • W

They have brisket, sausage, chicken, and pork ribs, plus homemade potato salad, slaw, and beans. It was named best barbecue in Texas by *Texas Monthly* magazine in 2008, a bodacious claim, given all the other great barbecue in Texas, but Snow's is still among the best.

ANNUAL EVENT

MAY

Lexington Homecoming • First weekend in May • Free • W

Barbecue, gospel singing, and a rodeo are just a few of the events in this annual welcome home party for everybody who's ever lived in Lexington, or wanted to.

From the museum, return to Rockdale and turn right. Stay on FM 696 east/Loop 123/Rockdale through the rest of town until you hit the US 77 intersection. Here FM 696 joins US 77 briefly before resuming its lone path eastward. Following the highway signs, turn left onto US 77; then turn right several hundred feet later, staying on FM 696 as it leaves US 77.

East of Lexington on FM 696, you enter old String Prairie, not leaving it till you turn south onto SH 21. This is one of Texas' oldest and most illustrious roads, the Old San Antonio Road, or El Camino Real, as documented by the old granite marker in the roadside park a mile or so south of the junction of FM 696 and SH 21. Actually, there were at least three documented branches of this road from San Antonio to Nacogdoches. The branch you are on now—the Old San Antonio Road of 1795—is followed almost exactly by SH 21 to the Brazos River.

HRANICE

Lee County • About 20 miles from Lexington

It was here, around two centuries ago, that Indians ambushed a Spanish pack train carrying a payroll of gold destined for the forts and missions of East Texas. Surrounded by Indians, with most of their comrades lying dead at their feet, the surviving soldiers scratched out a hole and dropped the gold into it. This task accomplished, they attempted to escape from the ring of Indians. Only one made it back to San Antonio with the bad news. Treasure hunters have been looking for the $90,000 in gold (pre-inflationary value) ever since. Some say it lies at the bottom of Suehs-Gest Lake; others say it rests somewhere on the old Kutej farm. Still others say a hired hand found the gold, split the loot with his boss, and then split the scene.

At Suehs Lake near Hranice, passenger pigeons were so numerous that they broke tree branches with their weight. Many natural lakes like this are associated with springs in Lee County. These lakes often have peat bogs next to them, and the peat moss eventually changes to the lignite, or brown coal, that is so common here. Fifteen thousand years ago, during the full glacial period, spruce, maple, dogwood, alder, and birch grew here.

Hranice was first settled by Anglos before the Civil War, but the 1880s saw the beginning of a massive influx of Czech and Moravian immigrants, when a land development firm bought land from Stephen Austin's heirs and sold it to Czechs and Moravians from Fayette County. Land in Fayette County was scarce, and the immigrants were drawn to the cheaper land in northern Lee County. Many of them came from a village in Moravia named Hranice, which means "watershed" or "dividing place."

During its peak years, between 1900 and 1920, Hranice had two saloons, a store, a blacksmith shop, a gin and sawmill, six molasses mills, two gristmills, a cloth loom, and a threshing machine. A school was open by 1897, when it had thirty-eight students. It had a Moravian Brethren church and a Catholic church. Hranice declined with the growth of New Dime Box.

OLD DIME BOX

Lee County • About 20 miles from Lexington

Old Dime Box—now a wide spot along SH 21 located just south of the turn-off to New Dime Box—started life as Brown's Mill, the second oldest town in Lee County. Joe Brown built a gristmill here, then a sawmill and cotton gin, before the Civil War. Soon Brown's Mill had a post office. Once a week the postmaster would ride to Giddings to pick up the town's mail. Locals would leave their letters in the mill's mailbox along with a dime for carrying charges. Sometime around the turn of the century, postal authorities told Brown's Mill to change its name because mail for Brown's Mill and Brownsville kept getting mixed up. A town meeting was held, and a local wag suggested "Dime Box," in honor of the old mailing custom. The new name floated, and when the town moved three miles east to the newly laid Southern Pacific tracks in

1913, the name Dime Box went along. So today we have Old Dime Box and New Dime Box. To further confuse matters, Hranice is sometimes referred to as Dime Box. New Dime Box enjoyed a flurry of nationwide fame during World War II when it was chosen for the starting point for the 1944 March of Dimes fund-raising drive.

Not surprisingly, there are several variations on the story of how Dime Box was named, the most colorful of which was committed to print by folklorist J. Mason Brewer. Aunt Dicy Johnson, a freedwoman of mythic character and ways, settled with her family in Lee County after the Civil War. She moved off her old plantation in an adjoining county to work on a German family's small farm. They had been there a month, and Aunt Dicy was feeling pretty dicey about the move, mostly because it was almost impossible to get her Levi Garrett snuff. At least there had been a commissary on the plantation; the Schultze farm was ten miles from nowhere. One Saturday, she saw the mailman from Lexington coming down the lane toward the Schultze family's mailbox. She scurried out to meet him.

Reaching him just in time, she handed him a dime and asked if he would bring her a dime box of snuff from Lexington the next time he delivered the mail. On Monday morning, Aunt Dicy met him at the mailbox for her dime box of Levi Garrett. And so, on every Saturday thereafter, for as long as she lived on the Schultze place, Aunt Dicy gave the postman her dime and waited for the Monday mail. Everyone in the area knew of Aunty Dicy's arrangement with the postman, and at a meeting one night they voted to name their growing little settlement Dime Box of Snuff, later shortened to Dime Box.

In an era when white Texans expected blacks to know their lowly place and stay there, Aunt Dicy deferred to no one, not even to the high judge in the Lee County courthouse. Her son Pomp had been arrested for shooting dice, and when trial day came, Aunt Dicy went to the courthouse to pay Pomp's fine. Aunt Dicy always took a paper bag to spit snuff juice into when she went to public places. But that court day, she forgot her bag. Once seated in the courtroom, she took a healthy dip and at the appropriate time spat heartily onto the floor. One of her neighbors noticed and asked her if she didn't know that spitting on the courthouse floor was a five-dollar offense.

Aunt Dicy said she didn't know and pulled three five-dollar bills out of the old kerchief that served as her purse, handing them to the man and telling him to take the fifteen dollars and give them to the judge "right now," because she planned on spitting two more times before she left the building.

A faithful member of Mount Zion Baptist Church in Dime Box, Aunt Dicy didn't believe that dipping would keep her out of Heaven, despite the preacher's threats of hell for snuff dippers as well as drunkards, liars, and gamblers. "Look here, Reverend, you've done stopped preaching and done started meddling," she would shout back.

One time Pastor Jackson called her to task for dipping when he saw her standing within spitting distance of some fresh brown evidence. She began to laugh, and in between fits of laughter, she explained that, on doctor's orders, she had been chewing Hershey's chocolate bars instead of dipping snuff, and she had to spit the vile stuff out on account of its evil flavor.

To get to New Dime Box, turn left on FM 141.

NEW DIME BOX

Lee County • 300 (approximate) • (979) • About 23 miles from Lexington

Oil stirred things up quite a bit in New Dime Box in the late 1970s and early 1980s, but things have declined since, and several of the vintage stores and beer joints have closed, although the buildings still stand. For now, Dime Box is comfortably weather-beaten and slightly frayed at the edges, rather like your favorite pair of comfortable old jeans. The brick buildings facing the railroad tracks on Guy M. Bryan Avenue were built by Vinc Balcar just after New Dime Box was established. He always closed his store and saloon on the Lord's Day, and children—his own included—were never permitted inside the saloon. One of Balcar's twelve children passed his lunch to him each day at the front door.

The Dime Box area bore its share of lynchings and outlaw troubles during the 1860s and 1870s. Dan Hensley, whose previously quoted eloquence helped him narrowly escape lynching, hailed from this area, as did the Irvin boys, John Tom and Little Tom. In the good old days, Old Man Irvin of the Salem Community near Dime Box owned five hundred to six hundred cattle. They had two slaves. They had lots of good grassland, unlike their Knobbs neighbors.

They were universally respected by their neighbors as a good family. But then old man Irvin was killed, and the negroes were blamed. They were hanged and buried at Salem Cemetery. Since the two boys, Jim Tom and Little Tom, were too young to assume their father's duties, cattle began to disappear.

One day, Jim Tom rode to Ledbetter for supplies. The Lee County sheriff persuaded him to gamble, and he lost his money. He grumbled about losing his money and not being able to bring any supplies home. Sheriff told him to go sell some cattle, and he'd win that money too. When the sheriff turned to walk away, Jim Tom shot him in the shoulder and thus began his career as outlaw on the run. After their mom died, Tom joined Jim Tom. None of their neighbors would help them because they were afraid of the sheriff. The boys had no way to earn money, so they began to steal from those they thought had stolen from them.

When Captain McNelly of the Rangers was going to Cuero to settle a feud, he told Jim Tom that he could join the Rangers. He didn't have a warrant for his arrest and would be glad to have him. Jim Tom was to meet them at La Grange. The Rangers went on to Cuero and made some arrests. A judge came, and they held court on the second floor of a two-story building. Jim Tom volunteered to search everyone and take their arms, but McNelly told his men to form a half circle around the room and have their guns drawn to shoot anyone who tried to draw a weapon. They had a peaceful court, hanged a few people, settled the feud, established law and order, and came home.

The Irvins and their friends hid out in the Nails Creek and Yegua Creek bottomland near Flagpond. Their last raid was planned to steal some horses and mules near Burton and take them north to start a new life. They stole a racehorse from Bill Deaver of Brenham and a mule from Bill Henley of Burton. The men from Burton trailed the Irvins to Groesbeck and captured them in early 1876.

On March 1, 1876, the *Austin Statesman* reported,

Two Irwins and a Shaw were taken from the Giddings jail. The Irwins were hanged. Shaw was shot to death. They were accused of stealing stock and had been arrested in Limestone County a few days before. A 14 year old boy named Wilkerson was spared because of his youth. Disguised men forced the jailer to give them the key. Rumor in Giddings that two men had been hung a few miles away the day before.

DIME BOX HERITAGE SOCIETY MUSEUM

FM 141, downtown • 884-0182, 884-4110 • Generally open weekends; call ahead for hours

The museum features local memorabilia and displays, and is a good genealogy resource as well.

THE BLACK BRIDGE

Guy M. Bryan Ave./County Rd. 425, 2.5 blocks north of FM 141

Sitting in a lot across from the railroad tracks and next to the picturesque SPJST lodge picnic grounds, this hundred-year-old iron, single-span truss bridge stood hidden from public view until recently, spanning the old H&TC tracks on private property a mile east of Dime Box. When the railroad was built, it divided the Asa Moses farm. To lay the track, much dirt had to be removed, which was dumped and piled up high on either side of the tracks. The dirt blocked Moses' path across the track to the rest of his farm. To appease Moses, the railroad dug him a cut through the dirt heaps. And thus E. B. Cushing, the railroad's inspector, found himself at the Moses farm. Not content with mere cuts, Moses put Cushing into his buggy for a visit to the farm across the track. When they came to the cut in the dirt dump, they found a train well on its way and narrowly escaped with their lives. Cushing wasted no time in locating a spare bridge the railroad wasn't using. It soon came by flatcar from a place somewhere beyond Hearne and was hoisted into place. This, at a time when the Dime Box area didn't have even one public road!

Private property it was, but Dime Box's young folks soon made it their own. Courting couples called it the Black Bridge, probably because it was only seen in the dark. On Sunday afternoons, teenagers would gather at the depot, select a partner, and walk the path to the bridge, where they enjoyed each others' company and took snapshots with their Kodaks.

DIME BOX MEAT MARKET

FM 141, on the outskirts of town • 884-3535 • Open Monday through Saturday, closed Sunday • W

The Meat Market makes an all-pork, old-style Deutscher-Tex ring sausage, perfect for barbecuing.

ANNUAL EVENT

OCTOBER

DIME BOX HOMECOMING

First Saturday in October • Free • W

Homecoming events include a mini-marathon in the morning; a barbecue cook-off, games, and crafts booths during the day; and a street dance at night.

Return to SH 21 via FM 141 and continue south toward Lincoln.

Just before you reach Lincoln, you cross West Yegua Creek. While the surrounding countryside now looks peaceful and bucolic, back in the 1880s it was something close to a living hell for workers building the San Antonio and Aransas Pass railroad line from Waco to Giddings. This line paralleled what is now US 77 from Waco down through Rockdale, Lexington, and Lincoln, to Giddings, passing through the Yegua Creek bottoms. A worker named George described the area as "a veritable wilderness, forested with post oaks, black jack and cedars, interspersed with dense thickets. This wilderness sheltered a variety of wild animals such as wolves, wild hogs, alligators and panthers." George said his uncle was killed and eaten by timber wolves. They also had to endure "the extremes of heat and cold, frequent rains, and at times a great number of hungry mosquitoes. In those days all railroad construction was performed by beast and man. The animals pulled the scoops and slips, while the men toiled mightily with pick, shovel, spike maul, and wheelbarrows."

LINCOLN

Lee County • 300 (approximate) • About 12 miles from Dime Box

Lincoln owes its name not to the sixteenth president but to a Campbellite preacher by the name of John A. Lincoln. Born in 1850 in Lincoln County, Tennessee, he moved to Texas in 1859. John joined the Confederate Army and conducted camp churches and prayer meetings. His first wife died. In 1879, he moved to Evergreen and bought a farm. He married again and had five children. He was county evangelist for Milam County and promoted churches in nearby communities such as Cameron and Rockdale. His friends and neighbors expressed their admiration for him by naming their new town, brought by the advent of the railroad in 1890, after him. The town rapidly became a regional shipping and supply center with several general stores, saloons, blacksmith shops, and the like.

Turn right from SH 21 at the Post Office sign onto Fifth Street.

Not much is left of old downtown Lincoln. Old man Wendel's store sits across from the post office, just north of Fifth Street, by where the railroad tracks used to run, crumbling slowly, leaning more every year, and nearly covered over by vines and other vegetation. The old frame Lincoln post office was torn down in the early 1990s. It sat next to the present post office, built in 1967.

The Lincoln Community Center grounds and baseball fields at the other end of town are charmingly quaint and from another era, and the barbecue that cooks on the pits at community picnics is first class. Come spring, the ball field sports one of the region's best wildflower displays. Electrically colored phlox, from the deepest of blood-red purples to the whitest of pale pinks, dot the diamond in pointillistic fashion, supported by lesser numbers of primroses, morning flowers, winecups, and spiderworts.

ANNUAL EVENT

AUGUST

LINCOLN COMMUNITY CLUB PICNIC

Usually third Sunday in August • Free • W

Lincoln's population increases several fold once a year for the community picnic, held under the graceful, spreading oaks of the community-center grounds. Activities include music, bingo, and various other games, but the stellar attraction is the barbecue—beef, pork, mutton, and Elgin sausage—some of the tastiest you'll find anywhere in Central Texas. It's sold by the pound, starting at 8:30 in the morning, and if you get here much past one in the afternoon, you'll have to settle for whatever is left on the pit.

There is another, similar picnic/barbecue held here annually (usually the third Sunday in May) to benefit St. John's Lutheran Church and school of Lincoln.

From Lincoln, continue south on SH 21. Old Evergreen, the town that Lincoln superseded, is just down SH 21 a bit and to your left on FM 1624.

EVERGREEN

Lee County • About 1 mile from Lincoln

Nothing remains but the old Evergreen oak, under whose branches pioneer justice was dispensed and from whose branches errants were hanged. Natives say a small fortune in lead could be mined from the tree, so numerous were the bullets fired into it.

Rattlin' Bill Longley, one of Texas' most notorious killers, hailed from Evergreen. Son of respected rancher-farmer Campbell Longley, Bill killed his first man at age fifteen. He notched up thirty-one more victims by his own admission, mostly blacks and Mexicans, and one woman, before he was hung at age twenty-seven. Longley was no robber or rustler; in between murders, he was content to work as a cowboy or to hoe his daddy's cotton patch. Bill's problem was that he couldn't abide insults: to his own honor, his family's honor, his friends' honor, Texas' honor, womankind's honor, or the white man's honor. Either the offender retracted the insult, or he died. It was as simple as that to Bill Longley. He was least tolerant of insults from African American men.

Longley's first victim was a burly drunken freedman who made the mistake of cursing white men in general, and Campbell Longley in particular, while galloping up and down the Camino Real, the old royal highway running through Evergreen. This was an unwise move, for although Longley was not yet old enough to shave, he was already "crack" enough with a gun to gallop his horse past the old Evergreen oak and put six balls into it without missing a shot. The offender swung his rifle up to shooting position after being called down by this young sapling of a boy. His rifle spat out one wild shot before Longley drilled a hole in the man's head with one shot from his Dance percussion-cap six-gun. Longley hurriedly buried his first victim in an unmarked grave.

Like Sam Bass, Bill had a weakness for fast horses and racing. He teamed up with friend Johnny McKowen, and together they raced their fast ponies at fairs and other gatherings all over the area. One fall day in 1866, they headed up to old Lexington for a day of racing. Blacks outnumbered whites at the races that day, and times being what they were, heated words were exchanged. Longley and McKowen headed back to Evergreen soon after their arrival. Word came back to Longley that afternoon that the blacks were celebrating "that white boy's" flight home. That was enough for Bill; he headed back to Lexington that night. The partying was at a high pitch by then, as were emotions. Longley studied the crowd for a moment and then galloped headlong into it with a rebel yell, both guns blazing. By the time young Longley had ridden out of the crowd, two men lay dead, and six were wounded. Bill suffered nary a scratch.

A few weeks later, three black men rode into Evergreen and stopped at a saloon to drink. As they returned to their horses, one of the men remarked that Evergreen was reported to be dangerous to the well-being of blacks and that he would be glad if someone would undertake to molest him. Longley overheard this, enlisted a couple of friends, and started after the trio. His intention was to disarm the freedmen and allow them to move on. They ignored his command to stop and surrender their arms, however, whereupon Longley and friends concentrated their fire on the man who had invited trouble at the bar. He fell dead into the dust.

Longley did not always shoot his insulters, to be entirely fair to the man. He once kicked a black porter off a traveling H&TC train because he had kicked Longley's feet into the aisle.

After that last killing on the road to Brenham, Longley had to go on the lam. The law was after him. He headed south to Gonzales County, where the Taylor-Sutton feud was beginning to heat up. Employed as a cowboy, he was riding along one day when a detachment of Yankee cavalry mistook him for Charlie Taylor, who was also on the dodge. Longley lit out, and the contingent of "bluebellies" followed. Soon it was a two-man race: Longley versus the detachment commander. Longley had fired five shots at his pursuers, none of which had taken effect. He had dodged over forty shots. That lone soldier overtook Longley, who had been saving his last shot. As they rode side by side, Longley rammed his pistol into the man's midriff and pulled the trigger, but the hammer had become entangled in the cavalryman's coat lapel. As he pulled the pistol back, the hammer was released, the shot was fired, and the bullet passed through the soldier's body.

After this affair, young Bill headed for Arkansas, where he teamed up with East Texas guerrilla-band captain Cullen Baker, the "Great Granddaddy of Six-Shooterology," the first man to master the quick draw. Baker's band roamed northeastern Texas and southern Arkansas, ambushing Yankee occupation-troop supply trains, firing their supply warehouses, and generally making life deadly miserable for the occupying troops.

Texas was under martial law during those years. It was during this period that Bill Longley had his first taste of the hangman's noose. Captured by vigilantes who suspected him of being a cattle rustler (he was in the company of one that night), he and recent acquaintance Tom Johnson were strung up from the same tree. Upon leaving the scene, one of the vigilantes emptied his pistol into the pair. One shot bounced off Longley's money belt; another struck him in the jaw, breaking one of his teeth; and the third cut through the two strands of rope from which he hung. Johnson's thirteen-year-old brother stumbled onto the necktie party just as the rope around Longley's neck broke. The lad cut the ropes from Longley's hands and neck and helped him to a safe place. Tom Johnson was already dead when cut down. Longley got his revenge a bit later on the vigilante who had fired upon him and Johnson as they swung helplessly. He hanged the man from the very same tree and emptied his pistol into the fellow.

Longley left Baker after a few more months and took to the road, returning to Evergreen periodically to visit friends and kin. In the meantime, he ranged through Llano, Burnet, Gillespie, and the rest of the frontier counties of Texas before heading for the Utah territory. He killed in the Dakotas, Kansas, and Utah. He was thrown in jail several times for his misdeeds but managed to escape every time.

He was finally captured for good in Louisiana in 1877, accused of the murder several years earlier of boyhood friend Will Anderson. Longley believed Anderson had murdered his cousin, Caleb "Little Cale" Longley. Most folks around Evergreen believed Little Cale's death was accidental—that as he and Anderson were on their way home from a day of drinking in Giddings, Caleb's horse bolted and he was knocked from his runaway mount by a low-hanging tree limb, whereupon Anderson picked the dead boy up and carried him home. Egged on by Cale's grieving father, Longley went to the field where Anderson was working and shot him with a double-barreled shotgun.

His trial began on September 3, 1877. A motion for continuance was overruled, the counsel for the defense having failed to allege the facts to be proved by an absent witness. A jury was selected from a special venire of fifty men. Longley's shackles were removed, being as Sheriff Brown had summoned a numerous guard of resolute men, who were well armed with shotguns and six-shooters. The courthouse was densely packed, and interest was intense; the concourse was the largest ever in attendance upon court at this place. Longley exhibited or affected exuberant spirits.

The court clerk read the indictment to the prisoner, who pleaded not guilty.

The night before, all the prisoners, twenty-four in number, escaped from the La Grange jail. One was recaptured and one killed.

Rattlin' Bill was convicted of Cale Longley's murder on the afternoon of September 6 and sentenced to death by hanging. While in jail, Bill wrote many letters that described his complex mentality. One written to Sheriff Jim Brown went like this:

Septober the 41st, 7777
DevilsPass, Hells half acre

I was at my home and my own Dear Father told me never to put my foot in his house again and Brother Jim quit me and said I was too bad for him and my kins-folk is all so G—— D—— cowwardly they don't want me to come about them so I still alone tread the living land destitute of Friends, but G—— D—— the world and every son of a bitch that don't like me for I am a wolf and it is my night to howl. I expect to get killed some time but you may bet your sweet life that I will keep the flies off of the son of a bitch that does it while he is at it.

Longley appealed his death sentence to the court of appeals, which upheld it in March 1878, sealing his doom.

The twenty-seven-year-old died by the hangman's noose in downtown Giddings on October 1, 1878, and he was buried just outside the boundaries of the Giddings cemetery, a piece of petrified wood marking his grave. Wild stories of his escape from the noose at Giddings abound.

Some claim that Sheriff Jim Brown was paid off to help Longley fake his hanging. They say that a harness worn under his clothes kept him from dying when the trap sprang and that his casket was really filled with rocks. From there he disappeared, to Central America or Louisiana. The fact that his coffin was closed during his funeral and was not opened before burial reinforced rumors that he had escaped. The controversy did not die with time; in the 1980s, Louisiana resident Ted Wax asked Douglas Owsley, a forensic anthropologist at the Smithsonian Natural History Museum, to help confirm whether or not his grandfather, Captain John Calhoun Brown, had really been Bill Longley. He had supposedly chosen the name Brown in honor of the Lee County sheriff who helped him fake the hanging. Several attempts were made to locate Longley's grave and exhume the remains. The trouble was no one knew exactly where he was buried. As was the custom with outlaws, Longley had been buried outside the boundaries of the cemetery, and his grave was marked by a piece of petrified wood, which was moved several times and eventually disappeared. Sixty graves were identified, and twenty-four were opened, but none of the remains matched Longley's description.

Finally, in 1997, using computer-graphic and remote-sensing techniques, Owsley found a grave that contained the remains of a six-foot-tall man in his mid-20s with tobacco-stained teeth and several artifacts resembling those Longley was wearing just before the hanging, a Catholic medallion and a celluloid rosette pinned on Longley's jacket by his niece. Owsley performed forensic analysis on the skeleton, including a DNA test that matched with the DNA of a descendant of Longley's sister. Wax refused to accept Owsley's conclusions, saying that the actual grave lay 250 feet from the one identified by Owsley.

But given contemporary accounts of his hanging, Longley's escape seems unlikely. When the trapdoor opened, Bill fell twelve feet, until his feet dragged the ground. The hanging rope had slipped. He writhed about as the sheriff and aides struggled to take up the rope's slack and raise him up into the air again to finish the strangulation process. After about ten minutes of this, he was pronounced dead by the execution's three doctors, who had been charged with verifying that the sentence had been successfully carried out. They turned his head 180 degrees in one direction, then 180 degrees in the other direction as proof. One of his guards that day said that the rope had buried itself in the side of his neck and had to be cut out.

For many years after Bill Longley's death, negroes living around Evergreen claimed that in the middle of the night they had seen a great horse go by, in the saddle the giant figure of Bill Longley, a six-shooter in each hand.

MANHEIM

Lee County • 40 • About 6 miles from Lincoln

Manheim (pronounced "Mon-heim") was founded by Adolph Wachsmann and largely settled by German immigrants. Wachsmann named the community after his parents' original home, Mannheim, Germany. A post office opened in 1900 with Wachsmann as postmaster. He also ran a combination general store, cotton gin, real estate office, and saloon. There was also a public school. The population in 1914 was estimated at fifty, about the same population as nearly one hundred years later.

Wachsmann's store was Manheim's only business for more than fifty years until it closed in 2009 upon the death of its owner. This sprawling barn of a grocery and feed store had one of the finest collections of cobwebs and vintage beer signs in Central Texas. At least half the beers advertised on the walls aren't made anymore.

Manheim Lutheran Church on SH 21 is the heart of the devout little community.

A little over eleven miles down SH 21 from Lincoln are two signed turnoffs for downtown Paige: Main Street/County Road 173 and Gonzales Street/County Road 175, which run parallel to each other, just a few yards apart, for the short distance into Paige.

PAIGE

Bastrop County • 275 • About 12 miles from Lincoln

Paige was established as a station on the H&TC railroad in 1871 and was named for H&TC engineer Norman Paige. The new town was settled for the most part by German immigrants, who began to pour into Texas once again with the end of the Civil War. At the turn of the century, Paige counted a pickle factory as one of its most prominent industries. Old downtown Paige was located along the railroad tracks; new downtown Paige is lined up along busy US 290.

Old Paige is slowly disappearing; many of the old houses and businesses have been torn down in recent years, and the old hotel by the railroad burned down. One of the old downtown store buildings has recently been moved to US 290 to a location just east of the Paige sign.

PAIGE HISTORICAL MUSEUM

South side of US 290 at Main; from old downtown Paige, take Main St. south across US 290 to the grounds of the Paige Community Center and Historical Museum

The Paige Community Center, a large, whitewashed frame hall with a high tin roof that is about ninety years old, fronts US 290. The Paige Historical Museum consists of the old Paige train depot and the Doris Goerner Laake building, an old-looking frame house built from recycled Victorian-era building materials. Both are filled with local memorabilia. No regular hours.

From Paige, return to SH 21 on either Main or Gonzales. Turn left onto SH 21. As you approach the SH 21/US 290 intersection, you will see a Texas Department of Transportation sign reading "Old Hwy 20." Turn right as per the sign. A few feet later, you will come to a Y intersection. Don't turn right onto County Road 160, aka Paint Creek Road, which runs off to the north. Continue forward on Old Highway 20, the old road to McDade. The old highway parallels US 290 and the railroad tracks. The quality of Old Highway 20 is very uneven. If the weather is bad, or you're just not adventuresome, you can get to McDade on US 290. Just take SH 21 to the intersection, turn right onto US 290, drive about ten miles, and turn right into McDade on Loop 223.

As you drive along through this sparsely settled ranching and watermelon country, you can see why early-day train robbers had such an easy time of it. The thickets of brush along the railroad right-of-way obscure the tracks much of the time, even though the tracks are never more than a few yards away from the road. The dense forests on the south side of the road enhanced the bandits' chances for a quick, safe getaway. A rattlesnake farm was once located along this road; the snakes were milked for their venom, which was used in the manufacture of patent medicines.

Once in the town of McDade, County Road 333 is called Old 20 S.

MCDADE

Bastrop County • 345 • About 10 miles from Paige

The McDade area was settled in the 1840s by farmers and planters from the Old South. In 1859, a post office was established at "Potters Shop," with James W. Allen as postmaster. But it was discontinued after a few months.

The town site itself was not settled until 1869, when the route of the Houston-to-Austin railroad was announced. The original route was to have passed through Bastrop, but the great Colorado River flood of 1869, which inundated Bastrop, prompted the road's builders to shift the route northward, to higher ground. A town site covering 640 acres was drawn up in August 1871 and was designated McDade, to honor the late ex-senator James W. McDade, the leading citizen and Brenham lawyer who was one of the original incorporators of the Western Branch of the Houston and Texas Central Railroad Company. On

October 8, 1871, the construction train on the Central Railroad made a trial trip to McDade. Twelve miles of the track nearest to McDade was found to be hastily and badly constructed and had to be relaid, which caused a detention of ten or twelve days.

On November 11, a person leaving Austin by stage in the morning could take the ten o'clock train at McDade and reach Houston for breakfast on the following morning; two competing stage lines began running hacks to and from Austin. From McDade, the railroad tracks were advancing at about a half mile a day, reaching the Hogeye neighborhood by the first week in November, Wheeler's Store by the first week in December, and Austin in the waning hours of Christmas Day.

In the early days, folks also referred to McDade as Tie City because it was a collection center for ties and logs cut for the railroad. Because Bastrop was bypassed by the railroad, McDade became the region's freight and cotton-shipping center. McDade was officially incorporated on May 3, 1873. McDade was also home to Bastrop County's oldest industry, a pottery factory using clay from Alum Creek. Mule power turned the mills that ground the clay, and the potters turned out urns, furnaces, milk crocks, mixing bowls, jugs, and flowerpots, all of them fired with a special salt glaze. Some of these pieces can be seen in the little museum located in the Old Rock Saloon at the west end of Old Highway 20 S.

A 1936 article in the *Elgin Courier* recounted the history of the pottery industry in McDade and the rest of Bastrop County.

There seems to be no definite information relative to the beginning of the pottery industry in or near McDade and it is therefore probably as old as the town itself and perhaps much older. No relics of Indian pottery have so far been unearthed in this vicinity. Most of the tribes who inhabited this section were of a roving type and naturally carried few of their belongings with them. Such as were carried would have been items not so easily broken. Nevertheless, there are evidences of Indian villages near the sources of clay in this locality and it may yet be discovered that the Indians were the first makers of earthenware near McDade. At any rate the early pioneers were obliged to rely on the natural resources of the country and whether they or the Indians discovered the possibilities of the clay, it is evident that they used bowls, pans, churns, jugs, etc., made from local clays from the beginning of civilization in this locality.

Scattered about over the country are the ruins of several kilns and a quantity of broken salt-glazed pieces of ware. Some of these have been identified and others have not. There is one that is known to have been operated by a Mr. Dunkin, which is probably the first about which there is any definite knowledge. Another was owned by Mr. Allen, and a few pieces of the ware from this pottery and the Dunkin shop are still in evidence in the homes of some of our oldest citizens. Another jug shop (as they were called) was operated by Mr. M. R. Stoker on Alum Creek. After operating this shop for a time, Mr. Stoker moved to McDade and built his factory in the townsite. Clay was secured from the same source as today. The ware burned to a light red body and was salt glazed. Later a deeper strata of clay was found which made a very hard body and was of a gray color. Salt glazing was done in a ground hog kiln, a low structure dug out of the earth and arched over with a smokestack at one end. The ware was placed in the back end of the kiln and the fire applied by means of wood at the front end. At the end of the burn, the whole front was covered until it became cool enough to enter. In such kilns ware in the front end would be very hard and well glazed. In the rear, however, it was often soft and unsatisfactory. Colors were varied from the same kiln but this ware served the purpose (and there was) a ready demand.

In 1888 R. L. Williams, a young potter who had migrated from Pennsylvania to Colorado and then to Texas, came over to Austin from Elmendorf to see the new capitol building and to attend the dedication services. While in Austin he heard of the Stoker pottery at McDade and decided that since he was close he would come on down and see what the possibilities were here. Mr. Stoker was so impressed with the man and his work that he immediately offered him a more remunerative job than the one at Elmendorf. Mr. Williams accepted and became the potter at this shop. He was pleased with his work and the new boss and decided to remain for some time. In 1889 Mr. Williams married Annis Clopton of Elgin. A small 2-room house was built near the Stoker shop and in a few years this couple had saved the sum of $500.00. With this amount Mr. Williams bought half interest in the Stoker pottery. A short time later Mr. Stoker decided to move to West Texas and sold the entire interest to Mr. Williams. As the Stoker lease expired on the land at the old location at about that time, Mr. Williams bought the present site and moved the pottery to its present location.

A new building was erected and the first piece of ware turned in the new shop by Mr. Williams was dated Jan. 26, 1892. The name of the new business was McDade Pottery. The first ware was made by hand and consisted mainly of stoneware, salt glazed. This was applied by throwing salt on the fires at the end of burning. The salt, vaporizing, settled on the ware and made an everlasting glaze. Mr. Williams did most of the work himself, first making the ware, then burning, and later selling it by peddling over the surrounding territory. Often Mr. Williams was obliged to trade his ware for bacon and other farm products, which he sold to others for cash.

Clay was hauled to town by a team of oxen, where it was prepared by placing it in a crude mill, the power being furnished by a blind horse. The horse was hitched to a long pole extending from the mill shaft and traveled around and around a well beaten path. A blind horse was used because he would not get drunk.

Although stoneware was the principal item manufactured for many years, probably the greatest volume of profitable business came with the making of clay furnaces. Mr. Williams secured a patent on a press for forming the shapes and practically eliminated competition in Texas. Many carloads were shipped throughout Texas and some into adjoining states. This business continued good until about 1929, when the convenience of electricity seemed to threaten to destroy it entirely. Within the past four years, however, the various uses of charcoal have been so highly advertised by manufacturers that the demand for clay furnaces is again rapidly increasing each year. In 1935, something over 20,000 of these clay pots were shipped from McDade to Texas and Louisiana points.

In about the year 1927 competition on stoneware became so keen that it was decided to discontinue those items and make flower pots instead. A good business was established with the florists and nurserymen of Texas and Louisiana and the volume of this business together with that on clay furnaces is now keeping the plant running full time with prospects of greater business than ever. It is expecting a great boom in the future.

The charcoal furnace is a versatile contrivance. Women cooked and also heated their irons on them. They heated rooms, or at least parts of them. They were used to great advantage when it was preserving time. At the height of summer, preserving sessions usually took place in the backyard, where agarita berries, dewberries, peaches, mulberries, grapes, plums, and figs would bubble away atop charcoal furnaces. Many old-timers maintain that preserves cooked over a charcoal furnace take on an added and desirable flavor from simmering over the charcoal.

The furnace is basically a glorified clay bucket, often bound in heavy tin with a metal loop handle. It has two elevations, with a day grate, which lets air breathe in from below through a ventilation hole. Old charcoal furnaces are collector's items and are priced accordingly, especially McDade stoves. But if you just want something to cook your preserves on, a hibachi will do nicely. The product line diversified as charcoal stove sales declined. For instance, art deco lamp bases were produced, but it was to no avail; the pottery closed not too long after the *Elgin Courier* article appeared.

McDade's railroad-derived prosperity and the proximity of the Yegua Knobbs brought trouble to the little town. McDade's citizens suffered from the widespread robbing, rustling, hijacking, and killing that pervaded the area from the days of Reconstruction through the 1880s. With the end of the Civil War, a gang of thieves got a foothold in the wild country where Bastrop, Lee, and Williamson counties now converge.

By 1868, stories were going around the state that there were "quite a number of these horse thieves in the cedar brakes of Bastrop and Burleson counties, and it may be unsafe for horsemen to travel, without being well armed. We will state that a large number of citizens of Bastrop and vicinity, have offered their services to the sheriff, whenever called upon, to search after thieves and lawless characters generally, and that class of nuisances will fare badly if they are caught" (*Galveston News*, April 22, 1868). When the H&TC railroad established its railhead at McDade in the fall of 1871, boomtown life added to the previously mentioned problems.

Since McDade was a commercial and shipping center, much money was spent there. Saloons and gambling places stayed open twenty-four hours a day. Thugs began preying on anyone with money. Men who won at the gambling tables in the back room of the Rock Front Saloon were often waylaid on their way home, as were farmers who had sold their cotton and were returning home. Stock stealing was ubiquitous; the big stockmen employed cowboys who didn't much care which brands were on the steers they were rounding up. And the little guys similarly filched from the big herds to even things out.

One of McDade's most prominent citizens at that time was George Milton, who came to Tie City in 1868 as the official agent to sell land. Milton had resided in Brownsville at the outbreak of the Civil War, being twenty-two years old and serving as a deputy under the late Sheriff Jeff Bartolow. Milton went into the Confederate Army as a volunteer, serving in Captain John Littleton's company with Colonel Rip Ford's brigade. The sale of land was not too good, so Milton opened a saloon and then a store at McDade. He met his wife Emeline in Brenham. He made occasional trips to Taylor and stayed with the Olives. He was friends enough with the Olives to have named one of his sons (George Prentice Milton, born in 1877) for Print Olive.

Milton's saloon, which was a converted boxcar, was in between the two trees across the street from the store. The two big trees were in front of the saloon, which had no stools or brass foot rail, but did have two pool tables, three poker tables, a kitchen, and a back door. Across the street from the Rock Front Saloon was a two-story dance hall complete with girls of the evening.

Jeptha Billingsley wrote in 1936:

At that time McDade was a thriving little city—it was the loading and unloading point for all the cotton and freight that went to and from Smithville and Bastrop, as the Katy track through Elgin did not operate until 1886. Great freight wagons drawn by as many as six or seven yokes of oxen often made the overland trips adjoining cities, and a stage-coach was run regularly between McDade and connecting points. As the town was such a commercial center, much money was spent in McDade. Some five or six stores, two drug stores and a blacksmith shop or two, one meat market, two or three saloons, two hotels and several other business houses did a thriving business. Flour could be bought a dollar a barrel cheaper in McDade than in Bastrop, where the freight charges had to be added. Saloons did a big business and gambling was wide open. Many tricksters and desperados naturally drifted in and made this vicinity their headquarters. The dense post oaks sections and big Yegua bottoms in this neighborhood were further conducive to secretive conduct. Thieving, stealing and shooting were almost weekly occurrences, and the better element in the community seemed powerless at times to remedy the solution.

On Saturday, May 4, 1874, a black man was hanged in McDade for the killing of a white man. That afternoon, five railroad workers were eating lunch when the black man approached asking to play cards. They declined and sent him away, but not before he threw his dirty sock in their cooking pot. He returned with a gun and shot one of the white men, killing him instantly. The black man was apprehended by H. A. Highsmith and W. A. Plummer, taken to the marshal, and placed in irons. While the marshal was escorting the man to the Bastrop jail, a number of unknown persons took him and hanged him.

During the same week, Thomas Null, charged under indictment with cattle stealing, was arrested by Deputy Zeno Hemphill near McDade. Null tried to shoot Hemphill; Hemphill shot back, striking Null in the hip.

On July 31, 1874, Turk Turner, A. Batey, W. Batey, John Allen, Jack Batey, and Calvin Null were indicted for theft of meat cattle. Based on these indictments and others, it appears that Turner, and the Null and Batey brothers, were considered by many to be part of the same rustling gang.

Then came the bloody week in September 1875. First, prominent McDade merchant Charles Kirk was murdered by Henry M. Carothers. Kirk was married, with one child and four stepchildren. Carothers was a fourth-class merchant, a liquor dealer by the quart in Bastrop County.

A couple of days later, Turk Turner ambushed and killed W. B. Craddock, known as Pea Eye because of his close-set eyes. Craddock had been willing to testify several times against Turner, who was regarded by many as a notorious cattle rustler. Now he had seen Turner stealing his cattle and had gone to file charges. The case against Turner was so strong that Turner's lawyer advised him to kill the witness.

Craddock, who had been to McDade with a load of country produce that he had disposed of, was returning home in an ox wagon when he was killed within a half mile of his residence. He was shot with a double-barreled shotgun, the entire discharge of buckshot lodging in his body. He fell instantly dead in his wagon. The oxen carried the wagon home and stopped in front of the gate. Mrs. Craddock had prepared the evening's supper and saw the wagon. Becoming impatient at the delay of her husband in coming in, she went out to the wagon to see what was detaining him. When she looked in the wagon, she was astonished to see her husband's body stretched out cold in death. Jack Beatty, who hauled Craddock to the graveyard the next day, was a distant relative of Craddock's but a friend of Turner's.

These two murders prompted a mass meeting of outraged area citizens, as mentioned earlier, in which attendees vowed to "bring to justice all offenders against the laws of our land."

On Saturday, February 12, 1881, between two and three o'clock p.m., Dave Cartwright and John Nash killed young T. J. Davis, about four miles south of McDade on the McDade and Bastrop road. Davis was about twenty years of age, son of Mr. B. F. Davis, who was under contract to build four bridges in Bastrop County. Davis had a pistol and a gun that he allegedly swindled someone out of. Nash obtained from Esq. W. H. Coulson a writ of sequestration to get possession of the gun and pistol. This writ was placed in the hands of Dave Cartwright, who had been summoned by Constable Bishop to execute it, he summoning John Nash, son of Mr. Oscar Nash, to assist him. They overtook Davis on the road, who refused to surrender and fired on the posse.

Nash and Cartwright fired back, killing Davis. The deceased's father took his son's body to Corsicana for interment. Thomas Bishop, constable of the precinct, said in part, "The writ of sequestration was sued out by Horace Nash. Horace is the uncle of John Nash. I don't know what right Horace Nash claimed to the gun. He said it was on account of some money he had loaned the deceased on the gun." Nash and Cartwright came in and surrendered during the investigation, under a $1,000 bond each, and were released from custody.

A fire in McDade on February 25, 1881, destroyed Tom Bishop's saloon, the Cohen Brothers Store, H. K. Barbee's house, and Oscar Nash's saloon. The fire started, it is supposed by an incendiary, at 2 a.m. in the back of Constable Tom Bishop's saloon. Was it revenge for the death of young Davis?

On August 1, 1882, Jeff Wheeler, a black man, was shot in McDade just as the train was getting into McDade at ten o'clock Sunday night. The unknown assailant used a shotgun, probably double barreled, because seven shots were lodged in his body. It was said that he had quarrels with several people around the depot, and on that night had a heavy coupling pin in his overcoat, which he no doubt intended to use to wreak vengeance on one of his enemies. It was supposed that he would live.

In October 1882, Neil F. Campbell's McDade cotton gin was burned. There was no doubt of its being set on fire. Some eight bales of cotton were burned. The property was insured for $2,600, but the insurance did not cover the loss.

S. B. Johnson was robbed by the side of the road three miles from McDade, a quarter mile from Jack Beatty's house, on February 1, 1883. Johnson couldn't identify the robber because his hat was low, his handkerchief covered his face, and there wasn't any moonlight to help him see. Marion Beatty was charged with the crime, tried, and convicted, but the conviction was later overturned by the Texas Supreme Court, and Bob McLemore was then arrested, tried, and convicted.

Later that year, Jeff Fitzpatrick, John Bloodworth, and Woods Puckett robbed and killed an old Dutchman at the Yeguas. The robbery was blamed on Bloodworth.

On August 23, 1883, Bob Young wounded George Milton at McDade and was shot, in turn, by Milton. The same day, John Bloodworth, who had recently been pardoned out of the pen to testify against Jeff Fitzpatrick, was assassinated. The two of them had been indicted for robbing and shooting the old German man. No one knew for sure who killed him, but everyone assumed it was Jeff Fitzpatrick.

Things were beginning to come to a head in McDade; folks were fed up with the ongoing violence.

At about 8:30 in the evening on November 22 or 25, 1883, three unknown men entered Keiffel's store in Fedor and demanded that Keiffel give them the store's money. Two other Germans were in the store at the time. Keiffel gave all he had, seventy-three dollars. The robbers then starting shooting, killing Keiffel and his clerk. The third man escaped by running out the back door. Keiffel was shot in the mouth, so close that there were powder burns on his face. Clerk Mansk was shot through the heart.

It was supposed that at least one of the robbers had an idea that he was recognized and killed the men to save himself. The robbers mounted their horses and rode into the darkness. Keiffel's house was nearby, and his wife ran to the store after hearing the shots to find her husband a corpse. She was so frightened that she didn't inform anyone until the next morning. A posse was organized and followed the horse tracks leading in the direction of Lexington.

On December 3, 1883, Lee County deputy sheriff Isaac Heffington, popularly known as "Bose," was shot. Heffington was in McDade, supposedly seeking information about the Keiffel murder and wanted to see Bill Mundine. Not locating Mundine, he started to leave, when he was shot somewhere north of the railroad tracks, supposedly by Jeff Fitzpatrick.

A group of citizens decided something had to be done. "Two hundred men met December 8 at McDade's only church," the *Galveston News* reported. "The people of this section are thoroughly aroused and determined to stop the frequent killings and robberies which have recently occurred in this vicinity."

The Citizens Committee for Law and Order was formed as a result of the meeting. During the next two weeks, names circulated among the vigilantes, and a date and method for revenge was chosen: a Christmas Eve lynching. George Milton and his friend and business partner Thomas Bishop were two of the prime instigators.

Heffington had bled to death in the parlor of Milton's home, and Milton and Bishop declared publicly that his death would not go unpunished. They believed that Jeff Fitzpatrick had done the shooting and that Heywood Beatty had helped him get away. The lynching committee met on the evening of December 23 in the cemetery just north of the Milton house. Two of the Olive brothers were part of Tom Bishop and George Milton's vigilance group. One of the Olive daughters married one of Milton's sons.

Details of, and motivations for, what went down that night vary depending on which side is telling the story, but certain facts are incontrovertible, as told in this story that ran statewide the next day:

McDade, Tex., December 25—Last night about 7:30 o'clock, Henry Pfeiffer, Wright McLemore and Thad McLemore were taken out of the saloon here by masked men and carried about a mile in the brush and hanged to a tree. Thad McLemore had been arrested late in the evening on a charge of burglary made by E. G. Walker, of McDade. He was under arrest at the time the masked men took him, while the other two parties happened to be present. Pfeiffer was charged with horse theft in this county. The party that did the hanging was about forty or fifty men, well armed.

On Christmas Day morning, six men who were friends and relatives of the hanged men came into town, and a gunfight erupted between Az Beatty, Jack Beatty, Charlie Goodman, Burt Hasley and Robert Stevens on one side, and George Milton and Thomas Bishop on the other side. Az Beatty and Jack Beatty were killed, as was Willie Griffin, a young man who was either an innocent bystander or trying to help Milton and Bishop, depending on who you believe.

Haywood Beatty was shot seventeen times, but survived.

The mob had expected to find Heywood in the saloon on Christmas Eve. The Milton side said the Beatty bunch were members of the Notchcutters gang who had come into town looking for trouble. Bob Stevens and Heywood Beatty both said that they thought Milton and Bishop to be good friends of theirs.

Governor John Ireland ordered the Brenham Grays to report to McDade, in full uniform and equipment, with ammunition, at once. Detachments from the Johnston Guards, Hempstead, and Brenham Grays, Brenham, arrived on December 26 and returned the same morning as their services were not needed.

The examining trial of George Milton and Thomas Bishop, for the killing of Az Beatty and Jack Beatty began on December 27, the state being represented by the County Attorney and the defendants by Major Joseph Sayers, future governor of Texas.

The examining trial found that:

Az Beatty, Jack Beatty, Charlie Goodman, Burt Hasley and Robert Stevens came into McDade yesterday morning. Az and Jack Beatty went to Milton's store. Milton being engaged at his desk writing, and Bishop sitting in a chair on the gallery. Milton's desk is at the rear end of the store.

Jack Beatty went up to Milton and began a conversation in reference to what had been rumored as to his brother's connection with the murder of Deputy Sheriff Heffington three weeks ago, in McDade. It appears that Az Beatty, who was not on good terms with Bishop, made the attack on him and succeeded in forcing Bishop off the gallery, Bishop falling upon the ground, and Beatty on top, both grasping a pistol.

In the scuffle, Beatty on top and Bishop under, the pistol was fired and Az Beatty fell back dead. In the meantime Jack Beatty, hearing the report of the pistol, rushed to the front door with knife in hand, Milton following him.

Just then Hayward Beatty ran up and fired upon Bishop, the latter returning the fire with effect. Just at this moment, William Griffin, a kinsman of Bishop, came running up to the assistance of Bishop, when he (Griffin) was dangerously wounded in the head and will probably die to-night. When Milton reached the front he began firing, and Jack Beatty was killed.

It is said that it will be proved that Goodman Hasley and Stevens were shooting at Milton and Bishop from a distance. In all there were from sixty to one hundred shots fired. When the firing ceased it was found that Az Beatty and Jack Beatty were dead, Griffin mortally wounded, Hayward Beatty badly wounded, Stevens and Goodman slightly wounded. Hasley escaped but is supposed to be also wounded. The escape of Bishop from being killed may be considered almost a miracle.

The Beatty's are brothers and Hasley and Stevens are connected with them by marriage.

Willie Griffin died on the morning of December 28 at 4 o'clock. Hayward Beatty, Robert Stevens and Charlie Goodman were arrested by Sheriff Jenkins and were placed in jail at Bastrop. The two former were wounded. The jury of inquest found that Willie Griffin came to his death by a pistol shot fired by Hayward Beatty.

Public sympathy locally appeared to be with Bishop and Milton and on December 28 Milton and Bishop were placed under a bond of $1,500 for the killing of the Beattys.

But the *Galveston Daily News,* on December 28, was anything but sympathetic to the vigilantes.

The deplorable occurrences, on Christmas eve, at the town of McDade, are of such a character that they can not, and should not, with propriety, be passed over in silence, either by the civil authorities, state or county, the press, or the people whom the press represents. And they are not likely to do so. The work of the mob of masked men who hung Pfeiffer and the McLemores is, unfortunately, of too startling a nature, too flagrant a disregard of law, to escape attention in this state, or denunciation abroad. A tragedy in which, from first to last, five men were killed, is something more than the ordinary run of criminal sensations with which the papers are now filled, and can not be ignored even by those who are victims of the fallacy that the hiding and covering up of crime are its best remedy. According to the best information at hand, no reason is given for the action of the mob, nor for deliberately taking the lives of three men, who do not appear to have been proved guilty of any crime. It is, however, stated in connection with the lynching, that one of the McLemores had been arrested on a charge of burglary just previous to the hanging, and that Pfeiffer was charged with horse-theft in Bastrop County. It is not stated that Wright McLemore was charged with anything. It does not appear to be the fact that the charges stated were the ground, and the only ground, upon which the lynchers proceeded to take the lives of these men, without the shadow and even the pretense of any form of legal justice or constituted authority. Even supposing Pfeiffer and the McLemores were horse-thieves and burglars, fairly convicted before the law, according to no statute of the State of Texas were they worthy of death; and had they been charged with higher crimes, they were entitled to a fair hearing and an honest trial by judge and jury. Practically the McDade mob was an organized rebellion against the laws of the State and a defiance of its authority, the leading object of which is the protection of the weak against the strong. The spirits which actuated the McDade lynchers should be promptly and effectually rebuked both by official authority and the public opinion back of it. If it is not checked, it is impossible to say how far it may proceed in the present state of popular irritation on account of fence-cutting. If the McDade mob can, with impunity, hang three men, who may have been innocent, the law becomes a mockery and the state government a standing and miserable joke.

It was commonly believed that the killings were related to the recent killing of Bose Heffington. And coincidentally or not, the fence-cutting mania had invaded the area. A Mr. Blackburn's fence was demolished for two or three miles on the night of the hangings.

Milton was no coward, but as his son Melbourn remembered years later, "I never saw a light in our house at night for ten years, and when 'Hello' was answered it would be from upstairs off the porch, and from behind the barrels of the old ten gauges." Milton and Bishop would carry guns for the rest of their lives. By August 1886, Milton was a Bastrop County deputy sheriff. In July 1891, the Texas Building and Loan Association had organized a branch in McDade with George Milton and Allen Wynn as founders; Milton also received his notary public commission. In October 1894, Milton was among the founders of a Joe Sayers democratic club. In August 1895, Milton was one of three men appointed as jury commissioners to select county court jurors for the next six months. Bishop eventually became a deputy United States marshal in the Rio Grande valley. Milton died in 1919 and is buried in the McDade city cemetery.

Jeptha Billingsley, who was no prize pig himself (he had been arrested for horse theft and assault with intent to murder), was to be taught a lesson, and the vigilantes made him cut down the McLemores. Tom Milton said that they made him do so because he was friends of the other people that were hanged and they wanted to teach him a lesson. He later left McDade also. A blacksmith and cobbler named Howery and Preacher Frank Fleming also had to help or get shot. Preacher Fleming, being a Baptist minister, had refused to take sides. Howery said that he had to pull the rope when the men were hanged. Thomas Bishop cursed him, stuck his pistol in his back, and told him to pull the rope.

Captain M. B. "Kige" Highsmith was one of the many witnesses. He told the *Bastrop Advertiser* that two of the masked men on Christmas Eve told him "Hands up," and that he did as commanded and did it quickly, remaining quiet as a little lamb for fifteen minutes, probably an hour. In fact he pledged his sacred word of honor that he doesn't know how long he remained seated on that bench, long enough to think of all the meanness he had ever done in his life, wishing that he could be hidden away in the water tank, and imagining the tickling sensation of a rope around his neck, and he was surprised and happy to find himself in the land of the living and that no rope had encircled his neck all that time. The *Advertiser* closed the story with an admonition: "Kige, this should be a warning. Keep away from saloons."

A few days after the killing at McDade, Marion Beatty, brother of Jack and Az Beatty, left for parts unknown, alleging as his reason that because of his relationship to the dead men, he feared for his personal safety. His whereabouts remained a secret for several weeks, when he was discovered at Taylor, in Williamson County. Sheriff Jenkins, of Bastrop, telegraphed the marshal of Taylor to arrest Beatty on the charge of robbery, which was done, and Beatty was brought to Austin that evening in charge of Marshal Olive.

The marshal received a telegram asking him to bring Beatty to Bastrop. This he declined to do, and he would not consent to turn him over to any subordinate officer or committee. Sheriff Jenkins would either take him in person or he would turn him loose. Marshal Olive feared violence to Beatty if he should attempt to carry him to Bastrop by way of McDade. Felix McLemore, brother to the men hanged at McDade, was with Beatty when the latter was arrested at Taylor. Milton and Bishop, concerned in the shooting at McDade, were also at Taylor when Beatty was apprehended, demanding that Beatty be turned over to them. The prisoner was held subject to Sheriff Jenkins' demand in person.

As to Bose Heffington, it is interesting to note that Lee County sheriff Jim Brown swore in court in *State of Texas vs. Jeff Fitzpatrick* that at the time of his killing, Heffington was not a deputy sheriff of Lee County or any legal officer of the state of Texas, and several people claimed that Heffington had journeyed to McDade with the express purpose of killing Jeff Fitzpatrick.

Fifty years later, dispute over the hangings and gun battle still simmered, and Jeptha Billingsley felt compelled to set the record straight as he saw it once and for all, in an article titled "McDade Lynchings Fifty Years Ago Remembered," published in the *Elgin Courier*, May 21, 1936.

> There were a good many folks in town that Christmas Eve, doing their last minute trading, drinking, etc. As I was going home that night, a little past sundown, two men invited me to go with them to the Christmas Tree at Oak Hill [a nearby community located where Camp Swift is now—ed.] , but I declined, saying I would

have my Christmas at home. The men evidently didn't get off as early as they planned because one of these men was among those hanged that night. Next day when I got to town I was told that a "Committee" of some 80 men or more had gone to Oscar Nash's Saloon and had called out the three men they wanted . . . victims and had trooped out of town with them to about a mile away; they stopped near a branch under a big tree—I believe it was a blackjack—and in a short time the lives of these three marked men were snuffed out. As seems to happen to all trees on which men are hanged, it wasn't long before the tree died. It was not until this Christmas Eve hanging that the Vigilance Committee finally "got" one of the men who had participated in the previously mentioned attack on Allen Wynn.

McDade, on that Christmas morning, presented a group of people with set faces. The action of the committee on the previous night began to be broadcast, and those who would dare arrived and came in to get particulars. The bodies were still hanging from the tree where they had been strung—waiting for the Sheriff from Bastrop to come and handle the matter. About the middle of the morning, Deputy Sheriff Sid Jenkins, Will Bell, and H. N. Bell arrived, and a large crowd of us went along to witness the proceedings, Sheriff Bill Jenkins arrived later in the day. I was in the crowd and helped cut the ropes the men were hung by—I knew all three of these men pretty well and the sight of them with their twisted faces and the nooses hanging at different angles about the victims' necks was about the most gruesome thing I have ever witnessed—I don't ever want to see anything like that again.

Deputy Sheriff Sid Jenkins and Will Bell returned to McDade to get a wagon to take the bodies of the hung men, while constable Scruggs, Deputy Sheriff H. N. Bell and Joe Simms stayed with the dead bodies. The wagon to carry the dead bodies arrived in about one hour. The wagon belonged to Jack Nash and was driven by Pat Murphy. At the arrival of the wagon, Pat Murphy viewed the bodies, exclaimed, "Bejesus, if Thad had been one foot higher, he would have been a living man yet." The hands of the men hung were tied behind them, and a loop had been slipped around their necks—they were strangled to death.

. . . I happened to be present when the wife of one of the brothers arrived. They lived quite a piece out in the country, and it was some little time before she came. She knelt down sobbing beside the dead form of her husband and prayed one of the most beautiful prayers I have ever heard.

For some days thereafter the residents of McDade lived in a tension. Parents would not let their children out of their sight, and some folks deliberately left town, to be gone until matters had been cleared up. Louis Bassist, who lived in Elgin, was one of the latter. He had been in this country only three months, and the gruesome tales and things he heard tell of, and the constant sight of quickly whipped out guns and pistols filled him with a feeling that is indescribable. Such wild and "uncivilized" life was so new and strange to him after being accustomed to the strict military conduct of the citizens in the city he had lived in while in Germany, that he was at a loss as to what to do about it all. At any rate, he took the first train out of McDade that Christmas Day, and went to Elgin where he stayed a week before venturing back to resume his work in the P. Bassist Store.

People who were at all subject to superstition were sure a curse was on the town and its inhabitants, and that the ghosts of the dead men would be certain to put in their appearance.

In 1884, Jeff Fitzpatrick was indicted for the murder of Bose Heffington. At a new trial in April of 1887, he was found not guilty. Witnesses said that Heffington was in a conspiracy to kill Jeff Fitzpatrick. Family members, including Sam Mundine's own wife, say he killed Heffington, skipped out of town, and went by the alias of Sam Bender.

After the Christmas massacre, the McDade troubles began winding down, albeit slowly, as illustrated by this July 1884 letter between members of the Turner family:

Well Marg times is pretty squaley here yet. They have comensed taken men from behind the brush. Pete Allen was waylayed and shot killed dead. They got the horse the man was a riding that done the work. The poney was turned over to the constable for safe keeping and the man com that night and got the poney. [Pete] had been to Simins Store after medicen for his sick child and on his way home was killed.

Henry Jackson had shot and killed Andrew J. "Pete" Allen, son of James W. and Sarah Dunkin Allen on July 14, 1884, near Blue. Both of the Allen men had signed the McDade mass meeting declaration of 1875 in response to the murders of Charles Kirk and Pea Eye Craddock. The killing of Pete Allen in 1884 and of Frank Renault in 1886 are supposed to have been the final acts in this feud.

Like Haywood and Marion Beatty, Felix McLemore chose to leave the area after the lynching of his two brothers. He headed for the gold mine country of Montana. He had no illusions about life or justice in the McDade/Knobbs country, as evidenced in this May 1885 letter to his wife:

In your last letter you sayed that Capt. Nash sayed that I owed him 30 or 40 dollars. I don't owe him a cent and don't you pay him a single cent and find out who he sold that cow to for he had no right to the cow or any authority from me to take or dispose of her. He had as well have stole her and it is nothing more or less and I will see what can be done with him when I come home if he sold the cow anywhere in the county and you can find her go on send and get her for he has no right to her for Capt. Nash can't take my property and sell it without my permission. He thinks as his sone Horace did in taking Blaches [?] hogs that thear is no one to hinder him. I know thear is no Law for me or justice to be had in the dam county and Nash thinks so too or he would never have dared to have taken that cow. But I will show him that I will not stand to be robbed by him because he knows he has the advantage of my circumstances. He thinks I am afraid to come back or ask for my rights. He knows that I have always been a friend of his although I always knew he was a dam rascal and many others knows so too.

On a grudge, George Duncan, who had left the McDade area after the Christmas massacres, followed Heywood Beatty up to Parker County, Texas, to kill him. There are two stories as to why: (1) the two had fought as boys at the Knobbs school, and Duncan could not let the fight rest; and (2) Duncan wanted recognition for killing the gamest man around (Haywood had taken seventeen bullets on Christmas Day and lived; he carried five bullets in his body until his death), and he had been bragging around town that he was going to kill Beatty. At any rate, Duncan confronted Beatty after a Sunday baptism, and a chase ensued. Beatty had the faster horse and beat Duncan home. Dashing inside, Beatty grabbed his Winchester and stood ready for Duncan beside a window. Duncan rode up, gun in hand, and was promptly shot dead by Beatty on October 26, 1889.

OLD ROCK FRONT SALOON

Old 20 S. at Waco • No set hours, open during Watermelon Festival and by appointment

The Old Rock Front Saloon, which was later covered with stucco, now serves as local museum. It is the westernmost building in one-block-long, downtown McDade. McDade's hotel stood directly across from the Old Rock Saloon by the tracks. McDade is considerably tamer now, over 120 years after the troubled times. The train station has been moved across the tracks from its original site. In the string of store buildings between the Mc-Dade store and the saloon, Dungan's Drug Store closed in about 1993, and the wonderful old Underwood Pharmacy signage ("J. B. Underwood Prop., Dr. E. S. Mullen, Prescriptions, Patent Medicines, Stationery, Candies") has been painted over. About the only good news is that the old McDade Guaranty State Bank building, a simple, square, one-story, red-brick affair, has been undergoing restoration. It is located on Bastrop Street, behind the post office. The bank building dates to about 1910; the bank itself closed during the Depression.

ANNUAL EVENT

JULY

WATERMELON FESTIVAL

Downtown McDade • Second Saturday in July • W

The festival includes a parade, a dance, good barbecue, an auction of the area's largest watermelons, and free watermelon for all.

Locals brag on the size of their watermelons; according to them, Luling's melons are marble sized in comparison. McDade is now most famous for its watermelons, which are as tasty and famous as those grown in Luling, but grapes were a major crop by July 1888, when S. Kujowski had started shipping his harvest. He had expected to ship ten or twelve thousand pounds of grapes and make the largest part of his crop into wine.

Great preparations were being made that same month for a July 21 barbecue, and as McDade was noted for its hospitality, good attendance was expected. Farmers Alliance president Evan Jones was keynote speaker and was staying with George Milton, Esq.

To leave McDade, take Old 20 S. east to Loop 223. Turn right on Loop 223, which takes you to US 290. Along the way is the McDade Cemetery, where some of the feud partici-pants are buried. Cross US 290 here and continue south toward Bastrop on what becomes FM 2336.

CAMP SWIFT

About 7.5 miles from McDade

FM 2336 skirts the eastern edge of Camp Swift, built at the beginning of World War II as an infantry training center. It now serves as a National Guard reservation.

When FM 2336 runs into SH 95, turn left on SH 95 to reach Bastrop. About seven miles later, turn right on Loop 150, which takes you to downtown Bastrop.

BASTROP

Bastrop County Seat • 8,500 (approximate) • (512) • About 9 miles from Camp Swift

The town we now call Bastrop started as a Spanish fort, established to protect commerce on the Old San Antonio Road, which crossed the Colorado River here. It was to have been the nucleus of a colony established by Felipe Enrique Neri, self-styled baron de Bastrop, but was abandoned shortly after its settlement in 1823 because of Indian attacks. Stephen F. Austin next attempted to settle the area, starting in 1829. The Anglos first called their settlement Bastrop in honor of the man who did so much to facilitate Moses and Stephen Austin's dealings with the Mexican government regarding their colonization projects.

The *Handbook of Texas* tells the following story of Bastrop's life:

> Felipe Enrique Neri was born Philip Hendrik Nering Boegel in Dutch Guiana in 1759. He moved to Holland with his parents in 1764, and in 1779 he enlisted in the cavalry of Holland and Upper Issel. He married Georgine Wolffeline Francoise Lijcklama Nyeholt in 1782; they had five children. Boegel served as collector general of taxes for the province of Friesland. In 1793, he was accused of embezzlement of tax funds and fled the country before he could be brought to trial. The Court of Justice of Leeuwarden offered a reward of one thousand gold ducats to anyone who brought him back.
>
> By April 1795, he had arrived in Spanish Louisiana, where he represented himself as a Dutch nobleman, the baron de Bastrop, who had fled Holland because of the French invasion. During the next decade, he received permission from the Spanish government to establish a colony in the Ouachita valley and engaged in several business ventures in Louisiana and Kentucky. After Louisiana was sold to the United States in 1803, Bastrop moved to Spanish Texas and was given permission to establish a colony between Bexar and the Trinity River. In 1806, he settled in San Antonio, where he had a freighting business and gained influence with the inhabitants and officials. In 1810, he was appointed second alcalde, or vice mayor, of Ayuntamiento de Bexar (Bexar County, which at the time encompassed all of Central Texas).
>
> One of his most significant contributions to Texas was his intercession with Governor Antonio Maria Martinez on behalf of Moses Austin in 1820, just before Mexico gained its independence. Because of Bastrop, Martinez approved Austin's project to establish an Anglo-American colony in Texas. After Moses Austin's death, Bastrop served as intermediary with the Mexican government for Stephen F. Austin, who would have encountered many more obstacles if not for Bastrop's assistance.

In July 1823, Bastrop was appointed commissioner of colonization for the Austin colony, with authority to issue land titles. In September 1823, the settlers elected Bastrop to the provincial deputation at Bexar, which in turn chose him as representative to the legislature of the new state of Coahuila and Texas in May 1824.

During his tenure as representative of Texas at the capital, Saltillo, Bastrop sought legislation favorable to the cause of immigration and to the interests of settlers, secured passage of the colonization act of 1825, and was instrumental in the passage of an act establishing a port at Galveston. His salary, according to the Mexican system, was paid by contributions from his constituents. The contributions were not generous; Bastrop did not leave enough money to pay his burial expenses when he died, on February 23, 1827. His fellow legislators donated the money to pay for his funeral. Bastrop was buried in Saltillo.

Even in his last will and testament, Bastrop continued to claim noble background. Some of his contemporaries believed him to be an American adventurer; historians have thought him to be a French nobleman or a Prussian soldier of fortune. Only within the last half century have records from the Netherlands been found to shed light on Bastrop's mysterious origins. While many of his peers doubted his claims of nobility, he earned respect as a diplomat and legislator. Bastrop, Texas, and Bastrop, Louisiana, as well as Bastrop County, Texas, were named in his honor.

But Vito Alessio Robles, a respected historian in the Mexican state of Coahuila, has a different story to tell of the baron of Bastrop. And when you read it, you will see that there is a certain poetic justice in Bastrop's impoverished death, when you consider the extent of the dastardly deeds he committed in life, not the least of which was his role as the Judas of the Mexican War of Independence.

Mexico's fight for independence began on September 16, 1810, in the village of Dolores, near San Miguel de Allende, when Father Miguel Hidalgo urged his poor, Indian, and mestizo parishioners to throw out the Spaniards. That night, a rebel army formed and began marching, overrunning the haciendas of the Spanish and capturing San Miguel, Celaya, Guanajuato, and Valladolid, under Hidalgo's command. Other sympathetic uprisings occurred across Mexico, including Saltillo. Failing to capture Mexico City, the rebels moved on to Guadalajara. Defeated there by the Spanish Army in January 1811, the rebels headed for Saltillo. General Ignacio Allende now commanded what was left of the rebel army. Father Hidalgo, Allende, and the other rebel leaders decided to march to the United States, via San Antonio, in order to buy the arms that they couldn't get in New Spain, so that they could continue the fight. They also hoped to recruit land-hungry North Americans to fight with them, dangling before them the prospect of settling Texas' vast lands in return for their services. In the first days of March, two men came to Allende who claimed to be fervently addicted to the cause of independence. They claimed to know well the road between San Antonio and Louisiana and offered their services as guides. From that point on, they had access to all of the leaders' meetings.

One of them was a Dutchman named Felipe Enrique Neri, baron de Bastrop. He had served as a soldier of fortune for Frederick the Great and then entered the Spanish Army, which sent him to Mexico with a special commission. When Louisiana was ruled by Spain, he obtained a concession of lands between the Mississippi and Red rivers, and when France, and then the United States, obtained Louisiana, he went to Texas. The other guide was Sebastian Rodriguez. But Bastrop and Rodriguez were really spies for a royalist junta that had formed in Monclova. Unbeknownst to the rebels, the provincial capitals of San Antonio, Texas, and Monclova, Coahuila, had changed sides from rebel to royalist. The rebel commander in Monclova, Captain Elizondo, had been insulted by Allende's refusal to make him a lieutenant general. So he turned coat again, back to the Spanish, determined to achieve generalcy one way or the other.

On March 17, 1811, the rebels, guided by Bastrop and Rodriguez, left Saltillo for the United States. That same day, the royalists began assembling an ambush. The rebels would have to march past Monclova on their way north, and Bastrop suggested the water hole at Bajan as a good spot for an ambush. The rebel caravan, which stretched out more than sixteen kilometers, proceeded slowly and disorderly up the narrow valley toward Bajan and Monclova. On March 20, the rebels marched for fifty-six difficult kilometers without food or water. But there was the hope and expectation of meeting up with friendly troops at Bajan. So on the morning of March 21, the rebels picked up and continued the march north. Incredibly, General Allende had not sent out a recon patrol ahead of the main column.

At Bajan, the road makes a turn to go around a low hill now known as the Loma del Prendimiento, or Capture Hill. Here, hidden behind the hill waited the royalist forces. As the elements of the rebel caravan made the turn, they were apprehended. Father Hidalgo was in the fourth carriage, Allende and Jimenez in the fifth. Allende declared that he would die before he would surrender and fired a shot from his pistol before the royalists opened fire and killed him.

Bastrop and Rodriguez followed in another carriage. When a group of six hundred rebel prisoners had been assembled, including Father Hidalgo, they were marched to captivity in Monclova, on the morning of March 22. From there, the leaders were taken to Chihuahua City, where Father Hidalgo was executed on July 30, 1811. An Indian was paid twenty pieces of silver to cut off his head, which was taken to Guanajuato and hung in an iron cage for all to see and abhor.

Bastrop profited greatly from his perfidy.

He died in Saltillo on February 23, 1827, while serving as a deputy in the Congress of Coahuila y Texas. According to his will, written in Saltillo a month before his death, he owned large tracts of land in the states of Virginia and Louisiana, as well as several properties in Texas.

Austin's colonists began pouring into Bastrop in 1829, and the town served as a jumping-off point for many western-bound Texans, including Noah Smithwick, William "Uncle Billy" Barton (of Austin's Barton Springs fame), and Reuben Hornsby.

The Mexican government changed the town of Bastrop's name to Mina in 1834 to honor the patriot Francisco Javier Mina. This name change did not set well at all with the Texans. Santa Anna burned the town in 1836. In 1837, the Republic of Texas changed the town's name back to Bastrop and made it seat of Bastrop County, one of Texas' original twenty-three counties, which encompassed all or parts of fifteen present-day counties.

Bastrop prospered after the Texas War for Independence, boasting a newspaper, library, and several schools by the 1850s. The newspaper—the *Bastrop Advertiser*—is the oldest still-publishing weekly in Texas, dating back to March 1, 1853. Bastrop's economy was supported by cotton, naturally, but also by coal mining, brick making, and lumbering in the Lost Pines. Bastrop pine was used in the construction of Austin's first capitol building and in many other Austin and Central Texas buildings. Steamboats plied the Colorado River in those days, carrying cotton and lumber down to the coast and bringing back all manner of highly demanded consumer goods.

In those antebellum days, one of Bastrop's most visible visitors was Andy Potter, who was later to become the "Fightin' Parson." Potter was a heathen back then, though, and was invited to visit the mayor's office almost every time he hit Bastrop, for he was forever being charged with violating some law, particularly the one forbidding fighting. Mayor/Judge O'Connor, being a hot-tempered Irishman himself, generally let Potter off with a moderate fine. This happened so many times that Potter was going broke, and the town coffers were becoming full of his fines. Therefore, Potter devised a plan to soak the town of Bastrop and get his money back.

Potter's plan involved a concert, and the only townspeople let in on the secret were the printer and the doorkeeper he hired for the occasion. Potter had printed and distributed the following playbill:

Signor Blitz, from the London and New York theatres, informs the citizens of this place that he will give one of his celebrated entertainments at the courthouse, at early candle-lighting Saturday night—the extraordinary vocal powers of Signor Blitz have been the theme of universal commendation throughout the North and in Havana, as well as in Europe, where his concerts have been honored with the presence of royalty. Admittance fees: For grown persons, $1; for man and wife, $1.50, for children and servants, half price. Front seats reserved for ladies.

The house was packed for Signor Blitz's show; there had been a horse race in town earlier that day. Potter blacked his face and, arming himself with a bowie knife and pistol, walked out on stage and announced that Signor Blitz had failed to arrive, but that he would substitute for the great Signor. Potter then burst forth into a black minstrel song. A prominent doctor approached the stage with pistol in hand and demanded to know who the singer was. Potter pulled his own pistol and waved the doctor back to his seat. Then he told them who he was. The crowd roared, laughed, and stomped as if to tear down the house, then carried Potter up on their shoulders to a barroom and made him sing till one in the morning. Potter was the only man in Bastrop who could have pulled such a trick; anyone else would have been arrested or abused within an inch of his hoaxing life.

Early in 1854, the *Bastrop Advertiser* weighed in on the state of civilization in Bastrop:

Private parties are getting to be quite common in Bastrop, we understand. Several very creditable candypullings are said to have come off during the Christmas week, at which we had not the good fortune to be present. We notice these parties, for they are important to a good state of society in any place. Bastrop for two years past enjoyed no enviable reputation in this respect, and yet Bastrop has more material than any town of its size in Texas. The substantial and wealthy citizens of a place—the merchants—the church members, whose interest as well as duty it is to improve society, should wake up on this matter. Let them give such magnificent entertainments as was given by Mr. and Mrs. C. K. Hall, on the 3rd inst. Liberality is not lost upon the young; and the liberal, social, and generous merchant will always succeed best, other things being equal.

Keeping the young folks properly entertained and out of mischief in a small Texas town is not a new problem, as the newspaper goes on to say:

> It is true that young people will have amusements, and to this end they will seek some kind of society. If the advantages of good association are denied them they often turn aside to evil practices and bad examples. Christmas week last year was one continual scene of mischief and drunken uproariousness all about town. Plows were perched to roost on the tops of houses. Signs changed their locations, and effigies of good and pious men were posted along the streets. This year all was peaceful, orderly, and quiet.
>
> The reason of this difference is obvious. This year the thoughts have been directed in a civil channel by parties and balls. The Citizens' Ball, given at the Nicholson House, on the 29th, convened an array of beauty and loveliness seldom surpassed. The rough sex, when enjoying such society, forget the moods which would lead to shameful excesses. But speaking of the ball—the supper prepared by Mrs. Beachboard gave perfect satisfaction, the music was excellent, and everything went off harmoniously. But alas, how time flies when shuffled off by nimble feet. The clock struck two, and all were obliged to take note of time "from its loss."

The Nicholson House, a hotel, was run by James Nicholson, who was born in England in 1814. He moved to Bastrop in 1839, opened a store, and became town clerk in June 1839. His family joined him in 1840. Nicholson served as mayor in 1844. In 1864, after service in the Confederate Army, he went to Mexico, but returned after the war. Nicholson died at Bastrop on April 29, 1885.

One of Nicholson's most illustrious guests was Sam Houston. After General Houston's election as governor in 1859, he brought his young son, Sam, to Bastrop to place him in Colonel Allen's Bastrop Military Academy. Future governor Joseph Sayers was captain of the cadets, and Houston inspected his company during that visit, handling every gun. General Houston for several days lodged at Nicholson's hotel. Houston, having just been elected governor, was in a cheerful mood, and being in the company of gentlemen who had canvassed for him, he entertained them until midnight with interesting events of his career.

One evening, Houston was seated opposite a desperate man named Ham White at Nicholson's dining table. Ham White had during his early life been a Texas Ranger and had sworn he would kill Houston on sight, because Houston had said during the "Archive War" after the Mexican invasion of Vasquez in 1842 that the people of the upper Colorado were horse thieves. White's threat was known, and Houston had been warned. While seated opposite each other at the dining table, White made a very insulting remark intended for the general. All heard it and expected trouble; no answer was made, but Houston, after laying down his knife and fork, straightened up in his chair and looked with defiant gaze straight at Ham White, who dropped his head and continued eating. Not a word was spoken, but anyone who had ever seen a powerful mastiff cow a barking dog with a mere look could understand the scene, one of their fellow diners remembered, years later.

When he brought young Sam to the military academy, Governor Houston pronounced his views of education. He wanted his son to be well grounded in the history and constitution of the United States, to continue his study of English grammar, and to have daily practice in writing until he could write well, to cypher to the "single rule of three," and learn how to calculate interest so as to protect himself in business, and did not wish him to "waste time" on Greek and Latin, nor keep him at school for years to learn the higher branches of mathematics. "For what profit," he asked, "is there in learning to tell how long it will take a ray of light from some distant star to reach our planet?" He wished to take Sam from school before he was twenty years old and place him in a clerk's office, or store, to come in contact with men and learn the "great book of human nature." He said that if Sam was kept at school until he was older in order to study Greek, Latin, and advanced mathematics, he would return home "a graduated fool."

By the start of the Civil War, Bastrop's business district was one of the state's biggest, consisting of two blocks of two-story wooden buildings on the banks of the Colorado River, along the same stretch of Main Street that comprises downtown today. At the time, it was one of the most imposing business districts anywhere in the state. The great fire of 1862 burned down almost all of downtown. The 1852 Union Hall (813 Main) is the only antebellum business building standing today.

In 1853, C. V. Shafer, owner of the *Union Hall Bar-Room Exchange*, announced:

To the Drinking Public.
    The subscriber would say that for their accommodation he has fitted up an establishment second to none anywhere. He only solicits such a share of patronage as he may be thought to be entitled to by those who will give him a call.

The Union Hall played a prominent role in Bastrop's earliest and highest-profile lynching. In July 1858, the *Waco Democrat* reported that a gang of horse thieves and robbers had been discovered in the upper portion of Navarro County. Two bad characters named Bill Mitchell and Jim Warren were captured and volunteered the names of the gang, which included several men from the Bastrop and future Lee County areas, most notably Tom Middleton.

In 1858, Tom Middleton was notorious enough that Governor Hardin Runnels had ordered his arrest, and various rewards amounting to between $2,000 and $3,000 had been posted for his apprehension and return to Bastrop County. The sheriffs of Austin and Burleson counties had been tracking him for several months in the fall of 1858 and finally found him in Shreveport, where he was arrested. They and a number of other people, acting as guards, brought him into Bastrop in late December 1858. Bastrop County sheriff John J. Moncure was gone, having gone down to Walnut Creek to arrest another man. He was putting the other man away when he found out about Middleton's arrival. He told Middleton's escorts to deliver him to the county jail, which they refused to do, stating that they would keep him at the place where they had stopped, that being the Union Hall at Pine and Main.

Sheriff Moncure went to Union Hall, where he received the prisoner and summoned a number of citizens of Bastrop, together with the guards who had escorted the prisoner to Bastrop, to assist in confining the prisoner in jail. But the crowd, numbering between 75 and 125 persons, who had assisted in escorting Middleton to Bastrop, forcibly rescued the prisoner from Moncure, placed him on a horse and conducted him about a mile and a half from town, and swung him between the heavens and earth from a post oak limb until he was dead. Moncure tried to stop them but was overwhelmed by the crowd. The hanging took place on the main road to La Grange, at the top of the hill overlooking Bastrop (near the present-day American Legion Hall).

The *Bastrop Advertiser* wrote the following:

Middleton was allowed sufficient time to make all the confessions he should wish.
. . . But he said he would never divulge a sentence to implicate a single person—
only stated that he knew he was a bad man. . . . We have been informed that he
was guilty of murder. He had been the dread of good citizens of Burleson, Washington and Bastrop and a number of counties for years past. He was a thief, well
educated in his profession and we do not suppose there is a man in Western Texas
that regrets his untimely death.

He has escaped the vigilance of justice time and again, and the people were
determined to execute their own will this time. Everything was done calmly and
with a determination which showed a revenge of good citizens who have been
outraged too often to have their rights trampled upon by nefarious swindlers,
cowards and horse thieves. We are not acquainted with but a few of the gentlemen
who executed Middleton; but all who brought him here, bore the appearance of
highly intelligent gentlemen, of noble bearing, and true courage.

At the time of his death, he was a fugitive from two indictments in Bastrop
County: April 1858, for threatening to kill, and October 1858, for assault with
intent to kill and murder. He failed to appear in court, forfeiting a $500 bond.

Moncure resigned a few months later, disgusted and disappointed with the
number of vigilantes that he knew. He knew he no longer had their support.

Milt Morgan was famous for the number of men his mob had hanged, including Tom Middleton. He also enjoyed tracking down escaped or stolen slaves.

In 1860, he was hunting a negro thief who had stolen two small negro boys
from Colonel Tom Moore who lived in Winchester in Fayette County, with
the help of a Fayette deputy and a couple of young men from near Lexington.
Roddy and Martin, the two young men, captured the thief, while Morgan and
the others went after the boys. When they returned to the road with the thief,
Morgan already had a noose ready. Roddy and Martin had promised him a
fair trial and refused to hand him over. Despite several more attempts to lynch
him, they finally got him to Winchester. There, one of Moore's sons denounced
Morgan and prevented yet another attempt to lynch the man, who was eventually tried, convicted, sent to the pen, and then pardoned to go and serve in the
Confederate Army, where he was lost to history. Morgan served as well, as a
captain, and Roddy ended up for a while under his command.

War fever was high in Bastrop in April 1861. On Saturday, April 27, 1861,
four companies of volunteers gathered and organized, one of them being the
Yegua Notchcutters. But that was not the day's only excitement. One of the
town's merchants had on his sign "New York Cheap Store." A ladder was raised
and placed against his business house under the sign, and then a man mounted
with a bucket of red paint and painted out the words "New York." Some of
the crowd hollered out, "Blow the house up." Others said to take the damned
abolitionist out to Middleton Hill and hang him on the same tree that the mob
hanged Tom Middleton on two years before.

The Confederate cause nationwide was plagued by poor and inadequate
armaments for its troops. N. B. Tanner got a state contract for five hundred
Mississippi-type rifles to be made at his factory at the corner of Water and Government streets. Rifles were rolling off the line with cheerful regularity, but the
inspector was rejecting an excessive percentage of them. Some of Tanner's rifles,
after being accepted by ordinance inspectors, burst in the field. His first delivery

of acceptable guns was in 1862. He was able to produce about one gun per day before production declined. The last delivery of guns was May 20, 1863, when thirty-one rifles were accepted; he delivered 264 rifles in all to Texas.

Bastrop County's plantation economy was in shambles by war's end, and the town struggled to rebuild. The Reconstruction years in Bastrop and Bastrop County were difficult and often violent, as evidenced by the troubles in Cedar Creek, detailed in the *Shiner-Lockhart Pilgrimage*.

When brought to the attention of Reconstruction governor Edmund Davis that a number of violent acts against blacks were being committed in Bastrop County (schools were a favorite target), the governor threatened to impose martial law and ordered that a grand jury convene to ascertain if the Ku Klux Klan were committing these crimes. The grand jury, which included two African Americans, reported that it found no evidence that the Ku Klux Klan existed in the county. Unsatisfied with the findings, Governor Davis continued to threaten martial law.

White Republicans and African Americans were elected or appointed to many prominent positions of power and responsibility in Bastrop County after the Civil War, which did not sit well with the white men who had formerly run things. The *Bastrop Advertiser* wrote in 1869 or 1870 that the "Negro-Radical Barbecue—Sat. last . . . featured a parade headed by two hacks, one occupied by Judge C. C. McGinnis with District Clerk Robert F. Campbell; the second driven by Sheriff Jo Jung with Judge Schutze, District Attorney B. Trigg, J. Duve, and the colored representative Jeremiah J. Hamilton."

That's right, Bastrop's representative in the Texas legislature was an ex-slave. Jeremiah J. Hamilton was born a slave in 1838 in Tennessee. He arrived in Texas in 1847. After emancipation, he married a woman named Ellen in 1867, and they had seven children. The Hamiltons lived in Bastrop County, and Jeremiah became a spokesman for black workers as early as 1866. He acquired land in the county and served as a land trustee for blacks. He learned to read and write as a slave and established a school for African Americans after the Civil War. In 1866, he served as a secretary for the Texas State Central Committee of Colored Men, which opposed white paternalism and worked with the Freedmen's Bureau. He was selected for the board that registered voters in Bastrop County during 1867. He ran successfully in 1869 for the Texas House of Representatives in the Twelfth Legislature as a Republican. As a legislator, he generally favored bills to advance law enforcement, education, and civil rights.

After his legislative term, Hamilton remained in Austin, where he worked as a carpenter before entering the newspaper business; he was owner and editor of the *Austin Citizen* in the mid-1880s and the *National Union* in the early 1890s, which circulated primarily in the black community. Hamilton also remained active as a leader in political and civic affairs. His date of death is unknown.

Hopes were buoyed by the prospect of the new Houston-to-Austin railroad coming through town, but those hopes were washed away by the great Colorado River flood of 1869, which left downtown Bastrop awash in several feet of water. Fearful of future floods, the Houston and Texas Central railroad chose a more upland route through northern Bastrop County, which spawned the towns of Elgin, McDade, and Paige in 1871. Goods had to be hauled to and from the station at McDade, fifteen miles to the north. This limited Bastrop's growth.

But 1887 would bring great changes when the Missouri-Kansas-Texas (MKT) railroad came to town. Bastrop quickly blossomed as a commercial center, as a look at the old downtown district indicates. Most of the buildings were built after 1887. The same may be said of old Bastrop's residential district. A few homes date to the 1830s, but most houses (and certainly the fanciest ones) postdate the railroad's arrival.

Bastrop's most famous son (or daughter) was Joseph Draper Sayers, born in 1841 in Mississippi. In 1851, he came to Bastrop with his father. He attended the Bastrop Military Institute from 1852 to 1860. He served in the Confederate Army during the Civil War, after which he returned to Bastrop and began to study the law. He was elected to the Texas legislature and was then elected lieutenant governor. Next, Sayers was elected to the U.S. Congress. He resigned from Congress to run for governor in 1898. He won and was reelected in 1900. His administration is remembered chiefly for the disasters that occurred during that time, such as the burning of the state penitentiary in Huntsville, the great Brazos River flood of 1899, and the great Galveston hurricane and flood of 1900. In retirement, he served as a regent of the University of Texas and on various state regulatory boards. Sayers died in 1929.

Through the years, Bastrop has been able to retain much of its old-time flavor. Unfortunately, Texas' oldest pharmacy—Erhard and Son—started in 1847, burned down in 1980. Cayton Erhard was born in Munich, Bavaria, in 1822. With his parents and younger brother, Adolph, he entered Texas at Galveston in 1839. The family made its way up the Colorado River to Bastrop. In January 1840, both parents died, and the boys were informally adopted by the James Nicholson family.

In 1841, Cayton joined the ill-fated Santa Fe expedition. Along with others, Erhard was captured by Mexican troops and spent the next two years as a prisoner in Mexico.

In March 1843, Erhard rejoined the Nicholson family in Bastrop. Four years later, with his own savings and a loan from friends, he moved to San Marcos, where he helped organize the Hays County government. He was elected the first county clerk and served as the first postmaster. In 1847, he opened a store in San Marcos that sold a large assortment of drugs and nostrums. This date marks it as the first drugstore in the state. Erhard was married to Harriet Smith in 1851, and they had nine children. Erhard prospered during his eighteen years in San Marcos. He bought several lots in San Marcos and Bastrop and several slaves.

When his business foundered in San Marcos, he moved his store to Bastrop, where he remained the rest of his life. After Reconstruction, Erhard again began to prosper. Erhard had been a typical Texas Democrat until Texas' secession in 1861. But as business conditions and public order deteriorated during the war, his political convictions began to change. His conservative and nonradical political stance attracted notice in Austin. In 1872, he was appointed a municipal elections judge for Bastrop, a position of influence normally reserved for supporters of Radical Republican governor Edmund J. Davis. Erhard's political position was sufficiently acceptable to the citizens of Bastrop for him to be elected a delegate to the Constitutional Convention of 1875. Erhard died at his home in 1884 and is buried in the city cemetery.

If Erhard were to return to the Bastrop of today, he wouldn't have much trouble finding his way around; much of Bastrop remains almost as it was a hundred years ago. Over 130 homes and buildings are listed in the National Register of Historic Places. Long a slumbering little town, Bastrop awakened in the 1980s as Austin-related growth began to spill over into Bastrop County. In 1985, the City of Austin and Bastrop County went toe to toe in court as Austin tried to extend its territorial jurisdiction into Bastrop County.

But while Bastrop County was able to keep Austin government out of Bastrop, it wasn't able to keep Austinites from moving to Bastrop. The most famous of these was Dr. Gerald Wagner, who was the catalyst behind the renovation of much of Bastrop's venerable business district in the 1980s. Wagner discovered Bastrop in 1982, at a time when an ambitious development project of his in Austin was going sour. He had been looking for alternative sites, and two of Bastrop's stately homes happened to be for sale. Wagner snapped them up and didn't stop buying until he owned several dozen buildings downtown and elsewhere in Bastrop. A dozen old cabins, barns, and other buildings were moved into town from their original sites in Bastrop and nearby counties, placed in a plantation-like arrangement, and meticulously restored.

BASTROP COUNTY COURTHOUSE

Courthouse square, Pine at Water • 321-2579 • Monday through Friday • W

J. W. Preston designed this three-story brick courthouse. It was built in 1883 and contains 1,383,512 bricks. During a subsequent, post–World War I remodeling, the exterior brick walls were covered over with stucco, the clock tower was reduced in size, and some of the Victorian ornamentation was removed, which gave the courthouse its current Mission Revival appearance.

OLD BASTROP COUNTY JAIL

Courthouse square • 321-2419

Built in 1891–1892 in the Second Empire style, this building looks more like an old city hall or bank than a jail. The jail moved out in 1974. A recent refurbishment converted much of the old jail space into county offices and a jury room, but a few of the original cells remain on display. The intricate lever-action cell-locking mechanism ("1874, Pauly Jail Bld'g & Lever; Lock Patd. Sept. 15, 1874, St. Louis Mo.") still works, and the thick metal straps used in lieu of bars remind you of being imprisoned inside a woven basket. The cells are low slung and cramped. They must have been hellishly uncomfortable on one of our sultry Central Texas summer days.

From the jail, walk on over to Main and the Bastrop County Historical Museum.

BASTROP COUNTY HISTORICAL MUSEUM

702 Main • 321-6177 • Open Monday through Friday afternoons • Fee • W

The museum is located in the Cornelson-Fehr house, built in 1850 and enlarged in 1854. It sits on the site of the old Spanish fort, Puesta del Colorado. The museum has rare manuscripts and miscellaneous pioneer and Indian artifacts. Notable among the contents are some silver spoons supposedly fashioned from coins taken from Santa Anna after his capture at San Jacinto. Recently added exhibits examine the lives of African Texans and the Tonkawa tribe in Bastrop County.

From the museum, stroll up Main to old downtown Bastrop.

ELZNER COTTAGE

802 Main • Private residence

The gingerbreaded P. O. Elzner cottage is a few feet north of the museum, built around 1876 with Bastrop pine. It stayed in the Elzner family until 1968. We'll say more on Elzner in a moment.

THE OLD BRIDGE

The 1923 Parker-style, arched steel-truss highway bridge over the Colorado River at Chestnut Street was recently retired from four-wheel service and has been integrated into the city parks system as a walkway. This type of bridge was commonly built in the 1920s and 1930s to cross long expanses. It has been added to the National Register of Historic Places, along with another Parker-style bridge (on SH 16) that crosses the Llano River in Llano.

LOCK DRUG STORE

1003 Main • 321-2422 • Open Monday through Saturday • W

A favored local hangout since 1905, when it was built by W. J. Miley, Lock Drug's soda fountain serves juices, coffee, ice cream cones, sodas, and banana splits from one of the few old-time soda fountains still in use in Central Texas. Sit at the bar and admire the marble fountain and stained-glass cabinets. If there's no room at the fountain (which is often the case), sit at one of the round tables in one of the old curved-wire chairs. Notice the pressed-tin ceiling and the old pharmacy drawers lining the walls. The W. J. Miley house, built in 1860, is located at 509 Spring. Before the drugstore was built, Dr. David Sayers, father of turn-of-the-century Texas governor Joseph D. Sayers, practiced medicine here.

ELZNER'S CORNER

Main at Spring

The corner of Spring and Main has been known as Elzner's Corner since the 1890s. For years, P. O. Elzner was Bastrop County's best-known merchant, and at its zenith, his little empire stretched east to the opera house and south half a block to the liquor store. "Elzner's got 'em" was a commonly heard phrase around these parts, as evidenced by this story told a few decades back in the *Bastrop Advertiser*:

If a stranger came to town and didn't know his way around, he soon found out where to go.

"Where can I buy a pair of good boots?" the outlander would ask.

The local citizen would point to the corner of the block. "Elzner's got 'em."

"And I have to get a load of groceries."

"Elzner's got 'em."

"Yes, but I haven't got a wagon yet."

"Buy one at Elzner's."

Elzner sold nearly everything: dry goods, groceries, hardware, furniture, farm machinery, and liquor. Bruno Elzner later took over the corner, and you see signs from his era painted on the backs and sides of the Elzner Corner buildings.

BASTROP CHAMBER OF COMMERCE VISITOR INFORMATION CENTER

1016 Main

The center is located in the old First National Bank building, which still contains many of its original bank fixtures.

BASTROP OPERA HOUSE

711 Spring • 321-6382

P. O. Elzner and D. S. Green built the opera house in 1889. It is two stories, stucco over brick. Elzner became sole owner in 1901. But he went bankrupt soon after, and the opera house got new owners. It was converted into a movie theater sometime after 1910. For years the pride of Bastrop, the opera house eventually lost its luster, and by 1978 it was threatened with demolition. But a group of concerned citizens decided it should be restored instead and launched a campaign that year to restore the house to its former glory. Plays and musicals are staged throughout the year. Dinner-show packages are available.

CALVARY EPISCOPAL CHURCH

603 Spring, one block west of Main

Calvary's cornerstone was laid in 1881. The bricks were locally made. Its simple Gothic exterior hasn't been altered since its construction, and the interior has been only slightly altered. The church was also the first building in Bastrop to get a Texas Historic Medallion. The interior is similarly dark, massive, and Gothic, with hand-carved pews, altar, vaulted ceiling, and exposed wood beams. The stained-glass windows are especially beautiful.

The streets with the greatest number of vintage commercial buildings and homes are Main, Church, and Pecan streets. Church runs parallel to Main one block west. Pecan runs parallel to Main two blocks east.

The Jenkins house (1710 Main) began as a log home in 1832 and was expanded over the years. The ornate porch was added at the height of the Victorian era. The Greenleaf Fisk house (1005 Hill) is a frame house with a heavy skeleton of hand-hewn logs, a building method that goes back to medieval England. German immigrants settled here in number as well, and built houses similar to those in the fatherland, but the last of these was razed in the 1970s. Most of Bastrop's old homes are in the Greek Revival style and the later, more exuberant Victorian styles. At 1703 Wilson Street is the home of Texas governor Joe Sayers, which was built in 1868. But the best known of Bastrop's stately old homes is the Wilbarger House on Main Street, four blocks north of downtown.

WILBARGER HOUSE

1403 Main • Private residence

This stately Greek Revival house was built sometime between 1842 and 1847. In 1850, James Wilbarger bought it. James was the son of Josiah Wilbarger, whom you will encounter later on this trip. Josiah came to Texas late in 1827 from Missouri with his bride Margaret. After a year at Matagorda, Wilbarger moved to what would soon become La Grange, in Austin's Colony. A year or so later, he moved farther west, into Bastrop County, where he established a plantation and sawmill on the Colorado River about ten miles upstream from Bastrop. Son James built upon his father's enterprises after blazing a trail that would later be called Wilbarger's Trace, which led from the plantation to Columbus and eventually Galveston. Along this "road," James drove ox wagon trains loaded with cotton, hides, and lumber. He returned with sugar, flour, yard goods, and supplies for the store he operated at Wilbarger's Bend on the Colorado River. The Wilbargers were lavish entertainers, and Governor Sam Houston and future Governor Joe Sayers were among their guests. The house remained in the Wilbarger family for four generations until the late 1970s.

LCRA RIVERSIDE CONFERENCE CENTER

1500 Wilson

The Crocheron Compound was acquired by the Lower Colorado River Authority and serves as a conference center, complete with dormitories and a dining room. The only vintage building original to the site is the Crocheron-McDowall home, built in 1857. This two-story Greek Revival home is furnished with period antiques and is available for small meetings.

DINING

CARTWRIGHT'S BBQ

409 SH 71 • 321-7719 • Open daily, lunch and dinner • W

They have good brisket, chicken, pork ribs, and sausage, but strictly pedestrian side dishes. Love that runny, vinegary sauce, though.

LAKE BASTROP

To reach North Shore Park, take TX 95 north from SH 71 about 3 miles to FM 1441, then right (east) on FM 1441 • To reach South Shore Park, take TX 95 north from SH 71 about 1.5 miles, then right on SH 21 to South Shore Rd. (CR 352) • 800-776-5272, ext. 1922 • Open daily • Fee • W variable

This 906-acre lake offers recreational facilities in two parks for boating, sailing, fishing, swimming, water-skiing, picnicking, and camping. Since the lake water is used to cool an electric power generation plant, it is warmer than other Central Texas lakes that merely impound water. This means that it is tolerable for swimming earlier in the spring than other lakes, but uncomfortably warm (ninety degrees) in the summer. Fishing is good. A twelve-pound Florida large-mouth bass and a fifty-six pound catfish have been pulled from the lake; species include black striped bass, Florida largemouth, crappie, channel, yellow, blue, and flathead catfish, and perch. The best bass fishing is December through March. Minicabins and canoe rentals are available at South Shore Park, which is the more popular of the two parks. An observation-picnic area adjacent to the power plant is open, free of charge, from 8 a.m. to sundown daily, from March to mid-September. To reach it, take the Plant Access Road off TX 21.

BASTROP STATE PARK

One mile east of town on SH 21; take Chestnut St. (Loop 150) from downtown • 321-2101 • Open daily • Fee • W variable

This is one of Texas' most beautiful state parks; many visitors return year after year. This pine-oak woodland covers approximately seventy square miles and is part of the most westerly stand of loblolly pines in the state, separated from the main body of East Texas pines by approximately one hundred miles of rolling, post oak woodlands. These "Lost Pines" were once part of a vast prehistoric pine forest that covered most of Texas. This forest was sustained by extensive rainfall caused by glacier activity that extended as far south as Kansas. As the glaciers subsided and the land dried out, most of the pines west of the East Texas pine belt died out. But this stand of loblolly pines remained, due to gen-erous rainfall, acidic soil, and good drainage. White-tail deer, rabbits, squirrels, opossums, and armadillos scurry through the woods. A checklist of the birdlife in Bastrop and Buescher state parks is available at the park headquarters.

Bastrop State Park comprises 5,926 acres. The land was acquired from the city of Bastrop and private owners, and the park opened in 1937. The Civilian Conservation Corps built the original park facilities. Park activities include backpacking, camping, picnicking, fishing, swimming, golfing, bicycling, wild-life viewing, hiking, and special tours. The endangered Houston toad lives in the park; call for information on guided toad tours.

The park has an 8.5-mile hiking trail, 3.5 additional miles of hiking trails, a golf course, and rustic cabins, which overlook a small lake. They are very popu-lar, and reservations often must be made months in advance. The park has a large freshwater swimming pool. There is a Texas Park Store. Wireless Internet access (Wi-Fi) is available.

A marker at the entrance of Bastrop State Park just off US 95 commemorates early settler James Goacher, who first settled in southern Lee County in 1828. He was commissioned by Stephen F. Austin to blaze a road linking Austin's lower colony at San Felipe to the upper colony at Bastrop. In return, Goacher received a league and a labor of land. Goacher chose as his smaller plot of land a worthless-for-farming section on Rabbs Creek. Why did he choose such an apparently worthless piece of land? Legend has it that Goacher had stumbled onto a lead mine on the tract in the process of laying out the "trace" (road) that bore his name. J. Frank Dobie wrote of James Goacher's lost lead mine in *Coronado's Children:*

When settlers came to Goacher's home to buy lead, so legend remembers, he would, if he did not have a sufficient supply on hand, insist on their staying at the house while he went for some. He always reappeared from a different quarter from that in which he had gone out. Sometimes he would be gone for hours, again, only for a short time. He guarded the secret of his lead ore as jealously as though it had been a trove of precious gems. Only three souls shared with him knowledge of the whereabouts of the mine, they were his two sons and a son-in-law named Crawford. One day about two years after they had settled on Rabbs Creek [1837], all four of the men met death while rushing to the house, unarmed, to repel a horde of savages. These savages, so it is claimed, knew the whereabouts of the lead, knew the fatal worth of lead bullets, and in annihilating the Goacher men and carrying off the women and children they did not kill, were but following a plan to render the colonists less formidable. Perhaps, after the massacre, they covered up all traces of the lead mine, so remote was the Goacher homestead that other settlers knew nothing of the havoc until several days later.

The mine has never been found, although several locals over the years have found large chunks of lead in and around the Rabbs Creek/Goacher area.

Head west toward Austin from Bastrop on SH 71. Two miles later, turn right onto FM 969, once the road of westward-pushing Austin colony pioneers.

Bastrop was just this side of a pipe dream in Stephen F. Austin's mind when land-hungry colonists began inching their way west toward what would become the capital city. By 1828, Leman Barker, his son-in-law Josiah Wilbarger, and their families had built a little stockade ten or so miles up the Colorado River from Bastrop on the bend of the river that still bears Wilbarger's name. These little family fortresses were a necessity, for Indian raids continued through the 1850s in these parts. The first settlement west of Bastrop on what we now call FM 969 was Utley.

UTLEY

Bastrop County • 30 • About 9.5 miles from Bastrop

Utley started as a trading post run by James Wilbarger, son of Josiah. Utley today is actually up the road a bit from the time-honored crossing of the Colorado where the hamlet first started. A smattering of houses is located at the original town site, at the top of the hill. The rich bottomland this road traverses was highly prized by early settlers. Take a drive out here during the spring and you will see why. The soil that produced bountiful crops of cotton and corn now produces bowers of flowers, starting with bluebonnets, paintbrushes, and primroses. Prickly poppies, phlox, verbena, gay feathers, winecups, ragworts, and lazy daisies pop out to reinforce the early bloomers, and about the time the first wave begins to fade, along come the gaillardias, horsemint, day flowers, wild petunias, trompillos, and the rest of the hot-weather flowers. Such a thorough mix of species comes only with age, and the roadside from Bastrop to Austin is a riot of color from early March through June.

Wells Prairie was the next settlement west on FM 969, generally in the area of Cedar Valley and the FM 1704 turnoff, about two miles from Utley. Martin

Wells settled here in 1831. The next road to your right is the Old Upper Elgin River Road. You continue west on FM 969.

Close by the Upper Elgin River Road turnoff on your left are the Robert Coleman historical markers. Colonel Robert M. Coleman and his family settled here in the early 1830s. Coleman was clearly a man going places in early Texas. He was the first president of the municipality of Mina in 1834. In the summer of 1835, Coleman commanded one of four volunteer companies organized to fight the Tawakoni Indians. Later that year, he commanded the Mina Volunteers, who played a supporting role in the Texas siege of Bexar (San Antonio). Coleman was a signer of the Declaration of Independence at Washington-on-the-Brazos and served as aide-de-camp to General Sam Houston at San Jacinto. Following his army discharge, Coleman commanded a company of Texas Rangers at the fort bearing his name, located in what is now east Austin. But then Coleman's luck began to run out, and not without irony. He was not too popular, it seems, with many of the men under his command. He was relieved from his Ranger command after the death of one of his men; he had encountered the subordinate in a dead-drunk state and had the man bound to a tree, supposedly till he sobered up. The man did not sober up; he was strangled to death by his bindings. Coleman had to go down to Velasco to await the decision on his case. While at Velasco, he drowned while bathing in the Brazos River in 1837. This bad luck dogged his family. His wife and oldest son were killed by marauding Indians here in 1839. A younger son was taken prisoner.

Just inside the Travis County line, about two miles from the Coleman markers, is the entry to pecan-shaded Webberville County Park on the Colorado River. It has a boat ramp, a fishing dock, softball fields, basketball courts, a hike and bike trail, and picnic facilities.

At the Blake-Manor Road turnoff, you enter Webberville, one of Travis County's earliest and wildest settlements. Stay on FM 969 through town.

WEBBERVILLE

Travis County • 350 (approximate) • About 8 miles from Utley

Webberville was first known as Webber's Prairie, after its first Anglo settler, "Dr." John F. Webber, Vermont native and War of 1812 veteran, who settled and built a stockade here before the Texas Revolution. Webber was—to say the least—an interesting character. His "doctor" title dated back to the 1820s, when on a tobacco-smuggling expedition to Mexico with Noah Smithwick he acted as a doctor for the duration of his stay, in order to divert suspicion from his real activities. It took time to disperse the tobacco, since it had to be sold in small lots so as not to arouse suspicion. American doctors were held in high esteem by the Mexicans, so Webber's services were in great demand. He achieved great fame as a healer during his lengthy stay, despite his inexperience.

Born in 1793, Webber was in Texas as part of Austin's Colony by 1826. He was granted land in the Webberville area in 1832. At some point, he married a slave, Silvia Hector. In 1834, her master, John Cryer, emancipated Silvia and her children. She and Webber would have eight more children. Even though his marriage to Silvia was very unorthodox for the time, most of his early neighbors took a live-and-let-live attitude; after all, Webber had been the first Anglo settler here. And everyone was busy enough as it was already, fighting off the Indians and trying to scratch out a living. What your neighbor did was pretty much his own business as long as it did not directly impinge on your own existence. Noah Smithwick explained:

> Webber having become entangled in a low amour, the result of which was an offspring, which, though his own flesh and blood, was yet the property of another, without whose consent he could not provide for nor protect it, he faced the consequences like a man. Too conscientious to abandon his yellow offspring and its sable mother to a life of slavery, he purchased them from their owner, who, cognizant of the situation, took advantage of it to drive a sharp bargain. Building himself a fort in the then unsettled prairie, Webber took his family home and acknowledged them before the world. The Webber family of course could not mingle with the white people, and, owing to the strong prejudice against free negroes, they were not allowed to mix with the slaves, even had they so desired; so they were constrained to keep to themselves. Still there wasn't a white woman in the vicinity but knew and liked Puss, as Webber's dusky helpmeet was called, and in truth they had cause to like her, for, if there was need of help, Puss was ever ready to render assistance, without money and without price, as we old timers know. Webber's house was always open to any one who chose to avail himself of its hospitality, and no human being ever went away from its doors hungry if the family knew it. The destitute and afflicted many times found an asylum there. One notable instance was that of a poor orphan girl who had gone astray and had been turned out of doors by her kindred. Having nowhere to lay her head, she sought refuge with the Webbers. Too true a woman to turn the despairing sinner away, Puss took her in, comforting and caring for her in her time of sorest trial. Beneath that sable bosom, beat as true a heart as ever warmed a human body. At another time they took in a poor friendless fellow who was crippled up with rheumatism and kept him for years. By such generous acts as these, joined to the good sense they displayed in conforming their outward lives to the hard lines which the peculiar situation imposed on them, Webber and his wife merited and enjoyed the good will, and, to a certain extent the respect, of the early settlers. The ladies visited Puss sometimes, not as an equal, but because they appreciated her kindness. At such times she flew around and set out the best meal which her larder afforded; but, neither herself nor her children offered to sit down and eat with her guests, and when she returned the visit she was set down in the kitchen to eat alone.

Their generosity even extended to the Tonkawa Indians who roamed the area, according to Smithwick:

> Having fleeced off the flesh of the dead Comanche, they borrowed a big wash kettle from Puss Webber, into which they put the Comanche meat, together with a lot of corn and potatoes—the most revolting mess my eyes ever rested on. When the stew was sufficiently cooked and cooled to allow of its being ladled out with the hands the whole tribe gathered round, dipping it up with their hands and eating it as greedily as hogs. Having gorged themselves on this delectable feast they lay down and slept till night, when the entertainment was concluded with the scalp dance.

This easygoing attitude no doubt contributed to the growth of Webber's Prairie. By 1840, James Manor and Frank Nash had opened up a store and saloon here, and Webberville became known as Hell's Half-Acre, or Half-Acre for short. Hard liquor flowed at several saloons, and there was little interference from the organized constabulary. A man might just ride through the saloon's front door and out the back if he had a mind to, and if he was man enough to deal with any objections to such a move. Anyone looking for a lively time came to Webberville. Lyman Wight and his band of Mormons lived here for a while before moving to Austin, spurred on by threats of tar and feathers, and rails and ropes.

A post office was established at Webber's Prairie in the 1840s. Noah Smithwick, who moved to Webber's Prairie in 1839, was the first postmaster. For this reason, the settlement was sometimes referred to as Smithwick. Smithwick also became the area's first justice of the peace. A practical and open-minded man, Smithwick explained his judicial philosophy and most interesting case:

People were all poor and struggling for a foothold in the country and I disliked to see them wrangling and wasting their slender substance in suits at law, so my usual plan was to send out my constable, Jimmie Snead, and have the contending parties brought before me, when I would counsel them to talk their difficulties over between themselves and try to arrive at a satisfactory settlement, a plan which was generally agreed to, thereby throwing the burden of costs on the judge and constable.

The most perplexing case I ever had to deal with was one in which I really had no jurisdiction. Three worthless scamps made a raid on the Lipan Indians and stole a number of their best horses. The Indians missed them almost immediately, and getting track of them, came to me to assist them in their recovery. I took the responsibility of sending two white men, Captain Beach and Andy Cryor, along with Chief Castro and a posse of Indians. They overtook the thieves down near La Grange. The ringleaders decamped, leaving a half-witted fellow to bear the consequences. The captive was brought back to me. In a quandary as to what to do with him, I turned to old Castro.

"What shall I do with him?" I asked. The old chief looked contemptuously at the poor trembling wretch, who frightened out of what little wit he ever possessed, was literally crying.

"Oh," said he, "turn him loose." I gave the young man some wholesome advice and let him go. Old Castro gave each of his white assistants a pony to compensate them for their services, and I got nothing. I have often contrasted the conduct of old Castro on that occasion with that of white men under similar circumstances. When an Indian stole a white man's horse, hanging was the penalty if he could be caught.

When my time expired my constituents were anxious to again invest me with the judicial ermine; but as I had never collected a dollar from the office, I told them I thought it should go round, and when it came my turn again I would take it. Peter Carr was the next incumbent. I was also elected lieutenant-colonel of militia when it was organized, and so held three offices at one time, but as there wasn't a cent profit in any of them, and the trust only nominal, any man could safely assume as many offices as he chose. The fees were small at best, and when paid in commonwealth paper would not keep a man in tobacco. Offices went begging. Coin there was absolutely none, and the constantly downward tendency of the commonwealth paper kept it moving lively, something like the old play, "If Jack dies in my hand, packsaddle me." I received a hatful of new, crisp, one-dollar bills in payment for a horse lost in the San Saba Indian fight.

Note that in the above case, Lipan Apaches had lodged a complaint with Smithwick against white horse thieves. In those early days, Anglo Texans often enjoyed good relations with tribes such as the Lipan Apaches and Tonkawas, united by their common enemy, the Comanches.

Smithwick described Anglo-Indian relations at Webber's Prairie in the early 1840s:

I had a gunshop in Webber's Prairie, where the friendly Indians were wont to congregate, and as they spoke very little English, using the Spanish language in their intercourse with the whites, I, having acquired a fair knowledge of the latter tongue, was often appealed to in matters of importance.

The Tonks took much interest in the social affairs of their white neighbors, attending every gathering that came to their knowledge, without waiting for an invitation. On one of the rare occasions that brought the people together for preaching, a lot of Indians assembled around the door, watching and listening as intently as if fully understanding all that was being said. At last a squaw, weary of holding a chubby baby boy in her arms, stood him up in the door where his highly original costume, consisting of a tiny bow of pink ribbon in lieu of the traditional fig leaf, attracted much attention.

A laughable little comedy enacted by a Tonkawa buck and his squaw at Half Acre affords a good example of the lofty forbearance of the Indian lord of creation toward the weaker vessel. A lot of Indians were in and around the store when one of the squaws, becoming irritated, presumably over the propensity of her lord for gambling off everything he could get his hands on, proceeded to give him a genuine tongue lashing, to judge by the volume and intensity of it. The buck only laughed at first, but becoming weary of the harangue, lit out at the door and started on a dead run. His long queue floating back was grasped by the squaw and away they went, followed by the applause of the spectators.

The friendly relations between the whites and Tonkawas was never seriously disturbed, the only cause of dissension being the pecan crop, from which the Indians derived quite a revenue, but with reckless prodigality they persisted in killing the goose that laid the golden egg, in chopping off the limbs of the trees to facilitate the gathering. This the owners of the land on which the trees grew objected to. The objection not being regarded, it was found necessary to sustain it with a shot gun in one or two instances, a proceeding that might have been productive of serious consequences had not the old chief, Placido, stood in the breach. It was old Placido's proudest boast that he had "never shed a white man's blood."

Another source of income after settlers became more numerous was game which, frightened away from its old feeding ground, was less easily obtained than formerly. Venison was the meat most frequently for sale. A lady who was in the habit of buying game once asked the vendor why he didn't bring in turkeys, they being quite numerous.

"Oh," said he, "turkey too hard to kill. Injun crawl along in the grass, deer, he say 'Maybe so, Injun, maybe so, stump' and then he go on eat. Injun crawl a little closer and shoot him. Turkey look, 'Injun, by God,' and he duck his head and run."

At the head of the Lipan tribe was old Chief Flacco, whose son, young Flacco, was the idol of the tribe. Brave and unswerving in his fidelity to the whites, his many services had likewise won him the friendship of all who knew him. In recognition of his service the Texas government presented him with a full colonel's uniform, including sword and plumed cocked hat and bestowed on him the title of "colonel." One of the department clerks taught him to write his name, which he persisted in doing according to the Spanish method, placing the adjective after the noun—Flacco Colonel. Old Flacco and his wife were often at my house, bringing presents of game and little beaded moccasins for my little boy.

Many of the newcomers to Webber's Prairie after 1840 were from the Deep South and did not approve of Webber's unusual marriage. Noah Smithwick explained:

After the Indians had been driven back, so that there was comparative safety in Webber's prairie, a new lot of people came—"the better sort" as Colonel Knight styled them—and they at once set to work to drive Webber out. His children could not attend school, so he hired an Englishman to come to his house and teach them, upon which his persecutors raised a hue and cry about the effect it would have on the slave negroes, and even went so far as to threaten to mob the tutor. The cruel injustice of the thing angered me, and I told some of them that Webber went there before any of them dared to, and I, for one, proposed to stand by him. I abhorred the situation, but I honored the man for standing by his children whatever their complexion. But the bitter prejudice, coupled with a desire to get Webber's land and improvements, became so threatening that I at length counseled him to sell out and take his family to Mexico, where there was no distinction of color.

Increasingly ostracized and living in fear of "blackbirders," those men who made a living by kidnapping free people of color and selling them into slavery, Webber finally sold out his holdings and moved the family down to South Texas, near Donna, in 1853, where they farmed in poverty on "Webber's Ranch." A Unionist, he fled to Mexico during the Civil War, returning in 1865. But try as they could, the Webbers could not avoid the war, as John S. "Rip" Ford related in his memoirs:

In response to the Federal invasion at Brownsville, the Confederates marched from the Ringgold Barracks in June 1864. Ford's troops marched down the river road. They reached the ranch of John McAllen, located below Edinburg. Just below McAllen's ranch was the ranch of John Webber. His house was visited. He closed the doors, refused admission until Ford came. His sons were made prisoners. One of them escaped and went to Fort Brown. He told the Federals that Ford had but sixty odd men. He saw no more. Accordingly, Federal authorities forwarded orders to Captain [Philip G.] Temple, commanding him to engage Ford and defeat him; and Temple could then have an easy time procuring supplies and equipments from loyal Confederate citizens in the area.

Webber died in 1882; Silvia died in 1891.

In her book, *Tales from the Manchaca Hills,* Edna Turley Carpenter wrote of her grandmother's and mother's relationship with the Webbers at Webberville, where they lived for a few years beginning in about 1846:

My mother and her mother never seemed to feel the violent resentment toward the "peculiar Webber situation" that most of their acquaintances expressed. Puss was noted throughout the region for her charity to the poor; she never refused a call for help to nurse the sick or feed the hungry—and she was personable and competent. Mr. Webber had been Grandma's neighbor before her marriage, and each spring she had always bought several bushels of peaches from him. She dried this fruit and used it during the winter to make delectable peach cobblers. She saw no reason why "the situation" should alter this traditional procedure. She held that Mr. Webber's domestic relations were none of her business and that he doubtless had reasons, unknown to her, for his behavior.

Three of Grandma's daughters, including Ma, accompanied her on one of these trips to Webberville. After the peaches had been packed it was lunchtime, and Mr.

Webber told her that he would be honored to have them as his guest. Although Grandma had brought along a box lunch, she accepted the invitation. As she and her children sat down to the savory meal, she saw that neither Puss nor any of the Webber children had any notion of joining them. It was an embarrassing plight.

Grandma said, "Well, Aunt Puss, if you're good enough to be Mr. Webber's wife, then surely you're good enough to sit down to the repast you have spread. So why don't you join us?"

Puss replied with dignity that she'd be much happier waiting on the table. "But," she added, "you're a truly great lady."

Ironically, the settlement's name was officially changed to Webberville the same year that the Webbers left for South Texas. A Colonel John Banks bought the Webber tract, established a plantation, and laid out a town site. After the Civil War, Webberville was elated at the prospect of a Houston-to-Austin railroad, but elation turned to consternation when the original route through Webberville was moved upland to the present Giddings-Elgin-Manor route. The Webberville route was too easily flooded by the Colorado River. Bypassed, Webberville lost any chance it had at long-term prosperity. By the 1880s, it boasted steam-powered gristmills and cotton gins, two churches, a school, four general stores, and 200 residents. By 1900, the population was up to 382. But the post office was discontinued in 1903, and Webberville started its gradual slide downward.

The county park on the river makes a pleasant stop. To get there, turn left (south) off FM 969, proceed several hundred feet, and follow the sign. When you leave the park, backtrack to FM 969 and head for Deatsville.

DEATSVILLE

Travis County • About 2 miles from Webberville

Farther toward Austin on FM 969 is a collection of houses known as Deatsville, which was the far western edge of old Webberville. This was the home of Peter Carr (Kerr), Travis County's first mailman. Carr would stop often along his route to entertain his friends with a tune or two. But his conviviality didn't stop there, explained Noah Smithwick:

> I was appointed postmaster [at Webberville], with a certain percentage of all the money I took in to pay me for my trouble. That was long before the advent of postage stamps, and the charge for letters was twenty-five cents, payable at either end of the line. Letters were consequently few and far between. An occasional newspaper strayed into the office and did duty for the whole neighborhood.
>
> Peter Carr was the first mail carrier, making weekly trips from LaGrange up to Austin on horseback with the mail, which was an imperceptible addition to the load, tied up in a buckskin wallet. Peter was very accommodating and when occasionally some one would meet him on the road and inquire: "Hello, Pete! Got anything for me?" Pete would reply: "I dunno; I can see." And down he would get, untying the mail sack and emptying the contents on the ground, where he would look it over and if there was anything for the inquirer, hand it out, free of charge. Peter's rural delivery system had been in operation some little time before it came

to my knowledge. I then straight-way notified the postal department that unless they would furnish a locked pouch I would throw up my commission. I served a year or more, using my dwelling house as an office, and never got a cent either for my services or office rent. I might have eventually gotten a few worthless shin-plasters, but the records of the department were lost during the archive war and my reports among them.

Carr was also one of Texas' earliest cattlemen, raising cattle at Deatsville and branding them with his registered brand KER. Many wild cattle were found in the thickets here along the Colorado River. Noah Smithwick, who lived for a time at Webberville, wrote of them as "handsome brutes, coal black and clean limbed, their white horns glistening as if polished."

Continue on FM 969.

MUD CITY

Travis County • About 6 miles from Webberville

You see no highway sign for Mud City anymore. Mud City was once a proud little community with a sense of humor. A few houses and an abandoned cotton gin still stand today. Mud City—or just plain Mud for short—grew up in the 1880s as a spillover from Hornsby Bend. Old-timers say a constantly overflowing creek nearby was responsible for the name. It made a perpetual bog out of this stretch of the Austin-to-Bastrop road, and travelers were constantly cursing the mud. Locals liked the name others used in anger, so Mud it was. Mud City even had a baseball team, named the Daubers.

Continue on FM 969.

HORNSBY BEND

Travis County • 20 • About 8 miles from Webberville

Hornsby Bend is Travis County's oldest settlement. Travis County's original surveyor, Reuben Hornsby, settled here with his family in 1832 when this was the very edge of the frontier. Life was not easy here, for the Indians attacked often, and civilization—at Bastrop—was a couple of days away. When the menfolk were away, Reuben's wife Sally had to fend off the Indians by herself. She accomplished this one time by dressing the women in men's clothes and parading them around with broomsticks on their shoulders. The ruse worked; the Indians left. Other times they were not as lucky. Violent deaths were a sad but unavoidable part of life. John Williams and Howell Haggett were killed while hoeing corn in Hornsby's field in 1836. Daniel Hornsby and William Atkinson were killed by Indians while fishing in the Colorado in 1845.

The best Indian story of all involves Josiah Wilbarger, who, you will remember, settled back toward Bastrop on the Colorado. In 1830, he, Reuben Hornsby, John Webber, Martin Wells, William Barton, and Jesse Tannehill had surveyed the north bank of the Colorado between Bastrop and Austin and then selected their head-right claims. In 1833, Wilbarger came up to Hornsby's Bend, where he was joined by William Strother, James Standifer, Thomas Christian, and John Haynie. Together they rode off for a look at the land northwest of Hornsby's grant, in the Pecan Springs area of Austin. The party had found Indian tracks but failed to find the Indians, so they gave up the search and stopped for a bit of lunch before heading back for Hornsby's place. Wilbarger, Christian, and Strother unsaddled and hobbled their horses, but Standifer and Haynie left their mounts saddled and staked. As they ate, a band of Indians attacked. Haynie and Standifer leapt for their horses and escaped, leaving the others to fend off the Indians as best they could. Strother and Christian were killed; Wilbarger took arrows in both legs and a rifle ball in his scalp. But Wilbarger was not dead. He was in fact conscious but was paralyzed by the rifle ball. He could feel no pain as the Indians ripped off his scalp; he could only hear the sound of it, a sound like thunder. He had been stripped naked except for one sock. Wilbarger was soon able to move again, and he crawled a few hundred yards toward Hornsby's before he was forced to stop, exhausted. He lay down under an oak tree and fell asleep at nightfall.

During his fitful sleep, his sister Margaret—who had died the day before in Missouri, although Wilbarger had no way of knowing this—came to him in a dream and told him not to despair; help would come. She then disappeared in Hornsby's direction. In the meantime, Standifer and Haynie had reached the Hornsby cabin and reported the deaths of Strother, Christian, and Wilbarger.

That night, Sally Hornsby dreamed twice that Wilbarger was not dead but badly wounded and lying under a tree. The next morning, she insisted that the men go rescue Wilbarger. They were reluctant to sally forth, but Hornsby prevailed. A search party went out, and advance scout Joe Rogers sighted Wilbarger first, sitting under the oak tree. He was so sunburned that Rogers first mistook him for an Indian and started to shoot, but the wounded man managed to shout out, "Don't shoot. It's Wilbarger." He was carried back to Hornsby's Bend, where he was nursed back to health. Wilbarger lived thirteen years after the scalping, but his scalp wound never healed completely, and he wore a cap of black silk over the area for the rest of his life. His death was reportedly hastened as a result of bumping his wounded head on the doorway of his home. Wilbarger died at his home on the Colorado and is now buried in the state cemetery in Austin.

At the intersection of FM 969 and FM 973 is a historical marker that tells the Hornsby saga. Most of the Hornsby family, including the Indians' victims and baseball great Rogers Hornsby, are at rest in the nearby Hornsby Cemetery. Farther on, Wilbarger's discoverer, Joe Rogers, is buried on the hill bearing his name. Rogers was himself the victim of an Indian ambush in 1837.

Two miles east of the Wilbarger marker, you pass by the Travis State School (on your left) and descend down Rogers Hill. Austin lies spread out before you, and Joe Rogers lies forever at rest in a thicket a few hundred feet north of FM 969, across from the school. Old-timers will remember Rogers Hill by another name: Hungry Hill. An anonymous *Austin Statesman* reporter went searching for Hungry Hill in 1935 and reported:

A negro settlement, Hungry Hill was so named because its soil was thin and unproductive. The stranger pulling up the hill in second gear and stopping to inquire directions gets an almost inevitable reply, "Yas suh, this is Hungry Hill and I'se the hungry man." All of which leads to the passage of a quarter from one palm to the other and silent gratitude that no hungrier hill lies beyond.

After six miles, you are back in Austin. It is unlikely that any of these pioneers—even in their wildest dreams—would have foreseen the Austin of today.

CENTRAL TEXAS STEW

....

APPROXIMATELY 165 MILES

....

V Americe tam je blaze,
Tam tece pivo po podlaze,
Krasna Amerika.

There's happiness there in America,
Beer flows on the floor there,
Beautiful America.

"Krasna Amerika," a popular nineteenth-century Czech song still sung in Texas, expresses the attraction that Texas and the United States held for millions of Central Europeans. Of all the European peoples who migrated to Texas between 1836 and World War I, the Germans came in the greatest numbers. Germans led the first European exodus to Texas, beginning in the 1830s. Thousands of their Slavic neighbors—Bohemians, Moravians, Silesians, and Wends—followed, seeking better lives, religious freedom, and liberation from their German and Austrian rulers.

The Civil War only temporarily interrupted the stream of immigrants. The flow resumed in 1866 and continued until World War I started. Germans of every faith, social class, and job category settled in Texas, but the Slavs were almost exclusively farmers and mostly Catholic. Czechs and Wends generally settled on farms in the country, rather than in the towns (like La Grange, Schulenburg, and Giddings), where many Germans settled. Today, communities with Old World names like Hostyn, Moravia, Dubina, Praha, and Serbin dot the Central Texas countryside. At their center is the church. Church steeples rise above the rolling farmlands of these immigrants' descendants, who still gather to celebrate feast days and holidays. Given Eastern Europeans' love of music, dancing, and food, at least one Slavic fest, feast, picnic, or dance occurs nearly every weekend somewhere in Texas. Most of the Catholic parish feast days fall between May and October, but other festivals and events commemorating German and Slavic heritage take place throughout the year.

CENTRAL TEXAS STEW

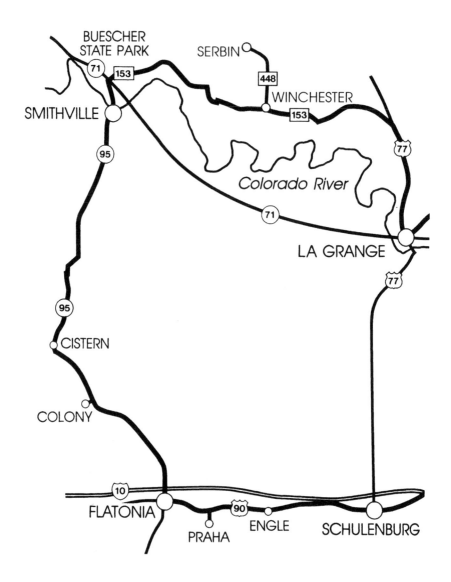

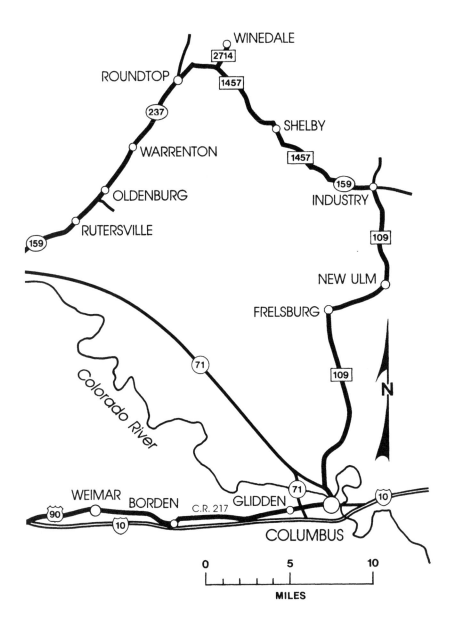

WINEDALE

2714

ROUNDTOP

1457

237

SHELBY

WARRENTON

1457

OLDENBURG

159

INDUSTRY

RUTERSVILLE

159

109

NEW ULM

FRELSBURG

71

Colorado River

109

N

WEIMAR

BORDEN

C.R. 217

GLIDDEN

71

10

90

10

COLUMBUS

0   5   10

MILES

This trip takes you through an area of Central Texas in which many Germans and Czechs settled. Much of the territory was originally settled by Anglo, Southern immigrants who came here as members of Austin's colonies. A decidedly German flavor still pervades towns and villages like Round Top and Winedale. The Czech presence is strong in Fayetteville and Praha. They commingle in La Grange and Schulenburg. Several area Lutheran churches still hold German-language services on a regular basis, and several area radio stations play polka music. Popular Tex-Czech groups such as the Red Ravens and Djuka Brothers play several times a month around greater Central Texas, at church and Czech heritage festivals, weddings, and SPJST halls.

Perhaps as much as faith and food, fraternal lodges have helped preserve Czech identity. The Slavonic Benevolent Order of the State of Texas (Slovanska podporujici jednota statu texas), or SPJST, began in La Grange in 1897 by a group of immigrants who felt that the national group, the Czech-Slovakian Fraternal Union, did not meet their needs. Nonpolitical and nonreligious, the SPJST provided social activities for Czech-Texans and assured its members help in case of sickness or need of a decent burial. It has lodges all over Texas and maintains the Czech Heritage Museum at its headquarters in Temple. Another organization, the Czech Catholic Union of Texas (Katolicka jednota texaska), or KJT, founded at Hostyn in 1889, also has lodges all over Texas. The Texas Germans, for their part, have their shooting clubs, singing societies, and Sons of Hermann lodges.

For my money, the best sausage and smoked meats in Texas come from this region, and you'll find a wide variety of other locally grown or homemade products for sale at local businesses, or from the farmer or butcher himself: honey, molasses, bread, kolaches, noodles, sauerkraut, flour, pickles, eggs, and butter.

Regrettably, this distinctive flavor fades a little more every year as the old-timers pass on. We begin in Smithville.

To reach Smithville from Austin, take SH 71 east about forty miles; then take Loop 230 (old SH 71) into downtown Smithville.

SMITHVILLE

Bastrop County • 4,000 (approximate) • (512) • About 40 miles from Austin

Dr. Thomas Gazley and family settled in the area in 1827 or 1828. He placed his headright—which was a patent to a league of land—on an expanse located on the creek now named for him, Gazley Creek. Gazley Creek flows through southwestern Smithville, entering the Colorado River just west of the Loop 230 (Old SH 71) bridge.

Frank Smith, for whom the town was eventually named, came to this area at about the same time as Gazley. The little settlement that would become Smithville began around Frederick W. Grasmeyer's trading post and ferry across the Colorado, at the Bastrop-Fayette county line, about two miles east of present-day Smithville. The little village at Grasmeyer's Crossing grew steadily. This village had several dry goods stores, a Masonic Lodge, and a post office by the centennial year of 1876. That same year, Murray Burleson bought most of the land on which Smithville now stands.

But Smithville didn't really take off until the arrival of the Taylor, Bastrop, and Houston railroad. On August 27, 1887, the first train blew its way into little Smithville. This train, a long line of flat cars with planks nailed across for seats, came from Taylor and brought passengers from every town along the route. People came from miles around to see the wonderful sight. Many of the children who had come to see their first train become frightened and ran away. The band boys stepped from the train and burst forth into a spirited march. The excited crowd joyously followed the band to the great grove of oak trees on Gazley Creek where a big barbecue was spread in celebration.

At this time, the town relocated along the newly laid tracks. Murray Burleson donated the land for the first railroad station, and a movement was afoot to re-name the town Burlesonville in his honor. Legend has it that the name dispute was settled by a coin toss; Burleson lost. The still-publishing *Smithville Times* was born in 1893. Town incorporation came in 1895, as did the Bank of Smithville, now the First State Bank.

In several years, the Missouri-Kansas-Texas (MKT) had incorporated the Taylor, Bastrop, and Houston road into its system and built a branch road to San Antonio. In 1894, it became a division point on the MKT when the road moved its regional shops here, with a working force of five hundred men. Overnight, Smithville's population doubled. Every family shared their homes with the newcomers, and still men were forced to sleep on porches, in boxcars, and on the railroad platforms. Houses sprang up like mushrooms, and in a few years the population had reached three thousand.

Smithville was home to the MKT's great regional railroad shop complex until 1957, when the MKT closed its shops. Smithville struggled for years to re-cover. The First Bank of Smithville, however, has managed to hold on through the fall of King Cotton, the Great Depression, and the railroad's pullout.

The great fire of January 16, 1896, almost wiped the town out of existence. It broke out in rear of Holmes' Grocery on Front Street at 7 p.m., and the flames quickly spread to buildings on either side, rapidly enveloping the whole block. Monday's Saloon was the second building to go, followed by the Wise Hotel, a large two-story building on the opposite side of the Holmes building. The hotel was raging with fire while firefighters tried to save the New York store behind the hotel. It was the key to controlling the conflagration, and they did it. A line was formed, water was secured from across the street, and a constant stream was kept upon the building.

Main Street, Smithville's traditional business artery, begins at the railroad tracks and goes north across Loop 230. "Downtown" Main Street is a quaint, three-block stretch of late-Victorian commercial buildings. Over thirty of these were built between the years 1895 and 1910, Smithville's golden era. A number of them still look pretty much like they did when first built. The city has in-stalled old-fashioned streetlamps. While none of the buildings are individually impressive, together they make for one of the most complete late-Victorian commercial districts in this region of Texas.

The Old Masonic Lodge (301 Main at Loop 230), a three-story red-brick building built in 1902, towers over the rest of Smithville. Its south side bears fading, painted advertising that dates back to well before World War II. Across the street, the old Rabb-McCollum building (302 Main) is Smithville's most ornate commercial building. Built in 1907, this red-brick building has buff brick trim and a simple but imposingly large cast-metal pediment.

In the Smithville post office, 400 N. Main Street, western and Depression-era art aficionados can see and enjoy the mural "The Law: Texas Rangers," by Minette Teichmueller.

SMITHVILLE RAILROAD MUSEUM AND PARK/ SMITHVILLE CHAMBER OF COMMERCE

First St., at the foot of Main St., by the railroad tracks • 237-2313 • www .smithvilletx.org • Park open daily

Smithville would be nowhere without the railroad, so the town pays homage to the iron horse with this little, though growing, museum. Kids love going through the old cabooses and motorcar outside. The museum is inside an authentic reproduction of an 1895-era station built with recycled vintage materials. It is full of early railroad artifacts, photos, logs, schedules, and such. The chamber of commerce building is also located inside the museum building.

Just south of the museum and park, where the MKT roundhouse was located, the Lower Colorado River Authority (LCRA) maintains its Smithville Railcar Facility, where the LCRA's fleet of one-thousand-plus railcars are maintained. The cars annually haul millions of tons of coal from Wyoming to LCRA's Fayette Power Plant near La Grange.

Smithville has around thirty Victorian-era homes scattered about the residential district between Loop 230, the Colorado River, and Garwood Street to the east. To start your exploration, drive north on Main from downtown to its dead end at a quaint little Colorado River overlook, and then branch out from there. In 1995, the Smithville Residential Historic District was created. It includes the area of town from First Street to the Colorado River, an area of about fifty city blocks.

SMITHVILLE HERITAGE SOCIETY HOUSE AND MUSEUM

602 Main • Open Tuesdays, during citywide events, and by appointment • Donations

This two-story frame house was built in 1908 by an MKT employee. Another metal building out back holds additional items of local history.

Other houses of note are the Burleson house (207 E. Eighth), a two-and-a-half-story Queen Anne style house built in about 1899 for Murray Burleson; the D. O. Hill house (502 Olive), built between 1856 and 1865, moved here by ferry across the Colorado River in 1891 and enlarged; and the 1915 Classical Revival Chapman-Trousdale house (201 E. Eighth).

RIVERBEND PARK

Off SH 71 • 237-3282

Located on the Colorado River, the park offers boating, a fishing pier, camping (including full RV hookups), and picnicking. There are barbecue pits. Lots of spreading oak trees provide welcome summer shade. Local celebrations are held here.

ZIMMERHANZEL'S BAR-B-QUE

Loop 230, just east of the Colorado River bridge, on the west edge of town • 237-4244 • Open Monday through Saturday 10–5 • No Cr. • W

We've had some of the best ever brisket here, very lean and flavorful. They make their own lean all-beef sausage. Chicken and lean, meaty pork ribs all cooked over oak make up the meat menu. Homemade slaw, macaroni salad, potato salad, and pinto beans are worthy accompaniments. No beer.

The best place in Smithville to stop for a cold one and for some local color is Huebel's, located at the corner of W. Second and Cleveland. Take Cleveland off Loop 230 and go one block south.

HUEBEL'S

W. 2nd and Cleveland • 237-2221 • Open daily • W

Huebel's is housed in a Depression-era gas station and garage. The main repair room has been cleaned out in favor of an assortment of tables and chairs for patrons. A jukebox with a good mix of country-and-western and polka blasts out from over by the door. There is an outdoor beer garden. The place really starts to hop in the afternoon when the domino games get going. The patrons are a good combination of old and young.

LODGING

THE KATY HOUSE BED AND BREAKFAST

201 Ramona • 237-4262 • katyhouse.com

Dry goods merchant J. H. Chancellor built this, the first two-story brick house in Smithville, in about 1909. In 1941, Dr. J. D. Stephens, MKT railroad surgeon, bought it and converted part of the ground floor into a clinic and laboratory. Now a B&B, the spacious Italianate-styled home features late-Victorian details such as leaded-glass double windows, marble wainscoting on bathroom walls, and sliding oak double doors in both of the living room inside walls. It is decorated in American antiques and railroad memorabilia. All five guest rooms offer a queen-sized bed, private bathroom, wi-fi, and cable TV. A full country breakfast is served in the main dining room every morning.

ANNUAL EVENT

APRIL

SMITHVILLE JAMBOREE

Crockett Riverbend Park • 237-2313 • First weekend after Easter • Fee • W

This community festival is complete with a carnival, a youth parade, a livestock show, a pet show, horseshoe pitching, volleyball, softball, fireworks.

From Main Street in Smithville, take Loop 230 back toward Austin a few hundred yards until you come to the intersection with SH 95. Travel south a little over fourteen miles on SH 95 to Cistern.

CISTERN

Fayette County • 75 • (361) • About 14 miles from Smithville

Cistern was settled in the early 1850s. The community was known by a variety of names during the early years, but when locals applied for a post office, they had to come up with one permanent name. At first they submitted Whiteside Prairie, after an early pioneer family. The post office nixed this name, as well as the next two proposed, Cockrill's Hill and Milton. In desperation, the locals submitted a name descriptive of the community's most distinctive feature: the cisterns dotting each yard. Local well water contained so much iron and sulfur that it was undrinkable, and each family had to build a cistern to catch their drinking water as it fell from the heavens. The post office authorities liked the name. Cistern made history in 1886 when a hailstorm ruined all the area crops, demolished every roof in the community, and killed every animal caught outside during the storm.

Back in the days of Reconstruction, some of the most largely attended public events were the Democratic barbecues. One of these great barbecues was given near Cockrell's Hill in Fayette County on July 4, 1871. There was a "tournament" in the morning, followed by a barbecue lunch, with speech making in the afternoon.

The tournament was a riding contest that gave great zest to many a neighborhood occasion, and every youth at some stage of his pilgrimage had to go through the exercise to prove himself worthy of the foemen who gathered to test his mettle. Poles were erected at certain distances apart; these poles had arms, to which rings would be attached or hung on nails. Each rider, sporting a spear, would successively gallop past these poles, the object being to catch these rings on the spear. This was great sport and was indulged in by the cowboy gentry of that period with great avidity. On nearly every barbecue occasion, there would be a tournament in the morning or in the afternoon, and the victorious knight would be privileged to crown his sweetheart queen of the occasion. The exercise called not only for expert horsemanship, but great marksmanship, because taking aim at these rings was just about like taking aim at any kind of game. Well-trained tournament horses were much in demand. The man who went into a tournament without a trained mount would always lose.

"Downtown" Cistern today consists of the V and V Sausage Company and the Cistern Country Store (361-865-3655, www.cisternstore-bar.com), located across from each other on SH 95. The one-hundred-year-old Country Store is a pleasant place to stop for a cold beer or soda water on a hot afternoon. There is some good barbecue on Saturdays: brisket, pork ribs and butt, chicken, and sausage.

ANNUAL EVENT

JULY

Cistern Catholic Church Picnic • First Sunday in July

Food is the big reason to show up in Cistern this particular Sunday noon. Sausage, stew, and all the homemade trimmings round out the menu.

From Cistern, continue south on SH 95 into Flatonia.

COLONY

Fayette County • About 5 miles from Cistern

The Colony community was established in the 1870s by former residents of Mississippi and was originally called Mississippi Colony. Three churches, several stores, and a post office once served the community. John and Margaret Young donated land in 1876 for a Methodist church and cemetery, which became the community's primary burying ground. The earliest known grave is of Methodist minister Samul J. Brown, who died in 1879. The cemetery, which is located just west of SH 95 on Colony Cemetery Road, is about all that is left of the Colony.

FLATONIA

Fayette County • 1,400 (approximate) • (361) • About 12 miles from Cistern

The present town of Flatonia has had two predecessors: Oso, which you passed through coming into Flatonia from the north, and Old Flatonia, aka Flatonia Junction, located a mile or so south.

Oso was a bustling little farm settlement with three stores, a mill, a gin, a tannery, and a blacksmith shop before the Galveston, Harrisburg, and San Antonio (GH&SA) railroad was built to Flatonia. With the railroad's arrival, Oso moved to the new town site lock, stock, and barrel.

Ditto for Old Flatonia. In the early days of Anglo Texas, Flatonia Junction was a stopping point on the old wagon road between La Grange and Gonzales. The village was named for F. W. Flato, who came to Texas in the 1840s as a ship captain. In that capacity, he carried hundreds of Texas-bound Adelsverein immigrants. Eventually he settled down at this wagon road junction and opened up a store.

In the early 1870s, Flato caught wind of plans by the GH&SA railroad company (later the Southern Pacific railroad) to extend their line from Alleyton to San Antonio. In 1873, Flato, John Lattimore, and John Kline bought the present Flatonia town site from the Faires brothers and offered GH&SA president T. W. Peirce one-half interest in the new town if Peirce would route his new line through the town. Peirce accepted, and when the railroad came in 1874, the whole population of Old Flatonia loaded their houses and goods on wagons and moved en masse to the new town site.

The first train arrived at Flatonia on the evening of Saturday, April 18, and trains began running back and forth daily two days later.

Incorporated in 1875, Flatonia immediately boomed. For a time after the railroad's arrival, Flatonia served as its western terminus. During that time, Flatonia was a crossroads market for cattle and produce. The town was full of cowboys and gandy dancers whose idea of a good time was drinking, gambling, whoring, and shooting up the town whenever the urge struck them, much to the consternation of the law-abiding Flatonians. Things eventually calmed down as the railroad progressed westward to San Antonio. But Flatonia continued to prosper.

By May 1877, Flatonia had an estimated population of one thousand souls. Being situated near the north line of Lavaca and Gonzales counties, many of their inhabitants came to Flatonia to purchase their supplies. Flatonia had about twenty stores, several saloons, two hotels, one livery stable, one bakery—and soon another—one millinery establishment, two blacksmith shops, two drugstores, two saddlery shops, one tin and stove establishment, three shoemakers, a Masonic and Odd Fellows' hall, and a schoolhouse.

The Germans of Flatonia and the vicinity held their first Mai Fest on May 1, 1877, at the schoolhouse at Old Flatonia. The morning opened bright, and at an early hour the farmers and citizens from the surrounding country began to pour in, so that by nine o'clock, Flatonia was full of men, women, and children. The procession was formed by the marshal, A. Linkilstein of Flatonia, and C. Brunnel of New Prague, and marched through the principal streets, headed by the High Hill brass band. They then marched to New Prague (Praha) and from thence to the schoolhouse at Old Flatonia, where the day and night were spent in true German style.

The procession was one and a half miles long. All the wagons were decorated with the German and American flags. The first car contained emigrants coming to Texas. This car represented Germans with families and baggage checked to Flatonia and was drawn by four yoke of oxen.

The second car represented ten years later and was drawn by mules. This car was fitted up with a parlor set of black walnut furniture and was intended to show the progress they had made in ten years. It carried an elegant family.

The third car represented mechanics at work. It contained blacksmiths, tinsmiths, carpenters, painters, harness makers, shoemakers, and barbers.

The fourth car represented the City Market, and it contained beef, vegetables, bread, and cake.

The fifth car contained Old Flatonia schoolchildren and was beautifully decorated.

The sixth car contained the queen, Miss Eda Koch. This car was most gorgeously fitted up, and the maids of honor surrounded the queen.

The seventh car contained the old and the new way. The old way, in front, was loaded with lager beer, wines, and the like, and the new way, at the back, had cold water drawn from a new well on the car.

The eighth car was loaded with Flatonia schoolchildren and teachers.

The ninth car was full of little boys and was tastefully decorated.

The tenth car was drawn by three teams nicely decorated and contained the schoolchildren of New Prague.

After this came citizens in carriages, in wagons, and on horseback. They reached the grounds at 1 p.m., where dinner was awaiting them. After dinner, Miss Eda Koch, of New Prague, was introduced and crowned. After the coronation, all took part in tripping the light fantastic toe until a late hour.

The celebration at Flatonia on the Fourth of July was a success, with from five thousand to seven thousand people being present, but the best order was observed, Sheriff Rabb having a large squad of extra policemen on duty.

Colonel Pocahontas Edmondson founded what is now the *Flatonia Argus* on January 1, 1875, in Schulenburg, and the paper moved here in March 1878. It is still published weekly, Fayette County's oldest paper and Flatonia's oldest continuous business.

That year, folks were predicting that Flatonia would soon become the new county seat for Fayette County, or even a new county.

E. J. Hartrick, a prominent scientist of the day, and his wife, of Galveston, spent the summer of 1878 in Flatonia to develop the mineral properties of nearby Ameler's Wells, which was hotly anticipated as the promised rival of Burditt's Wells near Luling.

Flatonians were overjoyed in 1880 when the San Antonio and Aransas Pass railway announced its plans to build a new line from Waco to the Gulf Coast, smack-dab through Flatonia. The town envisioned itself as the future rail center of Texas.

In 1880, Flatonia was a booming town with two thousand inhabitants. Two Vienna-trained pharmacists opened up a drugstore. Fur buying was a brisk industry, and tens of thousands of pounds of cotton were ginned and shipped out. Many substantial brick-and-limestone buildings were erected. Flatonia now had a furniture store, a community dance hall, and an opera house. Many of the commercial buildings from Flatonia's golden era still stand, but at least 40 percent of them are deserted today.

The SA&AP came through in 1888, but its arrival had just the opposite effect from the anticipated one. Instead of unparalleled growth, business fell off in the town. The farmers and ranchers who used to come in from miles around to trade in Flatonia started going instead to the new towns that sprang up along the railroad. In just a few years, the population dropped to eight hundred. Flatonia has not yet recovered; in 2000 it had about 1,400 citizens.

But Flatonia is not dead by any means. The "Twinkle in the Lone Star," as the town calls itself, is home to several industries, the most interesting of which is the mining of fuller's earth. The countryside around Flatonia is full of fuller's earth, and the material plays several very important roles in our lives, roles that not many of us are aware of. Fuller's earth serves the oil-drilling industry as a well filler and sealer. A coarser, granular grade of fuller's earth serves the average American as an oil absorber for garage floors and as kitty litter.

Downtown Flatonia has two main streets: North Main, which is US 90, and South Main, which parallels US 90 on the south side of the railroad tracks. SH 95 becomes Penn Street within Flatonia. Many of Flatonia's oldest buildings are located on North Main, South Main, and Penn.

ARNIM AND LANE MERCANTILE

102 W. North Main at Penn

The 1886 Arnim and Lane Mercantile building is one of Flatonia's most attractive and enduring commercial buildings. Essentially unaltered over the years, it is a great example, inside and out, of brick commercial architecture from that era. E. A. Arnim and Jonathon Lane founded the store in 1878. Most all of the fixtures are more than a century old, including the cast-iron rope dispensers. The wraparound interior balcony was added in the early 1920s. E. A.'s son, Doug, kept the store open until his death in 2001, not to make money, but more like a public service gesture on his part. The store was truly a step back in time. Doug Arnim was a 1930 UT Law School graduate.

E. A. ARNIM ARCHIVES AND MUSEUM

101 N. Main at Penn, across from Arnim and Lane Mercantile • 865-3720, 865-3368, 865-3643 • Open Sunday 9–3 • Donations • W partial

This museum is based upon the extensive collections of Douglas Arnim's brother, the late E. A. Arnim Jr., known as "Uncle Sam." E. A. Arnim Sr. had wanted to name him Ulysses Samuel Arnim so that his initials would be U.S.A. Mrs. Arnim vetoed that, but people began calling him Uncle Sam anyway. He grew up to be a lawyer and Fayette County judge, but his great passion was scouring the countryside collecting things, with the idea of establishing a museum in Flatonia. Out back of the museum is a nineteenth-century livery stable crammed with his accumulation of early farm machinery, tools, and household items.

Continue on Penn across US 90 to South Main. Once you are across the railroad tracks, you will see two wooden buildings on your right.

The larger, two-story building, Flatonia Tower No. 3, was built in 1902 by the Southern Pacific to control the GH&SA/SA&AP interlocker, where the two sets of tracks crossed. One of the SP's last manually controlled towers (workers pushed and pulled levers to switch the tracks), it was retired in 1996 and moved here from its original location just west of town. It has been repainted in standard SP colors, mustard yellow with brown trim. Restoration is ongoing. For an update on the status of this and other Flatonia attractions, visit www.flatonia-tx.com. Vintage SP buildings like this along the historic "Sunset Limited" route are now few and far between. Southern Pacific enthusiasts can get an idea of what Flatonia's SP complex looked like in 1902 by visiting Sanderson, in Terrell County, which has one of the state's best collections of original SP buildings, beginning with the 1883 depot. Visit the website at www.sandersontx.org to see photos, or better yet, ride out on the Amtrak's Sunset Limited from San Antonio.

The smaller, maroon-with-black-trim structure is the old Flatonia city jail, as you might guess from its small, barred windows and stout door.

The 100 blocks of E. and W. South Main have several interesting buildings.

OLD POST OFFICE

116 E. South Main

Flatonia's old post office is also of the Commercial Classical school, but not nearly so striking in its simplicity, due in part to the use of dark red brick. But it has its charm—note the complete absence of pressed-metal gaiety in the roofline: it's all brick, except for the coffeepot center finial and flanking volute.

FOSTER BUILDING

120–122 E. South Main

Down at the east end of the block is the 1886 Foster building, home of the Lyric Theater, a two-story, fortresslike building with Gothic overtones. But the Foster building is most notable for the fading old signs painted on its western wall: "Piedmont: The Cigarette of Quality, 10 for 5 cents" and "Meet Me at the Happy Hour Theatre Tonight." Once a favorite advertising medium, the walls of buildings stand increasingly pristine these days (except for the work of vandals), and the signs that remain fade a little more each year. At press time, happily, restoration of the "Meet Me at the Happy Hour Theatre Tonight" signage had commenced.

CITY MARKET CAFE

124 E. South Main • 865-3384 • Open Tuesday through Sunday, lunch only • No Cr. • W

At one time a grocery store, the City Market is now a restaurant with a good, down-home lunch buffet and a few antiques and collectibles on the side.

OLD HOSPITAL AND OPERA HOUSE

109 W. South Main

A block west of the City Market is the Old Flatonia Hospital and Opera House. Dr. George Washington Allen founded Flatonia's first hospital in 1896 and built this brick, Romanesque Revival building in 1897 to house it. In 1910, the opera house was established upstairs. The building was sold in 1914 and has housed a variety of businesses since.

MILLER BUILDING

214 S. Penn, just south of South Main

The *Flatonia Argus*, Flatonia's oldest ongoing business, is published inside this little 1886 brick building. The *Argus* is now printed on computerized presses, but the old ones are still inside, gathering dust.

FRIENDLY TAVERN

216 S. Penn, just south of South Main • Open daily • No Cr. • W
Here you will find cheap, cold beer and friendly service.

Flatonia's old home district is located behind S. Main; the greatest concentration of Victorian and pre–World War I homes are on S. Penn, S. Market, and S. Converse. S. Market and S. Converse run parallel to S. Penn.

OLLE HOTEL

218 S. Market Ave. • 361-772-0310 • www.ollehotel.com
They have ten rooms in a homey atmosphere, and one nearby apartment. Rooms feature antique and antique-looking furnishings with modern amenities, like wireless Internet, cable TV with DVD players, and locally baked Czech-Tex delicacies for breakfast.

ANNUAL EVENT

OCTOBER

CZHILISPIEL

Downtown • 865-3920 • Last weekend in October • Most events free • W variable
Flatonia's big annual blowout is the Czhilispiel, a three-day Czhili cook-off-cum-everything-else affair. A Biergarten, a carnival midway, and street and folk dances are just a few of the Czhilispiel's draws.

Leave Flatonia on US 90, heading east toward Schulenburg.

As you drive through these gently rolling hills, now rather thickly covered with trees, reflect on this fact: When the railroad came through this then sparsely populated territory, scarcely a tree grew as far as the eye could see, just a sea of chest-high wind-waving grass.

Not quite three miles out of Flatonia, you come to the FM 1295 intersection, and if you look right down that road, you'll see the tall Gothic steeple of St. Mary's Catholic Church in Praha (one of Fayette County's four "painted" Catholic churches) about a mile south of you. Go south on FM 1295 to reach Praha.

PRAHA

Fayette County • 25 • (361) • About 3 miles from Flatonia

Anglo Texans like James Duff and the Criswell brothers—William and Leroy—first settled this area. These Texas Revolution vets called the place Mulberry, a name that stuck through at least the late 1870s. With the arrival of an outlaw gang who made this pretty little valley their new base of operations, the place was more notoriously known as Hottentot. Little information has survived about this supposed gang, but we do know that in May 1875, the body of a stockman, styling himself G. A. Duncan of Dogtown, was found in Hottentot Cemetery, one mile west of Praha, with a bullet hole through his head. He was supposed to have been murdered. His true name was later ascertained to be Cass Perry, from Dallas, and his death was probably the result of an old quarrel. The unknown man who was shot in Schrip's Saloon in October died soon after.

Six months later, some stock men of Goliad County reported to Inspector G. W. Bell that a herd of cattle had been taken out of the county without inspection. Mr. Bell summoned a party to go in pursuit, and they found the cattle, some sixty or seventy in number, in the hands of one Mr. Perkins and a couple of other hands, all of Goliad County, at Praha. The men and cattle were taken charge of and brought back, and affidavits were made out against Mr. Perkins, who claimed to be only a boss hand for one Mr. J. H. Martin. Perkins was put under a bond for $3,000 and Martin for $6,000.

During the mid-1850s, a Bohemian immigrant named Mathias Novak arrived. After working for the American settlers, he saved enough money to buy one hundred acres of land and build a house where early masses were celebrated with other Bohemian immigrants who began to move here in about 1858. They renamed the hamlet Praha after their capital and cultural center in the homeland. It was also called Maticka Praha ("Mother Prague") because it was the mother parish for surrounding towns.

To the outside world, the village was known as New Prague from the mid-1870s until about 1885, when they too began calling it Praha.

In October 1878, an Anglo visitor described his visit to New Prague, a "Bohemian" town:

> The country around for seven miles is settled up with Bohemians. All of them have small farms, and judging by the outward-appearance of their fields they are undoubtedly successful farmers. They are a hard working, industrious and sociable people. While passing through here yesterday I found the town full of men, women and children. All came to attend church in the morning, and after church they do their shopping, talk about their crops and enjoy a social glass, and not unfrequently the young people get up a hop and spend the evening in tripping the light fantastic toe. As this is a busy season with them they don't have time during the week to attend political meetings.

The Bohemians had a grand ball at New Prague every Sunday night, which was well attended, as a rule, by young men from Flatonia. Generally they got along well. But one Sunday night in 1882, there was quite a delegation from Flatonia, who reported matters as having been very lively. Pistol shooting was the principal sport of the occasion. A gentleman residing near the place said it sounded just as though a battle was progressing.

In 1892, at a Saturday night dance, John Bacha was shot and instantly killed by Anton Bohuslau. The row originated over the question of who should dance with a certain girl.

The parish of St. Mary's at Praha was first served by Father Victor Gury, who came from Frelsburg. The first sanctuary was a small frame structure built in 1865. Mass was first offered there on Christmas Day 1865. It was replaced in 1866 by another frame church building, then by another in 1876. The current, soaring Saint Mary's sanctuary was built in 1895 and is commonly regarded today as the mother church for Texas Czechs. It cost $12,000 and took five years to build. Back then, Praha also boasted America's first Czech parochial school and close to seven hundred people lived around here.

In November 1891, large quantities of building stone from the Muldoon quarries were being shipped to Flatonia and hauled to Praha for use in the construction of the church. The cornerstone was laid on May 1, 1892.

November 20, 1895, was the grandest day in Praha's history. The occasion was the dedication of the present-day Catholic church. About ten thousand people were present, consisting principally of Germans and Bohemians. The dedication services were performed by Rt. Rev. Bishop J. A. Forest of San Antonio, assisted by about twenty priests. The church was described as "a fine structure, built of rock and will last for all time. It will seat about 1,000 people but only a small portion of the crowd could gain access yesterday." The reception accorded to Bishop Forest was flattering in the extreme. When the Southern Pacific train arrived from San Antonio, the bishop was met at the Flatonia depot by a large crowd of people in buggies, wagons, and on horseback. The Flatonia city band was also in attendance, dressed in their fine new uniforms. The procession, led by one hundred horsemen, then began the march to Praha, distant about three miles from Flatonia. After the dedication services, three sermons were preached, one in German, one in Bohemian, and one in English. There were people present from Fayette and several adjoining counties, and altogether the occasion was one long to be remembered by those participating.

The church exterior is spare, void of gargoyles and other gewgaws, but a Gothic masterpiece nonetheless, thanks to the religious paintings that adorn the interior walls and ceilings.

In 1895, Godfrey Flury was commissioned to paint the interior of St. Mary's Church. Born in Switzerland in 1864, he came to the United States with his family at age sixteen. After stays in New York, Kansas City, and San Antonio, he ended up in nearby Moulton in 1892, where he painted church and home exteriors and interiors. The St. Mary's commission produced the most important work of his career. He painted the tongue-and-groove plank ceiling sky blue and emphasized the church's classic vault with trompe l'oeil ribs that echoed medieval stone vaulting. The wooden columns received painted Gothic capitals. The ceiling was divided into panels ornamented with painted vines, flowers, curving gold scrolls, and symbols such as a chalice, a star, and an eye within a radiant triangle. Above the altar, Flury painted the great cathedral in Prague and a well-known convent outside Prague. At the highest point above the altar, he painted three angels around a jeweled cross.

His work won Flury other commissions, such as the sheet-steel ceilings of the Lavaca County courthouse, the interior of St. John's Church (near Schulenburg), and the interior of the church in Cestohowa, but evidence of his work has disappeared or been painted over. The painted ceilings in several Flatonia homes have been attributed to Flury.

Like many other Texas farming towns, Praha slowly declined, and the school closed in 1973. Praha today consists of St. Mary's Church, the old school, a couple of houses, and Felix Hajek's old garage ("Since 1931"), which is now a Tex-Czech exhibit ("Automotive: A Family Tradition"), opened limited hours (call 361-865-2512 or 979-249-6242, weekends). But Praha is more than just a tiny town; it is a community whose citizens live all over Texas. These Czechs and their friends—over five thousand of them—squeeze into Praha every year to celebrate Czech homecoming at the Praha Homecoming.

ANNUAL EVENTS

AUGUST

PRAHA HOMECOMING

St. Mary's Catholic Church, FM 1295 • 865-3560 • August 15 • Meal and dance tickets • W

Since 1855, thousands of Czechs from across Texas have been returning to "Maticka Praha" on August 15 to celebrate the church's feast and to participate in *Prazska pout* ("Praha Homecoming"). The celebration is always held on this date, regardless of the day of the week, and Praha is said to be the only Roman Catholic parish in the United States with such a custom. The celebration begins with a march from the parish hall to the church, where three masses are said throughout the day. From noon on, there's food and drink (most prominently a dinner of picnic stew, fried chicken, and sausage, and naturally lots of beer (or *pivo*), merriment, reminiscing, game booths, entertainment by Czech dancers and singers, and music (Czech and country-western) for dancing late into the night.

In 1935, Governor James V. Allred addressed the crowd, estimated at between six thousand and seven thousand people, and commended them on the fine citizenship their community represented. After his address, two dances were given. The crowd was estimated as being the largest in the history of the celebration.

NOVEMBER

VETERANS DAY MEMORIAL CEREMONIES

St. Mary's Catholic Church, FM 1295 • 865-3560 • November 11 • Free • W

Texas Czechs are proudly patriotic, and their annual Veterans Day ceremonies are among the largest and most impressive in the country. Thousands of visitors come to praise and remember our soldiers. Ceremonies usually include a twenty-one-gun salute, silver taps with echo, a missing-man formation flown by the U.S. or Confederate Air Force, bands, speakers, an air show, a dinner, and of course beer.

ENGLE

Fayette County • 106 • About 4 miles from Flatonia, excluding Praha side trip

The next little burg down US 90 is Engle. The area was thinly settled by Bohemian and Czech immigrants in the 1850s, but their community focus was at Praha to the southwest. In 1874, Engle was established as a stop on the Galveston, Harrisburg, and San Antonio railway, named after railroad engineer J. E. Engle. A post office was established in 1888, and the first store in 1890. By 1900, Engle had three saloons, two stores, a blacksmith shop, a tinsmith shop, a lumberyard, and a photography studio. Sometime after 1930, its post office closed. By 1950, six businesses served a population of 250. When this book first came out in 1983, the chief (and only) attraction at Engle was the Jerry Simek Place (long closed), a humble little beer joint notable for serving the cheapest Shiner beer in Texas, in addition to local homemade noodles and fresh churned butter. The little whitewashed frame building still stands.

Five miles east of Engle, turn left on FM 2672 to reach the old High Hill community, approximately four miles north of US 90.

HIGH HILL

Fayette County • 116 • About 9 miles from Engle

Starting in about 1844, German immigrants established three small settlements in this part of southern Fayette County: Blum Hill, Oldenburg, and Wursten. Blum Hill, in what is now the southern part of High Hill, was named for German left-wing political activist Robert Blum, who was assassinated in 1848. Oldenburg, in what is now the northern part of High Hill, was named for a German province. Wursten is an area in the north German low country near Bremerhaven (although some say that Wursten got its name from the good sausage, or *wurst*, made by the Anders Meat Market). Henry Ebeling opened a store in Oldenburg in 1847, and John F. Hillje was operating a cotton gin and saw/gristmill. In either 1858 or 1860, a post office was established, and the three communities combined under the post office's name, High Hill. The Germans were supplanted by a wave of Czech immigrants starting in 1860.

In 1860, several families from the towns of Neudek and Bolten in Moravia were inspired to make the long perilous journey to Texas. The group included Joseph and Anna Heinrich, Franz and Anna Wick, Anton and Anna Bednarz, and Andreas and Anna Billimek. First they traveled to Bremen, Germany. On September 15, 1860, the group boarded the sailing ship *Jeverlin* at Bremen; they arrived at Galveston on November 19. From Galveston they made their way by oxcart to Fayette County. The carts had wooden frames covered with rawhide, and the wheels were slabs cut from large-diameter trees, with boards fastened across them to keep them from falling apart; they were pulled by two or more oxen.

This group stopped at Dubina, and after a few days of visiting and resting with the Czech families living there, they traveled the last few miles west to High Hill, where they camped under a cluster of large trees. The countryside was mostly prairie, with timber starting a short distance toward the west. Wild game was plentiful, and local streams supplied fish. The new settlers cleared the land for farming and built rail fences to keep the cattle out of their fields. Families raised one cash crop, usually cotton. The proceeds of its sale were spent on necessities that could not be grown or manufactured at home.

Most of the recent arrivals were Catholic and were disappointed that they would not be able to celebrate their first Christmas in the usual manner. They heard of the Catholic settlement of Frelsburg about twenty-five miles to the northeast, and some of the men decided to walk over there and talk to the pastor, Father Victor Gury. They arrived in time for Christmas Mass. They arranged for Father Gury to come to High Hill three or four times a year to celebrate Mass. The first such Mass was celebrated in 1861 in the Andreas Billimek home. Later, the Franz Wick cabin was used for regular services until the first church was built.

The first funeral was for five-year-old Joseph Bednarz, who had been playing in a cotton field while his parents burned the stalks. His clothes caught fire, and he was badly burned. He died two days later.

When the Civil War broke out in 1861, some of the men joined the Confederate Army, others escaped into Mexico, and some went to New Orleans and joined the Union Army. Still others hid in the woods when Confederate soldiers appeared in the neighborhood to conscript additional men for the army. Some men dressed in women's clothing and continued their farming chores under the noses of the soldiers.

High Hill was the only town in south Fayette County until after the Civil War. With two private schools drawing students from all over the state, High Hill was a center of culture for the region. The local choir and orchestra were in great demand at Saengerfests throughout Texas. In 1869, High Hill had six stores, three blacksmith shops, a couple of grocery stores and saloons, a hotel, a shoe shop, and a brewery among its business establishments.

Two major roads crossed at High Hill. The road running from east to west was the main road from San Antonio to Houston, traveled by stagecoaches and wagons that carried passengers, mail, and freight. The north-south road was the stage road from Victoria to La Grange and points farther north.

By 1870, around three dozen Catholic families lived in the High Hill area. They wanted a proper church, so they hauled lumber by oxcart from Columbus and sawed it at the Hillje sawmill. The whole community pitched in to build the church, which was located on nine acres of donated land. Christian Baumgarten supervised construction of that first church, which was blessed on September 8, 1870. This church was originally named "Nativity of Mary, Blessed Virgin" but is now generally just called St. Mary's. In 1875–1876, a larger church was constructed, and the smaller one became St. Mary's School. The second church was torn down to make way for the present sanctuary.

T. W. Peirce and James Converse passed through the area in 1873 looking for a route to San Antonio for their GH&SA railroad. They were interested in establishing a station in High Hill, a prominent stagecoach stop on the overland mail route between Washington, D.C., and San Francisco. But their request for a right-of-way through High Hill was rebuffed.

"Railroads are just a fad," it is said High Hillers told them. "We don't want to ruin our country with a railroad. We can go off and leave our houses unlocked. We won't be able to do that if your railroad comes through." So the GH&SA line went through two miles south of High Hill. In just a few years, High Hill was on the road to becoming a ghost town, as folks began moving to Schulenburg and the railroad, rolling their houses and businesses over on logs.

In 1884, the town had two hundred residents, four schools (including a Catholic parochial school), two saloons, two general stores, a church, and a steam gristmill and cotton gin. In 1900, the population was 134. The post office closed in 1907, and by 1940, High Hill had a population of 75 and three businesses.

Despite the population decline, there were enough people in the neighborhood to build St. Mary's Catholic Church, a red-brick Gothic Revival sanctuary, in 1906. One of the "painted" churches of Fayette County, it is partially built with material from the sanctuary it replaced. Its interior has some of the most elaborate and sophisticated decorative painting to be found in Texas churches. All the ceiling, walls, and columns are painted. The nave is separated from the two side aisles by octagonal wooden columns painted to look like marble. The ceilings and walls are painted with Greek and religious motifs. San Antonio artists Ferdinand Stockert and Hermann Kern did the work in 1912, combining freehand painting with stenciling. The High Hill cemetery (one mile south) has many old stones with Czech and German inscriptions.

A few dozen yards north and west of the church stood Texas' first cottonseed oil mill, a barnlike structure of stucco over brick built in 1866 by Frederick Hillje. Hillje first used a modified sugar beet crusher imported from Germany. Later, he installed regular cottonseed-milling machinery. But the mill failed after just a few years, for cottonseed oil was then an almost unknown commodity. High Hill Springs are on the east side of the settlement and once supplied a brewery. Their flow is now greatly reduced.

From High Hill, return to US 90 on FM 2672 and continue east on US 90 into Schulenburg.

SCHULENBURG

Fayette County • 2,700 (approximate) • (979) • About 13 miles from Flatonia, excluding Praha side trip

Schulenburg, which in German means "city of schools," was a child of the GH&SA railway. As was often the case all over Texas, the railroad spawned one town and killed off another; Schulenburg was born at High Hill's expense. Schulenburg was part of a 4,428-acre tract of land granted to Kesiah Crier by the Mexican government in 1831, which ran along the West Navidad River. After 1845, the Crier family began to sell off pieces of the league, which brought more population to the southern half of Fayette County.

In 1873, the railroad bought Louis Schulenburg's 450-acre farm, along with tracts owned by Franz Stanzel and Christian Baumgarten. Since the railroad's depot was to be located on Schulenburg's land, Christian Baumgarten suggested that the new town should be named after him. The passenger and freight depots opened for business on December 8, 1873, and on December 31, the first passenger train chugged into Schulenburg. Lawrence Keller was the first stationmaster. Just a few months later, he was crushed to death between two boxcars and buried in the High Hill cemetery, since Schulenburg didn't have one yet.

The town may have been named for Louis Schulenburg, but Christian Baumgarten was the "Father of Schulenburg." The Baumgarten Lumber Company was the first business in Schulenburg, located at the railroad tracks on N. Main at Wolters.

Baumgarten built Schulenburg's first frame, stone, and brick buildings; established furniture and hardware stores, a cotton gin, a mill, and a sash and door factory; and initiated the first commercial manufacturing of curly pine furniture in Texas. The working of curly pine is now an extinct art, but a prime example of the wood's beauty can be found at the Sisterdale General Store in Sisterdale.

But Baumgarten is most famous for his work with cottonseed oil. Baumgarten and his son Gus built a cottonseed oil mill here in 1883. Gus took up where his father left off, building oil mills in Hempstead, Rockdale, Caldwell, Taylor, Kyle, Luling, and Hallettsville. Gus Baumgarten worked tirelessly promoting cottonseed oil as a cooking fat. The result was a revolution in American cooking; housewives began to use vegetable fats in their kitchens rather than the traditional butter and animal fats, a trend that has continued right into the 1990s and 2000s.

Gus Baumgarten also developed a starch-free flour from cottonseed meal, which is useful for diabetics. His Baumgarten Process Allison Flour has five times the nutritive value of wheat flour. While government chemists were in Schulenburg studying the Baumgarten flour-making process in 1917, Gus Baumgarten effected another revolutionary change in the American kitchen. Baumgarten had been fiddling around with a thermometer in his home oven. He invented controlled-heat baking in the process. Herbert Hoover, who had sent the government chemists down to the Schulenburg mill, heard of Baumgarten's experiments and wrote asking if he would please instruct by mail 2,385 home economists, who would then demonstrate this new baking method all over the country. The end result was a thermostat on almost every oven subsequently produced in America. These days it's hard to imagine an oven without one.

Born in Prussia in 1836, Christian Baumgarten was a carpenter by age fourteen and an orphan by eighteen. Thereupon he set sail for America, landing at Galveston, where he worked till he had saved enough money to move inland. Baumgarten came to Fayette County in 1857, buying land in this area shortly thereafter for ten dollars an acre. Its value mushroomed when Schulenburg was born.

Baumgarten built the Immigration House in 1875 for Franz Russek. Russek, who was immigration agent for the railroad, helped bring hundreds of newly immigrated German and Czech families to the area. Most of the Czechs were farmers, and Schulenburg served as a trading center for them. They and other local farmers raised many bumper crops of cotton from the rich soil. Schulenburg had one of the area's biggest cotton presses. From here, the bales went by train to the great ports of Houston and Galveston.

In 1875, Schulenburg incorporated. During its time as the railroad's western terminus, Schulenburg attracted its share of opportunistic scalawags and was a rowdy town until the law-abiding citizens hired a man named Jamison to bring law and order to town. He "had to shoot and stab some of the bad men," but he succeeded, and Schulenburg has led a peaceful existence for the most part since.

In his 1883 best seller, *On a Mexican Mustang through Texas*, humorist Alex Sweet visited Schulenburg.

Schulenberg [*sic*] is a small town on the railroad. Almost all the inhabitants are Germans—thrifty, hard-working people, who attend to their own business with more enthusiasm than the native American can ever be accused of doing.

They have a mayor and a board of aldermen in Schulenberg, and city ordinances are made by the aldermen. Those that are not vetoed by the mayor are broken by vagrant hogs, stray cows, and inebriated cowboys. There is a newspaper published in Schulenberg. Its columns are devoted to the mayor's proclamations, the railroad time-table, patent-medicine advertisements, and reports of aldermanic discussions on municipal affairs. The absorbing topic at Schulenberg, when we were there, was, "Shall we continue to employ our present efficient police-force?"

The "efficient police-force" consisted of a large man, whose clothes had apparently been made for a smaller policeman. He was armed with a very large revolver. His trousers did not quite reach his ankles; they had evidently been pulled before they were ripe.

By 1885, Schulenburg had more than one thousand inhabitants, 90 percent of whom were foreign born, mostly Czech and German. But a handful of families were Jewish. One hundred years ago, Jewish communities flourished in many small towns throughout Texas, such as Schulenburg, Luling, Gonzales, and Columbus. Most are gone today, their descendants having moved to Texas' largest cities. At the turn of the century, this area's congregation began meeting in the Odd Fellows Hall in Hallettsville, twenty miles south of Schulenburg. Jews from the surrounding towns, such as Flatonia, La Grange, Columbus, and Weimar, would gather to celebrate religious holidays. After World War II, it became apparent that the locus of membership had moved north, and members decided to build a synagogue in Schulenburg, which was dedicated in 1951. Hirsch Schwartz, born here in 1909, served as Schulenburg's mayor from 1963 to 1981. Today, Schulenburg's Temple Israel is one of the few remaining Jewish synagogues in small-town Central Texas.

Schulenburg has always been an industrious little town. Texas' first evaporated-milk plant (begun in 1929), the Oak Ridge Smokehouse, poultry and egg processing plants, and the Victor Stanzel Company (maker of model airplane kits) have been just a few of Schulenburg's industries over the years.

The best of Schulenburg's old commercial buildings are located on N. Main, two blocks south of Summit/US 90.

To get to N. Main from Summit/US 90, go south on Kessler/US 77. After one block, the road bifurcates: US 77 continues straight, passing under N. Main, the railroad tracks, and S. Main, while Kessler veers to the right, dead-ending one block later at N. Main. You follow Kessler's veer, then turn right on N. Main.

Main Street Schulenburg is a riot of elaborate brick arches, gingerbread, and frosting. Schulenburg was a prosperous town almost immediately, and substantial business buildings and homes began to be erected almost as soon as the town was created. Several of the buildings on the east end of N. Main date to the 1870s. In 1893, the Great Fire of Schulenburg destroyed a half block of buildings that had been built in 1874, specifically buildings from the west half of N. Main, along Upton Avenue, to the west portion of Anderson.

SCHAEFER BUILDING

N. Main at Kessler

Sigmund T. Schaefer built this brick building with fanciful, pinnacled roofline in 1896 to house his hardware and building supply store. He was also an undertaker; this was a common business combination in those days. The Palace was located in the eastern corner; "Palace Saloon" is still painted over the building's back entrance, which you see just before you turn onto N. Main. The *Schulenburg Sticker* newspaper (established in 1894) is now located here.

The 500 block is notable for several buildings, including the 1894 building that now houses the Upstairs at the Downstairs club (525 N. Main, 743-4040, beer, pool, darts, and dance floor). The brickwork on this two-story building is a decorative exercise in geometry and repetition that creates buff brick icing on a red-brick cake.

SENGELMANN HALL

531 N. Main • 743-2300 • www.sengelmannhall.com

The red-brick Sengelmann Brothers building, built in 1894, is downtown's tallest and one of its most elaborate buildings, newly remodeled and reopened (June 2009) as a restaurant, bar, and dance hall by a descendant of Gus Cranz.

SCHULENBURG TOURIST INFORMATION CENTER

618 N. Main • 743-4514 • Open Monday through Friday

Even when the center is closed, you can pick up an informative area guide from the rack of brochures outside.

SCHULENBURG HISTORICAL MUSEUM

631 N. Main • 743-3023 (chamber of commerce) • Open Sunday afternoons • Donation • W

Located in the 1886 C. Bohms building, the museum depicts life in Schulenburg's early days. There's a lot to see.

BAUMGARTEN COTTON GIN

700 block of N. Main

This compact, square brick building on your right was built in the mid-1870s. The bricks were made at Baumgarten's nearby brick kiln. It originally housed his mule-powered cotton gin. Such a gin might take up to three hours to compress one bale of cotton. Located at this site, at one time or another, have been a mattress factory, a wire basket works, and Gus Russek's Enterprise Bottling Works.

Continue on N. Main to West Avenue and turn right on West. One block north, at the corner of West and Anderson, is one of Schulenburg's most elaborate residences.

GUS CRANZ HOUSE

701 West at Anderson • Private residence

Whoever coined the term gingerbread for elaborate building ornamentation could have been looking at this house styled after an Austrian villa. The full-length front porch and twin staircases leading up to it are lined by balustrades comprised of dozens of balled balusters. The porch is curved to create twin porticoes, and its roofline is trimmed with an overhang of dozens more balled balusters. The gable windows are leaded glass; the foundation is covered with panels of whitewashed wood-strip fretwork. Dating to 1874, the house was meticulously built, down to its mitered and doweled joints. Builder Gus Cranz later acquired a son-in-law of some note, Hugh Roy Cullen, who became a leading Texas oil man.

BAUMGARTEN HOME

607 West

This home encases the original cedar log cabin built by John Christian Baumgarten in 1850, which was the first home built in what is now Schulenburg. The home was enlarged over the years as the family grew. The oak tree in the yard is estimated to be over four hundred years old.

Continue north, across US 90, on West Avenue to see two more of Schulenburg's old Victorian-style homes.

The Gus Russek home (409 West) is an elaborate two-story showplace built in 1909 by this business magnate of early-day Schulenburg who also served in the Texas Senate for ten years. At the far north end of West Avenue (just after it becomes County Road 415), on your left, is the two-story Ignac Russek home, built in 1893.

Finally, Schulenburg is famous as the home of the jumbo hamburger. They were ten cents a shot when longtime local restaurateur Frank Tilicek invented them during the Depression as a way to get travelers to stop at his place. Frank's Restaurant, a Schulenburg institution for over fifty years, is still open and still serving jumbo burgers.

To get to Frank's Restaurant, take Kessler/US 77 north from US 90. Turn left on Kessler and travel about a mile to the intersection with I-10.

FRANK'S RESTAURANT

I-10 and US 77 • 743-3555 • Open daily • Breakfast, lunch, and dinner • MC, V • W

Frank and Rozine Tilicek founded this place way back when US 90 was the main drag through town. They were right there, ready to cater to the hungry traveler. When I-10 lifted the traffic burden from US 90, the Tiliceks moved with the traffic. The building may be devoid of the old roadhouse charm of earlier Frank's establishments, but the food is the same: steaks, chicken, Mexican food, homemade bread and pies, and of course those venerable jumbo hamburgers. They also serve a good weekday blue-plate lunch.

CITY MARKET

Kessler/US 77 at College St., between Frank's Restaurant and Summit/ US 90 • 743-3440 • Open Monday through Saturday 7:30–5:30 • W

The City Market is one of Central Texas' best meat markets, offering their own smoked pork loin, jerky, bacon, sausage, wieners, and barbecue as well as fresh meats. Pick your barbecue off the pit in the back room and pay for it in the meat market up front. You can sit down and eat it here or take it with you.

KOUNTRY BAKERY

Kessler/US 77 at College St., across from City Market • 743-4342 • Open Monday, Tuesday, Thursday, and Friday 5:30–5, Saturday 5:30–2:00, closed Sunday and Wednesday • W

Good kolaches (I'm partial to the cream cheese and the poppy seed; there is also a variety of fruit fillings), pigs in a blanket, bread, pies, cookies, and apple strudel. Old-fashioned hamburgers and sandwiches are also served. Kolaches freeze well, so you can take a dozen home with you.

HARLAN'S SUPERMARKET

236 College • 743-4866

Harlan's is noteworthy because of its Saturday-only barbecue to go: brisket, pork ribs, chicken, and sausage. They are often sold out before 11:30.

LODGING

VON MINDEN HOTEL

607 Lyons (US 90 at Lyons) • 743-3493

Built in 1927, this building contains both a forty-room hotel that still has much of its original furnishings and a movie theater that still shows first-run movies. The Cozy Theatre opened in November 1927; the hotel in May 1928. It has a reputation for being haunted; ask the staff for the story. The hotel has a restaurant that serves pizza and American home-style cooking.

OTHER SIGHTS AND ATTRACTIONS

SAINT ISIDORE SCULPTURE

1010 Lyons Ave., southeast of St. Rose Catholic Church

The importance of agriculture and God in the lives of Schulenburgers is expressed by this sculpture, which memorializes Saint Isidore, patron saint of farmers. The sculpture was created by local artist Gene Mikulik and was dedicated in 1982. The parish celebrates the feast day of Saint Isidore every year on May 15.

STANZEL MODEL AIRCRAFT MUSEUM

311 Baumgarten St. • 743-6559 • www.stanzelmuseum.org • Open daily June and July; open Wednesday through Sunday rest of year

The museum features interactive exhibits and static displays that depict the history of model aircraft in general and the Stanzel brothers in particular. Born on a Schulenburg farm, Victor and Joe Stanzel became fascinated with aviation at an early age. Whenever a plane flew over Schulenburg during the 1920s, both boys would stop their chores to gaze up and imagine what adventures lay ahead for the lucky pilot. Victor was seventeen when Charles Lindbergh crossed the Atlantic, and the epic flight inspired him to construct and sell airplane models. Beautifully made, they cost as much as most working men earned in a week. And because of all the work involved, Victor made very little profit. Joe, eight years younger than Victor, stepped in to help. Soon they began to produce do-it-yourself balsa-wood kits that could be sold cheaply. As visitors see, the kits were very labor intensive and the results very fragile. And what's worse, they just sat there, or hung there, depending on how you displayed them.

The Stanzel brothers wanted to offer their customers the thrill of flight. For the 1936 Texas State Fair carnival, they built a Buck-Rogers-style rocket ship ride that held up to six passengers and simulated flight via an ingenious tower-and-beam system that used a water-tank counterbalance system. Water flowed back and forth in pipes from the water tank on one end of the beam to the rocket ship on the other end. The resulting weight changes caused the ship to swoop up and down like an airship. The Stanzel brothers built a similar, airplane ride that seated two. Folks came from all over the region to Schulenburg to take the ride, which also traveled the carnival circuit.

Their biggest development came in 1939, with the first control-line flying model airplane kit, the Tiger Shark. Now enthusiasts could fly their favorite models. During World War II, they invented and built a flying model plane that could be used for antiaircraft gunnery practice. Balsa-wood construction eventually gave way to injection-molded plastics. Unlike so many other small toy companies that went out of business in the 1950s, 1960s, and 1970s, the Stanzel brothers continued to produce all manner of flying planes, helicopters, racing cars, and shooting spaceships. Their factory was located two blocks south of the museum on the west side of Kessler/US 77, across the street from the Knights of Columbus Hall.

The museum's factory wing gives visitors an idea of the manufacturing process of model aircraft and rocketry at the factory.

The simple white frame house next to the museum was built in about 1870 by Victor and Joe's grandparents, Franz and Rozina Stanzel. It has been moved here from its original location outside of town. The museum docents are happy to give tours of the house, which has been restored and filled with period furnishings. Note the wall stenciling in two of the rooms, reminiscent of that seen in the Painted Churches of Fayette County.

WOLTERS PARK

West Ave., 4 blocks south of US 90; follow signs • Open daily • Free

Schulenburg's city park is named after R. A. Wolters, who donated the land in 1936. The first building moved here was Turner Hall, built in 1886 and originally located at Summit and Upton streets. It was put on logs and rolled across town to the park. Turner Hall is now the American Legion Hall. In 1941, a log cabin built by Jacob Wolters at Industry in 1835 was moved here. The spacious tree-shaded grounds are perfect for picnicking. The 112-year-old Hermis Road bridge over Mulberry Creek (about three miles southwest of Schulenburg) has been moved to Wolters Park.

ANNUAL EVENTS

SCHULENBURG FESTIVAL

Last weekend in July • Wolters Park • www.schulenburgfestival.org

Featured are a rodeo, live music, and entertainment, as well as barbecue and chili cook-offs, a biergarten, festival foods, and more.

ST. JOHN'S PARISH PICNIC

St. John's Catholic Church grounds, 6 miles southwest of Schulenburg on FM 957 • Every July 4th • W

St. John's Parish is over one hundred years old; parishioners and guests have been celebrating on July Fourth for almost as long. The day starts with 9:30 Mass and a flag-raising ceremony, and then the fun and feasting begins. Dinner is stew, fried chicken, and all the trimmings. Popular polka groups play all afternoon for your dancing and listening pleasure. There are lots of games for kids, a cakewalk, an auction, lots of cold German soda water, and more.

Leave Schulenburg on US 90 and head east toward Weimar. Five miles east of Schulenburg, turn left on FM 1383 to reach the picturesque hamlets of Dubina and Ammannsville. In 2.5 miles, you come to Dubina. Turn left on Fayette County Road 480.

DUBINA

Fayette County • About 7.5 miles from Schulenburg

"Dubina" is the Czech word for oak grove. The area was first settled in late 1856 by seven Bohemian emigrant families who spent their first night here huddled under a large oak tree.

In 1906, August Haidusek, a member of Dubina's founding group, described their arrival.

> It was in the afternoon at the end of the month of November, a brisk norther was blowing, it was raining and sleeting, when we arrived by wagon at a spot studded with oaks. Here, soaked with rain, we were left at the mercy of the weather; the only protection was the branches of the spreading oaks. There were no houses for miles around and the wagon driven by Charles and Joseph Brasher returned to La Grange. The good women wept for fear of freezing to death. The men took the situation in hand the best they could by building a huge fire. After supper which was served later, a long night vigil followed. No one slept because of the cold and rain. The next day the weather cleared up and an improvised shelter was made out of a log frame-work overlaid with grass. This served as a shelter for the next six months until Francis Kossa built a log cabin.
>
> In the following fall only one bale of cotton was made by the whole group. It was loaded on a sled and pulled by oxen to La Grange where it was sold. By now the savings brought from Europe were spent. Flour was $20 a barrel and an epidemic broke out caused by hard work and contaminated water. But God was with us. The following year crops were better and with the kind help of those of English-speaking extraction we became firmly established.

In 1860, one of Valentin's classmates from Moravia, having recently arrived in the New World, cast a critical eye over Haidusek's three-year-old cabin at Dubina. He remarked, "My dear Valento, you had a better pigsty at home."

Haidusek replied, "I would rather live in this cabin as an American citizen than live in a palace and be subject to the ruler of Austria."

The community that grew up here was also known as Navidad, Bohemia Navidad, and East Navidad, owing to its location near the Navidad River and its overwhelmingly Bohemian population.

August Haidusek was born in Moravia in 1845. He was elected mayor of La Grange in 1876, state representative from Fayette and Lee counties in 1880, and county judge in 1884. He later bought and published *Svoboda*, a Czech weekly newspaper.

While they were against slavery, all the able-bodied men of the settlement served in the Confederate forces. After the war, bandits attacked several families and plundered their homes. But life got better, and the village began to prosper, servicing about six hundred families by the turn of the century, with a cotton gin, grocery, meat market, saloon, gristmill, blacksmith, and post office, all owned and operated by Joseph Peter Jr.

Next to the Peter store, under the shade of the live oaks, was a platform and bandstand for dances. The meals were often free at these events. As many as fifteen steers might be butchered and barbecued, because appetites were so hearty, and cattle were so plentiful and cheap. Charlie Adamcik remembered the platform as measuring fifty by seventy-five feet, built off a hill. There were two rows of wooden seats for spectators, who paid ten cents. The dancers paid twenty-five cents.

One of the jolliest crowds a man ever saw went to Joe Peter's park at Dubina on Palm Sunday, 1910, to spend the day in social intercourse. There was enough to eat for about twice the crowd, consisting of the following menu: roast turkey, roast beef, fried chicken, chicken salads, oysters on the half shell and fried, roast pork, veal loaf, hamburger steak, cold tongue, tongue salad, stuffed eggs and boiled eggs, salmon salad, Irish and sweet potato salad, baked Irish potatoes, boiled ham, tomatoes, rice, cabbage slaw, coffee, catsup, crackers, pickles, and several different varieties of pies and cake. E. F. Leidolf was the chief oyster opener, but he said he didn't mind opening oysters for a man that has had his dinner. Adolf Schindler received the medal for eating the most raw oysters; he only ate eleven dozen.

In 1912, two fires destroyed Josef (Joe) Peter's house, gin, mill, blacksmith shop, and store. He rebuilt the store that same year, which still stands near the church on the way to the piano-wire bridge. But the bloom was off Dubina as a commercial center, and the store had closed by the 1940s. Only two hundred people live in the area today, and the only active institution is the Saints Cyril and Methodius Catholic Church.

SAINTS CYRIL AND METHODIUS CHURCH

Open daily • Donations accepted • W with help

Josef Peter Sr. built a log house in 1858 that was first used for church. Two or three times a year, Father Vic Gury of Frelsburg came to say Mass and administer the sacraments. People would begin to arrive on Saturday. After service on Sunday, everyone enjoyed a hearty meal and discussed their joys and woes.

Finally, in 1876 or 1877, a church was built that looked very much like the present one. Bishop Pellicer came from San Antonio for the dedication, and a great feast was served in the old log house, which was so small that honored guests ate inside while everyone else ate outside. All the food, including noodle soup, was cooked over the fireplace. The bread was baked in Dutch ovens covered with hot coals.

At its peak, about 1900, the church served a parish of more than six hundred families.

The first church was flattened by a tropical storm in late July 1909. The parishioners began building the present church later that year, but it was not finished until October 1911. The cross atop the steeple was salvaged from the original church. It was made by Tom Lee, a former slave who worked for Josef Peter as the town's blacksmith. The church is most notable for its stenciled and painted interior walls and vaulted ceiling, stained-glass windows, and Gothic altar. The church is open for viewing daily from nine to five.

Besides the church and some aging local farmhouses, all that remains of Dubina today are the old Josef Peter saloon/post office/store (long closed) and the local KJT Lodge, No. 6. KJT stands for "Katolik Jednota Texaska," or Catholic Union of Texas, similar to the SPJST. The signs on the whitewashed outhouses behind the hall still say "Muzke" (men) and "Zenske" (women). The adjacent cemetery has many tombstones inscribed in Czech. The Czech legend at the cemetery entrance translates roughly as "Here lies a large number of us who were sent to God. If you don't want to pray for us, then leave us alone."

The parish hall next to the church is the site of the parish's annual picnic and Feast Day, held the first Sunday in July. It's similar to the Shiner Catholic Church picnic. Mass is still celebrated regularly, and on Christmas Eve, the carols are still sung in Czech, German, and English.

If you continue on County Road 480 for another 0.75 miles, you will cross a quaint one-lane bridge, then another one that dates to 1885, built by the King Iron Bridge Company of Cleveland, Ohio, for $3,000. This truss "piano-wire" bridge is one of the few of its type still in use in Central Texas. The bridge was built, in part, because of the supplications of Father Joseph Chromcik. Father Chromcik, an ecclesiastical judge for the Catholic Church, was based out of St. John's Church in Fayetteville. His mission trips by buggy or horseback to surrounding communities, including Ellinger, Bluff, Round Top, Dubina, and Warrenton, led him to request that passable roads and bridges between communities be built. Because many Texas Czechs had difficulty obtaining life insurance from eastern companies, Chromcik suggested establishing an insurance and fraternal group to serve Czech Catholics, and so, in 1889, the KJT was established. Chromcik was the KJT's chaplain from 1890 to 1894, from 1896 to 1898, and from 1901 to 1910; he was also made director and counselor for life.

From the bridge, return to the church. From Dubina, continue north five more miles on FM 1383 to Ammannsville.

AMMANNSVILLE

Fayette County • About 5 miles from Dubina

Ammannsville was named for its first settler, Andrew Ammann, who arrived in 1870. He was a farmer and architect. Other German and Czech immigrants followed, establishing farms on lands originally allotted to the Fayette County schools. In 1876, the first business opened, and by 1879, the town had a post office and a public school. St. John the Baptist Catholic Church and a German private school were established in 1890. In 1900, Ammannsville had three stores and saloons, two blacksmith shops, one drugstore, one physician, and two gins. Several of the old commercial storefronts still stand. The post office was discontinued in 1906. The public school closed in 1909. The First State Bank of Ammannsville was chartered in 1914, when the population of the extended community was estimated at eight hundred, with one hundred living in town.

ST. JOHN THE BAPTIST CHURCH

Open daily • Donations accepted • W

For about the first twenty years of Ammannsville's existence, the faithful attended Mass at neighboring parishes. The first church, built in 1890, was destroyed by the same storm that blew down the Dubina church in 1909, and was rebuilt. In 1917, the church was again destroyed, by fire, and was replaced by the present wooden sanctuary in 1919. Several of the statues of the saints in the present church were carried out of the burning second church by parishioners.

The interior is outstanding, with its Gothic altars and intricately stenciled walls and vaulted ceilings. A European drifter is said to have done the decorative painting. St. John's is the fourth of the Schulenburg area's Painted Churches, along with those previously described at Dubina, High Hill, and Praha, all true Texas treasures. The church is open for viewing daily from nine to five.

The local KJT hall, or *beseda* (Czech for "get-together"), has served over the years as church, school, and library, and is still used for local weddings, reunions, meetings, and the St. John's Parish annual picnic and feast day, held each Father's Day in June. This picnic, or any of the German-Czech Belt's parish picnics, is a lot of fun, with plenty of Czech-Tex food, polka dancing, and such.

From Ammannsville, return to US 90 and continue east toward Weimar.

WEIMAR

Colorado County • 2,000 (approximate) • (979) • About 8 miles from Schulenburg

Weimar is a German and Czech community located in the rolling hills of Colorado County. Weimar started out as the Jackson's Ranch Settlement, named after the man who owned much of the local land. When the GH&SA railroad came through in 1873, the name was altered slightly to Jackson's Station.

There are two stories as to how Jackson's Station became Weimar. The first story says that in 1882, members of the local German club, Verein Frohsinn, gathered for the purpose of renaming the town. All suggestions were written on slips of paper and dropped in a hat, and then the winning name, Weimar, submitted by a Bohemian clerk, was drawn.

Story number two has a GH&SA engineer rolling into town one day and telling the folks of Jackson's Station they should rename their town Weimar. It seems the engineer had a son enrolled at a school in Weimar, Germany. In letters home, the son had described the countryside around Weimar in detail, and the engineer thought his son's description of the German town's terrain fit Jackson's Station to a tee. The German and Czech settlers agreed and accordingly renamed their town.

These are nice stories, but whatever the reason for the name, Jackson's Station was being called Weimar by September 1877, described in such a way by the *Galveston News* that one can reasonably infer that the name change had recently taken place: "The town of Weimar is pleasantly situated on an undulating plain, with groves of beautiful live oaks adjacent. The place contains twelve stores, two millinery establishments, six saloons, one hotel, two lumberyards, two blacksmith and wagon shops, one church, Odd Fellow and Masonic halls, also a public hall, fitted up with stage and scenery, where hold all public reunions."

On November 16, 1880, the Colorado River at Weimar was so thick with ice that a wagon with a double team of horses could cross safely. An enterprising Weimar photographer was sharp enough to record this once-in-a-century occurrence for posterity. During the same blue norther, the snow stood four and five inches thick on level ground. Cattle edged up against the recently introduced barbed wire fences and froze to death by the hundreds.

Weimar has always been a God-fearing little town, but it has known its moments of violent passion and cold-blooded murder. On January 10, 1895, two prominent Weimar physicians, Drs. J. E. Grace and Eugene Pottost, met on one of the town's principal streets, whipped out their revolvers, and settled their differences with a burst of gunfire. Grace was killed, struck by two bullets. Pottost was hit three times but survived. A contemporary newspaper account further describes the Grace-Pottost confrontation: "The affair was caused by a little difficulty between the two men about a small matter about two weeks ago, in which a blow or two was passed. It seems they met this evening for the first time since. Insults were passed and soon the shooting began. The affair is much regretted and has caused great excitement."

But Weimar settled down and became a livestock and poultry processing center, and for years it even had a pickle factory. Weimar's most prominent edifice is the soaring St. Michael's Catholic Church, whose steeple you saw coming into town. To get there from US 90, turn left on Center Street.

ST. MICHAEL'S CATHOLIC CHURCH

410 N. Center, 4 blocks north of US 90 • 725-6714 • W with assistance

The imposing, Gothic St. Michael's was completed in 1913. Brick from Elgin was used in its construction. Inside, the high vaulted ceiling and elaborately carved altar and statuary tend to leave the viewer breathless, then contemplative.

From St. Michael's, double back on Center toward US 90, but turn left on Post Office Street. Post Office runs north of and parallel to Main Street/US 90.

SUSIE'S BAKERY

124 E. Post Office • Monday through Saturday 7–5:30 • No Cr. • W

Located on Post Office Street (the post office is now located on Main) is Susie's Bakery, purveyor of cheap and tasty kolaches in various guises (try the poppy seed and cheese ones), white and whole wheat bread, filled doughnuts, sweet rolls, cookies, and pigs in blankets.

KASPER MEAT MARKET

119 E. Post Office • 725-8227 • Open Monday through Saturday • No Cr. • W

The place has been run by the Kasper family for several generations, long enough for them to perfect their art; over a ton of sausage is sold every Saturday. They put out hogshead sausage, beef-and-pork sausage, pork sausage, and smoked hams year-round, and smoked turkey in season. The Kaspers also smoke some pretty good beef jerky. Patrons sit on old handmade cedar furniture while they wait for their orders to be filled.

Just south of the railroad tracks, the 100 block of E. Jackson sports several old commercial buildings. The old train station now houses the public library. It's just across the street, on the north side of E. Jackson, and faces the opera house.

WEIMAR HERITAGE SOCIETY MUSEUM

125 E. Main (US 90) • Open Wednesday and Sunday afternoons • W

Exhibits trace the city from its beginnings. There is a turn-of-the-century doctor's office, farm implements, photos, and more. One room is dedicated to veterans of World War I, World War II, the Korean conflict, and the Vietnam War.

From Weimar, go south on FM 155, then right on FM 532.

SIDE TRIPS

OAKLAND

Oakland, located ten miles south of Weimar, dates to the early 1840s and was originally called Prairie Point. In order to get a post office, developer A. C. Herford lured a nearby postmaster into moving his post office to Herford's site, on the condition that the post office retain the name "Oakland," after the name of David G. Burnet's home. From 1849 until the Civil War, John Duff Brown practiced medicine and operated a plantation at Oakland. Oakland never incorporated and has never counted more than about three hundred inhabitants. The current population is about eighty.

Oakland's most famous citizen was Robert Lloyd Smith, distinguished black educator, entrepreneur, and politician. Born a free negro in Charleston, South Carolina, in 1861, Smith earned a B.S. from Atlanta University in 1880 and taught school in Georgia and South Carolina for five years. Smith served as an aide to Booker T. Washington and espoused Washington's philosophy of accommodation and self-help. In 1885, he moved to Oakland to serve as principal of the Oakland Normal School, training young African Americans to be teachers. He once said that he left South Carolina because of social pressure placed on him for having married a woman of dark complexion.

Oakland was not a pretty sight in 1885. Most of the town's blacks were ex-slaves who rented dilapidated shacks from the white inhabitants. They were segregated, and there was no grade school for blacks, only for the whites.

Smith didn't like what he saw, observing that "the negro problem was to teach him how to live and how to take hold of the things about him." So, in 1890, Smith organized the Village Improvement Society of Oakland in order to boost "the American Negro up to a high standard of citizenship." At first, the society encouraged only home beautification projects, but it soon began teaching improved farming methods and cooperative buying. The results were nothing short of spectacular; by 1894, according to Smith, you could not "pick out the location of the homes of the races by the exterior, or, for that matter, the interior of their dwellings." The roads had been repaired, and the blacks had their own grade school as well. Despite their antipathy toward African Americans in general, many whites in Colorado County couldn't help but be impressed by what Smith had done.

Smith's success in Oakland led him to found the Farmers' Home Improvement Society, a farmers' association for negroes, whose purpose was to guide its members out of the serflike sharecropping/credit cycle and into economic self-sufficiency through home and farm ownership. Society members learned about crop diversification and other improved farming methods, cooperative buying and selling, and how to raise most of their own food. With Smith as president, the society sponsored agricultural fairs and provided sick and death benefits. It began with fourteen members. In 1900, it claimed eighty-six branches and 2,340 members. By 1909, it had 21,000 members in Texas, Arkansas, and the Oklahoma Territory. By 1912, the society owned seventy-five thousand acres of land valued at more than one million dollars. The group's enterprises included a truck growers' union, an agricultural college at Wolfe City in 1906, and the Woman's Barnyard Auxiliaries, with membership in twenty counties, which specialized in better egg, poultry, and butter production and the raising of improved swine for the market. The society even had its own bank, the Farmers' Improvement Bank, founded in 1911 in Waco. But the society was chronically in financial trouble, mostly because of its overly generous benefits package.

The chief attraction in Oakland today is the old Oakland Normal School building. Founded in 1882, the Oakland Normal School provided professional training for black schoolteachers for three decades. G. R. Townsend served as first principal, but for most of the school's existence it was directed by Robert L. Smith. Conducting classes during spring and summer vacation periods, Oakland Normal School provided educational opportunities to teachers from seven southeast Texas counties. It was considered one of the finest institutions of its kind in the state. But the obstacles were great; of twenty-five negroes who applied for teacher certification in Colorado County in 1893, only twelve met the certification qualifications.

Schools like the Oakland Normal School represented the second step in the evolution of public education for black Texans, which began during the Reconstruction period after the Civil War. In 1865, the United States Congress instituted the Freedmen's Bureau (officially known as the Bureau of Refugees, Freedmen, and Abandoned Lands), a temporary agency under the jurisdiction of the United States Army. The bureau's primary function was to supervise and coordinate a vast educational enterprise located in Texas and the other Southern, slaveholding states. Beyond education for blacks, it tried to provide relief to the thousands of refugees, black and white, who had been left homeless by the Civil War; to supervise affairs related to newly freed slaves in the southern states; and to administer all land abandoned by Confederates or confiscated from them during the war. It also insisted that the courts give blacks the same legal rights enjoyed by whites.

The schools offered classes from the elementary level through college, with a formal curriculum of arithmetic, reading, writing, history, and geography. A practical curriculum of civics, politics, home economics, and vocational training was also provided. At first, most teachers came from the northern states, supplied by the American Missionary Association. A few Southern whites and educated African Americans were recruited to teach. In January 1866, Texas had ten day and six night schools; ten teachers had 1,041 students, many of whom were adults.

On July 1, 1866, the Freedmen's Bureau in Texas had ninety schools (day, night, and Sabbath schools), forty-three teachers, and 4,590 students.

Schools staffed by Northern white missionaries were not acceptable to many ex-Confederate Texans. Some of them manifested their resentment by burning schools and intimidating the missionary teachers. Gradually, however, the opposition declined. In his last report, the superintendent of the Texas schools reported that "the burning of school houses and maltreatment of teachers so common at the commencement of the Bureau operations, have almost entirely ceased."

In December 1868, the bureau halted all but its educational efforts in Texas, and the local offices were closed. By July of 1870, the last month of the bureau's activities, 150 schools enrolled 9,086 black students. By the end of 1870, there were eighty-eight day and night schools, eighty-five teachers (forty-four African Americans), and 4,478 students, as well as twenty-seven Sabbath schools with twenty-eight teachers (twenty-three African Americans) and 1,350 students.

In 1871, Texas organized a public school system. The succeeding system, formed under the Constitution of 1876, reestablished racial segregation. Between 1873 and 1893, at black state conventions, African Texans met to express opinions, delineate needs, and shape educational policies.

The Teachers State Association of Texas was founded in 1884 by thirteen colleagues who met at Prairie View Normal School to promote quality education for blacks and good working conditions for black teachers. In 1885, the group reorganized as the Colored Teachers State Association of Texas. The all-volunteer association worked to better organize blacks and to stop the deterioration of black political power in Texas. Because it sought to bring together black teachers and politicians, the association was considered a primarily political organization. It fought for adequate state legislative support for Prairie View Normal College and for the black university provided for in the 1876 constitution; without a university for graduate and professional study, black teachers and their students could not gain equal status with their white counterparts.

By providing long-term protection for freedmen and promoting peace and goodwill, it was felt that the Freedmen's Bureau would be able to establish a free agricultural labor system and a system of good schools for the freedmen. The Freedmen's Bureau operated in Texas from late September 1865 until July 1870, run by a series of assistant commissioners who were Union Army officers.

The assistant commissioner relied on local agents, who toured their districts urging freedmen to work hard and fulfill their contracts. Agents helped blacks search for relatives from whom they had been separated while slaves. When a local agent aided local authorities in disarming blacks who were in town, one assistant commissioner ordered the agent to return the weapons unless the law also disarmed whites.

The bureau enjoyed little success in Texas, defeated by the size of the state, its poor transportation and communication networks, limited resources, and white hostility. Because the Freedmen's Bureau was a U.S. Army agency, white Texans associated it with the policy of Reconstruction imposed on them by the vengeful North. Plus the bureau envisioned a role for blacks in Texas society that whites believed they were incapable of filling.

Local agents were U.S. soldiers, Northern citizens, or Texans; army officers were preferred. Few officers were willing to serve as agents. Civilians who served before 1867 did so as volunteers, because the bureau lacked funds to pay them. Assistant commissioners hesitated to use civilians because they had less control over them. Assistant commissioners were especially suspicious of Texans, who were assumed to have no sympathy for the freedmen. But at least a few civilians and Texans were employed at any given time; from April 1867 through December 1868, about half of the agents were civilians.

One of those agents was George Thompson Ruby, a black born free in New York in 1841. After acquiring a liberal arts education, he worked as a correspondent in Haiti. He returned to the United States and in 1864 settled in Louisiana, where he was a schoolteacher. He left Louisiana in September 1866 after being beaten by a white mob while trying to establish a common school. He joined the Freedmen's Bureau at Galveston and began administering the bureau's schools. He then became a traveling agent for the bureau, visiting Austin, Bastrop, Fort Bend, and other counties to establish Union League chapters and temperance societies.

Many agents operated with little or no military support, which emboldened their enemies. Two agents were killed on duty, and a third was killed en route to his post. At least three others were shot and wounded, two more escaped attempted assassinations without serious injury, and two others, finding themselves surrounded by a hostile populace and threatened with death, ran. Then there was the yellow fever epidemic of 1867, which forced several local offices to close and caused the death of General Griffin, assistant commissioner at the time, and four of his local agents.

Leave Weimar on US 90, heading east toward Columbus.

BORDEN

Colorado County • About 5 miles from Weimar

Borden is named for and founded by Gail Borden. Jack-of-all-trades and inventor, Borden arrived at Galveston Island on Christmas Eve, 1829. He spent time ranching, surveying for Austin's colony, and publishing a newspaper before becoming the first collector of the port of Galveston. He next served as land agent, Sunday school teacher, and Galveston city alderman. In 1836, he bought five hundred acres on the east bank of the Colorado above Bastrop.

Borden started inventing in the 1840s, creating among other things a "terraqueous machine," a sort of prairie schooner that could travel on land or water. By 1849, Borden had perfected his "meat biscuit," a dehydrated meat patty compounded with flour. He spent the next few years traveling all over the world trying to sell it, mostly to the war ministries of various countries, as the ideal traveling ration for armies on the move. But it tasted awful, and it didn't keep well in damp coastal climates. In his effort to market the meat biscuit, Borden moved to New York in 1851. By 1853, he had invented a process for condensing milk.

But financial success eluded him, so in 1854, Borden was in Texas selling land to pay debts and stay afloat financially. He had just written a newspaper article telling how to fight corn weevils and build corncribs. He toyed with a plan to mill lumber on his Bastrop County land. That year he went to visit Noah Smithwick at Mormon Mills, saying that he had heard rumors of gold on his Burnet County lands. The rumor was false. Son Henry Lee Borden was ranching in Texas.

After two failed attempts at establishing a condensing factory, Borden managed to open one and keep it running in Connecticut in 1858. The Civil War and the resulting upsurge in demand for condensed milk made Borden a wealthy man. Along the way, he also invented processes for condensing fruit juices, coffee, and extracts of beef.

In February 1867, Borden moved his meat business to Texas. His Bastrop sawmill produced lumber, shingles, tubs, and cooperware pails. His other facility tanned and dressed hides. Most of the beef extract business was moved to Borden where sons Lee and John had homes. By 1871, he owned 1,600 acres around Borden and built a small house overlooking Harvey's Creek. He preferred to spend the winters here, not in cold New York. The house was surrounded by acres of orchards and flower and vegetable gardens, in accordance with his motto: "Beautiful surroundings for home and work."

In the spring of 1873, he built a school for freedmen, organized a negro day school and Sunday school, built a school for white children, and designed a church, all at Borden. He also helped build five other churches. The first locomotive that traveled the twelve miles from Columbus was called the Gail Borden, as was the station. He died of pneumonia at his Harvey Creek home on January 11, 1874. He was shipped back to New York State for burial.

The plants shut down soon thereafter. His home burned to the ground in 1885. As time marched on the old factory buildings were torn down, with some of the materials used to build the bustling town of Weimar.

Borden these days consists of the Borden Store.

Turn left at the Borden Store onto County Road 217. Resume your course east on US 90 when County Road 247 rejoins it.

GLIDDEN

Colorado County • 255 • About 8 miles from Borden

Glidden, which is now a suburb of Columbus, was founded in 1887 and was named for railroad engineer F. J. Glidden.

COLUMBUS

Colorado County Seat • 4,000 (approximate) • (979) • About a mile from Glidden

Columbus started life as an Indian village located on the banks of the Colorado River, identified on old Spanish maps as Montezuma. Montezuma happened to be located in the western corner of the two-hundred-thousand-acre area of Texas along the Brazos and Colorado rivers granted to Moses and Stephen F. Austin for the purpose of settling American immigrant families. The first white settlers in the Montezuma area were Robert and Joseph Kuykendall and Daniel Gilleland, who arrived around Christmas 1821. In August 1823, Stephen F. Austin and the Baron de Bastrop, Felipe Enrique Neri, surveyed 170 acres here on the Colorado River. This plot, the present site of Columbus, was to be capital and headquarters for the Austin colony. But Austin relocated his capital to a similar spot on the Brazos River, due to the frequency of Indian attacks here and the fact that most of the settlers had already located along the Brazos.

But the settlers here stayed on. That same year, 1823, W. B. DeWees, commonly regarded as the founder of Columbus, married the daughter of Leander Beason and built a home here. Others joined the Gillelands, Kuykendalls, and DeWeeses, and the little settlement was first known as Beason's Ferry.

Austin's contract with the Mexican government called for the family to be the basic unit of settlement. Each family that farmed and raised stock was to receive a minimum land grant of one square league (4,428 acres). Because of the vagueness of the Mexican grant to Austin, the money that settlers paid for their land ranged from nothing to about three cents an acre. In order to gain legal title to the land, settlers had to satisfy a number of requirements, including such quaint practices as walking the land's perimeters while shouting out the transfer of title from the Mexican government to the settler, pulling up herbs, throwing stones, and setting out stakes. They also had to cultivate the land and build a residence within two years of the grant.

By 1835, the village of Columbus had been laid out and named, and Texas was on the brink of rebellion. The village sent a contingent of men to Gonzales that fall, where they took part in the Battle of Gonzales. The war came to Columbus the next spring, as the Republican Army under the command of Sam Houston retreated from Gonzales. The Mexican Army was in hot pursuit.

By March 6, 1836, Houston's troops were camped on the east bank of the Colorado near Columbus. Here Houston tried to train his raw troops in the fine art of organized warfare. By March 24, the Mexican Army was camped on the west bank of the Colorado, reinforced by the arrival of Santa Anna.

Most of the Texans wanted to do battle then and there, but Houston counseled caution, saying he wanted to wait for the proper time and place, and this was neither. So the Republican Army burned every building in Columbus to the ground and hightailed it east, where they finally confronted and whipped Santa Anna at San Jacinto on April 21, 1836.

With the cessation of hostilities, the Anglo Texans began to drift back to the homes and settlements they had abandoned in the face of the Mexican Army's rampage. Their hasty and ungainly retreat is known today as the Runaway Scrape.

In the early days of June 1837, a "Citizen of Ohio" visited Columbus, which he described for a series of articles that ran in an Ohio monthly called the *Hesperian*:

> Columbus, a small town consisting of two public houses, two small stores and a half-dozen shanties, stands upon the west side of the Colorado River about one hundred miles from its mouth. Since the expulsion of the Mexicans, quite a settlement has been made in the vicinity of Columbus, consisting of twenty or thirty families who in their collected strength, aided by the citizens of the town, think themselves able to resist any predatory or general attack of the Indians. The people in this settlement had more the appearance of industry than any I had yet seen, and with the exception of gambling, the besetting sin here as everywhere else in Texas, there would be little to complain of more than is common among men anywhere.

The anonymous author remained in Columbus for several days, preparing for a journey to San Antonio. It would be no casual lark, as the author related:

> All began to prepare for war. Rifles and pistols were put in order, bullets run, and powder distributed. Our wallets were filled with dodgers, and everything attended to necessary for a regular Indian campaign. A course was laid down to regulate our conduct so as to avoid danger to ourselves and especially to our horses during the night, the time when there was the greatest reason for fear. The plan was the same that is most in practice by those who are in the frequent habit of traveling from the coast to the interior. It is to stop about dark, build up a fire and prepare something to eat, to remain in this situation until ten o'clock, then after replenishing the fire, to depart with great secrecy and travel eight or ten miles on the course. To make assurance doubly sure, it is then customary to ride three or four miles either to the right or left and go quickly to sleep. But it is common, after all this precaution, for the party to take turns in watching during the night.
>
> A number of discharged Mexican prisoners had been collecting for some days from every part of the country until they amounted to near forty, and these were making similar preparations with ourselves to meet the dangers of the unsettled country. A prospect of once more seeing their native land made their hearts glad with joy. The kindness of the citizens had furnished the company which was now preparing to proceed to Mexico a number of muskets to kill game and defend themselves in case of attack, as well as many other things that would be required along the way.

Colorado County was organized in the spring of 1837, and the first court session was held under a giant live oak, since all the town buildings had been burned during the Runaway Scrape, and the new courthouse had literally slipped through the fingers of its builders. Preparations had been made for the construction of a county courthouse here. Lumber had been cut upriver at Bastrop and then floated to Columbus, but the obstruction built across the river to catch the lumber failed to hold, and the timber continued merrily on to the Gulf. The court was presided over by Judge Robert McAlpin Williamson, more colorfully known as "Three-Legged Willie," by virtue of the wooden leg he had attached to the knee of his withered left leg. The lower, natural half of that leg he left protruding rearward, and he had all his pants tailored accordingly.

Justice in those days was of a no-nonsense nature. In May 1838, Wilson H. Bibbs was charged with grand larceny (probably cattle theft). Pleading guilty as charged, Bibbs threw himself on the mercy of the court. The court's mercy consisted of the following sentence: "That Wilson H. Bibbs should receive on this day 39 lashes on his bare back and be branded on the right hand with the letter T." The T presumably stood for "thief." He was also to be held in "outside" until a $500 fine was paid, but this portion of the sentence was later remitted when it was shown that the sum of $500 was not to be found anywhere west of the Colorado River. Bibbs was then released "from outside," where he had presumably been chained to a tree, there being no jail built as yet.

Columbus eventually got its courthouse and jail built and proceeded to grow into a prosperous little city.

In February 1846, German scientist Dr. Ferdinand Roemer passed through Columbus on his way from Houston to New Braunfels. He counted eighteen to twenty frame houses with wide porches, three stores, two taverns, and a smithy standing charmingly in the shade of old live oaks.

We found the place in great excitement. A number of horses were tied to the low branches of the live oak trees near the two taverns; in the entrance hall of the taverns, groups of men were standing, carrying on excited conversations. We learned the cause of this excitement: a horse race had just taken place and the result of the race formed the topic of their animated conversation. The wagers are sometimes quite large, single bets in a little place like Columbus amounting to as much as five hundred dollars. We had some difficulty in persuading the smith, who took part in the discussions at one of the taverns and who drank one glass of whiskey after another in the heat of the conversation, to drop his "hippological" discussions in order to repair the damage done to our wagon.

Colorado County grew dramatically in the 1850s as a cotton plantation economy emerged. New communities were founded at Osage and Oakland. Getting the cotton to market was easier said than done. Colorado County depended on the Colorado River for transporting its cotton and other crops to market, first aboard keelboats and flatboats; by the 1840s, the *Moccasin Belle* and other steamboats carried the county's cotton most of the way downriver to the port of Matagorda.

Before 1853 (when service commenced on Texas' first railroad, a twenty-mile stretch of the Buffalo Bayou, Brazos, and Colorado Railway Company between Harrisburg and Stafford's Point), transportation in Texas was confined to keelboat and steamboat traffic along the coast and through the lower reaches of a few rivers, and to animal-drawn vehicles on the few and primitive roads to the interior. Only a handful of Texas rivers were even close to being navigable by anything larger than a canoe, and the Colorado offered formidable obstacles, as we shall soon see. Despite all the problems, river navigation played an important role in the development of Texas before the Civil War, and by 1860, there were a number of steamboats on each of the most important rivers, despite water so shallow that schedules were frequently interrupted.

In 1821, Stephen F. Austin had planned to sail the schooner *Lively* up the Colorado with supplies for his colony of three hundred families, but after mistaking the mouth of the Brazos for the Colorado, it wrecked on Galveston Island. Henry Austin's *Ariel* was the first steamboat to travel a Texas river. Following a few months' unsuccessful operation on the Rio Grande, the *Ariel* was moved to the Brazos in August 1830, and in December 1830, after several attempts to make New Orleans, the *Ariel* was laid up to rot near Harrisburg.

In April 1835, the legislature of the state of Coahuila y Texas granted exclusive rights for ten years to Ben Milam to (1) clear and otherwise make navigable the Colorado River up to Mina (now Bastrop), and (2) establish shipping companies to ply the river. A few years earlier, Milam had removed the great Red River raft of debris, which for years had blocked traffic in the upper part of the Red River for all vessels except canoes and small, flat-bottomed boats. He then purchased a steamboat, the *Alps*, the first of its kind to pass through the channel. But in December 1835, Milam was killed leading the Texian army charge to capture San Antonio from the Mexicans.

The *David Crockett*, a keelboat, was the first large craft known to navigate the Colorado River. On April 11, 1838, it arrived at the head of "the raft on the Colorado," ten miles above the port of Matagorda, after averaging more than sixty miles a day of daytime navigation. "The raft on the Colorado" was a jam of logs six miles long caused by the Colorado's slow current. Teamsters unloaded cargoes from vessels above the raft and carried them by wagon ten to twenty miles down to the port of Matagorda, where they were loaded onto ships that traveled the last few miles down the Colorado to the Gulf of Mexico and then headed for Galveston and other Gulf ports. Despite this considerable inconvenience, the *David Crockett* and other keelboats and flatboats of light draft were busy operating above the raft. Columbus served as a shipping point for inland farm products from a wide surrounding area and as a supply center for wagon trains headed west.

In 1838, the Colorado Navigation Company was chartered to remove the raft and otherwise promote the use of the river for transportation. In 1839, William Wallach made a hydrographic survey of Matagorda Bay and was employed by the Colorado Navigation Company to make a survey of the Colorado River raft that hindered navigation.

In June 1844, the *La Grange Intelligencer* announced that local merchant Samuel Ward was going to build a steamboat for use on the Colorado, which was supposed to be in operation by November 1. The *Intelligencer* article praised Ward for helping sell stock in the Colorado Navigation Company, which had been rechartered in January 1844 for the purpose of clearing the raft. Ward evidently had partners, for other contemporary newspaper accounts say the boat was owned by "Messrs. [George W.] Ward and Robinson" or by "Mr. Ward and Co. of Matagorda and a Mr. Robertson of Columbus." The *Kate Ward*, named for Ward's sister, was a side-wheel steamer with two engines rated at seventy horsepower each, about 110 feet long and 24 feet across at the beam, and capable of carrying six hundred bales of cotton. It was reckoned that with such a cargo she would draw three feet of water, but at her launching she was said to draw only five inches. Such a shallow draft would help the boat avoid the many snags and sandbars found in the river channel below Columbus. The boat was assembled on the coast at Matagorda from parts purchased and sent from Pittsburg, Pennsylvania.

After several months of delays, the *Kate Ward* finally steamed upstream from Matagorda Bay, somehow managed to get past the raft, and arrived in Austin on March 8, 1846, her first and only visit to the capital. She was the first steamboat to operate on the Colorado River. On March 11, she took a party of citizens, legislators, and U.S. Army personnel several miles upriver to visit Mormon Falls. At this time, the boat was described as having a draft, "with wood, water, etc.," of eighteen inches. The steamer stayed above the raft from 1846 to 1848. High water on the Colorado in the summer of 1848 cut a temporary channel around the raft, and the *Kate Ward* was finally able to return to Matagorda Bay. From 1848 or 1849 to 1850, the *Kate Ward* plied the Guadalupe River, where it made thirty trips.

In September 1850, a new version of the Colorado Navigation Company was organized to promote Colorado River traffic and commerce. They hired William Whiting to help clear the Colorado River raft. During the 1850s, Whiting was involved in engineering projects in California, Texas, North Carolina, South Carolina, Georgia, and Florida. In his report of December 9, 1852, to the Corps of Engineers in Washington, he reported favorably on the work already done by the Colorado Navigation Company. He recommended a plan of action that was adopted by the secretary of war. In 1852, the *Kate Ward* worked as a snag boat on the Colorado in the cleanup project that cleared a twenty-mile stretch from the mouth upstream. The Colorado Navigation Company appears to have owned the boat at this time. The United States government bought the *Kate Ward* in July 1853 and had her repaired that fall. In November, she was back on the Colorado, where United States Army engineers used her to help dig a channel around the raft. What later became of the steamer is unknown.

But the cleanup project only removed the biggest obstacle to efficient navigation; plenty of smaller ones remained. The *Colorado Ranger* was a side-wheel steamer that operated on the Colorado River between Columbus in Colorado County and the head of the Colorado raft in Matagorda County during the early 1850s. Its cargoes of Colorado County cotton were unloaded there and carried by wagons around the raft to Matagorda. The steamer made a trip to Austin and arrived on April 7, 1851, amid public fanfare. On March 5, 1853, it hit an obstruction, tore its hull, and sank ten miles southeast of La Grange. Another steamboat, the *Flying Jenny*, ran from Robson's castle in Columbus up the Colorado to Austin.

For lack of maintenance, the raft quickly reassembled. By 1858, the situation in Matagorda and Wharton counties had become so bad that the state appropriated funds for the construction of a new channel around the raft. But the Civil War soon interrupted the project.

One of the town's more memorable settlers during the plantation era was Colonel Robert Robson, who hailed from Dumfries, Scotland. Once in Columbus, Robson erected a castle of homemade lime and gravel on the south side of the Colorado, on the site where Austin had planned to establish his colonial headquarters. Robson's three-story fortress was surrounded by a moat, and the entrance was gained via a drawbridge. Most of the rooms were twenty feet by twenty feet, with a grand ballroom three times the length of the other rooms. The castle is said to have been the first building in Texas to have running water and a roof garden. Colonel Robson also introduced the Mexican huisache tree to Texas. The Robson house was undermined by a severe river flood in 1869 and was torn down in 1883 to make way for Bob Stafford's beef-processing plant.

By 1860, the county's population numbered 7,885, including 3,559 African Americans. Fourteen Colorado County men had fortunes of $100,000. That year, the county had 397 farms and 306 slaveholders; 160 men owned fewer than five slaves, while 12 had fifty or more, and 4 had more than a hundred. Colorado County had the fifth-largest cotton crop of all Texas counties in 1860, more than fourteen thousand bales. With almost thirty thousand head, cattle ranching began to assume an important role in the county economy.

One of the slaveowners' most persistent fears was the possibility of slave insurrection. They attempted to prevent such uprisings by a variety of practices, such as denying their chattel any formal education or the right to congregate except in small, supervised groups. But plots were concocted among the slaves despite their masters' efforts.

According to several contemporary newspaper accounts, Colorado County was very nearly laid to waste in September 1856. On September 9, 1856, the Vigilance Committee of Colorado County wrote the following report for the *Galveston News*:

> The object of this communication is to state to you all the facts of any importance connected with a recent intended insurrection. Our suspicions were aroused about two weeks ago, when a meeting of the citizens of the county was called, and a committee of investigation appointed to ferret out the whole matter, and lay the facts before the people of the county for their consideration. The committee

entered upon their duties, and, in a short time, they were in full possession of the facts of a well-organized and systematized plan for the murder of our entire white population, with the exception of the young ladies, who were to be taken captives, and made the wives of the diabolical murderers of their parents and friends. The committee found in their possession a number of pistols, bowie-knives, guns, and ammunition. Their passwords of organization were adopted, and their motto, "Leave not a shadow behind."

Last Saturday, the 6th inst., was the time agreed upon for the execution of their damning designs. At a late hour at night, all were to make one simultaneous, desperate effort, with from two to ten apportioned to nearly every house in the county, kill all the whites, save the above exception, plunder their homes, take their horses and arms, and fight their way on to a "free State" (Mexico).

Notwithstanding the intense excitement which moved every member of our community, and the desperate measures to which men are liable to be led on by such impending danger to which we have been exposed by our indulgence and lenity to our slaves, we must say the people acted with more caution and deliberation than ever before characterized the action of any people under similar circumstances.

More than two hundred negroes had violated the law, the penalty of which is death. But, by unanimous consent, the law was withheld, and their lives spared, with the exception of three of the ringleaders, who were, on last Friday, the 5th inst., at 2 o'clock p.m., hung, in compliance with the unanimous voice of the citizens of the county.

Without exception, every Mexican in the county was implicated. They were arrested, and ordered to leave the county within five days, and never again to return, under the penalty of death. There is one, however, by the name of Frank, who is proven to be one of the prime movers of the affair, that was not arrested; but we hope that he may yet be, and have meted out to him such reward as his black deed demands.

We are satisfied that the lower class of the Mexican population are incendiaries in any country where slaves are held, and should be dealt with accordingly. And, for the benefit of the Mexican population, we would here state, that a resolution was passed by the unanimous voice of the county, forever forbidding any Mexican from coming within the limits of the county.

Peace, quiet, and good order are again restored, and, by the watchful care of our Vigilance Committee, a well-organized patrol, and good discipline among our planters, we are persuaded that there will never again occur the necessity of a communication of the character of this.

The September 11 issue of the *Galveston News* contained the following update:

We learn, from the *Columbian Planter*, of the 9th, that two of the negroes engaged in the insurrection at Columbus were whipped to death; three more were hung last Friday, and the Mexicans who were implicated were ordered to leave the country. There was no proof against these last beyond surmises. The band had a deposit of arms and ammunition in the bottom. They had quite a number of guns, and a large lot of knives, manufactured by one of their number. It was their intention to fight their way to Mexico.

The September 5 issue of the *La Grange True Issue* reported,

We noticed last week the rumor that a large number of slaves, of Colorado County, had combined and armed themselves for the purpose of fighting their way into Mexico. Developments have since been made of a much more serious nature than our information then indicated. It is ascertained that a secret combination had been formed, embracing most of the negroes of the county, for the purpose of not fleeing to Mexico, but of murdering the inhabitants—men, women, and children promiscuously. To carry out their hellish purposes, they had organized into companies of various sizes, had adopted secret signs and passwords, sworn never to divulge the plot under the penalty of death, and had elected captains and subordinate officers to command the respective companies. They had provided themselves with some fire-arms and home-made bowie knives, and had appointed the time for a simultaneous movement. Some two hundred, we learn, have been severely punished under the lash, and several are now in jail awaiting the more serious punishment of death, which is to be inflicted today. One of the principal instigators of the movement is a free negro, or one who had been permitted to control his own time as a free man.

Columbus and Colorado County voted for secession in 1861, although the predominantly German town of Frelsburg voted against it. Hundreds of able-bodied men marched off to war. The very old and very young men stayed at home serving in the Home Guard, or "Heel Flies."

Fighting never reached Colorado County, but the war devastated the county's plantation economy, which depended so heavily on slave labor that the value of county farms dropped from $3,066,070 in 1860 to $493,890 by war's end. The value of livestock fell by about half during the 1860s, and the value of overall farm property fell by more than 80 percent.

The Reconstruction years were turbulent and sometimes violent. At war's end, the newly freed slaves came to the courthouse square in great jubilant crowds singing, "Lincoln rode de big black horse, Davis rode de mule, Lincoln wuz de nobleman and Davis wuz de fool." Naturally, the recently subdued white Rebels didn't take to this behavior too well. Federal troops occupied Columbus in June 1865, and troops were garrisoned there through 1870. The Yankee occupation troops put the freedmen in uniform and commissioned them to keep the peace in Colorado County. Freedmen's Bureau agents stationed in Columbus opened schools for black children and attempted to mediate labor contracts between planters and freedmen.

An organization in the spirit of the Ku Klux Klan composed of Colorado and Fayette county men, and formed around a nucleus of Confederate veterans, was active in the county in the late 1860s. These unreconstructed Rebels would ride into town, fire a couple dozen shots, and then dash back into the wooded night. The bluebellies would then halfheartedly pursue the raiders a mile or two before turning back. Federal authorities and county officers often clashed.

There were new fortunes to be made now that the war was over. In 1869, the railroad finally came to Columbus, and the Colorado River immediately ceased to be a factor in transportation. The Buffalo Bayou, Brazos, and Colorado railway had reached Alleyton (three miles east of Columbus) by 1860, but the Colorado River still stood in the way. After the war, the Buffalo Bayou, Brazos, and Colorado railway reorganized as the Galveston, Harrisburg, and San Antonio railway and finally made the big leap over the Colorado and into Columbus. The railroad made it much cheaper to ship out Colorado County cotton and to bring in all sorts of consumer goods. But instead of riding the rails to market, Colorado County cattle were trailed north. At least one man, Robert Earl "Bob" Stafford, made a million dollars from Texas longhorns, which were almost as numerous as grasshoppers in the region after the war. But prosperity did not bring peace to Colorado County.

During the pre-barbed-wire days of free range and wild cattle (about 1875), a feud developed between the Townsend family—longtime pillars of Colorado County—and the Staffords, relative Johnny-come-latelys who had wasted little time in getting wealthy. No one knows exactly how the feud got started, but once it got going, it was a hot one. Things came to a head when J. L. "Light" Townsend was elected county sheriff. The Stafford faction tried to unseat him at succeeding elections, but failed.

The Townsend clan (Asa and Rebecca Harper Townsend and their nine children) had come to Columbus in 1838. Asa was involved in Texas politics by 1845, when he served on a committee involved with the annexation of the Republic of Texas to the United States. He was also director of the Colorado (River) Navigation Association and an active Mason.

Robert Stafford, born in Georgia in 1834, came to Texas in 1856 and settled in Colorado County, where he farmed and raised livestock on a small scale, using the I.C.U. brand. At the start of the Civil War, Stafford joined Hood's Texas Brigade but soon returned home and spent the rest of the war years building up his herd. After the war, Stafford, who was the oldest child in his family, was joined by five of his brothers, six or seven sisters, and assorted other relatives.

Cattle rustling was common, and the Stafford clan and their employees gained a reputation as people not to be crossed. At least once, and probably twice, the Staffords sent their cowboys into the countryside to kill whomever they suspected of rustling. A good many people ended up dead. Retaliation was inevitable; one of the Stafford brothers was shot dead, and another was wounded. But the violence didn't hinder Bob's empire building.

In 1869, he drove a herd of cattle to Kansas. Emboldened by his success, he bought up all the brands in his section of the county that were for sale. In 1872, he contracted to deliver beef to Havana, Cuba. He also sold cattle that went to pacified Indians out west. His fortune increased rapidly, to the point that he organized his own bank in 1882. The following year, Stafford realized that he and his fellow stockmen could make more money by shipping dressed, chilled beef to distant markets than by driving live cows up the long and arduous Chisholm Trail. He organized the Columbus, Texas Meat and Ice Company and built a $250,000 three-story plant on the site of the old Robson Castle in 1884. At the time, it was one of only three packing houses in Texas. The plant could process either 125 or 250 head of cattle per day, depending on whom you believe, and could make forty tons of ice daily. The company filled an order for an English syndicate and also shipped dressed carcasses to Chicago, New Orleans, Galveston, and other points via the new refrigerated rail cars that were the wonder of the age. The plant closed in 1891 and was later torn down.

In 1889, a group of Colorado County citizens decided that the little 1855 courthouse no longer befitted a town of Columbus' stature, and they persuaded county commissioners to build a new one. Despite considerable opposition from county citizens who lived outside Columbus, the commissioners went ahead with their plans. But the project was plagued by delays. Citizens demanded that the brick be manufactured in Colorado County, so the schedule was relaxed. By April 1890, the foundation had finally been poured. The county decided to incorporate the laying of the new courthouse's cornerstone into the county's traditional July Fourth celebration. But that date couldn't be met, so it was delayed until July 7, 1890. At eleven that morning, about three thousand folks from around the county began gathering on the north side of Columbus for a barbecue. At about five that afternoon, they assembled in parade formation and marched down Milam Street to the courthouse square. The Masons of Caledonia Lodge No. 68 conducted the cornerstone laying and ceremony, and then the group paraded back to the barbecue grounds. At this point, the crowd began to disperse. Many went off to prepare for the big dance to be held that night at the opera house.

About an hour before the dance was to start, Bob Stafford got into an argument with City Marshal Larkin Hope, who was Sheriff Townsend's son-in-law, about the arrest of Bob Stafford's son, Warren, earlier that afternoon for drunkenness. Bob Stafford had had an understanding with Sheriff Townsend and Hope that whenever Warren tied one on, he would be dealt with discreetly instead of taken to jail like a common criminal. But this time Larkin and Marion Hope had arrested Warren and paraded him down the street in handcuffs. Family friends persuaded them not to jail Warren, but the damage had been done. Bob Stafford was fit to be tied at this insult to his family's dignity.

What exactly transpired between them depends on whose side you're on, and some folks in Columbus still take sides over 120 years later. At any rate, the argument ended when Larkin Hope and his brother Marion shot and killed Bob Stafford and his younger brother John in front of Nicoli's Saloon on the southwest corner of the courthouse square. Their funeral procession was a mile long.

With the death of Bob Stafford, Colorado County went into rapid economic decline. The new courthouse had been meant to be a symbol of the prosperity that Columbus had come to enjoy. Stafford's death ended any chance for the future success of the meatpacking plant, opera house, and a host of other endeavors associated with him. Within twenty years, there would be little of the Stafford fortune in Columbus.

There was considerable outrage over the Stafford killings, and many called for Townsend's removal, but this was not effected until his death several years later. The Stafford-Townsend feud expanded into what became known as the Colorado County Feud, involving more than half a dozen area families; the Townsends, Reeses, Burfords, Clementses, Hopes, and Lessings were all related to each other, either directly or through marriage.

After Townsend's death in 1894, his relatives squabbled over who would be his successor as sheriff. His deputy and cousin by marriage, Samuel Houston Reese, a well-to-do landowner from Oakland, took over and held the post for four years. The 1898 Colorado County sheriff's race pitted incumbent sheriff Sam Reese against his deputy and one-time Columbus City marshal, Larkin Hope. Former state senator Mark Townsend, who directed a political machine that had backed the winning candidate in each of the last nine sheriff's elections, dropped his backing of Reese and endorsed Hope. Hope's victory was practically assured.

But on the night of August 3, 1898, someone killed Hope in downtown Columbus. Suspicion centered on Jim Coleman, a close friend of Reese's sons, Walter and Herbert. Townsend picked a new candidate, his brother-in-law, farmer Will Burford. Reese was not implicated in the shooting, but he lost the election to Burford.

In the early evening of March 16, 1899, Sam Reese was killed in a gun battle on Milam Street in front of Brunson's Saloon, near where Hope died. Stray bullets killed Charles Boehme, an innocent bystander, and wounded a boy named Johnny Williams. Will Clements, Marion Hope, and Mark Townsend were among those shooting. Walter Reese, who had been in a nearby store, ran to his father. He cradled Sam's head in his lap and vowed to get the man who had killed his father.

Accounts of how the battle started are in conflict, but it appears that Reese had provoked the fight in which he was killed. The killings had two important consequences for Columbus, according to the late Columbus historian Bill Stein. First, despite strong evidence to the contrary, Reese's children regarded their father's death as a cold-blooded, premeditated assassination and spent years exacting their revenge. In five more gunfights (May 17, 1899; January 15, 1900; July 31, 1900; June 30, 1906; and May 17, 1907), five men were killed, and several others were wounded. The dead included Reese's brother Dick, Burford's son Arthur, Will Clements' brother Hiram, and Jim Coleman. One of the dead was an innocent bystander. No one was ever convicted of any of the murders. Those accused included Mark Townsend, Jim Townsend, Step Yates, Will Clements, Walter Reese, Joe Lessing, Frank Burford, and Marion Hope.

Second, the killing of Boehme, a farmer in town on business, and the continued atmosphere of violence in Columbus, persuaded many of his fellow farmers to take their business elsewhere, severely damaging the town's economy. People commonly referred to Columbus as Hell's Half-Acre, and many travelers skirted the town altogether for years thereafter.

The death of Boehme and the wounding of Williams prompted townspeople to call for the Texas Rangers. Captain Bill McDonald boarded a train for Columbus and arrived first. He found members of both factions milling about on opposite sides of the courthouse square, armed and spoiling for action. He visited the district judge who advised McDonald not to do anything until he was reinforced by more Rangers. The judge was amazed that McDonald had come alone; he thought that it would take twenty-five Rangers to lay down the law. McDonald replied that two more men would arrive tomorrow and that he wanted to stop the fighting before it started. McDonald started by facing down the Townsend crowd, which included the Colorado County sheriff. He called to Sheriff Burford asking him to stop the needless killing that was sure to come. Burford replied that such words would fall on deaf ears, so McDonald said that he would disarm the mob himself. Shamed by such bravery, the sheriff asked his friends to accompany him inside the courthouse to confer with McDonald. He talked to the Townsend partisans calmly, showing neither fear nor anger, and threatening no one. After speaking his peace, he invited them, "Here boys, come and stack your guns in this wardrobe. It's a good safe place for them. They won't be likely to go off and hurt anybody here." They pondered his words awhile and acceded. McDonald then locked up the wardrobe and went outside. He toted his Winchester over to the Reeses and told them that the governor had sent him to stop the trouble, and that they would have to disarm and go home, as the other side had done. One fellow replied that Captain Bill would play hell getting his gun, whereupon McDonald shoved the Winchester under the man's nose and threatened to take him to jail. The man dropped his gun, and the Reese leader told his men to obey Bill, who marched them to a store, where they disarmed and left their guns with the store's clerk. The other two Rangers arrived the next day, and the three men were conspicuous around town for several, peaceful weeks before returning to camp.

After their departure, Columbus didn't keep the peace for long. On May 17, 1899, Sam Reese's brother, Dick Reese, and Dick Gant, his black driver from Alleyton, were shot and killed by deputy sheriffs Step Yates and Jim Townsend. The deputies claimed that Dick Reese had drawn his pistol when they tried to halt him from crossing the Colorado River bridge. The Reeses didn't accept that excuse.

County Judge Mansfield called the Rangers back to keep a lid on the simmering hatred. After a few months' calm, the gun battles resumed and spilled over into neighboring counties. Early in 1900, four men from Company F were sent to Bastrop, where Jim Townsend was being tried for the murder of Dick Reese. Try as they might, they weren't able to keep Walter Reese, Jim Coleman, and some other friends from ambushing and killing Arthur Burford and wounding Will Clements. Within twenty minutes of the killing, Ranger Captain J. A. Brooks left one of his men to guard the prisoners at the jail and to keep the Townsend men away, while he and the other two Rangers began to arrest and jail seventeen Reese supporters. When the habeas corpus hearing for the indicted Reese murderers came up, sixteen Rangers were in Bastrop to disarm both sides and prevent any fighting. They gathered up every weapon in sight and worked with local freight and railroad employees to examine every bag and parcel that entered town and to confiscate every weapon sent to either side. A trunk mailed to one of the Townsends was found to be full of guns, as was a large package mailed to a Reese supporter.

The cases against Jim Townsend, Walter Reese, and Jim Coleman eventually ended up in San Antonio courts, where they were dropped.

Walter Reese moved to Rosenberg, about fifty miles east of Columbus. But trouble was just a train ride away, and the Townsends regularly passed through Rosenberg on their way to and from Houston. On July 31, 1900, Walter and Jim Coleman were standing on the station platform when Willie Clements, Mark Townsend, and Frank Burford rode through on the train. Shots were exchanged, and both Coleman and Reese were badly wounded. Townsend and Burford were arrested in Houston, but the case evidently derailed and disappeared.

But this period of trial and tribulation was not without its humorous incidents. At the north end of Columbus, the Colorado River makes a big loop north, returning to the south end of Columbus some six miles later. During the 1880s, a young man was paddling down the Colorado on his way to the sea. When he reached Columbus from the northwest, he discovered an iron bridge, indicating that he had reached a town of some importance.

On investigation, he discovered Mr. Encke's store a block from the north bridge. That night, he entered Mr. Encke's store and left with a quantity of pocketknives, butcher knives, and other valuable articles. He returned to his boat and continued his ride down the river. The next morning, after drifting with the flow of the stream, he discovered a railroad bridge and a wagon bridge. This indicated a town of more considerable importance, which he assumed to be Wharton. He walked west a couple of blocks to the main street and was soon selling pocketknives and butcher knives at prices lower than any honest merchant could match.

Sheriff J. Light Townsend soon learned of the young man and sought him out. He took the young man to Encke's store, where Encke at once recognized his stolen property. The young man was horrified to discover that after several hours of boat travel, he was whisked in a few moments to the store he had visited the night before. After a lengthy sojourn, enduring the hospitality of the Colorado County jail, his journey's final destination was the state prison in Huntsville.

As the Stafford-Townsend/Colorado County feud dragged on through the 1890s, frustrated townspeople called for its end. In an attempt to restore order, they demanded that the office of town marshal be reinstated. A couple of years earlier, the town had dissolved the police force as a cost-cutting measure. The mayor was in agreement, but the money-conscious city council refused. In desperation, the citizens forced, by signed petition, an election to consider dissolving the city government so that the county sheriff would have full jurisdiction in the town. The measure passed overwhelmingly, and so in 1906, the city of Columbus (incorporated in 1866) was voted out of existence. It would be twenty-one years before the town reincorporated. It is said that a Texas Ranger was permanently stationed here to help enforce the peace. With that, the feud was pretty much over—at least the shooting part. Eight men had died in the process.

Many of the feud's other participants died violent deaths. In 1911, Marion Hope was killed in an accident in Gonzales County, Will Clements was shot from ambush in Matagorda County by a Bohemian blacksmith with whom he had had an altercation a few days earlier, and Jim Townsend was killed in a gun battle with a saloon keeper in Louise. Herbert Reese was killed in 1912, when a gun he was cleaning in his Columbus home accidentally discharged. Walter Reese died as a result of injuries received in an automobile accident in El Paso in 1919.

But the Stafford-Townsend/Colorado County feud was only one facet of a larger conflict that wracked the county, one that also pitted whites against blacks.

In spite of the county economy's decline during the 1860s, the population continued to grow, reaching 8,326 in 1870. The black population grew as well, reaching a peak of 46 percent of the county population in 1880; thereafter, while continuing to grow in absolute numbers, African Americans declined in relative terms to 43 percent of the whole by 1900.

These numbers translated into political strength; several blacks from Colorado County held state and county office during and immediately after Reconstruction, including county commissioner Isaac Yates, state representative B. F. Williams, and county commissioner Cicero Howard. A group of Colorado County whites attempted to intimidate black voters in 1873 by killing two freedmen. As a result, four hundred blacks armed themselves out of self-defense. When the whites discovered this, they moved to disarm them. In the melee that resulted, "several" blacks died, and many others fled the county. Federal authorities investigated but found no one willing to file an affidavit. The county nevertheless voted for Republican governor Edmund J. Davis that year and supported Republican presidential candidates from 1872 to 1884. In spite of the growth of the White Man's Union Association in the late 1870s, blacks continued to hold county office through the 1880s.

In 1881, Edmund Eason was elected Columbus alderman. Columbus had a negro firefighting company, but it had no say in selecting the town's fire chief and assistant chief. In 1892, the Populist Party in Colorado County was almost equally divided black and white in membership numbers. Two of the three county chairmen were black, as well as three precinct chairmen. Black voters also helped to repeatedly reelect Sheriff James Light Townsend, who, despite an apparently good record in office, was widely criticized for appointing family members to many law enforcement positions and for failing to suppress, if not actually fostering, a climate of violence in the county.

In the state elections of 1894 and 1896, the white voters of Colorado County split into Democratic and Populist party factions. The result? Both times, Robert Lloyd Smith, an African American Republican living in Oakland in southwestern Colorado County, was elected to serve Colorado County in the Texas House of Representatives. His was a lonely life, being one of only two black men in the Texas legislature during the 1895 session, and the only black in the 1897 session. But it was a delightful irony for Smith, representing a county that had cruelly shut down the putative mass rebellion scheme of 1856, a county with a majority-white population, during times when blacks and Republicans seldom held any public office in Texas. While it would be an exaggeration to say that Smith was widely respected among Texas whites, even the conservative Democratic *Houston Post* endorsed his candidacy. After Smith's win in 1896, seventy years would pass before another black Texan (Barbara Jordan) was elected to the Texas legislature.

In the Texas House, Smith worked to improve educational opportunities for black Texans, especially the advancement of Prairie View Normal School (now Prairie View A&M University). He also struggled to protect the civil rights of black Texans, which were being steadily eroded by the discriminatory "Jim Crow" laws that were then being enacted throughout the South. For instance, in 1895 he attacked (unsuccessfully) a bill calling for separate white and colored waiting rooms. He also unsuccessfully fought the establishment of the poll tax. But that same year, his bill to allow colored schools to elect their own trustees (who in turn managed and controlled the colored schools) was passed and signed into law.

White resentment to the continued black political power in Colorado County culminated in the establishment of the White Man's Reformation Association in 1894 and the White Man's Party in 1902. Leaders of the White Man's Party reached an agreement with the local Democratic Party leaders in which the latter stipulated that the White Man's Party nominees for local offices would automatically be nominated by the Democrats, effectively eliminating the Democratic primary. Since only white men were allowed to vote in the White Man's Party primary, blacks were effectively disenfranchised.

Robert Lloyd Smith's career of public service wasn't over; it just shifted gears and locales. A nationally respected Republican, he sought a post in the United States Treasury Department, only to have the appointment blocked by another black Texas Republican, Charles Ferguson. Smith was appointed deputy U.S. marshal for the Eastern District of Texas by President Theodore Roosevelt and served from 1902 to 1909, when he was removed in the early days of the Taft administration. During these years, Smith began a factory for manufacturing overalls. He was elected the first president of the Texas branch of the National Negro Business League when it was organized in 1907. Smith called himself a "practical sociologist." He was married to Ruby Cobb, and the couple adopted two children. In 1915, while at Prairie View, he became the first director of the state's Cooperative Extension Program for Negroes and began teaching improved agricultural methods to black farmers. That same year, he publicly denounced the blockbuster motion picture *Birth of a Nation* for its inaccurate and biased portrayal of slaves and the plantation system. He died in 1942 in Waco, where he and Ruby had lived for a number of years.

In 1898, William Dunovant, who owned a plantation near Eagle Lake, planted the county's first rice crop. Buoyed by his success, he and others quickly converted vast acreages in the southern part of the county to the cultivation of rice. More recently, the gravel and oil industries have supplanted Colorado County's traditional sources of agricultural income.

Today, Columbus is considerably more peaceful, but a person brought up in those wild and woolly days would not have too much trouble finding his or her way around, so much remains of old Columbus—enough, in fact, to merit a small book all its own. Many of these old-timers now reside in the town's two cemeteries.

In the Old City Cemetery (1300 Walnut) are Benjamin Beason, W. B. Dewees, Dr. John Logue (who opened the first drugstore in Texas), Columbus Tap Railway president E. P. Whitfield, and Dilue Rose Harris. The Stafford brothers and Larkin Hope rest in the Odd Fellows Rest Cemetery (1500 Montezuma), as well as Wells Thompson, who served as Texas lieutenant governor from 1878 to 1880. Then there is Ike Towell, whose epitaph reads, "Here rests Ike Towell— An infidel who had no hope of heaven nor fear of hell, was free of superstition, to do right and love justice was his religion."

R. B. "Bob" Johnson left Colorado County in the spring of 1870 with a herd bound for Abilene, Kansas. Soon after reaching Abilene, he died. The body was embalmed, put in a metal casket, and buried at Abilene about the last of July 1870. The following September, a young black cowhand named George Glenn, whom Johnson had raised on his ranch, came to Abilene with a Studebaker wagon, the body was disinterred, and Glenn began the long journey home with his ex-master's body. The trip took forty-two days; Glenn slept each night in the wagon next to the casket. Once back at Columbus, Johnson was laid to permanent rest beside his wife.

Near the city cemetery is the one-acre Hebrew Benevolence Society Cemetery, at Montezuma and FM 806, established in 1879 with the burial of M. A. Levy. By that time, Columbus counted twelve Jewish families, several more Jewish single men, and a B'nai B'rith Lodge. As Jewish families began to settle in nearby Wharton in the 1880s, families in both towns began to worship together, eventually organizing Congregation Shearith Israel in Wharton in 1913. Among the town's Jewish citizens buried here are two infants who died in the 1880s, and merchant Louis Rosenstein. The last burial, of Pauline Lewin Nussbaum, occurred in 1938. Abandoned for many years, the cemetery was restored in 1988 by Boy Scouts from Houston's Beth Israel congregation.

From the western outskirts of Columbus, continue east on US 90 past the old city cemetery. US 90 becomes Walnut once you are in Columbus. The courthouse square is located six blocks east of the US 90/SH 71B junction at Walnut and Milam.

Columbus' *Talking Houses* audio driving tour program puts local history as near as your radio dial. Many of the town's historic sites are equipped with radio transmitters that operate on a specified AM frequency. The transmitter broadcasts a prerecorded message that provides interesting information about the site over the car radio; you stay in your vehicle and listen, making it easy to explore the major historic sites. Look for the audio driving tour symbol at these sites; the sign lists the appropriate frequency.

COLORADO COUNTY COURTHOUSE

Walnut and Milam • 732-2604 • Monday through Friday • W

Built of locally made brick with Belton limestone trim in the Second Empire style, this is the courthouse whose cornerstone played a catalyst role on the bloody day of July 7, 1890. In November 1890, the commissioners voted to install a clock in the tower. Even this caused controversy. The city of Columbus provided about 25 percent of the purchase price and an employee to maintain it, but many rural Colorado Countians were against the "Columbus town clock," saying among other things that the county paid too much for it. The courthouse was finally completed in February 1891, and a grand ball on February 24 inaugurated it.

The Neoclassical copper dome that now tops the courthouse replaced the original bell tower, which was knocked to the ground by the hurricane of 1909. The clock was never replaced, and so the clock winder lost his fifteen-dollar-a-month job.

Step inside for a look at the district courtroom, most notable for its Tiffany-style stained-glass dome and matching lampshade. The courtroom looks just as it did when first built, down to the hard-backed wooden spectators benches, pine wainscoting, and wreathed ceiling. Stained-glass enthusiasts come from all over the country to see the dome.

1883 CONFEDERATE MEMORIAL MUSEUM

Southwest corner of courthouse square, Spring and Milam • 732-5135 • Open Monday through Saturday and by appointment • Fee • W variable

Located on the southwest corner of the courthouse square is the old water tower. The tower was built in 1883 using four hundred thousand bricks. A wooden water tank up top and a horse-drawn fire wagon beneath comprised Columbus' first fire department. The tower served in that capacity until 1912. The town tried to demolish it a few years later, but the thirty-two-inch-thick walls proved indestructible. In 1926, it became the local Daughters of the Confederacy museum.

STAFFORD OPERA HOUSE AND COLUMBUS CHAMBER OF COMMERCE

425 Spring at Milam • 732-8385 • www.columbustexas.org • Monday through Saturday • Fee • W

Located across from the courthouse and next to the Bob Stafford house is the Stafford Opera House, built by Bob Stafford in 1886 for the princely sum of $50,000. Stafford acquired the property after fire destroyed Bond's Hotel, which had previously occupied this corner. He planned to build two commercial buildings, but he was asked by local citizens to build something large enough to host theatrical productions and other social events. Stafford acceded to their wishes, and prominent Galveston architect Nicholas J. Clayton designed the opera house in the French Second Empire style. The bricks were made south of town. Bob's Stafford Bank (capitalized at $50,000) and the Senftenberg Mercantile Company occupied the first floor, with the elaborate opera house upstairs. It was lit by gas-burning chandeliers. The curtain, wings, and additional stage equipment cost Stafford $10,000. One thousand people filled the hall on opening night; special trains were run to bring in folk from surrounding counties. Stafford could watch the shows from his bedroom next door. The marble cornerstone of "R. E. Stafford's Building," depicting a steer roped by the horns, the rope being held by a single right hand, is one of the more unusual cornerstones you'll ever see. After Stafford's death, the bank, store, and opera house continued to operate until the building was sold in 1916. The last show upstairs was held in 1916. The first floor housed the local Ford dealership from 1918 to 1974. The upstairs was used as a boxing arena, for basketball games, and as a roller-skating rink. The stage was torn out in World War II, and the area converted into eight apartments in response to the wartime housing shortage. Finally it became a tire storage area.

Preservation-minded citizens purchased the building in 1972 and spent $1.3 million restoring it. Plays and other live entertainment are presented on a regular basis. The chamber of commerce offices are located downstairs, where you can obtain information about opera house events and tours, as well as a variety of informative local literature, including self-guided tours of historic Columbus. Guided tours of historic Columbus are given on the first and third Thursdays and third Saturday of each month. There are over seventy historical markers scattered about town.

Group tours of museums and specialty shops are available to meet the needs and abilities of everyone, including those with hearing or other impairments, slow walkers, and wheelchair travelers. Theme tours include Texian Heritage, Frontier (Reconstruction) Heritage, Victorian Heritage, Arts Heritage, and Collections Heritage.

R. E. "BOB" STAFFORD HOUSE

400 block of Spring, next to the opera house • Private residence

Stafford built his residence next door to his bank and opera house. This two-story, cypress-and-pine frame house with a cupola on top is a good example of the Carpenter Gothic style, with ornate, jigsaw-cut porch-column brackets, fascia, and balustrades. At the time of his murder, Bob Stafford's range extended from Colorado County to the Gulf of Mexico, and his herd numbered somewhere between fifty thousand and seventy-five thousand head. He had a horse ranch in Presidio County and about ninety thousand acres of various properties in other counties and in the San Antonio area.

From the Stafford Opera House, head north on Milam.

EHRENWERTH-RAMSEY-UNTERMEYER BUILDING

1120 Milam

Built in 1875 with bricks from a local kiln and being one of Columbus' oldest commercial buildings, this is about the most elaborate business structure downtown. Ehrenwerth built it to house his mercantile store, but it housed L. G. Smith's Red Elk Saloon and Gambling Hall during the 1880s. The Untermeyer Hardware Store was here for nearly seventy years, beginning in 1925.

BRUNSON BUILDING

1014 Milam

Charles Brunson built the building which bears his name in 1891. A native of Westphalia, Germany, Brunson came to the United States in 1845 at age fifteen.

After driving stagecoaches and mule teams for years, he settled in Columbus in 1866 and went into the saloon business, at which he prospered. In the early days, the second story of his saloon served as an opera house and theater. In 1896, he built the structure at 1010 Milam, which was later known as the Wald-vogel building. The Brunson building was used as a saloon until Prohibition and has since housed a variety of businesses. On the morning of March 16, 1899, Sam Reese tied his horse to the hitching rail in front of Brunson's Saloon and was shot dead moments later. Except for the lowering of the canopy and some changes in the windows, it has maintained its original style, down to the cast-iron porch columns and step-up out front.

PRESTON KYLE SHATTO WILDLIFE MUSEUM

1002 Milam • 732-5135 • Open first and third Thursdays and for group tours; closed July and August • Fee

Wildlife from around the world are on display; the collection was gathered over the years by two local families. There are more than sixty-five species from North America, Africa, Australia, and New Zealand, ranging from bull elk to elephant, rhinoceros, lion, leopard, and cape buffalo.

HANCOCK-HELLER HOME

934 Milam • Private residence

One of Columbus' more unique homes is the Hancock-Heller home. It was built in 1865 by county tax collector John Hancock as a simple one-story dogtrot house with cypress walls and cedar floors. The house received its current, radical face-lift in 1884, when another owner added the gable with its sinfully rich scroll-work bargeboards, the equally elaborate porch fascia, the lacy porch-column brackets, and the ball-and-spindle porch balustrade. Seldom do you see so much gingerbread on a small one-story house. You gain weight just looking at it.

SIMPSON-YOUENS-HOPKINS HOUSE

617 Milam • Private residence

Joseph Hopkins had this cottage built after the Civil War. James Simpson, the county's first banker, bought it in 1875. It has a local-brick foundation and is constructed of pine and cypress. Cypress is a very durable wood, especially impervious to moisture; cypress and cedar were used extensively in many of the old homes still standing today.

Double back to Walnut; then turn right on Walnut to reach the next three attractions.

GANT HOUSE

936 Bowie • Currently not open to the public; audio tour only

This German cottage built in 1860 features original wall stenciling and decorative painting. It has been featured in *Country Living*, and the stenciling in one room was copied for the Texas Room in the DAR Museum in Washington, D.C.

ILSE-RAU HOME/RAUMONDA

1100 Bowie at Walnut • Private residence

Another of Columbus' showcase homes is the graceful Ilse-Rau home, built by farmer-rancher-saloonkeeper Henry Ilse in 1887. Constructed in a symmetric Carpenter Gothic style, the two-story home is cypress with wood floors, and a roof of stamped-metal rectangles. The porch balustrades are of an elaborate interlocking circle design.

TATE-SENFTENBERG-BRANDON HOUSE MUSEUM

616 Walnut (US 90), between Bowie and Live Oak • 732-5135 • Open for group tours and special events • Fee

This house started as a simple one-story, four-room Greek Revival cottage with four fireplaces and a basement made of handmade brick. It was remodeled by the Senftenberg family in the 1880s to its present two-story, ornate Victorian appearance. Kenneth Brandon bought the house in 1900 and added the northeast wing. The Magnolia Homes Tour Inc. acquired the house in 1968. The museum depicts life in Columbus in the late nineteenth century and includes many antique items donated by local families, including crazy quilts from the Bob Stafford family.

Now take Live Oak back to Spring, where you turn left, past the Townsend-West-Stiles home.

TOWNSEND-WEST-STILES HOME

634 Spring

This Eastlake-style house was built in 1890 for Marcus and Annie Burford Townsend, on the site of the old Southern Pacific Railway Hospital, which burned down in 1886. Marcus was one of the principals in the Stafford-Townsend feud; he served as state representative from 1883 to 1885, and state senator from 1889 to 1893. Townsend's main legislative accomplishments amounted to sponsoring the bill for the state to buy the Alamo and another bill to name a county after his law partner, Robert Foard. Built in the shape of a cross, it features ornate lacy gingerbread trim along the roofline and gables, a ball-and-spindle porch balustrade, intricately carved doors and woodwork, and stained-glass windows. The house also features ten-foot-tall windows that go to the floor; some say Townsend had the windows installed that way so he could easily watch for potential assailants. Thurman West bought the place from Townsend in 1906, and the West family occupied the house until 1989.

Head back toward the courthouse square. At Bowie, turn right to reach the Alley Log Cabin, Dilue Rose Harris House, and Mary Elizabeth Hopkins Santa Claus Museum.

ALLEY LOG CABIN AND ANTIQUE TOOL MUSEUM

1224 Bowie • 732-5135 • Monday through Friday • Fee

In 1822, eighteen-year-old Abraham Alley and three brothers came to Texas from Missouri to join their older brother, Rawson, who had settled in Colorado County the year before as a member of Austin's "Old Three Hundred." A farmer, Abraham also participated in several campaigns against the Waco, Tawakoni, and Comanche Indians as far away as San Saba during the 1820s. Alley built this cabin from oak logs in late 1836 to replace the cabin burned during the Runaway Scrape; he and his wife Nancy raised five children in it. The cabin was moved here from its original site at nearby Alleyton in 1976. It is furnished with period antiques. Alleyton was named for the Alley brothers, all of whom settled near each other about three miles east of Columbus. Brother William donated land for the town site in 1859. In 1860, Alleyton became the terminus of the Buffalo Bayou, Brazos, and Colorado railroad and was briefly the biggest town in the county.

Not to be outgunned by Columbus, Alleyton had its own feudists, the most infamous of whom were Dallas Stoudenmire and Tuck Hoover.

Dallas was born in 1845 in Alabama and served in the Confederate Army. In about 1867, he came to Columbus, where he farmed and reputedly killed several men. He briefly served with the Texas Rangers and then returned to Colorado County to work as a carpenter and wheelwright at the German settlement of Mentz, near Alleyton. On September 14, 1876, he sat on a jury that tried an outhouse for being a nauseating annoyance. The jury found the privy to be a public nuisance and ordered the proper authorities to have it cleaned. He loved women, drinking, horse races, and dogfights. He is said to have trained a stallion to attack on command, biting adversaries on the leg, according to Robert Fleming, president of the Colorado County Historical Society. "He was a man who laughed a lot and what he said made others laugh too."

In 1876, while riding the range in Colorado County, he met up with someone he had been arguing with for several months. They hurled insults from a distance and then fired some shots at each other that fell short. As they closed in on each other, Dallas fired and hit his opponent and then strolled on over to watch him die. In 1877, he was at a large party at Alleyton when a shooting brawl flared up. He wounded several adversaries, but he was himself shot, captured, and bound up. But his guard went to sleep, and Dallas freed himself and escaped. A grand jury convened but indicted no one.

Buck and Tuck Hoover were Stoudenmire's best friends. Tuck Hoover was an Alleyton rancher. Dallas and the Hoover brothers loved to dance, and Buck, a fiddler, was in constant demand at parties; they traveled to parties as far as forty miles away. Dallas didn't hesitate to ask any girl to dance. A Mrs. Clapp said years later that Dallas once asked her to dance. She told him that she would dance with any man who wore his pants in his boots. Dallas replied that he would dance with her if her pants were in her boots.

In 1878, Tuck Hoover, Dallas Stoudenmire, and some other friends got into an argument near Alleyton with a rival group of cattlemen, led by the Sparks brothers of Eagle Lake, about the ownership of some cattle. When the shooting was over, two members of the Sparks faction were dead, and one of the Sparks brothers was wounded.

By 1880 Dallas was in the merchandising business in Llano County, where he had a "serious difficulty" that sent him to Dr. John Herff in San Antonio. Dr. Herff was frequently mentioned in the *Colorado County Citizen* in the 1870s, so it's possible that they knew each other from those days. No record exists of Dallas' problem or Herff's treatment, though.

Evidently the mercantile business was not in Stoudenmire's blood, for he became El Paso city marshal in 1881. Within days of his appointment, he was involved in two bloody shootouts, killing four men, including former city marshal Bill Johnson, who had tried to assassinate him. Stoudenmire returned to Columbus in February 1882 to marry Isabella "Belle" Sherrington but was soon back in El Paso with his bride. He began feuding with the Texas Rangers, local politicians, and newspapers. He especially hated the Manning brothers (Doc, Frank, and James), who owned two saloons. James Manning had recently killed Samuel Cummings, Dallas' brother-in-law. El Pasoans insisted that Dallas and the Mannings sign a peace treaty, which was published in the *El Paso Herald*. An alcoholic who cheated on his wife, he was censured after several absences because of drinking. He resigned after a year and became deputy U.S. marshal but continued to drink. On September 18, 1882, James and Doc Manning killed him in an El Paso saloon. The Mannings were acquitted of murder charges, and Stoudenmire's body was shipped to Columbus for burial in Alleyton.

Belle wanted him buried in Columbus, but he had died with no money and lots of debt, so Mason Lodge 130, which had awarded Dallas his third degree in January 1882, paid for his coffin and a suit of clothes. He was shipped by rail to Columbus and then taken to Alleyton where he laid in state for a couple of days. Stoudenmire was buried at the Alleyton cemetery, where his grave is prominently marked.

In 1894, Tuck Hoover got into a fight with an Alleyton saloon keeper named Burtshell. Shooting started, and Burtshell was killed. Hoover was released on bond, but soon after, he was accosted on an Alleyton street by Jim Coleman, a young local tough. Coleman shot Hoover to death. He would go on to participate in the Reese-Townsend feud before being killed in San Antonio.

DILUE ROSE HARRIS HOUSE MUSEUM

602 Washington • 732-5135 • Open for group tours and special events • Fee

Dilue Rose Harris came to Texas as a young girl in 1833. She married Ira Harris in 1839 at the tender age of thirteen, and they moved to Columbus in 1845. Ira served as county sheriff and city marshal. They built this house in 1858. It has masonry walls of gravel and lime, plastered over and scored to resemble stone blocks, and is decidedly uncharacteristic of the era. Ira died in 1869, leaving her and nine children behind. Intimately acquainted with the leaders of the Texas Revolution and the Republic, Dilue wrote extensively of her early life in Texas. Historians have relied on her reminiscences ever since. The house is filled with personal effects and period furnishings. She died in nearby Eagle Lake in 1914.

MARY ELIZABETH HOPKINS SANTA CLAUS MUSEUM

604 Washington • 732-5135 • www.santamuseum.org • Monday and Thursday and group tours • Fee

Over one thousand representations of Santa are on display. There are Santa music boxes, banks, creamers, pitchers, salt and pepper shakers, cookie jars, and homemade Santas. The collection memorializes Mary Elizabeth Hopkins, who got her first Santa in 1913. After her death in 1990, her husband donated the collection to the Magnolia Homes Tour Inc., which led to the creation of the museum.

NESBITT MEMORIAL LIBRARY

529 Washington • 732-3392 • www.columbustexas.net/library • Monday through Saturday

This public library is enhanced by a collection of old dolls and kids' toys donated by Miss Lee Nesbitt. The library is also notable for its Texas history and genealogy archives.

OTHER ATTRACTIONS

KEITH-TRAYLOR HOUSE

806 Live Oak

This gingerbread-festooned cottage was built around 1871 by John Keith, a Civil War veteran who moved here in 1870 and became a lumber dealer. Charles and Lura Traylor bought it in 1875. In 1896, one of the Traylor daughters married a son of the Keith family in the same room of the house in which both were born.

TAIT TOWN HOUSE

526 Wallace

Born in Georgia, Dr. Charles Tait (1815–1878) came to Texas from Alabama in 1844. A former U.S. Navy surgeon who also had a civil engineering degree, Tait surveyed land for a railroad company and was paid with a six-thousand-acre tract of land south of Columbus. He used the land to establish a plantation he called Sylvania that was headquartered about ten miles south of Columbus. The plantation grew corn, cotton, and cane, and produced lime. Slaves hewed the logs and fired bricks in the plantation's kiln that they used to build the plantation house in 1847. Tait fought in the Mexican War of 1846–1848, serving as surgeon with Jack Hays' Texas Mounted Cavalry. In 1848, he married Louisa Williams of Bastrop. He was elected to the state legislature in 1853 and 1855. But by 1856, Tait had decided to move his family into town; he felt that the damp river-bottom climate was dangerous to their health, and he wanted his children to attend a good school. So construction began in 1856 on a town house located on a 640-acre tract on the edge of Columbus. Bricks for the two-story Greek Revival house were made at the plantation. Stone quarried there formed the foundation. The lumber came from trees cut at Sylvania, cut by a saw powered by the engine of a small steamboat that had gotten stuck in the silt-laden Colorado River near the plantation. The *Moccasin Belle* had carried Tait's cotton to Galveston. Tait bought the marooned boat and salvaged what he could. The pine flooring and window frames came by boat from Bastrop. The family moved into the house in 1859, but it wasn't finished until Dr. Tait returned from service with the Confederate Army. From the high widow's walk, Tait could see all the way to his plantation. Dr. Tait died in 1878, but members of the family have continued to live in the house ever since. The anchor from the *Moccasin Belle* still sits in the front yard.

MONTGOMERY HOUSE

1419 Milam

This L-shaped cottage was built in 1867 by land agent A. J. Gallilee. It has a handmade-brick foundation, native oak sills, and pine flooring. The siding, doors, and window shutters are cypress. J. T. and Fanny Montgomery bought it in 1876.

SECOND-LARGEST LIVE OAK

1218 Walnut, across from Post Office

This venerable, low-spreading tree is recognized as the second-largest recorded live oak in Texas by the Texas Forest Service. It is also recorded in their Registry of Champion Big Trees in Texas. It tops out at 75 feet and has a trunk circumference of 310 inches.

DINING

SCHOBEL'S RESTAURANT

2020 Milam at SH 71B, just north of I-10 • 732-2385 • Open daily, breakfast, lunch, and dinner • DC, MC, V • W

Located in a modern prefab building, which fortunately does not reflect upon the down-home food, Schobel's has a basic Texas rural cafe menu: steaks, seafood, fried chicken, and Mexican food. They serve homemade bread and pie. Beer, wine, and mixed drinks are also on the menu.

KEYSER'S MEAT MARKET

1116 Milam, on the courthouse square • 732-2658

This is an old-fashioned meat market offering smoked meats, ham, turkey, and sandwiches.

MIKESKA'S BAR-B-Q

4053 Hwy. 90 East, along westbound I-10 • 732-2293, 800-524-7613 • www.jerrymikeska.com • Open daily, lunch and dinner

Jerry Mikeska based the building's somewhat octagon shape on an old dance hall. This trip is short on barbecue places, so if you missed Zimmerhanzel's in Smithville, Mikeska serves acceptable brisket, pork ribs, sausage, and chicken. The vast collection of exotic animals on display makes it as much a museum as a restaurant, if you didn't get your fill of stuffed animals at the Preston Kyle Shatto Wildlife Museum.

LODGING

The Columbus area has a number of B&Bs. Call 732-5135 for current establishments and reservations.

MAGNOLIA OAKS AND THE LITTLE RED HOUSE BED AND BREAKFAST

634 Spring • 732-2726 • www.magnoliaoaks.com

This 1890 Eastlake Victorian mansion has six units with private baths. It is shaded by massive oak and magnolia trees and is beautifully decorated. Sitting next to Magnolia Oaks is the charming 1860s German saltbox cottage named the Little Red House. The cottage has a suite with a sunny sitting porch and bath, and accommodates two or four people. The upper room has two double beds with a bath downstairs. The Little Red House common room has a historic painted ceiling of Texas wildflowers and the Texas Star.

AREA PARKS

BEASON'S PARK

US 90 at Colorado River bridge, east of town • W

This park has primitive camping and picnic areas, playing fields, swimming in the river, canoeing, and fishing for catfish, perch, gasper goo, and bass.

OTHER ATTRACTIONS

ATTWATER PRAIRIE CHICKEN NATIONAL WILDLIFE REFUGE

Take SH 71 south to US 90A, then east to FM 3013 at Eagle Lake, then east (left) about 7 miles to the refuge • 234-3021 • Open daily dawn to dusk • Free • W variable

During mating season, male prairie chickens make a mating call that sounds like someone blowing across the mouth of a bottle. You can watch this endangered species' mating dance and hear the male's "booming" mating call from late February to early May in this eight-thousand-acre U.S. Fish and Wildlife Service refuge. Write PO Box 519, Eagle Lake 77434.

ANNUAL EVENT

MAY

SPRINGTIME FESTIVAL

732-5135 • Third weekend in May • Fee for some events • W

Featured are street dances and live music, antique cars, an arts-and-crafts show, live entertainment at the Stafford Opera House, a beer garden, and the famous Magnolia Homes Tour, featuring several of Columbus' historic old homes and buildings, often private homes that folks would otherwise never get a chance to see.

To leave Columbus, proceed west on Walnut/US 90 from the courthouse square; then turn right on SH 71B toward La Grange. As you cross the Colorado River, you pass by the site of the fabulous Robson castle, located on your right on the south bank of the river. Nothing remains of the castle. A little more than a half mile from the river bridge, turn right on FM 109 to Frelsburg.

The graceful spreading live oak at the SH 71B/FM 109 intersection has a dark history that has prompted some to demand that it be destroyed. On the night of November 12, 1935, two black teenagers, Benny Mitchell Jr. and Ernest Collins, were hanged from the tree's limbs. They were about to stand trial for the murder of a local white girl a month earlier. They had been taken to Houston for their safety and were brought back to Columbus the night before the trial. But an armed mob of white men snatched them from the sheriff's car and lynched them here.

ZIMMERSCHEIDT SCHOOL

Zimmerscheidt Community • About 8 miles from SH 71 and 3 miles south of Frelsburg

Just before the four-way intersection with Zimmerscheidt Road, you'll see on your left the one-room, white frame Zimmerscheidt School, one of the few one-room schools left standing in Central Texas. In 1855, Frederick Zimmerscheidt donated an acre of land so that a school might be established to educate local children. That school served the community that took on Zimmerscheidt's name from the time of its establishment in 1857 till its consolidation with the Columbus Independent School District in 1948. The building then served as community center until 1962. The doors are locked, but if you look in through the windows, the interior looks just like it did when they closed the doors for the last time.

FRELSBURG

Colorado County • 75 • About 12 miles from Columbus

Frelsburg was named for John and William Frels, pre-Adelsverein German immigrants who settled here in the early 1830s. There's not much to see or do in Frelsburg these days, but if things had worked out a little differently, Frelsburg might be a bustling college town today. Frelsburg, you see, was to be the home of Hermann's University, an institute of higher learning that would offer German instruction in liberal arts, theology, medicine, and the law. The Republic of Texas Congress chartered the university in 1844 and donated a league of land. The school was to be financed by sales of stock shares, at fifty dollars a pop. But evidently Texans deemed the price too steep, and at any rate the Civil War came along and disrupted plans. Hermann's University was reincorporated in 1870, with twenty-five dollar shares, a league of land donated by the state in Gillespie County, and an actual building site located at Frelsburg. A two-story building was erected here, but classes were never held. The act of incorporation was repealed in 1871, and the Frelsburg public school inherited the building.

SAINTS PETER AND PAUL CATHOLIC CHURCH

Church Lane, east side of FM 109, 0.5 miles south of the intersection with FM 1291

Established in 1847 by German Catholics, it is one of the state's oldest Catholic parishes. The current sanctuary was built in 1912 and features ornate statuary. Its Greek Revival, temple-style facade gives it a unique look among Central Texas Catholic churches.

TRINITY LUTHERAN CHURCH

FM 1291, just off FM 109, several hundred feet west of the Frelsburg store

In 1855, William Frels donated land for a cemetery and church. A Lutheran congregation was formed, as well as a day school. English-language services were not conducted here until 1932, so overwhelmingly German was the membership. The present, white frame sanctuary (built in 1927) reflects the basic philosophy of its congregation. The structure is severely straightforward, of minimal physical ornamentation save the gables projecting from the tinned steeple. The steeple is covered with embossed tin, the pattern of which looks like nothing so much as the Pentecostal water-droplet symbol. It is capped by a crucifix resting atop a ball (the earth). Even the stained-glass windows are mostly black and white and a somber, severe green.

Porch railings are no-nonsense plumbing pipe. The inscription "Evan. Luth. Trinity Congregation Frelsburg" is executed in stained glass over the front entrance.

At Frelsburg, follow FM 109's path east, then north into New Ulm.

NEW ULM

Austin County • 650 • About 4 miles from Frelsburg

New Ulm was originally known as Duffs Settlement after James Duff, to whom this land was granted in 1841. After 1845, the area's population became increasingly German, many of them coming here from the previously established communities of Nassau, Shelby, and Industry. They renamed the community after the city of Ulm in Württemberg, Germany. New Ulm has been, and continues to be, a prosperous farming community, with its very own bank. And by virtue of its pioneer architecture, New Ulm is one of Central Texas' most unique communities.

As Texas towns developed during the last half of the nineteenth century, they went through several transformations. Almost always, the first permanent commercial buildings to be erected were small, one-story, wood-framed shotgun affairs. The omnipresent gabled roof was always hidden by a false front. The front entrance was always symmetrically arranged, with centered double doors flanked by single windows or display bays. You've seen these buildings in countless Hollywood westerns, but you hardly ever see them in real life anymore.

Almost universally, time has been harsh to these structures. Those that remain are found only in isolated communities and are usually abandoned and decaying. But in New Ulm, a few of these frontier relics are alive and well. One of Central Texas' most timeless communities, New Ulm is full of turn-of-the-century houses and commercial buildings.

As small as the town is, it's hard to get lost, and it's pretty easy to find places despite the less-than-comprehensive street signing. Every north-south street that concerns us is marked along FM 1094 (Bastrop, New Ulm's principal east-west artery). In order, from west to east and starting with FM 109 (the principal north-south artery), they are FM 109, Elm, Pecan, Walnut, and Main. Cross streets (running east to west) as you come into New Ulm from Frelsburg are Front, Taylor, and Bastrop (FM 1094).

All of the buildings of interest are within the confines of this twelve-block area. The buildings seemingly dot the blocks at random, punctuating the gridded grasslands rather than obliterating them, just as they have done for the last century. In this rare collection, one home stands out from the rest as an exercise in fanciful deception.

FINK HOUSE

315 Walnut at Bastrop/FM 1094 • Private residence

Built in 1893 for the Fink family, who moved here from Bastrop, this interesting house has a facade in the shingle style of architecture. True shingle-style houses have floor plans that feature irregular rooms freely grouped around a large hall. The rooms open up to each other in a continuous flow of space, and the theme of spatial flow and unity continues outside, with wide porches encircling most of the house. Broad horizontal lines on the exterior emphasize the theme of interior flow by the use of huge, massive roofs, horizontal bands of windows, and the fusion of roof shingles and shingles as wall surface, creating a house with sprawling, lazy lines. The Fink House features a broad, massive roof that unites with a portholed, shingled front porch, but the floor plan is traditionally symmetrical. Altogether, the house is a unique exercise in Swiss-flavored geometric gingerbread and shingle styling.

Another nice housing compound is at 302 Houston at Cedar, featuring a two-story lap-board main house, a smaller one-story lap-board house, a small log cabin, and a gazebo.

Most of commercial New Ulm is vacant (though recently renovated), but a few businesses hang on in the old storefronts. Good examples of frontier shotgun buildings are located in the 600 block of Taylor east of FM 109, the 800 block of Pecan (two blocks east of FM 109), and the 200 block of Walnut. These locations include both freestanding structures and strings of three or more contiguous buildings. The old creamery complex stands at the corner of Taylor and Main, four blocks east of FM 109 and one block south of Bastrop/FM 1094.

To reach Fireman's Park, follow the signs from FM 109.

FIREMAN'S PARK

One mile west of town on Taylor • Open during daylight hours • Free • W

This park/baseball diamond/picnic area is quiet, secluded, shaded, and big enough to let the kids run around in. Community baseball league games take place here every Sunday afternoon in the summer.

Retrace your route back to town from the park. Continue north on FM 109 from New Ulm to Industry.

As you leave New Ulm, you will notice more of New Ulm's old homes and the Lutheran church atop the gently rising hill to your left.

INDUSTRY

Austin County • 475 • About 6 miles from New Ulm

Industry can properly be regarded as the first German settlement in Texas, and the beginning of the great German migrations to Texas can properly be dated to the 1831 arrival of Friedrich Ernst and Charles Fordtran. Ernst, a former postal clerk, and Fordtran, a tanner from Westphalia, met in New York and joined forces to find a new home. Their search led them to Texas, where Ernst, as a married man with a family, was eligible for a full league of land in Austin's colony. The single Fordtran was eligible for only one-quarter league. The two settled as neighbors here in the

Mill Creek valley, in the northwest corner of present-day Austin County. Ernst, the "Father of German Immigration in Texas," was ill-prepared for his new pioneer lifestyle. He did not know how to build a cabin, he hated guns, and he had brought none of the equipment necessary for clothing his family out here on the fringe of civilization. Still, he had a boundless love for his new homeland with its rich soil, mild climate, political freedom, and unlimited opportunities. He poured out all these feelings in an eloquent letter to a friend back home in Oldenburg. The friend passed Ernst's letter to a friend, who copied the letter and passed it on to others, who did the same. Ernst's enthusiasm spread to the letter's many readers, and the stream of German migration to Texas commenced.

Meanwhile, Ernst and Fordtran were adapting to life out here on the frontier and were beginning to prosper. Ernst improvised a gristmill by fashioning a mortar from a tree stump, after the fashion of Indian stump mills. Softened corn was placed in the mortar and ground into meal. It served several families until a better mill was constructed.

Ernst laid out a town site on his land in 1838. He had invited all German immigrants who so desired to stop at his estate until they had selected land of their own. A number of them chose to settle down here. Some of these visitors suggested that Ernst make cigars from the tobacco grown in his garden, and the cigar-making industry that developed gave the town its name. The industrious Germans would spend their lunch breaks from the fields rolling cigars; their Anglo American neighbors were so impressed with the Germans' industriousness that they referred to the village accordingly.

In 1846, William Hermes, a German immigrant who had just arrived at Galveston, heard about the sickness and death then plaguing other German immigrants camped at Indianola and traveling the road to New Braunfels,

> So, with a fellow traveler I decided to take passage on the mail-coach to Industry about which we had heard and read quite laudable reports.
> The mail-coach did not touch at Industry but within a few miles of the place we got off the coach and reached our destination on foot. The so-called City of Industry at the time consisted of three buildings: Sieper's store, the Squire Ernst inn, and a small building in which three young unmarried doctors resided; the Doctors Ricklessen, Schade, and Sigismund. A few yards from there and on the road to Mr. Walter's farm, a Mr. Knolle was in the act of building a house for himself with whom I found employment as a handy-man for a short time.

Industry prospered as a farm community, with its own gin and sawmill, well into the twentieth century. After a bit of a nap during the last half of the twentieth century, Industry is getting lively again, thanks to the spillover from Houston and Austin.

To get to the heart of old downtown Industry, turn right off FM 109 onto Main, the first street after the FM 109/SH 159 intersection, by the post office.

WEIGE BUILDING

1500 block of Main St. at Weige, 1 block north of SH 159

The Weige building, on your left, was built in 1888. The Weige Store closed in 1973. A third of the building was detached and moved a short distance away, where it became Assman's Cafe. Before it was detached, it had housed the Industry Bottling Works (1903–1928), which bottled soft drinks, as well as a saloon. The bar was still in use when Assman's Cafe burned down several decades ago. It was not the first time that fire ravaged downtown Industry. In 1917, the other side of Main Street burned down. The only survivor was the small old wooden store across the street from Weige's store.

Behind the Weige building, practically obscured from sight by another small building in front of it, is a small, simple, one-room white frame commercial building, moved from its original location on Main, across from Firemen's Park. It was originally the saddle shop of Ferdinand Ernst, grandson of Friedrich Ernst. Later, it was a weekend meat market. You get a slightly better glimpse of it from behind, on Bermuda Street, one block north of Main.

A few yards east of the Weige building and on the other side of Main Street is another 1917 fire survivor, the old, abandoned wood-frame George Kollatschny store, which was a combination garage, convenience store, and beer joint before it closed in the 1970s. The men's and women's bathroom doors in the back still say "For whites only." If there were bathrooms for other races, they no longer exist.

Continue east on Main to the modern Immaculate Conception Catholic Church to see the "East End" of old Industry. Of the various old houses strung out along this section of Main, the most interesting is the Schramm House, which is also the last house, as the town plays out, located at the corner of Main and the first cross street running to your right, just before you reach the cotton gin, and then Immaculate Conception Church.

SCHRAMM HOUSE

Private Residence

This large two-story white frame house with the massive pillared plantation-style front porch was built by German businessman C. C. Koch in the 1860s. After his death in 1891, his widow converted the house into a hotel. It reverted to a family residence in 1908. A detached building behind the house (you can see it as you double back into town) is supposedly a pre–Civil War kitchen, back when kitchens were separated from the main house because of fire hazards.

From Immaculate Conception Church, backtrack on Main, past the Weige building, to the intersection with FM 109. Continue west on Main to see the "West End" of old Industry. Follow the sign, to your right, to Industry Methodist Church.

INDUSTRY METHODIST CHURCH

The simple whitewashed wooden sanctuary behind the newer church was built in 1867. Men from the congregation did most of the construction work, since hard money to pay professional carpenters was almost nonexistent after the Civil War. The adjacent Pilgrims' Rest Cemetery offers one of the best panoramic views of the bucolic countryside in Austin County. Friedrich Ernst's widow and children are buried here. Farther west on Main, after you cross FM 159, is the 1899 Lindemann Home and store, and a historical marker describing the family's prominent role in Industry's business life. The old, rusting, corrugated metal shed next to Zaskoda Funeral Chapel was Industry's last blacksmith shop. It closed in 1972.

INDUSTRY POST OFFICE

Friedrich Ernst Park, Schroeder Lane, just off FM 109, about 0.5 miles north of the FM 109/FM 159 intersection; turn left at the Friedrich Ernst Park signs • Always open • No fee • W

As best as anyone can tell, this small, one-room rock building was built from locally quarried stone in 1838 as a store for Friedrich Ernst and his son-in-law, John Sieper. It was also the area post office, supposedly the first post office in Texas west of Galveston. The adjoining park is a good picnic spot.

From Ernst Park, return to the FM 109/FM 159 intersection. Head west on FM 159 (toward Fayetteville and La Grange). In 2.5 miles, turn right onto FM 1457 toward Shelby.

ECKERMANN'S MEAT MARKET

FM 1457, about 4.5 miles from Industry • 979-836-8858 • eckermanns meatmarket.com • Open Monday through Saturday • W

It seems like every neighborhood big enough to have a name in this part of Texas has a meat market or a local sausage maker, and Shelby is no exception. Eckermann's makes two kinds of pork/beef sausage (one with garlic, one without), liver sausage, bacon, and ham, all locally popular. If you want to cook your sausage the way the natives do, try this recipe, given to me by Shelby's master sausage chef, who has been doing it for over thirty years at Shelby's annual wingding. You can shop online.

Place sausage links in a large pot with enough water to cover. To the water, add a couple of bay leaves, garlic, the juice of a couple of fresh lemons, and a couple of tablespoons of pickling spice tied up in cheesecloth. Simmer slowly for an hour and a half. Do not bring to a hard boil or you'll split the sausage casings. It's important that the casing not burst, he emphasized. This recipe is good for about five pounds of sausage. Adjust accordingly for larger or smaller portions.

SHELBY

Austin County • 175 • About 6.5 miles from Industry

Shelby is named for David Shelby, who settled here in 1822 as one of Stephen F. Austin's "Old Three Hundred." (The Old Three Hundred were the settlers who filled Austin's quota of three hundred families to settle his first land grant.) The village did not really come into existence until Otto von Röder built a gristmill, which attracted prospective settlers. The village took on a decidedly German flavor after 1845, being known for a time as Rödersmuhle. David Shelby became the village's first postmaster in 1846. The Germans' desire for a cultured life led to the founding of an agricultural society, singing society, school, and band by the start of the Civil War. Shelby had two hundred residents and a dozen businesses by 1900. By 1940, the number of commercial establishments was down to seven. Today there are two, as the farm life has given way to the city.

The cemetery is nice, with its collection of graceful cedars and German tombstones, and there are a couple of aging gabled Victorian farmhouses, but not much else here.

The rustic log chapel on Voelkel Road was built in 1988, but it gives you an idea of how the early churches looked. Just a few yards down FM 389 (to your left), you'll see the whitewashed Harmonic Hall. The Harmonic (singing) Society was established here in 1875 and began work on this hall soon after. Every German community of any size had a Harmonic Society, or something like it, and they all built sprawling wooden pavilions like this in which to hold their functions. This hall is still used; its events include a spring antique show that draws dealers from all over the state.

SHELBY AREA HISTORICAL SOCIETY MUSEUM

6755 Skull Creek Road, 0.25 miles north of FM 1457

Located just north of the present-day St. Paul Lutheran Church is the old wood-frame, whitewashed St. Paul Lutheran Church, built in 1903 and now a museum. The front doors are generally left unlocked during the day for visitors' appreciation. The interior of the church is unchanged from a century ago, down to the unpadded wood bench seats, wooden altar, baptistery, and pulpit. The newest items are the hymnals, copyright 1930. The old Hinner's pump organ is in an adjoining room.

About five miles west of Shelby on FM 1457, you see a historical marker, which tells the story of the Nassau Farm and the early days of the Adelsverein.

NASSAU FARM HISTORICAL MARKER

FM 1457 at Wolff Rd. • About 5 miles from Shelby

Books and novels about Texas had captured the fancy of Germans by 1842, among them fourteen noblemen who met to form an informal society "for the purpose of purchasing landed property in the Republic of Texas." The day they met to organize—April 20, 1842—the nobles decided to send two of their group as delegates to Texas to investigate the land, the people, and the climate, and to report back with their findings. Counts Boos-Waldeck and Victor Leiningen left for Texas in May.

In February 1842, Sam Houston, the president of the Republic of Texas, had been authorized by the Congress to grant, under certain conditions, entire tracts of land to contractors who would colonize the land. Count Leiningen negotiated with President Houston, but being inexperienced in legal matters and lacking in counsel, he made demands that could not be granted without nullifying the legality of the contract, changes that even the president could not make.

The Congress did not see fit to alter its colonization law to fit Leiningen's desires, so no agreement was reached. But when he returned to Germany in 1843, Leiningen submitted a favorable report for a large-scale colonization project.

Meanwhile, Count Boos-Waldeck had acquired a beautiful league of land in Fayette County, with rich soil, good water, and heavy forests. The 4,428 acres had cost a little over $3,000; the big house, outbuildings, slaves, and equipment were to cost another $18,000. The Nassau Farm was the showplace of the region. Boos-Waldeck returned to Germany in January 1844 opposing large-scale colonization because of insufficient funds. His advice went unheeded.

Count Castell, one of the society's leaders, had plans for an enterprise like the British East India Company. By July 1843, a joint stock company had been formed "for the purchase and colonization of land grants in the Republic of Texas."

That summer, society members had been approached by Alexander Bourgeois d'Orvanne, a French flimflam man who, with his wealth of Texas knowledge, soon gained the confidence of the society's directors. The commoner Bourgeois had added the title "d'Orvanne" to his name in order to facilitate his approach to the society of German noblemen. By mid-September 1843, he had conned the society into the tentative purchase of his colonization rights in Texas, although the rights were to expire only three months later. His contract with the republic had called for the arrival of four hundred families in Texas within an eighteen-month period, but it expired in December 1843 without his having settled a single colonist. At that time, d'Orvanne had not yet moved the slow-acting German nobles to a final purchase of his contract, either.

By the time the nobles finally ratified the purchase agreement in April 1844, d'Orvanne no longer had any colonization rights to sell. But the nobles knew nothing of this; in the six months spent mulling over the purchase, they had apparently failed to inform themselves fully of the contract's ramifications. Any hope of negotiating an extension on the contract was lost by February 1, 1844, for the Texas Congress had passed a law nullifying all unfulfilled contracts and prohibiting any extensions favorable to the contractors. If Castell and Leiningen, the society's major leaders, knew anything of this law, they probably expected the society's good reputation to ensure renewal of the d'Orvanne contract.

By the time the society was officially chartered as the Adelsverein on May 3, 1844, d'Orvanne was colonial director for the organization, at the disposal of the commissioner general, Prince Carl of Solms-Braunfels. Both men left for Texas later that month. Once in Texas, d'Orvanne pleaded, in vain, with President Houston for a contract extension. When Prince Carl understood the true state of affairs, he wrote back to Germany telling of the difficult situation he was in: the arrival of immigrants was expected soon, and there was no land on which to settle them.

By this time, the society had been approached by another con artist, Henry Fisher, who talked the nobles into buying his colonization contract, the infamous Fisher-Miller contract, for $9,000. Again, the society had neglected to find out what it was getting itself into. Meanwhile, d'Orvanne was canned unceremoniously in August 1844.

Under the terms of the Fisher-Miller contract, the society was bound by law to settle six thousand immigrants on land that was 300 miles from the coast, 150 miles from the closest settlement, completely unexplored, and in the hands of hostile Indians. The Adelsverein believed it held title to the land; all it really held was the right to settle the land. It was responsible for surveying the land and dealing with the Indians. The nobles did not know it, but they had acquired an albatross, and Messrs. Fisher and Miller had extricated themselves from an impossible-to-fulfill contract, with $9,000 to boot.

Nassau Farm remained in the hands of the Adelsverein and would have made an ideal mid-journey way station for the German immigrants bound for the interior of Texas, but Prince Carl rejected this idea. He feared that the plantation's close proximity to non-German settlements would cause the immigrants to lose their native culture. For the first way station north, he chose instead the tract of land we now call New Braunfels. Prince Carl did, however, use the Nassau Farm as a place for personal rest and recreation, especially horse racing. The big house, two stories of solid oak, had two glass windows, when glass was a true frontier luxury. Prince Carl's successor as commissioner general, John Meusebach, also used the farm as a vacation spot. When the Adelsverein went bankrupt in 1848, the Nassau Farm was sold to Otto von Röder, who sold some of the land and eventually lost the rest in a lawsuit. Thereafter, the farm was gradually broken down into smaller plots. All that remains today are the old cemetery and two large, weathered barns which stand atop the high hill to the south of the historical marker. To see the barns, turn left off FM 1457 on Wolff Road and drive to the crest of the hill. You can see them, some distance away, atop the next hill south. To get a better view, continue on Wolff Road, through the hard left turn and then the hard right turn, to the property's entrance.

Turn right on FM 2714 to reach Winedale.

WINEDALE

Fayette County • (979) • About 7 miles from Shelby

Although the Nassau Farm was never used by the Adelsverein for colonization, it nonetheless acted as a magnet to many German immigrants who settled in the fertile rolling countryside surrounding the plantation. Winedale was founded by one of those German settlers, Charles Windewehen, about 1870. The village's original name of Truebsal ("trouble" in English) was changed to Winedale because of the wine industry that resulted from abundant crops of grapes.

WINEDALE HISTORICAL CENTER

3738 FM 2714 • 278-3530 • www.cah.utexas.edu/museums/winedale.php • Tours by appointment • Fee • W variable

Winedale is best known as home of the Winedale Historical Center and the annual summer Shakespeare workshops taught by UT professor James Ayres. The historical center is a collection of restored farm buildings and their furnishings, donated by the late philanthropist Miss Ima Hogg to the University of Texas in 1965. The centerpiece is the Lewis House, built by William Townsend in about 1834 as a one-room cabin with a sleeping loft, using locally cut cedar timber. Sam Lewis acquired the property in 1848 and enlarged the cabin to its present state sometime during the 1850s. With two stories, eight rooms, a galleried porch across the front, and a dogtrot through the center, the building reflects both Anglo American and German influences. The room arrangement, with a wide central hall and double gallery, is typically southern, while the steeply pitched roof, small windows, and other structural details reflect the work of German craftsmen.

The Lewis House's most outstanding feature is the decorative painting found inside, executed by the locally renowned Rudolph Melchior. A successful artist in Germany, Melchior immigrated to Texas in 1853. Two of the rooms contain his stenciled borders and freehand over mantle paintings. One of the rooms also contains a ceiling painting full of Neoclassic details—medallions containing symbols of the four seasons and in the center, a green parrot.

The Lewis place became a stage stop and popular overnight stop for travelers when the road from Brenham to La Grange was relocated to run past the Lewis farm in 1859. Joseph Wagner bought the house and surrounding farmland in 1882.

Miss Ima acquired the property in 1963 and supervised the painstaking restoration of the Lewis home and two handsome barns. The larger barn was converted into the present theater. Several more buildings were added after 1965. The old Winedale schoolhouse has also been moved to the compound.

Behind the Lewis House are a log kitchen and smokehouse, moved to Winedale during restoration and placed on the sites of similar structures which were torn down in the 1920s. A nineteenth-century vegetable and flower garden faces the buildings. The theater barn was built in 1894 from cedar beams salvaged from an animal-powered cotton gin dating to the 1850s. It served as Wagner's hay barn. The other barn was for the animals. Hazel's Lone Oak Cottage is a typical Texas dogtrot home, built about 1855 by German immigrant Franz Jaentschke on Jack's Creek, about two miles south of Winedale. It was moved here in 1965, the gift of Miss Ima's friend, Mrs. Hazel Ledbetter.

The McGregor-Grimm House is a two-story Greek Revival farmhouse built in 1861 by Washington County planter and land speculator Dr. Gregor McGregor for his bride, Anna Portia Fordtran. It was moved here in 1967 from the Wesley community, fifteen miles to the east, and has been furnished to reflect the lifestyle of a wealthy Anglo-German family of the 1860s. The rooms contain several more examples of decorative wall stenciling and painting believed to have been done by Rudolph Melchior.

The Lauderdale house, an 1858 Greek Revival farmhouse, served as a dormitory and conference center until it burned in 1981; only the twin brick chimneys are left standing.

Behind the theater barn in the shade of four large post oak trees, black tenant farmers had an outdoor dancing platform at the turn of the century.

Winedale draws students, tourists, and program participants who attend its various public programs and continuing education seminars.

ANNUAL EVENTS

APRIL

SPRING HISTORY SYMPOSIUM ON TEXAS FURNITURE

278-3530 • First Saturday in April • W variable

This event features traditional German/Texas crafts and the best in contemporary crafts (juried show, by invitation). Watch demonstrations of blacksmithing, soap making, quilting, goose plucking, and more. There is live folk music, and food served on the grounds. A traditional German play opens the festival on Friday night.

APRIL OR MAY

EEYORE'S BIRTHDAY

278-3530 • End of April or beginning of May • Free

University of Texas students began the tradition of celebrating the rites of spring in a city park with a party marking the birthday of lonesome Eeyore from *Winnie the Pooh*. Later, part of the fun moved to Winedale. Much the milder of the two parties, the Winedale celebration features maypoles, games, and a costume contest.

JULY AND AUGUST

SHAKESPEARE AT WINEDALE

278-3530 • Weekends in late July and August • Write or call Winedale Historical Center for reservations • W

Each summer, a special group of UT-Austin students comes to live Shakespeare out here at Winedale. And at the end of the session, the troupe presents several selections from the master's catalogue, a different program each weekend.

DECEMBER

CHRISTMAS OPEN HOUSE

Second Sunday • 278-3530 • W variable

Experience an 1800s Christmas with period decorations; folk-life demonstrations of whittling, quilt making, weaving, spinning, blacksmithing, and basket weaving; and examples of Civil War military life. Weihnachtmann (Santa Claus) gives out candy coins to children. There are stagecoach and covered-wagon rides, farm animals for the kids to pet, German singers, an oompah band, dulcimer players, fiddlers, children's choir, Shakespeare players, and more.

From Winedale, return to FM 1457, turn right, and head for Round Top.

Tidy old German farmhouses dot the gently rolling hills along the way. Just before you enter Round Top, you pass the collection of neatly kept, whitewashed buildings that comprise the Round Top Rifle Association, which has been in existence since 1873.

ROUND TOP

Fayette County • 80 (approximate) • (979) • About 4 miles from Winedale

Round Top occupies a unique spot in Texas. For many years the state's smallest incorporated city, Round Top has managed to maintain a certain rural German antiquity while resisting both the charm-sapping growth that has plagued Fredericksburg and New Braunfels and the decline that has killed many other German hamlets.

The Townsends were the first white settlers here, and the locality was known as Townsend for several years due to the presence of five families by that name. But the post office created here during the republic days was known as the Jones post office, after postmaster John Jones, brother of the republic's postmaster general.

With the coming of the stagecoach that ran from Goliad to Washington-on-the-Brazos, the area became known as Round Top after the distinctive house with the round top built by German immigrant Alwin Soergel in 1847. Originally settled by Southern Anglos, many of whom fought in the Texas Revolution, Round Top was heavily German by the Civil War. It was then a prosperous village of three hundred, including doctors, lawyers, teachers, carpenters, blacksmiths, painters, two ministers, a saddle maker, a cabinet-maker, a bookbinder, and a cobbler. The town even had a brewery and a cigar factory.

The Round Top Academy was operated on the nearby Ledbetter Plantation from 1854 until 1867. The curriculum included the three Rs, plus advanced studies in philosophy, chemistry, algebra, Latin, German, Spanish, and French.

Round Top's Lutheran church was organized in January 1861. During the Civil War, the town served as Confederate Army recruiting station for northern Fayette County. Round Top contributed two companies—the Round Top Mounted Infantry and the Round Top Guerrillas—to the Confederate war effort. Federal troops were stationed here at war's end. Local citizens organized a community militia to combat postwar lawlessness and applied for a town charter in 1870, which was not approved until 1877.

Round Top continued on as a sleepy little farm town until the 1960s, when Houstonians discovered its charms and began buying up the many old buildings here and restoring them. For a small city, Round Top has an awful lot to see.

The Round Top area has long been prime antiquing territory. In addition to area shops that are open year-round, seasonal antique shows and sales take place in Round Top, Fayetteville, and Warrenton on the first weekend of April (except when Easter is that weekend) and the first weekend in October each year. Dealers come from all over the country; traffic is heavy, and parking places are scarce.

FM 1457 dead-ends into FM 237 at the Round Top town square.

ROUND TOP VISITORS CENTER

South side, town square • Open daily

The visitors center is built on the ruins of Round Top's first brewery, built in the 1860s. The only original part of the building is the basement, which was carved out of the native sandstone bedrock. Faith P. Bybee, who established the Texas Pioneer Arts Foundation and Henkel Square, bought the property in the 1970s and had a facsimile of the brewery built upon the original foundation. Inside are information and displays about area history and attractions.

ROUND TOP AREA CHAMBER OF COMMERCE

249-4042, 888-368-4783 • www.roundtop.org • PO Box 216, Round Top 78954

HENKEL SQUARE

FM 1457 • 249-3308 • www.texaspioneerarts.org/henkel_square.html • Open Thursday through Sunday, noon to 5 • Fee

Henkel Square is a collection of local and imported early Texas structures administered by the Texas Pioneer Arts Foundation. Most of the buildings are furnished with period pieces. Among the highlights here are the stenciled walls in the Schumann and Henkel homes, the bluing walls inside the old Muckleroy log cabin (imported from Frelsburg), and the German-language sign inside the Haw Creek schoolhouse and church, which translated into English reads, "I call the living to church and the dead to the grave." "Squire" Henkel laid out the town of Round Top, and his old home is the centerpiece of the collection. For more information about Henkel Square, write PO Box 82, Round Top 78954.

BETHLEHEM LUTHERAN CHURCH

Southwest of the town square, 409 South White St., 1 block west of FM 237 • 249-3686 • Open • W variable

Follow the signs and white steeple to the Bethlehem Lutheran Church, built in 1866 of limestone from the hill on which the church stands and local cedar. Construction was supervised by Carl Siegismund Bauer, a local stone mason. The church was dedicated on October 28, 1866, and cost $2,400 to build.

Johann Traugott Wantke built a native-cedar pipe organ for the church, which is still played the fourth Sunday of each month. The church interior features native cedar floors and doors and traditional German Lutheran fittings. Only three Wantke cedar pipe organs are known to exist, and this one took over two years to build. Wantke built it on the premises. He had no tuning fork. Local legend has it that to tune the organ, Wantke would play a note on his piano at home, then scurry down to the church with the note fresh in his mind to tune the corresponding pipe on the organ. Wantke's distinctive one-story stone home still stands a block north of the church, a block west of FM 237. The old cigar factory stands a few yards south and east of Wantke's house, a small brown-painted frame building whose back overlooks FM 237. It is inside a white picket fence, in a compound with several other old frame buildings. It still contains the original cigar-making equipment.

ROUND TOP HISTORICAL SOCIETY MUSEUM

SH 237, just off the town square • 888-368-4783 • Open Saturday and Sunday

The museum is filled with items of local historical significance.

ROUND TOP FESTIVAL-INSTITUTE

248 Jaster Rd., off SH 237, 0.5 miles north of the town square • 249-3129 • www.festivalhill.org • Fee • W

The International Festival-Institute at Round Top was founded by American concert pianist James Dick in 1971. The project began in a small converted school building on a six-acre campus. Today, continually expanding, the two-hundred-acre-plus campus is dotted with several beautifully restored mansions, gardens and fountains, and the massive, thousand-seat Festival Concert Hall.

The Institute offers advanced young musicians an intensive summer education program that includes public performances of chamber, vocal, and orchestral works. The faculty includes distinguished musicians and teachers from the United States and abroad. The student body is similarly international.

The institute has two performance seasons. The first, summer season, takes place during June and July, with concerts presented by festival participants, faculty members, and the Texas Festival Orchestra. The second, the August-to-April benefit season, features faculty members and visiting artists who perform solo and chamber music each month. Proceeds go to the scholarship fund.

Other special events, exhibits, and forums presented throughout the year, such as the annual herbal forum in March, explore various facets of culture and the arts. A Christmas open house and concert are held in December.

The one-story frame Clayton House was built in 1885 near La Grange and was moved here in 1976, where it underwent restoration and enlargement. The C. A. Menke House was built in 1902 at Hempstead and was moved here a few years after the Clayton House. The restored house is a tribute to Dick's other passion, the preservation of fine carpentry and woodworking skills. The interior of the great concert hall features an intricate inlaid, patterned-wood ceiling.

The wooden, Carpenter Gothic-style Travis Street United Methodist Church, built in 1883 at La Grange, was moved here in 1994 and was renamed the Edythe Bates Old Chapel, honoring the woman who made the church's restoration possible. The chapel houses a manual pipe organ built in about 1835 by New Yorker Henry Erben, with fourteen half stops and 484 pipes of both wood and metal. The chapel serves as a center for chamber music, organ recitals, lectures, and seminars.

The Log House was inspired by "Al Araf," a home built by George J. Jenks on the shore of Lake Huron at Harbor Beach, Michigan, between 1896 and 1923. The house is furnished with original materials from "Al Araf," including Stickley furniture crafted between 1902 and 1920. The Log House provides faculty residences, guest housing, music rehearsal rooms, and a permanent repository for historic Jenks and Ilsley family collections.

The romantic and beautiful Herzstein Memorial Plaza covers an enormous area adjacent to the Edythe Bates Old Chapel and the limestone-paved swimming pool garden enclosure with its late nineteenth-century fountain and Russian-styled onion-domed gazebo. The architectural features of the Herzstein Memorial Plaza include a dramatic stone-columned entrance to an underground Stone Room (the Kaffe Kaffein), beneath the Edythe Bates Old Chapel, flanked by two rushing waterfalls. The Herzstein Memorial Plaza is used for and is available for large open-air gatherings, such as reunions and many other private and Institute events.

The replica "Roman ruins," in a garden setting, comprise two walls and a tower, and were built of rough-cut limestone blocks using no mortar.

Tours of the facility may be arranged by appointment for any number of people.

SHOPPING

ROUND TOP GENERAL STORE

SH 237, on the west side of the town square • 249-3600

On the square since 1848, the general store features antiques, gifts, and fudge made on the premises.

DINING

ROYERS' ROUND TOP CAFE

Town square • 249-3611 • www.royersroundtopcafe.com • **Open Thursday through Sunday, lunch and dinner • Beer and wine • W**

The *Houston Chronicle* has called it the best country cafe in Texas, and I won't argue. It's a mix of country and city cooking. Local ingredients are used, and the cafe makes its own breads, rolls, pies, and such. Old country standards such as steak and grilled pork chops and quail are joined by city favorites like grilled salmon and fresh pastas. Fabulous sandwiches, plus soups and salads, round out the menu.

LODGING

ROUND TOP FARMS

301 S. Washington (SH 237) • 249-3977 • Checks OK

This 1852 house is two blocks from the town square. Fishing, hiking, wi-fi.

HEART OF MY HEART RANCH

403 Florida Chapel Rd., off SH 237 • 249-3171

All guest rooms in this comfortable Victorian-style home have private baths, and those on the ground floor have separate entrances. Or you can stay in an 1839 log cabin with a stone fireplace and complete kitchen. There is a pond you can fish or float in, or you can walk through the woods down to Cummins Creek. In the morning, there's a hearty country breakfast that features locally grown or produced foods.

ROUND TOP INN

407 S. White St., SH 237, 3 blocks south of the town square • 249-5294 • www.andersonsroundtopinn.com

The inn is a collection of old pioneer buildings (1840–1879) spread out over a city block that have been restored and refurbished with modern conveniences; there are seven guest rooms with private baths.

ANNUAL EVENTS

MARCH AND OCTOBER

ANTIQUE SHOPS

First weekend of each month

Several antique shows put on by different promoters occur from Shelby to Round Top down to Warrenton. It's best to check with the Round Top Area Chamber Of Commerce (888-368-4783, www.roundtop.org) for year-to-year details.

JULY

FOURTH OF JULY CELEBRATION

Round Top Rifle Association Hall • July 4 • W

Round Top's celebration of our national day of independence dates back to 1826 and is believed to be the oldest Fourth of July fest west of the Mississippi. These celebrations have been widely publicized since 1851. In 1876, for example, the featured speaker was local Texas Revolution veteran Joel Robison, who transported the captured Santa Anna to General Sam Houston. For his services, Robison received Santa Anna's gold brocaded vest. It became customary for the young men of Fayette County to borrow this vest for their wedding day.

These days, the Glorious Fourth is marked by a trail ride from Carmine to Round Top, speeches at the town square, and a parade out to the Rifle Association Hall, the start of which is signaled by a shot from the town's Civil War cannon. Barbecue is served at the hall, and the Round Top Brass Band and a variety of polka and country-and-western bands play throughout the day and well into the night.

DECEMBER

ROUND TOP CHRISTMAS

Downtown • Usually first weekend in December • 249-4042, 888-368-4783 • Free • W

The celebration includes Christmas carols, tree lighting, Santa's arrival, and open house at local shops.

Leave Round Top via SH 237 south, toward La Grange.

Vintage German farmhouses continue to line the road south of Round Top to Warrenton.

ST. MARTIN'S CHAPEL

SH 237, about 4.5 miles from Round Top on the west side of the road

St. Martin's Chapel is called the world's smallest Catholic church. The history of St. Martin's goes back to 1886, when it served one hundred families. It was a mission of the Fayetteville parish then, as it is now. In 1915, the parish built a schoolhouse in Fayetteville. Since many Warrenton families were moving to Fayetteville, the Warrenton church was torn down so its lumber could be used to build the new school. Just enough wood was retained to build this tiny twelve-pew chapel. Mass is celebrated here once a year, on All Saints Day. The bell in the steeple still works.

WARRENTON

Fayette County • 50 • (979) • About 5 miles from Round Top

Warrenton was founded by William Neese, a German immigrant who bought land here in 1854 from Conrad Tiemann. The land had been owned originally by John G. Robison, who was killed by Indians one mile east of here in 1837. His son was Joel Robison, captor of Santa Anna.

Neese married Tiemann's daughter Wilhelmine on New Year's Day 1855. He had just built Neese's Store a few months earlier, and so became the settlement's first merchant and postmaster. It was first named for his store, but finally was permanently named for his friend and neighbor Warren Ligon, who had bought five hundred acres here in 1852. Ligon wanted to call the settlement Neeseville; Neese favored Warrenton.

Neese also built a cotton gin. He bought local cotton, ginned it, and hauled it to Galveston for sale. In 1868, he started building the two-story sandstone house that stands across the road and a few yards north from the current Warrenton Store. He meant for it to be the finest home between Brenham and La Grange. The Neese family was still living in a double-pen log cabin at the time. The sandstone came from a quarry five miles east, toward Willow Springs. The double-column two-story portico with iron banister came from New Orleans.

He didn't enjoy his new house for long. On the evening of October 3, 1872, Neese returned from visiting his brother-in-law and noticed a light on in his store, which stood opposite his house just a few feet south of the current Warrenton Store. He went to investigate, opened the door, and was gunned down by the robber. The murderer escaped to La Grange on horseback but was caught and later convicted of first-degree murder. Curiously, he was not hanged—which was the common practice of the time—but was sent instead to the penitentiary at Huntsville. Neese was buried at the Drawe Cemetery two miles east of Warrenton.

The open area directly across the road from the Warrenton Store was originally laid out as the town square. Today it is just a pleasant field, well shaded by live oaks and surrounded by a half dozen or so old farmhouses, several of which now house antique shops. Several of Warrenton's old commercial buildings are closed and moldering, but Charles Brendle's 1898 Harmonie Hall, a combination dance hall and saloon, has been renovated. It stands a few dozen yards south of the old Warrenton Store. The Baca Pavilion was moved to its present location from Fayetteville.

The old Krause place, which originally was a grocery store and bar, is now the Warrenton Inn, a B&B (4339 S. SH 237, 249-3074, www.hillcrestinnat warrenton.com).

OLDENBURG

Fayette County • 54 • About 3.5 miles from Warrenton

Oldenburg was founded in 1836 by Johann Schmitt; it was named by Gus Stenken in honor of the German duchy from which he and many of his neighbors came. They felt very much at home in this alternately open and forested, well-watered, rolling countryside. Oldenburg's decline paralleled that of Texas agriculture.

Just south of Oldenburg, SH 237 ends at SH 159. Continue south toward La Grange on SH 159.

RUTERSVILLE

Fayette County • 72 • About 2 miles from Oldenburg

Rutersville is the next wide spot on the road to La Grange, but it was once the home of the first institute of higher education in Texas. Martin Ruter, who came to the state in 1837 as superintendent of the Methodist mission in Texas, dreamed of a university that would be the "Athens of the South," located near the geographic center of Texas' already existing settlements and accessible from all directions. Within ninety days of his arrival in Texas, Ruter had established twenty missions. He made public his dream in a sermon to the Congress of the Republic of Texas, whereupon several landowners made him offers of land. Ruter selected the name Bastrop University, wrote a charter, and rode across Texas soliciting money and students. He died at Washington-on-the-Brazos in May 1838, his dream as yet unfulfilled.

Others carried on his dream. A group of men acquired title to a tract of land here in June 1838 and began the sale of town lots later that fall. They commenced a promotional campaign and by April 1839 had sold one hundred lots.

Meanwhile, the newly organized Texas Conference of the Methodist Episcopal Church appointed a president for the embryonic university and renamed it Rutersville College. Granted a charter in 1840, the school opened that same year with sixty-three students. The founders of Rutersville had given fifty-two acres for the college's male department and twenty-four for the female department. One visitor to Rutersville that first year was A. B. Lawrence, author of *Texas in 1840: The Emigrant's Guide to the New Republic.* Lawrence, who was preparing to move his family to Texas from the east, praised the little town of God as follows:

> There appears a peculiar appropriateness in the name of this town, when it is remembered that it is intended to be consecrated specially to literature and religion, and that from it all gambling, and the sales of spirituous liquors, are strictly excluded. Situated at a distance from navigable waters, or extended water power, the place seems not especially adapted to commercial enterprise, but well fitted for retired literary and scientific pursuits.

As the college grew, so grew Rutersville. By 1841, the college had one hundred students and four leagues of land at its disposal, courtesy of the Republic of Texas. Peak enrollment was 194, during the 1844–1845 term. Indian attacks, the departure of students for the Mexican War, and the establishment of Baylor University caused a decline in enrollment. The school's decline was accelerated by questions of trustee impropriety, faculty misconduct, and the establishment of rival schools.

By 1856, the school's properties merged with the Texas Military Institute. Caleb Forshey, the Texas Military Institute's founder, was born in 1812 in Pennsylvania. He attended the United States Military Academy but apparently didn't graduate. He was professor of mathematics and civil engineering from 1836 to 1838 at Jefferson College in Mississippi. Forshey next worked on engineering projects along the Mississippi River. In 1848, he constructed a hydrologic station at Carrollton, Louisiana, that measured the river's flow from 1848 to 1855 for the federal government's Mississippi Delta Survey.

In 1853, Forshey moved to Texas to become chief engineer of the newly chartered Galveston, Houston, and Henderson railroad. In 1854, Forshey founded the Texas Military Institute in Galveston. In 1856, Forshey moved the school to Rutersville, where it consolidated with Rutersville College and the Texas Monumental Committee of La Grange. During its first term at Rutersville, the school counted fifty-eight cadets. Besides traditional military-school studies, the school taught German, zoology, mechanics, and road and railroad courses. Forshey and the cadets made astronomical observations and collected biological specimens, mostly in Fayette County, for the Smithsonian Institution and for academies and museums in Boston and Philadelphia. Forshey wrote scientific articles that appeared in many leading journals of the time, and he contributed articles on Texas meteorology and climate to the *Texas Almanac* in 1860 and 1861.

The cadets appear to have eaten better than many other Texans; in an October 1858 diary entry, Forshey noted that the supper menu was cornbread, cold beef, peach preserves, fresh butter, coffee, and water. But discipline was strict; when one cadet was found absent from quarters between taps and reveille, he was sentenced to compulsory resignation without honorable discharge. Forshey served as superintendent until he closed the school in 1861.

As an officer in the Engineering Corps, C.S.A. (Confederate States of America), Forshey worked on Texas coastal defenses. On December 25, 1862, he ordered the outfitting of the Confederate "cotton-clad" gunboats that were used successfully at the battle of Galveston on January 1, 1863. Three Civil War songs by Forshey were included in Francis D. Allan's collection, *Allan's Lone Star Ballads* (1874). After the war, Forshey was an engineering consultant to the city of Galveston. He worked along the Red River in 1874–1875 and eventually returned to the Mississippi River delta, where he died in 1881.

Rutersville followed the school's decline. Present-day Rutersville, located about a half mile west of the college site, developed with the construction of modern highways.

Rutersville's most famous resident was Asa Hill, the Paul Revere of the Runaway Scrape. A member of the Republican Army in 1836, General Sam Houston sent Hill to warn all the people in Santa Anna's path. Hill and sons Jeffrey and John later joined the ill-fated Mier Expedition of 1842, detailed later in this chapter. Both Asa and Jeffrey were captured and imprisoned. But Mexican general Pedro Ampudia adopted fourteen-year-old John and sent him to school in Matamoros and then to Santa Anna in Mexico City, where he was instrumental in gaining the release of his father and older brother from prison. Asa and Jeffrey immediately returned to Texas, but young John stayed in Mexico for nearly forty more years, not returning to Texas until 1880. Asa Hill died here shortly after his return and is buried nearby.

There are quite a few 'Three-Legged Willie" Williamson stories, and one of the best concerns an incident in Rutersville. A camp meeting was going on, and Williamson—being mistaken for a preacher—was asked to pray. As a drought was then gripping the countryside, the day had been set aside for rain prayers. Willie acquiesced to the worshippers' request and began praying: "Lord, we have met today to pray for rain. Lord thou knowest how much we need rain for man and beast. We need copious rains, real copious rains: rootsoakers, gully-washers. Lord we ask thee not to send us little sunshowers that will make our corn produce nubbins that all hell couldn't shuck." At this point his prayer was drowned out by a deafening sea of amens from the horrified congregation. It is not recorded how soon thereafter the next gully-washer fell.

The Texas Jersey Cheese Company makes various cheeses from Jersey milk from the Frerichs Dairy on FM 159, just north of La Grange. Visitors can take guided and self-guided tours, milk a cow, feed and pet the other animals, and more. Kids are especially welcome. Learn more at www.texasjersey.com.

Continue on SH 159 into La Grange.

LA GRANGE

Fayette County Seat • 4,500 (approximate) • (979) • About 5.5 miles from Rutersville

Well before the first Europeans visited Texas, Indians had established an east-west trade route that crossed the Colorado River near Monument Hill and thence to the Guadalupe along an open high ridge defining the Navidad River and Peach Creek watersheds that led past present-day Shiner.

When Alonso de Leon, governor of Coahuila (which included Texas at the time) left Monclova in 1689 to search for La Salle's French colony in Texas, his journey led to an Indian village located near the Colorado River crossing, across from modern-day La Grange. They found several Tejas Indians and two Frenchmen. One claimed to be a survivor of La Salle's expedition who had become ill during La Salle's overland search for the Mississippi River. He and several other sick men were left with the Tejas in east Texas as La Salle pressed on to the northeast. The other had been one of the 250 men who founded the French colony on Matagorda Bay. The Spanish would have traveled farther, except that the Colorado River was too high to cross. In 1690, De Leon crossed the Colorado again at the same place, on his way to establishing the first Spanish mission in east Texas.

La Grange's first white settler was the legendary Aylett C. "Strap" Buckner, who built a trading post nearby in 1819. He had come to Texas as early as 1812 as a member of the Gutierrez-Magee Expedition. He was back again with Francisco Xavier Mina in 1816 and again in 1819 with Dr. James Long. Each of these expeditions had entered Texas for the purpose of carving out a republic. In a letter to Stephen F. Austin, Buckner claimed he had been the first person to build a cabin on the Colorado River, that he had kept an open house ever since he came, and that he had lost more property to Indian raiders than anyone else on the river. He became one of Austin's Old Three Hundred with the establishment of that colony. Austin sent him to make a treaty with the Waco and Tawakoni Indians near the present site of Waco in 1824.

Austin could not have sent a more imposing representative. Buckner had quite a reputation. Legend says he possessed the strength of ten lions, and that he used it like ten lions. Kind natured, he had a pride in his strength that eventually became ungovernable. He had a queer penchant, one story goes, for good-naturedly knocking men down. He knocked down every man in Austin's colony at least thrice, including Austin himself. Strap would not hesitate to knock down anything; it was a merry pastime with him to knock a yearling bull stark dead with his fist. Once Strap confronted a great black bull that had been terrorizing the colonists. They had named him Noche. The bull charged Strap on the field of combat, and Strap met Noche with a blow to the frontlet from his bare fist, which sent the bull staggering back on his haunches and caused the blood to flow in rivers from his smoking nostrils. Recovering from his surprise, Noche turned tail and ran, never to be seen again.

After next impressing the Indians residing nearby with his strength, Buckner got gloriously drunk and declared himself "Champion of the World" and challenged anybody and everybody to fight him, even the Devil himself. At this point, a terrible tempest arose, during which the air was filled with smoke and fire and brimstone, and the Devil himself appeared. He took Strap up on his challenge, and the ensuing battle lasted a day and a night. In the end, the Devil conquered and carried Strap away on a cloud of pale blue smoke.

In another story, Strap was bothered by the thieving and general cussedness of two tribes that frequented his neighborhood, so he got each tribe mad at the other and told each chief he ought to fight the other tribe. Strap secretly gave each tribe powder and bullets and sat back to watch the fun. Both tribes came into view whooping and decorated in war paint and feathers. They started shooting at the other side as soon as they saw each other, while they were still out of range. They fired all their ammunition at each other and then rode off, without a man hurt on either side. The only loser was Strap, who was out the powder and bullets.

A ferry once stood on the Colorado where the road that ran through Strap Buckner's country to San Antonio crossed. A celebration took place in the ferry house, and everyone was pretty drunk. Strap got mad at the ferryman for something and chased him into the cattle pen, where the man hid behind the meanest ox in the settlement. Strap yelled, "You would hide behind your ox, but your ox will pay the penalty," and he crushed the ox's skull with one blow. Some burros were in the next pen, and one of them looked over the fence to watch the drama and gave a little burro laugh. Strap, his rage still unsated, shouted at the burro, "You would laugh at me, would you?" and the next moment the burro was lying on the ground with a broken skull.

Strap took a breather, and the ferryman, who had climbed on the fence in the meantime, now yelled defiance at Strap. Strap moved toward him but was blocked by Bruno, a huge black man, who stepped in front of him. Strap aimed a mighty blow at Bruno's head, but Bruno ducked and hit Strap head on. The crash was terrible, and Strap fell backward with blood streaming from his head. As Strap lay on the ground, Bruno stood over him and said in German, "You can knock an ox down and you can cave in the skull of a burro, but you cannot hurt old Black Bruno." A German named Herman von Snitzendahl used to tell this tale.

Another tale placed Strap at a bee cave west of present-day Round Rock, where at certain times of the year, a peculiar cloud was visible over a bluff. Strap investigated and found that bees were coming out of a hole in the ground on top of a bare limestone ridge. He knew there must be a cavity below. In a ravine far down the slope, he found a small opening that led to the concealed cave. After trying for several days to enlarge the opening, he got mad and knocked out the whole side of the cliff with one blow from his fist.

So much for legend. In real life, Buckner quarreled openly with Austin, and then became his fast friend and ally. Never one to pass up a good fight, Buckner was killed at the Battle of Velasco in 1832. A creek that empties into the Colorado on the western outskirts of La Grange bears his name.

The first building located within the present-day city limits was a twin blockhouse built by James Ross in 1826. John Moore killed Ross in 1826 and took possession of the fort, renaming it Moore's Fort. Neighboring settlers often came to the fort for refuge from Indian attacks. La Grange had the semblance of a town by 1831 but was not surveyed and platted until 1837, when it became the county seat of the newly created Fayette County. The county was named for the Marquis de Lafayette, the city for Lafayette's estate in France. La Grange means "the meadow."

Moore was the dominant force in early La Grange. Persons who opposed Moore's dream of making La Grange the most important town in Fayette

County founded the rival Colorado City, located at the La Bahia Road river crossing, directly across the river from La Grange. Colorado City was unanimously selected by the Second Congress of the republic for the capital of Texas, but the bill was vetoed by President Sam Houston. A Colorado River flood destroyed what there was of the city, and the Fayette County court abolished the city in 1841.

La Grange became a center for education in the 1840s and 1850s, with such schools as the La Grange Collegiate Institute, the La Grange Female Institute, the La Grange Male and Female Seminary, and the La Grange Select School. Livestock and cotton, much of the latter grown under the plantation system, sustained the county's economy before the Civil War.

La Grange citizens, along with boosters in Columbus, promoted the clearing of the Colorado River between Austin and the Gulf of Mexico. The *La Grange Intelligencer* was one of the project's most vocal supporters. This short-lived but lively weekly started publishing in January 1844 with the motto, "Westward! the Star of empire takes its way." Editor Smallwood S. B. "Steamboat" Fields announced plans to devote a part of each issue to information on "Politics, Science, Agriculture, Religion, Foreign Affairs, Miscellaneous Items, and Domestic Matters" but reserved the right to "animadvert freely" on government practice.

Steamboat Fields, a lawyer, had moved to Fayette County when the county was organized. He practiced law in La Grange and served as county tax assessor from 1840 to 1849. In 1842–1843, he represented Fayette County in the Texas House of Representatives. He was a member of the La Grange Company under William M. Eastland but did not participate in the Mier Expedition.

The September 12, 1845, issue of the *Intelligencer* reported "Hard times! Hard times! and the scarcity of money is wrung upon us at every turn and corner of life." Fields asked for the friends of the paper to support it with "corn, fodder, potatoes, meat, lumber, cattle, or anything from a dozen eggs to a stick of firewood" to keep it from closing. His appeal was in vain, for the paper folded after its September 19, 1845, issue. Fields died in Austin in April 1846.

Fayette County voted against secession by a narrow margin in 1861, but 1,300 Fayette County men marched off to war under the Bonnie Blue Flag nonetheless. Special county war taxes provided relief for the families of soldiers at the front. Freighters carried cotton from La Grange and Round Top to Mexico, where the bales were exchanged for desperately needed supplies. La Grange's position on both the river and the La Bahia Road made it a prime shipping center. Teamsters often sang among themselves to make the long drives less boring, and one of their favorite songs went as follows:

Hollered at the mule and the mule wouldn't mind: Well, I whopt him in the head with the leadin' line. And it's, "Go on, mule, you better stop saddlin'." Hollered at the mule and the mule wouldn't gee. Well, I tuck him in the head with the singletree. And it's "Go on, mule, you better stop saddlin'."

Unionist Germans in neighboring Austin County were in near revolt by December 1862 because of Confederate attempts to register German men for the draft. The Germans beat one draft officer and manhandled several others. They refused to serve without adequate protection of their homes and property. The area's draft officer recommended that a cavalry regiment be sent there to quell incipient violence. The district militia commander reported that the Germans had threatened to kill loyal citizens who registered for the draft. By January 1863, General Magruder decided to place Austin, Colorado, and Fayette counties under martial law. Lieutenant Colonel Hardeman was sent to Alleyton and then to La Grange, where he made many arrests. By the time he got to Bellville, the Germans were not making any problems.

La Grange, like much of the rest of Texas, suffered from shortages of essential and luxury goods during the Civil War, but it experienced no violence until the Confederate veterans began returning home. At La Grange, the county's returned soldiers held a mass meeting on May 27, 1865, damned the politicians and the cotton speculators, and appointed a committee to gather up all Confederate government property in the county and distribute it, paying special attention to the needs of indigent soldiers or their families. The soldiers felt they had suffered great hardships during their service and had not been adequately supported by the folks at home, and that the country's resources had been wasted by the incompetent or unprincipled men who had controlled them. Many people felt that the soldiers had more right to Confederate property than anyone else. But the soldiers didn't stop there; that same month, returning Confederate veterans robbed local German businesses, provoked arguments and fights, and on one occasion threatened to burn the town. Federal troops occupied La Grange in 1866, and a Freedmen's Bureau office was opened to protect the rights and welfare of the freed slaves. Friction between federal authorities and ex-Confederates led to a number of altercations that at times "reached the proportions of a first-class riot," according to one contemporary.

Supposedly no Klan organization existed in Fayette County after the Civil War, but violence indicative of Klan activity did exist. In one instance, a "big octoroon Negro from up north came to our county to preach equality to our colored citizens. This copper colored agitator was quietly taken out on the Fayetteville-Rutersville Road one night and hanged to a willow tree. A warning sign was left pinned on him." The teller of the above story also said that Colorado and Fayette county Klansmen reciprocated in their necktie parties (each group hanged victims from the other group's county) so that their respective identities might better be kept secret.

Despite these activities, Fayette County blacks exercised some political power until the 1890s. M. M. Rodgers was elected La Grange alderman in 1887 and served two terms. But in 1878, Constable Perry Dobbins of Fayette County was sentenced to prison for cattle theft. In the 1892 gubernatorial election, B. W. Carter, a community leader in West Point, wrote Democratic candidate Jim Hogg that his folks weren't especially fond of Hogg's opponent Clark, but that they had been offered rewards for their support. He proposed, "If you [Hogg] put up the rite purse we will [cast] our ticket for you and carry my beat."

The 1860s were arguably the cruelest decade in La Grange's history. As if the Civil War's ravages weren't enough, there was the great Colorado River flood of 1869 and the yellow fever epidemic of 1867.

Central Texas, along with the rest of the state, experienced numerous epidemics during the nineteenth century. Cholera, yellow fever, smallpox, dengue fever, measles, influenza, diphtheria, and whooping cough afflicted Texans in different locales at different times. Between 1836 and 1867, yellow fever epidemics occurred somewhere in Texas nearly every year, mostly in a yellow fever "belt" that covered all of Texas east of the Balcones Escarpment. Galveston experienced at least nine yellow fever epidemics between 1839 and 1867.

Yellow fever epidemics terrified everyone. You could be healthy one day and dead three days later. Victims first experienced debility, fever, and pains in their extremities and loins. Then they began vomiting blood clots (called "black vomit"). Jaundice followed, and often death.

No one understood the mosquito's role in transmitting the yellow fever virus. Many believed that garbage heaps and stagnant ponds produced particles in the air, called miasmata, which caused the disease. Doctors and town leaders advocated sanitary cleanups when epidemics appeared or threatened. Others believed that sick people transmitted the disease directly to others and urged quarantines to prevent the spread of this communicable disease. During an 1839 epidemic in Galveston, Dr. Ashbel Smith tasted the "black vomit" of patients and did not become sick. He believed that yellow fever was not contagious and that Galvestonians should not quarantine incoming ships.

Texans were confused because improved sanitation and enforced quarantines did not prevent or curb epidemics. During an 1853 yellow fever epidemic in Galveston, approximately 60 percent of the five thousand residents became sick, and 523 persons died. During Galveston's last yellow fever epidemic in 1867, thousands were afflicted, and approximately 725 residents had died by early September.

The 1867 yellow fever epidemic was one of the worst in Texas history, affecting an area ranging from Corpus Christi up the Texas coast to Galveston, and inland more than one hundred miles. Central Texas was especially hard hit. From August to December 1867, the yellow fever epidemic killed at least 240 people in La Grange—about 20 percent of its population. More may have died and not been reported, amid the chaos created by the epidemic. Also hard hit were the nearby towns of Brenham and Chappell Hill. The high mortality of the 1867 yellow fever epidemic caused many surviving residents to flee to the countryside to live in tents.

Prisoners in the Fayette County jail were either removed or discharged. The supply of coffins soon ran out. At the height of the epidemic, victims were placed in hastily made wooden boxes, were stacked in piles inside the cemetery fence, and were buried en masse, six or seven per grave. There are several stories as to how the yellow fever virus arrived in La Grange. Some said a peddler brought the virus. Others claimed it came in a box of books shipped from New Orleans.

In 1874, Edward King visited Texas for *Scribner's Monthly* and described a hanging he saw one morning, somewhere "on the banks of the beautiful Colorado River" between Austin and Columbus.

A ghastly cross-tree affronted the sky, while around the platform a great throng of white and black, and brown men, American, and negro, and Mexican, gathered to see two men die. He will remember how the criminals came to the gallows and gazed round the scaffold in search of some sympathetic desperado to help them; how, in his despair at finding none, one of them, in derision, broke into a shuffling dance, and after making a blackguard speech, fainted as the rope was placed about his guilty neck; how the crowd jeered at and mocked the two men until the scene was over, leaving the gallows to stand as a perpetual warning.

By 1882, La Grange had attained increased importance as a regional shipping center. It was now the terminus of a Galveston, Harrisburg, and San Antonio branch line that joined the main GH&SA tracks at Glidden, west of

Columbus. The first train had arrived on New Year's Eve, 1880. The business day ended early as crowds gathered to await its arrival, which was greeted with the firing of more than a hundred guns. Just a week later, the *La Grange Journal* reported, "Already our town is taking on a new appearance, dozens of new and strange faces are to be seen on the street and the hotels are full of guests from everywhere." The Missouri-Kansas-Texas railroad came through on its way to Houston a couple of years later.

By 1884, La Grange had four churches, three schools, an opera house, an oil factory, a bank, and 1,800 citizens. Two weekly newspapers, the *Journal* and the *Slovan* (a Bohemian paper), were being published. Two more banks were established during the late 1880s, strengthening the city's position as a regional business and shipping center. By 1896, the city had electric service and a water-works, as well as an opera house, two bridges, four schools, five churches, three gristmills and cotton gins, and three newspapers, including the *Deutsche Zeitung*, a German-language publication. By 1900, nearly 2,400 people lived in La Grange.

The town declined during the first two decades of the 1900s but grew again during the late 1920s, reaching an estimated population of 2,800 in 1929. During the Great Depression, the number of businesses dropped, and the population declined. By 1939, however, La Grange had begun to recover. Declining cotton production after World War II threatened the city's traditional economic base. By the early 1970s, all but one of the cotton gins had closed, and there were few job opportunities for young people; many left the city after graduating from high school. La Grange civic leaders began efforts to attract small industries. La Grange received national attention during the late 1970s and early 1980s, when the story of the Chicken Ranch was publicized through the Broadway production of *The Best Little Whorehouse in Texas* and by a Hollywood film of the same name.

La Grange's courthouse square has a number of centenarian buildings; some are modernized, and others have been restored or were never altered. The Dyers Building, 101 N. Main at Travis, was built around 1885 and has been a dry goods store, pharmacy/confectionary, and courthouse annex. Much of downtown La Grange dates back to the prosperous times at the turn of the twentieth century.

To get downtown, turn right on SH 71B at its intersection with SH 159. Proceed west on SH 71B, which is called Travis Street. A couple of blocks past the railroad tracks, you pass La Grange High School on your left. One block past the high school, turn right on Monroe and go one block to see St. James Episcopal Church.

ST. JAMES EPISCOPAL CHURCH

156 N. Monroe at Colorado • 968-3910

The 1885 St. James sanctuary is a good example of that period's American brand of Queen Anne Revival design. Queen Anne Revival as practiced in England was a style of half-timber work, brick, hung tile, and stucco. After its migration to America during the 1870s, the Queen Anne style was often executed in wood alone, the walls being covered with shingles. Richard Upjohn designed the church; his father was a renowned designer of churches and founder of the American Institute of Architects.

Shingles cover most of the walls and the steeply pitched roof of this wooden-framed building. The vastness of the roof is relieved by little gable "eyebrows." The square base of the bell tower is covered with horizontal boards, articulated with diagonal boards as if to simulate half-timbering. Just above are two bands of panels in a repeating quatrefoil design. Tudor spindles, also characteristic of the Queen Anne Revival style, support the porch roof.

Continue west toward downtown on Colorado. Three blocks west of the St. James church is the La Grange post office.

LA GRANGE POST OFFICE

113 E. Colorado at Jefferson

This muted example of Art Moderne architecture—Texas Centennial style—is lifted from anonymity by the bas-relief carvings that decorate the exterior; three separate panels depict the steamship, airplane, and railroad locomotive in their respective 1930s zenith forms. Inside, art aficionados will find the mural "Horses," painted by Tom Lewis in 1939.

The post office's rural free-delivery (RFD) system began here on August 1, 1889, when the nation's first RFD route began operating out of La Grange. Prior to this, farmers had to trek to the nearest post office, which wasn't always very close, to pick up and drop off mail.

In another block, you're at the courthouse square. Park here and take a stroll around the square.

DAWSON OAK

Colorado and Washington

A centuries-old oak tree stands at the corner of Colorado and Washington, in front of the bank. The granite marker beside it tells the tragic, heroic story of Captain Nicholas Mosby Dawson and his company. When news hit La Grange of the Mexican invasion of Texas and the capture of San Antonio on September 11, 1842, Captain Dawson rallied a group of about sixteen men here under the oak. Leaving La Grange on September 16, they marched toward San Antonio to reinforce the volunteer Texans attempting to recapture the city. Along the way, Dawson's force swelled to fifty-four strong. They pressed on toward San Antonio as fast as their fatigued horses could carry them.

On September 18, seven days after Mexican General Adrian Woll's capture of San Antonio, Colonel Mathew "Old Paint" Caldwell and his Texans lured the main force of the Mexican invaders into a trap at Salado Creek just north of San Antonio. There the Texans won a decisive victory, checking the Mexican advance and preventing the capture of the Republic capital at Austin.

As Caldwell's troops were whipping the Mexicans, they were unaware of the tragedy occurring just two miles away. Dawson and his men had been intercepted by a force of Mexican cavalry, just minutes away from joining their Texan comrades in battle. Dawson's exhausted Texans took cover in a mesquite thicket and prepared to resist attack. But the Mexicans withdrew from rifle range and brought up two cannons, showering the Texans with death. Soon half the force lay dead or dying. Dawson raised a white flag of surrender, realizing that the Texans' cause was hopeless against such odds. As the Texans lay down their arms, the Mexican cavalry charged. Of the fifty-three men, Dawson and thirty-four more were slain. Fifteen were captured, three escaped.

Colonel Caldwell and his troops arrived at the scene the next day to discover a field littered with the stripped and mutilated bodies of their fellow Texans. Heavy rains overnight had bleached the nude corpses to a ghastly white. Caldwell's men buried their unidentifiable bodies in a makeshift mass grave.

As news of the invasion and butchery spread across the republic, there were demands for retaliation, which led to the ill-fated Mier Expedition of Christmas 1842. Again, patriotic Fayette County residents rallied at the oak tree and joined the avenging march to Mexico. The Texan force had captured Laredo and Guerrero by mid-December but had failed to engage the Mexican Army. Recognizing that the expedition was a failure, General Alexander Somervell ordered his army to march home. But only 189 of the men obeyed his order. The remaining 308 troops elected a new commander and chose to attack the border town of Mier on the afternoon of Christmas Day 1842. Outnumbered ten to one, they nonetheless killed six hundred Mexicans and wounded two hundred more, while suffering only thirty casualties. But by the afternoon of December 26, the Texans were hungry, thirsty, and low on powder, and their discipline had begun to crack. Mexican commander General Pedro Ampudia sent a white flag to the Texans and boldly demanded their surrender, saying that he had just been reinforced by a large Mexican contingent. This was a lie, but the Texans' commander fell for the ruse and ordered his troops to lay down their arms without agreeing on any terms of capitulation. As soon as the Texans were in Mexican hands, orders for their mass execution were issued. Ampudia reversed these orders, though, and marched the able-bodied Texans over a tortuous route to Salado, Mexico. There the Texans escaped and headed for the Mexican mountains, where they became hopelessly lost. Many died of exposure and starvation, 176 were recaptured, and only five made it back to Texas.

The recaptured party was marched back to Salado, where Santa Anna decreed that every tenth man would be shot. The result was the Black Bean Episode, in which 159 white beans and 17 black beans were placed in a jar. Each Texan was blindfolded and ordered to draw a bean. Those drawing black beans were marched to the Salado prison's outer wall and shot in the back.

The remaining prisoners were marched to Mexico City, where Captain Ewen Cameron, mastermind of the Salado escape, was executed. Most of the Texans were placed in the Perote prison. Sixteen of these prisoners tunneled their way out; eight escaped to Texas, and eight were recaptured. Over the next year, many died in prison, and a few were released at the request of the U.S. government. The remaining prisoners were released by Santa Anna in September 1844, in accordance with the deathbed wish of his wife. The Dawson Oak stands as a living tribute to the indiscriminate bravery of these men.

Continue along Colorado; then take a left on Main.

LUKAS BAKERY

135 N. Main, on the square • 968-3052 • Monday through Friday 5:30–6:30, Saturday 5:30–2 • No Cr. • W

Lukas Bakery supplies many local restaurants with their "homemade" bread, and while bread is the bakery's bread-and-butter product, it also puts out a variety of tasty kolaches, cookies, and pastries guaranteed to do maximum damage to your waistline while inflicting minimum damage to your pocketbook.

Cross Travis/SH 71 and head east on Travis to continue your tour around the courthouse square.

OLD COUNTY JAIL/TOURIST INFORMATION AND CULTURE CENTER

171 S. Main, behind Prause's Market, 1 block south of the courthouse square • (800) 524-7264 • www.lagrangetx.org • Open daily

This picturesque stone, Gothic castle dates to 1881. The stone was quarried in nearby Muldoon. The jailer and his family lived in an apartment downstairs. In 1995, the La Grange Chamber of Commerce moved in, and the Tourist Information and Culture Center was established here as well. You can take a tour of the cell block and look through the guards' peepholes. There is no gallows, but the official La Grange hanging rope is on display. It was used in the only two legal hangings in Fayette County, which took place in July 1899 and January 1909. Sheriff August Loessin, who served as Fayette County sheriff for twenty-five years, presided over both executions. The hangings took place outside on the jail grounds. An admission ticket to one of the hangings, signed by the sheriff, is also on view. The simple concrete block building with small barred windows on the north edge of the property was the hoosegow, where drunks were thrown in to cool off, instead of being arrested and put into the county jail.

The center features information about each community in Fayette County and displays of Fayette County sheriff history, including Sheriff Jim Flournoy, who had the distinction of solving every murder and bank robbery in Fayette County during his thirty-four years in office. Ironically, his relationship with the Chicken Ranch of "Best Little Whorehouse" fame was a key to his crime-fighting success.

The "Chicken Ranch" was perhaps the oldest continuously running brothel in the nation, the *Handbook of Texas* tells us. Institutionalized prostitution in La Grange goes back at least to 1844, when a widow, "Mrs. Swine," brought three young women from New Orleans and settled in a small hotel near the saloon. Madame Swine began a tradition of interaction with the community and local lawmen that lasted almost 130 years. Swine and her ladies of the night used the hotel lobby for entertaining and a room upstairs for customer service until the Civil War, when she and a faithful employee were run out of town as Yankees and traitors. After the war, prostitution continued to operate in conjunction with La Grange saloons, but no official records were kept. By the end of the century, prostitution had moved out of the hotels and into a red-light district on the banks of the Colorado River, where Miss Jessie Williams bought a small house soon after her arrival from Waco in 1905. She maintained good relations with the law and ran the district's only respectable house; she admitted politicians and lawmen but excluded drunkards. When Miss Jessie learned of an impending crusade against the red-light district, she bought two buildings and eleven acres outside the city limits and two blocks from the Houston-Galveston highway. This would become the Chicken Ranch.

Automobiles made Miss Jessie's establishment accessible to many more customers. To meet the demand, more prostitutes were added, necessitating more rooms. The rooms were built onto the main house in a haphazard fashion as needed. Miss Jessie ruled the house with a firm hand. Nothing exotic was allowed, and none of the bedroom doors had locks on them. Miss Jessie walked the halls, and if she heard a customer abusing one of her girls, she chased him out with an iron rod. Social contact between the girls and the residents of La Grange was forbidden, girls saw the doctor weekly, and commodities and supplies were bought from local stores on a rotating basis.

Sheriff Will Lossein visited every evening to pick up gossip and get information on criminals who had visited the whorehouse and bragged of their exploits. He solved many crimes this way.

With the Great Depression, customers were not so plentiful and had less cash. Miss Jessie began the "poultry standard" of charging "one chicken for one encounter." Soon chickens were everywhere, and the establishment became known as the Chicken Ranch. The girls were never hungry, and Miss Jessie sold the surplus chickens and eggs. When the Civilian Conservation Corps began construction of Camp Swift near Bastrop, the shortage of men and money declined. With World War II, the ranch began a full-blown economic recovery. On some weekends, there was a line at the front door. By this time, Miss Jessie was confined to a wheelchair by arthritis, but she still ruled the roost. She did so into the 1950s before moving in with a wealthy sister in San Antonio where she died in 1961 at age eighty.

Edna Milton came to the Chicken Ranch in 1952 at age twenty-three, took over the management chores for Miss Jessie, and eventually bought the ranch for $30,000. She had a good relationship with the new sheriff, T. J. Flournoy, who had been elected in 1946. He put in a direct phone line to the Chicken Ranch so he could call the ranch nightly instead of visit. Edna continued Jessie's custom of giving money to local civic causes.

A door attendant admitted only white, presentable, and sober men into the parlor, where they waited their turn. No cursing or drinking was allowed. The standard fee was fifteen dollars for fifteen minutes. A girl would have from five to twenty customers a day. The ranch's annual income was probably more than $500,000 a year. Edna took an estimated 75 percent off the top, but the girls still made $300 a week and had no expenses. Edna took care of all the bills. All new employees were fingerprinted and photographed by Sheriff Flournoy, and a criminal record prevented their employment. Flournoy caught a few wanted women this way.

The Chicken Ranch operated until mid-1973, when Houston TV reporter Marvin Zindler ran a weeklong exposé on the ranch. He claimed that the Texas Department of Public Safety and local law officers had failed to combat organized crime and corruption at the ranch. His charges were unproven, but Governor Dolph Briscoe ordered the house closed. Sheriff Flournoy, along with some La Grange citizens, saw little reason to close the ranch, but he did so anyway. Edna got married and moved to East Texas.

Two Houston lawyers bought the Chicken Ranch in 1977 and moved part of the building to Dallas for the Chicken Ranch restaurant, which opened in September 1977 with Miss Edna as hostess and a menu of mainly chicken dishes. The restaurant closed in January 1978. Sheriff Flournoy resigned in 1980, saying that he and his wife were sick of hearing about the Chicken Ranch and did not want to hear that name again. When he died in 1982, Lieutenant Governor Bill Hobby and nearly one hundred lawmen attended his funeral.

PRAUSE'S MEAT MARKET

W. Travis at Main, on the square • 968-3259 • Open Monday through Saturday • W

This La Grange institution offers all-star pork and beef-pork sausage, smoked ham, Canadian bacon, and pork tenderloin, in addition to a complete line of fresh meats and larruping good, oak-smoked barbecue, by the pound or plate. The standard sides include three kinds of potato salad. Many locals will go nowhere else for their meat. Stepping inside is like stepping into a set from *The Last Picture Show*, with the beautiful old Friedrich Floating Air refrigerators up front and the cowboy mural on the back wall. The Prause family has operated the market since at least 1904, when the shop was located on the north side of the courthouse square.

La Grange's reputation for great barbecue goes back at least to August 19, 1843, when the town threw a great wingding for the republic's ex-president, General Mirabeau Lamar. Beeves, pigs, venison, and poultry were slaughtered in numbers, and that morning the cooking commenced. Great piles of wood were burnt down to coals, which were shoveled into trenches, across which the viands were roasted. The meat was accompanied by heaps of corn cakes, sweet potatoes, beetroot, tomatoes, butter, and the like, but no booze—just barrels of water.

OLD VON ROSENBERG STORE

245 W. Travis • W

Now a modern-day men's clothing store, the interior is still largely original, with beadboard walls, interior atrium, and skylight, with surrounding second-story walkways. Just east of the front doors embedded in the store's wall is the high-water marker stone for the great 1869 flood.

Turn left on Washington to complete your tour of the courthouse square.

OLD HERMES DRUG STORE

148 N. Washington • W

Hermes Drug Store (now an antiques shop) was Central Texas' most antiquely ornate drugstore, as well as its oldest drugstore. The elaborate patterned-tin ceiling is a riot of intricate lyre-and-rose-pattern squares. Wood-and-glass cabinets ornately carved in the Greek Revival style line the north and south walls, highlighted by Ionic columns and oval beveled mirrors. Each set of cabinets rests atop a wall-length line of wooden drawers stacked three high. Each of the several dozen drawers has its own labeled square ceramic knob. "Sulphur," "Suppositor," "SODA Bibor P.V.," "Insect Guns," "Artists Brushes," "Rubber Bands," "Nux Vomica," "Sundries," "Lamp Black"—these are just a few of the graceful hand-painted inscriptions on the drawer knobs.

Hermes Drug Store began operation in 1855, when William Hermes opened for business in a log cabin. He had come from Germany in late October 1846, just in time for the deadly wave of infectious disease that swept first through New Braunfels and then Fredericksburg. Unlike hundreds of his less-fortunate compatriots, Hermes survived the plague. After living a while in Fredericksburg, he moved to Castell, and finally to La Grange. Somewhere along the way, Hermes became a medical doctor. He was obsessed with the nature of the mysterious disease that had devastated the German colonies. He read every medical book he could find looking for similar cases. The Adelsverein's physician had diagnosed the epidemic as scurvy of the mouth and prescribed wild purslane as a remedy. Hermes concluded that they really suffered from petechial fever, also called epidemic cerebro-spinal meningitis. He felt that the disease could have been cured with a diet of good, wholesome food, including meat.

Built in 1907, this two-story Romanesque Revival structure appears at first to be constructed of rough-cut red sandstone or painted limestone blocks. But take a closer look, specifically at the southernmost second-story column, and you'll see that what appears to be stone is merely stucco over red brick, sculpted and dimpled to look like stone. The contrasting ivory-color window lintels, first-story columns and arches, and cornice trim are also painted stucco. H. W. Speckels was the architect responsible. The one other prominent example in Central Texas of this articulated stucco facade style is the castle-like Old General Land Office building (1857) on the state capitol grounds in Austin.

Just around the corner from the Hermes building, at 135 W. Colorado, is another two-story Speckels building of similar stucco-over-brick construction, sculpted to look like limestone blocks.

FAYETTE COUNTY COURTHOUSE

Courthouse square, 151 N. Washington • 968-3251 • Monday through Friday 8–5 • Free • W

The most visually arresting building on the square is the Fayette County courthouse, built in 1891 for $96,000. The exterior walls are Belton white limestone, complemented with blue sandstone quarried at nearby Muldoon. Red Pecos sandstone stringcourses (decorative horizontal moldings) and pink Burnet granite columns and steps form rich accents. At the base of the clock tower is a large stone slab on which is carved a large American eagle. Above this, at the tower's four corners, are carved griffins. The roof is covered with slate and Spanish tile. The building originally had an open court in the center, but it was converted into a vault and offices during the 1940s.

Take Main north from the courthouse square to its dead end to see four of La Grange's best remaining Victorian gingerbread houses, some restored, some not. From the courthouse square, head east to Jefferson/US 77 and proceed south. Eight and a half blocks south of the intersection

of US 77 and SH 71, you see the Faison home on your right and the Fayette County Library and Museum on your left.

N. W. FAISON HOUSE AND MUSEUM

822 S. Jefferson • 968-5756 • faisonhouse.org • Group tours by appointment • Contributions accepted

This house started life in 1841 as a two-room structure made of local pine. It was acquired and enlarged in 1855 by S. S. Munger. Nathaniel Faison acquired the home in 1866. Faison had been a member of the ill-fated Dawson Expedition, one of the fifteen men taken prisoner on the battlefield near San Antonio. After the battle, his Mexican captors demanded his gold ring. He pretended it wouldn't come off, until one of the Mexicans produced a knife and threatened to start cutting. Faison then discovered that the ring would come off very easily. Faison was pardoned by Santa Anna and returned to La Grange in 1843. Elected county clerk that year, he worked tirelessly to have the bones of his slain comrades returned to Fayette County. Faison passed away in 1870, but his family owned the house until 1961, when the La Grange Garden Club acquired it, restored it, and turned it into a museum.

FAYETTE HERITAGE MUSEUM AND ARCHIVES

855 S. Jefferson • 968-3765 • cityoflg.com • Open Tuesday through Sunday • Free • W first floor only

Directly across Jefferson from the Faison home is the Fayette Heritage Museum and Archives. The museum houses a collection of Fayette County memorabilia and artifacts.

From the library and museum, continue south on US 77 out of town, across the Colorado River, to Monument Hill State Historical Park.

Texas is famous for its spring wildflowers, which is the best season for Sunday drives in the country. The roadsides are brimming over with color in a good year, thanks partially to the Texas Department of Transportation, which has scattered wildflower seeds each year since the 1930s. Gibb Gilchrist, state highway engineer at the time, promoted the practice, in addition to preserving and planting roadside trees and shrubbery. According to Gilchrist, William Pape Sr., District Thirteen section foreman (1924–1940), was the first to scatter wildflower seeds on the highway roadside, in Fayette County from the Colorado River at La Grange south to Monument Hill on US 77.

By 1934, Gilchrist was recommending that his engineers take note of areas adjacent to highways where there were large concentrations of wildflowers, to locate the owners of those properties, and, where possible, to get written permission from them to enter the properties to gather seeds for planting along the highway right-of-way. He also directed in May of that year that "promiscuous mowing of the right of way should be delayed until the flower season is over."

Gilchrist also credited Pape for inventing the roadside park in the United States. "This was started in the early thirties," he said.

A chap in Fayette County named William Pape Sr. was county foreman on a road [SH 71] near Smithville where there were some beautiful live oak trees along a creek. He accepted the tract of land [1.31 acres] and built some tables and benches and things of that kind that would cause people to stop. I found out about it and determined that I either had to fire him or join him. So we joined him and everybody in the Highway Commission pushed along the idea of beautification until all engineers became advocates.

The park still sits under the oaks, on SH 71 west of La Grange, between West Point and Smithville.

A mile south of the river, turn right on Spur 92, which leads to the park.

MONUMENT HILL AND KREISCHE BREWERY STATE HISTORICAL PARKS

Take SH 77 south across the Colorado River, and then 0.4 mile on Spur 92, west to the park entrance • 968-5658 • www.tpwd.state.tx.us • Open daily, except Christmas Day • Fee • W variable

Here rest the Battle of Salado's martyrs and the victims of the Mier Expedition's Black Bean Episode. The land for these parks was acquired by the state over a lengthy period, beginning in 1907.

During the Mexican War in 1847, Texas Rangers (including Captain John Dusenberry, a "white bean veteran" from La Grange) retrieved sixteen of the seventeen remains buried at Hacienda Salado. After being carried around on packhorses until the end of the war, Dusenberry brought the bones to La Grange in 1848. That year, La Grange and Fayette County men retrieved the remains of Captain Dawson and his men from their Salado Creek burial site near San Antonio. The remains of these two groups were reburied with full military honors on September 18, 1848 (the sixth anniversary of the Dawson massacre), in the tomb on Monument Hill on a beautiful bluff overlooking the Colorado River and the City of La Grange. The site was specially selected for its grandeur and to appease Fayette County for the earlier, failed attempt to locate the republic's capital here. Sam Houston and a host of other dignitaries and citizens from all over the state attended the ceremonies.

The state erected a monument to these fallen men on the courthouse square in 1884. A new granite vault was built over the tomb in 1933, and the monument marking the site was erected in 1936 for the Texas Independence Centennial.

THE KREISCHE BREWERY AND KREISCHE HOME COMPLEX

H. L. Kreische immigrated to Texas in 1846 through Galveston. He purchased this property in 1849. A master stonemason, he lived on this bluff overlooking the Colorado River with his wife, Josepha, and six children. Kreische constructed his large three-story stone and wooden home in the hillside, finishing the first portion around 1855 and completing the rest of the home in 1857. Kreische's sons and daughters lived in the house until the last daughter, Miss

Julia Kreische, died in 1952. The house was still largely intact, with few modern modifications.

Between 1860 and 1870, Kreische devoted most of his attention to brewing beer, and his brewery was one of the first commercial breweries in Texas. He could brew seven hundred barrels in a good year. By 1879, his brewery was Texas' third-largest-producing brewery. Kreische died in 1882 after an accident, and the brewery was out of business by 1884. Today, the stabilized brewery ruins consist of two masonry levels; a third story made of wood is missing. A barrel-arched vault is located on the lowest level, where Mr. Kreische produced a lager beer, during at least part of the year. Lager brewing requires lower temperatures. Kreische made his lager before artificial refrigeration made the practice more common in Texas. He did this by harnessing cold spring water from Monument Springs (which issue nearby from the steep sandstone bluff) and channeling cooled air drafts into the fermentation area to keep it cool. The second floor is composed of levels, stairs, and rooms of varying sizes. A museum in the park's headquarters building interprets the Kreische family, the brewery, and the home.

In 1838, the five commissioners charged with finding a new seat of government for the republic recommended a site across the river from Monument Springs. In 1840, George Bonnell wrote,

> Just below the mouth of this [Buckner's] creek, upon the west side of the river, is a high bluff known in the neighborhood by the name of Mount Maria. It is about 500 feet in height, and commands a magnificent prospect. Upon the top of the hill is a spring, the water of which, in its descent, forms a beautiful cascade. At this cascade is found a great abundance of limestone spar—the most beautiful of all mineral formations. With proper improvements this would be one of the most magnificent situations in any country.

Bonnell's description was pretty accurate, except that they issue from about halfway up the bluff, about 130 meters. The springs have since all but disappeared.

Park activities include picnicking, nature study, and historical study. Contact the park staff to schedule weddings and group functions. The Trail of Lights is held during the first half of December on selected evenings, where visitors can experience a beautifully decorated trail with Christmas lights. It follows the bluff and proceeds through the Kreische home, which is traditionally decorated with Christmas trees, wreaths, lamps, and candles.

The brewery is open for guided tours on Saturday and Sunday afternoons (October–May) and Saturday morning (June–September). Kreische house tours are scheduled on selected weekends, typically on the first and second Sunday afternoon of each month. Special weekday group tours of Monument Hill, the brewery, or the Kreische house can be arranged in advance through the park headquarters. Larger groups enjoy a special overview of the park on a historical, scenic guided tour along the park's interpretive trail (with kolaches and refreshments as an option).

The bluff at Monument Hill is the northern limit of the Oakville Escarpment of Miocene-era bearing sandstone. This escarpment, or "cuesta," marks the boundary between the Upland Post Oak Woodlands and the Fayette Prairie environments. Here, along the bluff, eastern plant and animal communities of the woodlands and prairie coexist with an isolated colony of western species. The Colorado River, located at the base of the two-hundred-foot bluff, has transported and deposited numerous plants and animals common to the limestone-based soils of the Hill Country here. Mr. Kreische's old roads, trails, retaining walls, and buildings add beauty and places of shelter to the environment. The park's nature trail has a list of more common plant and animal species and is available at the park headquarters.

DINING

WEIKEL'S STORE AND BAKERY

2247 SH 71B, across from McDonald's at the intersection with SH 71 bypass, on the far west side of La Grange • 968-9413 • Open daily • W

This is a convenient gas stop on the far west side of town, but the real reason to stop is the baked goods: all sorts of kolaches, cinnamon rolls, pigs in blankets, homemade bread, and the like. It is an obligatory stop for many travelers.

OTHER AREA ATTRACTIONS

LA GRANGE RAILROAD MUSEUM

206 N. Washington at Lafayette, one block north of courthouse square

The old MKT station, which has waiting rooms, an office, and a freight area, was completed in November 1897 by the Taylor, Bastrop, and Houston Railway Company to replace the first station, which burned earlier that year. The TB&H was soon taken over by the Missouri-Kansas-Texas railroad. Passenger service continued until the 1950s, and freight service into the 1970s. Museum furnishings include the original potbelly stove, an MKT safe, and a stationmaster's desk, as well as historic photographs and a gold-headed cane presented to James Converse in 1880 in appreciation of his successful efforts to bring a railroad to La Grange. There also are hands-on exhibits for adults and children. The exterior has the original passenger and freight signs, and there is a "Chessie" line caboose on display next to the depot.

TEXAS CZECH HERITAGE AND CULTURAL CENTER

Fayette County Fairgrounds • Open Monday through Friday

Fayette County has the largest Czech-origin population (per capita) and the most Czech communities in Texas, and is considered to be the cradle of Czech culture in Texas. The Texas Czech Heritage and Cultural Center preserves the history, language, culture, and heritage of Texans who trace their ancestry to Bohemia, Moravia, Slovakia, and Silesia.

Attractions include the Kalich house, moved here from near Engle, an old farmhouse that symbolized the progress of the Texas Czech immigrants. The house was built in three to four stages, starting with a one-room cabin at its core. Others include the Migl House (built in 1890 near Praha); the Fair Pavilion, built in 1925, which over the years has served as a place for people of La Grange and the surrounding area to gather for dances and other gatherings; an amphitheater; a bell and belfry from the Czech Republic; a gift shop featuring books, handicrafts, and recorded music; and the Polka Lovers Club of Texas Museum, located in the restored late-1870s Hoelscher house.

The Czech immigrants who came to Central Texas were proud people who yearned to be free. The Austrian government, which had ruled Bohemia and Moravia since 1526, discouraged use of the Czech language and prohibited Protestantism. Most Czechs were Roman Catholics. The Bohemians and Moravians, who together form the Czech people, especially hated compulsory service in the Austrian army, where foot soldiers earned only six cents a day.

More importantly, people overflowed the Czech countryside, which was so subdivided that in some instances it was claimed that a person could clear a man's farm with one leap. Most Czech immigrants to Texas were *chalupnici*, or cottagers (families owning fewer than twenty acres), from the Moravian side of the Moravian/Bohemian border. To people who lived ten or more to a one- or two-room cottage, the lure of one hundred acres in Texas proved irresistible. About forty thousand Bohemians and Moravians came to Texas between about 1851 and 1939.

The father of Czech immigration to Texas, the Reverend Josef Arnost Bergmann, settled at Cat Spring in today's Austin County, around 1850, where he served as pastor and teacher to the area's Protestant Germans. His enthusiastic letters to friends about life in Texas, copied and passed around northeastern Bohemia and Moravia like holy relics, inspired the first mass Czech migrations to Texas.

Early groups entered Texas at Galveston, made their way to Cat Spring, and began to fan out across Austin and Fayette counties. By 1856, Czech communities existed at Fayetteville, Dubina, Bluff (renamed Hostyn in 1925 by Father Paul Kasper, after the town of Hostyn, Moravia), and Mulberry (now known as Praha).

During the 1870s and 1880s, E. J. Spacek of Fayetteville helped many Czechs of primarily Moravian descent find homes and farms, earning Fayetteville the title "Cradle of Czech Immigration to Texas." By 1900, a "Czech Belt" stretched across Texas' fertile Blackland Prairies, from the town of West southward two hundred miles to Victoria. After 1900, the Czechs began to settle the coastal prairie, from Victoria east to Brazoria County. "Family hearth above gold" and "A farmer's eyes guard his home," two old Czech proverbs, illustrate the love of family. Respect for land and reverence for the church form the other linchpins of Czech society in Texas.

Czech settlers constructed the sprawling rock grotto at Hostyn's Holy Rosary Church (about 5.5 miles south of La Grange; take US 77 south to FM 243 and turn right to reach Hostyn) in 1925 to thank God for bringing an end to the great drought of 1924–1925. It and the parish's other shrines made Hostyn a mecca for thousands of visitors annually. At the same site stands a full-size model of Hostyn's first Catholic church, a log cabin built in 1856. After the wooden building deteriorated, the congregation decided to build a more lasting monument, constructing in its place a stucco replica that echoes the original church, down to its knotholes. The Holy Rosary Czech Catholic Cemetery is filled with old-style tombstones inscribed in Czech. Buried side by side here are Joseph Lidiak and his son, John, who fought during the Civil War on opposite sides. The present church was built in 1966 and is of little interest to the average visitor.

Though officially Roman Catholic, some Czechs who came to Texas had secretly followed the teachings of Jan Hus, a Bohemian reformist priest burned at the stake as a heretic in 1415. Suppressed at home, the Brethren, as they called themselves, worshiped openly in Texas, holding their first service in 1855 near the present location of the Fayetteville Brethren Church. Eventually, the Czech Brethren in Texas formed an independent denomination, the Unity of the Brethren, which now counts about two dozen congregations. The first congregation organized in 1864 at Vesely ("happy" in Czech), later called Wesley. The original mother church, built in 1866, boasts an unusual interior created in 1890 by the congregation's pastor, Bohuslav Lacjak. He painted bricks and Ionic columns onto the interior walls of the wooden church and covered the ceiling with stars of David and geometric stenciling. Unfortunately, Lacjak died in a hunting accident in 1891, never having explained his mystical work.

Most Czech immigrants, however, remained Catholic and expressed their faith by building churches as grand as they could afford. The first permanent Catholic church for Czechs in Fayette County was established in 1855 near today's Ellinger and was later moved to a rise above the town of Live Oak Hill. As late as 1870, no Czech-speaking priest served Czechs in Texas. After Konstantin Chovanec petitioned the bishop in 1872, Father Joseph Chromcik arrived on Christmas Eve of that year and celebrated the first Texas Mass in Czech on Christmas Day.

Nothing brings church members or the family together better than a shared meal, and Czech proverbs exalt such occasions: "Where there is good cooking, there is happiness"; "Good food, good drink—the basis of all living."

Czech food is simple, flavorful, and hearty. An "official" Czech meal would include roast pork with dumplings, gravy, and sauerkraut. Although roast goose, another popular Czech dish, didn't become part of the Tex-Czech diet, noodles, kolaches, and sausages did. Today, the smoky aromas of sausages, bacon, ham, pork tenderloin, and beef jerky draw many to meat markets in the Czech Belt. Sweets also enliven the Czech menu. Fruit-filled kolaches lure many a traveler to Weikel's in La Grange. Fayetteville folks like to brag that Brenham's Blue Bell Creameries used recipes from Rudolph Baca's ice cream parlor on Fayetteville's square for some of its popular flavors.

Fayetteville (about fifteen miles east of La Grange on FM 159) proudly chronicles its Czechness in displays at the Fayetteville Museum, with particular emphasis on the Frank J. Baca family. For nearly one hundred years, generations of the Baca Family Orchestras and Bands played all over Texas, and their recordings are still sold in area stores.

Against the odds, the Czech language endures in Texas. A nineteenth-century poem by Czechoslovakian nationalist Svatopluk Cech says, "What has protected us like a shield in battle? Our language." Since Czech language was prohibited in the Old Country, immigrants reveled in their New World freedom to speak and write as they pleased. Before World War II, Texas counted more than two dozen Czech-language publications.

Few Texans under age seventy speak Czech fluently, but the language will persist a while longer, thanks to the efforts of folks like Joe Vrabel, who publishes *Nasinec*, the only weekly Czech-language newspaper in Texas. Founded in 1914, *Nasinec* claimed 1,750 subscribers when Joe took over the paper in 1981;

now fewer than eight hundred subscribe, and the list keeps shrinking. Though letters from readers and funeral notices fill most of *Nasinec's* pages today, Vrabel views his work as a calling. "I'll keep publishing as long as I get enough support to keep going. It's my gift to readers and to the Czech people."

Groups such as the Moravian Heritage Singers, the Fayette Czech Singers and Dancers, the Happy Czech Singers, the Praha KJZT Junior Czech Singers, and Kovanda's Czech Band perform traditional Czech music and dances. On any given weekend, Czech-Tex groups play at dances across the state, mostly at SPJST, lodges, and celebrations like the Texas Folklife Festival at San Antonio's Institute of Texan Cultures. Such musical fervor isn't surprising, in light of the Czech proverb: *Kazdy Cech, je muzikant!* (Every Czech a musician!)

WHITE ROCK PARK

On the left, approximately one mile south on US 77, downstream of the US 77 bridge in La Grange • 968-5805

This 23.5-acre day-use park was developed by the Lower Colorado River Authority and is operated by the City of La Grange. Facilities include a canoe launch area, baseball fields, a playground, picnic areas, restrooms, and a fishing pier.

ANNUAL EVENT

SEPTEMBER

FAYETTE COUNTY FAIR

Fayette County Fairgrounds, US 77 • Labor Day weekend • Fee • W

The fair features entertainment, horse racing, tractor pulls, livestock exhibitions, agricultural and home economics displays, a parade, and dances.

Leave La Grange on US 77 north. Seven miles north of La Grange, turn left on FM 153. FM 153 winds its way to Winchester through thick stands of fragrant, tall pines.

WINCHESTER

Fayette County • 50 • About 16 miles from La Grange

Winchester was originally settled by John Ingram, who came to Texas at the age of thirteen. After he came of age, he was granted a one-fourth-league tract in Austin's second colony. A veteran of the Battle of Gonzales, the siege of Bexar, and the Battle of San Jacinto, he received a total of nearly two thousand acres from the republic and the State of Texas for his wartime services.

The town proper was laid out in 1851 by John Gromme and was named for Winchester, Tennessee, birthplace of some of the early settlers. The SA&AP railroad had reached Winchester by 1890, turning the town into a regional shipping center. But with the decline of the railroad and the family farm system, and the growth of the modern highway system, Winchester found itself off the beaten track and has since slipped into a peaceful somnolence. Today, Winchester is a collection of mostly pre–World War I houses and abandoned, slowly decaying frame commercial buildings.

After crossing the railroad tracks, turn right on Front Street, which parallels the railroad tracks, for a tour of old downtown Winchester. The long-closed Dew Drop Inn sits on the corner of FM 153 and Front. A block and a half later, at 211 Front, is a classic, turn-of-the-century, wooden, shotgun-style store with rectangular false front—the old Brahm store and saloon. It was most notable for the segregation line painted on the floor; blacks stayed on one side of the line, whites on the other.

Until recently, it had a twin on its north side, which started life as Winchester's bank. When the bank went bust in 1932, the post office moved in and stayed over fifty years. A few yards to the south and west of Brahm's store, at the corner of Nueces and Thomas streets, one block north of FM 153, is the old Schmidt Store, the only brick commercial building in town. C. H. Schmidt built this brick, one-story store in 1913, during Winchester's halcyon days. It was his third store here. He came from Germany in 1890 and built his first store in 1892. Outgrowing that wooden building, he built another, larger store in 1908, which he outgrew only four years later. Schmidt sold everything but coffins. At the time, Schmidt competed with half a dozen other general merchandise stores in town. He died in 1921, and his daughter and son-in-law took over the store. Grandson Calvin Harris took over the store in 1973 and ran it until 1989. It has changed owners and names several times since, and it housed the post office and a steakhouse at press time.

ST. MICHAEL'S LUTHERAN CHURCH

North edge of town • Sunday worship service 9 a.m.

Set on Winchester's "hill," St. Michael's Church with its whitewashed spire is easily visible. The congregation dates to 1876, but not by that name. On St. Michael's Day 1887, members gathered to choose a name for their congregation, and that's what they chose. The current wooden sanctuary dates to 1906. The spare interior's most ornate features are the white altar imported from Germany and the baptismal built long ago by a congregation member. The pipe organ in the loft dates to the sanctuary's construction and is played every Sunday.

The big red house just west of the church is the old Ramsey Hotel, built by Mr. and Mrs. Alex Ramsey sometime during the 1890s in downtown Winchester. He was also postmaster. The hotel had six rooms downstairs and six more upstairs. After the Ramseys died, Ben Noack bought it. Several years later, he had it torn down and reassembled as before at its current location. It has been remodeled several times since and is currently a private residence.

OTHER ATTRACTIONS

SERBIN

Take FM 448, which intersects FM 153 on the outskirts of Winchester just before you cross the railroad tracks, north to the intersection with FM 2239; turn left on FM 2239 to reach Serbin.

Winchester is also the southernmost tip of the tiny "Wendish Belt" in Central Texas. The Wends are a Slavic people who live in Lusatia in eastern Germany. Unlike the Czechs and Poles, who retained their Slavic cultural identity, the Texas Wends adopted the ways of their German neighbors. The Wends are one of the smallest European ethnic communities in the United States, having immigrated here en masse only once. In 1854, a congregation of nearly six hundred Wendish Lutherans, led by Pastor Johann Kilian, sailed aboard the ship *Ben Nevis* to Galveston. Mostly farmers, they came to Texas seeking a better life and the right to practice their Lutheran beliefs. Once in America, they affiliated with the Lutheran Church, Missouri Synod, which had recently been founded in St. Louis.

The Wends, who came to the United States to escape Prussian domination, bought a 4,254-acre tract of poor-quality, sandy, post oak land in a German-settled area in Lee County. Better land was available at higher prices, but the Wends didn't have money, wagons, work animals, gold, or other substantial material possessions. They had to settle where they could harvest wood for houses, fences, and fuel and dig some shallow water wells for themselves and the few animals they brought. They set aside land for a church and, in 1855, founded Low Pinoak (the name was changed to Serbin, meaning "Wendish Land," in 1860). Because earlier settlers already owned most of the arable ground in the vicinity, many Wendish families moved to better land as soon as they could afford it. They founded the nearby villages of Fedor, Loebau, and Warda. Later, Wends settled in towns throughout Texas, including Vernon, Thorndale, Copperas Cove, and Bishop.

Established in 1855, St. Paul Lutheran Church is the mother church to Texas' Wends. Dedicated in 1871, the current church closely resembles Pastor Kilian's former church in Kotitz, Germany. While the stenciling, paintings, and faux-marble columns of St. Paul's are simpler than the adornment of the painted Catholic churches of Fayette County, the decorations reflect a Slavic love of religious art that even the somber Lutheran ethic could not quell. Johann Kilian, the only Missouri Synod preacher in Texas from 1854 to 1868, also served at New Ulm, Louis Settlement, Swiss Alp, Röder's Mill (Shelby), and Bastrop.

The Wends soon replaced their native Wendish (a Slavic language closely related to Czech) with German as their language of everyday use. Though today few speak fluent Wendish, many older Wends converse in German, and St. Paul Lutheran Church still conducts one service a month in German.

Bypassed by the railroad and paved highways until as late as the 1970s, Serbin dwindled over the years to a collection of farmhouses clustered around St. Paul's Church and school. A cultural reawakening began in the late 1960s, and the Wends formed the Texas Wendish Heritage Society, which founded the Texas Wendish Heritage Museum, now housed in a complex that includes an interpretive center, a research library, and two nineteenth-century log structures. The highlight of the year is the annual Wendish Fest, held the last Sunday of September on the grounds of the museum and the St. Paul Lutheran Church picnic grounds, with food, music, demonstrations, and activities for adults and children.

From Winchester, continue west on FM 153, which in June 1883 was described by Mrs. Joseph D. Sayers as the worst road in the United States. She had come from Bastrop to visit the mineral wells at Winchester for their curative powers. It has improved considerably since then.

In a little over three miles, you cross back into Bastrop County. Before you get to SH 71 and Smithville, there are two more points of interest along FM 153.

ROCKY HILL RANCH

Off FM 153 (north side), about 9 miles from Winchester • 512-237-3112 • www.rockyhillranchtexas.com • Open daily • Fee • W variable

Rocky Hill Ranch has over thirty miles of mountain bike trails over several different types of terrain; there are rocks, sand, dirt, pine forest, canyons, hills, and creek crossings. The trail system is graded according to the individual rider's skill level. Tour de France champion Lance Armstrong has ridden and raced here. Helmets are required. Families are welcome. Hikers are also welcome. Other diversions include sand volleyball, fishing, horseshoe pitching, and washers. You can camp at a historic spring-fed waterhole where Indians and wagon trains once camped. The Rocky Hill Cafe and Saloon serves cold drinks, beer, burgers, and sandwiches and features rock and country bands on weekends. Sunsets from the saloon's front porch are great.

BUESCHER STATE PARK

Park Rd. 1, off FM 153, about 10 miles from Winchester • 512-237-2241 • Open daily • Fee • W variable

Buescher State Park measures 1,016 acres and is named for Emile Buescher, who donated 318 acres to the state in the 1930s. After his death, his heirs donated more land, and the rest of the parkland came from the city of Smithville. The original park improvements were made by the Civilian Conservation Corps. A scenic road connects Buescher State Park with Bastrop State Park, traveling through the Lost Pines, a remnant of what was probably once an extensive pine and oak forest that covered much of Central Texas during a time when ice-age glaciers reigned not too far to the north.

Activities include biking, boating, fishing, lake swimming, nature study, camping, and hiking. The thirteen-mile-long, winding, and hilly road between Buescher and Bastrop state parks is ideal for biking. Approximately six miles between the parks is private land; do not camp between parks or trespass on private land. The beautiful wooded setting, which includes a lake, makes for fruitful birding; some 250 species of birds spend time in or inhabit the park over the course of a year.

Not far away to the west is the old Alum Creek Settlement (Craft's Prairie), where Andy Potter, who would become known across Texas as the Fightin'

Parson, got religion. Potter, who once called himself "the ringleader in sin," at first found Alum Creek an ideal place to live, but later he called it the worst community he had ever seen. On the Sabbath, he and his crowd would assemble at the grocery, get drunk, fight, and gamble. He and Noah Smithwick had a particular affinity for each other, never forsaking each other even in the direst of circumstances. But after a bloody fight that pitted the two of them against a dozen or more men, Smithwick told him, "Potter, it is time to stop; it is time to reform." He went to the Methodist camp meeting going on at the time and was converted. Potter's comment: "I had lost my strongest brother in sin."

Indignant over the conversion of his friend Smithwick, Potter attended the next meeting, with no good purpose. But instead of busting up the services, Potter was won over to the Lord by the Reverend J. G. John's sermon and was led to the altar by Smithwick. Potter now felt he had to be a leader in the new life. So even though he could not write and had only read a few chapters from the Bible, he entered the itinerant ministry, a profession that took him all over Texas and the frontier.

INDEX